# Rick Steves®

# FLORENCE
# & TUSCANY

Rick Steves & Gene Openshaw

# CONTENTS

# Welcome to Rick Steves' Europe

Travel is intensified living—maximum thrills per minute and one of the last great sources of legal adventure. Travel is freedom. It's recess, and we need it.

I discovered a passion for European travel as a teen and have been sharing it ever since—through my bus tours, public television and radio shows, and travel guide-books. Over the years, I've taught millions of travelers how to best enjoy Europe's blockbuster sights—and experience "Back Door" discoveries that most tourists miss.

Written with my talented co-author, Gene Openshaw, this book offers a balanced mix of Florence's rich cultural heritage and the romantic charm of Tuscany's time-passed villages. It's selective: Rather than listing dozens of hill towns, we recommend only the best ones. And it's in depth: Our self-guided  museum tours and city walks provide insight into the region's vibrant history and today's living, breathing culture.

We advocate traveling simply and smartly. Take advantage of our money- and time-saving tips on sight-seeing, transportation, and more. Try local, characteristic alternatives to expensive hotels and restaurants. In many ways, spending more money only builds a thicker wall between you and what you traveled so far to see.

We visit Tuscany to experience it—to become temporary locals. Thoughtful travel engages us with the world, as we learn to appreciate other cultures and new ways to measure quality of life.

Judging by the positive feedback we receive from readers, this book will help you enjoy a fun, affordable, and rewarding vacation—whether it's your first trip or your tenth.

*Buon viaggio!* Happy travels!

*Rick Steves*

# FLORENCE & TUSCANY

Florence is Europe's cultural capital. As the home of the Renaissance and the birthplace of the modern world, Florence practiced the art of civilized living back when the rest of Europe was rural and crude. The proud and energetic Florentines of the 1400s championed democracy, science, and literature as well as painting, sculpture, and architecture.

When the Florentine poet Dante first saw the teenaged Beatrice, her beauty so inspired him that he spent the rest of his life writing poems to her. In the same way, the Renaissance opened people's eyes to the physical beauty of the world around them, inspiring them to write, paint, sculpt, and build.

The result is that Florence today offers you a brimming bucket list of art, topped by Michelangelo's *David* and Botticelli's *Birth of Venus*. As for architecture, nothing tops the Duomo's heavenly dome, designed by Brunelleschi. Gilding the lily, Ghiberti created the glorious Gates of Paradise for the church's Baptistery.

Blessed with a wealth of riches, Florence has historic churches (like Santa Croce), masterpiece chapels (Michelangelo's Medici and Masaccio's Brancacci), palaces large and small (Pitti and Vecchio), and a surprising range of museums (from Fra Angelico's San Marco monastery, to Ferragamo fashion, to the Galileo Science Museum).

The city has so many sights and tourists that at times it feels like a Renaissance theme park. But where else can you stroll the same pedestrian streets walked by Michelangelo, Leonardo, and Botticelli while savoring Italy's best gelato?

Look beyond the sights to experience the city, too, with its lively squares and bustling markets, such as Mercato Centrale, a produce and foodie hall all in one. Head across the historic, shop-lined Ponte Vecchio bridge spanning the Arno River to explore the bohemian Oltrarno neighborhood and glimpse artisans at work. Above it all is Piazzale Michelangelo, awarding visitors with a stunning view of the city's tiled rooftops, elegant bridges, and sublime dome.

Florence is a different city at night—it feels smaller, quieter, and more romantic. For dinner, stroll the back streets to find that perfect wine bar or restaurant. Try hearty Tuscan specialties: bean soup *(ribollita),* wild boar *(cinghiale),* and T-bone steak *(bistecca alla fiorentina).*

The city's compact urban center, short on open spaces, can easily exhaust travelers who feel obligated to see as many museums as possible. Sightsee selectively. And to round out your trip, leave the city behind and explore the green, serene Tuscan countryside. Breathe...slow down...enjoy.

Tuscany is our romantic image of Italy, with manicured fields, rustic farms, cypress-lined driveways, and towns clinging to nearly every hill. This is one part of Italy where I recommend traveling by car—it's the best way to lace together the views, villages, and vineyards.

The region's sunny, wine-soaked villages each have their own appeal and claim to fame: Volterra (Etruscan ruins), San

*Florence has Italy's best gelato. Piazzale Michelangelo awards visitors with a stunning panorama.*

# Experiencing Italy's Renaissance

Imagine: In Florence you can sleep in a 16th-century monastery-hotel that's just a block from Michelangelo's *David*, around the corner from Brunelleschi's famous cathedral dome, and down the street from the tombs of the great Medici art patrons. Florence boasts more artistic masterpieces per square mile than any place I can think of.

Before the Renaissance, Europeans spent about 1,000 years in a cultural slumber. Most art was made to serve the Church, and man played only a bit part—typically as a sinner. But around 1400, starting in Florence, everything began to change. The new "Renaissance Man" shaped his own destiny and was no longer a mere plaything of the supernatural. Belief in the importance of the individual skyrocketed.

Wealthy families—like the Medici, who ruled Florence for generations—showed their civic pride by commissioning great art. Never before had artists been asked to do so much or given so much money and freedom.

The most successful artists—like Leonardo, Michelangelo, Botticelli, and Raphael—achieved celebrity status. In their pursuit of realism in painting and sculpture, these Renaissance greats merged art and science. They studied anatomy like doctors, nature like biologists, and the laws of perspective like mathematicians. With the Renaissance, artists rediscovered the beauty of the human body, expressing the optimism of this new humanistic age. ◼

*Michelangelo's* David *exudes Renaissance confidence, while Botticelli's* Spring *radiates beauty.*

*Tuscany's tranquil countryside;
Siena's thrilling Palio race*

Gimignano (towers), Montepulciano (artisans), Pienza (tidy Renaissance-planned streets), and Montalcino (wine). Connoisseurs visit Tuscany to sample the great local wines at classy wineries elegantly tucked into rolling hills.

Tuscany's cities are equally engaging. Sprawling Siena, huddling around one of Italy's coziest squares and finest cathedrals, hosts the flag-twirling, no-holds-barred Palio horse race that shows off its medieval roots. Pisa boasts the Field of Miracles, famous for its Leaning Tower, an icon of all Italy. Lucca is graced with churches, towers, and a delightful city wall-turned-city park that's ideal for a stroll or pedal.

To connect with Tuscany's rural charm, stay on a farm—an *agriturismo*. These rural guesthouses provide a good home base for relaxing and exploring as much or as little as you want. Your hosts may even offer you a "zero kilometer" meal, serving food produced right on the farm.

The small island of Elba in the Tuscan archipelago is worth a visit for its beaches, fresh fish dinners, and a trio of 16th-century fortresses.

You'll discover that peaceful Tuscan villages and bustling Florence—with its rough-stone beauty, art-packed museums, children chasing pigeons, students riding Vespas, artisans sipping Chianti, and supermodels wearing Gucci—offer many of the very things you came to Italy to see.

# Tuscany's Top Destinations

*Salute!* Let's toast to Tuscany, which offers a heady mix of experiences. This overview categorizes the top destinations into must-see places (to help first-time travelers plan their trip) and worth-it places (for those with extra time or special interests). I've also suggested a minimum number of days to allow per destination.

**PLACES COVERED IN THIS BOOK**

▲▲▲ Must See
▲▲ Try Hard to See
▲ Worthwhile

LUCCA

PISA

FLORENCE

T U S C A N Y

SAN GIMIGNANO

VOLTERRA

*Ligurian Sea*

SIENA

CORTONA

C R E T E
S E N E S I

HEART OF TUSCANY

ELBA

*Tyrrhenian Sea*

N

30 Kilometers

30 Miles

## MUST-SEE DESTINATIONS

Tuscany's two major cities—Florence and Siena—are the perfect introduction to medieval and Renaissance Italy. From there, escape to the heart of Tuscany for a sampler of rural delights.

### ▲▲▲Florence (allow 3 days)

This compact, bustling, and culturally rich city stars Michelangelo's *David*, Brunelleschi's dome, and a treasure trove of Renaissance artworks. The historic city, bisected by the Arno River and spanned by the irresistible Ponte Vecchio, is loaded with marvelous sights, churches, markets, and squares.

### ▲▲▲Siena (2 days)

This hilltop city is known for its medieval pageantry, Palio horse race, and stunning traffic-free main square—great anytime but best after dark. This is the ultimate hill town, with red-brick lanes cascading every which way and a proud spirit any visitor can enjoy. It's also a fine jumping-off point for exploring the Tuscan countryside with a driving tour of the Crete Senesi region.

### ▲▲▲Heart of Tuscany (2-3 days)

Several picturesque villages cluster like grapes on a stem: medieval Montepulciano (a good home base for drivers); pint-sized Pienza with Renaissance architecture; and Brunello-fueled Montalcino (a manageable home base for nondrivers). Enjoy the region's serene scenery by following one of my self-guided driving tours (Heart of Tuscany or Brunello Wine Country) or by joining a minibus wine tour.

*Botticelli's* Birth of Venus *(opposite); Florence's Duomo; peaceful Pienza; wine tasting in Montalcino; practicing for Siena's Palio*

Pisa's Leaning Tower; alabaster workshop in Volterra;
tower-topped San Gimignano;
Lucca's wall promenade

## WORTH-IT DESTINATIONS

You can weave any of these destinations—rated ▲ or ▲▲—into your itinerary. It's easy to add some destinations based on proximity (if you're going to Florence, Pisa is next door), but some out-of-the-way places can merit the journey, depending on your time and interests.

### ▲▲Pisa (half-day)
Pisa is famous for its iconic Leaning Tower, but it has other equally impressive monuments on its gleaming Field of Miracles. Those must-see sights are reminders of Pisa's long-ago sea-trading wealth (which evaporated when its port silted up). Today's arcaded old town is fun to wander and delightfully tourist-free.

### ▲▲Lucca (1 day)
This charming town has a lively (and flat) town center, ringed by Europe's mightiest Renaissance wall. That still-intact wall makes a rampart wide enough for biking and strolling. Without major monuments or museums, Lucca is pleasant for just hanging out, with cafés and shops for whiling away your time.

### ▲▲Volterra (half-day)
Off the beaten path, this authentic, walled hill town has a long Etruscan history and established alabaster workshops—a heritage that makes for unusually interesting sightseeing for a small town.

### ▲San Gimignano (half-day)
San Gimignano is the epitome of a hill town, spiked with 14 medieval towers. By day it's packed with tourists who crowd the narrow, shop-lined lanes, but a stroll through its core in the

shadow of those towers is worth it. At night, it's an evocative, traffic-free delight.

## ▲Cortona (half-day)

Basking under the Tuscan sun, enjoyable Cortona is home to grand churches, museums of Etruscan artifacts and Renaissance art, and an archaeological park. Nestled in hills on the fringe of Tuscany, it's an easy stop for drivers heading to or from neighboring Umbria.

## ▲Elba (2 nights/1 full day)

This small island—a one-hour ferry ride from the mainland—combines a rugged and mountainous landscape, twisty drives to charming beach towns, and echoes of Napoleon's famous 10-month exile here, adding up to an inviting seaside "vacation from your vacation."

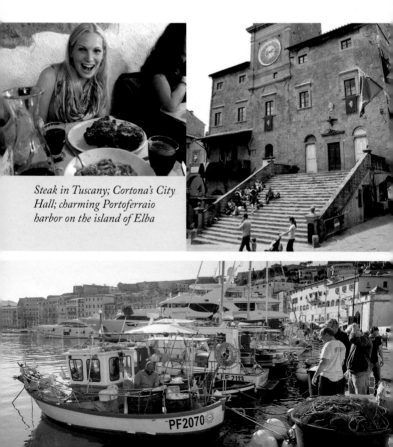

*Steak in Tuscany; Cortona's City Hall; charming Portoferraio harbor on the island of Elba*

# Planning Your Trip

To plan your trip, you'll need to design your itinerary—choosing where and when to go, how you'll travel, and how many days to spend at each destination. For my best general advice on sightseeing, accommodations, restaurants, and more, see the Practicalities chapter.

## DESIGNING AN ITINERARY

As you read this book and learn your options...

### Choose your top destinations.

My recommended itinerary (see the sidebar on page 18) gives you an idea of how much you can reasonably see in 13 days, but you can adapt it to fit your own interests and time frame. If you like Renaissance art and enjoy museums, linger longer in Florence. If you've always wanted to ascend Pisa's Leaning Tower, now's the time for the climb (and relaxing, low-pressure Lucca awaits nearby).

Stay overnight in at least one hill town. While most of the towns are undeniably touristy by day, in the evening they become the domain of locals, who polish the cobbled streets with convivial promenades. For medieval pageantry and pride, nothing beats Siena. Wine lovers savor Montalcino. Remote Volterra (with Etruscan sights) is the least touristy of the towns I recommend.

Exploring Tuscany's hill towns could easily take up to two weeks, especially if you relax into an *agriturismo* guesthouse. With its scenery, abbeys, and wineries, Tuscany is a fine place to slow down—what's the rush?

## Decide when to go.

Tuscany's best travel months (also its busiest and most expensive) are April, May, June, September, and October. These months combine the conveniences of peak season with pleasant weather.

The most grueling thing about travel in Tuscany is the summer heat in July and August, when temperatures hit the high 80s and 90s. Most midrange hotels come with air conditioning—a worthwhile splurge in the summer—but it's often available only from June through September. August is vacation time for Italians, with cities emptying out for a week before and two weeks after the August 15 Ferragosto holiday (marking the Assumption of Mary). City hotels consider this period low season.

In April and October, you'll generally need a sweater or light jacket in the evening. In winter the temperatures can drop to the 40s or 50s. Off-season has none of the sweat and stress of the tourist season, but sights may have shorter hours, lunchtime breaks, and fewer activities. Confirm your sight-seeing plans locally, especially when traveling off-season. For weather specifics, see the climate chart in the appendix.

## Connect the dots.

Link your destinations into a logical route. Determine which

*Staying in an* agriturismo *(farmhouse B&B); traveling through Tuscany by train*

Treno **63**

cities you'll fly into and out of. Begin your search for transatlantic flights at Kayak.com.

Decide if you'll travel by car or public transportation, or a combination. A car is particularly helpful for exploring the villages of Tuscany (where public transportation can be sparse and time-consuming), but is useless in Florence and Siena—rent one before or after you visit these bigger cities.

Florence, Pisa, Lucca, and Siena are readily linked by public transportation. The smaller hill towns are more of a challenge. Plan on using a mix of trains and buses, as not all hill towns have rail service. Allow more time in your itinerary—bus service is spotty on weekends. For efficiency, consider taking regional minibus tours to the countryside from Florence or Siena.

To determine approximate travel times between destinations, study the driving map in the Practicalities chapter or check Google Maps; visit Trenitalia.it for train schedules. Compare the cost of any long train ride with a budget flight; check Skyscanner.com for intra-European flights.

## Write out a day-by-day itinerary.

Figure out how many destinations you can comfortably fit in your time frame. Don't overdo it—few travelers wish they'd hurried more. Allow enough days per stop (see estimates in

## Tuscany's Best 13 Days

| Day | Plan | Sleep |
|-----|------|-------|
| 1 | Arrive in Florence | Florence |
| 2-4 | Sightsee Florence | Florence |
| 5 | Bus to Siena (1.5 hours) | Siena |
| 6 | Siena | Siena |
| 7 | Rent car, drive Crete Senesi route to Montepulciano | Montepulciano |
| 8 | Take Heart of Tuscany Drive, with a stop in Pienza | Montepulciano |
| 9 | Take Brunello Wine Country Drive | Montepulciano |
| 10 | To San Gimignano for a short stop, then Volterra | Volterra |
| 11 | Volterra | Volterra |
| 12 | To Lucca, drop car | Lucca |
| 13 | Day-trip to Pisa by bus | Lucca |
|  | Fly home |  |

**Notes:** To rely solely on public transportation, modify this itinerary. On day 7, bus from Siena to Montalcino (stay here three nights). On day 8, take the Brunello Wine Bus tour. On day 9, day-trip by bus to Montepulciano or Pienza. On day 10, take the early bus from Montalcino to Volterra (transfer in Siena). Spend day 11 in Volterra; on day 12, bus to Lucca; and on day 13, day-trip to Pisa.

Drivers visiting the neighboring region of Umbria can easily stop in Cortona en route. If you'd prefer beach time, head to Elba from Montepulciano, then head to Lucca.

"Tuscany's Top Destinations," earlier). Minimize one-night stands. It can be worth taking a late-afternoon drive or train ride to settle into a town for two consecutive nights—and gain a full uninterrupted day for sightseeing. Include sufficient time for transportation; whether you travel by train, bus, or car, it'll take you a half-day to get between most destinations.

To get over jet lag, consider starting your trip in a smaller town (like Lucca or Siena) before tackling Florence.

Staying in a home base (like Florence) and making day trips can be more time-efficient than changing locations

and hotels. The relative compactness of Tuscany is a plus for day-tripping.

Take sight closures into account. Avoid visiting a town on the one day a week its must-see sights are closed. Check if any holidays or festivals fall during your trip—these attract crowds and can close sights (for the latest, visit Florence's tourist website, www.feelflorence.it). Note major sights where advance reservations are smart or a free Rick Steves audio tour is available.

Give yourself some slack. Every trip, and every traveler, needs downtime for doing laundry, picnic shopping, people-watching, and so on. Pace yourself. Assume you will return.

*Siena's Campo; Galileo Science Museum in Florence; hanging out in Lucca; pasta-making class*

## Trip Costs Per Person

Run a reality check on your dream trip. You'll have major transportation costs in addition to daily expenses.

**Flight:** A round-trip flight from the US to Florence costs about $900-1,500, depending on where you fly from and when.

**Public Transportation:** Most of compact Florence is walkable, but if you opt for taxis, allow at least $80-100 for a one-week visit (taxis can be shared by up to four people). Round-trip, second-class train transportation to nearby destinations is affordable (about $11 by train or bus to Pisa, Siena, or San Gimignano). You'll usually save money buying train tickets in Italy, rather than buying a rail pass before you leave home. For a one-way trip between Florence's airport and the city center, allow $2 by tram, $8 by bus, or $25 by taxi.

**Car Rental:** Allow $300-500 per week (booked well in advance), not including tolls, gas, parking, and insurance (theft insurance is mandatory in Italy).

AVERAGE DAILY EXPENSES PER PERSON

**$175**
Applies to cities, figure on less for towns

**Lodging**
Based on two people splitting the cost of a $180 double room with breakfast
**$90**

**Meals**
$15 for lunch, $30 for dinner, and $5 for gelato
**$50**

**City Transit**
Buses, trams, or taxis
**$10**

**Sights and Entertainment**
This daily average works for most people.
**$25**

## Budget Tips

To cut your daily expenses, take advantage of the deals you'll find throughout Tuscany and mentioned in this book.

In Florence, making advance reservations and purchasing combo-tickets will save you valuable time, and a little money too. For more tips specific to Florence, see the "Affordable Florence" sidebar in the next chapter. Throughout Tuscany, prioritize the sights you most want to see, and seek out free sights and experiences (people-watching counts). ▶▶▶

## Rick Steves Florence & Tuscany

▶▶▶ Some businesses—especially hotels and walking-tour companies—offer discounts to my readers (look for the RS% symbol in the listings in this book).

Reserve your rooms directly with the hotel. Some hotels offer a discount if you pay in cash and/or stay three or more nights (check online or ask). Rooms can cost less in spring and fall (April-June and Sept-Oct). And even seniors can sleep cheaply in hostels (most have private rooms) for about $30 per person.

Or check Airbnb-type sites for deals.

It's no hardship to eat inexpensively in Tuscany. You can get tasty, affordable meals at cafés, self-service cafeterias, sandwich shops, and pizzerias. Cultivate the art of picnicking in atmospheric settings.

When you splurge, choose an experience you'll always remember, such as a cooking class or concert. Minimize souvenir shopping; focus instead on collecting wonderful memories. ◼

*Reserve tickets for the Uffizi Gallery; join a walking tour in Florence; enjoy local food.*

## BEFORE YOU GO

You'll have a smoother trip if you tackle a few things ahead of time. For more details on these topics, see the Practicalities chapter and RickSteves.com, which has helpful travel-tip articles and videos.

**Make sure your travel documents are valid.** If your passport is due to expire within six months of your ticketed date of return, you need to renew it. Allow six weeks or more to renew or get a passport (www.travel.state.gov). Check for current Covid entry requirements, such as proof of vaccination or a negative Covid-19 test result.

**Arrange your transportation.** Book your international flights. Overall, Kayak.com is the best place to start searching for flights. You won't want a car in Florence (driving is prohibited in the city center), but if you'll be traveling beyond Florence, figure out your transportation options: bus or train (and either a rail pass or individual train tickets), rental car, or a cheap flight. (You can wing it in Europe, but it may cost more.) Drivers: Consider bringing an International Driving Permit (sold at AAA offices in the US, www.aaa.com) along with your license.

**Book rooms well in advance,** especially if your trip falls during peak season or any major holidays or festivals.

**Reserve ahead for key sights.** For Florence, consider reservations mandatory for the Uffizi Gallery (Renaissance paintings) and Accademia (Michelangelo's *David*). You'll also need a reservation for the Duomo's dome climb (make it when you buy the Duomo complex Brunelleschi Pass). If you want to climb Pisa's Leaning Tower, reserve up to 20 days in advance.

It's also good to book ahead for wine-tasting tours in the countryside, but generally one to two days ahead is sufficient.

**Consider travel insurance.** Compare the cost of insurance to the cost of your potential loss. Check whether your existing insurance (health, homeowners, or renters) covers you and your possessions overseas.

**Call your bank.** Alert your bank that you'll be using your debit and credit cards in Europe. Ask about transaction fees, and, if you don't already have one, get a "contactless" credit card (request your card PIN too). You don't need to bring euros for your trip; you can withdraw euros from cash machines in Europe.

**Use your smartphone smartly.** Sign up for an international service plan to reduce your costs, or rely on Wi-Fi in Europe instead. Download any apps you'll want on the road, such as maps, translators, transit schedules, and Rick Steves Audio Europe (see the sidebar).

**Pack light.** You'll walk with your luggage more than you think. I travel for weeks with a single carry-on bag and a day pack. Use the packing checklist in the appendix as a guide.

## Rick's Free Video Clips and Audio Tours

Travel smarter with these free, fun resources:

**Rick Steves Classroom Europe,** a powerful tool for teachers, is also useful for travelers. This video library contains about 500 short clips excerpted from my public television series. Enjoy these videos  as you sort through options for your trip and to better understand what you'll see in Europe. Check it out at Classroom. RickSteves.com (just enter a topic to find everything I've filmed on a subject).

**Rick Steves Audio Europe,** a free app, makes it easy to download my audio tours and listen to them offline as you travel. For this book (look for the Ω), these audio tours include my Renaissance Walk and  tours of the Accademia, Uffizi Gallery, Bargello, and Museum of San Marco in Florence, and my City Walk in Siena. The app also offers interviews from my public radio show with experts from Europe and around the globe. Find it in your app store or at RickSteves.com/AudioEurope.

# Travel Smart

If you have a positive attitude, equip yourself with good information (this book), and expect to travel smart, you will.

**Read—and reread—this book.** To have an "A" trip, be an "A" student. Note opening hours of sights, closed days, crowd-beating tips, and whether reservations are required or advisable. Check the latest at RickSteves.com/update. Saving Michelangelo's *David* for your trip finale is risky, and impossible on Mondays, when Florence's major sights are closed. If you visit Siena as a short day trip, you'll miss the city's medieval magic at twilight.

**Be your own tour guide.** As you travel, get up-to-date info on sights, reserve tickets and tours, reconfirm hotels and travel arrangements, and check transit connections. Visit local tourist information offices (TIs). Upon arrival in a new town, lay the groundwork for a smooth departure; confirm the train, bus, or road you'll take when you leave.

**Outsmart thieves.** Pickpockets abound in crowded places where tourists congregate. Treat commotions as smokescreens for theft. Keep your cash, credit cards, and passport secure in a money belt tucked under your clothes; carry only a day's spending money in your front pocket or wallet. Don't set valuable items down on counters or café tabletops, where they can be quickly stolen or easily forgotten.

**Minimize potential loss.** Keep expensive gear to a minimum. Bring copies or take photos of important documents (passport and cards) to aid in replacement if they're lost or stolen. Back up photos and files frequently.

**Beat the summer heat.** If you wilt easily, choose a hotel

## Florence's Top Spots

### Best Views

For panoramic views of the city's skyline, head to Piazzale Michelangelo and, above it, San Miniato Church. Within the city center, climb the Campanile (bell tower next to the Duomo), the Duomo's dome, or the tower at the Palazzo Vecchio. Or have a drink at a rooftop café.

### Best Outdoor Hangouts

The city's most atmospheric places include the main drag, Via dei Calzaiuoli, which connects the Duomo with the Palazzo Vecchio on Piazza della Signoria. Piazza della Repubblica is a more modern scene (usually with a fun carousel). Touristy by day, Ponte Vecchio (the old-time bridge) becomes romantic by lamplight at night.

### Best Escape from the City

Relax at the Boboli Gardens with a picnic. The hilly suburb of Fiesole is a fine place to catch the sunset and dinner, with a view of Florence. But your best escape is the Tuscan countryside, dotted with cypress trees and sprinkled with hill towns.

### Best Church Art

Many masterpieces still hang in the churches for which they were created. At Santa Maria Novella, you'll see Masaccio's *Trinity* and Giotto's magnificent *Crucifix;* Santo Spirito has a sculptural *Christ on the Cross* by a young Michelangelo; and the life of St. Francis is told in a Giotto fresco cycle in Santa Croce. In some churches, great artwork hides in dark side chapels; look for light boxes that you activate by depositing a euro coin or two. ▪

*Atop Florence's Duomo; Piazza della Signoria; Boboli Gardens; Santa Croce Church*

with air-conditioning, start your day early, take a midday siesta, and resume your sightseeing later. Churches offer a cool haven (though dress modestly—no bare shoulders or shorts). Take frequent gelato breaks. Join the *passeggiata*, when locals stroll in the cool of the evening.

**Guard your time and energy.** Taking a taxi can be a good value if it saves you a long wait for a cheap bus or an exhausting walk across town. To avoid long lines, follow my crowd-beating tips, such as making advance reservations, or sightseeing early or late.

**Be flexible.** Even if you have a well-planned itinerary, expect changes, strikes, closures, sore feet, bad weather, and so on. Your Plan B could turn out to be even better.

**Attempt the language.** Many Italians—especially in the tourist trade and in cities—speak English, but if you learn some Italian, even just a few pleasantries, you'll get more smiles and make more friends. Apps such as Google Translate work for on-the-go translation help, but you can get a head

*Join Florence's passeggiata—the evening stroll. Learn some Italian gestures, like the cheek screw (meaning good, beautiful, or clever).*

start by practicing the survival phrases near the end of this book.

**Connect with the culture.** Interacting with locals carbonates your experience. Enjoy the friendliness of the Italian people. Ask questions; most locals are happy to point you in their idea of the right direction. Set up your own quest for the best gelato, piazza, *enoteca* (wine bar), or Renaissance painting or sculpture. When an opportunity pops up, make it a habit to say "yes."

Tuscany...here you come!

uoli. This central axis—Duomo to the Palazzo Vecchio to the Arno River—is the spine for Florentine sightseeing and the route of my self-guided Renaissance Walk. To the west of this axis is a glitzy shopping zone, and to the east is a characteristic web of narrow lanes.

**Accademia/San Lorenzo** (North of the Duomo): The area north of the Duomo is less atmospheric but has several crucial sights. From the Duomo, Via Cavour runs north, bisecting the neighborhood. To the east lie the Accademia and the Museum of San Marco. The western part clusters around the Basilica of San Lorenzo, with its Medici Chapels. The area near San Lorenzo teems with tourists: There are the vendor stalls of San Lorenzo Market, the lively Mercato Centrale, and many hotels and trattorias that cater to out-of-towners—convenient, if not fully authentic.

**Train Station/Santa Maria Novella** (West of the Duomo): The area near the train station and Church of Santa Maria Novella is somewhat urban and dreary, but has inexpensive hotels and characteristic eateries. Closer to the river (near Palazzo Strozzi) is a posh shopping zone, with a more affordable mix of shops lining Via del Parione and Borgo Ognissanti.

**Santa Croce** (East of the Duomo): A 10-minute walk east from the Palazzo Vecchio leads to the neighborhood's main landmark, the Church of Santa Croce. Along the way is the Bargello sculpture museum. This neighborhood is congested with tourists by day (as cruise-ship buses use the nearby riverbank as their depot) and students partying by night. But the area stretching north and west from Santa Croce is increasingly authentic and workaday, offering a glimpse at untouristy Florence.

**Oltrarno** (South of the River): Literally the "Other Side of the Arno River," this neighborhood reveals a Florence from a time before tourism. Many artisans still have workshops here, and open their doors to passing visitors.

The Oltrarno starts just across Ponte Vecchio (jammed with tourists and tackiness) and stretches south to the giant Pitti Palace and surrounding gardens (Boboli and Bardini). To the west is the rough-but-bohemian Piazza di Santo Spirito (with its namesake church) and the lavishly frescoed Brancacci Chapel. To the east of Pitti, perched high on the hill, is Piazzale Michelangelo, with Florence's most popular viewpoint. Tucked between there and the river is the little San Niccolò neighborhood, with its lively bars and eateries.

**Farther Out:** Everything mentioned above is within about a 30-minute walk of the Duomo. To venture farther, one popular choice is the adjacent hilltop town of Fiesole, easily reached by public bus or taxi, with its archaeological sites and fine views.

ORIENTATION

# Florence Overview

To Airport

MERCATO CENTRALE

SAN LORENZO

To Museum of San Marco

CAVOUR

RICASOLI

ACCADEMIA (DAVID)

MAIN TRAIN STN.

CERRETANI

DUOMO

DUOMO MUSEUM

SANTA MARIA NOVELLA

AREA OF ANCIENT ROMAN TOWN →

Piazza della Repubblica

VIA DEI CALZAIUOLI

BARGELLO

PALAZZO VECCHIO

RITZY SHOPPING ZONE

Piazza della Signoria

SANTA CROCE

UFFIZI

PONTE VECCHIO

LUNGARNO

BRANCACCI CHAPEL

OLTRARNO

Arno River

SANTO SPIRITO

PITTI PALACE

GUICCIARDINI

SAN NICCOLO

To Piazzale Michelangelo

Not to Scale

Boboli Gardens

## PLANNING YOUR TIME

Set up a good itinerary in advance. Get the latest opening hours from the TI's website (see later). Use the "Daily Reminder" later in this chapter to plan which sights are open on which days. In general, Sundays and Mondays are not ideal for sightseeing, as many places are either closed or have shorter hours. Sights may also have shorter hours off-season.

Most importantly, use my strategies to avoid wasting hours in long lines. This is especially true for peak season (April-Oct), holidays and weekends, and for the big attractions—the Uffizi, Accademia, and Duomo complex. Make reservations well in advance for the first two (see the next chapter for details).

The following day plans are jam-packed but doable if you're well-organized. With more time, spread out these priorities to give yourself some breathing room. No matter how you plan your visit, unless you're here for only one day, do my Renaissance Walk (ideally, using the free audio version on my Rick Steves Audio Europe app), either in the morning or late afternoon to avoid heat and crowds.

## Florence in One Brutal Day

8:15    Uffizi Gallery (finest paintings)—with a reservation.

11:00   Bargello (great statues) or explore and shop San Lorenzo/Mercato Centrale area, lunch.

13:00   Renaissance Walk through heart of old town.

15:00   Duomo Museum (great bronze work).

17:30   Accademia *(David)*—with a reservation.

19:30   Cross Ponte Vecchio for dinner and Oltrarno Walk.

## Florence in Two Days
**Day 1**

9:00    Accademia—with a reservation.

10:30   Museum of San Marco (art by Fra Angelico).

12:00   Explore Mercato Centrale and have lunch nearby.

14:00   Tour Church of Santa Maria Novella for its art.

16:00   Free time (or tour Palazzo Vecchio).

18:00   Renaissance Walk through heart of old town.

20:00   Dinner in the old center.

**Day 2**

9:00    Bargello.

10:30   Duomo Museum (statues by Donatello and Michelangelo) or Galileo Science Museum (if art's not your thing).

12:30   Lunch, then wander and shop.

14:00   Take a walking tour.

16:30   Uffizi—with a reservation.

19:00   Cross Ponte Vecchio for dinner and Oltrarno Walk.

## Florence in Three (or More) Days
**Day 1**

9:00    Accademia—with a reservation.

10:30   Museum of San Marco.

| 12:00 | Medici Chapels (Michelangelo) or explore San Lorenzo Market area, have lunch near Mercato Centrale. |
| 14:00 | Basilica of San Lorenzo. |
| 16:00 | Free time or Baptistery and Duomo interior, or climb the dome (reservation required) or Campanile. |
| 18:00 | Renaissance Walk through heart of old town. |
| 20:00 | Dinner in the old center. |

**Day 2**

| 9:00 | Bargello. |
| 11:00 | Duomo Museum or Galileo Science Museum. |
| 13:00 | Lunch, then wander and shop. |
| 15:30 | Uffizi—with a reservation. |
| 18:00 | Cross Ponte Vecchio for dinner and Oltrarno Walk. |

**Day 3**

| 10:00 | Tour Church of Santa Maria Novella. |
| 12:00 | Free time for shopping and wandering. |
| 13:00 | Lunch. |
| 14:00 | Pitti Palace and gardens. |
| 17:00 | Tour Palazzo Vecchio or taxi to San Miniato Church and Piazzale Michelangelo (city views), walk back into town. |

**Day 4**

Side-trip to Siena (sights open daily; 1.5 hours away by bus or train).

# Overview

## TOURIST INFORMATION

The city TI's main branch is across the square from the **train station** (Mon-Sat 9:00-19:00, Sun until 14:00; at the back corner of the Church of Santa Maria Novella at Piazza della Stazione 4; +39 055 212 245, www.feelflorence.it). Museum hours in Florence are constantly changing. Check the TI's website or stop by and pick up a current timetable as you confirm your sightseeing plans.

A less crowded TI (covering both the city and the greater province of Florence) is a couple of blocks **north of the Duomo,** just past the Medici-Riccardi Palace (Mon-Fri 9:00-13:00, closed Sat-Sun, Via Cavour 1 red, +39 055 290 832). There's also a TI booth at the **airport.**

At any TI, you can pick up a city map. For goings-on around town, ask for a copy of *The Florentine* newspaper, which has great articles with cultural insights (in English, published monthly and updated online every other Thu at www.theflorentine.net).

## ARRIVAL IN FLORENCE

For a rundown on Florence's train, bus, and tram stations; airport; cruise ship arrival at the Livorno port; and information for drivers; see the Florence Connections chapter.

## HELPFUL HINTS

**Sightseeing Tips:** Everyone—and I mean everyone—visiting Florence wants to see the **Uffizi** and the **Accademia,** and  climb the Duomo's **dome.** It's flat out stupid to attempt a visit to any of these without a reservation. The process for making reservations is clearly explained in the next chapter.

As for the **Duomo** itself, anyone can wait in the long line to go inside—it's free to enter—but you can get in faster with one of the Duomo complex passes (covered in the next chapter). The only way to see the Baptistery, climb the Campanile, or climb the dome is with one of these passes. The Duomo Museum has no line concerns.

**Theft Alert:** Florence has hardworking gangs of thieves who hang out near the train station, the station's underpass (especially where the tunnel surfaces), around Mercato Centrale, and at major sights. American tourists are considered easy targets. Some thieves even dress like tourists to fool you. Any crowded bus likely holds at least one thief.

**Medical Help: Medical Service Firenze** provides 24/7 phone consults; they also do house calls in English or will see you at their walk-in clinic (clinic closed Sun—check website for hours, Via Roma 4, between the Duomo and Piazza della Repubblica, +39 055 475 411, www.medicalservice.firenze.it).

**Dr. Stephen Kerr** is an English doctor specializing in helping sick tourists (drop-in clinic open Mon-Fri 15:00-17:00, other times by appointment, Piazza Mercato Nuovo 1, between Piazza della Repubblica and Ponte Vecchio, +39 055 288 055, mobile +39 335 836 1682, www.dr-kerr.com). The TI has a list of other English-speaking doctors.

There are 24-hour **pharmacies** at the train station and near Palazzo Vecchio (at Via dei Calzaiuoli 7).

**Visiting Churches:** Modest dress is required in some churches, including the Duomo, Santa Maria Novella, Santa Croce, Santa Maria del Carmine/Brancacci Chapel, and the Medici Chapels (see page 663 for details). Be respectful of worshippers and the paintings; don't use a flash. Many churches, though

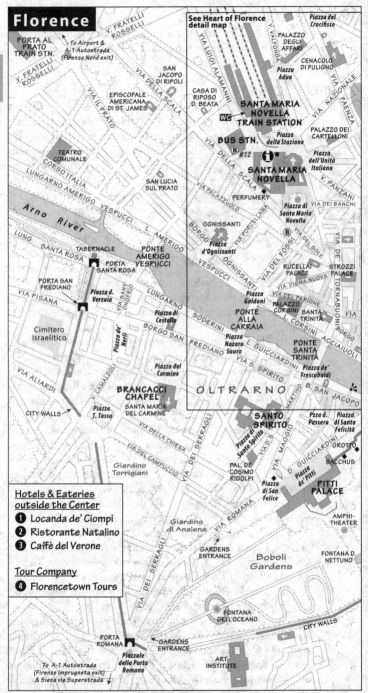

# Florence

See Heart of Florence detail map

**PORTA AL PRATO TRAIN STN.**

V. FRATELLI ROSSELLI

To Airport & A-1 Autostrada (Firenze Nord exit)

V. FRATELLI ROSSELLI

V. DELLA SCALA

SAN JACOPO DI RIPOLI

EPISCOPALE AMERICANA DI ST. JAMES

VIA IL PRATO

CASA DI RIPOSO D. BEATA

TEATRO COMUNALE

CORSO ITALIA

LUNGARNO AMERIGO VESPUCCI

SAN LUCIA SUL PRATO

VIA DELLA SCALA

VIA PALAZZUOLO

PERFUMERY

Piazza del Crocifisso

VIA VALFONDA

PALAZZO DEGLI AFFARI

CENACOLO DI FULIGNO

Piazza Adua

VIA LUIGI ALAMANNI

**SANTA MARIA NOVELLA TRAIN STATION**

WC

VIA NAZIONALE

VIA FAENZA

PALAZZO DEI CARTELLONI

**BUS STN.** B #12

Piazza della Stazione

i ■

Piazza dell'Unità Italiana

V. PANZANI

**SANTA MARIA NOVELLA**

VIA DEI BANCHI

Arno River

LUNG. SANTA ROSA

TABERNACLE

PORTA SANTA ROSA

**PONTE AMERIGO VESPUCCI**

L. AMERIGO

VIA SANT' ONOFRIO

LUNGARNO

VESPUCCI

OGNISSANTI

Piazza d'Ognissanti

BORGO OGNISSANTI

Piazza di Santa Maria Novella

VIA PORCELLANA

Piazza di Santa Maria Novella

B

VIA DEL SOLE

VIA DEL FOSSI

RUCELLAI PALACE

VIA VIGNA NUOVA

STROZZI PALACE

VIA DE' TORNABUONI

PORTA SAN FREDIANO

VIA PISANA

Piazza d. Verzaia

Cimitero Israelitico

VIA ALIARDI

CITY WALLS

Piazza de' Nerfi

Piazza di Cestello

BORGO SAN FREDIANO

SODERINI

LUNGARNO

L. GUICCIARDINI

Piazza Nazaro Sauro

VIA S. SPIRITO

Piazza Goldoni

PALAZZO CORSINI

**PONTE ALLA CARRAIA**

VIA DEL PARIONE

SANTA TRINITA

L. CORSINI

**PONTE SANTA TRINITA**

Piazza de' Frescobaldi

ACCIAIUOLI

BORGO

VIA

**BRANCACCI CHAPEL**

SANTA MARIA DEL CARMINE

Piazza del Carmine

Piazza T. Tasso

VIA CAMALDOLI

VIA DELLA CHIESA

VIA DEI SERRAGLI

**OLTRARNO**

B SAN JACOPO

V. MARTINO

**SANTO SPIRITO**

Piazza di Santo Spirito

Pzza d. Passera

Piazza di Santa Felicità

GROTTO

BACCHUS

VIA MAGGIO

VIA D. 9

D. GUICCIARDINI

Piazza di Pitti

**PITTI PALACE**

PAL. DE COSIMO RIDOLFI

Piazza di San Felice

Giardino Torrigiani

VIA DEL CAMPUCCIO

VIA ROMANA

Giardino di Analena

GARDENS ENTRANCE

AMPHI-THEATER

FONTANA D. NETTUNO

**Boboli Gardens**

ART INSTITUTE

FONTANA DELL'OCEANO

CITY WALLS

PORTA ROMANA

GARDENS ENTRANCE

Piazzale della Porta Romana

To A-1 Autostrada (Firenze Impruneta exit) & Siena via Superstrada

## Hotels & Eateries outside the Center

**1** Locanda de' Ciompi
**2** Ristorante Natalino
**3** Caffè del Verone

## Tour Company

**4** Florencetown Tours

ORIENTATION

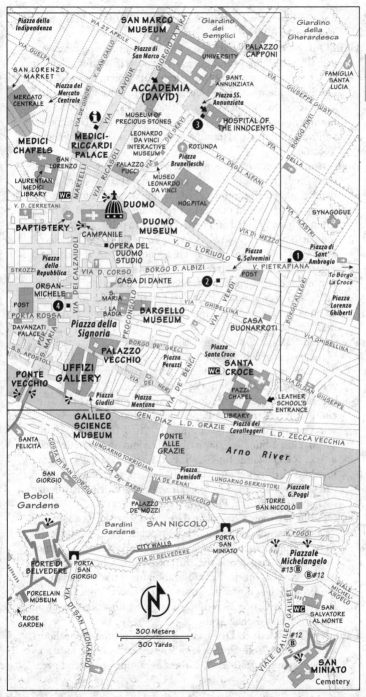

Piazza della Indipendenza

Giardino dei Semplici

Giardino della Gherardesca

VIA 27 APRILE

SAN MARCO MUSEUM

VIA GIORGIO LA PIRA

PALAZZO CAPPONI

VIA GUELFA

Piazza di San Marco

UNIVERSITY

V. SAN GALLO

VIA GIUSEPPE GIUSTI

FAMIGLIA SANTA LUCIA

SAN LORENZO MARKET

CAVOUR

SANT. ANNUNZIATA

ACCADEMIA (DAVID)

Piazza del Mercato Centrale

MERCATO CENTRALE

VIA DE' GINORI

Piazza SS. Annunziata

BORGO PINTI

HOSPITAL OF THE INNOCENTS

❸

MUSEUM OF PRECIOUS STONES

VIA DEI SERVI

MEDICI CHAPELS

MEDICI-RICCARDI PALACE

VIA RICASOLI

LEONARDO DA VINCI INTERACTIVE MUSEUM

ROTUNDA

DELLA

SAN LORENZO

Piazza Brunelleschi

VIA DEGLI ALFANI

LAURENTIAN MEDICI LIBRARY

MARTELLI

PALAZZO PUCCI

MUSEO LEONARDO DA VINCI

VIA PILASTRI

WC

V. D. CERRETANI

DUOMO

HOSPITAL

SYNAGOGUE

BAPTISTERY

CAMPANILE

DUOMO MUSEUM

VIA DI MEZZO

Piazza della Repubblica

OPERA DEL DUOMO STUDIO

V. D. L'ORIUOLO

Piazza G. Salvemini

V. PIETRAPIANA

Piazza di Sant' Ambrogio ❶

STROZZI

VIA D. CORSO

BORGO D. ALBIZI

POST

To Borgo La Croce

ORSANMICHELE

CASA DI DANTE

❷

VIA VERDI

Piazza Lorenzo Ghiberti

POST

VIA DEI CALZAIUOLI

S. MARIA LA BADIA

VIA GHIBELLINA

PORTA ROSSA

❹

PROCONSOLO

BARGELLO MUSEUM

CASA BUONARROTI

DAVANZATI PALACE

Piazza della Signoria

VIA GHIBELLINA

POR S. MARIA

S.S. APOSTOLI

PALAZZO VECCHIO

BORGO DE' GRECI

Piazza Peruzzi

Piazza Santa Croce

VIA PISAN

VIA GIUSEPPE

PONTE VECCHIO

UFFIZI GALLERY

VIA DEI NERI

SANTA CROCE

WC

Piazza Giudici

Piazza Mentana

VIA DE' BENCI

PAZZI CHAPEL

LEATHER SCHOOL'S ENTRANCE

GALILEO SCIENCE MUSEUM

GEN. DIAZ

L.D. GRAZIE

LIBRARY

Piazza dei Cavalleggeri

L.D. ZECCA VECCHIA

SANTA FELICITÀ

PONTE ALLE GRAZIE

Arno River

LUNGARNO TORRIGIANI

Piazza Demidoff

LUNGARNO SERRISTORI

COSTA DI SAN GIORGIO

VIA DE' BARDI

VIA DE' RENAI

Piazzale G. Poggi

SAN GIORGIO

Boboli Gardens

PALAZZO DE' MOZZI

VIA SAN NICCOLÒ

TORRE SAN NICCOLÒ

V. POGGI

Bardini Gardens

SAN NICCOLÒ

CITY WALLS

VIA DI BELVEDERE

PORTA SAN MINIATO

Piazzale Michelangelo
#13 Ⓑ Ⓑ#12

FORTE DI BELVEDERE

PORTA SAN GIORGIO

VIALE MICHELANGELO

PORCELAIN MUSEUM

VIA DI SAN LEONARDO

WC

SAN SALVATORE AL MONTE

ROSE GARDEN

N

Ⓑ #12

300 Meters

300 Yards

VIALE GALILEO GALILEI

SAN MINIATO Cemetery

not the biggies we mention, close from 12:00 or 12:30 until 15:00 or 16:00.

**Chill Out:** Schedule several breaks into your sightseeing when you can sit, pause, cool off, and refresh yourself with a gelato or coffee. Carry a water bottle to refill at Florence's twist-the-handle public fountains (around the corner from the "Piglet" at Mercato Nuovo, or in front of the Pitti Palace). Try the *fontanello* (dispenser of free cold water) on Piazza della Signoria, behind the statue of Neptune (on the left side of the Palazzo Vecchio).

**Addresses:** Florence has a confusing system for street addresses, with "red" numbers for businesses and "black" (sometimes blue) numbers for residences, though the red numbers are slowly being phased out. Street signs are indeed red or black (though usually faded and hard to read); in print, addresses are indicated with "r" (as in Via Cavour 2r) or "n" (for black—*nero*, as in Via Cavour 25n). Red and black numbers are interspersed together on the same street; each set goes in roughly consecutive order, but their numbers bear no connection with each other. I'm lazy and don't concern myself with the distinction (if one number's wrong, I look nearby for the other) and easily find my way around.

**Pedestrian Safety:** Once nightmarish for pedestrians, the city is increasingly delightful on foot, though even in traffic-free zones delivery trucks and nearly silent hybrid taxis nudge their way through crowds. Stay alert as you walk.

**Bookstores:** For a good selection of brand-name guidebooks (including mine), try these: **Paperback Exchange** has the widest selection of English books, new and used (Mon-Sat 10:00-19:00, closed Sun, just south of the Duomo on Via delle Oche 4 red). **RED** (stands for "Read, Eat, Dream"), a flagship store for the Feltrinelli chain (the Italian Barnes & Noble) with a café and restaurant, has a small selection of English books (daily 9:00-20:00, on Piazza della Repubblica).

**WCs:** Public restrooms are scarce. Use them when you can, in any café or museum you patronize. Pay public WCs are typically €1. Convenient locations include: at the Baptistery ticket office (near the Duomo); near the entrance to the Church of Santa Maria Novella; inside the train station (near track 5 and in the food court); just down the street from Piazza Santa Croce (at Borgo Santa Croce 29 red); on Piazza Santo Spirito; and up near Piazzale Michelangelo.

**Laundry:** The **Wash & Dry Lavarapido** chain offers long hours and efficient, self-service launderettes at several locations (generally daily 7:30-23:00). These locations are close to rec-

**ORIENTATION**

ommended hotels: Via del Sole 29 red and Via della Scala 52 red (this location is a Speed Queen, between train station and river), and Via Ghibellina 143 red (Palazzo Vecchio). On the Oltrarno side, there's one at Via dei Serragli 87 red (Santo Spirito area).

**Bike Rental:** I don't recommend biking in the city as it's so jam-packed with pedestrians. But if you must, **Florence by Bike** rents two-wheelers of all sizes (€12/day and up depending on type of bike, includes bike lock and helmet; Mon-Sat 9:00-13:00 & 15:30-19:30, Sun until 15:00, closed Sun Nov-March; a 15-minute walk north of the Duomo at Via San Zanobi 54 red, +39 055 488 992, www.florencebybike.it).

**Travel Agencies:** Travel agencies can be helpful for getting both domestic and international tickets and reservations. Convenient travel agencies in the town center are **Intertravel Viaggi** (Mon-Fri 9:00-12:00 & 14:00-17:00, closed Sat-Sun, south of Piazza della Repubblica at Via de Lamberti 39 red, +39 055 280 706) and **Florentour** (Mon-Fri 9:30-13:30, closed Sat-Sun, Via dei Servi 23 red, a block off the Duomo, +39 055 292 237). For locations of both, see the map on page 58.

## GETTING AROUND FLORENCE

I organize my sightseeing geographically and do it all on foot. I think of Florence as a Renaissance tread-mill—it requires a lot of walking. You likely won't need public transit, except maybe to head up to Piazzale Michelangelo and San Miniato Church for the view, or to Fiesole. For major bus and tram stop locations, see the map on page 58.

### By Bus

The city's full-size buses don't cover the old center well (the whole area around the Duomo is off-limits to motorized traffic). Pick up a map of transit routes at the bus station; you'll also find routes online (www.at-bus.it/it/orari).

Buy bus tickets at tobacco shops *(tabacchi)*, newsstands, or tram stops (€1.50/90 minutes). Be sure to validate your ticket in the machine on board (or risk a steep fine). Do this as you board, otherwise you're cheating. Inspectors fine even innocent-looking tourists €50. You can sometimes buy a ticket on board, but you'll pay more and may need exact change. Follow general bus etiquette: Board at front or rear doors, exit out the center.

ORIENTATION

# Daily Reminder

**Sunday:** The Mercato Centrale is closed (except the upstairs food court) as are the Duomo, the Basilica of San Lorenzo, and the Museum of San Marco. The Bargello closes on the second and fourth Sundays of the month and the Medici Chapels and Palazzo Davanzati close on the first, third, and fifth Sundays.

A few sights are open only in the afternoon: the Duomo's dome (12:45-16:30), Santa Croce Church (12:30-17:30), Brancacci Chapel (13:00-17:00), and Church of Santa Maria Novella (13:00-17:30).

**Monday:** The biggies are closed, including the Accademia and the Uffizi, as well as the Pitti Palace sights and the Palazzo Davanzati. The Pitti Palace's Boboli and Bardini Gardens close on the first and last Mondays of each month; the Bargello is closed on the first, third, and fifth Mondays; and the Museum of San Marco closes on the second and fourth Mondays.

Target these sights on Mondays: the Duomo, Duomo Museum, Campanile, Baptistery, Medici-Riccardi Palace, Brancacci Chapel, Mercato Nuovo, Mercato Centrale, Casa Buonarroti, Galileo Science Museum, the Palazzo Vecchio, and churches (including Santa Croce and Santa Maria Novella). Or take a walking tour.

**Tuesday:** Casa Buonarroti, the Brancacci Chapel, and the Medici

Of the many bus lines, I find these to be of most value for seeing outlying sights such as Piazzale Michelangelo or Fiesole, a small town with big views of Florence:

Bus **#12** goes from near Piazza d'Ognissanti, over the Carraia bridge to Porta Romana, then up to San Miniato Church and Piazzale Michelangelo (3/hour). Bus **#13** makes the return trip down the hill.

Bus **#7** goes from the Largo Alinari stop across from the train station (near McDonald's) to Fiesole.

The train station and Piazza San Marco are two major hubs near the city center; to get between these two, either walk (about 15 minutes) or take bus #1 or #6 (from side of station), or #23 (from front of station); from San Marco, buses heading toward the station leave from the front of the monastery or around the corner on Via Cavour.

Fun little **minibuses** (many of them electric—*elettrico*) wind through the tangled old center of town and up and down the river—just €1.50 gets you a 1.5-hour joyride. These buses, which run every 10 minutes from 7:00 to 21:00 (less frequent on Sun), are popular with sore-footed sightseers and eccentric local seniors. The minibuses also connect many major parking lots with the historic center (buy tickets from machines at lots).

Chapels are closed. The Duomo Museum is closed on the first Tuesday of the month. The Galileo Science Museum closes early (13:00).

**Wednesday:** The Medici-Riccardi Palace and Brancacci Chapel are closed.

**Thursday:** The Brancacci Chapel is closed and the Palazzo Vecchio closes early (14:00).

**Friday:** All sights are open, but the Duomo's dome closes earlier than usual (17:15).

**Saturday:** All sights are open except the Basilica of San Lorenzo, and the Duomo's dome closes earlier than usual (16:30).

**Early Closing Warning:** Some of Florence's sights close surprisingly early, as early as 14:00 for the following sights—the Bargello (later for special exhibits), Palazzo Vecchio (on Thu), Palazzo Davanzati (Tue-Thu, open later Fri-Sun), and the Museum of San Marco (on weekdays only, open later Sat). Mercato Centrale's lower level closes at 14:00 (except on Sat, when it stays open until 17:00).

For all sights, be advised the last entry is usually 30 to 60 minutes before posted closing times.

Bus **#C1** stops behind the Palazzo Vecchio and Piazza Santa Croce, then heads north, passing near San Marco and the Accademia before heading up to Piazza Libertà. On its southbound route, this bus also stops near the train station, the Basilica of San Lorenzo, and the Duomo.

Bus **#C2**, if operating, twists through the congested old center from the train station, passing near Piazza della Repubblica and Piazza della Signoria to Piazza Beccaria.

Bus **#C3** goes up and down the Arno River, with stops near Piazza Santa Croce, Ponte Vecchio, the Carraia bridge to the Oltrarno (including the Pitti Palace), and beyond.

Bus **#C4** goes from near the Duomo to the train station, crosses the Carraia bridge, and cruises through the Oltrarno (passing the Pitti Palace) before heading into the San Niccolò neighborhood.

### By Tram

The T1 and T2 tram lines are cheap, easy, and frequent. For travelers, they're generally most useful for service between the airport (T2) or the big park-and-ride lots at Villa Costanza (T1) near the town of Scandicci to the train station (€1.50, 25 minutes; www.gestramvia.com; see the Florence Connections chapter for map and more details). The T1 line from Villa Costanza is a great option for day-trippers coming from southern Tuscany.

## By Taxi

The minimum cost for a taxi ride is about €7 (more after 22:00 and on Sun); rides in the center of town should be charged as tariff #1. The flat rate for the airport is €22 plus €1 per bag if the driver puts them in the trunk (also more on nights and weekends). Taxi fares and supplements (e.g., €2 extra to call a cab rather than hail one) are clearly explained on signs in each taxi. Look for an official, regulated cab (white; marked with *Taxi/Comune di Firenze*, red fleur-de-lis, and one of the official phone numbers: 4390 or 4242). Before getting in a cab at a stand or on the street, ask for an approximate cost (*"Più o meno, quanto costa?"* pew oh MEH-noh, KWAHN-toh KOH-stah). If you can't get a straight answer or the price is outrageous, wait for the next one. It can be hard to find a cab on the street, but they stop and sometimes wait in taxi ranks near the major tourist sights (marked by orange *Taxi* signs). To call one, dial +39 055 4390 or +39 055 4242 (or ask your waiter or hotelier to call for you). Uber does not operate in Florence.

# Tours in Florence

For extra insight with a personal touch, consider the tour companies and individual Florentine guides listed here. Hardworking and creative, they offer a worthwhile array of organized sightseeing activities. Many tour companies (such as Florencetown) offer regularly scheduled group tours that anyone can sign up for. This is usually the cheapest option for individual travelers. But families and small groups can book a private guide for a similar price (since rates are hourly for any size of group).

Some tour companies offer bus excursions that go out to smaller towns in the Tuscan countryside. The most popular day trips are Siena, San Gimignano, Pisa, and into Chianti country for wine tasting. To see Florence itself, it's clearly best on foot.

Since traffic restrictions keep buses out of the center, hop-on, hop-off bus tours make no sense. Vespa and classic-car tours are dangerous for rookie drivers, and companies reportedly make more money off of tourists paying for dents than the actual service.

⌂ To sightsee on your own, download my **free audio tours** that illuminate some of Florence's top sights and neighborhoods.

# Affordable Florence

Follow these sightseeing and eating tips to stretch your euro:

## Sightseeing

**Free Sights:** There is no entry charge for the Duomo, Santo Spirito, and San Miniato churches. It's free to visit the leather school at Santa Croce Church and the perfumery near the Church of Santa Maria Novella. The three markets (Centrale for produce, San Lorenzo and Nuovo for goods) are fun to browse.

**Free Public Spaces:** Visit courtyards at the Uffizi, Palazzo Vecchio (with a small exhibit of historic maps and scenes of old Florence), Medici-Riccardi Palace, and Palazzo Strozzi; the art-filled loggia on Piazza della Signoria; the quintessentially Renaissance square Piazza Santissima Annunziata; and Piazzale Michelangelo, with glorious views over Florence. A walk across the picturesque Ponte Vecchio costs nothing at all, and a stroll anywhere with a gelato in hand is an inexpensive treat.

**Free Music:** In the evening, street musicians often perform on the Piazza della Signoria and Ponte Vecchio.

## Dining

**Don't Over Order:** Servings are often big—and splittable. While restaurants frown on a couple splitting just one dish, if you order a selection and enjoy them family-style, you can sample several things, save some euros, and still have room for gelato.

**Grab-and-Go Food:** Takeaway sandwich shops and food carts abound in Florence's old center, making it easy to grab a €4-5 lunch to enjoy on a picturesque piazza. Or order takeout from delis. Many shops have ready-to-eat entrées and side dishes, and will heat them up and provide plastic cutlery and napkins.

**Aperitivo Happy Hour:** For a cheap, light dinner, head to an *aperitivo* happy hour. All over town, bars—many of them very elegant with fine views—attract customers with free little buffets of light bites. Buy a drink, and make it a meal—a practice locals call *"apericena"* (combining the word *aperitivo* with *cena*—dinner). For a €10 cocktail or glass of wine, you'll enjoy a light meal for no extra charge.

# WALKING TOURS

While I've outlined the general offerings for each company, check their websites or pick up their brochures for other tour options and to confirm specific times and prices.

Many also offer food tours (see the end of this section) and cooking classes, sometimes including a shopping trip to pick up ingredients at a local market. This can be fun, educational, efficient (combining a meal with a "sightseeing" experience)...and delicious. For more on cooking classes, see page 321.

## Artviva

Artviva offers an intriguing variety of tours (guided by native English speakers). Popular choices include their small-group overview tour ("Original Florence" 3-hour town walk); and private tours including "Florence in One Glorious Day," which combines the town walk and tours of the Uffizi and Accademia (6 hours total). They also have standalone Uffizi and Accademia tours, cooking classes, art classes, food tours, tours around Tuscany and to the Cinque Terre, and more (RS%—10 percent discount with this book, use the password "reader"; +39 055 264 5033, www.artviva.com).

## Florencetown

This company offers English-language tours and experiences on foot or by bike. Their most popular offerings are "Walk and Talk Florence" (€35, 2.5 hours, April-Oct daily at 10:00 and 15:00, basic stops including the Oltrarno) and "I Bike Florence" (€39; 3 hours on one-speed bike, 15-stop blitz of town's top sights, helmets optional; in bad weather it goes as a walking tour). They also offer cooking classes and wine tours. Their booking office is at Piazza Mentana (see "Florence" map earlier in this chapter); they also have a "Tourist Point" kiosk on Piazza della Repubblica, under the arches at the corner with Via Pellicceria (RS%, +39 055 281 103, www.florencetown.com).

## Florentia

Top-notch private walking tours—geared for thoughtful, well-heeled travelers with longer-than-average attention spans—are led by Florentine scholars. The tours range from introductory city walks and museum visits to in-depth thematic walks, such as the Oltrarno, Jewish Florence, or the Medici dynasty; they also offer family-oriented tours (€250 and up, includes planning assistance by email, www.florentia.net).

## Context Florence

This scholarly group of graduate students and professors leads small-group or private "walking seminars," such as a 3.5-hour study of Michelangelo's work and influence and a two-hour evening orientation stroll. See their website for pricing and other innovative offerings: Medici walk, family tours, private fresco workshop, and more (www.contexttravel.com).

## Walks Inside Florence

Two art historians—Paola Barubiani and Francesco Calanca—and their 15 partners provide quality private tours at a discounted rate for my readers (RS%—€200/group for three-hour intro tour, up to 6 people). Their "Florence in a Day" tour gives you the essentials in four hours (€265/group, up to 6 people, museum admissions extra—they make the reservations so there's no waiting in line; tour starts at the Accademia, follows with a historic town walk, and finishes at the Uffizi, leaving you inside after a tour of the highlights). Other offerings are described on their website (e.g., shopping tour featuring select artisans, guided evening walk, and cruise excursions from the port of Livorno; +39 333 483 1431, www.walksinsideflorence.it).

## Exclusive Connection

This smart, high-end, and well-connected agency offers an impressive list of services in Florence and around Italy, including specialized tours and museum bookings. Both Lucia Montuschi and Cora Ferroni have a passion for history, art, and culture, and love sharing it with visitors (+39 055 200 1586, www.exclusiveconnection.it).

## Food Tours of Florence

Most tour companies (including Florencetown) offer food tours, as do countless food lovers who simply offer their services on various online-booking sites. Typically, tours last 3-4 hours and make 5-6 stops as you walk, munch, and learn with small groups of 6-8 people (a natural limit since hole-in-the-wall bakeries and wine bars are tiny). I enjoy Toni Mazzaglia's **Taste Florence Food Tours.** A native of North Carolina, Toni's been in Florence for 20 years, and does a fine tour in and around the Mercato Centrale ($109, RS%, most days at 10:00, 4 hours, 6 stops, www.tasteflorence.com).

## LOCAL GUIDES

**Vanessa Garau** is an enthusiastic young guide with good connections in the Oltrarno and an infectious love of Florence (half-day private tours for €180, +39 349 133 6894, garau.vanessa@gmail.com).

**Alessandra Marchetti,** a Florentine who has lived in the US, gives private walking tours of Florence and driving tours of Tuscany. Her passion is Michelangelo (from €60-85/hour, +39 347 386 9839, www.tuscanydriverguide.com, alessandramarchettitours@gmail.com).

**Paola Migliorini** and her partners offer museum tours, city walking tours, family tours, private cooking classes, wine tours,

ORIENTATION

and Tuscan excursions by van—you can tailor tours as you like (€65/hour without car, €70/hour in a van for up to 8 passengers, minimum 3 hours, +39 347 657 2611, www.florencetour.com). They also do cruise excursions from the port of Livorno (€600/up to 4 people, €680/up to 6, €780/up to 8).

**Elena Fulceri,** specializing in art, history, and secret corners and gardens, is a delightful and engaging guide. She organizes tailor-made private tours, has good Oltrarno artisan connections, and enjoys family tours (from €60/hour for 2 people, +39 347 942 2054, www.florencewithflair.com).

# SIGHTS IN FLORENCE

In this chapter, some of Florence's most important sights have the shortest listings and are marked with a 📖. That's because they are covered in much more detail in one of the self-guided walks or tours included in this book. A 🎧 means the walk or tour is available as a free audio tour (via my Rick Steves Audio Europe app—see page 24). Some walks and tours are available in both formats—take your pick.

For general tips on sightseeing, see the Practicalities chapter. Remember to check RickSteves.com/update for any significant changes that have occurred since this book was printed.

**Opening Hours:** Check opening hours carefully online and plan your time well. Many museums have erratic hours (for example, closing on alternating Sundays and Mondays), and Florence—more than most cities—has a tendency to change these hours from season to season.

**Avoid Free-Entry Crowds:** For most of the year, state museums are free on the first Sunday of each month (no reservations are available). In Florence, this includes the Uffizi Gallery, Accademia (Michelangelo's *David*), Pitti Palace and gardens, and the Bargello. Free days are actually bad news—they attract crowds, especially at the Uffizi and Accademia. Make a point to avoid these days.

## ADVANCE RESERVATIONS AND SIGHTSEEING PASSES

While mobs of visitors line up for (literally) hours throughout the year to ogle *David* in the Accademia, tour the Uffizi Gallery, and climb the Duomo's dome, the rest of the city is easy without reservations.

Consider reservations mandatory for the **Uffizi** and **Accademia.** For the **Duomo complex** (cathedral, cathedral crypt,

SIGHTS

# Florence at a Glance

▲▲▲**Accademia** Michelangelo's *David* and powerful (unfinished) *Prisoners*. Reserve ahead. **Hours:** Tue-Sun 9:00-19:00, closed Mon, may stay open later in peak season. See page 57.

▲▲▲**Uffizi Gallery** Greatest collection of Italian paintings anywhere. Reserve well in advance. **Hours:** Tue-Sun 8:15-18:30, closed Mon, may stay open later in peak season. See page 71.

▲▲▲**Bargello** Underappreciated sculpture museum (Michelangelo, Donatello, Medici treasures). **Hours:** Daily 8:15-14:00; may close on second and fourth Sun and first, third, and fifth Mon of each month. See page 76.

▲▲▲**Duomo Museum** Freshly renovated cathedral museum with the finest in Florentine sculpture. **Hours:** Daily 9:00-19:45, closed first Tue of each month. See page 57.

▲▲▲**Pitti Palace** Several museums in lavish palace plus sprawling Boboli and Bardini Gardens. **Hours:** Palatine Gallery, Royal Apartments, Treasury, Museum of Costume and Fashion, and Gallery of Modern Art open Tue-Sun 8:15-18:50, closed Mon; Boboli and Bardini Gardens, and Porcelain Museum open daily June-Aug 8:15-19:00, April-May and Sept-Oct until 18:30, Nov-March until 16:30; closed first and last Mon of each month. See page 79.

▲▲**Duomo** Gothic cathedral with colorful facade and the first dome built since ancient Roman times. **Hours:** Mon-Sat 10:15-16:45, closed Sun. See page 53.

▲▲**Museum of San Marco** Best collection anywhere of artwork by the early Renaissance master Fra Angelico. **Hours:** Mon-Fri 8:15-14:00, Sat until 17:00, closed Sun; also closed second and fourth Mon of each month. See page 61.

▲▲**Medici Chapels** Tombs of Florence's great ruling family, designed and carved by Michelangelo. **Hours:** Sat-Mon 8:15-13:50, Wed-Fri 13:15-18:50; closed Tue and first, third, and fifth Sun of each month. See page 65.

▲▲**Palazzo Vecchio** Fortified palace, once the home of the Medici family, wallpapered with history. **Hours:** Museum and excavations open daily 9:00-19:00 except Thu until 14:00; shorter hours off-season; shorter hours for tower. See page 72.

▲▲**Galileo Science Museum** Fascinating old clocks, telescopes, maps, and three of Galileo's fingers. **Hours:** Daily 9:30-18:00 except Tue until 13:00. See page 73.

**▲▲Santa Croce Church** Precious art, tombs of famous Florentines, and Brunelleschi's Pazzi Chapel in 14th-century church. **Hours:** Mon-Sat 9:30-17:30, Sun from 12:30. See page 77.

**▲▲Church of Santa Maria Novella** Thirteenth-century Dominican church with Masaccio's famous 3-D painting. **Hours:** Mon-Thu and Sat 10:00-17:00, Fri from 11:00, Sun from 13:00. See page 78.

**▲▲Brancacci Chapel** Works of Masaccio, early Renaissance master who reinvented perspective. **Hours:** Fri-Sat and Mon 10:00-17:00, Sun from 13:00, closed Tue-Thu. See page 81.

**▲▲San Miniato Church** Sumptuous Renaissance chapel and sacristy showing scenes of St. Benedict. **Hours:** Daily 9:30-13:00 & 15:00-19:00, closed sporadically for special occasions. See page 83.

**▲Climbing the Duomo's Dome** Grand view into the cathedral, close-up of dome architecture, and, after 463 steps, a glorious city vista. Reservations required. **Hours:** Mon-Fri 8:15-19:30, Sat until 17:15, Sun 12:45-16:30. See page 55.

**▲Campanile** Bell tower with views similar to Duomo's, 50 fewer steps, and shorter lines. **Hours:** Daily 8:15-19:45. See page 56.

**▲Baptistery** Bronze doors fit to be the gates of paradise. **Hours:** Doors always viewable; interior open daily 9:00-19:45. See page 56.

**▲Piazza Santissima Annunziata** Lovely square epitomizing Renaissance harmony, with Brunelleschi's Hospital of the Innocents, considered the first Renaissance building. See page 60.

**▲Medici-Riccardi Palace** Lorenzo the Magnificent's home, with fine art, frescoed ceilings, and Gozzoli's lovely Chapel of the Magi. **Hours:** Thu-Tue 9:00-19:00, closed Wed. See page 66.

**▲Ponte Vecchio** Famous bridge lined with gold and silver shops. See page 73.

**▲Piazzale Michelangelo** Hilltop square with stunning view of Duomo and Florence, with San Miniato Church just uphill. See page 82.

dome, Baptistery, Campanile, and Duomo Museum), the easy answer is to enjoy the complex from the outside and only go into the magnificent museum (with one of three Duomo passes—described later—which you can generally buy at the entrance with no serious line). To climb the Duomo's dome, you'll need a pass and a reservation.

Some of Florence's **other major sights**—including the Bargello, Medici Chapels, Pitti Palace, Museum of San Marco, and Medici Chapels—offer reservations, but they're generally not necessary. (A couple places require advance reservations even with no crowds.)

**Uffizi and Accademia Tickets:** To book your timed-entry tickets in advance for both of these museums, simply go to the **official website** at www.b-ticket.com/b-Ticket/uffizi and follow the prompts.

If there's no availability at this site, you can try **for-profit vendors** such as Florence.net or Tickitaly.com, which may have time slots available, though you'll pay about €5 more per ticket. Various private companies—including those listed on page 44—sell tours that include a reserved museum entry. If you're booking a private guide well in advance, they are often happy to obtain tickets and reservations for your tour with them.

If you show up in Florence without reservations, **Opera Your Preview** is a handy little ticket office that can book for you in-person what most will just do online (Uffizi and Accademia only, €4/museum extra, daily 10:00-17:45, 50 yards before Ponte Vecchio on Via Por Santa Maria, www.operayourpreview.com).

The ticket office at the **Orsanmichele Church** is another place to make reservations for the Uffizi and Accademia (Mon-Sat 9:00-16:00, closed Sun).

**Uffizi/Pitti Palace/Boboli Gardens Combo-Ticket:** This pass, officially called "PassePartout," is valid for five consecutive days and offers admission to these sights at a €12 savings (€38 March-Oct, €18 Nov-Feb, requires Uffizi reservation). Purchase the pass in advance at www.b-ticket.com/b-Ticket/uffizi.

**Duomo Complex Tickets**: See the next section.

## THE DUOMO COMPLEX

Florence's most distinctive monuments—the Duomo (cathedral), Baptistery, and Campanile—are gathered around the pedestrian-only Piazza del Duomo. Just behind the Duomo, the excellent

Duomo Museum holds many of the original treasures from these monuments. The Duomo complex also includes the crypt beneath the cathedral and the dome climb.

📖 The Renaissance Walk chapter and my 🎧 free audio tour connect the Duomo sights.

**Duomo Complex Tickets:** Three passes (named for the artists Ghiberti, Giotto, and Brunelleschi) cover the various Duomo sights. The cathedral itself is free to enter, but has extremely long lines to get in. The only way to avoid these lines is to buy one of the passes: They all include the cathedral's crypt, which has a separate entrance into the church with short lines.

The Duomo's dome climb can only be done with a reservation, which you get when you buy the Brunelleschi Pass. The Campanile, the Baptistery, and the Duomo Museum—the most important of these sights—never have long lines but require a pass (which you can easily buy at the Duomo Museum door).

The easiest approach: View everything from the outside and only go into the Duomo Museum. For anything more than that, sort through these three passes (each good for 3 days):

*Ghiberti Pass:* €15; includes entrance to the cathedral via the crypt (shorter line, near the Campanile), the crypt in the church, the Baptistery, and the Duomo Museum (no timed reservations required, just establish the first day).

*Giotto Pass:* €20; includes everything in the Ghiberti Pass plus the Campanile (having this pass is the only way to go up the tower).

*Brunelleschi Pass:* €30; includes everything in the Giotto Pass, plus a timed entry to climb the Duomo's dome (this is the only way to climb the dome). You'll choose your time slot when you buy the pass.

**Booking in Advance:** To arrive in Florence with your Duomo complex pass already in hand, book online at www.museumflorence.com. You'll get a bar code that you can print out or download to your phone to show at each automated entry.

SIGHTS

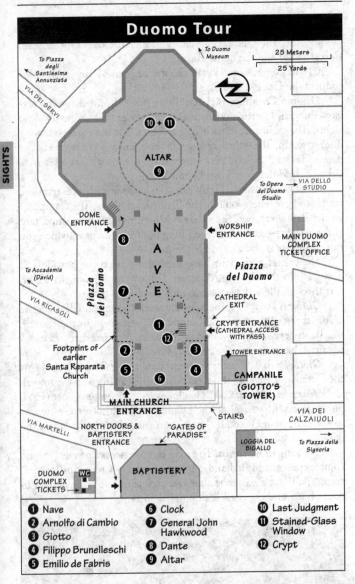

# Duomo Tour

To Duomo Museum

25 Meters
25 Yards

To Piazza degli Santissima Annunziata

VIA DEI SERVI

10 + 11

ALTAR

9

To Opera del Duomo Studio

VIA DELLO STUDIO

DOME ENTRANCE

WORSHIP ENTRANCE

MAIN DUOMO COMPLEX TICKET OFFICE

8

N A V E

Piazza del Duomo

Piazza del Duomo

To Accademia (David)

VIA RICASOLI

7

CATHEDRAL EXIT

1

CRYPT ENTRANCE (CATHEDRAL ACCESS WITH PASS)

12

TOWER ENTRANCE

Footprint of earlier Santa Reparata Church

2

3

5

4

CAMPANILE (GIOTTO'S TOWER)

6

VIA DEI CALZAIUOLI

MAIN CHURCH ENTRANCE

STAIRS

VIA MARTELLI

NORTH DOORS & BAPTISTERY ENTRANCE

"GATES OF PARADISE"

LOGGIA DEL BIGALLO

To Piazza della Signoria

DUOMO COMPLEX TICKETS

WC

BAPTISTERY

| | | |
|---|---|---|
| ❶ Nave | ❻ Clock | ❿ Last Judgment |
| ❷ Arnolfo di Cambio | ❼ General John Hawkwood | ⓫ Stained-Glass Window |
| ❸ Giotto | ❽ Dante | ⓬ Crypt |
| ❹ Filippo Brunelleschi | ❾ Altar | |
| ❺ Emilio de Fabris | | |

**Ticket Offices:** While it's easy to book your pass online, passes are also sold at three offices near the cathedral. The main ticket office faces the Campanile entrance (at #14 on the square, staffed counter; daily 8:00-19:00). There are also ticket counters in the Duomo Museum lobby and opposite the Baptistery (at #7). Some offices also have self-service machines (cash and credit card).

### ▲▲Duomo (Cattedrale di Santa Maria del Fiore)

Florence's Gothic cathedral has the third-longest nave in Christendom. The church's noisy Neo-Gothic facade (from the 1870s) is covered with pink, green, and white Tuscan marble. The cathedral's claim to artistic fame is Brunelleschi's magnificent dome—the first Renaissance dome and *the* model for domes to follow. While viewing the Duomo from the outside is well worth ▲▲, the massive but empty-feeling interior is lucky to rate ▲—it doesn't justify the massive crowds that line up to get inside.

**Cost and Hours:** Free to enter the cathedral, Duomo complex pass required for crypt; open Mon-Sat 10:15-16:45, closed Sun; open hours sometimes change due to religious functions, modest dress code enforced, +39 055 230 2885, www.museumflorence.com.

**Lines:** Because the church is free, lines to get in can be very long. Buy a pass to avoid them by entering through the crypt.

**Mass:** The church is open to all for Mass: English Mass on Sun at 17:00 and old-school Latin Mass with Gregorian chants on Sun at 10:30.

**❷ Self-Guided Tour:** Enter the Duomo (from Latin *domus*, as it's the "house" of God) and make your way to the nave (if you entered through the crypt, it's up the stairs).

Survey the huge **❶ nave**—it's 500 feet long and 300 feet wide. The structural elements are unabashedly highlighted by the gray stone and cream-colored filling. While the dome is famously Renaissance, the church itself is medieval. In medieval times, engineers weren't accustomed to spanning such distances, so they used iron support bars between the columns to ensure stability. A church has been on this spot since the fall of Rome c. AD 500. (You can see part of the earlier church at the end of this tour.)

While there are no tombs here, the church honors its great

architects with four small, round *(tondo)* memorials on either wall near the rear of the nave. In 1296, the present church was begun under **❷ Arnolfo di Cambio** (shown here holding the Duomo's blueprint), who also built the Palazzo Vecchio and Santa Croce Church. **❸ Giotto** started the church's Campanile in 1334.

By 1420, the nave was done, except for a 140-foot-wide hole in the roof over the altar. ❹ **Filippo Brunelleschi** covered that with the famous dome that helped define the Renaissance. Finally, in the 19th cen-

tury, the church was completed with a multicolored facade by ❺ **Emilio de Fabris.**

Above the main entrance is a ❻ **huge clock,** painted by Paolo Uccello (1443). It still works. It's a 24-hour clock, starting with sunset as the first hour, and turning counterclockwise.

As you stroll down the nave, notice the equestrian portraits on your left. The church, originally financed by the city of Florence, honors great (secular) men, such as ❼ **General John Hawkwood** (on horseback; 1436, it's the second horse picture, colored green). Paolo Uccello wowed Florence by creating this 3-D illusion of an equestrian statue on the flat wall. Farther up the left (north) wall is a painting of Florence's great poet ❽ **Dante,** in a frilly stone frame. He holds his *Divine Comedy,* points toward Hell (Inferno), puts his back to Mount Purgatory (a spiral with souls working their way out of limbo, upward to heaven), and turns toward Paradise—its skyline none other than that of Florence (circa 1465).

Continue all the way up to the very front of the church, beneath the brightly painted dome. The ❾ **altar** area is octagonal, echoing the shape of the Baptistery. At the base of the crucifix

is a high-backed wooden chair—the cathedral of Florence's bishop, which makes the Duomo a "cathedral." Looking up, notice how the dome stretches halfway into the transepts— that was one big hole Brunelleschi had to cover. Look up 300 feet, into the dome, to see the expansive (if artistically uninteresting) ❿ *Last Judgment* by Giorgio Vasari and Federico Zuccari. From their graves, the dead rise into a multilevel heaven to be judged by a radiant Christ. Beneath Christ, Mary intercedes. Below them is the pagan god Kronos with the hourglass and a skeleton—symbolizing that mankind's time is up, and they (we) are entering eternity.

Just below that, on the base that supports the dome, is a ❶ **round stained-glass window** by Donatello, showing the coronation of the Virgin—demonstrating that human beings can eventually be exalted through the Christian faith.

Follow the crowds back toward the exit. If you have a Duomo complex pass, take a quick visit to the ❷ **crypt,** an archaeological cross-section of 1st- to 14th-century Florence, with the footprint and miscellaneous historical fragments of an earlier church called Santa Reparata. (As there's little to see and it's sparsely explained, the crypt is skippable. Brunelleschi's tomb is tucked unceremoniously—and free to view—in a corner of the crypt's bookstore.)

### ▲Climbing the Duomo's Dome

For a grand view into the cathedral from the base of the dome, a chance to see Brunelleschi's "dome-within-a-dome" construction, and a glorious Florence view from the top, climb 463 steps up the dome. The claustrophobic one-way route takes you up narrow, steep staircases and walkways to the top—but it's well worth the climb.

**Cost and Hours:** Covered by the Brunelleschi Pass (see earlier); Mon-Fri 8:15-19:30, Sat until 17:15, Sun 12:45-16:30.

**Reservations:** You must reserve your dome-climb entry when you purchase your pass. If possible, visit at sunset for a romantic experience. If you can't get a reservation, consider buying the Giotto Pass and ascend the Campanile instead: It rarely has a line, is far less claustrophobic, and has a terrific view of the dome.

**Getting In:** Enter the dome climb from the north side of the church (get in line about 15 minutes before your reservation time).

**Climbing the Dome:** While waiting to enter at your reserved time, spend a few minutes studying the side-entrance door, called the Porta della Mandorla ("Almond Door"). Just above the delicately carved doorframe is a colorful Annunciation mosaic by Nanni di Banco, and above that, in a sculpted almond-shaped frame, the Madonna is borne up to heaven by angels. If you look up from here you'll see an empty pedestal atop the transept. Michelangelo's *David* was originally destined to adorn one of these.

The climb is long but there are small landings where you can pull over and take a breather. Halfway up, you'll stroll on the walkway high above the altar where you can get a close-up of Vasari's *Last Judgment* ceiling (especially the ghoulish lower portion, filled with scenes of eternal torment) and a vertigo-inducing view of the nave. After a few tight, winding staircases and a steep final climb, you'll pop out of the hatch on the crowded terrace with a grand city view.

📖 For more on the dome, see page 97 of the Renaissance Walk chapter.

### ▲Campanile (Giotto's Tower)

The 270-foot bell tower has 50-some fewer steps than the Duomo's dome (but that's still 414 steps—no elevator); offers a faster, less-intense climb (with typically short lines); and has a view of that magnificent dome to boot. On the way up, there are several intermediate levels where you can catch your breath and enjoy ever-higher views. The stairs narrow as you go, creating a mosh-pit bottleneck near the very top—but the views are worth the hassle. While the viewpoints are enclosed by cage-like bars, the gaps are big enough to snap great photos.

**Cost and Hours:** Covered by the Giotto Pass (see earlier); daily 8:15-19:45, last entry 40 minutes before closing.

📖 For more on the Campanile, see page 94 of the Renaissance Walk chapter.

### ▲Baptistery

Michelangelo said the bronze doors of this octagonal building facing the Duomo were fit to be the Gates of Paradise. Check out the gleaming copies of Lorenzo Ghiberti's bronze doors (the originals are in the Duomo Museum). Making a breakthrough in perspective, Ghiberti used mathematical laws to create the illusion of receding distance on a basically flat surface.

The doors on the north side of the building (around to the right from the Gates of Paradise) were designed by Ghiberti when he was younger; he'd won the honor and opportunity by beating Brunelleschi in a competition (the rivals' original entries are in the Bargello).

Inside, sit and savor the medieval mosaic ceiling, where it's always Judgment Day and Jesus is giving the ultimate thumbs-up or thumbs-down.

**Cost and Hours:** Covered by all three Duomo passes (see earlier); interior generally open daily 9:00-19:45. The (facsimile) bronze doors on the exterior are always viewable.

☐ For more on the Baptistery, see the Renaissance Walk chapter. For more on the famous doors, see the Bargello Tour chapter and the Duomo Museum Tour chapter.

### ▲▲▲Duomo Museum (Museo dell'Opera del Duomo)

The often-overlooked but superbly presented cathedral museum is filled with some of the best sculpture of the Renaissance, including a late Michelangelo *Pietà* and statues from the original Baptistery facade. Remarkably, it's almost never crowded. It also holds Brunelleschi's models for his dome, Donatello's emaciated *Mary Magdalene* and playful choir loft, and Ghiberti's original bronze Gates of Paradise doors with all the panels (the ones on the Baptistery's doors today are copies).

**Cost and Hours:** Covered by all three Duomo passes (see earlier); daily 9:00-19:45, closed first Tue of each month, last entry one hour before closing; one of the few museums in Florence open every Mon; behind the church at Via del Proconsolo 9, +39 055 230 2885, www.museumflorence.com.

☐ See the Duomo Museum Tour chapter.

## NORTH OF THE DUOMO
### ▲▲▲Accademia (Galleria dell'Accademia)

This museum houses Michelangelo's *David,* the consummate Renaissance statue of the buff, biblical shepherd boy ready to take on the giant. Nearby are some of the master's other works, including his powerful (unfinished) *Prisoners* and *St. Matthew,* as well as a *Pietà* (possibly by one of his disciples). Florentine Michelangelo Buonarroti, who would work tirelessly through the night, believed that the sculptor was a tool of God. He would chip away at the stone to let the intended sculpture emerge. Beyond the magic marble are

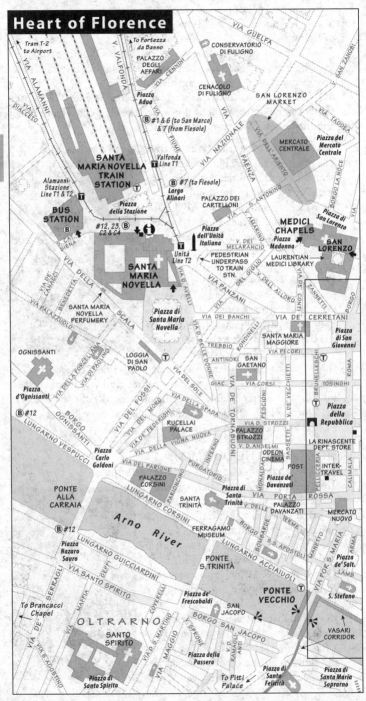

# Heart of Florence

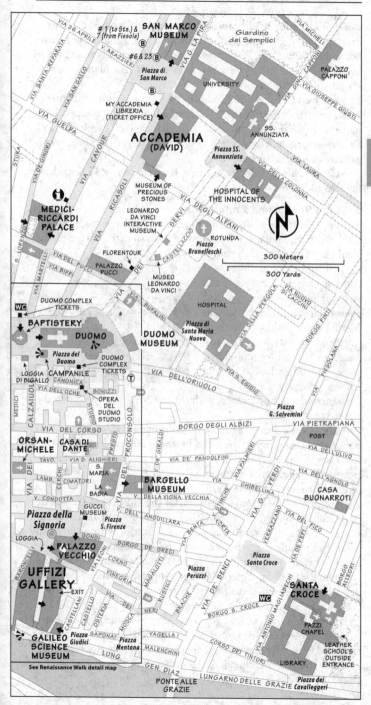

SIGHTS

some mildly interesting pre-Renaissance and Renaissance paintings, including a couple of Botticellis, the plaster model of Giambologna's *Rape of the Sabine Women*, and a musical instrument collection with one of the very first-ever pianos (the pianoforte was invented here in Florence).

**Cost and Hours:** €12, additional €4 for recommended reservation; Tue-Sun 9:00-19:00, closed Mon, may stay open later in peak season; audioguide-€6, Via Ricasoli 60, +39 055 294 883; reservations: www.b-ticket.com/b-Ticket/uffizi, info: www.galleriaaccademiafirenze.it/en.

📖 See the Accademia Gallery Tour chapter or 🎧 download my free audio tour.

### ▲Piazza Santissima Annunziata

The most Renaissance square in Florence is tucked just a block behind the Accademia. It's like an urban cloister (the image of the ideal city) from the 15th century, with three fine buildings—a convent church, a hospital, and an orphanage—ringing a fine equestrian statue of Ferdinand, a Medici grand duke of the then-independent state of Tuscany. Stand in the center and slowly spin, imagining being here in 1500 as you survey the only Re-

naissance square in Florence, with the towering Duomo down the street.

The 15th-century **Santissima Annunziata church** (with its patronage attribution to the Pucci brothers: Alexander and Roberto) is worth a peek. The welcoming cloister has early-16th-century frescoes by Andrea del Sarto, and the church's interior is slathered in Baroque—rare in Florence.

Filippo Brunelleschi's **Hospital of the Innocents** (Ospedale degli Innocenti), built in the 1420s, is considered the first Renaissance building. Its graceful arches and columns, with each set of columns forming a square, embody the quintessence of Renaissance harmony and typified the new aesthetic of calm balance and symmetry. It's ornamented with terra-cotta medallions by Luca della Robbia—each showing a different way to wrap an infant (swaddled—meant to help babies grow straight, and practiced in Italy until about a century ago). Terra-cotta—made of glazed and painted clay—was a combination of painting and sculpture, durable and economic. For three generations, the Della Robbia family guarded the secret recipe and made their name by bringing this affordable art medium to Florence.

With its mission to care for the least among society (parentless or unwanted children), this hospital was also an important symbol of the increasingly humanistic and humanitarian outlook of Renaissance Florence. For four centuries (until 1875), orphans would be left at the "wheel of the innocents" (the small, barred window at the far left of the porch).

The **Museum of the Innocents** fills the hospital. For centuries, since the first newborn was abandoned here in 1445, this "institute of the innocents" cared for unloved babies. Today, a fine and earnestly explained-in-English exhibit tells the story of these nursed and swaddled infants with artifacts (like a huge chest of drawers, each drawer containing half a piece of jewelry possessed by each child to help identify split families) that help you imagine what it was like living here. It also houses some fine art, including several iconic glazed terra-cotta medallions by the Della Robbia family (€8, Wed-Mon 11:00-18:00, closed Tue, audioguide-€3, +39 055 203 7301, www.museodeglinnocenti.it).

**Eating: $$ Caffè del Verone,** on the top terrace, offers a nice, peaceful break with rooftop views. Enter from the Museum of the Innocents (no ticket required) or from the square outside; just catch the elevator—it's to the far right as you face the building (daily 16:00-20:00, Sat-Sun until 21:00, +39 392 498 2559).

## ▲▲Museum of San Marco (Museo di San Marco)

One block north of the Accademia, this 15th-century monastery houses the greatest collection anywhere of frescoes and paintings by the early Renaissance master Fra Angelico. The ground floor features the monk's paintings, along with works by Fra Bartolomeo.

Upstairs are 43 cells decorated by Fra Angelico and his assistants. While the monk/painter was trained in the medieval religious style, he also learned and adopted Renaissance techniques and sensibilities, producing works that blended Christian symbols and Renaissance realism. Don't miss the cell of Savonarola, the charismatic monk who rode in from the Christian right, threw out the Medici, turned Florence into a theocracy, sponsored "bonfires of the vanities" (burning books, paintings, and so on), and was finally burned himself when Florence decided to change channels.

**Cost and Hours:** €8; Mon-Fri 8:15-14:00, Sat until 17:00, closed Sun; also closed second and fourth Mon of each month;

reservations possible but unnecessary, on Piazza San Marco, +39 055 238 8608.

📖 See the Museum of San Marco Tour chapter or 🎧 download my free audio tour.

## Museum of Precious Stones
## (Museo dell'Opificio delle Pietre Dure)

This unusual gem of a museum features room after room of exquisite mosaics of inlaid marble and other stones. The Medici loved *pietre dure* (semiprecious stone) and founded an art workshop just for the production of mosaic tabletops and floors in this durable material. You'll even find detailed landscapes and portraits made from inlaid stone (find Cosimo I in Room I). Upstairs, you'll see tools and examples of the trade, including wooden workbenches from the Medici workshop (1588), complete with foot-powered saws and drills. Rockhounds can browse 500 different stones (lapis lazuli, quartz, agate, marble, and so on) and the tools used to cut and inlay them. Borrow the English descriptions in each room.

Today, Florence is known less for artistic production, but continues its tradition of craftsmanship as a world leader in restoration technique. While not accessible to the public, the rooms off the humble courtyard serve as an active workshop and the center of the city's preservation work. Here Ghiberti's famous bronze doors from the Baptistery were restored, as were Andrea Pisano's south doors. It bears remembering that revenue from sight admission tickets helps preserve Florentine masterpieces for future generations.

**Cost and Hours:** €4, Mon-Sat 8:15-14:00, closed Sun, around corner from Accademia at Via degli Alfani 78, +39 055 265 1357, www.opificiodellepietredure.it.

## Basilica of San Lorenzo

The Basilica of San Lorenzo—on the site of the first Christian church in Florence—was built outside the Roman walls and consecrated in AD 393, then rebuilt in the early 1400s. That's when Filippo Brunelleschi was hired to replace a Romanesque church that stood here. Brunelleschi designed the building, and Donatello worked on the bronze pulpits inside (among other things). Adjacent to the church is a cloister where you can visit

the crypt and the Michelangelo-designed library. (The famed Medici Chapels, with Michelangelo's tomb sculptures, are part of the church complex but have a separate ticket; see next listing.)

**Cost and Hours:** €9 for the church and crypt, buy ticket just inside cloister to the left of the facade; €4 for library only (purchase upstairs); church and crypt open Mon-Sat 9:30-17:30, closed Sun, shorter hours off-season; library Mon-Fri 10:00-13:30, closed Sat-Sun; Piazza di San Lorenzo, +39 055 214 042, basilica: www.sanlorenzofirenze.it, library: www.bmlonline.it.

**Visiting the Basilica:** The exterior of San Lorenzo is rough and exposed brick—unfinished because the Church pulled the plug on the project due to dwindling funds—after Michelangelo had labored on a facade plan for four years, from 1516 to 1520. (Throughout the following decades, the square in front of the church was a literal marble yard with the materials stacked and awaiting construction. That marble was finally sliced up and used to pave the floor of the Duomo.)

Inside though, things are finished and you feel the spirit of Florence in the 1420s, with gray-and-white columns and arches in perfect Renaissance symmetry and simplicity. The simple color scheme seems designed to show off the architectural lines. Brunelleschi designed the interior to receive an even, diffused light. This is a post-Gothic church—with clear rather than  stained glass. The Medici coat of arms decorates the ceiling, and everywhere are images of St. Lawrence, one of the Medici patron saints (who was martyred on a grill).

The highlights of the church include two finely sculpted Donatello pulpits overlooking the nave. One, on the left dating from 1466, shows scenes from the Passion. Donatello heightens the drama by compressing the depth. The dramatic Deposition panel to the right of the Crucifixion zooms in on the pietà drama.

On the wall behind this pulpit is the big, dramatic *Martyrdom of St. Lawrence* by Bronzino. The vivid colors, musculature, and twisted poses are clues that Bronzino must have seen and been inspired by Michelangelo's Sistine Chapel (done during the same period).

The high altar features exquisite inlaid stonework. Look closely at this 17th-century *pietre dure* work, uniquely Florentine and a favorite way for the Medici to show off. The round inlaid marble in the floor before the main altar marks where Cosimo the Elder—Lorenzo the Magnificent's grandfather—is buried. His actual tomb is immediately under the altar (viewable in the crypt, described later), where he physically supports the church (like his money supported Florentine culture).

The Martelli Chapel (left wall of the left transept) has Filippo Lippi's *Annunciation* (c. 1440), featuring a graceful angel greeting Mary in a 3-D courtyard.

The Old Sacristy (a separate room in the far-left corner as you face the front altar), designed by Brunelleschi and decorated by Donatello and Luca della Robbia, was the burial chapel for Giovanni di Bicci, the first Medici who made all the money and the family's patriarch (Cosimo the Elder's father). His tomb is in the center, under what looks like a fancy marble ping-pong table. Overhead, the dome above the altar shows the exact arrangement of the heavens on July 4, 1442, leaving scholars to hypothesize about why that particular date was used.

**Cloister, Crypt, and Library:** Outside the church, just to the left of the main door, is a cloister with peek-a-boo Duomo views (free entry, just walk past the church ticket line) and two worthwhile sights: the crypt (included with church entry) and library (separate ticket required).

The crypt features the tomb of Cosimo the Elder, who died in 1464. A great patron of the arts, he was fabulously wealthy and powerful. The tomb is past the black gate, directly under the church's high altar (again, as if supporting the entire thing). Cosimo's friend Donatello (a cultural soul mate) is buried nearby under a simple tombstone (near where you entered). The adjacent treasury has fine reliquaries, a holy Whitman's Sampler of saintly bones. Outside the treasury stands a white plaster statue of Anna Maria Luisa de' Medici (died 1743). The last of the family line, she willed all Medici art to the city with the legal obligation to keep it here in order to "provoke the interest and curiosity of the foreigners." Without this "family pact," signed in Vienna in 1737, many of the Renaissance treasures of the Medici would have ended up in Habsburg palaces and museums in Vienna and elsewhere. Anna Maria Luisa is particularly appreciated by Florentine guides, whose steady work is due to her visionary will.

The **Laurentian Medici Library,** designed by Michelangelo and finished by others, is worth a look (from the cloister, climb upstairs). It stars Michelangelo's impressive staircase and vestibule. Viewed from the top of the staircase, it almost seems that Michelangelo woke from a stormy architectural dream and threw together a nonsensical warehouse of elements—empty niches, scrolls, oddly taper-

ing pilasters—in a way that was revolutionary in 1520. Enter the Reading Room—a long, rectangular hall with a coffered-wood ceiling—designed to host scholars enjoying the Medici family's collection of manuscripts. It has the feel of a Renaissance church, with its high ceiling, rows of ergonomic "pews," and stained-glass windows. But instead of religious scenes, the windows are filled with Medici heraldic emblems. Knowledge is power, and this was like a public library—but the Medici were firmly in control. Various books were literally chained to the pews as the information was organized by subject (notice the proto-"index cards" at the front of each pew). The library includes special exhibits on historic books (in back room).

**Nearby:** Around the back end of the church is the entrance to the **Medici Chapels** and the New Sacristy, designed by Michelangelo for a later generation of dead Medici. And the lanes leading to Mercato Centrale (one block north) are clogged with the vendor stalls of **San Lorenzo Market.**

## ▲▲Medici Chapels (Cappelle Medicee)

The burial site of the ruling Medici family in the Basilica of San Lorenzo includes the dusky crypt; the big, domed Chapel of Princes; and the magnificent New Sacristy, featuring architecture, tombs, and statues almost entirely by Michelangelo. The Medici made their money in textiles and banking, and patronized a dream team of Renaissance artists that put Florence on the cul-

tural map. Michelangelo, who spent his teen years living with the Medici, was commissioned to create the family's final tribute.

**Cost and Hours:** €9; Sat-Mon 8:15-13:50, Wed-Fri 13:15-18:50; closed Tue and first, third, and fifth Sun of each month; reservations possible but unnecessary, audioguide-€6, modest dress required, +39 055 294 886, www.bargellomusei.beniculturali.it.

📖 See the Medici Chapels Tour chapter.

## ▲San Lorenzo Market

Florence's vast open-air market sprawls in the streets just north of the Basilica of San Lorenzo, between the Duomo and the train station (daily 9:00-19:00). You'll find the highest concentration in the streets ringing Mercato Centrale, a block away.

More popular with tourists than locals, it's a hodgepodge of vendors selling T-shirts, scarves, cheap souvenirs, and leather goods of varying quality. Many of the leather stalls are run by

Iranians selling South American leather that was tailored in Italy; a few more-established, more-reputable leather shops with permanent addresses are nearby. At stalls or shops, prices are soft—don't be shy about bargaining. (For advice about shopping for leather—including recommendations for specific shops—see the Shopping in Florence chapter.) Every night, in a poignant little parade that feels centuries old, the merchants fold their wares into their wheeled wooden stalls and push them through the city streets to their overnight parking spaces.

### ▲Mercato Centrale (Central Market)

Florence's giant iron-and-glass-covered central market was constructed around 1865 as part of the city remake during the unification of Italy, when Florence was, for a few years, the capital of the newly formed country. Stand back and see it as an Industrial Age triumph...a temple of commerce and good food. Then step in and explore the fragrant and picturesque wonderland of produce. While the nearby San Lorenzo Market—with its garment and souvenir stalls in the streets—feels only a step up from a haphazard flea market, Mercato Centrale retains a Florentine elegance.

Downstairs, you'll see parts of the cow (and bull) you'd never dream of eating (no, that's not a turkey neck), enjoy free samples, watch pasta being made, and have your pick of plenty of fun eateries sloshing out cheap and tasty pasta to locals (Mon-Fri 7:00-14:00, Sat until 17:00, closed Sun).

Upstairs, the restored glass roof and steel rafters soar over a modern and extremely touristy food court (daily 10:00-24:00). For eating ideas downstairs, upstairs, and around the market, see the Eating in Florence chapter.

### ▲Medici-Riccardi Palace (Palazzo Medici-Riccardi)

Lorenzo the Magnificent's home is worth a look for its art. The tiny Chapel of the Magi contains colorful Renaissance gems such as

*The Journey of the Magi* frescoes by Benozzo Gozzoli. The former library has a Baroque ceiling fresco by Luca Giordano, a prolific artist from Naples known as "Fast Luke" *(Luca fa presto)* for his speedy workmanship. While the Medici originally occupied this 1444 house, in the 1700s

it became home to the Riccardi family, who added the Baroque flourishes.

**Cost and Hours:** €10, Thu-Tue 9:00-19:00, closed Wed; ticket entrance is off the central courtyard, enter from Via Cavour 3 or sometimes from Via de' Ginori 2; +39 055 276 0552, www. palazzomediciriccardi.it.

☐ See the Medici-Riccardi Palace Tour chapter.

### Leonardo Museums

Two different-but-similar entrepreneurial outfits—with confusingly similar names—are around the corner from one another and show off reproductions of Leonardo da Vinci's ingenious inventions. While there are no actual historic artifacts, each museum has working models of dozens of Leonardo's inventions and experiments. You might see a full-size armored tank, walk into a chamber of mirrors, operate a rotating crane, or watch experiments in flying. The exhibits are described in English, and you're encouraged to touch and play with many of the models (great for kids). The Museo Leonardo da Vinci Firenze has larger scale models; the Leonardo da Vinci Interactive Museum is more kid-friendly and has better visitor information. Either is fun for anyone who wants to crank the shaft and spin the ball bearings of Leonardo's fertile imagination.

**Cost and Hours:** Admission to each museum is €8 for adults, €7 for kids 5-18, free for kids 4 and under (daily 10:00-19:00, shorter hours off-season, last entry one hour before closing). **Museo Leonardo da Vinci Firenze,** Via del Castellaccio 1 red, +39 055 295 264, www.museoleonardodavincifirenze.com. **Leonardo da Vinci Interactive Museum,** Via dei Servi 66 red, +39 055 282 966, www.leonardointeractivemuseum.com.

## BETWEEN THE DUOMO AND PIAZZA DELLA SIGNORIA

### Casa di Dante (Dante's House)

Dante Alighieri (1265-1321), the poet who gave us *The Divine Comedy,* is the Shakespeare of Italy, the father of the modern Italian language, and the face on the country's €2 coin. However, most Americans know little of him. Unfortunately, this small museum (in a building near where Dante likely lived) is not the ideal place to start. Even though it has English information, the museum assumes visitors have prior knowledge of the poet. It's not a medieval-flavored house with period furniture—it's just a small, uninspiring museum about Dante. Still, Dante lovers can trace his interesting life and works through pictures, models, and artifacts, and learn about the medieval city Dante lived in.

**Cost and Hours:** €8, daily 10:00-18:00, closed Mon Nov-March; near the Bargello at Via Santa Margherita 1, +39 055 219 416, www.museocasadidante.it.

**Visiting the Museum:** As you traverse the three floors, you'll walk through Dante's life—from starry-eyed youth to bitter exile, to the beatific legacy of his po-etic genius. Some call Dante the father of the Renaissance. If you're new to the poet, the following information may help the museum seem less Dante-ing.

**First Floor:** Begin in Room 1 (straight ahead from the ticket desk). Dante was born into the noble Alighieri family (see his family tree). He married Gemma Donati, but his first love, Beatrice Portinari, remained his muse, inspiring him to give up medicine in favor of writing lofty poetry. The touchscreen on the wall provides "virtual volumes" about Dante's life.

Continue into Room 2, behind the curtain, to learn about the decisive Battle of Campaldino (on "San Barnaba Saturday"). Florence's army (including Dante) won, establishing the city's dominance, and elevating Dante to a prominent ambassadorship. Now 35 years old—"midway along the journey" of a traditional 70-year lifespan—Dante was at his peak. Then it all went bad.

In Room 3 you'll find the coats of arms of various influential Florentine guilds. To participate in the political life of the city, membership was required.

In Room 4, an interactive map of Dante's Florence shows the evolution of the city in the 13th century and the main buildings of medieval Florence. As the city grew, new walls and neighborhoods *(sestieri)* were built to house feuding Monatague and Capulet-type clans.

**Second Floor:** Head upstairs into Room 5. Dante became ensnared in confusing political battles between the pope (Boniface VIII) and the Holy Roman Emperor (Henry VII)—between the Black Guelphs and the White Ghibellines. Dante's side lost. Suddenly, politically incorrect Dante was exiled—see the *Book of the Nail ("Libro del Chiodo")* that condemned him. He would never again see his beloved Florence.

Opposite the book, inside a reconstruction of a medieval bedroom (Room 6), there's a painting of Dante—in red, forlorn, having received the news of his exile, with his distinctive ear-flap cap, hooked nose, and jutting chin.

In exile, Dante completed his magnum opus, *The Divine Comedy*. Room 7 houses a collection of the famed book written in 49 languages and 22 dialects. Displays bring the poem to life. *The Divine Comedy* tells the story of a lost pilgrim who must journey through Hell (*inferno*, a spiral-shaped hole through the Earth), Purgatory (*purgatorio*, a spiral-shaped mountain),  and Paradise (*paradiso*, the concentric orbits of satellites that surround Earth).

**Top Floor:** The top floor displays a depiction of Dante's Florence which looks very similar to the city you encounter today.

### ▲Orsanmichele Church

In the ninth century, this loggia (covered courtyard) was a market used for selling grain (stored upstairs). Later, it was enclosed to make a church. Focus on the exterior, with its dynamic, statue-filled niches, some with accompanying symbols from the guilds that sponsored the art. Donatello's *St. Mark* and *St. George* (on the northeast and northwest corners) step out boldly in the new Renaissance style.

The interior (open only two days a week) has a glorious Gothic tabernacle (1359), which houses the painted wooden panel that depicts *Madonna delle Grazie* (1346). The iron bars spanning the vaults were the Italian Gothic answer to the French Gothic external buttresses. The rectangular holes in the piers were once grain chutes that connected to the upper floors. The museum upstairs displays most of the original statues from the niches outside the building, including ones by Ghiberti, Donatello, Brunelleschi, and others.

**Cost and Hours:** €4, includes museum; Tue and Sat 10:30-18:00, closed Sun-Mon and Wed-Fri; ticket office open Mon-Sat 9:00-16:00, closed Sun, books concert tickets (see next) as well as Uffizi and Accademia tickets; www.bargellomusei.beniculturali.it.

**Evening Concerts:** You can give the *Madonna delle Grazie* a special thanks if you're in town when the church is hosting an evening concert (tickets sold on day of concert from door facing Via dei Calzaiuoli or, on Sun, from the doorway opposite the church entrance).

📖 See page 102 of the Renaissance Walk chapter.

### ▲Mercato Nuovo (a.k.a. the Straw Market)

This market loggia is how Orsanmichele looked before it became a church. Originally a silk-and-straw market, Mercato Nuovo still functions as a rustic yet touristy market (at the intersection of Via Calimala and Via Porta Rossa; daily 9:00-18:30). Prices are soft, but San Lorenzo Market (listed earlier) is much better for haggling. Notice the circled X in the center, marking the spot where people landed after being hoisted up to the top and dropped as punishment for bankruptcy (easiest to find when the market is closed and the vendors disappear). You'll also find *Il Porcellino* (a statue of a wild boar nicknamed "The Piglet"), which people rub and give coins to ensure their return to Florence. This new copy, while only a few years old, already has a polished snout. At the back corner, a wagon sells tripe (cow innards) sandwiches—a local favorite (for more on this Tuscan taste treat, see page 304).

### ▲Piazza della Repubblica

Lined with venerable cafés and high-fashion stores, this square has been the center of Florence for millennia. In Roman times, it was a fort at the intersection of the two main roads (marked today by the square's lone column). In 1571, Cosimo I de' Medici had the area walled in and made into the Jewish ghetto. If you venture outside the piazza, you get a sense of what the old neighborhood was like—a tangle of narrow, winding lanes dotted with medieval towers. In the late 19th century, the area was razed to create this spacious square, with a huge triumphal arch celebrating the unification of Italy.

Today, people sip drinks at outdoor cafes, shop at the local La Rinascente department store, or enjoy a reasonably priced coffee on the store's rooftop terrace, with great Duomo and city views.

For more about Piazza della Repubblica, 📖 see page 101 of the Renaissance Walk chapter.

**Nearby:** Between here and the river, you'll find characteristic parts of the medieval city that give a sense of what this neighborhood felt like before it was bulldozed. Back in the Middle Ages, writers described Florence as so densely built up that when it rained, pedestrians didn't get wet. Torches were used to light the lanes in midday. The city was prickly with scores of noble families' towers (like San Gimignano) and had Romeo and Juliet-type family feuds. But with the rise of city power (c. 1300), no noble family was allowed to have an architectural ego trip taller than the Palazzo Vecchio, and nearly all other towers were taken down.

## Palazzo Strozzi

The former home of the wealthy Strozzi family, great rivals of the Medici, offers a textbook example of a Renaissance palace (built between 1489 and 1538). It feels like an attempt to one-up the Medici-Riccardi Palace just a few blocks away. Step into its grand courtyard and imagine how well-to-do families competed to commission grandiose structures (and artistic masterpieces) to promote their status and wealth. The Strozzi were bankers. And, considering how the family name, Strozzi, gave Italian its words for loan shark *(strozzino)* and strangle *(strozzare)*, their loans (with notoriously high interest rates) must have come with some aggressive banking practices. Today the palace hosts top-notch special exhibitions on topics ranging from Renaissance times to contemporary artists. The courtyard also hosts a tranquil, shaded café.

**Cost and Hours:** Typically around €13—gallery price depends on changing exhibits, buy online to skip the queue; daily 10:00-20:00, Thu until 23:00, last entry one hour before closing; just west of Piazza della Repubblica at Piazza Strozzi, +39 055 264 5155, www.palazzostrozzi.org.

## ▲Palazzo Davanzati

This five-story, late-medieval tower house offers a rare look at a noble dwelling built in the 14th century. Like other buildings of the age, the exterior is festooned with 14th-century horse-tethering rings made from iron, torch holders, and poles upon which to hang tapestries and fly flags. Inside, though the furnishings are pretty sparse, you'll see richly painted walls, a long chute that functioned as a well, plenty of fireplaces, a lace display, and even an indoor "outhouse." You can borrow English descriptions in each room.

**Cost and Hours:** €6; Tue-Thu 8:45-13:30, Fri-Sun 13:45-18:30; closed Mon and first, third, and fifth Sun of each month; reservations possible but unnecessary; Via Porta Rossa 13, +39 055 238 8610, www.bargellomusei.beniculturali.it.

## ON AND NEAR PIAZZA DELLA SIGNORIA
### ▲▲▲Uffizi Gallery

This greatest collection of Italian paintings anywhere features works by Giotto, Leonardo, Raphael, Caravaggio, Titian, and Michelangelo, and a roomful of Botticellis, including the *Birth of Venus*. Start with Giotto's early stabs at Renaissance-style realism,

then move on through the 3-D experimentation of the early 1400s to the real thing rendered by the likes of Botticelli and Leonardo. Finish off with Michelangelo and Titian. Because only 600 visitors are allowed inside the building at any one time, there's generally a very long wait. The good news: no Vatican-style mob scenes inside. The museum is nowhere near as big as it is great. Few tourists spend more than two hours inside.

**Cost and Hours:** €20 plus €4 for recommended timed-entry reservation, cheaper in winter, covered by €38 Uffizi/Pitti Palace/Boboli Gardens "PassePartout" combo-ticket; open Tue-Sun 8:15-18:30, closed Mon, may stay open later in peak season, last entry one hour before closing; audioguide-€6, +39 055 294 883, reservations: www.b-ticket.com/b-Ticket/uffizi, info: www.uffizi.it.

📖 See the Uffizi Gallery Tour chapter or 🎧 download my free audio tour.

**Uffizi Courtyard:** Enjoy the courtyard (free), full of artists and souvenir stalls. (Swing by after dinner when it's crowd-free, and talented street musicians take advantage of the space's superior acoustics.) The surrounding statues honor earthshaking Florentines. The courtyard is covered on page 106.

### ▲▲Palazzo Vecchio

This castle-like fortress with the 300-foot spire dominates Florence's main square. In Renaissance times, it was the Town Hall, where citizens pioneered the once-radical notion of self-rule. Its official name—Palazzo della Signoria—refers to the elected members of the city council. In 1540, the tyrant Cosimo I made the building his personal palace, redecorating the interior in lavish style. Today the building functions once again as the Town Hall.

Entry to the ground-floor Michelozzo courtyard, with its arcade of intricately carved columns, is free, so even if you don't go upstairs to the museum, you can step inside and feel the essence of the Medici. There's also a fine little exhibit of scenes from old Florence (ground level in adjacent ticketing courtyard). Paying customers can see Cosimo's (fairly) lavish royal apartments, decorated with (fairly) top-notch paintings and statues by Michelangelo and Donatello. The highlight is the Grand Hall (Salone dei Cinquecento), a 13,000-square-foot hall lined with huge frescoes and interesting statues.

Across from the Palazzo, facing the square, is the **Loggia dei Lanzi,** where Renaissance Florentines once debated the issues of the day; a collection of Medici-approved sculptures now stand (or writhe) under its canopy, including Cellini's bronze *Perseus.*

**Cost and Hours:** Michelozzo courtyard-free, museum and tower climb (418 steps)-€12.50 each, excavations-€4. Museum and excavations open daily 9:00-19:00 except Thu until 14:00, may stay open later in peak season; tower keeps shorter hours (last entry one hour before closing) and closed in bad weather; last tickets for all sights sold one hour before closing; videoguide-€5, Piazza della Signoria, +39 055 276 8224, http://bigliettimusei.comune.fi.it.

📖 See the Palazzo Vecchio Tour chapter.

### ▲Ponte Vecchio

Florence's most famous bridge has long been lined with shops. Originally these were butcher shops that used the river as a handy

disposal system. Then, when the powerful and princely Medici built the Vasari Corridor over the bridge, the stinky meat market was replaced by more elegant gold-and-silver shops (some of which remain here to this day). The corridor, an elevated passageway above the bridge, was built so the Medici could commute comfortably between their Pitti Palace home and their Palazzo Vecchio offices (corridor may be closed for renovation when you visit). A statue of Benvenuto Cellini, the master goldsmith of the Renaissance, stands in the center of the bridge, ignored by the flood of tacky tourism.

📖 For more about the bridge, see the Renaissance Walk chapter and the Oltrarno Walk chapter.

### ▲▲Galileo Science Museum (Museo Galilei)

When we think of the Florentine Renaissance, we think of visual arts: painting, mosaics, architecture, and sculpture. But when the visual arts declined in the 1600s (abused and

# The Medici in a Minute and a Half

The Medici family- part Kennedys, part *Sopranos*, part John-D-and-Catherine-T art patrons—dominated Florentine politics for 300 years (c. 1434-1737). Originally a hardworking, middle-class family in the cloth, silk, and banking businesses, they used their wealth, blue-collar popularity, and philanthropy to rise into Europe's nobility, producing popes and queens.

## 1400s: The Princes

Lorenzo the Magnificent (ruled 1469-1492), Cosimo the Elder's grandson, epitomized the Medici ruling style: publicly praising Florence's constitution while privately holding the purse strings. A true Renaissance Man, Lorenzo's personal charisma, public festivals, and support of Leonardo, Botticelli, and teenage Michelangelo made Florence Europe's most enlightened city.

## 1494-1532: Exile in Rome

After Lorenzo's early death, the family was exiled by the Florentines. The Medici became victims of bank failure, Savonarola's reforms, and the Florentine tradition of democracy. They built a power base in Rome under Lorenzo's son (Pope Leo X, who made forays into Florence) and nephew (Pope Clement VII, who finally invaded Florence and crushed the republic).

## 1537-1737: The Grand Duchy/Mediocre Medici

Backed by Europe's popes and kings, the "later" Medici—descendants of Cosimo the Elder's brother—ruled Florence and Tuscany as just another duchy. Cosimo I was politically repressive but a generous patron of the arts, leaving his mark on the Palazzo Vecchio, the Uffizi, and the Pitti Palace. Cosimo II supported Galileo. Famous throughout Europe, the Medici married into Europe's royal families (Catherine and Marie de' Medici were queens of France), even while Florence declined as a European power.

co-opted by political powers), music and science flourished in Florence. The first opera was written here. And Florence hosted many scientific breakthroughs, as you'll see in this fascinating collection of Renaissance and later clocks, telescopes, maps, and ingenious gadgets. Trace the technical innovations as modern science emerges from 1000 to 1900. Some of the most talked about bottles in Florence are the ones here that contain Galileo's fingers. Exhibits include various tools for gauging the world, from a compass and thermometer to Galileo's telescopes. Other displays delve into

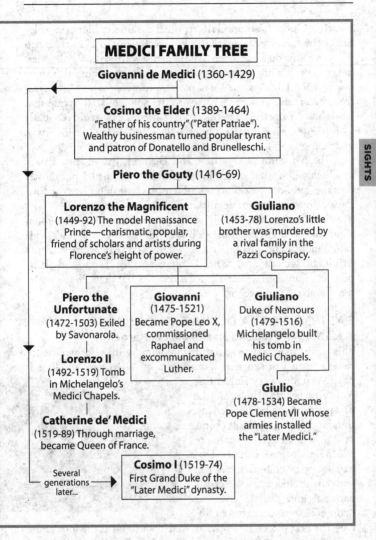

**MEDICI FAMILY TREE**

**Giovanni de Medici** (1360-1429)

**Cosimo the Elder** (1389-1464)
"Father of his country" ("Pater Patriae").
Wealthy businessman turned popular tyrant
and patron of Donatello and Brunelleschi.

**Piero the Gouty** (1416-69)

**Lorenzo the Magnificent**
(1449-92) The model Renaissance
Prince—charismatic, popular,
friend of scholars and artists during
Florence's height of power.

**Giuliano**
(1453-78) Lorenzo's little
brother was murdered by
a rival family in the
Pazzi Conspiracy.

**Piero the Unfortunate**
(1472-1503) Exiled
by Savonarola.

**Giovanni**
(1475-1521)
Became Pope Leo X,
commissioned
Raphael and
excommunicated
Luther.

**Giuliano**
Duke of Nemours
(1479-1516)
Michelangelo built
his tomb in
Medici Chapels.

**Lorenzo II**
(1492-1519) Tomb
in Michelangelo's
Medici Chapels.

**Giulio**
(1478-1534) Became
Pope Clement VII whose
armies installed
the "Later Medici."

**Catherine de' Medici**
(1519-89) Through marriage,
became Queen of France.

Several
generations
later...

**Cosimo I** (1519-74)
First Grand Duke of the
"Later Medici" dynasty.

SIGHTS

pumps, medicine, and chemistry. It's friendly, comfortably cool, never crowded, and just a block east of the Uffizi on the Arno River.

**Cost and Hours:** €10, daily 9:30-18:00 except Tue until 13:00, Piazza dei Giudici 1, +39 055 265 311, www.museogalileo.it.

▢ See the Galileo Science Museum Tour chapter.

**▲Fashion Museums**

Medici, Michelangelo, meh. Fashionistas who've had enough of 15th-century Florence enjoy delving into the 21st century at these exhibits. But I find them disappointing and prefer window shopping around Via de' Tornabuoni.

The **Gucci Garden Gallery,** on Piazza della Signoria, celebrates the famous designer Guccio Gucci, who, in 1921, founded the company that has been synonymous with style for decades. Seven rooms, while mostly holding temporary exhibits, also show off the company's unique Flora pattern, handbags and travel cases from every era, and evening wear. The suitably stylish café and bookshop are open even to those not visiting the museum (€8, daily 11:00-19:00, Piazza della Signoria 10, +39 055 7592 7010, www.guccimuseo.com).

The **Museum of Costume and Fashion,** in the Pitti Palace and included in that ticket, has a little fashion history but mostly contains temporary exhibits on contemporary fashion (see the Pitti Palace Tour chapter for details).

The **Ferragamo** flagship store has an interesting, nine-room **shoe museum.** The specific exhibit changes each year, but it's typically fanciful and imaginative (€9, daily 10:00-19:30, near Santa Trinità bridge at Piazza Santa Trinità 5 red, see map in the Shopping in Florence chapter for location, +39 055 356 2846, www.ferragamo.com/museo/en).

## EAST OF PIAZZA DELLA SIGNORIA
### ▲▲▲Bargello (Museo Nazionale del Bargello)

This underappreciated sculpture museum is in a former police station-turned-prison that looks like a mini-Palazzo Vecchio. It

has Donatello's very influential, painfully beautiful *David* (the first male nude to be sculpted in a thousand years), multiple works by Michelangelo, and rooms of Medici treasures. Moody Donatello, who embraced realism with his lifelike statues, set the personal and artistic style for many Renaissance artists to follow. The best pieces are in the ground-floor room at the foot of the outdoor staircase (with fine works by Michelangelo, Cellini, and Giambologna) and in the "Donatello room" directly above (including his two different *David*s, plus Ghiberti and Brunelleschi's dueling competition entries for the Baptistery doors—and yet another *David* by Verrocchio).

**Cost and Hours:** €9; usually daily 8:15-14:00—later for special exhibits; may close on second and fourth Sun and first, third, and fifth Mon of each month; last entry 50 minutes before closing; reservations possible but unnecessary, audioguide-€6; Via del Proconsolo 4, +39 055 238 8606, www.bargellomusei.beniculturali.it.

☐ See the Bargello Tour chapter or ∩ download my free audio tour.

## ▲▲Santa Croce Church

This 14th-century Franciscan church, decorated with centuries of precious art, holds the tombs of great Florentines. The loud 19th-century Victorian Gothic facade faces a huge square ringed with tempting shops and littered with tired tourists. Escape into the church and admire its sheer height and spacious-ness. Your ticket includes the Pazzi Chapel and a small museum; the com-plex also houses a leather school. It can be really crowded with tourists, as the bus depot for day-tripping cruise-ship travelers is just down the street.

**Cost and Hours:** Church—€8; Mon-Sat 9:30-17:30, Sun from 12:30; multimedia guide-€4, modest dress required, 10-minute walk east of the Palazzo Vecchio along Borgo de' Greci, +39 055 246 6105, www.santacroceopera.it. Leather school—free, use entry at the back of the church; Mon-Sat 10:00-18:00, closed Sun; https://leatherschool.biz.

☐ See the Santa Croce Tour chapter.

## ▲Casa Buonarroti (Michelangelo's House)

A property once owned by Michelangelo, this house was built after the artist's death by his grandnephew "Michelangelo the Younger," who turned it into a little museum honoring his famous relative. The highlights—Michelangelo's first sculptures and some sketch-es—are not must-sees in art-heavy Florence, but are appreciated by Michelangelo lovers. The place where Michelangelo actually grew up is only a few blocks from here, at 10 Via de' Bentaccordi.

**Cost and Hours:** €8, Wed-Mon 10:00-16:30, closed Tue, Via Ghibellina 70, +39 055 241 752, www.casabuonarroti.it.

**Visiting the Museum:** After browsing the ground floor (of Michelangelo the Younger's collection of ancient pottery), climb the stairs to the first-floor landing, where you come face-to-face with portraits (by his contemporaries) of 60-year-old Michelange-lo, the Buonarroti family walking sticks, and some leather slippers thought to be Michelangelo's.

The room to the left of the landing displays two relief pan-els, Michelangelo's earliest known sculptures and mainstays of Art History 101 classes. Teenage Michelangelo carved every inch of the *Battle of the Centaurs* (1490-1492). This squirming tangle of

battling nudes shows his fascination with anatomy and love of classical art. He kept this in his personal collection all his life. *The Madonna of the Stairs* (c. 1490) is as contemplative as *Centaurs* is dramatic. Throughout his long career, bipolar Michelangelo veered between these two styles—moving or still, emotional or thoughtful, pagan or Christian.

In an adjoining room behind you is the big wooden model of a project Michelangelo took on but never completed: the facade of the Basilica of San Lorenzo (which remains bare brick to this day). It wasn't the artist's fault—his patron, Pope Leo X, simultaneously tasked him with completing tomb statuary for the Medici Chapels.

You'll also visit a series of ornately paneled and frescoed rooms where Michelangelo the Younger lived, carrying on the legacy of his esteemed forebear.

Back near the landing, step into the darkened room with just a few Michelangelo sketches *(disegni)*. This is only a slice of the museum's once-vast collection (successive heirs sold off many drawings to pay their bills). Vasari claimed

that Michelangelo wanted to burn his preliminary sketches, lest anyone think him less than perfect.

Another room near the landing displays small clay and wax models—some by Michelangelo, some by pupils—used by the artist to sketch out ideas for his statues.

Back downstairs near the entrance, a room often hosts excellent temporary exhibits.

## NEAR THE TRAIN STATION
### ▲▲Church of Santa Maria Novella

This 13th-century Dominican church is rich in art. Along with crucifixes by Giotto and Brunelleschi, it contains the textbook example of the early Renaissance mastery of perspective: *The Trinity* by Masaccio. The exquisite chapels trace art in Florence from medieval times to early Baroque. The outside of the church features a dash of Romanesque (horizontal stripes), Gothic (pointed arches), Renaissance (geometric shapes), and Baroque (scrolls). Step in and look down the 330-foot nave for a 14th-century optical illusion.

SIGHTS

Next to the church are the cloisters and the **museum,** located in the old Dominican convent of Santa Maria Novella. The museum's highlight is the breathtaking Spanish Chapel, with walls covered by a series of frescoes by Andrea di Bonaiuto.

**Cost and Hours:** Church and museum-€7.50; Mon-Thu and Sat 10:00-17:00, Fri from 11:00, Sun from 13:00; multimedia guide-€3, modest dress required; main entrance on Piazza Santa Maria Novella across from the train station; +39 055 219 257, www.smn.it.

📖 See the Santa Maria Novella Tour chapter.

**Nearby:** Behind the church you'll find a top-of-the-line *parfumerie,* the **Farmacia di Santa Maria Novella,** which was founded by the Dominicans in 1612 (daily 10:00-19:00, Via della Scala 16). Even nonshoppers enjoy exploring its elegant halls and heaven-scent. For details, see the Shopping in Florence chapter.

## THE OLTRARNO (SOUTH OF THE ARNO RIVER)

📖 The Oltrarno Walk chapter connects several of these sights, including the Pitti Palace and Santo Spirito Church.

### ▲▲▲Pitti Palace

The imposing Pitti Palace, several blocks southwest of Ponte Vecchio, has many separate museums and two gardens. The main reason to visit is to see the Palatine Gallery, which houses a fine painting collection that picks up where the Uffizi leaves off.

**Cost and Hours:** The €16 **Pitti Palace** ticket covers the Palatine Gallery, Royal Apartments, Treasury of the Grand Dukes (silver museum), Museum of Costume and Fashion, and Gallery of Modern Art; open Tue-Sun 8:15-18:50, closed Mon, last entry one hour before closing. The €10 **Boboli Garden** ticket covers the Boboli and Bardini Gardens as well as the Porcelain Museum located in the garden; open daily June-Aug 8:15-19:00, April-May and Sept-Oct until 18:30, Nov-March until 16:30;

SIGHTS

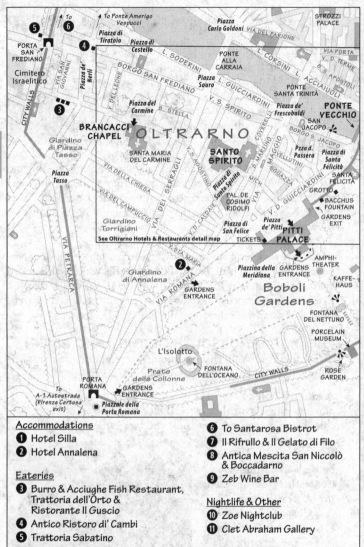

## Accommodations
1 Hotel Silla
2 Hotel Annalena

## Eateries
3 Burro & Acciughe Fish Restaurant,
   Trattoria dell'Orto &
   Ristorante Il Guscio
4 Antico Ristoro di' Cambi
5 Trattoria Sabatino

6 To Santarosa Bistrot
7 Il Rifrullo & Il Gelato di Filo
8 Antica Mescita San Niccolò
   & Boccadarno
9 Zeb Wine Bar

## Nightlife & Other
10 Zoe Nightclub
11 Clet Abraham Gallery

closed first and last Mon of each month, last entry one hour before closing. Reservations are possible but unnecessary.

The €38 **PassePartout** combo-ticket covers the palace, Boboli Gardens, and the Uffizi Gallery (purchase in advance at www.b-ticket.com/b-Ticket/uffizi).

**Information:** An €8 audioguide explains the sprawling palace. +39 055 238 8614, www.uffizi.it.

☐ See the Pitti Palace Tour chapter.

SIGHTS

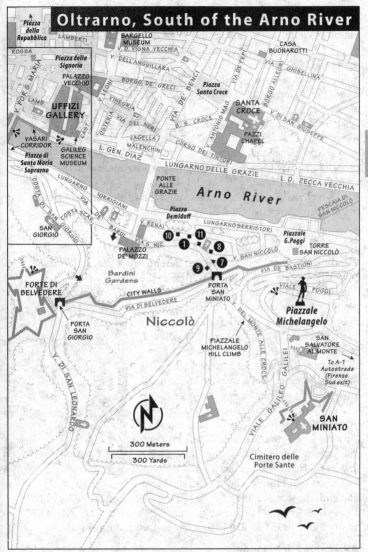

Oltrarno, South of the Arno River

## ▲▲Brancacci Chapel (Capella Brancacci)

For the best look at works by Masaccio (one of the early Renaissance pioneers of perspective in painting), see his restored frescoes here. Instead of medieval religious symbols, Masaccio's paintings feature simple, strong human figures with facial expressions that reflect their emotions. The accompanying works of Masolino and Filippino Lippi provide illuminating contrasts. The chapel may be undergoing restoration when you visit; if that's ongoing you may be able to climb the scaffolding and see the frescoes up close.

**SIGHTS**

**Cost and Hours:** €10; Fri-Sat and Mon 10:00-17:00, Sun from 13:00, closed Tue-Thu, reservations required; video-guide–€3, knees and shoulders must be covered, in Church of Santa Maria del Carmine on Piazza del Carmine; to reserve call +39 055 276 8224 or +39 055 276 8558, or email cappellabrancacci@musefirenze.it; www.musefirenze.it.

📖 See the Brancacci Chapel Tour chapter.

**Nearby:** The neighborhoods around the church are considered the last surviving bits of old Florence.

## Santo Spirito Church

This church has a classic Brunelleschi interior—enjoy its pure Renaissance lines (and ignore the later Baroque altar that replaced the original). Notice Brunelleschi's "dice"—the large stone cubes added above the column capitals that contribute to the nave's playful lightness.

The church's art treasure is a painted, carved wooden crucifix by 17-year-old Michelangelo. The sculptor donated this early work to the monastery in appreciation for allowing him to dissect and learn about bodies. The Michelangelo *Crocifisso* is displayed in the sacristy, which can be accessed from the nave (pop into the tranquil cloisters from the sacristy). Beer-drinking, guitar-playing rowdies decorate the church steps.

**Cost and Hours:** Church—free, Mon-Tue and Thu-Sat 10:00-13:00 & 15:00-18:00, Sun 11:30-13:30 & 15:00-18:00, closed Wed; crucifix of Michelangelo—€2; Piazza di Santo Spirito, +39 055 210 030, www.basilicasantospirito.it.

## ▲Piazzale Michelangelo

Overlooking the city from across the river (look for the huge bronze statue of *David*), this square has a superb view of Florence and the stunning dome of the Duomo. It's worth the 25-minute hike, taxi, or bus ride.

An inviting café (open seasonally) with great views is just below the overlook. The best photos are taken from the street immediately below the overlook (go around to the right and down a few steps). Off the west side of the piazza is a somewhat hidden terrace, an excellent place to retreat from the mobs. After dark, the square is packed with school kids licking ice cream and each other. About 200 yards beyond all the tour groups and teenagers is the stark, beautiful, crowd-free, Romanesque San Miniato Church (next listing). A WC is located just off the road, halfway between the two sights.

SIGHTS

**Getting There** (and Back): While you can catch bus #12 (from near Piazza d'Ognissanti, can be a long ride) or a taxi up to the piazza, the walk up from the Oltrarno neighborhood of San Niccolò is popular—especially in the early evening—and not that challenging (see the map).

Start at the intersection of Via San Niccolò and Via San Miniato, just below Porta San Miniato (scope out the restaurants and bars here, as you'll circle back to this spot in about an hour if you walk down). Point yourself uphill, head through the old gate, and continue until you reach a broad, terraced hill-climb to the left. The path becomes steep, but it's shaded and short: you'll make it to the top in no more than 10 minutes. If you need an excuse to stop and catch your breath, peek into the rose garden (Giardino delle Rose) that's on the way. Up top, Piazzale Michelangelo will be to your left, and San Miniato Church to your right.

When you're ready to leave, the hike down is quick and enjoyable (or take bus #13). You can retrace your steps, or you can turn this walk into a loop: From the parking lot, take the ramp leading down toward Ponte Vecchio (near the replica *David*). At the bottom of the ramp, cross the street and continue down the pathway. You'll cross one more street, then zigzag downhill toward the river. You are descending on the so-called Poggi ramps, developed in the late 19th century as a string of staircases, fountains, and grottos that embellishes (and stabilizes) the hillside. When you draw even with the big tower (Porta San Niccolò), turn left onto Via San Niccolò and make your way back to the group of lively cafés and restaurants where you started (for recommendations, see page 320).

### ▲▲San Miniato Church

According to legend, the martyred St. Minias—this church's namesake—was beheaded on the banks of the Arno in AD 250. He picked up his head and walked here (this was before the #12 bus), where he died and was buried in what became the first Christian cemetery in Florence. In the 11th century, this church was built to house Minias' remains. Imagine this fine church all alone—

without any nearby buildings or fancy stairs—a peaceful refuge where white-robed Benedictine monks could pray and work (their motto: *ora et labora*). The evening vesper service with the monks chanting in Latin offers a meditative worship experience—a peaceful way to end your visit.

**Cost and Hours:** Free, daily 9:30-13:00 & 15:00-19:00, closed sporadically for special occasions, +39 055 234 2731, www.sanminiatoalmonte.it.

**Getting There:** It's about 200 yards above Piazzale Michelangelo. Follow the walking directions in the Piazzale Michelangelo listing earlier, or take bus #12 to the San Miniato al Monte stop (hop off and hike up the grand staircase); bus #13 takes you back down the hill.

**Gregorian Chants:** To experience this mystical medieval space at its full potential, time your visit to coincide with a 30-minute prayer service in Latin with Gregorian chants. In general, these are held Mon-Sat at 18:00 and 18:30, and Sun at 17:30—but as the schedule is subject to change, double-check with any TI, the church's website, or call ahead.

**Saintly Souvenirs:** The monks make and sell beeswax candles as well as edible delicacies in their shop, which is generally open daily from 10:00-12:15 & 16:00-18:00.

**Visiting the Church:** For a thousand years, San Miniato Church—still part of a functioning monastery—has blessed the city that lies at the foot of its hill. Carved into the marble of its threshold on the left door is the Genesis verse *"Haec est Porta Coeli"* ("This is the Gate of Heaven").

The church's green-and-white marble **facade** (12th century) is classic Florentine Romanesque, one of the oldest in town. The perfect symmetry is a reminder of the perfection of God. The central mosaic shows Christ flanked by Mary and St. Minias. Minias, who was King of Armenia before his conversion, offers his secular crown to the heavenly king. The eagle on top, with bags of wool in his talons, reminds all who approach the church who paid for it—the merchants guild (which made money selling wool).

Stepping inside **the nave,** you enter the closest thing to a holy space that medieval

Florentines could create. The "carpet of marble" (with its zodiac wheel) dates from 1207. The wood ceiling is painted as it was originally. The glittering 13th-century golden mosaic that dominates the dome at the front of the nave repeats the scene on the church's facade: St. Minias offering his paltry secular crown to the king in heaven.

The Renaissance **tabernacle** front and center was commissioned by the Medici. It's a résumé of early Renaissance humanism, with experiments in 3-D paintings (including St. Minias, in red) and a plush canopy of glazed terra-cotta panels by Luca della Robbia.

On the left side of the nave is an exquisite **chapel** dedicated to Cardinal Jacopo of Portugal. When 26-year-old Jacopo died in Florence (1459), his wealthy family mourned him by adding a chapel to the church (by cutting a hole in the church wall) and hiring the best artists of the day to decorate it. The family could enter their private chapel, take a seat on the throne (on the left), and meditate on the tomb of Jacopo (on the right).

The church is designed like a split-level rambler, with staircases on either side of the altar, leading upstairs and down. Downstairs in the **crypt,** an alabaster window helps create a quiet and mysterious atmosphere. The forest of columns and capitals are all recycled...each from ancient Roman buildings and each different. The floor is paved with the tombstones of long-forgotten big shots. Look through the window in the marble altar to see St. Minias' name, carved on the box that holds his mortal remains.

At the **staircase** to the right of the main altar, notice the sinopia on the wall. A sinopia is a pattern that guides the fresco artist and also gives the patron a peek at what the artist intends to create before it's set in plaster. There's a sinopia behind every surviving fresco in Florence.

Step upstairs and enter the **sacristy** (the room on the right), which is beautifully frescoed with scenes from the life of St. Benedict (circa 1350, by a follower of Giotto). Drop €2 into the electronic panel in the corner to light the room for five minutes. The elegantly bearded patron saint of Europe was the founder of the vast network of monasteries that gave the Continent some cohesiveness in the cultural darkness that followed the collapse of Rome. Benedict is shown as an active force for good, with his arm always outstretched: busy blessing, being kissed, preaching, helping, chasing the devil, bringing a man (crushed by a fallen tower) back to life, reaching out even on his death bed. Notice Benedict on the ramp, scooting up to heaven to be welcomed by an angel. And, overseeing everything, in the starry skies of the ceiling, are the Four Evangelists—each with his book, pen, and symbolic sidekicks.

**Outside the Church:** Before leaving, stroll through the cemetery behind the church (go right as you exit the church and head through the passage) to marvel at the showy crypts and headstones of Florentine hotshots from the last two centuries.

To get to Piazzale Michelangelo, head out and back down the grand staircase, savoring views of Florence along the way. Or for a quieter walk, turn right from the cemetery and pass into the adjacent park; keep veering left and you'll emerge at the viewpoint.

## NEAR FLORENCE
### Florence American Cemetery and Memorial

The compelling sight of endless rows of white marble crosses and Stars of David recalls the heroism of the young Americans who fought so valiantly in World War II to free Italy (and ultimately Europe) from the grip of fascism. This cemetery is the final resting place of more than 4,000 Americans who died in the liberation of Italy. Climb the hill past the perfectly manicured lawn lined with grave markers to the memorial, where maps and a

history of the Italian campaign detail the Allied advance. A staff member is on duty in the visitors center to answer questions.

**Cost and Hours:** Free, daily 9:00-17:00, +39 055 202 0020, www.abmc.gov.

**Getting There:** The cemetery is eight miles south of Florence, off Via Cassia, which parallels the *superstrada* between Florence and Siena, 2 miles south of the exit signed *Firenze Impruneta* on A-1 autostrada. Bus #365A runs from the BusItalia Station near the train station to the cemetery; get off at "Cimitero Degli Americani" (hourly, 30 minutes, www.at-bus.it).

# Fiesole

Perched on a hill overlooking the Arno valley, the tidy little town of Fiesole (FEE-ay-zoh-lay), just north of Florence, gives weary travelers a break in the action and—during the heat of summer—a breezy location from which to admire the city below. It's a small town with a main square, a few restaurants and shops, a few minor sights, and a great view. It's fitting that the E. M. Forster novel and the Merchant-Ivory film adaptation *A Room with a View* both have ties here.

The ancient Etruscans knew a good spot when they saw one, and chose to settle here, establishing Fiesole about 400 years before the Romans founded Florence. The Romans—more concerned

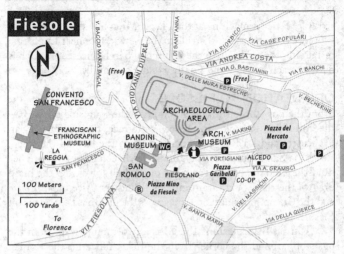

with water access than with Fiesole's strategic, sky-high position—shifted the region's focus down into the valley, allowing Fiesole to

evolve on a more relaxed track than bustling Florence. Wealthy Renaissance families in pre-air-conditioning days chose Fiesole as a preferred vacation spot, building villas in the surrounding hillsides. Later, 19th-century Romantics spent part of the Grand Tour admiring the vistas, much like the hordes of tourists do today. Most come here for the view and the smaller-scale, easy-to-visit attractions. Shutterbugs visit in the morning for the best light, while some prefer the evening for sunset.

## GETTING TO FIESOLE

It's only a half-hour from Florence by bus or taxi. Bus #7 departs from the Largo Alinari stop (across the street from the Florence train station's side entrance; return buses stop next to San Marco on Via Cavour and by the train station—see map on page 58; 3-4/hour, fewer after 21:00 and on Sun, 30 minutes, €1.50; tickets not sold on bus—buy at tobacco shops *(tabacchi)*, newsstands, or tram stops; validate on board). Relax and enjoy the ride to the last stop, in Fiesole's Piazza Mino.

As you climb up toward Fiesole, workaday apartment buildings give way to walled estates, small olive orchards, and Tuscan greenery. If you didn't buy a return bus ticket in Florence, there's a red ATAF ticket machine at the Piazza Mino bus stop. Taxis from Florence cost about €25-35 (ride to the view terrace near La Reggia restaurant, then hike up to the Church of San Francesco—which is hard to reach by car—and finally explore downhill).

## ORIENTATION TO FIESOLE

From the bus stop on Piazza Mino, face the long side of the Cathedral of San Romolo. The best view terrace, the Church of San Francesco, and La Reggia restaurant are to the left, up the steep, stone Via San Francesco. The TI and Archaeological Area are behind the Duomo, just to the right of the bell tower. Up the main drag to the right (Via Gramsci), you'll find the Alcedo *pasticceria* and the Co-op supermarket. And across the piazza is the restaurant Fiesolano.

**Tourist Information:** The TI is a two-minute walk from the bus stop, around the corner from the ticket office for the Roman Archaeological Area—just head behind the church (April-May daily 10:00-13:00 & 14:00-17:00, June-Sept Fri-Mon 10:00-13:00 & 16:00-18:00, closed Tue-Thu, open weekends only in Oct, closed Nov-March, Via Portigiani 3, +39 055 596 1311, www.fiesoleforyou.it).

**Market Day:** Fiesole weekends often come with markets—produce on Saturday mornings, antiques on the first Sunday of each month, and all-day artisan markets on some Sundays.

## SIGHTS IN FIESOLE
### On or Near the Main Square
#### Cathedral of San Romolo (Cattedrale di San Romolo)

While this church has a drab, 19th-century exterior, the interior is worth a look. The cool, clean architecture—with round Romanesque arches and narrow slits for light—is enlivened by some glittering Gothic altarpieces and a wood-beamed ceiling. Over the main door, look for the blue-and-white glazed Giovanni della Robbia statue of St. Romulus (not the founder of Rome, but Fiesole's patron saint). Then climb up the stairs past the altar and bear right to find the smiling, head-cocked tomb of Bishop Salutati, which was carved by Mino da Fiesole, a talented student of Donatello.

**Cost and Hours:** Free, generally daily 7:30-12:00 & 15:00-17:30, across Piazza Mino from the bus stop.

#### Archaeological Area and Museum
#### (Area Archeologica and Museo Civico Archeologico)

Florence has few visible Roman ruins—and archaeological finds are far more impressive elsewhere in Italy—but the archaeological area at Fiesole occupies one of the most beautiful spots in town. This pricey but well-presented complex features a largely intact

Roman theater, some less-intact fragments of a theater and baths, and a decent museum of local finds. And the valley view and peaceful setting are lovely. If you don't want to spring for the hefty entry fee, you can get a peek of the grounds from the on-site café terrace.

**Cost and Hours:** €10, €12 combo-ticket also covers Bandini Museum, includes excellent videoguide; daily 9:00-19:00, March and Oct 10:00-18:00; Nov-Feb Wed-Mon 10:00-15:00, closed Tue; behind the Duomo at Via Portigiani 1, www.museidifiesole. it.

**Visiting the Ruins and Museum:** When you buy your ticket, be sure to borrow the included tablet videoguide with a well-produced virtual tour of the ruins. Then head inside and proceed straight ahead.

At your feet is the area's chief attraction, its **Roman theater.** Occasionally used today for plays and concerts, the well-preserved theater held up to 2,000 people in its heyday. About half of what you see here has been rebuilt (the part to the left). More ruins sprawl nearby: To the right, marked by the three arches, are fragments of a bath complex; and to the left, in the trees, is what's left of a temple. While there's little to see, a pleasant loop walk connects everything.

The **museum,** located in the faux-temple within the Archaeological Area, imparts insight into Fiesole's Etruscan and Roman roots with well-displayed artifacts (borrow the English descriptions that supplement the videoguide). You'll see fragments of tombs (boxy bases and ornately decorated lids, depicting the departed lounging at an eternal banquet), appealing Etruscan bronze votive statues, and jewelry. Upstairs are Attica-style black-and-red pottery vases. As this look originated in ancient Greece, their existence here is evidence of widely traveled Etruscan traders (who brought this style home with them). You'll also see several *bucchero* vases—a method for turning red clay into shiny black pottery pieces, in order to resemble highly prized bronze.

### Bandini Museum (Museo Bandini)

This petite museum displays a small trove of paintings and sculptures from between 1000 and 1400. The ground floor shows a group of glazed terra-cotta figures by Andrea della Robbia, while the first floor displays the wooden panels of lesser-known Gothic and early Renaissance painters.

**Cost and Hours:** €5, €12 combo-ticket with Archaeological Area and Museum, Fri-Sun 9:00-19:00, closed Mon-Thu, shorter hours Oct-March, behind Duomo at Via Dupre 1.

## Up the Hill, at the Top of Town

To reach these sights, you'll have to huff your way about 10 minutes steeply up from the main square and bus stop. First you'll pass the recommended La Reggia restaurant, then the terrace, and finally (a few more vertical minutes up) the church complex.

### ▲▲Terrace and Garden with a View

Catch the sunset (and your breath) from the sweeping view terrace just above La Reggia restaurant. Florence stretches out from the Duomo's stately dome, with the Oltrarno and Piazzale Michelangelo in the background. And the hillsides all around are draped with vineyards and speckled with luxury villas of Renaissance bigwigs who knew how to maximize a great city view.

### Church and Convent of San Francesco
### (Chiesa e Convento di San Francesco)

Continue up from the view terrace to this charming church complex, with a tiny church, some monks' cells, two little cloisters, and a quirky museum of missionary souvenirs.

**Cost and Hours:** Church—free, daily 7:00-20:00 except closed Fri morning, Nov-March 7:30-19:00, +39 055 59 175; museum—free but donation suggested, same hours as church; both at Via San Francesco 13. There's a little refreshment stand on-site.

**Visiting the Complex:** In this peaceful place, you can see why the Franciscans sought out nature to foster contemplative thought. The church complex has a commanding view over the surrounding valley.

Before entering the church, poke in the doorway to the right for a look at a tranquil **cloister.** Climbing the nearby stairs, you'll find a hall of 15th-century monastic cells, where Franciscan monks lived in prayerful meditation.

Next head **inside** the church, with a simple, clean interior. To the left of the altar, find the door leading into another cloister, and the eclectic little **Franciscan Ethnographic Museum** (Museo Etnografico Francescano). Consisting primarily of items that Franciscan missionaries brought back from exotic lands, it features an Egyptian mummy, ancient coins, and Chinese Buddhas and vases. It all sits upon some very old history: One wall of the museum is actually part of the third-century-BC Etruscan town wall.

## EATING IN FIESOLE

The first restaurant is right on Piazza Mino, where the bus from Florence stops; the other is near the view terrace above town.

**$$ Fiesolano,** a local favorite, serves authentic Tuscan dishes, including Florentine steaks, at a fair price. Choose between the homey, cluttered interior, the few sidewalk tables facing the main square, or the shady garden terrace (daily 12:30-14:30 & 19:30-23:30, Piazza Mino 9 red, +39 055 59 143, Leonardo).

**$$$ Ristorante La Reggia degli Etruschi** has some of the

highest prices—and best views—in town, as long as you're willing to make the steep walk up. As you're paying for the panorama, reserve a table at a window or on their terrace to fully enjoy the vista (daily 12:00-15:00 & 19:00-22:00, Via San Francesco 18, +39 055 59 385, www.lareggiadeglietruschi.com).

**Picnics:** Fiesole is made-to-order for a scenic and breezy picnic. Grab a fresh-made panini from the food truck that's often set up on the square, or pick up a sandwich and pastry from Fiesole's best *pasticceria,* **$ Alcedo** (head up the main drag from the bus stop to Via Gramsci 39, closed Mon). Round out your goodies across the street at the **Co-op** supermarket (closed Sun) before backtracking to the panoramic terrace. Or, for more convenience and less view, picnic in the shaded park on the way to the view terrace (walk up Via San Francesco and climb the stairs to the right).

# RENAISSANCE WALK

*From the Duomo to the Arno*

After centuries of labor, Florence gave birth to the Renaissance. We'll start with the soaring church dome that stands as the proud symbol of the Renaissance spirit. Just opposite, you'll find the Baptistery doors that opened the Renaissance. Finally, we'll reach Florence's political center, dotted with monuments of that proud time. As great and rich as this city is, it's easily covered on foot. While these days many of the crowded and commercial streets of Florence have the elegance of an amusement park, you'll still find inspirational sights everywhere you look... assuming you know where to look.

The Duomo, the cathedral with the distinctive red dome, is the center of Florence and the orientation point for this walk. If you ever get lost, home's the dome. We'll start here, see several sights in the area, and then stroll down the city's pedestrian-only main street to the Palazzo Vecchio and the Arno River. Along the way, we'll pass elegant stores, lively eateries, and the parade of people that make up Florence today.

## Orientation

**Length of This Walk:** The walk is less than a mile long. Allow two hours, including a visit to the interior of the Baptistery.

**Duomo** (Cathedral): Free but long lines without a pass; Mon-Sat 10:15-16:45, closed Sun. A modest dress code is enforced.

**Campanile** (Giotto's Tower): Covered by Duomo's Giotto Pass, daily 8:15-19:45, 414 steps.

**Climbing the Dome:** Covered by Duomo's Brunelleschi Pass, must reserve dome-climb entry at time of purchase (see page 51).

**Baptistery:** Covered by all three Duomo passes, interior open daily 9:00-19:45. The facsimiles of the famous *Gates of Paradise* bronze doors on the exterior are always viewable (and free to see); the original panels are in the Duomo Museum.

**Palazzo Vecchio:** Michelozzo courtyard-free, museum and tower climb—€12.50 each, excavations—€4; museum and excavations open daily 9:00-19:00 except Thu until 14:00.

**Tours:** ♫ Download my free Renaissance Walk audio tour and I'll personally give you this tour.

**Services:** Pay WCs are at the ticket office opposite the Baptistery. Keep an eye out for public twist-the-handle fountains along this route where you can refill your water bottle.

**Eating:** You'll find plenty of cafés, self-service cafeterias, bars, and gelato shops along the route, including several recommended eateries (see the Eating in Florence chapter for details).

**Starring:** Brunelleschi's dome, Ghiberti's doors, and the city of Florence—old and new.

# The Walk Begins

Stroll around the piazza in front of the cathedral (the Duomo) and take in the sights. There's the church itself, with its ornate white, green, and pink facade. The Duomo is topped with a soaring red-and-white dome—though from close up, it's hard to even see the dome because the church itself is so big. To the right of the Duomo rises its skyscraping bell tower (the Campanile) with its Renaissance statues. In front of the church is the Baptistery, an octagonal, green-and-white stone building that's bigger than many churches.

The piazza is always buzzing with activity—tourists, horse buggies, and Florentines on their way to somewhere else—as this is one of the main intersections in town. Get a feel for the place, then let's explore.

## ❶ The Duomo

Florence's massive cathedral is the city's geographical and spiritual heart. Its dome, visible from all over the city, inspired Florentines to do great things. (Most recently, it inspired the city to make the area around the cathedral delightfully traffic-free.)

The church was begun in 1296, in the Gothic style. After generations of work, it was still unfinished. The facade was little more than bare brick, and it stood that way until it was completed in 1870 in the "Neo"-Gothic style. Its "retro" look captures the feel of the original medieval facade, with green,

white, and pink marble sheets that cover the brick construction. You'll see Gothic (pointed) arches and three stories decorated with mosaics and statues. This over-the-top facade is adored by many, while others call it "the cathedral in pajamas." The Duomo is dedicated to the Virgin Mary. Find her statue right in the center—above the main doorway but below the round window.

We won't go inside the church on this tour. It has a cavernous, bare interior with a few noteworthy sights. Entry is free, but there's often a long wait unless you buy a pass that allows you to enter through the crypt. For my brief self-guided tour of the interior, see page 53.

• *Now turn to the church's bell tower, to the right.*

## ❷ Campanile (Giotto's Tower)

The 270-foot bell tower was begun in the 1300s by the great painter Giotto. As a forerunner of the Renaissance genius, Giotto excelled in many artistic fields, just as Michelange-lo would do two centuries later. In his day, Giotto was called the ugliest man to ever walk the streets of Florence, but he designed what many call the most beautiful bell tower in all of Europe.

The bell tower served as a sculpture gallery for Renaissance artists. Find the four statues of prophets (about a third of the way up) done by the great Early Renaissance sculptor, Donatello. The most striking is bald-headed Habbakuk. At the lowest level are several hexagonal panels that ring the Campanile. These reliefs depict Bible scenes: God Creates Adam, then Eve, and they set to work. Then Jabal learns to till the soil while Jubal blows his horn...as if celebrating the cultural evolution of humanity. It was early Renaissance, heralding a new humanistic approach to God and the idea that the best way to glorify God was to use your God-given talents. The

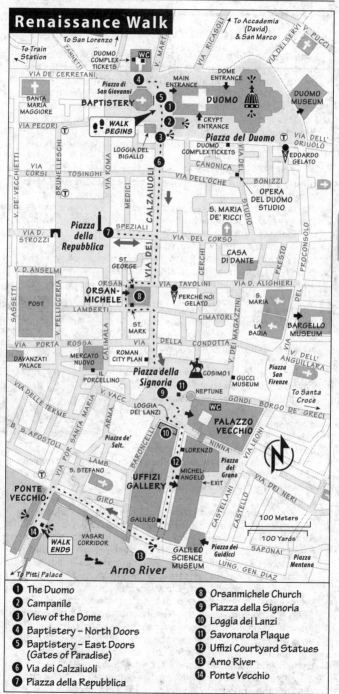

# Renaissance Walk

To Accademia (David) & San Marco

To Train Station

To San Lorenzo

DUOMO COMPLEX TICKETS

WC

SANTA MARIA MAGGIORE

Piazza di San Giovanni

BAPTISTERY

MAIN ENTRANCE

DOME ENTRANCE

DUOMO

DUOMO MUSEUM

CRYPT ENTRANCE

WALK BEGINS

LOGGIA DEL BIGALLO

Piazza del Duomo

DUOMO COMPLEX TICKETS

CANONICA

EDOARDO GELATO

VIA DELL' ORIUOLO

OPERA DEL DUOMO STUDIO

S. MARIA DE' RICCI

BONIZZI

Piazza della Repubblica

ST. GEORGE

ORSAN-MICHELE

LAMBERTI

ST. MARK

ROMAN CITY PLAN

POST

DAVANZATI PALACE

MERCATO NUOVO

IL PORCELLINO

Piazza della Signoria

COSIMO I

GUCCI MUSEUM

NEPTUNE

WC

PALAZZO VECCHIO

LOGGIA DEI LANZI

Piazza de' Salt.

S. STEFANO

BARONCELLI

LORENZO

MICHEL-ANGELO

EXIT

NINNA

Piazza del Grano

UFFIZI GALLERY

PONTE VECCHIO

WALK ENDS

VASARI CORRIDOR

GALILEO

GALILEO SCIENCE MUSEUM

Piazza dei Guidicci

To Pitti Palace

Arno River

CASA DI DANTE

PERCHÉ NOI GELATO

S. MARIA

LA BADIA

BARGELLO MUSEUM

Piazza San Firenze

To Santa Croce

BORGO DE' GRECI

100 Meters

100 Yards

Piazza Mentana

RENAISSANCE WALK

① The Duomo
② Campanile
③ View of the Dome
④ Baptistery – North Doors
⑤ Baptistery – East Doors (Gates of Paradise)
⑥ Via dei Calzaiuoli
⑦ Piazza della Repubblica
⑧ Orsanmichele Church
⑨ Piazza della Signoria
⑩ Loggia dei Lanzi
⑪ Savonarola Plaque
⑫ Uffizi Courtyard Statues
⑬ Arno River
⑭ Ponte Vecchio

# The Florentine Renaissance

In the 13th and 14th centuries, Florence was a powerful center of banking, trading, and textile manufacturing. The resulting wealth fertilized the cultural soil. Then came the Black Death in 1348. Nearly half the population died, but the infrastructure remained strong, and the city rebuilt better than ever. Led by Florence's chief family—the art-crazy Medici—and propelled by the naturally aggressive and creative spirit of the Florentines, it's no wonder that the long-awaited Renaissance finally took root here.

The Renaissance—the "rebirth" of Greek and Roman culture that swept across Europe—started around 1400 and lasted about 150 years. In politics, the Renaissance meant democracy; in science, a renewed interest in exploring nature. The general mood was optimistic and "humanistic," with a confidence in the power of the individual.

In medieval times, poverty and ignorance had made life "nasty, brutish, and short" (for lack of a better cliché). The Church was the people's opiate, and their lives were only a preparation for a happier time in heaven after leaving this miserable vale of tears.

Medieval art was the Church's servant. The noblest art form was architecture—churches themselves—and other arts were considered most worthwhile if they embellished the house of God. Painting and sculpture were narrative and symbolic, designed to tell Bible stories to the devout and illiterate masses.

As prosperity rose in Florence, so did people's confidence in life and themselves. Middle-class craftsmen, merchants, and bankers felt they could control their own destinies, rather than be at the whim of nature. They found much in common with the ancient Greeks and Romans, who valued logic and reason above superstition and blind faith.

Renaissance art was a return to the realism and balance of Greek and Roman sculpture and architecture. Domes and round arches replaced Gothic spires and pointed arches. In painting and sculpture, Renaissance artists strove for realism. Merging art and science, they used mathematics, the laws of perspective, and direct observation of nature.

This was not an anti-Christian movement. Artists saw themselves as an extension of God's creative powers. The Church even supported the Renaissance and commissioned many of its greatest works—for instance, Raphael frescoed images of Plato and Aristotle on the walls of the Vatican. But for the first time in Europe since Roman times, there were rich laymen who wanted art simply for art's sake.

After 1,000 years of waiting, the embers of Europe's classical heritage burst into flames right here in Florence.

realism of these groundbreaking works paved the way for Michelangelo and the High Renaissance generations later.

These are copies—the originals are at the excellent **Duomo Museum,** just behind the church. There you'll find more statues from the Duomo, plus displays on the dome, Ghiberti's bronze doors, and a late pietà by Michelangelo. (📖 See the Duomo Museum Tour chapter.)

You can climb the Campanile for great views. It doesn't require a reservation, just the Duomo's Giotto Pass (see page 51 for information about climbing the tower).

• *Now take in the Duomo's star attraction: the dome. The best viewing spot is just to the right of the facade, from the corner of the pedestrian-only Via dei Calzaiuoli.*

## ❸ View of Brunelleschi's Dome

The dome rises 330 feet from ground level. It's made of red brick, held together with eight white ribs, and capped with a lantern.

Though construction of the church began in 1296, by the 1400s there still was no suitable roof. (For a century, the old cathedral remained inside the new so people could still go to Mass.) City fathers intended to top the new church with a dome, but the technology to span the 140-foot-wide hole had yet to be invented. *Non c'è problema.* The brash Florentines knew that someday someone would come along who could handle the challenge. That man was Filippo Brunelleschi.

Brunelleschi had a plan. He would cap the church's octagonal hole-in-the-roof with a round Roman-style dome. It would be a tall, self-supporting dome as grand as that of the ancient Pantheon—which he had studied.

Brunelleschi used a dome within a dome. What you see is the outer shell, covered in terra-cotta tile. The inner dome is thicker and provides much of the structural support. The grand white skeletal ribs connect at the top, supporting each other in a way similar to a pointed arch. Hidden between them are interlocking bricks, laid in a herringbone pattern. Rather than being stacked horizontally, like traditional brickwork, the alternating vertical bricks act as "bookends." The dome grew upward like an igloo, supporting itself as it proceeded from the base. When the ribs reached the top, Brunelleschi arched them in and fixed them in place with a decorative, nonstructural architectural cherry on top—the lantern. His dome, built in only 16 years, was the largest since ancient Rome's Pantheon.

When completed in 1436, Brunelleschi's dome was the wonder of the age. It became the model for many domes to follow, from St. Peter's Basilica in Rome to the US Capitol. People gave it the ultimate compliment, saying, "Not even the ancients could have

done it." Michelangelo, setting out to construct the dome of St. Peter's, drew inspiration from the dome of Florence. He said, "I'll make its sister...bigger, but not more beautiful."

You can climb the dome for Florence's best views, but it requires a reservation and the Duomo's Brunelleschi pass (for details, see page 51).

• *Next up, the Baptistery. Step into the zone between the Duomo and the Baptistery that local tour guides call the "Piazza of Paradise."*

## Baptistery and Ghiberti's Bronze Doors

Florence's Baptistery is dear to the soul of the city. Built in the 11th century, atop Roman foundations, it's one of Florence's oldest surviving buildings—a thousand years old. In medieval and Renaissance times, the locals—eager to link themselves to the classical past—believed (wrongly) that this was actually an ancient Roman structure. And for a thousand years, most of the city's festivals and parades have either started or ended here.

The Baptistery is known for its doors. Andrea Pisano created the oldest set (from the 1330s, on the south side). The most famous ones are the East Doors, which face the cathedral, but let's start with the North Doors—around to the right, where tourists go in—which may be even more important. (Note that the doors on the Baptistery are copies. The originals are in the Duomo Museum and well worth seeing.)

❹ **North Doors:** The huge doors are made of rectangular panels that feature 28 scenes from the New Testament. For example, the second row from the bottom has the Four Evangelists: John (with his eagle), Matthew (inspired by an angel), Luke (just chilling), and Mark (with his flying lion).

Some say that these doors actually started the Renaissance. It was the year 1401, and Florence was holding a competition to find the best artist to make some doors for the Baptistery entrance. Florence had a long tradition of strong civic spirit, with different guilds (powerful trade associations) and merchant groups embellishing their city with superb art. All the greats entered the contest,

RENAISSANCE WALK

including Donatello and Brunelleschi. The winner was relatively unknown 24-year-old Lorenzo Ghiberti. (Brunelleschi—after losing the Baptistery gig—went to Rome with Donatello, studied the Pantheon, and returned to build the Duomo's dome.) Take a moment to appreciate the composition—impressive—but no background. On the left, eight feet up in the center with the turban, is the young artist Ghiberti.

For the next 25 years, Ghiberti worked on these North Doors, creating such realistic figures that all of Florence was astounded. But that was just the beginning.

• *Now return to the more famous doors facing the church—and see progress made in 25 years.*

**❺ East Doors** (Gates of Paradise): When the Baptistery needed another set of doors, this time there was literally no con-

test. Ghiberti's bronze panels for these doors added a whole new dimension to art—depth. Michelangelo said these doors were fit to be the "Gates of Paradise." Here we see how the Renaissance masters merged art and science. Realism was in, and Renaissance artists used math, illusion, and dissection to create it.

Find the Jacob and Esau panel (just above eye level on the left). The receding arches, floor tiles, and banisters create a background for a realistic scene. The figures in the foreground

stand and move like real people, telling the Bible story with human details. Amazingly, this spacious, 3-D scene is made from bronze only a couple of inches deep.

Find Ghiberti's tiny self-portrait (now 25 years older)—he's the bald guy in the center of the door's frame, atop the second row of panels. Ghiberti's groundbreaking use of 3-D and the laws of perspective went on to influence the next generation of painters and artists, who would usher in the full bloom of the Renaissance. (For a full description and diagram of the doors, see page 176.)

• *At some point in your visit, you'll want to go inside the Baptistery (covered by all three Duomo passes).*

**Inside the Baptistery:** The spacious interior, topped with an octagonal dome, features a fine example of pre-Renaissance mosaic art (1200s-1300s) in the Byzantine style. Workers from St. Mark's in Venice came here to make the remarkable ceiling mosaics (of Venetian glass) in the late 1200s.

*The Last Judgment* on the ceiling gives us a glimpse of the medieval worldview. Life was a preparation for the afterlife, when you

would be judged and saved, or judged and damned—with no in-between. Christ, peaceful and reassuring, blessed those at his right hand with heaven (thumbs up) and sent those on his left to hell (the ultimate thumbs-down), to be tortured by demons and gnashed between the teeth of monsters.

Look closely at hell. It's a chaotic tangle of mangled bodies, slithering snakes, and licking flames. In the center squats a bull-headed monster, with his arms outstretched like Christ's demonic doppelganger. He gorges on one poor soul, grabs the next course with his hands, and stomps on two more souls, while snakes sprout from his ears and tail to grab more victims. The anguished faces of the damned tell a sad story of eternal torment.

The whole hellish scene looks like something out of the *Inferno* by Dante, who was dipped into the baptismal waters right here.

The rest of the ceiling mosaics tell the history of the world, from Adam and Eve (over the north/entrance doors, top row) to Noah and the Flood (over south doors, top row), to the life of Christ (second row, all around) to the life, ministry, and eventual beheading of John the Baptist (bottom row, all around)—all bathed in the golden glow of pre-Renaissance heaven.

• *Now head south, down the busy pedestrian-only street that runs from here toward the Arno River.*

## ❻ Via dei Calzaiuoli

Via dei Calzaiuoli (kahlts-ay-WOH-lee), the former "street of the stocking makers," is today lined with shops that cater to the mobs

of tourists. This street has long been the main axis of the city, and it was part of the ancient Roman grid plan that became Florence. Around the year 1400, as the Renaissance was blooming, this street connected the religious center (where we are now) with the political center (where we're heading), a five-

RENAISSANCE WALK

minute walk away. Back then, the shops sold cheese, flags, and horse bridles. The street bustled with men in colorful Romeo-style tights, with swords in their belts, and caps with a feather in it. The women promenaded by in Juliet-style dresses with poufy sleeves and brocaded patterns, their elaborate braids tucked into hairnets.

Nowadays this historic core is home to tourists in shorts, licking the drips on their gelato cones. You'll pass an ever-changing array of *gelaterie* here and on adjoining streets—some old and venerable, some the trendy flavor of the month. Shops sell everything from high-fashion clothes to Florentine specialties: leather bags, gold-work jewelry, and *David* knickknacks.

Since most vehicles were banned a few years back, this street has been transformed into a pleasant place to stroll, people-watch, window-shop, and wonder why American cities can't become more pedestrian friendly.

• *Continue down Via dei Calzaiuoli. Two blocks down from the Baptistery, turn right on Via degli Speziali toward the triumphal arch that marks...*

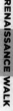

## ❼ Piazza della Repubblica

This large square sits on the site of the original Roman Forum. Florence was founded 2,000 years ago as a riverside garrison town, with its main square here at the intersection of the two main roads (Via Corso and Via Roma). The lone column that still stands here—nicknamed the "belly button of Florence"—once marked that intersection. If you look at a map of Florence today, you can make out the ghost of Rome in its streets: a rectangular grid-plan city center surrounded by a circular city wall.

By the 1500s, this square was the heart of the Jewish quarter. In 1571, Cosimo I had it walled in and made into a ghetto.

In the 1860s, the square got its magnificent triumphal arch. It celebrated the unification of Italy. In fact, from 1865 to 1870, Florence became the capital of the newly united nation of Italy. To live up to its role, the city was spiffed up: City walls were taken down, grand European-style boulevards were blasted through, and the Jewish ghetto was razed to create this imposing, modern forum surrounded by stately circa-1890 buildings. Notice the proud statement atop the triumphal arch, which proclaims, "The squalor of the ancient city is given a new life."

Venerable cafés and stores line the square. During the 19th

century, intellectuals met in cafés here. Gilli, on the northeast corner, is a favorite for its grand atmosphere and tasty sweets (cheap if you stand at the bar, expensive to sit down). The much-loved drink called Negroni (gin, vermouth, bitter Campari, and a slice of orange) was named for a local count who popularized it here.

The department store La Rinascente, facing Piazza della Repubblica, is one of the city's mainstays, and its rooftop **$$ Caffè Tosca & Nino** offers great Duomo and city views for the cost of a drink.

• *Return to the main street and continue walking toward the river. A block farther, at the intersection with Via Orsanmichele, is the...*

## ❽ Orsanmichele Church

The Orsanmichele Church provides an interesting look at Florence's medieval roots. It's a combo church/granary. Originally, this was an open loggia (covered porch) with a huge grain warehouse upstairs. Then, as you can see, the arches of the loggia were artfully filled in (14th century) to make walls, and the building gained a new purpose—as a church. This was prime real estate on what had become the main drag between the church and palace.

The 14 niches in the exterior walls feature remarkable-in-their-day statues paid for by the city's rising middle class of merchants and their 21 guilds. Florence in 1400 was a republic, a government working for the interests not of a king, but of these guilds (much as modern America is controlled by and caters to corporate interests). The guilds commissioned statues as PR gestures, hiring the finest artists of the time. As the statues were done over several decades, they function as a textbook of the evolution of Florentine art.

In earlier Gothic times, statues were set deep into church niches, simply embellishing the house of God. Here at the Orsanmichele Church, we see statues—as restless as man on the verge of the Renaissance—stepping out from the protection of the Church.

• *Circle the church exterior counterclockwise to enjoy the statues. While these are all copies, on some days you can see the originals in the church's top-floor museum. The original of the most famous of the statues (St. George) is in the Bargello Museum.*

*Starting on the church's right side (along Via Orsanmichele), in the third niche is...*

**Nanni di Banco's *Quattro Santi Coronati* (c. 1415-1417):** These four early Christians were sculptors martyred by the Roman emperor Diocletian because they refused to sculpt pagan gods. They seem to be contemplating the consequences of the fatal decision they're about to make. Their faces are classical—like their ancient inspiration. Beneath some of the niches, you'll find the symbol of the guilds that paid for the art. Art historians differ here. Some think the work was commissioned by the carpenters' and masons' guild. Others contend it was by the guys who did discount circumcisions.

• *While Banco's saints are deep in the church's niche, the next statue feels ready to step out. Just to the right is...*

**Donatello's *St. George:*** George is alert, perched on the edge of his niche, scanning the horizon for dragons and announcing the new age with its new outlook. His knitted brow shows there's a drama unfolding. Sure, he's anxious, but he's also self-assured. Comparing this Renaissance-style *St. George* to *Quattro Santi Coronati*, you can psychoanalyze the heady changes underway. This is humanism.

This *St. George* is a copy of the c. 1417 original (now in the Bargello; 📖 see the Bargello Tour chapter).

The predella (small carving below the statue) shows St. George slaying the dragon and saving the damsel, who's in a classic damsel-in-distress pose. It reminds viewers that this statue was brought to you by the sword-and-armor makers' guild. Art historians consider this relief (by Donatello, the apprentice of relief-maestro Ghiberti) a breakthrough in realism. Notice Donatello's mathematically correct receding colonnade (on the right) behind that delightful little S-shaped figure.

• *Walk across the back side of the church.*

***St. Matthew, St. Stephen,* and *St. Eligius:*** Three statues here are worth a look. *St. Matthew,* patron of bankers, and *St. Stephen,* patron of wool merchants (both by Ghiberti), are a reminder that banking and textiles were mainstays of the Florentine economy—and wealthy enough to actually pay for bronze statues rather than marble. Nanni di Banco's *St. Eligius,* patron of metalworkers, shows workers shoeing a horse.

• *Around the corner, the first niche you come to features...*

**Donatello's *St. Mark* (1411-1413):** The evangelist cradles his gospel in his strong, veined hand and gazes out, resting his weight on the right leg while bending the left. Though subtle, St. Mark's twisting *contrapposto* pose was the first seen since antiquity. Commissioned by the linen sellers' guild, the statue has elaborately detailed robes that drape around the natural contours of his weighty body. When the guild first saw the statue, they thought the oversized head and torso made it top-heavy. Only after it was lifted into its raised niche did Donatello's cleverly designed proportions look right—and the guild accepted it. Eighty years after young Donatello carved this statue, a teenage Michelangelo Buonarroti stood here and marveled.

• *The Bargello, with Florence's best collection of sculpture, is a few blocks east, down Via dei Tavolini. But let's continue down the mall 50 more yards, to the huge and historic square...*

## ❾ Piazza della Signoria

What a view! This piazza—the main civic center of Florence—is dominated by the massive stone facade of the Palazzo Vecchio, with a tower that reaches for the sky. The square is dotted with statues. The stately Uffizi Gallery is nearby, and the marble greatness of old Florence litters the cobbles. Piazza della Signoria, with the feel of an open-air museum of statuary, still vibrates with the echoes of the city's past—executions, riots, and great celebrations. There's even Roman history: Look for the **chart** showing the ancient city (20 steps into the square on the right). Today, it's a tourist's world with pigeons, selfie sticks, horse buggies, and tired spouses.

Before you towers the **Palazzo Vecchio,** the "old palace" and palatial Town Hall of the Medici—a fortress designed to contain riches and survive the many riots that went with local politics. The windows are just beyond the reach of angry stones, and the tower was a handy lookout post. Capping the tip of the tower is a lion weathervane. (Locals like to say "when the lion pees in the river, it's going to rain.") Justice was doled out sternly on this square. Until 1873, Michelangelo's *David* stood where you see the replica today. The original was damaged in a 1527 riot (when a bench thrown from a palace window knocked its left arm off), but it remained here for several centuries, before being moved indoors for protection.

Step past the fake *David* through the front door into the Palazzo Vecchio's courtyard (free). This palace was Florence's symbol of civic power. You're surrounded by art for art's sake—a cherub playing with a dolphin frivolously marks the courtyard's center, and ornate stuccoes and frescoes decorate the walls and columns. Such luxury represented a big change 500 years ago.

☐ For a self-guided tour of this palace, including more on this courtyard, see the Palazzo Vecchio Tour chapter.

• *Back outside, check out the arcade of three arches filled with statues.*

## ❿ Loggia dei Lanzi

This loggia, once a forum for public debate, was perfect for a city that prided itself on its democratic traditions. But later, when the Medici figured that good art was more desirable than free speech, it was turned into an outdoor sculpture gallery. Notice the squirming themes—conquest, domination, rape, and decapitation (don't mess with the Medici). The statues lining the back are Roman

originals brought back to Florence by a Medici when his villa in Rome was sold. Two statues in the front deserve a closer look.

At the right end of the loggia, *The Rape of the Sabine Women* (c. 1583)—with its pulse-quickening rhythm of muscles—is from the restless Mannerist period, which followed the stately and confident Renaissance. The sculptor, Giambologna, proved his mastery of the medium by sculpting three entangled bodies from one piece of marble. The composition is best viewed from below and in front. The relief panel below shows a wider view of the terrible scene. (In the Accademia, you can see the original plaster model of this statue that was used to guide Giambologna's workers in helping him create it.)

Benvenuto Cellini's *Perseus* (1545-1553), the loggia's most noteworthy piece, shows the Greek hero who decapitated the snake-headed Medusa. They say Medusa was so ugly she turned humans who looked at her to stone—though one of this book's authors thinks she's kinda cute. Cellini, a notorious braggart, placed his name prominently across the sash on the front and amazingly, included a secret self-portrait on the back of Perseus' head: His locks form the beard while the helmet frames the bushy brow and eyes.

• *Cross the square to Bartolomeo Ammanati's* big **fountain of Neptune.** *Florentines (including Michelangelo) consider this a huge waste of marble—though one of this book's authors...*

*Near the Neptune statue is a bronze* **equestrian statue.** *The guy on the horse is Cosimo I, the post-Renaissance Medici who commissioned the Uffizi. Find the round marble plaque on the ground 10 steps in front of the fountain.*

## ⓫ Savonarola Plaque

The plaque's inscription begins with the word *"Qui"*—"here." It explains that a crucial event in Florentine history happened right on this spot.

In the 1490s (when Michelangelo was a teenager) the Medici family was briefly thrown from power by an austere and charismatic monk named Savonarola, who made Florence a constitutional republic. He organized huge rallies lit by roaring bonfires here on the square where he preached. While children sang hymns, the devout brought their rich "vanities" (such as paintings, musical instruments, and playing cards) and threw them into the flames.

But not everyone wanted a return to the medieval past. Encouraged by the pope, the Florentines fought back and arrested

Savonarola. For two days, they tortured him, trying unsuccessfully to persuade him to see their side of things. Finally, on the very spot where Savonarola's followers had built bonfires of vanities, the monk was burned. The plaque, engraved in Italian *("Qui dove...")*, reads, "Here, Girolamo Savonarola and his Dominican brothers were hanged and burned" in the year "MCCCCXCVIII" (1498), ending his theocracy. Then—after 18 years in exile—the Medici returned to power and the Renaissance picked up where it left off. (For more on Savonarola, 🕮 see the Museum of San Marco Tour chapter.)

• *Stay cool, we have 200 yards to go. Follow the gaze of the fake David into the courtyard of the two-tone horseshoe-shaped building.*

## ⓬ Uffizi Courtyard Statues

The top floor of this building, known as the *uffizi* (offices) during Medici days, is filled with the greatest collection of Florentine

RENAISSANCE WALK

painting anywhere. It's one of Europe's top four or five art galleries (📖 see the Uffizi Gallery Tour chapter).

The Uffizi courtyard, free to enter and filled with vendors and hustling young artists, is watched over by 19th-century statues of the great figures of the Renaissance—all Tuscans. Tourists zero in on the visual accomplishments of the era, but let's pay tribute to the many other accomplishments of the Renaissance as well, as we wander through Florence's Renaissance Hall of Fame.

• *Stroll down the left side of the courtyard from the Palazzo Vecchio to the river, noticing the following greats.*

LORENZO IL MAGNIFICO

**Lorenzo the Magnificent,** the Medici ruler, was a great art patron and cunning power broker. Excelling in everything except modesty, he set the tone for the Renaissance. His statue is tucked under the arcade, by an Uffizi doorway.

**Giotto,** holding the plan to the city's bell tower (which is named for him) was the great pre-Renaissance artist whose paintings foretold the future of Italian art.

**Donatello,** the sculptor who served as a role model for Michelangelo, holds a hammer and chisel.

**Alberti** wrote a famous book, *On Painting,* which taught early Renaissance artists the mathematics of perspective.

**Leonardo da Vinci** was a scientist, sculptor, musician, engineer...and not a bad painter, either. This well-roundedness marked the epitome of a Renaissance genius.

**Michelangelo** ponders the universe and/or stifles a belch.

**Dante,** with the laurel-leaf crown and lyre of a poet, says, "I am the father of the Italian language." He was the first Italian to write a popular work *(The Divine Comedy)* in the Florentine dialect, which soon became "Italian" throughout the country (until Dante, Latin had been the language of literature).

**Petrarch,** the poet, wears laurel leaves from Greece, a robe from Rome, and a belt from Walmart.

**Boccaccio** wrote *The Decameron,* stories told to pass the time during the 1348 Black Death. He helped popularize literature in the people's language rather than Latin.

**Machiavelli** looks like he's deviously hatching a plot—his book *The Prince* taught that the end justifies the means, paving the way for the slick-and-cunning "Machiavellian" politics of today.

**Vespucci** (in the corner) was an explorer who gave his first name, Amerigo, to a fledgling New World.

NICCOLO MACCHIAVELLI

**Galileo** (in the other corner) holds the humble telescope he used to spot the moons of Jupiter. By the way, Galileo's actual fingers are preserved and on display in the Galileo Science Museum, a block from here (see page 73).

Before leaving the courtyard, look up and appreciate the architectural harmony. Created by Brunelleschi, it's symmetrical—with a rhythm, a geometrical logic, a classical order...and a Medici grand duke above the arch overseeing it all.

• *Now, head on out to the Arno River and a magnificent view of the Ponte Vecchio.*

## ⓭ Arno River

The Arno runs east to west. It starts in the Apennine Mountains that form the spine of Italy; 150 miles later, it spills out into the Mediterranean near Pisa. For centuries, the river was a crucial east-west trade route linking northern Italy. The north-south trade ran along a highway, from northern Europe to Rome, with Florence in between. So, since ancient times, a bridge has stood at this narrow spot in the Arno. When a flood washed away the old wooden bridge, this one was built in 1345, and is now called the Ponte Vecchio (Old Bridge). The Arno's last epic flood, back in 1966, caused so much damage to the city. Notice the windows running across the upper part of the buildings on the bridge. This is the Vasari Corridor—a protected and elevated passageway, built by the Medici. It led from the Palazzo Vecchio through the Uffizi, across Ponte Vecchio, and up to the immense Pitti Palace, four blocks beyond the bridge.

By the way, to get into the exclusive little park below (on the north bank of the river), you'll need to join the Florence rowing club.

• *Finish your walk by hiking to the center of the...*

## ⓮ Ponte Vecchio

In times past, the bridge's shops were inhabited by butchers and hide tanners—a natural fit, because they could empty their waste into the river below. In the 1500s, the Medici booted them out and installed gold-

and silversmiths who tempt visitors to this day. Fittingly, a famous goldsmith is honored with a fine bust at the central point of the bridge—the sculptor Benvenuto *("Perseus")* Cellini. (For more on this bridge, 🕮 see the start of the Oltrarno Walk chapter.)

Looking upstream and down, you have timeless views of the city. The neighborhood across the river, known as the Oltrarno, is more rustic and working-class. The other bridges are all modern replacements. During World War II, the local German commander was instructed to blow up all of Florence's bridges to cover the Nazi retreat. But even some Nazis appreciate history: He blew up the other bridges, and left the Ponte Vecchio impassable but intact.

The Ponte Vecchio is a romantic spot in the evening. The sun sets behind the hills, and the bridges cast their reflection on the flat water. Street musicians play and lovers hold hands. The city of Florence—born in Roman times, flourishing in the medieval age, and blossoming in the Renaissance—remains a vibrant cultural capital.

• *From the Duomo to the Arno, we've taken in sights from Florence's medieval roots and Renaissance greats. After this introduction, several of the finest museums in Europe await your discovery—or perhaps it's time for a nice espresso or gelato. Enjoy.*

RENAISSANCE WALK

# ACCADEMIA GALLERY TOUR

*Galleria dell'Accademia*

One of Europe's great thrills is seeing Michelangelo's *David* in the flesh at the Accademia Gallery (rated ▲▲▲). Seventeen feet high, gleaming white, and exalted by a halo-like dome over his head, *David* rarely disappoints, even for those with high expectations. And the Accademia doesn't stop there. With a handful of other Michelangelo statues and a few other interesting sights, it makes for an uplifting visit that isn't overwhelming. *David*, a must-see on any visit to Florence, is always mobbed with visitors. Plan carefully to minimize your time in line.

## Orientation

**Cost:** €12, additional €4 fee for recommended reservation.

**Hours:** Tue-Sun 9:00-19:00, closed Mon; may stay open later during peak season.

**Information:** +39 055 294 883; reservations: www.b-ticket.com/b-Ticket/uffizi, info: www.galleriaaccademiafirenze.it/en.

**Reservation Highly Recommended:** Any time of year, assume a reservation is necessary. Get your entry time online in advance. Take your receipt or confirmation number to the My Accademia Libreria reservation office across the street from the museum (at #105r), pick up your ticket, and join the line for those with a reservation. (Above the doorways, you'll see two red signs clearly marked *"reserved"* and *"not reserved."*)

**Getting There:** It's at Via Ricasoli 60, a 15-minute walk from the train station or a 10-minute walk northeast of the Duomo.

**Tours:** A €6 audioguide is available in the ticket lobby.

🎧 Download my free Accademia audio tour.

**Length of This Tour:** While *David* and the *Prisoners* can be seen in 30 minutes, allow an hour so you can linger and explore other parts of the museum.

**Security:** You'll pass through a metal detector and put your bag through a scanner (on crowded days, this can take up to 30 minutes). Leave pocketknives and corkscrews at your hotel. The museum has no bag-check service, and large backpacks are not allowed.

**Cuisine Art:** Plenty of fast and cheap places (to eat in or take out) face Piazza San Marco a block away. My favorite place for a nearby picnic is the picturesque Renaissance Piazza Santissima Annunziata (see recommendations for takeout and sit-down dining on page 311).

**Starring:** Michelangelo's *David* and *Prisoners.*

# The Tour Begins

• *From the entrance lobby, show your ticket, turn left, and look right down the long hall with* David *at the far end, under an illuminating circular skylight. Yes, you're really here. With* David *presiding at the "altar," the* Prisoners *lining the "nave," and hordes of "pilgrims" crowding in to look, you've arrived at Florence's "cathedral of humanism."*

*Start with the ultimate...*

## ❶ *David,* 1501-1504

When you look into the eyes of Michelangelo's *David,* you're looking into the eyes of Renaissance Man. This six-ton, 17-foot-tall symbol of divine victory over evil represents a new century and a whole new Renaissance outlook. This is the age of Columbus and classicism, Galileo and Gutenberg, Luther and Leonardo—of Florence and the Renaissance.

In 1501, Michelangelo Buonarroti, a 26-year-old Florentine, was commissioned to carve a large-scale work for the Duomo. He was given a block of marble that other sculptors had rejected as too tall, shallow, and flawed to be of any value. But Michelangelo picked up his hammer and chisel, knocked a knot off what became *David*'s heart, and started to work.

The figure comes from an Old Testament story. The Israelites, God's chosen people, are surrounded by the Philistines, barbarian warriors led by a brutish giant named Goliath. The giant challenges the Israelites to send out someone to fight him. Everyone is afraid except for one young shepherd boy—David. Armed only

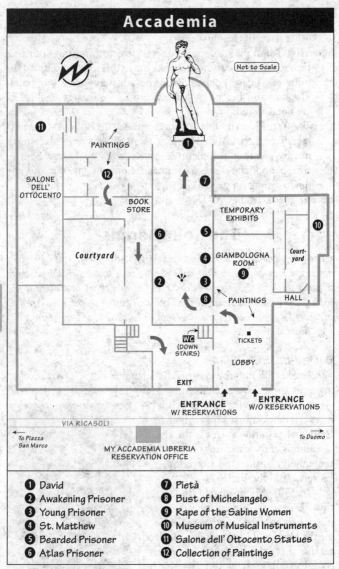

## Accademia

Not to Scale

PAINTINGS

SALONE
DELL'
OTTOCENTO

BOOK
STORE

Courtyard

TEMPORARY
EXHIBITS

GIAMBOLOGNA
ROOM

PAINTINGS

Courtyard

HALL

TICKETS

WC
(DOWN
STAIRS)

LOBBY

EXIT

**ENTRANCE
W/ RESERVATIONS**

**ENTRANCE
W/O RESERVATIONS**

VIA RICASOLI

To Piazza
San Marco

To Duomo

MY ACCADEMIA LIBRERIA
RESERVATION OFFICE

**❶** David
**❷** Awakening Prisoner
**❸** Young Prisoner
**❹** St. Matthew
**❺** Bearded Prisoner
**❻** Atlas Prisoner
**❼** Pietà
**❽** Bust of Michelangelo
**❾** Rape of the Sabine Women
**❿** Museum of Musical Instruments
**⓫** Salone dell' Ottocento Statues
**⓬** Collection of Paintings

with a sling, which he's thrown over his shoulder, David gathers five smooth stones from the stream and faces Goliath.

The statue captures David as he's sizing up his enemy. He stands relaxed but alert, leaning on one leg in a classical pose known as *contrapposto*. In his powerful left hand, he fondles the handle of the sling, ready to fling a stone at the giant. His gaze is steady—searching with intense concentration, but also with extreme confidence. Michelangelo has caught the precise moment when David is saying to himself, "I can take this guy."

While some think that he's already slain the giant, the current director of the Accademia believes, as I do, that Michelangelo has portrayed David facing the giant. (Unlike most depictions of David after the kill, this sculpture does not show the giant's severed head.)

*David* is a symbol of Renaissance optimism. He's no brute. He's a civilized, thinking individual who can grapple with and overcome problems. He needs no armor, only his God-given physical strength and wits. Look at his right hand, with the raised veins and strong, relaxed fingers—many complained that it was too big and overdeveloped. But this is the hand of a man with the strength of God on his side. No mere boy could slay the giant. But David, powered by God, could...and did.

Originally, the statue was commissioned to stand atop the roofline of the Duomo. But during the three years it took to sculpt, they decided instead to place it guarding the entrance of Town Hall—the Palazzo Vecchio. (If the relationship between *David*'s head and body seems a bit out of proportion, it's because Michelangelo designed it to be seen "correctly" from far below the rooftop of the church.)

The colossus was placed standing up in a cart and dragged across rollers from Michelangelo's workshop (behind the Duomo) to the Palazzo Vecchio, where it replaced a work by Donatello. There *David* stood—naked and outdoors—for 350 years. In the right light, you can see signs of weathering on his shoulders. Also, note the crack in *David*'s left arm where it was broken off during a 1527 riot near the Palazzo Vecchio. In 1873, to conserve the masterpiece, the statue was moved indoors and today resides under this wonderful Renaissance-style dome designed just for him, while a copy adorns Palazzo Vecchio.

Circle *David* and view him from various angles. From the front, he's confident, but a little less so when you gaze directly into his eyes. Around back, see his sling strap, buns of steel, and Renaissance mullet. Up close, you can see the blue-veined Carrara marble and a few cracks and stains. From the sides, Michelangelo's challenge becomes clear: to sculpt a figure from a block of marble other sculptors said was too tall and narrow to accommodate a human figure.

Renaissance Florentines could identify with *David*. Like him, they considered themselves God-blessed underdogs fighting their city-state rivals. In a deeper sense, they were civilized Renaissance people slaying the ugly giant of medieval superstition, pessimism, and oppression.

• *Hang around a while. Eavesdrop on tour guides. The barrier around the base of the statue is a reminder of an attack by a frustrated artist, who smashed the statue's feet in 1991.*

Lining the hall leading up to David *are other statues by Michelangelo—his* Prisoners, St. Matthew, *and* Pietà. *Start with the* Awakening Prisoner, *the statue at the end of the nave (farthest from* David*). He's on your left as you face* David.

### The Prisoners (Prigioni), c. 1516-1534

These unfinished figures seem to be fighting to free themselves from the stone. Michelangelo believed the sculptor was a tool of God, not creating but simply revealing the powerful and beautiful figures that God had encased in the marble. Michelangelo's job was to chip away the excess, to reveal. He needed to be in tune with God's will, and whenever the spirit came upon him, Michelangelo worked in a frenzy, without sleep, often for days on end.

The *Prisoners* give us a glimpse of this fitful process, showing the restless energy of someone possessed, struggling against the rock that binds him. Michelangelo himself fought to create the image he saw in his mind's eye. You can still see the grooves from the chisel, and you can picture Michelangelo hacking away in a cloud of dust. Unlike most sculptors, who built a model and then marked up their block of marble to know where to chip, Michelangelo always worked freehand, starting from the front and working back. These figures emerge from the stone (as his colleague Vasari put it) "as though surfacing from a pool of water."

The so-called ❷ *Awakening Prisoner* (the names are given by scholars, not Michelangelo) seems to be stretching after a long nap, still tangled in the "bedsheets" of uncarved rock. He's more block than statue.

On the right, the ❸ *Young Prisoner* is more finished. He buries his face in his forearm, while his other arm is chained behind him.

The *Prisoners* were designed for the never-completed tomb of Pope Julius II (who also commissioned the Sistine Chapel ceiling). Michelangelo may have abandoned them simply because the project itself petered out, or he may have deliberately left them unfinished. Having perhaps satisfied himself that he'd accomplished what he set out to do, and seeing no point in polishing them into their shiny, finished state, he moved on to a new project. Two slightly more completed statues from the same series are in the Louvre in Paris, while the much-scaled-down tomb, featuring another of his masterpieces, *Moses,* is in the church of St. Peter-in-Chains in Rome.

Walking up the nave toward *David,* you'll pass by Michelangelo's ❹ *St. Matthew* (1503), on the right. Though not one of

the *Prisoners* series, he is also unfinished, perfectly illustrating Vasari's "surfacing" description.

The next statue (also on the right), the ❺ *Bearded Prisoner,* is the most finished of the four, with all four limbs, a bushy face, and even a hint of daylight between his arm and body.

Across the nave on the left, the ❻ *Atlas Prisoner* carries the unfinished marble on his stooped shoulders, his head still encased in the block.

As you study the *Prisoners,* notice Michelangelo's love and understanding of the human body. His greatest days were spent sketching the muscular, tanned, and sweating bodies of the workers in the Carrara marble quarries. The prisoners' heads and faces are the least-developed part—they "speak" with their poses. Comparing the restless, claustrophobic *Prisoners* with the serene and confident *David* gives an idea of the sheer emotional range in Michelangelo's work.

• *The unfinished threesome closest to* David *is the...*

## ❼ Pietà

The figures struggle to hold up the sagging body of Christ. Michelangelo (or, more likely, one of his followers) emphasizes the heaviness of Jesus' dead body, driving home the point that this divine being suffered a very human death. Christ's massive arm is almost the size of his bent and broken legs. By stretching his body—if he stood up, he'd be more than seven feet tall—the weight is exaggerated.

• *After getting your fill of Michelangelo, consider taking a spin around the rest of the Accademia. Michelangelo's statues are far and away the highlight here, but the rest of this small museum—housed in a*

ACCADEMIA

### *David, David, David,* and *David*

Several Italian masters produced iconic sculptures of David—all of them different. Compare and contrast the artists' styles. How many ways can you slay a giant?

### Donatello's *David* (c. 1440, Bargello, Florence)

Donatello's *David* is young and graceful, casually gloating over the head of Goliath, almost Gothic in its elegance and smooth lines. While he has a similar weight-on-one-leg *(contrapposto)* stance as Michelangelo's later version, Donatello's *David* seems feminine rather than masculine. (For further description, see page 150 of the Bargello Tour chapter.)

### Andrea del Verrocchio's *David* (c. 1470, Bargello, Florence)

Wearing a military skirt and armed with a small sword, Verrocchio's *David* is just a boy. The statue is only four feet tall—dwarfed by Michelangelo's monumental version. (For more, see page 150 of the Bargello Tour chapter.)

*former convent—has a few bonuses. Head back toward the entrance. Near the* Young Prisoner *find a...*

### ❽ Bust of Michelangelo

The bronze bust depicts a craggy, wrinkled Michelangelo, age 88, by Daniele da Volterra. (Daniele, one of Michelangelo's colleagues and friends, is best known as the one who painted loincloths on the private parts of Michelangelo's nudes in the Sistine Chapel.) As a teenager, Michelangelo got his nose broken in a fight with a rival artist. Though Michelangelo went

### Michelangelo's *David*
### (1501-1504, Accademia, Florence)

Michelangelo's *David* is pure Renaissance: massive, heroic in size, and superhuman in strength and power. The tensed right hand, which grips a stone in readiness to hurl at Goliath, is more powerful than any human hand. It's symbolic of divine strength. A model of perfection, Michelangelo's *David* is far larger and grander than we mere mortals. We know he'll win. Renaissance Man has arrived.

### Gian Lorenzo Bernini's *David*
### (1624, Borghese Museum, Rome)

Flash forward more than a century. In this self-portrait, 25-year-old Bernini is ready to take on the world, slay the pretty-boy *Davids* of the Renaissance, and invent Baroque. Unlike Michelangelo's rational, cool, restrained *David,* Bernini's is a doer: passionate, engaged, dramatic. While Renaissance *David* is simple and unadorned—carrying only a sling—Baroque Dave is "cluttered" with a braided sling, a hairy pouch, flowing cloth, and discarded armor. Bernini's *David,* with his tousled hair and set mouth, is one of us; the contest is less certain than with the other three Davids.

To sum up: Donatello's *David* represents the first inkling of the Renaissance; Verrocchio's is early Renaissance in miniature; Michelangelo's is textbook Renaissance; and Bernini's is the epitome of Baroque.

on to create great beauty, he was never classically handsome.

• *Enter the room near the museum entrance dominated by a large, squirming statue.*

## Giambologna Room

This full-size plaster model of ❾ *Rape of the Sabine Women* (1582) guided Giambologna's assistants in completing the marble version in the Loggia dei Lanzi (on Piazza della Signoria, next to the Palazzo Vecchio, described in the Renaissance Walk chapter). A Roman warrior tramples a fighter from the Sabine tribe and carries off the man's wife. Husband and wife exchange one final, anguished glance. Circle the statue and watch it spiral to life around its axis. Giambologna was clearly influenced by Michelangelo's groundbreaking *Victory* in the Palazzo Vecchio (1533-1534, described in the Palazzo Vecchio Tour chapter). Michelangelo's statue of a man triumphing over a fallen enemy introduced both the theme and the spiral-shaped pose that many artists imitated.

Browse the room clockwise (from the entrance) to locate **minor paintings** by artists you'll encounter elsewhere in Florence. Domenico Ghirlandaio's paintings of Renaissance Florence are behind the altar of the Church of Santa Maria Novella (see the Santa Maria Novella Tour chapter). Francesco Granacci, a childhood friend of Michelangelo, assisted him on the Sistine Ceiling. Benozzo Gozzoli decorated the personal chapel of the Medici in the Medici-Riccardi Palace (see the Medici-Riccardi Palace Tour chapter). Filippino Lippi is known for his frescoes in the Brancacci Chapel (see the Brancacci Chapel Tour chapter) and Church of Santa Maria Novella. And Botticelli's *Birth of Venus* hangs in the Uffizi Gallery.

• *From the Giambologna Room, head down a short hallway leading to a few rooms containing the...*

## ❿ Museum of Musical Instruments

Between 1400 and 1700, Florence was one of Europe's most sophisticated cities, and the Medici rulers were trendsetters. Musicians like Scarlatti and Handel flocked to the court of Prince Ferdinando de' Medici (1663-1713). You'll see late-Renaissance cellos, dulcimers, violins, woodwinds, and harpsichords. (Listen to some on the computer terminals.)

As you enter, look for the two group paintings that include the prince (he's second from the right in both paintings, with the yellow bowtie) hanging out with his musician friends. The gay prince played a mean harpsichord, and he helped pioneer new variations. In the adjoining room, you'll see musical instruments from times past—some familiar, some weird and now obsolete.

The highlight is a room of several experimental keyboards, including some by Florence's keyboard pioneer, Bartolomeo Cristofori. As the exhibits point out, the breakthrough in keyboard technology was about how to make the string ring. The harpsichord plucked the string.

ACCADEMIA

# More Michelangelo

If you're a fan of Earth's greatest sculptor, you won't leave Florence until there's a check next to each of these:

**Bargello:** Several Michelangelo sculptures, including the *Bacchus* (pictured here; 🕮 see the Bargello Tour chapter).

**Duomo Museum:** Another moving pietà (see page 180).

**Medici Chapels:** The *Night* and *Day* statues, plus others done for the Medici tomb, located at the Basilica of San Lorenzo (see the 🕮 Medici Chapels Tour chapter).

**Laurentian Medici Library:** Michelangelo designed the entrance staircase and more, located at the Basilica of San Lorenzo (see page 64).

**Palazzo Vecchio:** His *Victory* statue (see page 194).

**Uffizi Gallery:** A rare Michelangelo painting (see page 136).

**Casa Buonarroti:** Built on property Michelangelo once owned, at Via Ghibellina 70, containing some early works (see page 77).

**Santa Croce Church:** Michelangelo's tomb (see page 229).

**Santo Spirito Church:** Wooden crucifix thought to be by Michelangelo (see page 82).

ACCADEMIA

By 1700, they'd invented the "pianoforte"—the piano, which used a padded hammer that could strike it either soft *(piano)* or hard *(forte)*. The tall piano on display (from 1739) is considered by some to be the world's first upright piano.

• *Head one more time back up the nave to say goodbye to Dave.*

## More Sights on the Way to the Exit

To the left of *David*, at the end of the hall, is the ⓫ **Salone dell'Ottocento**—a long room crammed with plaster statues and busts. These were the Academy art students' "final exams"—preparatory models for statues, many of which were later executed in marble. The black dots on the statues are sculptors' "points," guiding them on how deep to chisel. The Academy art school has been attached to the museum for centuries, and you may see the next Michelangelo wandering the streets nearby.

Finally, near *David* (in several rooms' adjoining halls) is the museum's pleasant-but-underwhelming ⓬ **collection of paintings.** You'll be hard-pressed to find even one by a painter whose name you recognize. As you look at these somber medieval altar-pieces, mentally contrast them with the confident optimism of Michelangelo's *David*, done a century later. It's a testament to how far Florence evolved from the depths of medieval despair to the full bloom of the Renaissance.

• *Our tour is finished. To exit, pass through the bookstore and use the free WC before heading into the open air, for some sun, peace, and quiet... aaaah.*

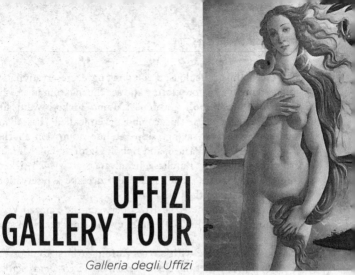

# UFFIZI GALLERY TOUR

*Galleria degli Uffizi*

In the Renaissance, Florentine artists rediscovered the beauty of the natural world. Medieval art had been symbolic, telling Bible stories. Realism didn't matter. But Renaissance people saw the beauty of God in nature and the human body. They used math and science to capture the natural world on canvas as realistically as possible.

The Uffizi Gallery (oo-FEET-zee, rated ▲▲▲) has the greatest overall collection anywhere of Italian painting. We'll trace the rise of realism and savor the optimistic spirit that marked the Renaissance.

> *My eyes love things that are fair,*
> *and my soul for salvation cries.*
> *But neither will to Heaven rise*
> *unless the sight of Beauty lifts them there.*
> —Michelangelo Buonarroti, sculptor, painter, poet

## Orientation

**Cost:** €20 plus €4 for recommended timed-entry reservation, cheaper in winter.

**Hours:** Tue-Sun 8:15-18:30, closed Mon; may stay open later in peak season; last entry one hour before closing.

**Information:** +39 055 294 883, reservations: www.b-ticket.com/b-Ticket/uffizi, info: www.uffizi.it.

**Reservations Required:** To skip the notoriously long ticket-buying lines, book your Uffizi entrance in advance online. You'll be emailed a voucher that you'll swap for an actual ticket 15 minutes before your visit at the reservation ticket office (across the courtyard from the museum entrance).

**When to Go:** While ridiculous, if you don't have a reservation, try going 90 minutes before closing and see the museum in a rush.

**Uffizi/Pitti Palace/Boboli Gardens Combo-Ticket:** Valid for five consecutive days, this combo-ticket (called "PassePartout") offers a cost-saving, skip-the-line admission to the Uffizi Gallery, Pitti Palace, and Boboli Gardens (€38 March-Oct, €18 Nov-Feb). Purchase in advance at www.b-ticket.com/b-Ticket/uffizi. You'll still need to make a reservation for an entry time at the Uffizi.

**Getting There:** It's on the Arno River between the Palazzo Vecchio and Ponte Vecchio, a 15-minute walk from the train station.

**Getting In:** If you arrive with a **reservation,** go first to door #3 to pick up your ticket (labeled *Reservation Ticket Office,* across the courtyard from doors #1 and #2). There you exchange your email voucher/confirmation number for a ticket. Tickets are available for pickup 15 minutes before your appointed time. Then, with ticket in hand, walk briskly past the looooong ticket-buying line—pondering the IQ of this gang—to door #1. Get in the queue for "individuals," not "groups."

To **buy a ticket on the spot,** line up with everyone else at door #2, marked *Main Entrance.* An estimated wait time is posted.

At especially busy times, expect long waits even if you have a reservation. There may be a queue to pick up your reserved ticket at door #3 and another wait to enter at door #1.

Just after the doors you'll pass through airport-type screening. Expect a slow shuffle into the crowded lobby, where you'll find a bag check, audio-guide rental, and guidebook sales. Next, everyone shows their ticket and climbs the stairs, and then our tour begins.

**Renovation:** The Uffizi recently completed a reorganization; pick up a map as you enter for the latest (some locations may vary from this tour).

**Tours:** The 2.5-hour audioguide costs €6. Or download my 🎧 free Uffizi Gallery audio tour.

**Length of This Tour:** Allow two hours. If you have limited time (or energy), concentrate on the top floor, especially Botticelli, Leonardo, and Michelangelo.

**Services:** All backpacks and large bags must be checked at the entrance lobby counter. A WC, post office, and extensive book/gift shop are in the entrance/exit hall on the ground floor.

UFFIZI

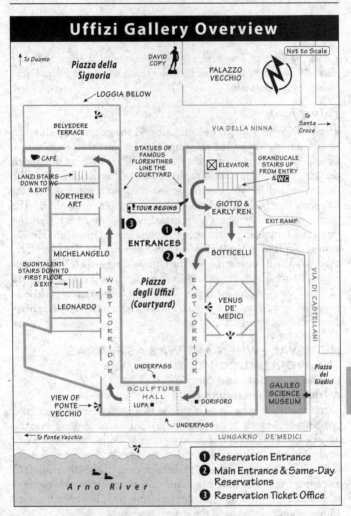

## Uffizi Gallery Overview

Not to Scale

To Duomo

*Piazza della Signoria*

DAVID COPY

PALAZZO VECCHIO

To Santa Croce

LOGGIA BELOW

BELVEDERE TERRACE

VIA DELLA NINNA

CAFÉ

STATUES OF FAMOUS FLORENTINES LINE THE COURTYARD

ELEVATOR

GRANDUCALE STAIRS UP FROM ENTRY & WC

LANZI STAIRS DOWN TO WC & EXIT

NORTHERN ART

TOUR BEGINS

GIOTTO & EARLY REN.

EXIT RAMP

❸

❶ ➤

MICHELANGELO

ENTRANCES

❷ ➤

BOTTICELLI

BUONTALENTI STAIRS DOWN TO FIRST FLOOR & EXIT

LEONARDO

*Piazza degli Uffizi (Courtyard)*

W E S T   C O R R I D O R

E A S T   C O R R I D O R

VENUS DE' MEDICI

VIA DI CASTELLANI

UNDERPASS

*Piazza dei Giudici*

VIEW OF PONTE VECCHIO

SCULPTURE HALL

LUPA ■

■ DORIFORO

GALILEO SCIENCE MUSEUM

UNDERPASS

To Ponte Vecchio

LUNGARNO DE'MEDICI

*Arno River*

❶ Reservation Entrance
❷ Main Entrance & Same-Day Reservations
❸ Reservation Ticket Office

UFFIZI

Once in the gallery, there are no WCs until near the end of our tour, either on the staircase leading down from the café or on the first floor.

**Cuisine Art:** The simple café at the top end of the gallery has an outdoor terrace with stunning views of the Palazzo Vecchio and the Duomo's dome. They serve pricey sandwiches, salads, and desserts, but a €5 cappuccino outside, with that view, is one of Europe's great treats. Plenty of handy eateries are nearby and described in the Eating in Florence chapter.

**Starring:** Botticelli, Venus, Raphael, Giotto, Titian, Leonardo, and Michelangelo.

# The Tour Begins

• *Walk up the four long flights of the monumental staircase to the top floor. (Those with limited mobility can take the elevator.) Catch your breath, then get oriented.*

## OVERVIEW

The Uffizi is U-shaped, running around the courtyard. This east wing contains Florentine paintings from medieval to Renaissance times. At the far end, you pass through a short hallway filled with the kind of ancient sculpture that inspired the Renaissance. The west wing (which you can see across the courtyard) has the Renaissance biggies—Leonardo, Michelangelo, and Raphael. The visit concludes downstairs with many more rooms of art, showing how the Florentine Renaissance morphed into Mannerism (Parmigianino), spread to Venice (Titian), and inspired the Baroque (Caravaggio). We'll concentrate on the Uffizi's forte—the Florentines.

• *Head up the long hallway, and enter the first door on the left, labeled Giotto (Room 4). You come face-to-face with a large painting of the Virgin Mary on a throne, by Giotto. It's flanked left and right by two similar works by other artists.*

## MEDIEVAL—WHEN ART WAS AS FLAT AS THE WORLD (1200-1400)

### Duccio, Cimabue, and Giotto: A Trio of Madonnas with Child

Mary and Baby Jesus sit on a throne in a golden never-never land symbolizing heaven. It's as if medieval Christians couldn't imagine holy people inhabiting our dreary material world. It took Renaissance painters to bring Mary down to earth and give her human realism. For the Florentines, "realism" meant "three-dimensional." The three similar-looking Madonna-and-Bambinos in this room—all painted within a few decades of each other, in about the year 1300—show baby steps in the march to realism.

❶ **Duccio**'s piece (on the left as you face Giotto) is the most medieval and two-dimensional. There's no background. The angels are just stacked one on top of the other, floating in the golden atmosphere. Mary's throne is crudely drawn—the left side is at a three-quarter angle while the right is practically straight on. Mary herself is a wispy cardboard-cutout figure seemingly floating just above the throne.

❷ **Cimabue,** on the opposite wall, mixes the iconic Byzantine style with budding Italian realism—as things get more lifelike. The large throne creates an illusion of depth; the angels alongside peek out from behind its massive architecture. Mary's foot actually sticks out over the lip of the throne. Still, the angels are stacked totem-pole-style, serving as heavenly bookends. Cimabue wowed the people of his day with his technique (including his much-loved crucifix for the Church of Santa Croce; see page 233), but he was quickly overshadowed by one of his students—Giotto—who grew to be more talented and famous.

❸ **Giotto** employs realism to make his theological points. He creates a space and fills it. Like a set designer, he builds a three-dimensional "stage"—the canopied throne—then peoples it with real beings. The throne has angels in front, prophets behind, and a canopy over the top, clearly defining its three dimensions. The steps up to the throne lead from our space to Mary's, making the scene an extension of our world. But the real triumph here is Mary herself—big and monumental, like a Roman statue. Beneath her robe, she has a real live body, with knees and breasts that stick out at us. This three-dimensionality was revolutionary in its day, a taste of the Renaissance a century before it began.

Giotto was one of the first "famous" artists. In the Middle Ages, artists were mostly unglamorous craftsmen, like carpenters or cable-TV repairmen. They cranked out generic art. But Giotto was recognized as a genius, a unique individual. He died in the plague that devastated Florence. If there had been no plague, would the Renaissance have started 100 years earlier?

• *Enter Room 5, featuring art from Siena. It's to the left as you face Giotto.*

### ❹ Simone Martini, *Annunciation*

Simone Martini (c. 1284-1344) depicts the Bible story of how Jesus's mom got the news that she was pregnant. He boils things

down to the basic figures needed to get the message across: (1) The angel appears to sternly tell (2) Mary that she'll be the mother of Jesus. In the center is (3) a vase of lilies, a symbol of purity. Above is (4) the Holy Spirit as a dove about to descend on her. If the symbols aren't enough to get the message across, Simone Martini has spelled it right out for us in Latin: *"Ave Gratia Plena..."* or, "Hail, favored one, the Lord is with you." Mary doesn't exactly look pleased as punch.

This is not a three-dimensional work. The point was not to re-create reality but to teach religion, especially to the illiterate masses. This isn't a beautiful Mary or even a real Mary. She's a generic woman without distinctive features. We know she's pure—

UFFIZI

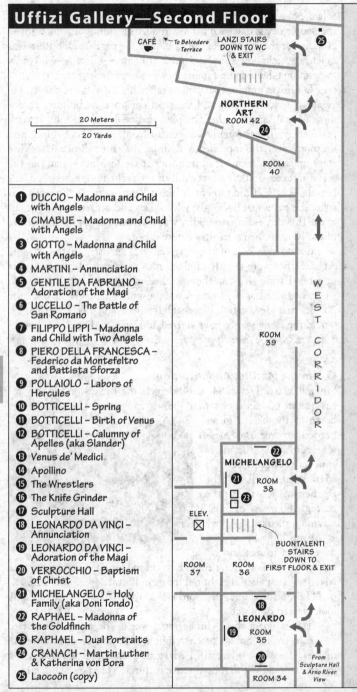

# Uffizi Gallery—Second Floor

CAFÉ → To Belvedere Terrace

LANZI STAIRS DOWN TO WC & EXIT

NORTHERN ART ROOM 42

ROOM 40

ROOM 39

WEST CORRIDOR

20 Meters
20 Yards

MICHELANGELO — ROOM 38

ELEV.

BUONTALENTI STAIRS DOWN TO FIRST FLOOR & EXIT

ROOM 37   ROOM 36

LEONARDO — ROOM 35

From Sculpture Hall & Arno River View

ROOM 34

UFFIZI

1 DUCCIO – Madonna and Child with Angels
2 CIMABUE – Madonna and Child with Angels
3 GIOTTO – Madonna and Child with Angels
4 MARTINI – Annunciation
5 GENTILE DA FABRIANO – Adoration of the Magi
6 UCCELLO – The Battle of San Romano
7 FILIPPO LIPPI – Madonna and Child with Two Angels
8 PIERO DELLA FRANCESCA – Federico da Montefeltro and Battista Sforza
9 POLLAIOLO – Labors of Hercules
10 BOTTICELLI – Spring
11 BOTTICELLI – Birth of Venus
12 BOTTICELLI – Calumny of Apelles (aka Slander)
13 Venus de' Medici
14 Apollino
15 The Wrestlers
16 The Knife Grinder
17 Sculpture Hall
18 LEONARDO DA VINCI – Annunciation
19 LEONARDO DA VINCI – Adoration of the Magi
20 VERROCCHIO – Baptism of Christ
21 MICHELANGELO – Holy Family (aka Doni Tondo)
22 RAPHAEL – Madonna of the Goldfinch
23 RAPHAEL – Dual Portraits
24 CRANACH – Martin Luther & Katherina von Bora
25 Laocoön (copy)

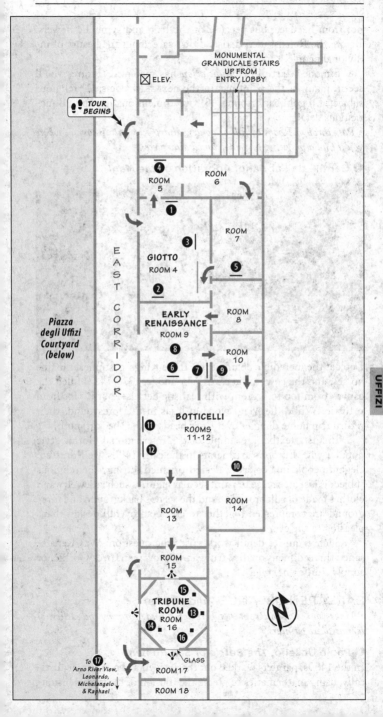

UFFIZI

MONUMENTAL
GRANDUCALE STAIRS
UP FROM
ENTRY LOBBY

ELEV.

TOUR
BEGINS

ROOM 5

ROOM 6

4

1

ROOM 7

3

GIOTTO
ROOM 4

5

2

*Piazza
degli Uffizi
Courtyard
(below)*

E
A
S
T

C
O
R
R
I
D
O
R

EARLY
RENAISSANCE
ROOM 9

ROOM 8

8

ROOM 10

6

7

9

BOTTICELLI
ROOMS
11-12

11

12

10

ROOM 13

ROOM 14

ROOM 15

TRIBUNE ROOM
ROOM 16

15

13

14

16

GLASS

To 17
Arno River View,
Leonardo,
Michelangelo
& Raphael

ROOM 17

ROOM 18

not from her face, but because of the halo and symbolic flowers. Before the Renaissance, artists didn't care about the beauty of individual people.

Simone Martini's *Annunciation* has medieval features you'll see in many of the paintings in the next few rooms: (1) religious subject, (2) gold background, (3) two-dimensionality, and (4) meticulous detail.

• *Pass through Room 6, full of golden altarpieces, into Room 7, where you'll find a magnificent gold-framed altarpiece...*

**❺ Gentile da Fabriano, *Adoration of the Magi***

Look at the incredible detail of the Three Kings' costumes, the fine horses, and the cow in the cave. Fabriano (c. 1370-1427) filled the canvas from top to bottom with realistic details—but it's far from realistic. While the Magi worship Jesus in the foreground, their return trip home dangles over their heads in the "background."

This is a textbook example of the International Gothic style popular with Europe's aristocrats in the early 1400s: well-dressed, elegant people in a colorful, design-oriented setting. The religious subject is just an excuse to paint secular luxuries such as jewelry and clothes made of silk brocade. And the scene's background and foreground are compressed together to create an overall design that's pleasing to the eye.

Such exquisite detail work raises the question: Was Renaissance three-dimensionality truly an improvement over Gothic, or simply a different style?

## EARLY RENAISSANCE (mid-1400s)

• *Make your way to Room 9, where you'll find works by the earliest of Renaissance painters.*

**❻ Paolo Uccello, *The Battle of San Romano***

In the 1400s, painters worked out the problems of painting realistically, using mathematics to create the illusion of three-dimension-

ality. This colorful battle scene is not so much a piece of art as an exercise in perspective. Paolo Uccello (1397-1475) has challenged himself with every possible problem.

The broken lances at left set up a 3-D "grid" in which this crowded scene is placed. The fallen horses and soldiers are experiments in "foreshortening"—diminishing the things that are farther away from us (which appear smaller) to create the illusion of distance. Some of the figures are definitely A-plus material, like the fallen gray horse in the center and the white horse at the far right walking away. But some are more like B-minus work—the kicking red horse's legs look like ham hocks at this angle, and the fallen soldier at the far right would be child-size if he stood up.

And then there's the D-minus "Are you on drugs?" work. The converging hedges in the background create a nice illusion of a distant hillside maybe 250 feet away. So what are those soldiers the size of the foreground figures doing there? And jumping the hedge, is that rabbit 40 feet tall?

Uccello almost literally went crazy trying to master the three dimensions (thank God he was born before Einstein discovered one more). Uccello got so wrapped up in it he kind of lost...perspective.

• *Also in Room 9, find a painting of Mary with her hands folded and Baby Jesus being lifted up by playful angel boys.*

### ❼ Fra Filippo Lippi, *Madonna and Child with Two Angels*

Mentally compare this Mary with the generic female in Simone Martini's *Annunciation*. We don't need the wispy halo over her head to tell us she's holy—she radiates sweetness and light from her divine face. Heavenly beauty is expressed by a physically beautiful woman.

UFFIZI

Fra (Brother) Lippi (1406-1469), an orphan raised as a monk, lived a less-than-monkish life. He lived with a nun who bore him two children. He spent his entire life searching for the perfect Virgin. Through his studio passed Florence's prettiest girls, many of whom decorate the walls here in this room.

Lippi painted idealized beauty, but his models were real flesh-and-blood human beings. You could look through all the thousands of paintings from the Middle Ages and not find anything so human as the mischievous face of one of Lippi's little angel boys.

• *Nearby is a freestanding double-portrait painting of a man and wife.*

### ❽ Piero della Francesca, *Federico da Montefeltro and Battista Sforza*

In medieval times, only saints and angels were worthy of being painted. In the humanistic Renaissance, however, even nonreli-gious folk like this husband and wife by Piero della Francesca (c. 1412-1492) had their features preserved for posterity. Usually the man would have appeared on the left, with his wife at the right. But Federico's right side was definitely not his best—he lost his right eye and part of his nose in a tournament. Renaissance artists discovered the beauty in ordinary people and painted them, literally, warts and all.

• *In Room 10, find the glass case with two tiny works by Pollaiolo.*

### ❾ Antonio del Pollaiolo, *Labors of Hercules*

Hercules gets a workout in two small panels showing the human form at odd angles. The poses are the wildest imaginable, to show how each muscle twists and tightens. While Uccello worked on perspective, Pollaiolo (c. 1431-1498) studied anatomy. In medieval times, dissection of corpses was a sin and a crime (the two were the same then). Dissecting was a desecration of the human body, the temple of God. But Pollaiolo was willing to sell his soul to the devil for artistic knowledge. He dissected.

There's something funny about this room that I can't put my finger on...I've got it—no Madonnas. Not one. (No, that's not a Madonna; she's a Virtue.)

We've seen how Early Renaissance artists worked to conquer reality. Now let's see the fruits of their work, the flowering of Florence's Renaissance.

• *Enter the large space (Rooms 11-12) where works by Botticelli are displayed. Stroll around and take it all in, as you think about the optimistic generation that produced such works of beauty.*

## THE RENAISSANCE BLOSSOMS (1450-1500)

Florence in 1450 was in a Firenz-y of activity. There was a can-do spirit of optimism in the air, led by prosperous merchants and bankers and a strong middle class. The government was reasonably democratic, and Florentines saw themselves as citizens of a strong republic—like ancient Rome. Their civic pride showed in the public monuments and artworks they built. Man was leaving the protection of the Church to stand on his own two feet.

Lorenzo de' Medici, head of the powerful Medici family, epitomized this new humanistic spirit. Strong, decisive, handsome, poetic, athletic, sensitive, charismatic, intelligent, brave, clean, and reverent, Lorenzo was a true Renaissance Man, deserving of the nickname he went by—the Magnificent. He gathered Florence's best and brightest around him for evening wine and discussions of great ideas. One of this circle was the painter Botticelli.

### ⑩ Sandro Botticelli, *Spring*

It's springtime in a citrus grove. The winds of spring blow in (Mr. Blue, at right), causing the woman on the right to sprout flowers from her lips as she morphs into Flora, or Spring—who walks by, spreading flowers from her dress. At the left are Mercury and the Three Graces, dancing a delicate maypole dance. The Graces may be symbolic of the three forms of love—of beauty, love of people, and sexual love, suggested by the raised intertwined fingers. (They forgot love of peanut butter on toast.) In the center stands Venus, the Greek goddess of love. Above her flies a blindfolded Cupid, happily shooting his arrows of love without worrying about whom they'll hit.

Here is the Renaissance in its first bloom, its "springtime" of innocence. Madonna is out, Venus is in. Adam and Eve hiding their nakedness are out, glorious flesh is in. This is a return to the pre-Christian pagan world of classical Greece, where things of the flesh are not sinful. But this is certainly no orgy—just fresh-faced innocence and playfulness.

Botticelli (1445-1510) emphasizes pristine beauty over gritty realism. The lines of the bodies, especially of the Graces in their see-through nighties, have pleasing, S-like curves. The faces are idealized but have real human features. There's a look of thoughtfulness and even melancholy in the faces—as though everyone knows that the innocence of spring will not last forever.

• *Now approach the room's most famous painting, thronged by admirers.*

### ⓫ Botticelli, *Birth of Venus*

According to myth, Venus was born from the foam of a wave. Still only half awake, this fragile, newborn beauty floats ashore on a clamshell, blown by the winds, where her maid waits to dress her. The pose is the same S-curve of classical statues (as we'll soon see). Botticelli's pastel colors make the world itself seem fresh and newly born.

This is the purest expression of Renaissance beauty. Venus' naked body is not sensual, but innocent. Botticelli thought that physical beauty was a way of appreciating God. Remember Michelangelo's poem: Souls will never ascend to heaven "...unless the sight of Beauty lifts them there."

Botticelli finds God in the details—Venus' windblown hair, her translucent skin, the maid's braided hair, the slight ripple of the wind god's abs, and the flowers tumbling in the slowest of slow motions, suspended like musical notes, caught at the peak of their brief life.

Mr. and Mrs. Wind intertwine—notice her hands clasped

UFFIZI

around his body. Their hair, wings, and robes mingle like the wind. But what happened to those splayed toes?

• *"Venus on the Half-Shell" (as many tourists call this) is one of the masterpieces of Western art. Take some time with it. Then find a small canvas nearby depicting a more turbulent scene.*

### ⑫ Botticelli, *Calumny of Apelles*, a.k.a. *Slander*

The spring of Florence's Renaissance had to end. Lorenzo died young. The economy faltered. Into town rode the monk Savonarola, preaching medieval hellfire and damnation for those who embraced the "pagan" Renaissance spirit. "Down, down with all gold and decoration," he roared. "Down where the body is food for the worms." He presided over huge bonfires, where the people threw in their fine clothes, jewelry, pagan books...and paintings.

*Slander* spells the end of the Florentine Renaissance. The architectural setting is classic Brunelleschi, but look what's taking place beneath those stately arches. These aren't proud Renaissance men and women but a ragtag, medieval-looking bunch, a Court of Thieves in an abandoned hall of justice. The accusations fly, and everyone is condemned. The naked man pleads for

mercy, but the hooded black figure, a symbol of his execution, turns away. The figure of Truth (naked Truth)—straight out of *The Birth of Venus*—looks up to heaven as if to ask, "What has happened to us?" The classical statues in their niches look on in disbelief.

Botticelli got caught up in the teachings of Savonarola. He burned some of his own paintings and changed his artistic tune. The last works of his life were darker, more somber, and pessimistic about humanity.

The 19th-century German poet Heinrich Heine said, "When they start by burning books, they'll end by burning people." After four short years of power, Savonarola was burned in 1498 on his own bonfire in Piazza della Signoria, but by then the city was in shambles. The first flowering of the Renaissance was over. When the cultural climate turned chilly, artists flew south to warmer climes. The Renaissance shifted—as we'll soon see—to Rome and beyond.

• *Enter the next room (#13) and continue straight ahead until you reach a small hallway with a glass barrier where you can look into the Tribune Room, or Tribuna (a.k.a. Room 16). Gazing inside, you'll see the famous Venus de' Medici statue. (If this little hallway is crowded, note that there are two other viewing spots: back out in the main hallway, and another farther on in Room 17.)*

## TRIBUNE ROOM
If the Renaissance was the foundation of the modern world, the foundation of the Renaissance was classical sculpture. Sculptors, painters, and poets alike turned for inspiration to these ancient Greek and Roman works as the epitome of balance, 3-D perspective, human anatomy, and beauty. The Tribune Room features several well-known statues. Start with the goddess of love.

### ⓭ *Venus de' Medici,* first century BC
Is this pose familiar? Botticelli's *Birth of Venus* has the same position of the arms, the same S-curved body, and the same lifting of the

right leg. A copy of this statue stood in Lorenzo the Magnificent's garden, where Botticelli used to hang out. This one is a Roman copy of the lost original by the great Greek sculptor Praxiteles. Balanced, harmonious, and serene, the statue embodies the attributes of Greece's "golden age," when balance was admired in every aspect of life.

Perhaps more than any other work of art, this statue *(Venere dei Medici)* has been the epitome of both ideal beauty and sexuality. In the 18th and 19th centuries, sex was "dirty," so the sex drive of cultured aristocrats was channeled into a love of pure beauty. Wealthy sons and daughters of Europe's aristocrats made the pilgrimage to the Uffizi to complete their classical education...where they swooned in ecstasy before the cold beauty of this goddess of love.

Louis XIV had a bronze copy made. Napoleon stole her away to Paris for himself. And in Philadelphia in the 1800s, a copy had to be kept under lock and key to prevent the innocent from catching the Venere-al disease. At first, it may be difficult for us to appreciate such passionate love of art, but if any generation knows the power of sex to sell something—be it art or underarm deodorant—it's ours.

### The Other Statues, first-second century AD
Check out some of the other ancient statues. Facing Venus—leaning on a tree trunk—is Venus' male counterpart, ⓮ *Apollino.* Affectionately called "Venus with a Penis," Apollino is also carved by that ancient Greek master of smooth, cool lines: Praxiteles.

These other works are later Greek (Hellenistic), when quiet

balance was replaced by violent motion and emotion. ⓯ *The Wrestlers,* to the left of Venus, is a study in anatomy and twisted limbs—like Pollaiolo's paintings a thousand years later.

The drama of ⓰ *The Knife Grinder* to the right of Venus stems from the offstage action—he's sharpening the knife to flay a man alive.

Now check out the room itself, gazing up into the dazzling dome. This fine room was a showroom, or a "cabinet of wonders," back when this building still functioned as the Medici offices. Filled with family portraits, it's a holistic statement that symbolically links the Medici family with the four basic elements: air (weathervane in the lantern), water (inlaid mother of pearl in the dome), fire (red wall), and earth (inlaid stone floor).

• *Exit into the main hallway. Breathe. Sit. Admire the ceiling. Look out the window. See you in five. Back already? Now continue strolling to the end of the hall, where a standing nude statue welcomes you to the...*

## SCULPTURE HALL

A hundred years ago, no one even looked at Botticelli—they came to the Uffizi to see the collection in the ⓱ **sculpture hall.** And today, these 2,000-year-old Roman copies of 2,500-year-old Greek originals are hardly noticed...but they should be. Only a few are displayed here now.

The most impressive is the male nude, *Doriforo* ("spear carrier"), a Roman copy of the Greek original by Polykleitos, located in the middle of the hallway, where it turns right.

The purple statue in the center of the hall—headless and limbless—is the Roman **"she-wolf"** (*Lupa,* c. AD 120) done in porphyry stone. This was the animal that raised Rome's legendary founders and became the city's symbol. The image was seen throughout the Roman Empire on coins, medallions, and statues in city squares. A thousand years later, Renaissance Florentines marveled at the ancient Romans' ability to create such lifelike, three-dimensional works. They learned to reproduce them in stone...and then learned to paint them on a two-dimensional surface.

• *Gaze out the windows from the hall. At the far end, enjoy the best...*

**View of the Arno:** This is my favorite view of the river and Ponte Vecchio. You can also see the red-tiled roof of the Vasari Corridor, the "secret" passage connecting the Palazzo Vecchio, Uffizi, Ponte Vecchio, and the Pitti Palace on the other side of the river—a half-mile in all. This was a private walkway for the Medici family's commute from home to work.

As you appreciate the view, remember that it's this sort of pleasure that Renaissance painters wanted you to get from their paintings. For them, a canvas was a window you looked through to see the wide world. Their paintings re-create natural perspective: Distant objects (such as bridges) are smaller, dimmer, and higher up the "canvas," while closer objects are bigger, clearer, and lower.

We're headed down the home stretch now. If your little U-feetsies are killing you, and it feels like torture, remind yourself that it's a pleasant torture and smile...like the *Marsia Rosso* statue hanging around next to you.

• *Round the bend and start down the far hallway. Skip the first two open doorways (on your left), then turn left into Room 35, with major works by one of Florence's brightest lights.*

## RENAISSANCE MASTERS
### ⓲ Leonardo da Vinci, *Annunciation*

A scientist, architect, engineer, musician, and painter, Leonardo da Vinci (1452-1519) was a true Renaissance Man. He worked at his own pace rather than to please an employer, so he often left works unfinished. The two paintings in this room aren't his best, but even a lesser Leonardo is enough to put a museum on the map, and they're definitely worth a look.

In the *Annunciation*, the angel Gabriel has walked up to Mary, and now kneels on one knee like an ambassador, saluting her. See

how relaxed his other hand is, draped over his knee. Mary, who's been reading, looks up with a gesture of surprise and curiosity.

Leonardo constructs a beautifully landscaped "stage" and puts his characters in it. Look at the bricks on the right wall. If you extended lines from them, the lines would all converge at the center of the painting, the distant blue mountain. Same with the edge of the sarcophagus and the railing. This subtle touch creates a subconscious feeling of balance, order, and spaciousness in the viewer.

Think back to Simone Martini's *Annunciation* to realize how much more natural, relaxed, and realistic Leonardo's version is. He's taken a miraculous event—an angel appearing out of the blue—and presented it in a very human way.

### ⑲ Leonardo da Vinci, *Adoration of the Magi*
Leonardo's human insight is even more apparent here, in this unfinished work. The poor kings are amazed at the Christ Child—

even afraid of him. They scurry around like chimps around a fire. This work is as agitated as the *Annunciation* is calm, giving us an idea of Leonardo's range. Leonardo was pioneering a new era of painting, showing not just the outer features but also the inner personality.

Nearby hangs the ⑳ *Baptism of Christ* by Andrea del Verrocchio, Leonardo's teacher. Leonardo painted the angel on the far left when he was only a teenager. Legend has it that when Verrocchio saw that some kid had painted an angel better than he ever would...he hung up his brush for good.

• *Continue a few steps more down the hallway to Room 38, with works by Michelangelo and Raphael. Start with the round painting in a gold frame.*

### ㉑ Michelangelo Buonarroti, *Holy Family*, a.k.a. *Doni Tondo*
This is the only completed easel painting by the greatest sculptor in history. Florentine painters were sculptors with brushes; this shows it. Instead of a painting, it's more like three clusters of statues with some clothes painted on.

The main subject is the holy family—Mary, Joseph, and Baby Jesus—and in the background are two groups of nudes looking like classical statues. The background

UFFIZI

represents the old pagan world, while Jesus in the foreground is the new age of Christianity. The figure of young John the Baptist at right is the link between the two.

This is a "peasant" Mary, with a plain face and sunburned arms. Michelangelo (1475-1564) shows her from a very unflattering angle—we're looking up her nostrils. But Michelangelo himself was an ugly man, and he was among the first artists to recognize the beauty in everyday people.

Michelangelo was a Florentine—in fact, he was like an adopted son of the Medici, who recognized his talent—but much of his greatest work was done in Rome as part of the pope's face-lift of the city. We can see here some of the techniques he used on the Sistine Chapel ceiling that revolutionized painting—monumental figures; dramatic angles (looking up Mary's nose); accentuated, rippling muscles; and bright, clashing colors (all the more apparent since both this work and the Sistine Chapel ceiling have recently been cleaned). These elements added a dramatic tension that was lacking in the graceful work of Leonardo and Botticelli.

Michelangelo painted this for his friend Agnolo Doni for 70 ducats. (Michelangelo designed, but didn't carve, the elaborate frame.) When the painting was delivered, Doni tried to talk Michelangelo down to 40. Proud Michelangelo took the painting away and would not sell it until the man finally agreed to pay double...140 ducats.

• *Also on display in Room 38 are several paintings by a young painter who learned tricks from both Leonardo and Michelangelo.*

UFFIZI

### ㉗ Raphael, *Madonna of the Goldfinch*

Raphael (Raffaello Sanzio, 1483-1520) brings Mary and Bambino down from heaven and into the real world of trees, water, and sky.

He gives Baby Jesus (right) and John the Baptist a realistic, human playfulness. It's a tender scene painted with warm colors and a hazy background that matches the golden skin of the children.

Raphael perfected his craft in Florence, following the graceful style of Leonardo. In typical Leonardo fashion, this group of Mary, John the Baptist, and Jesus is arranged in the shape of a pyramid, with Mary's head at the peak.

The two halves of the painting balance perfectly. Draw a line down the middle, through Mary's nose and down through her knee. John the Baptist on the left is balanced by Jesus on the right. Even the trees in the background balance each other, left and right.

These things aren't immediately noticeable, but they help create the subconscious feelings of balance and order that reinforce the atmosphere of maternal security in this domestic scene—pure Renaissance.

The **❷ dual portraits** nearby are of (the notoriously frugal) Agnolo Doni and his new bride, Maddalena Strozzi. They wear the rich clothes and jewelry befitting a wealthy textile merchant and his noble wife. Raphael borrowed Leonardo's technique of the slightly turned pose, his subjects resting casually on their elbows. Maddalena even has Mona Lisa's folded hands.

The Florentine Renaissance ended in 1520 with the death of Raphael. Raphael is considered both the culmination and conclusion of the Renaissance. The realism, balance, and humanism we associate with the Renaissance are all found in Raphael's work. He combined the grace of Leonardo with the power of Michelangelo. With his death, the High Renaissance ended as well.

• *But, for the rest of Europe, the Renaissance was only beginning. Return to the hallway and continue past special exhibits and rooms where masterpieces from closed rooms are temporarily displayed. Near the end you'll reach Room 42.*

## NORTHERN ART

What the Florentines began was soon trendy all over Europe. Northern artists learned the Italian techniques of creating 3-D scenes and realistic portraits. On display you may see a dual portrait of Martin Luther and his wife.

### ❷ Lucas Cranach the Elder, *Martin Luther* and *Katherina von Bora*

Martin Luther—German monk, fiery orator, and religious whistle-blower—sparked a century of European wars by speaking out against the Catholic Church.

Luther (1483-1546) lived a turbulent life. In early adulthood, the newly ordained priest suffered a severe personal crisis of faith, before finally emerging "born again." In 1517, he openly protested against Church corruption and was excommunicated. Defying both the pope and the emperor, he lived on the run as an outlaw, watching as his ideas sparked peasant riots. He still found time to translate the New Testament from Latin to German, write hymns such as "A

UFFIZI

Mighty Fortress," and spar with the humanist Erasmus and fellow Reformer Zwingli.

In Cranach's portrait, Martin Luther (at age 46) is easing out of the fast lane. Recently married to an ex-nun, he has traded his monk's habit for street clothes, bought a house, had several kids... and has clearly been enjoying his wife's home cooking and home-brewed beer.

How Luther met his wife "Katie" is a story in itself. When she decided to leave her convent, the famous Martin Luther agreed to help find her a husband. She rejected his nominees, saying she'd marry no one...except Luther himself. In 1525, the 42-year-old ex-priest married the 26-year-old ex-nun "to please my father and annoy the pope." Martin turned his checkbook over to "my lord Katie," who also ran the family farm, raised their six children and 11 adopted orphans, brewed good beer, and hosted Martin's circle of friends (including Cranach) at loud, chatty dinner parties.

· *Return to the main hall and, at the end of the hall, find a reminder of the original source of the entire Renaissance—the ancient world. The hard-to-miss statue is called...*

### ㉕ *Laocoön* (16th-century copy)

At the far end of the hall is a copy of the dramatic ancient Greek statue of *Laocoön* (the original is at the Vatican Museums). It depicts the moment when this priest of Troy is overcome by snakes, and he realizes his people are doomed. ("Snakes? Why did it have to be snakes?") One of the most famous statues of antiquity, it was discovered in 1506—just in time to inspire Renaissance greats like Michelangelo. After seeing *Laocoön*, Michelangelo began creating figures with more restless motion and tragic emotion. *Laocoön*'s anguished face may exude tragedy, but right now Mr. Laocoön seems to be saying, "Time for a coffee break." Just past him is a fine café and an open-air terrace where you can enjoy a truly aesthetic experience...

### Little Capuchin Monk (Cappuccino)

This drinkable art form, born in Italy, is now enjoyed all over the world. It's called the "Little Capuchin Monk" because the coffee's frothy, light- and dark-brown foam looks like the two-toned cowls of the Capuchin order. Sip it on the terrace in the shadow of the towering Palazzo Vecchio, and be glad we live in an age where you don't need to be a Medici to enjoy all this fine art. *Salute.*

· *If you're ready to leave, the stairs next to the café lead directly to a handy WC and an exit.*

*For those willing to linger longer, the*

*first floor is worth a look. It features work from after the Renaissance: Mannerism (such as Parmigianino), Venetian (that would be Titian—it rhymes), Baroque (Caravaggio), and finally Flemish and Dutch (Rubens and Rembrandt). To reach the first floor, retrace your steps to the staircase between the Leonardo da Vinci and Michelangelo galleries and head down. We'll breeze through quickly, making a few key stops along the way.*

## FIRST FLOOR—MORE ART ON THE WAY TO THE EXIT

The first floor is a tangled maze of galleries. Keep your focus on the artists below and enlist the help of museum staff, if needed.

• *Head left at the bottom of the stairs and chug through a few rooms until you reach Room D8, with a tall painting.*

### Parmigianino, *Madonna with the Long Neck*

Once Renaissance artists had mastered reality, where could they go next?

Mannerists such as Parmigianino (1503-1540) tried to go beyond realism, exaggerating it for effect. Using brighter colors and twisting poses, they created scenes more elegant and more exciting than real life.

By stretching the neck of his Madonna, Parmigianino gives her an unnatural, swanlike beauty. She has the same pose and position of hands as Botticelli's *Venus* and the *Venus de' Medici*. Her body forms an arcing S-curve—down her neck as far as her elbow, then back the other way along Jesus' body to her knee, then down to her foot. Baby Jesus seems to be blissfully gliding down this slippery slide of sheer beauty.

• *Double back past the stairs (pausing to check out the ❷ portraits by Bronzino in Room 14 of Duke Cosimo I de' Medici, his wife, Eleonora, their cute bird-holding son, and their daughters) and find Room D22, with a number of works by Titian.*

### ❸ Titian, *Venus of Urbino*

Compare this *Venus* with Botticelli's newly hatched *Venus* and you get a good idea of the difference between the Florentine and Venetian Renaissances. Botticelli's was pure, innocent, and otherworldly. Titian's should have a staple in her belly button. This isn't a Venus, it's a centerfold—with no purpose but to please the eye (and other organs). While Botticelli's allegorical *Venus* is a message, this is a massage. The bed is used.

UFFIZI

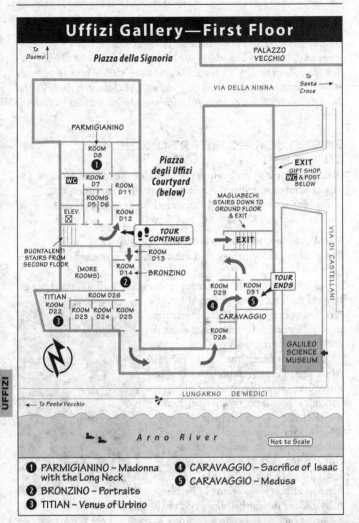

# Uffizi Gallery—First Floor

*Piazza della Signoria*

To Duomo ↑

PALAZZO VECCHIO

VIA DELLA NINNA

To Santa Croce →

PARMIGIANINO

ROOM D8  ❶

WC

ROOM D7

ROOMS D5 D6

ROOM D11

ELEV. ⊠

ROOM D12

*Piazza degli Uffizi Courtyard (below)*

BUONTALENTI STAIRS FROM SECOND FLOOR

(MORE ROOMS)

👣 TOUR CONTINUES

← ROOM D13

ROOM D14  ❷

BRONZINO

TITIAN ROOM D22  ❸

ROOM D26

ROOM D23  ROOM D24  ROOM D25

MAGLIABECHI STAIRS DOWN TO GROUND FLOOR & EXIT

EXIT

EXIT  GIFT SHOP, WC & POST BELOW

VIA DI CASTELLANI

ROOM D29  ❹

ROOM D31  ❺

TOUR ENDS

CARAVAGGIO

ROOM D28

GALILEO SCIENCE MUSEUM

LUNGARNO DE'MEDICI

← To Ponte Vecchio

*Arno River*

Not to Scale

❶ PARMIGIANINO – Madonna with the Long Neck
❷ BRONZINO – Portraits
❸ TITIAN – Venus of Urbino
❹ CARAVAGGIO – Sacrifice of Isaac
❺ CARAVAGGIO – Medusa

UFFIZI

Titian (c. 1490-1576) and his fellow Venetians took the pagan spirit pioneered in Florence and carried it to its logical hedonistic conclusion. Using bright, rich colors, they captured the luxurious life of happy-go-lucky Venice.

While other artists may have balanced their compositions with a figure on the left and one on the right, Titian balances his painting in a different way—with color. The canvas is split down the middle by the curtain. The left half is dark, the right half is lighter. The two halves are connected by a diagonal slash of luminous gold—the nude woman. The girl in the background is trying to find her some clothes.

In the Uffizi, we've seen many images of female beauty: from ancient goddesses to medieval Madonnas, from Parmigianino's cheesy slippery-slide to Michelangelo's peasant Mary, from Botticelli's pristine nymphs to Titian's sensuous centerfold. Their physical beauty expresses different aspects of the human spirit.

By the way, visitors from centuries past panted in front of this Venus by Titian. The Romantic poet Byron called it "*the* Venus." With her sensual skin, hey-sailor look, and suggestively placed hand, she must have left them blithering idiots.

• *Our tour is n-n-n-nearly over. Walk toward the long hallway and round the bend, with views of the Arno, before pausing to see works by* **Caravaggio,** *including the shockingly realistic* ❹ Sacrifice of Isaac *(Room D29) and the macabre head of* ❺ Medusa, *painted on a ceremonial shield (Room D31). (I think Medusa is screaming, "Agggh! Get me outta here.")*

*When you're ready to leave, the exit takes you back down to the WCs/bookstore/post office, and out to the street. You'll pop out behind the Uffizi, a block up from the river and very near the Galileo Science Museum and the Bargello (sculpture museum). Stepping back into the real world after your Uffizi experience, you may see it with new eyes.*

UFFIZI

# BARGELLO
# TOUR

The Renaissance began with sculpture. The great Florentine painters were "sculptors with brushes." You can see the birth of this revolution of 3-D in the Bargello (bar-JEL-oh), which boasts the best collection of Florentine sculpture (rated ▲▲▲). It's a small, uncrowded museum and a pleasant break from the intensity of the rest of Florence. You'll see 150 years of great statues, spanning the history of Florence's heyday. And it's all set in a rustic palazzo with a medieval atmosphere.

## Orientation

**Cost:** €9.

**Hours:** Daily 8:15-14:00—later for special exhibits; may close on the second and fourth Sun and first, third, and fifth Mon of each month; last entry 50 minutes before closing; reservations possible but unnecessary.

**Info:** +39 055 238 8606, www.bargellomusei.beniculturali.it.

**Getting There:** It's located at Via del Proconsolo 4, a three-minute walk northeast of the Uffizi. Facing the Palazzo Vecchio, go behind the Palazzo and turn left. Look for a rustic brick building with a spire that looks like a baby Palazzo Vecchio. If lost ask, *"Dov'è Bargello?"* (doh-VEH bar-JEL-oh).

**Tours:** Audioguides are €6 or 🎧 download my free Bargello audio tour.

**Length of This Tour:** Allow one hour. If your time is limited, be sure to see the Michelangelo statues on the ground floor and the Donatello *David* statues on the first.

**Cuisine Art:** Inexpensive bars and cafés await in the surrounding streets. See recommended eateries on page 309.

**Starring:** Michelangelo, Donatello, Brunelleschi, Ghiberti, and four different *David*s.

# The Tour Begins

## COURTYARD

• *Buy your ticket and take a seat in the courtyard.*

The Bargello, built in 1255, was Florence's original Town Hall and also served as a police station *(bargello)*, and later a prison. The heavy

fortifications tell us that keeping the peace in medieval Florence had its occupational hazards. While the stoniness of this building seems to fit its past, it is interesting to note that the independent Duchy of Tuscany abolished torture and capital punishment in the 18th century. They gathered the tools of torture and executions and burned them right here in this courtyard.

This cool and peaceful courtyard is at the center of the three-story rectangular building. The best statues are found in two rooms—one on the ground floor at the foot of the outdoor staircase, and another one flight up, directly above. We'll proceed from Michelangelo to Donatello and more.

But first, meander around this courtyard and get a feel for sculpture in general and the medium of stone in particular. Sculpture is a much more robust art form than painting. Think of just the engineering problems of the sculpting process: quarrying and cutting the stone, transporting the block to the artist's studio, all the hours of chiseling away chips, then the painstaking process of sanding the final product by hand.

A sculptor must be strong enough to gouge into the stone, but delicate enough to groove out the smallest details. Think of Michelangelo's approach to sculpting: He wasn't creating a figure—he was liberating it from the rock that surrounded it.

The Renaissance was centered on humanism—and sculpture is the perfect medium in which to express it. It shows the human form, standing alone, independent of church, state, or society, ready to fulfill its potential.

# Bargello—Ground Floor

*50 Feet*

To Duomo ↑

VIA GHIBELLINA

TOWER

TICKETS

ENTRANCE ►

EXIT

TEMPORARY EXHIBITS

VIA PROCONSOLO

COURTYARD

WELL

WC & ELEVATOR

COLUMN

STAIRS UP TO DONATELLO ROOM (FIRST FLOOR)

VIA DELLA VIGNA VECCHIA

To Santa Croce →

↓ To Palazzo Vecchio & Uffizi

❶ MICHELANGELO – Bacchus
❷ MICHELANGELO – Pitti Tondo
❸ MICHELANGELO – Brutus
❹ MICHELANGELO – David (Apollo)
❺ Copies of Michelangelo's Works
❻ DANIELE – Bust of Michelangelo
❼ CELLINI – Models of Perseus (2)
❽ GIAMBOLOGNA – Flying Mercury

Finally, a viewing tip. Every sculpture has an invisible "frame" around it—the stone block it was cut from. Visualizing this frame helps you find the center of the composition.

## GROUND FLOOR

• *Head into the room at the foot of the courtyard's grand staircase, turn left, and be greeted by a tall, marble party animal.*

### ❶ Michelangelo, *Bacchus,* c. 1497

Bacchus, the god of wine and revelry, raises another cup to his lips, while his little companion goes straight for the grapes.

Maybe Michelangelo had a sense of humor after all. Mentally compare this tipsy Greek god of wine with his sturdy, sober *David,* begun a few years later. Raucous *Bacchus* isn't nearly so muscular, so monumental...or so sure on his feet. Hope he's not driving. The pose, the smooth muscles, the beer belly, and the swaying hips look more like Donatello's boyish *David* (upstairs). The little satyr is considered the first such twisting serpentine figure since ancient times.

This was Michelangelo's first major commission. Check the date it was carved: c. 1497. The city of Florence was caught in the grip of the puritanical monk Savonarola. Meanwhile, young Michelangelo had fled to Rome, where he hobnobbed with the festive Medici exiles and created this ultra-pagan Bacchus. Michelangelo often vacillated—showing man either as strong and noble, or as weak and perverse. This isn't the nobility of the classical world, but the decadent side of orgies and indulgence.

• *Behind Bacchus' right cheek is a circular relief.*

### ❷ Michelangelo, *Madonna and Child with the Young St. John,* a.k.a. *Pitti Tondo,* c. 1505

By 1504, Michelangelo had just finished his monumental, heroic statue *David.* In a complete change of pace, he turned to this quiet, small-scale marble work.

The Virgin Mary sits reading a book, while Baby Jesus and (probably) John the Baptist look on. The round "tondo" format gave Michelangelo a compositional opportunity. He combined the vertical (the upright Madonna) and the horizontal (her forearms and thighs), all enfolded in a warm family circle. Jesus curves lovingly around his mom, casually glancing at her book. Another dimension to the composition is depth: The bench Mary sits on juts outward, and her face rises from the stone in a cameo effect. Finally, Michelangelo added an element of surprise to the standard tondo by letting Mary's head pop out from the top of the frame.

The tondo is unfinished, giving us a chance to look at Michelangelo's work process. He started first with the easy stuff—Mary's robe and the bench, which are nearly finished. Mary's blouse is still in rough form, being chiseled out in Michelangelo's cross-hatch technique. Find the little details beginning to emerge—the small child at left and the tiny face in Mary's diadem. But called away to a bigger project in Rome, Michelangelo abandoned the not-quite-finished tondo. Compare this ultra-sacred sculpture with the ultra-pagan Bacchus. Throughout his life, Michelangelo would veer between these two poles.

• *Farther back in the room, a marble bust against a square column is...*

### ❸ Michelangelo, *Brutus,* 1540

Another example of the influence of Donatello is this so-ugly-he's-beautiful bust by Michelangelo. His rough intensity gives him the look of a man who has succeeded against all odds, a dignified and heroic quality that would be missing if he were too pretty.

The subject is Brutus, the Roman who, for the love of liberty, murdered his friend and dictator, Julius Caesar *("Et tu...?")*. A Florentine in exile commissioned the bust after the 1537 assassination of a contemporary tyrant—the Medici Duke Alessandro. Michelangelo could understand this man's dilemma. He himself was torn between his love of the democratic tradition of Florence and loyalty to his friends the Medici, who had become dictators.

So he gives us two sides of a political assassin. The right profile (the front view) is heroic. But the hidden side (view from right), with the drooping mouth and squinting eye, makes him more cunning, sneering, and ominous. Michelangelo depicted a complex individual—a man who could bravely defend his Republic...and murder a close friend with a knife.

• *Nearby is...*

## ❹ Michelangelo, *David*, a.k.a. *Apollo*, 1530-1532

This restless, twisting man is either David or Apollo. (Is he reaching for a sling or a quiver?) Demure (and left unfinished), this stat-

ue is light years away from Michelangelo's famous *David* in the Accademia (1501-1504), which is so much larger than life in every way. We'll see three more *David*s upstairs. As you check out each one, compare and contrast the artists' styles.

In the glass cases in the corner are ❺ **small-scale copies** of some of Michelangelo's most famous works. In the center of the room, against a square column, look for a dark-bronze ❻ **bust of Michelangelo.** Made from his death mask by fellow sculptor Dan-

iele da Volterra, the bust (this one's a copy) captures his broken nose and brooding nature.

• *Circling back clockwise toward the entrance, look for two small statues in a glass case, by a pillar.*

## ❼ Cellini, Models of *Perseus*, 1545-1554

The life-size statue of Perseus slaying Medusa, located in the open-air loggia next to the Palazzo Vecchio, is cast bronze. Benvenuto Cellini started with these smaller models (one in wax, one in bronze) to master the difficult process of producing the first bronze statue of its kind in the Renaissance. Next to the statue, note the exquisite pedestal with four fine bronzes—built to support Cellini's statue of Perseus.

• *Take three steps toward the door to find...*

### ❽ Giambologna, *Flying Mercury,* before 1580

The messenger of the gods, naked from the winged helmet down, speeds off on his errands. The pose was made famous as a logo for

a well-known flower-delivery company. Despite all the bustle and motion, *Mercury* has a solid Renaissance core: the line of balance that runs straight up the center, from toes to hip to fingertip. He's caught in midstride. His top half leans forward, counterbalanced by his right leg in back, while the center of gravity rests firmly at the hipbone. Down at the toes, notice the cupid practicing for the circus.

• *We've seen statues from Florence's Renaissance heyday. Now, to see the roots of Florence's Renaissance, climb the court-yard staircase to the next floor up and turn right into the large Donatello room.*

## FIRST FLOOR

• *Entering the room, cross to the middle of the far wall, and check out the first of three* Davids *in this room (the marble one wearing the long skirt).*

### ❾ Donatello, *David,* c. 1408

This marble sculpture is young Donatello's first take on the popular subject of David slaying Goliath. His dainty pose makes him a little unsteady on his feet. He's dressed like a medieval knight—fully clothed but showing some leg through the slit skirt. The generic face and blank, vacant eyes give him the look not of a real man but of an anonymous decoration on a church facade. At age 22, Donatello still had one foot in the old Gothic world. *David*'s right leg makes his body sway in the Gothic style, while his left leg is planted in the *contrapposto* Renaissance. To tell the story of David, Donatello plants a huge rock right in the middle of Goliath's forehead. Stepping behind the statue, you see how flat it is—designed to be not freestanding but up against a wall, connected with a hook.

• *Nearby, find a smaller, black-metal statue. It's the same subject, of David, but by a different artist.*

# Bargello—First Floor

50 Feet

To Duomo

VIA GHIBELLINA

TOWER

CHAPEL

VIA PROCONSOLO

⑫
⑬
⑪ ⑭
⑩
DONATELLO ROOM
⑨

COURTYARD

ELEVATOR

STAIRS UP FROM GROUND FLOOR

UPPER LOGGIA

STAIRS UP TO SECOND FLOOR

VIA DELLA VIGNA VECCHIA

To Santa Croce

To Palazzo Vecchio & Uffizi

⑨ DONATELLO – David (c. 1408)
⑩ VERROCCHIO – David (c. 1470)
⑪ DONATELLO – David (c. 1440)
⑫ DONATELLO (or Desiderio) – Niccolò da Uzzano
⑬ DONATELLO – St. George
⑭ GHIBERTI & BRUNELLESCHI – The Sacrifice of Isaac (2 versions)

## ⑩ Andrea del Verrocchio, *David*, c. 1470

Verrocchio (1435-1488) is best known as the teacher of Leonardo da Vinci, but he was also the premier sculptor of the generation between Donatello and Michelangelo. Verrocchio's bronze *David* is definitely the shepherd "boy" described in the Bible. (Some have speculated that the statue was modeled on Verrocchio's young, handsome, curly-haired apprentice, Leonardo da Vinci.) *David* leans on one leg, not with a firm, commanding stance but a nimble one (especially noticeable from behind). Compare the smug smile of the victor with Goliath's "Oh, have I got a headache" expression.

• *Finally, a few steps away, is another shiny black-metal statue...*

## ⑪ Donatello, *David*, c. 1440

He's naked. Donatello sees David as a teenage boy wearing only a helmet, boots, and sword. The smooth-skinned warrior sways gracefully, poking his sword playfully at the severed head of the giant Goliath. His *contrapposto* stance is similar to Michelangelo's *David*, resting his weight on one leg in the classical style, but it gives him a feminine rather than masculine look. Gazing into his coy eyes and at his bulging belly is a very different experience from confronting Michelangelo's older and sturdier Renaissance Man.

Circle the statue clockwise. From the side, you see his ramrod-straight right leg. It's echoed by the sword he carries. Notice how *David*'s toes curl around the severed head of Goliath, drawing your attention to it. Around back, glance up at *David*'s neck. On the hair, there are still traces of the original gilding. Check out *David*'s prominent buttocks—clearly those of a young man, almost a boy. Notice the huge feather on the giant's helmet. It directs the viewer's eyes sensually up, up, up to *David*'s inviting back side. Now continue your circle and take in the whole statue.

This bronze *David* paved the way for Michelangelo's. Europe hadn't seen a freestanding male nude like this in a thousand years. In the Middle Ages, the human body was considered a dirty thing, a symbol of man's weakness, something to be covered up in shame. The church prohibited exhibitions of nudity like this one and certainly would never decorate a church with it. But in the Renaissance, a new class of rich and powerful merchants appeared, and they bought art for personal enjoyment. Reading Plato's *Symposium,* they saw the ideal of Beauty in the form of a young man. This particular statue stood in the palace of the Medici (today's Medici-Riccardi Palace)...where Michelangelo, practically an adopted son, grew up admiring it.

• *Along the wall behind the last* David *is...*

## ⓱ Donatello (or Desiderio da Settignano), *Niccolò da Uzzano,* after 1450

Not an emperor, not a king, not a pope, saint, or prince, this is one of Florence's leading businessmen, in a toga, portrayed in the style of an ancient Roman bust. In the 1400s, when Florence was inventing the Renaissance that all Europe would soon follow, there was an optimistic spirit of democracy that gloried in everyday people. Donatello (or his

## Donatello (1386-1466)

Donatello was the first great Renaissance genius, a model for Michelangelo and others. He mastered realism, creating the first truly lifelike statues of people since ancient times. Donatello turned out highly personal work. Unlike the ancient Greeks—but like the ancient Romans—he often sculpted real people, not idealized versions of pretty gods and goddesses. Some of these people are downright ugly. In the true spirit of Renaissance humanism, Donatello appreciated the beauty of flesh-and-blood human beings.

Donatello's personality was also a model for later artists. He was moody and irascible, purposely setting himself apart from others in order to concentrate on his sculpting. He developed the role of the "mad genius" that Michelangelo would later perfect.

student) portrayed this man as he was—with wrinkles, a quizzical look, and bags under his eyes.

• *In the niche in the wall stands...*

## ⑬ Donatello, *St. George,* c. 1417

The proud warrior has both feet planted firmly on the ground and stands on the edge of his niche looking out alertly. He tenses his

powerful right hand as he prepares to attack. George, the Christian slayer of dragons, was just the sort of righteous warrior that proud Renaissance Florentines could rally around in their struggles with nearby cities. Nearly a century later, Michelangelo's *David* replaced *George* as the unofficial symbol of Florence, but *David* was clearly inspired by *George*'s relaxed intensity and determination. (This is the original statue; a copy stands in its original niche at Orsanmichele Church—see page 102.)

The relief panel below shows *George* doing what he's been pondering. To his right, the sketchy arches and trees create the illusion of a distant landscape. Donatello, who apprenticed in Ghiberti's studio, is credited with teaching his master how to create 3-D illusions like this.

BARGELLO

• *On the wall next to* George, *you'll find some bronze relief panels. Don't look at the labels just yet.*

## ⓭ Ghiberti and Brunelleschi, Baptistery Door Competition Entries, 1401

*Ghiberti's panel, on the left, won.*

Some would say these two different relief panels represent the first works of the Renaissance. These two versions of *The Sacrifice of Isaac* were finalists in a contest held in 1401 to decide who would create the bronze doors of the Baptistery. The contest sparked citywide excitement, which evolved into the Renaissance spirit. Lorenzo Ghiberti won and later did the doors known as the Gates of Paradise. Filippo Brunelleschi lost—fortunately for us—freeing him to design the dome of the cathedral (or Duomo).

Both artists catch the crucial moment when Abraham, obeying God's orders, prepares to slaughter and burn his only son as a sacrifice. At the last moment—after Abraham has passed this test of faith—an angel of God appears to stop the bloodshed.

Let's look at the composition of the two panels: One is integrated and cohesive (yet dynamic), while the other is a balanced knickknack shelf of segments. Human drama: One has bodies and faces that speak. The boy's body is a fine classical nude in itself, so real and vulnerable. Abraham's face is intense and ready to follow God's will. Perspective: An angel zooms in from out of nowhere to save the boy in the nick of time.

Is one panel clearly better than the other? You be the judge. Pictured here are the two finalists for the Baptistery door competition—Ghiberti's and Brunelleschi's. Which do you like better?

It was obviously a tough call, but Ghiberti's was chosen, perhaps because his goldsmith training made him better suited for the technical work. (Ghiberti used the lost wax technique to cast his bronze panels. This was far cheaper than Brunelleschi's panels, which were molded with solid bronze. Economics may have entered into the decision-making process.)

Whatever the reason, Ghiberti got the gig, and that started a historic chain of events: Ghiberti went on to make the famous Baptistery doors, the ones so popular with tourists. Meanwhile, Brunelleschi was free to build his awe-inspiring dome. And Donatello graduated from Ghiberti's workshop to revolutionize sculpture. All three of these artists inspired Michelangelo, who built on their work and spread the Renaissance all across Europe. And it all started with these panels.

## THE REST OF THE BARGELLO

Our tour is done. But there's much more to see from the dynamic Renaissance. At the other end of this room are painted, glazed porcelains by the masterful Della Robbia family. Elsewhere on this floor, you can browse jewelry, ivories, and traditional Tuscan majolica ceramics. There's even an upper floor, with medallions, armor, colorful terra-cotta, and models of famous statues.

From swords to statues, from *Brutus* to Brunelleschi, from *David* to *David* to *David* to *David*—the Bargello's collection of civilized artifacts makes it clear that Florence was the birthplace of the Renaissance.

BARGELLO

# MUSEUM OF SAN MARCO TOUR

*Museo di San Marco*

Two of Florence's brightest lights lived in the San Marco Monastery, a reminder that the Renaissance was not just a secular phenomenon. At the Museum of San Marco (rated ▲▲), you'll find these two different expressions of 15th-century Christianity—Fra Angelico's radiant paintings, fusing medieval faith with Renaissance realism, and Savonarola's moral reforms, fusing medieval faith with modern politics.

## Orientation

**Cost:** €8.

**Hours:** Mon-Fri 8:15-14:00, Sat until 17:00, closed Sun; also closed second and fourth Mon of each month. Reservations are possible but unnecessary.

**Information:** +39 055 238 8608.

**Getting There:** It's on Piazza San Marco, a block north of the Accademia, and several long blocks northeast of the Duomo (head up Via Ricasoli or Via Cavour). Piazza San Marco is a hub for many buses.

**Tours:** ∩ Download my free Museum of San Marco audio tour and I'll personally walk you through this amazing place.

**Length of This Tour:** Allow one hour.

**Baggage Check:** Large bags are not allowed in the museum, and no baggage check is available (but the ticket taker might watch your bag if you ask).

**Starring:** Fra Angelico's paintings and Savonarola's living quarters.

## OVERVIEW

In 1439, Cosimo the Elder (the founder of the Medici ruling dynasty and Lorenzo the Magnificent's grandpa) hired the architect Michelozzo to build the monastery, and invited Fra Angelico's Dominican community to move here from Fiesole. (Being a moneylender, Cosimo had a big challenge: to give enough to charity to overcome his sinful occupation in order to earn salvation.) Fra Angelico (c. 1400-1455) turned down an offer to be archbishop of Florence, instead becoming prior (head monk) of this monastery. He quickly began decorating the monastery walls with frescoes.

The ground floor of this museum features the world's best collection of Fra Angelico paintings. The upstairs contains the monks' cells (living quarters), decorated by Fra Angelico, and the cell of the most famous resident, Savonarola.

# The Tour Begins

## GROUND FLOOR
• *Buy your ticket, and just inside the entrance, stop and take in...*

## The Cloister

Feel the spirituality of this place, a respite from the hubbub of modern Florence. A cloister like this is a private area in a monastery for mental and physical exercise. Monasteries often have two cloisters: one, more public and finely decorated, for pilgrims and visitors; the other, more private and deeper in the complex. This was the cloister where the public met the monastery.

Enjoy the calm, rhythmic symmetry of the stately columns and Renaissance arches, framing Gothic cross-vaulting. The proportion and harmony are very Renaissance. It just says 1439. This is an apt introduction to a monastery built during an optimistic time, when Renaissance humanism dovetailed with medieval spirituality.

• *Before hooking right into the first room, look down the corridor straight ahead. On the wall at the far end of the first corridor, in the corner of the cloister, is Fra Angelico's...*

### ❶ Crucifixion with St. Dominic (San Domenico in Adorazione del Crocifisso)

The fresco shows Dominic, the founder of the order, hugging the bloody cross like a groupie adoring a rock star. Monks who lived here—including Fra Angelico, Savonarola, and Fra Bartolomeo—renounced

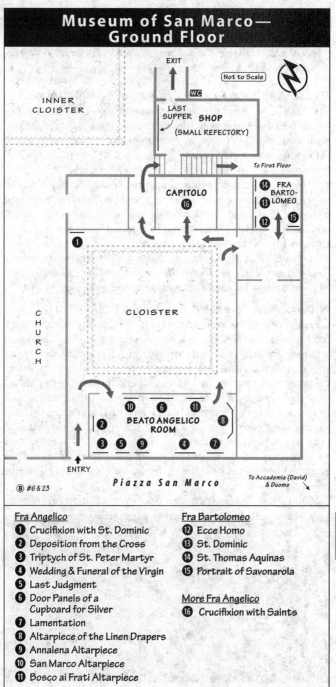

# Museum of San Marco—Ground Floor

EXIT

Not to Scale

INNER CLOISTER

WC

LAST SUPPER

SHOP (SMALL REFECTORY)

To First Floor

CAPITOLO

**1**

FRA BARTOLOMEO

**14**

**13**

**16**

**12**

**15**

CLOISTER

**2**

BEATO ANGELICO ROOM

**10**  **6**  **11**

**8**

**3**  **5**  **9**  **4**  **7**

CHURCH

ENTRY

*Piazza San Marco*

To Accademia (David) & Duomo

B #6 & 23

SAN MARCO

**Fra Angelico**
1 Crucifixion with St. Dominic
2 Deposition from the Cross
3 Triptych of St. Peter Martyr
4 Wedding & Funeral of the Virgin
5 Last Judgment
6 Door Panels of a Cupboard for Silver
7 Lamentation
8 Altarpiece of the Linen Drapers
9 Annalena Altarpiece
10 San Marco Altarpiece
11 Bosco ai Frati Altarpiece

**Fra Bartolomeo**
12 Ecce Homo
13 St. Dominic
14 St. Thomas Aquinas
15 Portrait of Savonarola

**More Fra Angelico**
16 Crucifixion with Saints

money, sex, ego, and pop music to follow a simple, regimented life, meditating on Christ's ultimate sacrifice.

• *Immediately to the right of the entry, a door leads into the Beato Angelico Room (Sala del Beato Angelico).*

## Beato Angelico Room: Fra Angelico Paintings

Fra Angelico—equal parts monk and painter—considered painting to be a form of prayer. He fused early-Renaissance technique with medieval spirituality, working to bridge the gap between the infinite (Christ) and the finite (a mortal's ability to relate to God) by injecting an ethereal atmosphere into his frescoes.

His works can be admired for their beauty or contemplated as spiritual visions. Browse the room, and you'll find serene-faced Marys, Christs, and saints wearing gold halos, evenly lit scenes, and meticulous detail—all creating a mystical world apart, glowing from within like stained-glass windows.

• *Start with the large three-peaked altarpiece. (While paintings periodically get rearranged, they should all be in this room. I've identified them by their shape, so you should be able to find them at a glance.)*

### ❷ Deposition from the Cross (Pala di Santa Trinità)

Christ's body is lowered from the cross, mourned by haloed women (on the left) and contemporary Florentines (right, likely the nobles who paid for this). There's a clearly defined foreground (the kneeling, curly-haired man and the woman with her back to us), background (the distant city and hills), and middle distance (the trees).

Though trained in medieval religious painting, Fra Angelico never closed his eyes to the innovations of the budding Renaissance, using both styles all his life. There are Gothic elements, such as the altarpiece frame, inherited from his former teacher (who painted the pinnacles on top). The holy wear halos, and the stretched-out "body of Christ" is symbolically "displayed" like the communion bread.

But it's truly a Renaissance work. The man in green, lowering

Christ, bends forward at a strongly foreshortened (difficult to draw) angle. Christ's toes, kissed by Mary Magdalene, cross the triptych wall, ignoring the frame's traditional three-arch divisions. Fra Angelico was boldly "coloring outside the lines" to create a single, realistic scene.

And the holy scene has been removed from its golden heaven and placed in the first great Renaissance landscape—on a lawn, among flowers, trees, cloud masses, real people, and the hillsides of Fiesole overlooking Florence (far right). Fra Angelico, the ascetic monk, refused to renounce one pleasure—his joy in the natural beauty of God's creation.

• *Find the triptych with three triangular peaks.*

### ❸ *Triptych of St. Peter Martyr (Trittico di San Pietro Martire)*

In this early, more "medieval" work, Fra Angelico sets (big) Mary and Child in a gold background flanked by (small) saints standing

obediently in their niches. When he joined the Dominican community in Fiesole, the artist took the name Giovanni (as he was known in his lifetime), and he wore the same attire as these famous Dominicans (including St. Dominic, far left, and St. Thomas Aquinas, far right)—white robe, black cape, and tonsured haircut.

Peter Martyr (on the right, next to Mary, with bloody head) exemplified the unbending Dominican spirit. Attacked by heretics (see the scene above Peter), he was hacked in the head with a dagger but died still preaching, writing with his own blood: *"Credo in Deum"* ("I believe in God").

• *Next find the two small panels sharing one long rectangular frame.*

### ❹ *Wedding and Funeral of the Virgin (Sposalizio, Funerali della Vergine)*

Fra Angelico's teenage training was as a miniaturist, so even these

small predella panels (descriptive lower panels of a larger altarpiece) are surprisingly realistic. The folds in the clothes, the gold-brocade hemlines, and the precisely outlined people are as though etched in glass. Notice the

Renaissance perspective tricks he was exploring, setting the wedding in front of receding buildings and the funeral (on the right) among candles that get shorter at the back of the scene.

• *Next up is a rectangular painting with three bloops on the top.*

### ❺ Last Judgment (Giudizio Universale)

Despite the Renaissance, Florence in the 1420s was still a city in the Christian universe described by Dante. Hell (to the right) is a hierarchical barbecue where sinners are burned, boiled, and tortured by a minotaur-like Satan, who rules the bottom of the pit. The blessed in heaven (left) play ring-around-the-rosy with angels. In the center, a row of open tombs creates a 3-D highway to hell, stretching ominously to that final Judgment Day. Notice the crowd of big shots—bishops, royals, monks of other orders—being herded to hell.

• *Find the set of 36 small square panels. Focus on the nine panels on the far left.*

### ❻ Door Panels of a Cupboard for Silver (Pannelli dell'Armadio degli Argenti)

The first nine scenes in this life of Christ (the big panel on the left end) are by Fra Angelico himself (the rest are by assistants). Like storyboards for a movie, these natural, realistic, and straightforward panels "show" through action, they don't just "tell" through symbols. (The Latin inscription beneath each panel is redundant.) The miraculous is presented as an everyday occurrence.

1. The Wheel of Ezekiel prophesies Christ's coming.
2. In the Annunciation, the angel gestures to tell Mary that she'll give birth.
3. Newborn Jesus glows, amazing his parents, while timid shepherds sneak a peek.
4. Precocious Jesus splays himself and says, "Cut me."
5. One of the Magi kneels to kiss the babe's foot.
6. In the temple, the tiny baby is dwarfed by elongated priests and columns.
7. Mary and the baby ride, while Joseph carries the luggage all the way to Egypt.
8. Meanwhile, innocent babies are slaughtered in a jumble of gore, dramatic poses, and agonized faces.
9. The commotion contrasts with the serenity of the child Jesus preaching in the temple.

This work by 50-year-old Fra Angelico—master of many

styles, famous in Italy—has the fresh, simple, and spontaneous storytelling of a children's book.

• *The largest horizontal rectangular frame in the room is...*

### ❼ Lamentation (Compianto sul Cristo Morto)

This painting of the executed Christ being mourned silently by loved ones was the last thing many condemned prisoners saw during

their final hours. It once hung in a church where the soon-to-be executed were incarcerated.

The melancholy mood is understated, suggested by a series of horizontal layers—Christ's body, the line of mourners, the city walls, landscape horizon, layered clouds, and the bar of the cross. It's as though Christ is being welcomed into peaceful rest, a comforting message from Fra Angelico to the condemned.

"Fra Angelico" (Angelic Brother) is a nickname that describes the artist's reputation for sweetness, humility, and compassion. It's said he couldn't paint a Crucifixion without crying. In 1984, he was beatified by Pope John Paul II and made patron of artists.

• *At the end of the room hangs the tallest painting with two panels opening like doors.*

### ❽ Altarpiece of the Linen Drapers (Tabernacolo dei Linaioli)

Check out the impressive size and marble frame (by Ghiberti, of baptistery-door fame), which attest to Fra Angelico's worldly success and collaboration with the Renaissance greats. The monumental Mary and Child, as well as the saints on the doors, are gold-backed and elegant, to please conservative patrons. In the three predella panels below, Fra Angelico gets to display his Renaissance chops, showing haloed saints mingling with

well-dressed Florentines amid local cityscapes and realistic landscapes.

• *Find three similar-looking altarpieces. Each of them is large and square, dominated by Mary in her blue robe in the center. They show how Fra Angelico, exploring Renaissance techniques, developed the theme of "Sacred Conversations" (Sacra Conversaziones) over his lifetime. These paintings show Mary and Child surrounded by saints "conversing" in-*

*formally about holy matters, inviting the viewer to join in. They represent an evolution of style, so it's worth seeing them in the order I present them.*

### ❾ Annalena Altarpiece (Pala d'Annalena)

In the *Annalena Altarpiece* (c. 1435)—considered Florence's first true *Sacra Conversazione*—the saints flank Mary in a neat line, backed by medieval gold in the form of a curtain. Everyone is either facing out or in profile—not the natural poses of a true crowd. There's little eye contact, and certainly no "conversation."

Mary and Jesus direct our eye to Mary's brooch, the first in a series of circles radiating out from the center: brooch, halo, canopy arch, and the imaginary circle that enfolds the group of saints. Set in a square frame, this painting has the circle-in-a-square composition that marks many *Sacra Conversaziones*.

• *Now find the largest of the three Sacred Conversations.*

### ❿ San Marco Altarpiece (Pala di San Marco)

Cosimo the Elder commissioned this painting (c. 1440) as the centerpiece of the new church next door. For the dedication Mass, Fra Angelico theatrically "opens the curtain," revealing a stage set with a distant backdrop of trees, kneeling saints in the foreground, and a crowd gathered around Mary and Child at center stage on a raised, canopied throne. The carpet makes a chessboard-like pattern to establish 3-D perspective. The altarpiece was like a window onto a marvelous world where the holy mill about on earth as naturally as mortals.

To show just how far we've come from Gothic, Fra Angelico gives us a painting-in-a-painting—a crude, gold-backed Crucifixion.

• *Finally, find the...*

### ⓫ Bosco ai Frati Altarpiece (Pala di Bosco ai Frati)

This altarpiece (c. 1450) is Fra Angelico's last great work, and he uses every stylistic arrow in his quiver: the detailed friezes of the miniaturist; medieval halos and gold backdrop; monumental, naturally posed figures in the style of Masaccio (especially St. Francis, on the left, with his relaxed *contrapposto*); 3-D perspective established by the floor tiles; and Renaissance love of natural beauty (the trees and sky).

Fra Angelico's bright colors are eye-catching. The gold backdrop sets off the red-pink handmaidens, which set off Jesus' pale skin. The deep blue of Mary's dress, frosted with a precious gold hem, turns out at her feet to show a swath of the green inner lining, suggesting the 3-D body within.

Despite Renaissance realism, Fra Angelico creates an ideal world of his own—perfectly lit, with no moody shadows, dirt, frayed clothing, or imperfections. The faces are certainly realistic, but they express no human emotion. These mortals, through sacrifice and meditation, have risen above the petty passions celebrated by humanist painters to achieve a serenity that lights them from within.

Before leaving, look for a portrait of Fra Angelico himself (a small, square, painting dominated by his black robe, hood, and solemn gaze).

• *Exit the room, returning to the open-air courtyard. Head for the far right corner, and enter the set of rooms marked* Lavabo e Refettorio. *To your right is the former monks' dining hall. Step inside. Above the door is the Risen Christ, reminding monks that every meal is a communion with God, a reenactment of the Last Supper. At the far end is a painting of the Last Supper. Like Leonardo's* Last Supper *in Milan, it's as if Jesus and the 12 apostles are dining with the monks. And, from the small balcony in the middle of the room, one monk would read from the Bible as the rest ate in silence.*

*Now enter the small room opposite the dining hall, with paintings by Fra Bartolomeo.*

## Room of Fra Bartolomeo Paintings

Fra Bartolomeo (1472-1517) lived and worked in this monastery a generation after the "Angelic" brother.

• *Locate the first small painting on the left.*

### ⓬ Ecce Homo

This shows the kind of Christ that young, idealistic Dominican monks (like Fra Bartolomeo) adored in their meditations—curly-haired, creamy-faced, dreamy-eyed, bearing the torments of the secular world with humble serenity.

• *The fourth panel to the right of Jesus is...*

SAN MARCO

### ⓭ *St. Dominic (San Domenico)*

St. Dominic holds a finger to his lips—"Shh! We have strict rules in my order." Dominic (c. 1170-1221), a friend of St. Francis of Assisi, formed his rules after seeing the austere *perfetti* (perfect ones) of the heretical Cathar sect of southern France. He figured they could only be converted by someone just as extreme, following Christ's simple, possession-free lifestyle. Nearing 50, Dominic made a 3,400-mile preaching tour—on foot, carrying his luggage—from Rome to Spain to Paris and back. Dominic is often portrayed with the star of revelation over his head.

• *Two more panels to the right is...*

### ⓮ *St. Thomas Aquinas (San Tommaso d'Aquino)*

St. Thomas Aquinas (c. 1225-1274, wearing a hood)—the intellectual giant of the U. of Paris—used logic and Aristotelian models to defend and explain Christianity (building the hierarchical belief system known as Scholasticism). He's often shown with a heavy build and the sun of knowledge burning in his chest.

• *As you face the door, to the left you'll see...*

### ⓯ *Portrait of Savonarola (Ritratto di Fra' Girolamo Savonarola)*

This is the famous portrait—in profile, hooded, with big nose and clear eyes, gazing intently into the darkness—of the man reviled as the evil opponent of Renaissance modernity. Would it surprise you to learn that it was Savonarola who inspired Fra Bartolomeo's art? Bartolomeo was so moved by Savonarola's sermons that he burned his early nude paintings (and back issues of *Penthouse*), became a monk, gave up painting for a few years...then resurfaced to paint the simple, sweet frescoes we see here.

• *Leaving the world of Fra Bartolomeo, return to the cloister, turn right, and continue to the next room.*

## Capitolo

This room contains Fra Angelico's ⓰ *Crucifixion with Saints (Crocifissione dell'Angelico)*. Set against a bleak background, this is one of more than 20 versions of Christ's torture/execution in the monastery. It was in this room that naughty monks were examined and judged.

Among the group of hermits, martyrs, and religious extremists who surround the cross, locate Dominic (kneeling at the foot of the cross, in Dominican white robe, black cape, and tonsured hair, with star on head), Peter Martyr (kneeling in right corner, with bloody head), and Thomas Aquinas (standing behind Peter, with jowls and sun on chest).

The old bell on display in the room is the original church bell. One night in 1498, this bell rang out, trying to warn Savonarola that a Florentine mob was coming to arrest him. (The mob was so mad at the bell, they whipped it in public and then, for good measure, exiled it for 10 years.) Ah, but we're getting ahead of the story. For that, we need to head upstairs.

• *Return to the cloister, and go through the next door. At the end of the short hall peek into the private, deeper cloister where the public wasn't allowed. This is the domain of the Dominicans, who still run this place 600 years after Fra Angelico. Then head upstairs.*

## FIRST FLOOR

• *At the top of the staircase, you'll come face-to-face with Fra Angelico's...*

### ❶ *Annunciation (Annunciazione)*

Sway back and forth and watch the angel's wings sparkle (from glitter mixed into the fresco) as he delivers "the good news" to

the very humble and accepting Virgin—particularly effective by torchlight and with a 15th-century mindset. Mary is under an arcade that's remarkably similar to the one in the cloister. Fra Angelico brings this scene home to the monks quite literally.

Paintings such as this one made Fra Angelico so famous that the pope called on him to paint the Vatican. Yet this work, like the other frescoes here, was meant only for the private eyes of humble monks. Monks gathered near this *Annunciation* for common prayers, contemplating Christ's life from beginning (*Annunciation*) to end (*Crucifixion with St. Dominic*, over your left shoulder). The caption reads: Remember to say your prayers.

• *From the* Annunciation, *take a few steps to the left, and look down the (east) corridor lined with...*

## The Monks' Living Quarters

This floor is lined with the cells (bedrooms) of those who lived in the monastery: monks, novice monks (farther down), and lay peo-

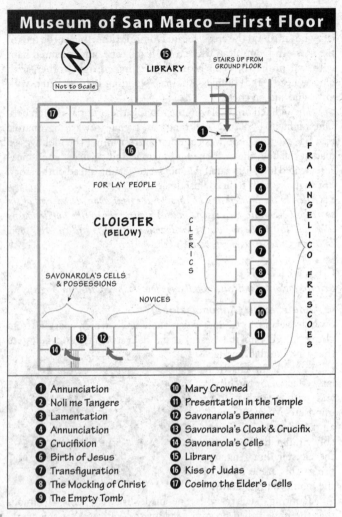

# Museum of San Marco—First Floor

Not to Scale

15 LIBRARY

STAIRS UP FROM
GROUND FLOOR

17

1

16

FOR LAY PEOPLE

2
3
4
5
6
7
8
9
10
11

F R A   A N G E L I C O   F R E S C O E S

CLOISTER
(BELOW)

C
L
E
R
I
C
S

SAVONAROLA'S CELLS
& POSSESSIONS

NOVICES

14   13   12

1 Annunciation
2 Noli me Tangere
3 Lamentation
4 Annunciation
5 Crucifixion
6 Birth of Jesus
7 Transfiguration
8 The Mocking of Christ
9 The Empty Tomb
10 Mary Crowned
11 Presentation in the Temple
12 Savonarola's Banner
13 Savonarola's Cloak & Crucifix
14 Savonarola's Cells
15 Library
16 Kiss of Judas
17 Cosimo the Elder's Cells

SAN MARCO

ple and support staff (to your right). We'll see Savonarola's quarters in the far corner, later on this tour. Each cell features a fresco by Fra Angelico or his assistants.

After a long day of prayer, meditation, reading, frugal meals, chopping wood, hauling water, translating Greek, attending Mass, and more prayer, a monk retired to one of these small, bare, lamplit rooms. His "late-night TV" was programmed by the prior—Fra Angelico—in the form of a fresco to meditate on before sleep. In monastic life, everything is a form of prayer. Pondering these scenes, monks learned the various aspects of worship: humility, adoration, flagellation, reflection, and so on.

Fra Angelico and his assistants decorated 43 cells in the early 1440s. Many feature a crucifix and St. Dominic, but each shows Dominic in a different physical posture (kneeling, head bowed, head raised, hands folded), which the monks copied to attain a more spiritual state.

• *Some of Fra Angelico's best work is found in the 10 cells along the left-hand side. Begin with the first of these cells and check out the entire lineup.*

❷ *Noli me Tangere:* The resurrected Jesus, appearing as a hoe-carrying gardener, says, "Don't touch me" and gingerly sidesteps Mary Magdalene's grasp. The flowers and trees represent the blossoming of new life, and they're about the last we'll see. Most scenes have stark, bare backgrounds, to concentrate the monk's focus on just the essential subject.

❸ *Lamentation:* Christ and mourners are a reverse image of the Lamentation downstairs. Christ levitates, not really supported by the ladies' laps. The colors are muted grays, browns, and pinks. Dominic (star on head) stands contemplating, just as the monk should do, by mentally transporting himself to the scene.

❹ *Annunciation:* The painting's arches echo the room's real arch. (And they, in turn, harmoniously "frame" the "arch" of Mary and the angel bending toward each other to talk.) Peter Martyr (bloody head) looks on.

You can't call these cells a wrap until you've found at least six crosses, three Dominics, three Peters, and a Thomas Aquinas. Ready...go.

❺ *Crucifixion:* That's one cross. And another Dominic.

❻ *Birth of Jesus:* And there's your second Peter.

❼ *Transfiguration:* Forsaking Renaissance realism, Fra Angelico emphasizes the miraculous. In an aura of blinding light, Christ spreads his arms cross-like, dazzling the three witnesses at the bottom of the "mountain." He's joined by disembodied heads of prophets, all spinning in a circle echoed by the room's arch. These rooms, which

housed senior monks, have some of the most complex and intellec-
tually demanding symbolism.

**❽ *The Mocking of Christ:*** From Renaissance realism to Dalí
Surrealism. Dominic, while reading the
Passion, conjures an image of Christ—
the true king, on a throne with a globe
and scepter—now blindfolded, spit upon,
slapped, and clubbed by...a painting of
medieval symbols of torment. This must
have been a puzzling riddle from the
Master to a fellow monk.

**❾ *The Empty Tomb:*** The worried
women are reassured by an angel that "he
is risen." Jesus, far away in the clouds,
seems annoyed that they didn't listen to him.

**❿ *Mary Crowned:*** ...triumphantly in heaven, while Dominic,
Peter, Aquinas, Francis, and others prepare to celebrate with high-
fives.

**⓫ *Presentation in the Temple:*** Baby Jesus is swaddled like a
mummy. And there's your final Peter.

• *Continue around the bend—Savonarola's three rooms are at the far
end of the corridor.*

## Savonarola's Cells (Celle del Savonarola)

Girolamo Savonarola (1452-1498) occupied the cluster of rooms at
the end of the hall. But before you climb the three steps to his cells,
stop at the last two rooms along the hall. Here you'll find a number
of his possessions, including **⓬** fragments of a Crucifixion **banner** carried during processions (labeled *Crocifissione* or *Lo Stendardo
del Savonarola*) and **⓭** his blue, hooded **cloak** and personal **crucifix.** Savonarola's life changed dramatically at 22, when he heard a
sermon on repentance. He traded his scholar's robes for the black
cloak of a simple Dominican monk. He quickly became known for
his asceticism, devotion, and knowledge of the Bible. His followers
rallied around this banner, painted with a gruesome Crucifixion
scene in the Fra Angelico style. They paraded through the streets
reminding all that Christ paid for their worldly Renaissance sins.

• *Now climb three steps and enter* **⓮** *Savonarola's Cells.*

### First Room

The **portrait bust** shows the hooded monk, whose personal charisma and prophetic fervor led him from humble scholar to celebrity
preacher to prior of San Marco to leader of Florence for four years
to controversial martyr. The **relief** under the portrait bust shows
Savonarola at his greatest moment. He stands before the Florence
city council and pledges allegiance to Florence's constitution, as-

suming control of the city after the exile of the Medici (1494). Reviled as a fanatical, regressive tyrant and praised as a saint, reformer, and champion of democracy, Savonarola was a complex man in a position of great power during turbulent times.

Various **paintings** depict Savonarola in action, including one by Federico Andreotti, which shows the powerful monk reproaching two troublemakers in his study.

• *The next room is Savonarola's...*

### Study (Studiolo)

Seated at this **desk,** in his ecclesiastical folding **chair** (built from several types of wood, as a diagram explains), Savonarola scoured his Bible for clues to solve Florence's civic strife.

In 1482 at age 30, the monk had come to San Marco as a lecturer. He was bright, humble...and boring. Then, after experiencing divine revelations, he spiced his sermons with prophecies of future events...which started coming true. His sermons on Ezekiel, Amos, Exodus, and the Apocalypse predicted doom for the Medici family. He made brazen references to the pope's embezzling and stable of mistresses, and preached hope for a glorious future after city and church were cleansed.

Packed houses heard him rail against the "prostitute church... the monster of abomination." Witnesses wrote that "the church echoed with weeping and wailing," and afterward "everyone wandered the city streets dazed and speechless." From this humble desk, he corresponded with the worldly pope, the humanist Pico della Mirandola, and fans, such as Lorenzo the Magnificent, who begrudgingly admired his courage.

Lorenzo died, the bankrupt Medici were exiled, and Florence was invaded by France...as Savonarola had prophesied. In the power vacuum, the masses saw Savonarola as a moderate voice who championed a return to Florence's traditional constitution. He was made head of a Christian commonwealth.

• *Finally, step into the...*

### Room with Savonarola's Possessions (Le Reliquie del Savonarola)

Savonarola's personal moral authority was unquestioned, as his simple **wool clothes** and **rosary** attest.

At first, his rule was just. He cut taxes, reduced street crime, shifted power from rich Medici to citizens, and even boldly proposed banning Vespas from tourist zones.

However, Savonarola had an uncompromising and fanatical side, as his **hair-shirt girdle** suggests. His government passed strict morality laws against swearing, blasphemy, gambling, and ostentatious clothes, which were enforced by gangs of thuggish teenagers. At the height of the Christian Republic, during Lent of 1497, followers built a huge "bonfire of vanities" on Piazza della Signoria, where they burned wigs, carnival masks, dice, playing cards, musical instruments, and discredited books and paintings.

In 1498, several forces undermined Savonarola's Republic: scheming Medici, crop failure, rival cities, a pissed-off pope threatening excommunication for Savonarola and political isolation for Florence, and a public tiring of puritanism. Gangs of opponents (called *Arrabbiati*, "Rabid Dogs") battled Savonarola's supporters (the "Weepers"). Meanwhile, Savonarola was slowly easing out of public life, refusing to embroil the church in a lengthy trial, retiring to his routine of study, prayer, and personal austerity.

Egged on by city leaders and the pope, a bloodthirsty mob marched on San Marco to arrest Savonarola. *Arrabbiati* fought monks with clubs (imagine it in the **courtyard** out the window), while the church bells clanged and the monks shouted, "*Salvum fac populum tuum, Domine!*" ("Save thy people, Lord!"). The *Arrabbiati* stormed up the stairs to this floor, and Savonarola was handed over to the authorities. He was taken to the Palazzo Vecchio, tortured, tried, and sentenced.

On May 23, 1498 (see the **painting** *Supplizio del Savonarola in Piazza della Signoria*), before a huge crowd in front of the Palazzo Vecchio (where today a memorial plaque is embedded in the pavement of the Piazza della Signoria), Savonarola was publicly defrocked, then publicly forgiven by a papal emissary. Then he was hanged—not Old West-style, in which the neck snaps, but instead slowly strangled, dangling from a rope, while teenage boys hooted and threw rocks.

The crowd looked upon the lifeless body of this man who had once captivated their minds, as they lit a pyre under the scaffold—see the **stick** *(palo)* from the fire. The flames rose up, engulfing the body, when suddenly...his arm shot upward!—like a final blessing or curse— and the terrified crowd stampeded, killing several. Savonarola's ashes were thrown in the Arno.

## THE REST OF THE MUSEUM

The corridor to the right of Fra Angelico's *Annunciation* is well worth a look.

**⓯ Library:** Also designed by Michelozzo, this room contains music and other manuscripts. Music hymnals needed to be large so the entire choir could read from one. Take a close look at the music pages, many made of vellum (sheep skin), gorgeously illuminated (painted), and with fancy leather bindings complete with buckles. Monks would chant, reading the rhythm (according to quarter notes, half notes, and so on), in a pitch relative to a C clef (rather than the G and F clefs that we are most familiar with). The C clef could slide depending on the range needed, marking middle C. A chest at the far end (well described in English) shows tools and ingredients for making, painting, and binding these fine books.

**⓰ *Kiss of Judas* Fresco:** In a cell a few steps past the library is Fra Angelico's *Kiss of Judas*. The theme proved prophetic, since it was outside that cell that Savonarola was arrested.

**⓱ Cosimo the Elder's Cells:** These are at the end of the corridor (right side). As the builder of this monastery, he often retired here for spiritual renewal. Inside, the painting of the Magi includes a kneeling king kissing the baby's little holy toes—a portrait of Cosimo. As at the Medici-Riccardi Palace, the family favored this Biblical scene, since it was one of the few in which it was acceptable to portray themselves as kings to showcase their wealth and power. Even in religious endeavors they constantly reminded people of their stature (you see their familiar coat of arms, with six balls, located over windows and doors throughout this building). After Cosimo financed the building of the complex, the pope granted him absolution for all his sins.

• *To exit, return to the stairway and descend. Take a right at the bottom into a bookshop decorated with a fine* **Ghirlandaio Last Supper** *fresco. It's no coincidence that the cherries on the table are reminiscent of the red balls of the Medici coat of arms.*

*Are you as tired as John is? WCs are immediately past the bookshop. Pass through corridors filled with a hodgepodge of architectural fragments (gathered from the ruins of the Jewish ghetto that stood on Piazza della Repubblica until the late 19th century) and on to the exit. On the street, turn right, then right again, and you'll see the Campanile of the Duomo.*

**SAN MARCO**

# DUOMO MUSEUM TOUR

*Museo dell'Opera del Duomo*

The Duomo Museum (rated ▲▲▲) makes the dazzling art of the cathedral accessible and easy to appreciate. Five centuries ago, Italian artists decorated Florence's Duomo, Baptistery, and Campanile with amazing art. Now these treasures are gathered inside, protected from the elements, in a marvelous museum.

Brunelleschi's dome, Ghiberti's bronze doors, and Donatello's statues. These creations define the 1400s (the Quattrocento) in Florence, when the city blossomed and classical arts were reborn. Copies of the doors and statues now decorate the exteriors of the cathedral, Baptistery, and Campanile, while the original sculptured masterpieces of the complex are now restored and thoughtfully displayed here. The museum also has two powerful statues by Florence's powerhouse sculptors—Donatello's *Mary Magdalene* and Michelangelo's *Pietà*, intended as his sculptural epitaph.

## Orientation

**Cost:** Covered by all three Duomo passes (Ghiberti-€15, Giotto-€20, and Brunelleschi-€30; see page 51).

**Hours:** Daily 9:00-19:45, closed first Tue of each month, last entry one hour before closing. This is one of the few museums in Florence that's open every Monday.

**Information:** +39 055 230 2885, www.museumflorence.com.

**Getting There:** The museum is across from the Duomo on the east side (the far end from the Baptistery), at Via del Proconsolo 9.

**Tours:** A free app for the Duomo Museum is available.

**Length of This Tour:** Allow 1.5 hours. With limited time, focus on Ghiberti's doors, Michelangelo's *Pietà*, Donatello's sculptures, and the pair of finely carved choir lofts *(cantorie)*.

**Services:** All backpacks must be checked, regardless of size; purses

and messenger bags are OK. Several WCs are available inside. The easiest is just after the museum entrance to the right.
**Starring:** Brunelleschi, Ghiberti, Donatello, and Michelangelo.

# The Tour Begins

## GROUND FLOOR

The museum presents the 2,000-year history of Florence's Duomo, Baptistery, and Campanile.
• *Scan your ticket, and pass the hall lined with names of the many great artists and architects who helped build the Duomo over the centuries. Enter Room 4, with a large...*

### ❶ Model of the Duomo's Medieval Facade

The model shows the church facade circa 1500, the era of Michelangelo. Notice that only the lower third of the facade is faced with

marble and statues. The rest was only bare brick. Church construction began in 1296, but after an initial burst of energy, petered out. The facade was meant to be a glorious showcase of great statues set into niches. Get close to the model and find a few: There's Mary-and-Babe over the central doorway. Above and to her left is a pope with a ridiculously tall hat. And below Mary are four big, seated Evangelists.

• *Now let's see those actual statues, and more from the medieval facade. Continue into the large hall, Room 6, dubbed the...*

### Hall of Paradise (Sala del Paradiso)

On one wall, this room re-creates that lower third of the facade we saw on the model. The opposite wall re-creates the Baptistery facade. Both buildings were a showcase of the greatest art of Florence from roughly 1300 to 1600. Now, in this room, the original statues, doors, and reliefs face each other again as they once did.

Start with the Duomo. Peruse the various statues, done by many different artists from different eras, and consider the church's long evolution. The Duomo began life in early medieval times as a humble church overshadowed by the more prestigious Baptistery. By the 1200s, the church wasn't big enough to contain the exuberant spirit of a city growing rich from the wool trade and banking. So in 1296, Florence set out to rebuild it, intending to make the finest church of the age.

Arnolfo di Cambio, the architect, began the construction and

DUOMO MUSEUM

# Duomo Museum—Ground Floor

STAIRS
UP TO
FIRST FLOOR

Room 9

Not to Scale

DUOMO FACADE

HALL OF PARADISE

BAPTISTERY FACADE

Room 7

Rm 12

Room 10

Room 4

STAIRS
& ELEV.

Room 5

Room 6

TEMPORARY
EXHIBITIONS

TOUR
BEGINS

SHOP

STAIRS

WC

TICKETS

LOBBY

ELEV.

COAT
ROOM

CAFE

ENTRANCE

To Duomo
Entrance

**Piazza del Duomo**

To Opera del
Duomo Studio

1 Model of the Duomo's Medieval Facade

2 ARNOLFO – Madonna with the Glass Eyes

3 DONATELLO – St. John the Evangelist

4 ARNOLFO – Pope Boniface VIII

5 GHIBERTI – "Gates of Paradise" Doors

6 GHIBERTI – North Doors

7 PISANO – South Doors

8 DONATELLO – Mary Magdalene

9 Relics

10 MICHELANGELO – Pietà

designed the facade. Arnolfo envisioned a three-story facade of pointed arches and white, pink, and green marble, studded with statues and gleaming with gold mosaics. In fact, it might have looked much like the Neo-Gothic version on the church today. For the next two centuries, great sculptors contributed to the facade. But, as we saw, it was never completed. Only the bottom third was faced with marble—the upper part remained bare brick.

Still, what they did complete is very impressive. It was a showcase for the city's top sculptors. In its niches were late Gothic and early Renaissance statues—some of the best of the age.

• *Let's get a closer look of some of the statues. Find the seated Madonna and Child, flanked by saints. The original is on ground level (so tourists can see it better), while a copy stands above, showing her original location on the facade.*

## ❷ Arnolfo di Cambio, *Madonna with the Glass Eyes (Madonna dagli Occhi di Vetro)*, c. 1300

This is the central figure over the cathedral's doorway. The building was dedicated to Mary—starry-eyed over the birth of Baby Jesus. She sits, crowned like a chess-set queen, framed with a dazzling mosaic halo. To the right is St. Zenobius, Florence's first bishop during Roman times. He raises his hand to consecrate the formerly pagan ground as Christian.

• *Flanking the Madonna in the four big niches are the Four Evangelists (left to right: Matthew, Luke, John, and Mark). Of the four, the most impressive is by Florence's first sculpting prodigy, Donatello.*

### ❸ Donatello, *St. John the Evangelist,* c. 1409

John the Evangelist and his mates would have made a solemn impression on worshippers as they filed through the church door for Mass.

John sits gazing at a distant horizon, his tall head rising high above his massive body. This visionary foresees a new age...and the coming Renaissance. With its expressive face, this work is a hundred years ahead of its time.

At 22 years old, Donatello (c. 1386-1466) sculpted this work just before becoming a celebrity for his inspiring statue of St. George (original in the Bargello, copy on the exterior of the Orsanmichele Church). Donatello ("Little Donato"), like most early Renaissance artists, was a blue-collar worker, raised as a workshop apprentice among knuckle-dragging musclemen. He proudly combined physical skill with technical know-how to create beauty (Art + Science = Renaissance Beauty). His statues are thinkers with big hands who can put theory into practice.

• *At the far left of the room is the original statue of the pope with the tall hat. The copy sits high up on the facade, just left of center.*

### ❹ Arnolfo di Cambio, *Pope Boniface VIII*

Despised by Dante for his meddling in politics, Pope Boniface paid 3,000 florins to get his image in a box seat high on the facade. While he looks stretched out when viewed at ground level, Arnolfo portrayed him out of proportion intentionally. His XXL shirt size looks right when he's up above and viewed from street level.

• Facing the facade of the church, as they did in the Middle Ages, are the famous doors of the Baptistery. Here's your chance to study the original panels of those famous bronze doors. The oldest doors on the left are by Pisano (South Doors, c. 1330-1336). The original competition doors on the right are the first ones done by Ghiberti (North Doors, 1403-1424). And in the center are the famous Gates of Paradise by Ghiberti (East Doors, 1425-1452). Start with the most famous of the three...

### ❺ Ghiberti's Gates of Paradise

The Renaissance began in 1401 with a citywide competition to build new doors for the Baptistery (see page 98 for more on this contest). Lorenzo Ghiberti (c. 1378-1455) won the job and built the

doors for the north side of the building. Everyone loved them, so he was then hired to make another set of doors for the east entrance, facing the Duomo. These bronze "Gates of Paradise" revolutionized the way Renaissance people saw the world around them.

Ghiberti, the illegitimate son of a goldsmith, labored all his working life (more than 50 years) on the two sets of Baptistery doors, including 27 years (1425-1452) working on the panels for the Gates of Paradise. The doors' execution was a major manufacturing job, requiring a large workshop of artists and artisans for each stage of the process: making the door frames that hold the panels, designing and forming models of the panels in wax (to cast them in bronze); gilding the panels (by painting them with powdered gold dissolved in mercury, then heating the panels until the mercury burned off, leaving the gold); polishing and mounting the panels; installing the doors...and signing paychecks for everyone along the way. Ghiberti was as much businessman as artist.

Each panel is bronze with a layer of gold on top. They tell several stories in one frame using perspective and realism as never before. Ghiberti poured his energy and creativity into these panels. That's him in the center of the door frame, atop the second row of panels—the head on the left with the shiny male-pattern baldness. His son (and assistant) is to his right.

These original 10 panels were moved

## Ghiberti's "Gates of Paradise"

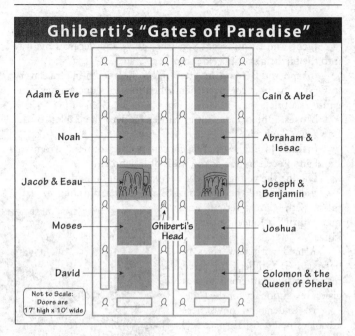

Adam & Eve ———→ | ←——— Cain & Abel

Noah ———→ | ←——— Abraham & Issac

Jacob & Esau ———→ | ←——— Joseph & Benjamin

↑ Ghiberti's Head

Moses ———→ | ←——— Joshua

David ———→ | ←——— Solomon & the Queen of Sheba

Not to Scale: Doors are 17' high x 10' wide

from the Baptistery to the museum to better preserve them. (Copies now adorn the Baptistery itself.) But even indoors, corrosive oxides gathered between the bronze panels and their gilding. Now they are under glass to protect against natural light and preserved in nitrogen to guard them from oxygen and humidity.

Moving from left to right and top to bottom, here are the Old Testament stories depicted in each panel:

**Adam and Eve:** God creates Adam, Eve, the snake, the apple, and original sin, then expels the humans.

**Cain and Abel:** Cain and Abel tend sheep, till the soil, and make a sacrifice, then Cain kills Abel and talks to God.

**Noah:** Noah and sons emerge from the ark (shown as a pyramid) after the flood, then Noah makes a sacrifice and gets drunk.

**Abraham and Isaac:** An angel prevents the sacrifice of Isaac.

**Jacob and Esau:** Isaac's son Jacob buys and deceives his way into the birthright of his elder brother, Esau.

**Joseph and Benjamin:** After his brothers sell him into slavery in Egypt, Joseph recognizes them when they visit and frames Benjamin as a thief.

**Moses:** Onlookers exult as Moses receives the Tablets of the Law from God.

**Joshua:** Joshua leads the chosen people into the Promised Land and in celebration as the walls of Jericho fall.

**David:** The young hero conquers the giant Goliath.

**Solomon and the Queen of Sheba:** After traveling to Jerusalem with a great retinue and many gifts, a queen meets a king.

Armed with new rules of perspective, Ghiberti rendered reality with a mathematical precision revolutionary for the time.

To understand how these advances made visual space feel more real than ever before, take a closer look at the following three panels:

The space created by the arches in the **Jacob and Esau panel** is as interesting as the scenes themselves. At the center is the so-

called vanishing point on the distant horizon, where all the arches and floor tiles converge. Those closest to us, at the bottom of the panel, are big and clearly defined. Distant figures are smaller, fuzzier, and higher up. Ghiberti has placed us as part of this casual crowd of holy people—some with their backs to us—milling around an arcade.

In the **Joseph and Benjamin panel,** notice how, with just the depth of a thumbnail, Ghiberti creates a temple in the round that's inhabited by workers. This round temple wowed the Florentines. Suddenly the world acquired a whole new dimension—depth.

The receding arches stretch into infinity in the **Solomon and the Queen of**

**Sheba panel,** giving the airy feeling that we can see forever. All the arches and steps converge at the center of the panel, where the two monarchs meet, uniting their respective peoples. Ghiberti's subject was likely influenced by the warm ecumenical breeze blowing through Florence in 1439, as religious leaders convened here in an attempt to reunite the eastern (centered on Constantinople) and western (Rome) realms of Christendom.

## Other Baptistery Doors

Displayed on either side of the Gates of Paradise you'll find the Baptistery's other doors.

**❻ North Doors:** Ghiberti made these doors after winning the 1401 competition, showing scenes from the life of Christ. Though they dazzled people at the time with their 3-D realism, they're most noteworthy today to illustrate how much further Ghiberti took the concept with the Gates of Paradise 25 years later.

**❼ South Doors:** These doors preceded Ghiberti and the Renaissance by 70 years. They tell stories from the life of St. John the Baptist, patron saint of Florence. Created by Andrea Pisano in the 1330s, they're not as renowned as Ghiberti's Renaissance doors—and with good reason: The static, expressionless Gothic figures make clear how revolutionary Ghiberti's enhancements in perspective and depth really were.

• *Before leaving Room 6, check out the* **Roman sarcophagi.** *They remind us that Florence's religious history stretches back to ancient times. The Baptistery (11th century) was likely built on the site of a pagan Roman temple. Exit the Hall of Paradise and pass through Room 7 and into Room 8 to find an evocative wooden statue of an emaciated woman.*

## ❽ Donatello, *Mary Magdalene (Santa Maria Maddalena),* c. 1455

Carved from white poplar and originally painted with realistic colors, this statue is a Renaissance work of intense devotion. Mary Magdalene—the prostitute rescued from the streets by Jesus—folds her hands in humble prayer. Her once-beautiful face and body have been scarred by fasting, repentance, and the fires of her own remorse. The matted hair sticks to her face; veins and tendons line the emaciated arms and neck. The rippling hair suggests emotional turmoil within. But in her hollow, tired eyes, you see a deep need for repentance, not idealized, praying to be forgiven. The rendering of her feet, arms, chest, and face make clear that

Donatello understood the body and had a passion to show it realistically.

• *Duck into Room 9 to see a collection of...*

### ❾ Relics

Impressive, shiny vessels contain the mortal remains of saints, which helped connect the devout to the long-dead. Among the reliquaries, you'll find a slender bronze pillar in the shape of a steeple. It holds John the Baptist's finger. This severed index finger of the beheaded prophet is the most revered relic of all the holy body parts in this museum. Also notice the large gem-studded gold cross that holds a purported fragment of the True Cross. Study the other exquisite containers, which illustrate the importance of holy relics in medieval times.

• *Backtrack into Room 8, pass Mary, and continue to Room 10 and meet the maestro...*

### ❿ Michelangelo, *Pietà*, 1547-1555

Three mourners tend the broken body of the crucified Christ. We see Mary, his mother (the shadowy figure on our right); Mary Magdalene (on the left, polished up by a pupil); and Nicodemus, the converted Pharisee, whose face is that of Michelangelo himself.

The polished body of Christ stands out from the unfinished background. Michelangelo (as Nicodemus), who spent a lifetime bringing statues to life by "freeing" them from the stone, looks down at what could be his final creation, the once-perfect body of Renaissance Man that is now twisted, disfigured, and dead.

A pietà—by definition—shows Mary mourning her dead son, taken off the cross. The theological point: Jesus died to save us. The artist's goal: to show him dead. Michelangelo made the dead weight of Jesus' body profound—you feel the downward pull. In fact, he sculpted Jesus in a Z-shape, taller than he probably was to accentuate the weight of his dead body. Notice also the intimacy of mother and son—Mary was with her son at his birth and at his death...struggling to support him.

The aging Michelangelo (1475-1564) designed his own tomb, with this as the centerpiece. He was depressed by old age, and the grim reality that by sculpting this statue, he was writing his own obituary. As it was done on his own dime, it's fair to consider this an introspective and very personal work.

• *Before leaving, look at the doorway to the left of the* Pietà *and find the tiny plaque indicating the level of the water during the terrible flooding*

DUOMO MUSEUM

*of the Arno on November 4, 1966. The flood damaged many of these works, then in their original setting inside the Duomo. After being restored, they were moved here to be kept in a more secure environment.*

*Now, exit through the doorway on the right to the staircase. Go up the steps and, at the top, turn right into the...*

## FIRST FLOOR
## Gallery of Campanile Decorations
## (Galleria del Campanile)

The Duomo's bell tower, designed by Giotto and augmented by Arnolfo di Cambio, also served as a colorful sculpture gallery. The museum has the original 16 statues (by several sculptors) from the bell tower's third story, where copies stand today. There are also small relief panels that once ringed the Campanile.

• *Start with the panels immediately on the left and work your way down the row. We'll focus on the statues later.*

### ⓫ Andrea Pisano (and Others), Campanile Panels, c. 1334-1359

These 28 hexagonal and 28 diamond-shaped, blue-glazed panels decorated the Campanile, seven per side. The original design scheme may have been Giotto's, but his successor, Andrea Pisano, and assistants executed the work.

The panels celebrate technology, showing workers, inventors, and thinkers. Allegorically, they depict humanity's long march to "civilization"—a blend of art and science, brain and brawn. But realistically, they're snapshots of the industrious generation that helped Florence bounce back ferociously from the plague, or Black Death, of 1348.

Start with the **hexagonal panels.** Reading left to right, you'll first see scenes from the Bible: God creates Adam, then Eve, who then get to work. Jabal learns to domesticate sheep while Jubal invents music on his horn. Tubalcain works as a blacksmith, and Noah invents—and gets blitzed on—wine. Next come scenes showing Florence's proto-scientific age: An astronomer charts the heavens and the (round, tilted-on-axis, pre-Columbian) Earth. Builders construct a brick wall. And a doctor holds a flask

of urine to the light for analysis (yes, that's what it is). Skipping ahead a dozen panels—just after the last door—find the famed invention of sculpture, as an artist chisels a figure to life.

# Duomo Museum—First Floor

**11** PISANO (& Others) – Campanile Panels
**12** DONATELLO – Jeremiah & Habakkuk
**13** Tools & Scaffolding
**14** BRUNELLESCHI – Models of the Cupola & Lantern
**15** Brunelleschi's Death Mask
**16** DELLA ROBBIA – Cantoria
**17** DONATELLO – Cantoria
**18** Evolution of the Facade

The upper **diamond-shaped panels,** made of marble on blue majolica (tin-glazed pottery tinged blue with cobalt sulfate), add religion (sacraments and virtues) to the march-of-civilization equation.

• *Now turn your attention to the other side of the room.*

This line of 16 **statues** once adorned the bell tower. Notice that the statues differ in quality, as they were made by different sculptors from different generations. The four statues closest to where you entered the room are some of the earliest, done by Nino and Andrea Pisano. They're less realistic, and more stylized and stiffer than those farther down the wall. The sixth and seventh statues in line, in particular, stand out. These are the prophets Jeremiah and Habakkuk by the early Renaissance master Donatello.

## ⑫ Donatello, *Jeremiah* (*Geremia,* 1427-1436) and *Habakkuk* (*Abacuc,* 1434-1436)

Donatello did several statues of the prophets, plus some others with collaborators. In the process, he developed the Renaissance style that Michelangelo would later perfect—powerful, expressive, and ultrarealistic, sculpted in an "unfinished" style by an artist known for experimentation and his prickly, brooding personality.

Start with *Jeremiah.* Watching Jerusalem burn in the distance, the prophet reflects on why the Israelites wouldn't listen when he

**DUOMO MUSEUM**

warned them that the
Babylonian kings would
conquer the city. He purses his lips bitterly, and his
downturned mouth is ac-
centuated by his plunging
neck muscle and sagging
shoulders. The folds in
the clothes are very deep,
evoking the anger, sorrow,

and disgust that *Jeremiah* feels but cannot share, as it is too late.
Movement, realism, and human drama were Donatello's great contributions to sculpture.

Next, find the bald prophet *Habakkuk*. Donatello's signature
piece shows us the wiry man beneath the heavy mantle of a prophet. From the deep furrows of his rumpled cloak emerges a bare arm
with well-defined tendons and that powerful right hand. His long,
muscled neck leads to a bald head (the Italians call the statue *Lo
Zuccone*, meaning "pumpkin head"). This is realism.

The ugly face, with several days' growth of beard, crossed eyes,
and tongue-tied mouth, looks crazed. This is no confident Charlton Heston prophet, but a man who's spent too much time alone,
fasting in the wilderness, searching for his calling, and who now
returns to babble his vision on a street corner.

Donatello, the eccentric prophet of a new style, identified with
this statue, talking to it, swearing at it, yelling at it: "Speak!"

• *Wander the rest of these statues and imagine them looking down on the
people of Florence from their bell-tower perches in 1400—at the dawn
of a new age.*

*Now pass into Room 15, with a large cutaway* **model of the dome**
*suspended from the ceiling.*

## Gallery of the Dome (Galleria della Cupola)

Room 15 is dedicated to the dome that defined the Florentine
Renaissance (and to the man who built it). Designed by Filippo
Brunelleschi (1377-1446), the dome was the final component of
the cathedral complex's construction. Start by watching a fine short
**video** about Brunelleschi's masterpiece (runs constantly, alternating between English and Italian).

• *Now find the following items.*

### ⓭ Tools and Scaffolding

The dome weighs an estimated 80 million pounds—as much as the
entire population of Florence—so Brunelleschi had to design special tools and machines to lift and work all that stone. (The lantern
alone—which caps the dome—is a marble building nearly as tall

## Pop. 100,000...But Still a Small Town

At the dawn of the Renaissance, Florence was bursting with creative geniuses, all of whom knew each other and worked together. For example, after Ghiberti won the bronze-door competition, Brunelleschi took teenage Donatello with him to Rome. Donatello returned to join Ghiberti's workshop. Ghiberti helped Brunelleschi with dome plans. Brunelleschi, Donatello, and Luca della Robbia collaborated on the Pazzi Chapel. And so on, and so on.

as the Baptistery.) You'll see sun-dried bricks, brick molds, rope, a tool belt, compasses, stone pincers, and various pulleys for lifting.

Although no scaffolding supported the dome itself, the stonemasons needed exterior scaffolding to stand on as they worked. Support timbers were stuck into postholes in the drum (some are visible on the church today).

The dome rose in rings. First, the workers stacked a few blocks of white marble to create part of the ribs, then connected the ribs with horizontal crosspieces before filling in the space with red brick, in a herringbone pattern. When the ring was complete and self-supporting, they'd move the scaffolding up and do another section.

### ⑩ Models of the Cupola and Lantern (Modello Architettonico della Lanterna della Cupola)

These wooden models, done by Brunelleschi, show the dome he was constructing, including the top portion that would cap it. Brunelleschi's actual dome, a feat of engineering that was both functional and beautiful, put mathematics in stone. It rises 330 feet from the ground, with eight white, pointed-arch ribs, filled in with red brick and capped with a lantern, or cupola, to hold it all in place.

In designing the dome, Brunelleschi faced a number of challenges. The dome had to cover a gaping 140-foot hole in the roof of the church (a drag on rainy Sundays), a hole too wide to be spanned by the wooden scaffolding that traditionally supported a dome under construction. (An earlier architect suggested supporting the dome with a great mound of dirt inside the church...filled with coins, so peasants would later cart it away for free.) In addition, the eight-sided "drum" that the dome was to rest on was too weak to support its weight, and there were no side buildings on the church on which to attach Gothic-style buttresses.

The solution was a dome within a dome, leaving a hollow space between to make the structure lighter. And the dome had to be self-supporting, both while being built and when finished, so as not to require buttresses.

Brunelleschi used wooden models such as these to demonstrate his ideas to skeptical approval committees.

• *Now consider the remarkable man who built the dome, by pondering his "portrait," made on his deathbed.*

### ⓯ Brunelleschi's Death Mask *(Maschera Funebre)*

Brunelleschi was uniquely qualified to create the dome. Trained in sculpture, he gave it up in disgust after losing the gig for the Baptistery doors. In Rome, he visualized placing the Pantheon on top of Florence's Duomo, and dissected the Pantheon's mathematics and engineering.

In 1420 Brunelleschi was declared *capomaestro* of the dome project. He was a jack-of-all-trades and now master of all as well, overseeing every aspect of the dome, the lantern (the decorative tip-top), and the machinery to build it all.

The dome was completed in 16 short years, capping 150 years of construction on the church. Brunelleschi enjoyed the dedication ceremonies, but he died before the lantern was completed. His legacy is a dome that stands as a proud symbol of man's ingenuity, proving that art and science can unite to make beauty.

• *With the dome nearing completion, the Florentines began to decorate the church interior. Let's see some exquisite pieces. Exit Room 15 into Room 22 and turn left into Room 23 to see the...*

## Room of the *Cantorie* (Sala delle *Cantorie*)

This room displays two marble choir lofts *(cantorie)* that once sat above the sacristy doors inside the Duomo. Both are from the 1430s. The one on the right is by Luca della Robbia, the one on the left by Donatello.

### ⓰ Luca della Robbia, *Cantoria*, 1430–c. 1438

After almost 150 years of construction, the cathedral was nearly done, and the Opera del Duomo, the workshop in charge, began preparing the interior for the celebration. Brunelleschi hired a little-known sculptor, 30-year-old Luca della Robbia, to make this *cantoria*, a balcony choir box for singers in the cathedral. It sums up the exuberance of the Quattrocento. The panels are elegant, composed, contained within their columns: a celebration of music, song, and dance performed by toddlers, children, and teenagers (originals are below).

The *cantoria* brings Psalm 150 ("Praise ye the Lord") to life like a YouTube video. Starting in the upper left, the banner reads *"Laudate..."*—"Praise the Lord"—while children laugh and dance to the sound of trumpets (*"sono Tubae"*) and guitars, autoharps, and tambourines (*"Psaltero...*

*Cythera... Timpano"*). In the next level down, kids dance ring-around-the-rosy, a scene in the round on an almost flat surface, showing front, back, and in-between poses. At bottom right, the Psalm ends: "Everybody praise the Lord!" Della Robbia's choir box was a triumph, a celebration of Florence's youthful boom time. (The Della Robbia family is best known for their colorful glazed terra-cotta, some of which you'll likely see here in the Duomo Museum and around town.)

## ⑰ Donatello, *Cantoria,* 1433-c. 1440

If Della Robbia's balcony looks like afternoon recess, Donatello's looks like an all-night rave. Donatello's figures are sketchier, murky and frenetic, as the dancing kids hurl themselves around the balcony. Imagine candles lighting this as the scenes seem to come to life.

Recently returned from a trip to Rome, Donatello carved in the style of classical friezes of dancing *putti* (chubby, playful toddlers). This choir box stood in a dark area of the Duomo, so Donatello chose colorful mosaics and marbles to catch the eye, while purposely leaving the dancers unfinished and shadowy, tangled figures flitting inside. In the dim light, worshippers swore they saw them move.

• *Now let's bring the Duomo up to the church we see today. Backtrack through Room 22, and down the corridor of Room 26. You'll pass by various diagrams, paintings, and photos that chart the multicentury...*

## ⑱ Evolution of the Facade

In 1587, the Duomo's medieval facade by Arnolfo di Cambio was considered hopelessly outdated and torn down like so much old linoleum. But work on a replacement never got off the ground, and the front of the church sat bare for nearly 300 years while church fathers debated proposal after proposal by many famous architects—that is, the designs in this room. Most versions championed the Renaissance style to match Brunelleschi's dome, rather than Gothic to fit the church. None of them were acted on.

Continue on, as the corridor turns into a series of alcoves (all part of Room 26) showing more designs. In the 1800s, as Italy was unifying and filled with a can-do spirit, there was a push to finish the facade. Toward the end of the corridor, you'll see a portrait of the mustachioed man (painted by Egisto Sarri) who brought the Duomo to completion—Emilio De Fabris.

A competition was held for the best design, and De Fabris made a bold entry. He proposed to build a Neo-Gothic facade that echoed the original work of Arnolfo. Critics charged that De Fabris' design was too retro and too ornate. But they had to admit it was the style beloved by no less than Ghiberti, Donatello, Brunelleschi, and the industrious citizens of Florence's Quattrocento, who saw it as Florence's finest art gallery. De Fabris was declared the winner. Everyone got on board with it, and the new-old facade was completed in a remarkably short time, and dedicated in 1887. After almost 600 years, the Duomo was finally done.

• *And so is our tour. But there are a couple other sights you might want to seek out.*

## REST OF THE MUSEUM

Don't miss the Terrazza Brunelleschiana on the third floor. (To get there, backtrack toward Room 15 and look for elevators and stairs nearby—see "Duomo Museum—First Floor" map.) You'll reach an **outdoor terrace** with an up-close, rooftop view of the very thing you've been learning about—the Duomo. It's an ideal place to pause at the end of your visit (and use the adjacent WC) and reflect on the engineering marvel that inspired so many other architects and marked the pinnacle of Renaissance achievement.

## ART STUDIO

After leaving the Duomo Museum, make one more stop for a fascinating behind-the-scenes peek at the Duomo's restoration workshop: Head to the left around the back of the Duomo to find Via dello Studio (near the south transept), then walk a block toward the river to #23a (freestanding yellow house on the right; see map on page 58). Here you can look through the window of

the **Opera del Duomo art stu-dio** and see workers sculpting new statues, restoring old ones, or making exact copies. It's run by the Opera del Duomo, the organization that does the continual work required to keep the cathedral's art in good repair (*opera* is Italian for "work"). They're carrying on an artistic
tradition that dates back to the days of Brunelleschi. The "opera" continues.

# PALAZZO VECCHIO TOUR

With its distinctive castle turret and rustic stonework, this fortified "Old Palace"—Florence's past and present Town Hall—is a Florentine landmark (rated ▲▲). The highlight of the interior is the Grand Hall: With a Michelangelo sculpture and epic paintings of great moments in Florentine history, it was the impressive epicenter of Medici power. The richly decorated rooms of the royal apartments—though hardly the most sumptuous royal quarters in Europe—show off some famous art, creative decorative flourishes, and aristocratic curiosities. It's often open late in summer, making it a fine after-dinner activity.

While there are several sightseeing options here, this tour focuses on the "museum" part of the palace.

## Orientation

**Cost:** Michelozzo Courtyard-free, museum and tower climb-€12.50 each, excavations-€4, free for kids 17 and under.

**Hours:** Museum and excavations open daily 9:00-19:00 except Thu until 14:00 (may stay open later in peak season); shorter hours off-season; tower keeps shorter hours (last entry one hour before closing) and closed in bad weather; last tickets for all sights sold one hour before closing.

**Information:** +39 055 276 8224, http://bigliettimusei.comune.fi.it.

**Crowd-Beating Tip:** Avoid midmorning and early-afternoon crowds. Tower tickets can sell out by midafternoon in peak season.

**Getting In:** On the ground floor, between the columned Michelozzo Courtyard and ticket office, are two staircases. One is designated for the museum and one for the tower—use the right one. If you have a museum ticket, you can ride an elevator partway up from the ticketing courtyard (near Tracce di Firenze exhibit).

**Tours:** A videoguide is available for €5 (€8/2 people).

**Length of This Tour:** One hour.

**Other Sights at the Palazzo Vecchio:** Besides visiting the museum, you can ascend Florence's landmark civic **tower** by climbing 418 steps (often requires a wait in line) for a great view over the city.

Underneath the Palazzo Vecchio are **Roman-era excavations**—the ruins of a 2,000-year-old theater from ancient Florentia. Other than heavily restored brickwork and an interesting 10-minute video about the city's evolution over 22 centuries, it's probably worthwhile only for antiquities enthusiasts, but serves as a reminder that underneath much of the city center lie the remains of its glorious origins.

Finally, in the ticketing courtyard, there's the free and interesting **Tracce di Firenze** exhibit (described later).

**Nighttime Terrace Visits:** In summer you can often join an escort for an unnarrated walk along the "patrol path"—the balcony that runs just below the crenellated top of the building (€5, no need to buy a museum or tower ticket, check online to confirm schedule). Note that this tour doesn't go to the top of the tower.

**Services:** Show your ticket to access the WCs, located on the ground floor, to the right of the ticket office.

**Starring:** The spacious grand hall known as the Salone dei Cinquecento, lavish royal apartments, and statues by Michelangelo and Donatello.

# The Tour Begins

• *Stand in Florence's main square, Piazza della Signoria, and take in the palace's grand facade.*

## Exterior

Around the year 1300, the citizens of Florence broke ground on a new Town Hall, designed by Arnolfo di Cambio, who also did the Duomo. Arnolfo's design expanded on an earlier palace on the site, turning its small tower into today's 308-foot spire and increasing the building's architectural footprint, which is why the tower ended up slightly off-center.

In Renaissance times, Florence was a proud, self-governing republic, and this

building is where its governing council met. The entrance sported a statue that symbolized the city's independent spirit—Michelangelo's *David*. (The statue standing here today is a copy— the original *David* was moved to the Accademia for safekeeping in 1873.) The palace's imposing, castle-like exterior announced to all of Europe's kings, popes, princes, and tyrants that Florence was determined to remain an independent city governed by its citizens.

But then came Cosimo I, who changed everything. (See a statue of him riding a horse, left of the palace.) In the 1530s, Cosimo assumed power and turned Florence's republic into a tyrannical dukedom. He and his wife Eleonora moved into the Palazzo Vecchio and transformed it from a symbol of the people to a luxury palace of the aristocracy. Let's go in and see what kind of extreme makeover they did to the place.

• *Enter the courtyard (free admission), walking past the fake* David.

## Michelozzo Courtyard

This courtyard, designed in 1470 by Michelozzo (a favorite architect of the Medicis), has long been a showcase for great Florentine art—art that made a statement to the city's populace.

Anchoring the courtyard is a copy of *Putto with Dolphin*, an innovative work of Renaissance 3-D by Verrocchio, Leonardo da Vinci's teacher (you'll see the original later, in the museum). With a twisting spiral form, this statue was one of the first intended to be equally enjoyable from any angle—an improvement on medieval statues that only worked when seen from the front.

Verrocchio's cherub took the place of Donatello's bronze *David* (now in the Bargello, and described on page 150), an even more groundbreaking statue—the first male nude sculpted in a thousand years. Donatello's *David* also made a bold populist statement, with an inscription on the base that said, "Behold, a boy defeated a tyrant, so fight on, citizens!"

Stroll around. The faded maps feature Austrian towns, designed to make the Habsburg princess feel welcome and at home

**Palazzo Vecchio—First Floor**

Not to Scale

50 Meters
50 Yards

STATUE OF LEO X

**GRAND HALL**
SALONE DEI CINQUECENTO

PISA

SIENA

Courtyard

MICHELANGELO'S VICTORY

COSIMO THE ELDER ROOM

LORENZO THE MAGNIFICENT ROOM

Piazza della Signoria

Courtyard

STAIRS UP FROM ENTRY COURTYARD

LEO X ROOM

APARTMENTS OF LEO X

SHADED AREA SHOWS ROOMS OPEN TO VISIT

STUDIO OF FRANCESCO I

STAIRS UP TO 2ND FLOOR

for her 1565 marriage into the Medici family. The squiggly wall painting (called "grotesque") was all the rage around 1500, inspired by ancient Roman art, which was being excavated at the time.

While the Palazzo Vecchio's exterior and courtyard reflect the tastes and ideals of the Florentine Republic (1200s to early 1500s), most of the interior decoration dates from a later era. When Florence came under the rule of Cosimo I de' Medici, he suspended the city council and ruled as a "grand duke." He transformed this building from a civic center of the people into his personal palatial residence.

• *Deeper inside the palace is an interesting and free history exhibit.*

The **Tracce di Firenze exhibit** is a peaceful room with an interesting collection of paintings showing historic views of Florence, and a fascinating set of maps (well described in English). Compare the big painting of the city "Fiorenza" (from 1490) with the version at the opposite end of the room (from 1936, notice the date: XII to XIV E.F., meaning the years 12 to 14 in the fascist era) to see how much—or how little—the city has changed over the centuries.

• *To see the rest of the palace, buy a ticket and head upstairs, following signs to the Museo. On the first floor, enter one of the highlights of the palace, the 13,000-square-foot...*

## Grand Hall (Salone dei Cinquecento)

This vast room—170' by 75'—is also called the Salone dei Cinquecento (Hall of Five Hundred). Originally built under Sa-

## Mannerism

While Florence is famous as the birthplace of the Renaissance, the art style that followed that period, Mannerism, is also showcased here—especially in the Palazzo Vecchio. It's hard to get a concise and clear definition of Mannerism. Michelangelo painted with bold colors and exaggerated the musculature and movement of the body in contrast to the mellow, graceful, and stable balance of the High Renaissance (think Raphael). Michelangelo died in 1564 and in the decades after that, artists tended to paint in the "manner" of the great master. No one could improve on Michelangelo, but you could enhance his bold, colorful, contorted muscular style. Call it "Mannerism."

vonarola in 1494 to house the Florentine Republic's 500 grand councilors, it was expanded under Cosimo I to accommodate 500

partygoers. The ceiling and huge wall paintings, all by Giorgio Vasari and his assistants, are a celebration of the power of Florence, specifically the power of the Medici. Consider this magnificent room in its proper context: In an age when there was no mass media to use as a mouthpiece, this was how a fabulously wealthy person waged a public-relations campaign (and kept the people down).

**Cosimo I** is the star here, looking down from the circular medallion in the center of the ceiling. He's dressed as an emperor, with

his highness-ness affirmed by the crown of the Holy Roman Emperor and blessed by the staff and cross of the pope. He's encircled by a kaleidoscope of symbols representing Florentine merchants' guilds, along with the shields of his domain—all asserting and celebrating his power.

In the square frame, find the letters "SPQF." In place of the Roman motto of SPQR (*Senatus Populusque Romanus*—the Senate and People of Rome), Cosimo used "SPQF," implying that Florence is the new Rome. From the stage at the far end of the room, Cosimo sat on his throne, overseeing his fawning subjects.

But now sitting in the front of the room is a statue of **Pope**

**Leo X,** looking down from his own throne. The son of Lorenzo the Magnificent, Leo X was the first of three Medici popes. When he became pope in 1513, the family suddenly had religious authority and some seriously good connections, helping them eventually become bankers to the Vatican and grand dukes of Tuscany. (Remember that 600 years ago Italy was a jumble of warring city states. Pisa rivaled Florence, and to this day Siena and Florence are football rivals.)

**Giorgio Vasari's wall paintings** show great Florentine victories: over Pisa in 1497 (on the left) and over Siena in 1555 (on the right). In the Pisa paintings, check out the painting closest to the front: In the upper-left corner you can see the Field of Miracles, with its church and Leaning Tower. In the Siena paintings, watch the Florentines storm Siena's gate by lantern light. Vasari's style features crowded canvases, contorted bodies in every imaginable pose, bright color, and a "flat" surface design. If you're into Mannerism, this is your Sistine Chapel.

While Vasari's battle scenes are impressive, they pale in comparison to what may lie beneath. Around 1500, this hall was the scene of a painting contest between two towering geniuses—young Michelangelo and aging Leonardo da Vinci. Unfortunately, Michelangelo never got around to starting his proposed *Battle of Cascina* (and his paper sketch of it is lost to history). But Leonardo likely started his *Battle of Anghiari* here. Now this famous-but-unseen Leonardo masterpiece may lie hidden beneath Vasari's *Battle of Marciano* (on the Siena wall, painting on far right). Vasari himself may have hinted at it to later scholars by painting an enigmatic clue: a banner (way up top, just right of the central farmhouse, hard to find without binoculars) that reads *Cerca trova*—"He who seeks, finds."

Underneath Siena, in the middle of the right wall, stands Michelangelo's statue of *Victory* (*La Vittoria*, 1533-1534), showing a young man triumphing over an older man. It was designed to ornament the never-finished tomb of Pope Julius II in St. Peter's Basilica in Rome. *Victory* was the prototype of the hall's many spiral-shaped statues by other artists. Taking their cue from Michelangelo, later artists twisted and contorted their sculpted figures into almost ridiculous acrobatics. Six of the statues are the *Labors of Hercules*. The

## Cosimo I de' Medici
### (1519-1574)

This palace is all about Cosimo I de' Medici. His presence is everywhere. In the famous statue on the square outside the palace, he sits like a Roman emperor astride a horse. Inside, in

the Grand Hall, he looms high above in a ceiling painting. And his aesthetic vision is on full display in the royal apartments, which were personally decorated with care by Cosimo and his high-maintenance wife Eleonora.

Cosimo's Medici forebears had been Florentine big shots, but Cosimo was the first to have a royal title, after the pope made him a grand duke in 1569. Don't confuse Grand Duke Cosimo I with his equally famous ancestor, Cosimo the Elder, who established the Medici dynasty a century earlier. To see how Cosimo I fits into the Medici family tree, see the chart on page 75.

Before Cosimo I took charge, the loggia in front of the palace (Loggia dei Lanzi) had been used as a gathering place, where Florentines discussed the issues of the day. Cosimo changed it into an art gallery, swapping out public discourse for statues that personified the power and strength of his family. Perseus, holding the head of Medusa, sent a clear message about how the Medici dealt with their enemies.

It was Cosimo I who moved the family out of the Medici-Riccardi Palace and into these digs—officially called Palazzo della Signoria. Cosimo left the exterior as-is, which is why it still looks like a medieval fortress. But he completely revamped the inside, updating it to match the outlook of the Renaissance. Later, when his wife Eleonora complained about needing a fancier place with a bigger yard, they moved across the river to the Pitti Palace, where she could stroll the sprawling Boboli Gardens. The Vasari Corridor was built over Ponte Vecchio to connect the two palaces. After they'd moved out, Palazzo della Signoria began to be known as the "old" palace—Palazzo "Vecchio."

Medici were quick to associate themselves with Hercules—who was not a god but a demigod, as close to divine as a mortal can get.

Before leaving for the ducal apartments, see if a small, richly ornamented room is open to the immediate right of where you entered. The Studio of Francesco I is an exquisite little room covered in fine and richly symbolic art. The commotion of tangled and contorted bodies is a good example of the Mannerist style (dating from the mid-16th century).

• *From the Grand Hall, we enter the royal apartments that housed Cosimo I and his family and guests.*

*Exit the Grand Hall through the door diagonally to the right of where you entered, go up the four steps, and turn immediately left into the first of the royal apartments, known as the...*

## Apartments of Leo X

In 1540, Cosimo I and his wife Eleonora of Toledo moved into the Palazzo Vecchio, turning the Town Hall into their private residence. They set about redecorating with frescoes and coffered ceilings in the Mannerist style. They wanted each room to have a theme. These rooms were dedicated to great members of the Medici family who preceded Cosimo I.

The first room honors Cosimo the Elder (portrayed on the ceiling, on horseback). One of the wealthiest men of his age, he launched the Medici dynasty in the 1400s. In another scene (above the exit door), he's the great patron of the arts overseeing Brunelleschi (kneeling) and Ghiberti as they rebuild Florence. The walls are decorated in the fanciful grotesque style popular in the late 16th century following the discovery of similar paintings underground in the ancient Roman ruins. You'll see similar motifs throughout Italy, including on ceilings of the Uffizi Gallery. The grotesques create a garden of exotic plants, frolicking fawns, airy cupids, and Venuses playing volleyball.

The next room is dedicated to the greatest of the Medici, Lorenzo the Magnificent, shown in the central ceiling painting. Lorenzo ruled Florence at its pinnacle. He sits on a throne in his purple robe (with his money-bag dangling from his belt) while the whole world comes to bring tribute, including exotic animals like lions and camels. (In fact, the giraffe, a gift from Tunisia, survived only a couple of months in the Medici court.) The ambassador from Rome offers Leonardo a cardinal's hat, which he'd give to his 13-year-old son...who's honored in the next room.

The room honors Lorenzo's son, who furthered the Medici legacy by becoming Pope Leo X. A wall painting shows Leo (far right) being carried on a litter during the triumphal parade through his hometown, culminating in the square outside the Palazzo Vecchio. Note Michelangelo's *David* guarding the entrance.

• *These apartments were largely ceremonial. Now we'll see Cosimo and Eleonora's more private living quarters. Go up the staircase to the second floor, then turn left, entering Cosimo's personal suite of rooms, called the...*

# Giorgio Vasari
## (1511-1574)

Giorgio Vasari—painter, architect, and writer—has been dismissed by history as a Renaissance hack, a man who was

equally mediocre at many things. But his influence on Renaissance history is undeniable.

During his lifetime, Vasari enjoyed respect and accumulated a considerable fortune. He was consistently employed by patrons in the Medici family in Florence and Rome. In Florence, you'll see his mark everywhere. His huge frescoes color the main hall of the Palazzo Vecchio and the dome of the Duomo (see page 53). His oil paintings hang in the Church of Santa Maria Novella (see page 224) and the Uffizi Gallery. He built the tomb for his hero Michelangelo in Santa Croce Church (page 229). As an architect, he designed the Uffizi Gallery and the Vasari Corridor over Ponte Vecchio, which connects the Uffizi with the Pitti Palace.

Vasari is most famous, though, as the first Italian art historian. His book, *The Lives of the Artists,* was an early work that chronicled the Renaissance (with a bias that favored Florentine painters, sculptors, and architects). For that classic alone, we can say, *"Grazie tante!"*

## Apartments of the Elements
## (Quartiere degli Elementi)

As Cosimo considered himself an enlightened Renaissance Man, he wanted his apartments decorated in the spirit of the classical world. Each of his personal living rooms has a name, usually derived from the ceiling and wall paintings.

The first room (with paintings by Vasari and assistants) depicts the four classical elements. On the far wall (as you enter) is "Water," showing the birth of a muscular (Mannerist) Venus from the foam of the waves. On the left wall is "Fire," with Vulcan at the forge hammering away while cupids pump the bellows and sharpen their arrows. On the third wall, "Earth" shows the abundant cornucopia of the world's produce. And on the ceiling, representing "Air," are scenes from the sky—the chariots of the sun and moon, and Cronos defeating Saturn to create the world.

Explore the rest of Cosimo's rooms. One room displays Verrocchio's original *Putto with Dolphin* (1476) from the courtyard downstairs. Cosimo I brought it to the Palazzo Vecchio from the

Medici family's rural villa. It may have captured the newlywed couple's innocent joy and abandon as they moved into their new home together. You'll reach a balcony (closed in off-season) that offers a stunning view of the surrounding hillsides and the steeple of Santa Croce Church.

• *Return to the top of the stairs and cross over to the Apartments of Eleonora of Toledo. On the way, you'll pass along a* **balcony** *overlooking the Grand Hall. Gaze out over the opulence and imagine it filled by a lavish Medici wedding celebration with a 500-person guest list. Now enter the apartments of the duchess, starting in the Green Room.*

## Private Apartments of Eleonora of Toledo

Eleonora di Toledo (1522-1562) married Cosimo I in 1539. Their marriage united the Medici clan with royal bloodlines all over Europe. The following year, the couple moved out of the Medici-Riccardi Palace (as it's now known) and settled in here. As Florence's "first lady," Eleonora used her natural grace and beauty to mollify Florentine democrats chafing under Cosimo's absolutist rule.

The Green Room (Sala Verde) was her living room. Her lively ceiling features vines, animals, and exotic birds. She'd read in the small side room and step into the adjoining Chapel of Eleonora to pray. Join Eleonora in the tiny chapel and meditate on the brightly painted symbolism by Agnolo Bronzino (1540-1565). After serving as their artistic wedding planner, Bronzino became Cosimo and Eleonora's court painter. The chapel's ceiling features St. Michael with a sword, battling a demon; St. John with his symbolic eagle; St. Francis receiving the stigmata; and St. Jerome with his companion the lion. In the center is the three-faced Trinity. The walls show scenes from the life of Moses, gathering manna (left wall) and crossing the Red Sea (right). If you're interested in what the Mannerist style was all about—you're looking at it. Bronzino and Vasari were the two big stars of Mannerism, and this palace was their enormous blank canvas.

Before leaving the Green Room, find a door, locked tight with a padlock, which leads onto the Vasari Corridor. From here, Eleonora and Cosimo could enter a private passageway that led through the Uffizi, across Ponte Vecchio, and into their other home across the river—the Pitti Palace.

Continue through the next half-dozen rooms. Each features virtuous women of history, thus putting Eleonora in their company. In the Room of the Sabines, the ceiling painting shows the

Sabine women bravely stepping between their men and the enemy Romans to appeal for peace. In the next room, Esther kneels before the Persian king to plead for her Jewish people. Along the tops of the walls, notice the fun panels with images of *putti* (chubby toddlers) playing in the letters: LEONORA on one side and, opposite, FLORENTIA. In the next room, Penelope spins at her wheel, faithfully awaiting the return of her lost husband Odysseus. The Penelope Room also has a *Madonna and Child* from the school of Botticelli.

• *Continue through these rooms (admiring some nice period furnishings, as well as* **Dante's Death Mask***) until you reach a large hall with a gilded ceiling. Pretty impressive. Then continue around the corner and into the next room, the...*

## Hall of Lilies (Sala dei Gigli)

The coffered ceiling (from the 1460s) sports the fleur-de-lis—the three-petaled lily that's the symbol of Florence. Check out the great view of the Duomo out the window. Now compare it with a painting on the wall (by Ghirlandaio) showing a similar glimpse of the Duomo, circa 1482. (Can't find the Duomo in the painting? Let the lion point the way.)

The room's highlight is Donatello's 11-piece bronze, *Judith and Holofernes*—cast in 1457, when the artist was in his prime. It

shows a Biblical scene easily interpreted by its Renaissance audience: the victory of the weak-but-virtuous Judith over Holofernes the tyrant. Over the years, various Florentines have used it as propaganda to trumpet their claim on power. Initially, the statue was commissioned by Cosimo the Elder as a fountain in the Medici-Riccardi Palace (note the holes in the cushion's corners). It stood there proclaiming the Medici as noble heroes slaying their (drunken, sleepy) enemies. But when Savonarola drove the Medici out, the statue was moved to the Palazzo Vecchio's main doorway (where the fake *David* now stands) as a symbol of their triumph over the corrupt family. A decade later, *Judith* was replaced as the city symbol altogether by Michelangelo's *David*, now the symbol of Florence victorious.

• *End your tour with a visit to two nearby rooms (starting at the far left from where you entered).*

## Old Chancellery and Hall of Geographical Maps

The **Old Chancellery** (Sala della Cancelleria) was once the office of Niccolò Machiavelli (1469-1527). Ponder the bust and portrait of the man who faithfully served the Florentine Republic as a civil servant from 1498 to 1512, while the Medici were exiled as tyrants. When the Medici returned to power (under Pope Leo X), they tortured and exiled Machiavelli. He then wrote *The Prince*, a poli-sci treatise about how a ruler can ruthlessly gain and maintain power. Ironically, Machiavelli's cautionary advice soon came to be exploited by the man who would end the Florentine Republic for good—Grand Duke Cosimo I.

Finally, the **Hall of Geographical Maps** (Sala delle Carte Geografiche, the palace's former wardrobe) is full of maps and globes made in a fit of post-1492 fascination with the wider world. Most date from about 1560 and show how serious cartography had become since Columbus landed in the New World. They say a great deal about what Europeans did—and didn't—know about faraway lands. For example, Cosimo's huge *mappa mundi* globe was obviously made before the discovery of Australia. On other maps, some Texans and Southern Californians can even find their hometowns (far right corner of the hall, upper level). Flo-

rentines excelled at creating and publishing maps—which is why, even though Columbus beat the Florentine Amerigo Vespucci to the New World, our continent isn't called "North Columbia."

• *Our tour is done. If you've only bought a museum ticket, follow signs to the exit. If you have a tower ticket, you'll find a staircase (often with a line), with more than 200 stairs up to the top of the* **tower**. *Whichever route, the exit will take you downstairs to the courtyard.*

*You're at the center of Florence—the city awaits.*

# MEDICI CHAPELS TOUR

*Capelle Medicee*

The Medici Chapels (rated ▲▲) contain tombs of Florence's great ruling family, from Lorenzo the Magnificent to those less so. The highlight is a chapel designed by Michelangelo when he was at the height of his creative powers. This is the Renaissance Man's greatest "installation," a room completely under his artistic control, featuring innovative architecture, tombs, and sculpture. His statues tell of a middle-aged man's brooding meditation on mortality, the fall of the Medici golden age, and the relentless passage of time—from *Dawn* to *Day* to *Dusk* to *Night*.

## Orientation

**Cost:** €9

**Hours:** Sat-Mon 8:15-13:50, Wed-Fri 13:15-18:50; closed Tue and first, third, and fifth Sun of each month; last entry 45 minutes before closing. Reservations are possible but unnecessary.

**Information:** +39 055 294 886, www.bargellomusei.beniculturali.it.

**Crowd Alert:** The bottleneck entrance (tickets and metal detector) can make for a slow entry.

**Dress Code:** No tank tops, short shorts, or short skirts.

**Getting There:** It's at the back (west end) of the Basilica of San Lorenzo—the one with the smaller dome on Florence's skyline (five-minute walk northwest of Duomo). See page 62 for more about the Basilica of San Lorenzo.

**Tours:** Audioguide rental is €6 (€10/2 people).

**Length of This Tour:** Allow 45 minutes. With limited time, make a beeline to Michelangelo's New Sacristy.

**Starring:** Michelangelo's statues *Day*, *Night*, *Dawn*, and *Dusk*.

## OVERVIEW

The Medici Chapels consist of three burial places: the unimpressive Crypt; the large and gaudy Chapel of Princes; and—the highlight—Michelangelo's New Sacristy, a room completely designed by him to honor four Medici. For a quick overview of the Medici family tree, see page 75.

# The Tour Begins

• *Enter the Chapel and buy tickets. Immediately after you show your ticket, you're in...*

## The Crypt

This gloomy, low-ceilinged room with gravestones underfoot reminds us that these "chapels" are really tombs. You'll see a few Lorenzos buried in this room (after all, "Laurentius," or Lawrence, was the family's patron saint)...but none that is "Magnificent" (he's later). The Medici buried here (and listed on the Crypt's family tree) come mainly from the later descendants who made little impact on history. The collection of ornate silver and gold reliquaries, with bone fragments of dead saints, is appropriately macabre.

• *Head upstairs via the righthand staircase. You enter a large, domed, multicolored chapel, which is not by Michelangelo.*

## Chapel of Princes
## (La Cappella dei Principi), 1602-1743

This impressive octagonal room echoes the octagonal Baptistery and the Duomo's dome base. The **chapel dome** overhead is, when seen from outside, the big, red-brick "mini-Duomo." The room is lined with six tombs of Medici rulers and is decorated everywhere with the **Medici coat of arms**—a shield with six balls thought to represent the pills of doctors *(medici)*, reputedly the family's original occupation. Along with many different-colored marbles, geologists will recognize jasper, porphyry, quartz, alabaster, coral, mother-of-pearl, and lapis lazuli.

**Sixteen shields** ring the room at eye level, each representing one of the Tuscan cities ("Civitas") ruled by Florence's dukes. Find Florence, with its fleur-de-lis ("Florentiae"), and Pisa ("Pisarum"), both just left of the altar.

The **bronze statues** honor two of the "later" Medici, the cul-

tured but oppressive dukes who ruled Florence after the city's glorious Renaissance. In the first niche to the right (as you face the altar) stands Ferdinando I (ruled 1587-1609), dressed in the Medicis' traditional ermine cape and jewels. Ferdinando's claim to fame is that he started the work on this Chapel of Princes and tore down the Duomo's medieval facade. His son, Cosimo II (ruled 1609-1621, to the right), was the man who appointed Galileo "first professor" of science at Pisa U., inspiring him to label the moons of Jupiter "the Medici Stars."

The **altar** is an awe-inspiring work of multicolored marble. (Or is it? It's actually painted wood.) It was made on the cheap, finished in 1939 for a visit from Hitler and Mussolini. The altar itself is the only Christian symbolism in this spacious but stifling temple to power, wealth, and mediocre Medici.

(*Psst.* Behind the altar are tiny rooms that display various relics, a processional banner, and the pastoral staff of Pope Leo X, who was Lorenzo the Magnificent's son and Michelangelo's classmate. It was Leo who hired Michelangelo to glorify the Medici—Michelangelo's adopted family—with a spruced-up burial place.)

• *Now let's see Michelangelo's work. Continue down the hall, passing statues of Roman armor with worms sprouting out, to Michelangelo's New Sacristy.*

### Michelangelo's New Sacristy (Sacrestia Nuova)

The entire room—architecture, tombs, and statues—was designed by Michelangelo over a 14-year period (1520-1534) to house the bodies of four of the Medici family. Michelangelo, who spent his teen years in the Medici household and personally knew three of the four family members buried here, was emotionally attached to the project. This is the work of a middle-aged man (he started at age 45 and finished at 59) reflecting on his contemporaries dying around him, and on his own mortality.

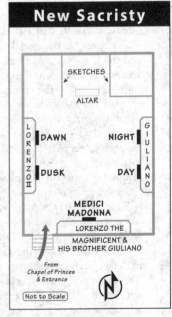

• *There are three tombs in this room. Start with the tomb on the left wall (as you enter and face the altar).*

### Tomb of Lorenzo II, Duke of Urbino

Lorenzo II—the grandson of Lorenzo the Magnificent—is not necessarily famous, but thanks to Michelangelo, his tomb is. (To find where Lorenzo II fits into the scheme of history, refer to the Medici family tree on page 75.) Lorenzo is shown as a Roman general, seated, elbow resting on a Medici-bank money box, and bowing his head in contemplation. He had been the model for Machiavelli's *The Prince,* and when he died at 27 (of tuberculosis and syphilis) without a male heir, the line of great princes stretching back to Cosimo the Elder died with him.

His sarcophagus, with a curved, scrolled lid, bears reclining statues. Michelangelo named the statues *Dawn* and *Dusk.* With

their counterparts on the opposite wall, the statues represented to Michelangelo the swift passage of time, from Dawn, to Day, to Dusk, to Night.

*Dawn* (the woman) stirs restlessly after a long night, with an anguished face, as though waking from a bad dream. *Dusk* (the man), worn out after a long day, slumps his chin on his chest and reflects on the day's events. These statues symbolize how quickly our time on earth passes, and how death makes our glorious deeds on earth fade.

Michelangelo sculpted these in a brooding mood. He was suffering through the deaths of his father and favorite brother, plus a plague that killed thousands. Nearing 50, he told friends he was feeling old, tired ("If I work one day, I need four to recuperate"), and depressed (he called it *mio pazzo,* "my madness"). He was also facing up to the sad fact that the Medici Chapels—plagued by delays—might never be completed.

Overachievers in severe midlife crises may wish to avoid the Medici Chapels.

• *On the opposite wall is the...*

### Tomb of Giuliano, Duke of Nemours

Overshadowed by his famous father (Lorenzo the Magnificent) and big brother (Pope Leo X), **Giuliano** led a wine-women-and-song life, dying young without a male heir. His statue as a Roman general, with scepter, powerful Moses-esque pose, and alert, intelligent face, looks in the direction of the Madonna statue, as though asking forgiveness for a wasted life. The likeness is not at all accurate. Michelangelo said, "In a thousand years, no one will know how they looked."

*Night* (the woman) does a crossover sit-up in her sleep, toning the fleshy abs that look marvelously supple and waxlike, not like hard stone. She's highly polished, shimmering, and finished with minute details. Michelangelo's females—musclemen with coconut bras—are generally more complete and (some think) less interesting than his men.

*Day* (the man) works out a crick in his back, each limb twisting a different direction, turning away from us. He looks over his shoulder with an expression (suspicious? Angry? Arrogant?) forever veiled behind chisel marks suggestive of Impressionist brush strokes. In fact, none of the four reclining statues' faces expresses a clear emotion, as all are turned inward, letting body language speak.

*Day, Night, Dawn,* and *Dusk*—brought to life in this room where Michelangelo had his workshop, and where they've been ever since—meditate eternally on Death, squirming restlessly, unable to come to terms with it.

• *On the entrance wall is the...*

### Tomb of Lorenzo the Magnificent and His Brother Giuliano

Michelangelo intended this to be the grand finale, a huge tomb to honor the greatest of the Medici, Lorenzo the Magnificent. Lorenzo was also the man who personally plucked a poor 13-year-old Michelangelo from obscurity to dine at the Medici table with cardinals and kings. But the tomb was never completed as hoped, and all that really marks where The Magnificent One's body lies is a marble slab, now topped with a statue of the Madonna flanked by saints.

Lorenzo is buried beside his

beloved younger brother, Giuliano, who died in 1478 in a "hit" by a rival family, stabbed to death before the altar of the Duomo during Easter Mass. (Lorenzo, wounded, drew his sword and backpedaled to safety. Enraged supporters grabbed the assassins—including two priests planted there by the pope—and literally tore them apart.)

If Lorenzo and Giuliano are looking down, they may be touched by Michelangelo's emotional **Medici Madonna.** Unlike many Michelangelo women, she's thin, vertical, and elegant, her sad face veiled under chisel marks. Aware of the hard life her son has ahead of him, she tolerates the squirming, two-year-old Jesus, who seems to want to breast-feed. Mary's right foot is still buried in stone, so this unfinished statue was certainly meant to be worked on more. The saints **Cosmas** and **Damian** were done by assistants.

• *Step into the apse—the area behind the altar.*

The doodles on the wall are presumably by Michelangelo and assistants. On the right wall, you can make out a horse, a nude figure crouching under an arch, a twisting female nude with her dog, and a tiny cartoon Roman soldier with shield and spurs. You get a sense of Michelangelo and staff working and just goofing off as the hammers pound and dust flies.

• *Now take in the whole thing—the tombs, the statues, the room, and the dome that tops it—and see how it all turned out.*

## The Whole Ensemble—Michelangelo's Vision

The New Sacristy was the first chance for Michelangelo to use his arsenal of talents—as sculptor, architect, and Thinker of Big Ideas—on a single multimedia project. It was essentially an "installation" (to use a 20th-century term) intended to produce a powerful overall effect.

He started with a plain white room, then lined it with gray stone columns, arches, and pediments. These may look like traditional Renaissance elements, but Michelangelo mixed and matched them like no one before, pointing the way toward the more ornate Baroque style.

The room is a cube topped with a Pantheon-style dome. There are three distinct stories—the heavy tombs at ground level, upper-level windows, and the dome. The whole effect draws the eye upward, from dark and "busy" to light and airy. (It's intensified by a clever optical illusion—Michelangelo made the dome's coffers, windows, and lunettes all taper imperceptibly at the top so they'd look taller and higher.)

Finally, Michelangelo wanted this room to symbolize the big philosophical questions that death presents to the living. Summing up these capital-letter concepts (far, far more crudely than was ever intended), the room might say:

Time (the four reclining statues) kills Mortal Men (statues of Lorenzo and Giuliano) and mocks their Glory (Roman power symbols). But if we Focus (Lorenzo and Giuliano's gaze) on God's Grace (Madonna and Child), our Souls (both Active and Contemplative parts) can be Resurrected (the Chapel was consecrated to this) and rise from this drab Earth (the dark, heavy ground floor) up into the Light (the windows and lantern) of Heaven (the geometrically perfect dome), where God and Plato's Ideas are forever Immortal.

# MEDICI-RICCARDI PALACE TOUR

*Palazzo Medici-Riccardi*

Cosimo the Elder, the founder of the ruling Medici family dynasty, lived here with his upwardly mobile clan, including his grandson, Lorenzo the Magnificent. Besides the immediate family, the palace (rated ▲) also hosted many famous Florentines: teenage Michelangelo, who lived almost as an adopted son; Leonardo da Vinci, who played the lute at Medici parties; and Botticelli, who studied the classical sculpture that dotted the gardens. The historical ambience is captured in a few well-preserved rooms and in a 15th-century fresco that brings the colorful Medici world to life.

## Orientation

**Cost:** €10, central courtyard and garden are free.

**Hours:** Thu-Tue 9:00-19:00, closed Wed.

**Information:** +39 055 276 0552, www.palazzomediciriccardi.it.

**Crowd Alert:** While the palace is rarely mobbed, you may encounter a slight bottleneck at the tiny Chapel of the Magi (Cappella di Benozzo Gozzoli). Only 10-15 people are allowed in at a time, but the line moves quickly.

**Getting There:** It's one block north of the Duomo at Via Cavour 3; you may also be able to enter through the garden courtyard at Via de' Ginori 2.

**Special Exhibits:** For a Renaissance palace, the Medici-Riccardi is surprisingly up-to-date in its choice of special exhibits included in your ticket (past offerings have included a retrospective of subversive street artist Banksy and an overview of David Bowie's photography). Fans of contemporary art should check to see what's on.

**Length of This Tour:** Allow 45 minutes. With limited time, focus on the Chapel of the Magi.

**Starring:** Cosimo the Elder and Lorenzo the Magnificent as depicted in Gozzoli's colorful Magi frescoes.

# The Tour Begins

### Exterior

Cosimo the Elder, the patriarch of the Medici dynasty, built the palace (1444). He hired the architect Michelozzo, whose three-story facade set the tone for the rest of Florence—rough stones at bottom, rising to smooth and elegant on top. Two generations later, Michelangelo added the distinctive "kneeling windows" (with scrolls), an innovation that later cropped up on palaces the world over. In the 1700s, the palace was extended northward (keeping the same style) by its next owners, the Riccardi family.

• *Enter the courtyard.*

### Courtyard

As with many Italian homes, the courtyard served as an open-air meeting point and "living room" for the extended family. The statue of Orpheus (who calmed wild animals with his harp) reminded visitors that the Medici family calmed wild Florence with civilized and soothing politics. Find the family shield above the arches, with the six pills of these doctors *(medici)*-turned-cloth merchants-turned-international bankers. The Riccardi family later gilded this Renaissance lily with Baroque decor and adorned this courtyard with their collection of classical sculpture. Temporary exhibits (covered by your ticket) often inhabit rooms adjoining the courtyard.

### Garden

Pop into the fragrant garden with its greenhouse that once housed lemon trees. This tiny oasis is a mere fraction of the once-spacious gardens that stretched for a city block to the north. In the past, the grounds were studded with many more fountains and statues, including the *Venus de' Medici* (Uffizi). Donatello's *David* (Bargello) likely stood in the courtyard. Teenage Michelangelo studied sculpture and liberal arts in the family school located in the gardens.

MEDICI-RICCARDI PALACE

In 1494, angry Florentine mobs exiled the Medici and looted the garden's precious statues.

On the right at the end of the garden and down the stairs is the easy-to-miss **Museo dei Marmi,** included with your ticket. At some point, you may want to visit its small collection of rare busts of ancient gods (like the bearded *Divinità Greca*), shaggy artists (the playwright Euripides), philosophers, emperors (cruel-looking Caracalla in a multicolored toga), and others (a *bambino* and the handsome *Sovrano Ellenistico*, a.k.a. Hellenistic Ruler).

• *Head back to the central courtyard and buy your ticket. Check out any temporary exhibits (in adjoining rooms). Then find the staircase in the corner of the courtyard that leads up to the...*

## Chapel of the Magi
## (Cappella di Benozzo Gozzoli)

This sumptuous little room was the nuclear family's private chapel, where they could kneel at the altar and pray to a *Madonna and Child* by Fra Filippo Lippi (where a copy stands now). At the time, it was rare and highly prestigious for a family to have a private chapel (this is one of only three in Florence). But Cosimo the Elder was the pope's banker—he even bankrolled one of the Crusades. He could afford it.

The three walls around the altar display *The Journey of the Magi* (the three kings—one king per wall) by Benozzo Gozzoli (1459).

On the biggest wall to the right of the altar, ❶ **a curly-haired young king,** dressed in gold and riding a white horse, leads a parade of men through a rocky landscape. (Some scholars have suggested that the young Magus may be Lorenzo the Magnificent, but others dismiss the idea. Lorenzo is pictured elsewhere—read on.) The scene takes you not to Bethlehem, but to 15th-century Medici-populated Tuscany. Riding behind the king is ❷ **Piero the Gouty,** Lorenzo the Magnificent's dad

(on a gray-white horse). Accompanying him is his father, ❸ **Cosimo the Elder,** who founded the family dynasty and hired Gozzoli to paint this room (in red hat, riding a modest brown donkey). In the line of young men behind them is Piero's 10-year-old son and future ruler—❹ **Lorenzo the Magnificent** (sixth in from the left, in red cap with scoop nose and brown bowl-cut hair; he looks to the right with an intense gaze).

Little Lorenzo grew up surrounded by these beautiful frescoes that celebrate the natural world. One day, he would commission his own great art.

Above Lorenzo (and slightly to the right) is ❺ **Gozzoli** himself. The sour-faced man in the brightest red cap above Gozzoli is ❻ **Pope Pius II,** often called "the first humanist" (see "Piccolomini Library" on page 397). Lost? Ask the attendant where they are: *"Dov'è* (doh-VEH) *Benozzo Gozzoli? Dov'è Cosimo? Dov'è Lorenzo?"*

The next wall (working clockwise) sets the king and his entourage in a green, spacious, and obviously Tuscan landscape. The stylish men wear colorful clothes that set trends throughout Europe. Every year on Epiphany (January 6), the Medici men would actually dress up like this and parade through the streets to celebrate the holiday of the three kings. The family invented this tradition to give them a chance to present themselves as royals to their citizenry.

On the last wall, notice that the white-bearded king on his white donkey (far left) got cut off when the room was later remodeled. But the fresco was preserved: Facing the fresco, back up and you'll find the horse's ass on the other side of the doorway.

Gozzoli's crystal-clear, shadowless scenes reflect the style of his teacher, Fra Angelico. The portraits are realistic, showing the leading characters of 1459 Florence.

The room itself functioned both as a chapel and as the place where Cosimo the Elder received VIPs. By portraying his own family in this religious setting, Cosimo made a classy display of cool power and sophistication. When learned rival powers came here, they thought, "Damn, these Medici are good."

• *Exit the Gozzoli room into several...*

## Palatial Rooms with Museum Exhibits

Though the displays change often, the rooms themselves give a small sense of the former luxury of the palace—chandeliers, tapestries, claw-foot chairs, coffered ceilings, and such. From roughly 1400 to 1700, the city of Florence set the tone for fashion and interior decor throughout Europe. This palace was ground zero of international style. For proof, check out the portraits (in the final rooms) of various Medici in their splendid clothes.

• *Eventually you'll reach a room displaying a painting in a glass case.*

### Fra Filippo Lippi, *Madonna and Child*

Lippi's cheek-to-cheek *Madonna and Child* demonstrates his specialty—humanizing the son of God and the Virgin. Baby Jesus' transparent shirt, Mary's transparent scarf, and their transparent halos make this late Lippi work especially ethereal. Mary's eyes are sad, while Jesus stares into his spiritual future. She gives him a tender hug before he's off on his mission.

• *Several rooms branching off the Lippi room are government offices.*

**MEDICI-RICCARDI PALACE**

### The Palace as Civic Center

Today, the palace is a functioning county government building. As you wander around, notice the bureaucrats at work. Occasionally, the provincial council meeting room (Sala Quattro Stagioni) is open for viewing. You'll see a few dozen modern-looking seats for the council members, amid chandeliered elegance. The tapestries on the wall depict the four seasons *(quattro stagioni).*

• *Complete your visit in the nearby...*

### Luca Giordano Room

This Baroque, Versailles-like former reception hall was added by the Riccardi family. All the elements—golden walls, mirrors, carved garlands, and ceiling fresco—were conceived together. The ceiling (*The Apotheosis of the Medici Family,* frescoed in 1685 by the Naples artist Luca Giordano) features Medici big shots (with starbursts over their heads) frolicking with Greek gods. Walk slowly toward the center of the room and watch as the Medici appear to rise up into heaven to be crowned by Zeus. Ring-

ing the base of the ceiling are various Greek myths. Find Poseidon (to the left) riding on a chariot of whitecap horses. On the right, Hades carries off Persephone, while Hercules stands near-by along with Charon, ferrying souls, and Cerberus, the three-headed canine guardian of hell. Claiming her place among the ancients, the blue-robed woman over the entrance is Florence, who re-birthed the classical world.

• *Your tour is done. Now head back out into the modern world and take your place among the ancients—and youth—of Florence.*

# SANTA MARIA NOVELLA TOUR

*Chiesa di Santa Maria Novella*

The Church of Santa Maria Novella, chock-full of groundbreaking paintings and statues (and rated ▲▲), is a reminder that the Renaissance was not simply a secular phenomenon. Many wealthy families paid for chapels inside this church. They were often bankers who made their money by charging interest—considered a sin by many Christians. Their need for forgiveness made their investment in a glorious chapel a very good value, and the results are the chapels that today are appreciated for their fine art.

Masaccio's fresco *The Trinity* (1427), the first painting of modern times to portray three-dimensional space, blew a "hole in the wall" of this church. From then on, a painting wasn't just a decorated panel, but a window into the spacious 3-D world of light and color. With Masaccio's *Trinity* as the centerpiece, Santa Maria Novella traces Florentine art from the medieval era to the Quattrocento (1400s) to the onset of Baroque.

## Orientation

**Cost:** €7.50 covers church and museum (in the adjoining cloister).

**Hours:** Mon-Thu and Sat 10:00-17:00, Fri from 11:00, Sun from 13:00.

**Information:** +39 055 219 257, www.smn.it.

**Dress Code:** No bare shoulders, short skirts, or short shorts for adults. Clothing must cover the knees. Free poncho-like coverings are available (worth keeping for other church visits).

**Getting There:** It's on Piazza Santa Maria Novella, across the street from (and south of) the train station.

**Getting In:** To buy tickets, enter the courtyard to the right of the church's main door.

You can also go in through the back door—facing the

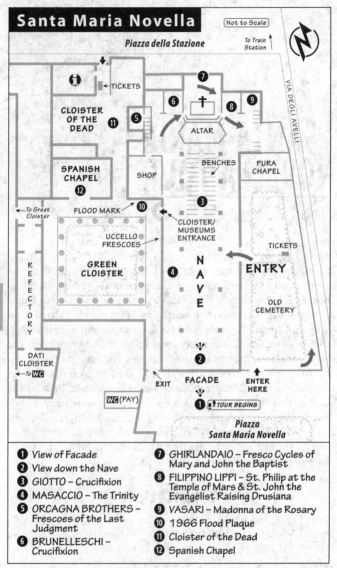

# Santa Maria Novella

Not to Scale

*Piazza della Stazione*

To Train Station

TICKETS

CLOISTER OF THE DEAD

SPANISH CHAPEL

ALTAR

BENCHES

PURA CHAPEL

SHOP

VIA DEGLI AVELLI

To Great Cloister

FLOOD MARK

UCCELLO FRESCOES

GREEN CLOISTER

CLOISTER/ MUSEUMS ENTRANCE

REFECTORY

N A V E

TICKETS

ENTRY

OLD CEMETERY

DATI CLOISTER

To WC

EXIT

FACADE

ENTER HERE

WC (PAY)

TOUR BEGINS

*Piazza Santa Maria Novella*

SANTA MARIA NOVELLA

❶ View of Facade
❷ View down the Nave
❸ GIOTTO – Crucifixion
❹ MASACCIO – The Trinity
❺ ORCAGNA BROTHERS – Frescoes of the Last Judgment
❻ BRUNELLESCHI – Crucifixion

❼ GHIRLANDAIO – Fresco Cycles of Mary and John the Baptist
❽ FILIPPINO LIPPI – St. Philip at the Temple of Mars & St. John the Evangelist Raising Drusiana
❾ VASARI – Madonna of the Rosary
❿ 1966 Flood Plaque
⓫ Cloister of the Dead
⓬ Spanish Chapel

train station at Piazza della Stazione 4. You'll enter directly into the Cloister of the Dead. (The church's back entrance is also the entry-point for the main TI.)

**Tours:** The multimedia guide is €3.

**Length of This Tour:** Allow 45 minutes.

**Eating:** For recommended restaurants in the area, see page 315.

**Nearby:** Across the square from the church is the **Museo Novecen-**

**to.** It's a must if you came to Florence to see 20th-century art by Italian artists you've never heard of..

**Starring:** The early Renaissance—Masaccio, Giotto, Brunelleschi, and Ghirlandaio.

# The Tour Begins

## ❶ Facade

There's a lot going on in Leon Battista Alberti's green-and-white marble facade (1456-1470), which contains elements of Florence's whole history: Romanesque (horizontal stripes, like the Baptistery), Gothic (pointed arches on the bottom level), and Renaissance (geometric squares and circles on the upper level). Note also the sundial sticking out.

The church itself is cross-shaped, with a high central nave and low-ceilinged side aisles. The scrolls on the facade help bridge the two levels.

Before stepping inside, turn around and survey Piazza Santa Maria Novella. This marked the Dominican Quarter, just outside the city walls, while the Franciscans flanked the city on the opposite side of town at Santa Croce. The monks here built a hospice (the fine arcade opposite the church), ran a pharmacy (around the corner), and for centuries provided a kind of neighborhood clinic (which still functions as an emergency room—notice the ambulances parked on the right).

The obelisks at either end of the square were commissioned by Cosimo I. His symbol was the turtle, and turtles seem to be holding up the obelisks, which served as end posts for a racetrack. Imagine high-energy, 16th-century horse races in this square as jockeys rode bareback to the delight of Florentine spectators.

• *Enter the courtyard to the right of the main door, passing through the cemetery, where you'll pay to enter. As you go inside the church, Masaccio's* Trinity *is on the opposite wall from the entrance. But we'll start our tour at the far end of the nave.*

## ❷ View Down the Nave

From the wall facing the altar, the long, 330-foot nave looks even

longer, thanks to a 14th-century perspective illusion. The columns converge as you approach the altar, the space between them gets smaller, the arches get lower, and the floor gets higher, creating the illusion that the nave stretches farther into the distance than it actually does. Gothic architects were aware of the rules of perspective and used them in their designs.

Notice the pulpit attached to a column partway up the nave on the left. The Dominicans who occupied this church stressed teaching, so they always had prominent pulpits. And from this particular pulpit, the astronomer and scientist Galileo was first accused of heresy.

• *Hanging from the ceiling in the middle of the nave is a painting by Giotto.*

### ❸ Giotto, *Crucifixion*

The altarpiece by Giotto (c. 1266-1337) originally hung above the iconostasis, which was removed in the 1500s after the Reformation. Stately and understated, it avoids the gruesome excesses of many medieval crucifixes. The tragic tilt of Christ's head, the parted lips, and the stretched rib cage tell more about human suffering than an excess of spurting blood.

On either side of the crossbar, Mary and John sit in a golden, iconic heaven, but they are fully human, turned at a three-quarter angle, with knowing, sympathetic expressions. Giotto, the proto-Renaissance experimenter in perspective, creates the illusion that Christ's hands are actually turned out, palms down, and not hammered flat against the cross. Still, it would be another century before painters could fully make 3-D realism a reality.

• *Masaccio's* Trinity *is on the left wall, about midway along the nave (opposite the entrance).*

### ❹ Masaccio, *The Trinity,* 1425-1427

In his short but influential five-year career, Masaccio (1401-1428) was the first painter since ancient times to portray Man in Nature—real humans with real emotions, in a spacious three-dimensional world. (Unfortunately for tourists, his best portrayal of 3-D space is here, but his best portrayal of humans is in the Brancacci Chapel across the river.)

With simple pinks and blues (now faded), Masaccio creates the illusion that we're looking into a raised, cube-shaped chapel (about nine feet tall) topped with an arched ceiling and framed at the entrance with classical columns. Inside the chapel, God the Father stands on an altar, holding up the cross of Christ. (Where's the dove of the Holy Spirit? Why is God's "white collar" crooked?) John looks up at Christ while Mary looks down at us. Note the realism in the face of Mary, now a 50-year-old mother. Two donors (husband and wife, most likely) kneel on the front step outside the chapel, their cloaks spilling out of the niche. Below this fake chapel sits a fake tomb with the skeleton of Adam; compare it with the real tomb and niche to the right.

The checkerboard-coffered ceiling creates a 3-D tunnel effect, with rows of panels that appear to converge at the back, the panels getting smaller, lower, and closer together. Earlier painters had played with tricks like this, but Masaccio went further, depicting the painting's imagery on at least five planes—the donors, Mary and John, Christ, God, and the background—and each one takes you deeper into the scene. He gave such thought to the proper perspective that we, as viewers, know right where we stand in relation to this 3-D virtual chapel.

Together, Masaccio and Brunelleschi did the math and developed the laws of perspective. Alberti (who designed the facade) codified the laws in his famous 1435 treatise, *On Painting*. Soon, artists everywhere were drawing Alberti checkerboards on the ground, creating spacious, perfectly lit, 3-D scenes filled with chess-piece humans.

• *The Orcagna Chapel is at the far end of the left transept. As you approach, view the chapel from a distance. This is the illusion that Masaccio tried to create—of a raised chapel set in a wall with people inside—using only paint on a flat surface. You can actually walk into this one.*

## ❺ Orcagna Brothers, Frescoes of the Last Judgment, 1340-1357

In 1347-1348, Florence was hit with the terrible Black Death (bubonic plague) that killed half the population. Here, in the Orcagna Chapel, the fading frescoes from that grim time show hundreds of figures, and not a single smile.

It's the Day of Judgment (center wall), and God (above the stained-glass window) spreads his hands to divide the good from the evil.

In Heaven (left wall), Hotel Paradiso is *completo*, stacked with gold-haloed saints. Hell (faded right wall) is a series of layers, the descending rings of Dante's Inferno. A river of fire runs through it, dividing Purgatory (above) and Hell (below). At the bottom of the pit, where dogs and winged demons run wild, naked souls in caves beg for mercy and get none. For something a bit lighter (flanking the stained glass windows), enjoy the hats, hairstyles, and clothing—all in vogue around 1350 in Florentine upper society.

*• Notice perhaps the most beautiful bookshop in the world, in the sacristy, as you return to the nave. Then, in a chapel to the left of the church's main altar, you'll find...*

### ❻ Filippo Brunelleschi, *Crucifixion*

Filippo Brunelleschi (1377-1446)—architect, painter, sculptor— used his skills as an analyst of nature to carve (in wood) a perfectly

realistic Crucifixion, neither prettified nor with the grotesque exaggeration of medieval religious objects. His Christ is buck naked, not particularly muscular or handsome, with bulging veins, armpit hair, tensed leg muscles, and bent feet. The tilt of Christ's head frees a tendril of hair that directs our eye down to the wound and the dripping blood, dropping straight from his side to his thigh to his calf—a strong vertical line that sets off the curve of Christ's body. Brunelleschi carved this to outdo a crucifix his friend Donatello had done elsewhere. He thought Donatello's Christ looked like an agonized peasant; Brunelleschi's was a dignified noble. (BTW, Donatello was impressed.)

*• In the choir area behind the main altar (the Tornabuoni Chapel) are Ghirlandaio's 21 frescoes, stacked seven to a wall. We'll concentrate on just the six panels on the bottom.*

### ❼ Domenico Ghirlandaio, Fresco Cycles of Mary and John the Baptist, 1485-1490

This well-preserved fresco cycle, one of the most complete in Florence, is by Domenico Ghirlandaio (1449-1494) and his workshop. This chapel was the choir where monks gathered to worship, chanting from huge illuminated hymnals that sat on the fine lectern (from 1615).

The 15th-century stained-glass window (lower left) shows the founder of the order, St. Dominic, and Dominican monks in their black robes. Above the window is the coronation of the Virgin Mary. The frescoes tell stories: the life of the Virgin (on the left), from Mary's birth to her assumption to heaven (on top), and the life of St. John the Baptist, the patron of Florence (on the right), which shows the angel announcing John's coming, his birth, his preaching, his baptism of Jesus, the banquet where Salome requests John's head (top), and so on.

At the peak of Florence's power, wealth, and confidence, Ghirlandaio painted portraits of his fellow Florentines in their Sunday best, inhabiting video-game landscapes of mixed classical and contemporary buildings, rubbing shoulders with saints and angels. The religious subjects get lost in the colorful scenes of everyday life—perhaps a metaphor for how Renaissance humanism was intertwining secular society with religion. Or perhaps it was simply more effective to communicate a message by using everyday scenes from contemporary and local life.

Here are a few panels worth a closer look:
• *Start with the left wall and work clockwise along the bottom. The first scene shows the...*

### Expulsion of Joachim from the Temple

Proud, young Florentine men (the group at left) seem oblivious to the bearded, robed saints rushing from the arcade. There's Ghirlandaio himself (in the group on the right) looking out at us, with one hand proudly on his hip and the other gesturing, "I did this." The scene is perfectly lit, almost shadow-free, allowing us to look deep into the receding arches.
• *The next scene, on the right, is the...*

### Birth of the Virgin

Five beautiful young women, led by the pregnant daughter of Ghirlandaio's patron, parade up to newborn Mary. Her mother,

Anne, is still in bed, overlooking the happy scene. The pregnant girl's brocade dress is a microcosm of the room's decorations. Dancing monochrome babies in the room's classical frieze celebrate Mary's birth, obviously echoing Donatello's beloved cantoria now housed in Florence's Duomo Museum.

True, Ghirlandaio's works are "busy"—each scene crammed

with portraits, designs, fantasy architecture, and great costumes—but if you mentally frame off small sections, you discover a collection of mini masterpieces.

• *On the lowest part of the center wall, flanking the stained-glass window, are two matching panels.*

### Giovanni Tornabuoni and His Wife Francesca Kneeling

Giovanni Tornabuoni, who paid for these frescoes, was a successful executive in the Medici Company (and Lorenzo the Magnificent's uncle). However, by the time these frescoes were being finished, the Medici bank was slipping seriously into the red, and soon the family had to flee Florence, creditors on their heels.

• *On the right wall...*

### Mary Meets Elizabeth

In a spacious, airy landscape (with the pointed steeple—now gone—of this church, Santa Maria Novella, in the distance), Mary and Elizabeth embrace, uniting their respective entourages. The parade of ladies in contemporary dress echoes the one on the opposite wall. This panel celebrates youth, beauty, the city, trees, rocks, and life. It also celebrates luxurious brocaded cloth, part of an industry that helped make Florence so wealthy.

A generation after Brunelleschi and Alberti, all artists—including the near-genius Ghirlandaio—had mastered perspective tricks. Here, Alberti's famed checkerboard is laid on its side, making a sharply receding wall to create the illusion of great distance.

Ghirlandaio employed many assistants in his productive workshop: "Johnson, you do the ladies' dresses. Anderson, you're great at birds and trees. And Michelangelo...you do young men's butts." The three small figures leaning over the wall (above Mary and Elizabeth) were likely done by 13-year-old Michelangelo, an apprentice here before being "discovered" by Lorenzo the Magnificent. Relaxed and natural, they cast real shadows, as true to life as anyone in Ghirlandaio's perfect-posture, face-the-camera world.

Ghirlandaio was reportedly jealous of talented Michelangelo (who in turn was contemptuous of Ghirlandaio), but, before they parted ways, Michelangelo learned how to lay fresco from the man who did it as well as anyone in Florence.

• *On the far right, find the...*

### Appearance of an Angel to Zechariah

In a crowded temple, old Zechariah is going about his business when an angel strolls up. "Uh, excuse me..." The event is supposedly miraculous, but there's nothing supernatural about this scene: no clouds of fire or rays of light. The crowd doesn't even notice the angel. Ghirlandaio presents the holy in a completely secular way. The cast here is the economic and social elite of late-15th-century Florence (wearing colors only the elites could afford—red and purple).

• *In the chapel to the right of the altar, Filippino Lippi did the frescoes on the left and right walls. Look first at the right wall, lower level...*

### ❽ Filippino Lippi

#### St. Philip at the Temple of Mars

In an elaborate shrine, a statue of the angry god Mars waves his broken lance menacingly. The Christian Philip points back up at him and says, "I'm not afraid of him—that's a false god." To prove it, he opens a hole in the base of the altar, letting out a little dragon, who promptly farts (believe it when you see it), causing the pagan king's son to swoon and die. The overcome spectators clutch their foreheads and noses.

If Ghirlandaio was "busy," Lippi is downright hyperactive, filling every square inch with something frilly—rumpled hair, folds in clothes, dramatic gestures, twisting friezes, windblown flags, and flatulent dragons.

• *On the left wall, lower level, is...*

#### St. John the Evangelist Raising Drusiana from the Dead

The miracle takes place in a spacious 3-D architectural setting, but Lippi has all his actors in a chorus line across the front of the stage. Filippino Lippi (1457-1504, the son of the more famous Fra Filippo Lippi) studied with and was influenced by Botticelli and exaggerated his bright colors, shadowless lighting, and elegant curves.

The sober, dignified realism of Florence's Quattrocento (the 1400s) was ending. Michelangelo would extend it, building on Masaccio's spacious, solemn, dimly lit scenes. But Lippi championed a style (later called Mannerism, which led to Baroque) that loved color, dramatic excitement, and the exotic.

• *In the next chapel to the right of the altar, on the central wall, find...*

### ❾ Giorgio Vasari, *Madonna of the Rosary*

The picture-plane is saturated with images from top to bottom. Saints and angels twist and squirm around Mary (the red patch in the center), but their body language is gibberish, just an excuse for Vasari to exhibit his technique.

Giorgio Vasari (1511-1574) was a prolific artist. As a Mannerist, he copied the "manner" of, say, a twisting Michelangelo statue, but violated the sober spirit, multiplying by 100 and cramming the canvas. I've tried to defend Vasari from the art critics who unanimously call his art superficial and garish... but doggone it, they're right. With Vasari, who immortalized the Florentine Renaissance with his writing, the Renaissance ended.

• *Exit the church out the left side, descending stairs into the museo part of the visit. Pause at the bottom of the steps and take in the peaceful Green Cloister.*

### Museum of Santa Maria Novella

The church was part of a Dominican monastery. Imagine monks circling this shaded courtyard (cloister), as well as several adjoining ones.

At the bottom of the steps to the Green Cloister, on the right, find a ❿ **small plaque** on the wall that marks the height of the 1966 flood ("Il 4 Novembre 1966..."). The horrendous flood of the Arno inundated the church and monastery with eight feet of water. It destroyed the precious frescoes by Paolo Uccello (1397-1475) that once lined the Green Cloister (so named for Uccello's dominant color). Today, most of the walls have been completely redone by other artists, but some of Uccello's original (and very faded) frescoes can be seen on the east wall and (later) in the museum collection. Ironically, these depict...the Great Flood. Nearby, check out the gravestones of the ⓫ **Cloister of the Dead**, filled with the leading patrons of this monastery.

The highlight of the museum is its breathtaking ⓬ **Spanish Chapel** (a.k.a. la Sala Capitular). Once the former chapter house of the monastery, the sheer size of the vault put this place on the map when it was built in the 1320s (it became known as the Spanish Chapel after Cosimo I gave it to his bride, Eleonora of Toledo). Covering the chapel's walls is Andrea di Bonaiuto's 14th-century fresco series, *Allegory of the Active and Triumphant Church and of the Dominican Order* (c. 1365). The fresco is a visual Sunday-school class—complete with Peter's fishing boat. Follow the long and tricky road to salvation, ending high above, where the saved are finally greeted by Peter at his gate (shown upstairs in the big yellow building).

On the left wall, find the 13th-century Dominican theologian Thomas Aquinas (in a dark robe and with the Bible he translated from Greek into Latin) seated in glory amid virtues, authors of books of the Bible, and angels. The central wall tells the Passion story: Christ carries his cross (lower left), is crucified between two thieves (center), then rises triumphant (right) to trample and spook the demons of death. On the right wall, the pinkish church was inspired by designs for the Duomo, which was then under construction (but shown before Brunelleschi's taller dome was envisioned). Along the bottom of the fresco, dogs fight off the wolves of heresy. They're led by St. Dominic, whose fiercely loyal Dominicans (Dominicanus in Latin) rightly earned their medieval play-on-words nickname of "Domini canes"—God's dogs.

• *A block away is the historic pharmacy of the monastery, today a fascinating perfume shop. From the piazza in front of the church, head west to Via della Scala 16.*

## Farmacia di Santa Maria Novella

Founded by the Dominicans of Santa Maria Novella back in 1612, this palatial perfumery and cosmetics shop started as the monk's herb garden. Thick with the lingering aroma of centuries of spritzes, it's well known even today for its top-quality products, and is extremely Florentine.

Beyond the salesroom is the Green Room, once a refined tea and chocolate room decorated with historic vases and 400 years of directors on its walls (with candles and incense on sale). To the right, a passage leading to a small sacristy offers a chance to get up close and personal with beautiful 600-year-old frescos by a follower of Giotto. Further on is a functioning herbal tearoom surrounded by a museum of historic perfume-making tools and distillation paraphernalia—an alchemist's dream come true.

Cross over to the other side of the Green Room (which is where the pharmacy was originally sited). From here, you can peek at one of Santa Maria Novella's cloisters with its dreamy frescoes and imagine a time before Vespas and tourists—600 years ago when monks tended their herbal garden (for more details and location, see the Shopping in Florence chapter).

# SANTA CROCE TOUR

*Chiesa di Santa Croce*

Santa Croce, one of Florence's biggest and oldest churches (rated ▲▲), gives us a glimpse into the medieval roots of the Renaissance. The church was the centerpiece of a monastery for Franciscans; it was designed by Arnolfo di Cambio (c. 1290), who also did the Duomo, and frescoed by Giotto, the proto-Renaissance pioneer.

In the cloisters is a small chapel that some consider the finest example of early Renaissance architecture. The church was host to many famous Florentines, including Michelangelo and Galileo, who are both buried here. Today, the church complex houses a leather school, reminders of the disastrous 1966 flood, and a museum housed in the monks' former dining hall.

## Orientation

**Cost:** €8 includes the church, Pazzi Chapel, museum, and cloisters. The leather school is always free.

**Hours:** Church—Mon-Sat 9:30-17:30, Sun from 12:30. Leather school—Mon-Sat 10:00-18:00, closed Sun.

**Information:** +39 055 246 6105, www.santacroceopera.it. The leather school has its own website (https://leatherschool.biz).

**Crowd-Beating Tips:** A limited number of people are allowed to enter the church at one time, sometimes resulting in long waits in summer and Sunday afternoons. Go early or late in the day, or buy a timed-entry ticket (€1 booking fee) online. The leather school is never crowded.

**Dress Code:** A modest dress code (no short shorts or bare shoulders) is enforced.

**Getting There:** It's a 10-minute walk east of the Palazzo Vecchio along the street called Borgo de' Greci.

**Tours:** Tablets loaded with a tour and lots of information rent for €4.

**Length of This Tour:** Allow one hour. With less time, focus on the tombs of VIFs (Very Important Florentines) and the Giotto frescoes.

**Eating:** Recommended eateries are nearby (see page 314).

**Shopping:** The church's famous leather school sells pricey jackets and handbags, but also souvenir-worthy catchalls, pouches, and wallets.

**Starring:** Tombs of Michelangelo and Galileo, Giotto's frescoes, and Brunelleschi's Pazzi Chapel.

# The Tour Begins

• *Begin on the square in front of the church.*

## Piazza Santa Croce

Santa Croce Church, the largest Franciscan church in the world, was built from 1294 to 1442. Architect Arnolfo di Cambio's design was so impressive, the city also hired him to do the Duomo and the Palazzo Vecchio.

The church's colorful marble facade, left unfinished for centuries, was finally added in the 1850s. A statue of the medieval poet Dante adorns the church steps.

The church presides over a vast square ringed with a few old palazzos, notably the late Renaissance building at the far end. Piazza Santa Croce has always been one of Florence's gathering spots, for Carnival, May Day, and community events. If you're here in the third week of June, the square is covered with dirt and surrounded by bleachers for an annual rugby-like contest that pits neighborhood against neighborhood, while commemorating games played here as long ago as the 16th century.

If you were here on November 4, 1966, you would have found the square covered with 15 feet of water. The Arno flooded that day, submerging the church steps and rising halfway up the central doorway (more on the flood later).

• *Buy your ticket and enter. Start at the far end of the nave (farthest from the altar). Face the altar and gaze down the long nave.*

## ❶ The Nave

The effect here is one of great spaciousness. Franciscans liked things bright and open. The nave is 375 feet long, lined with columns that are tall, slender, and spaced far apart, supporting wide, airy arches. The nave is spanned with massive wood beams. As in most Gothic churches, there's no attempt to hide

the structural skeleton of columns and pointed arches. Instead, they're the stars of this show, demonstrating the mathematical perfection of the design and the builders' technical prowess.

Although the building is much older, it is decorated (like many Florentine churches) in the 17th-century "Counter-Reformation" style: Colorful medieval frescoes that once adorned the walls were covered up, the wall dividing the people from the holy area behind the altar—where the religious heavy-lifting occurred—was removed so that priests could be closer to parishioners, and side altars were decorated with Mannerist paintings that preached Counter-Reformation, pro-Rome values.

## The Tombs

Hundreds of people are buried in the Santa Croce complex, including 276 of them under your feet, marked by plaques in the floor. More famous folk line the walls.

• *Near the rear of the nave, find the tombs of two particularly well-known people.*

On the left wall (as you face the altar) is the ❷ **tomb of Galileo Galilei** (1564-1642), the Pisan who lived his last years under house arrest near Florence. His crime? Defying the Church by saying that the earth revolved around the sun. His heretical remains were only allowed in the church long after his death. (For more on Galileo, see his relics in the Galileo Science Museum.)

Directly opposite (on the right wall) is the ❸ **tomb of Michelangelo Buonarroti** (1475-1564). Santa Croce was Michelangelo's childhood church, as he grew up a block west of here at Via dei Bentaccordi 15 (where nothing but a plaque marks the spot). He took Florentine culture and spread it across Europe. In his later years, Michelangelo envisioned that his tomb would be marked with a pietà he carved himself

# Santa Croce

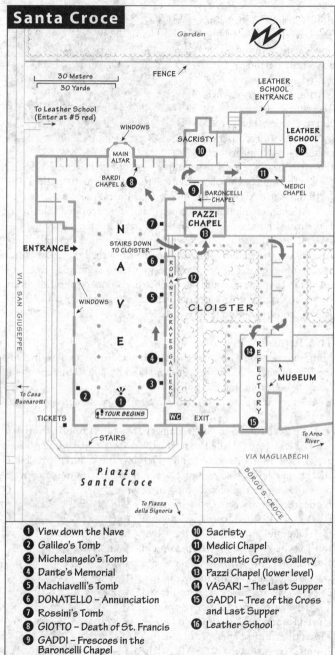

**SANTA CROCE**

Garden

FENCE

30 Meters
30 Yards

To Leather School
(Enter at #5 red)

WINDOWS

LEATHER
SCHOOL
ENTRANCE

LEATHER
SCHOOL  ⓰

SACRISTY  ❿

MAIN
ALTAR

BARDI
CHAPEL &  ❽

BARONCELLI
CHAPEL

❾

MEDICI
CHAPEL

⓫

N  A  V  E

ENTRANCE →

STAIRS DOWN
TO CLOISTER

WINDOWS

❼

❻

❺

❹

❸

ROMANTIC GRAVES GALLERY

PAZZI
CHAPEL

⓭

⓬

CLOISTER

⓮

REFECTORY

MUSEUM

⓯

VIA SAN GIUSEPPE

To Casa
Buonarroti

TICKETS

❷

❶

TOUR BEGINS

WC

EXIT

STAIRS

To Arno
River

VIA MAGLIABECHI

BORGO S. CROCE

Piazza
Santa Croce

To Piazza
della Signoria

❶ View down the Nave
❷ Galileo's Tomb
❸ Michelangelo's Tomb
❹ Dante's Memorial
❺ Machiavelli's Tomb
❻ DONATELLO – Annunciation
❼ Rossini's Tomb
❽ GIOTTO – Death of St. Francis
❾ GADDI – Frescoes in the
   Baroncelli Chapel

❿ Sacristy
⓫ Medici Chapel
⓬ Romantic Graves Gallery
⓭ Pazzi Chapel (lower level)
⓮ VASARI – The Last Supper
⓯ GADDI – Tree of the Cross
   and Last Supper
⓰ Leather School

(now in the Duomo Museum). The garish tomb he actually got—with the allegorical figures of painting, architecture, and sculpture—was designed by Michelangelo's great admirer, the artist/biographer Giorgio Vasari. (The portrait bust is considered an accurate likeness of Michelangelo.) Vasari also did the series of paintings that line the left side of the nave, using the twisting poses and bulky muscles that Michelangelo pioneered.

• *Stroll up the nave, finding more tombs and monuments along the right wall.*

At the memorial to the poet ❹ **Dante Alighieri** (1265-1321), there's no body inside, since Dante was banished by his hometown because of his politics and was buried in Ravenna. Exiled Dante looks weary, the Muse of Poetry mourns, and Lady Florence gestures to say, "Look what we missed out on."

Two tombs ahead, the ❺ **tomb of Niccolò Machiavelli** (1469-1527) features Lady Justice presenting a medallion with his portrait on it. Machiavelli, a champion of democratic Florence, opposed the Medici as tyrants. When they returned to power, he was arrested. He retired to his farm to write *The Prince,* a how-to manual on hardball politics—which later Medici rulers found instructive.

A few steps farther along, Donatello's carved gray-and-gold relief (1430-1435) depicting the ❻ **Annunciation** shows a kneeling angel gently breaking the news to Mary. An astonished Mary bends both away from and toward the angel, who cocks his head, fully understanding her confusion. Notable for its then-unprecedented realism, the wispy Mary (on the right) is considered one of the artistic breakthroughs that marked the beginning of the long-overdue Renaissance.

Two tombs up is ❼ **Gioacchino Rossini** (1792-1868), the Italian composer of many operas and the *William Tell Overture* (a.k.a. the *Lone Ranger* theme). Rossini died in Paris, but his body was later moved here, to his homeland, during a wave of Italian nationalism in the late 19th century.

• *Head for the main altar. On display in front of the altar is a **medieval*** *altarpiece, the Pala Bardi (c. 1250), with scenes from St. Francis' life. Look in particular at the scene of Francis' death—the third one up from bottom right. Compare this stiff, icon-like depiction with what we'll see next. In the first chapel to the right of the altar are the...*

## Giotto Frescoes in the Bardi Chapel (c. 1325)

The left wall has the famous ❽ *Death of St. Francis*. With simple but eloquent gestures, Francis' brothers bid him a sad farewell. One folds his hands and stares longingly at Francis' serene face. Another bends to kiss Francis' hand, while others raise their arms in grief. It's one of the first expressions of human emotion in modern painting. It's also one of the first to create a real three-dimensional grouping of figures. Giotto places three kneeling men (with their backs to us) in the foreground, puts some others standing behind Francis, and turns the rest to profile.

Giotto and his army of assistants were hired to plaster much of the church in colorful frescoes. But over the years, most were chiseled off, replaced by more modern works (like Vasari's). This chapel was only whitewashed over, and the groundbreaking frescoes were rediscovered in the 19th century.

• *Facing the altar, turn right, and head into the right (south) transept toward the chapel decorated with colorful frescoes.*

## ❾ Gaddi Frescoes in the Baroncelli Chapel (c. 1328-1338)

After assisting Giotto in the Bardi Chapel, Taddeo Gaddi (1300-1366)—Giotto's beloved godson—was charged with painting this chapel. His lively frescoes cover both the wall to the left (as you enter), and the wall straight ahead (with stained-glass windows by Gaddi and an altar by Giotto).

Start with the wall to the left. The story of Mary, the mother of Jesus, unfolds from top to bottom, left to right. At the very top (under the pointed arch) is a temple scene. Mary's future dad,

Joachim (with a beard and a halo), is turned away from the temple because he's childless. Ashamed, he retreats to the wilderness (right side), where an angel promises him a daughter. Overjoyed, Joachim rushes to his wife, Anna, and they embrace (next level down, left panel). Anna soon gives birth to baby Mary (badly damaged panel, right side). Still a child, Mary climbs the steps of the temple (bottom level, left panel; most of her body is missing from peeling plaster) to the chief priest (cone-shaped hat), who would raise her.

When it comes time for Mary to marry, the priest assembles all the eligible bachelors (bottom-right panel). Joseph's staff sprouts leaves and a dove (center of scene, to left of priest), signaling that he is chosen. In the foreground, a sore loser bends over and breaks his own staff.

Mary's life continues on the altar/stained-glass wall. At the top left, an angel swoops down to tell Mary that she'll give birth to Jesus. Perhaps Gaddi's most impressive scene is just below: A sleeping shepherd is awakened by an angel, who announces that Christ is born. Gaddi, an early pioneer in lighting effects, placed these windows where the natural light coming through would mix with the supernatural light from the radiant angel. Finally, Mary's story comes to its culmination (right of window): She gives birth to the Son of God in a stable.

• *From here, exit the chapel and do an immediate U-turn right, entering a hallway. Turn immediately left, into a big room—the Sacristy.*

## ⑩ Sacristy

The Sacristy (where priests get dressed for Mass) has an impressive wooden ceiling, decorated with Franciscan saints. The Franciscans who founded Santa Croce were dedicated to the principles of St. Francis, whose humanistic outlook and appreciation for the beauty of nature helped sow the seeds that would bloom into the Florentine Renaissance. On display (in a case along the wall) is a piece of Francis' robe, made of rough wool and tied with a rope belt, in keeping with his simple lifestyle.

**Cimabue's** *Crucifixion* (before 1288) hangs high overhead. Cimabue's

SANTA CROCE

## Floods in Florence

Summer visitors to Florence gaze at the lazy green creek called the Arno River and have a tough time imagining it being a destructive giant. But rare, powerful flooding is a part of life in this city. The Arno River washed away Ponte Vecchio in 1177 and 1333. And on November 4, 1966, a huge rainstorm turned the Arno into a wall of water, inundating the city with mud stacked as high as 20 feet. Nearly 14,000 families were left homeless, and tens of thousands of important frescoes, paintings, sculptures, and books were destroyed or damaged.

Almost as impressive as the flood was the huge outpouring of support, as the art-loving world came to the city's rescue. While money poured in from far and wide, volunteers, nicknamed "mud angels," mopped things up. After the flood, scientists made great gains in restoration techniques as they cleaned and repaired masterpieces from medieval and Renaissance times. Cimabue's *Crucifixion,* now displayed in Santa Croce's Sacristy, is a prime example.

You'll see plaques around town showing the high-water marks from 1966 (about six feet high at the Duomo). Now that a dam has tamed the Arno, rowers glide peacefully on the river, sightseers enjoy the great art with no thought of a flood, and locals...still get nervous after every heavy rain.

---

Christ isn't a remote figure, but a real man experiencing human suffering. The crucifix is a survivor of the terrible 1966 flooding of the Arno River that inundated Santa Croce and destroyed many priceless works of art throughout Florence. Cimabue's *Crucifixion* was one of the worst casualties, a poster child for the flood. Most of Christ's face and body were washed away. Rescued and restored (as best as possible), it became a symbol of revival and the international community's efforts to recover the city's historic artworks. (For more on the floods, see the sidebar.)

• *Return to the hallway, lined with more paintings destroyed in the flood that have now been laboriously restored and rehung here—at a safe height. At the end of the hall, enter the small...*

## ⓫ Medici Chapel

This was commissioned by Cosimo de' Medici the Elder in the 15th century so his family could have a private place of worship at this end of town. To design it, he hired his favorite architect, Michelozzo—who also built the Medici-Riccardi Palace.

The star here is Agnolo Bronzino's big colorful painting, *Descent of Christ into Limbo* (1522). Having just been resurrected, Christ picks up the flag of victory and goes to rescue souls in hell, where he's joyously welcomed by the grateful dead. In Bronzino's trademark Mannerist style, figures are posed at every conceivable angle, covering the canvas from top to bottom. Christ's female helper (at bottom) is especially well done.

• *Return to the church nave. Exit on the left between the Rossini and Machiavelli tombs, and descend the staircase into the delightful open-air cloister. At the bottom of the stairs, immediately to the right, is the doorway into the ⓬ Romantic Graves Gallery, a collection of 19th-century headstones. But let's go straight ahead to find (on your left), the entrance to the...*

## ⓭ Pazzi Chapel

Begun in 1430 by Brunelleschi, this small chapel captures the Renaissance in miniature. As with his Duomo dome, Brunelleschi was inspired by Rome's ancient Pantheon. The circle-in-square design reflects the ancient Romans' (and Renaissance Florentines') belief in the unity and harmony of perfect shapes. Notice how the color scheme of white plaster and gray sandstone accentuates the architectural lines so that only a little decoration is needed. The creamy colors help diffuse the light from the dome's windows, making the chapel evenly lit and meditative. The four medallions showing the Evangelists (at the base of the dome)

may be by Donatello; the medallions of apostles (on the walls) are by Luca della Robbia. While originally used as a monk's assembly room (chapter house), this later became the Pazzi family's private chapel. Imagine how modern this chapel—capped by a Brunelleschi dome—must have seemed. The chapel's portico is freshly restored thanks to a decidedly modern method of fundraising: A 2014 Kickstarter campaign quickly raised long-awaited funds, and the restoration was completed within months.

• *Exiting into the big cloister, toward the exit, is the entrance to the...*

## Museum and Refectory

Stroll through several rooms of paintings, statues, frescoes, and altarpieces by Andrea della Robbia until you come into the large room that was originally the monks' refectory, or dining hall, under heavy timber beams. The wall to the right as you enter displays Giorgio Vasari's ⓮ *The Last Supper*. Vasari was commissioned to paint this three years before he became better known for his tell-all biography, *The Lives of the Artists.* The bright colors, robust bodies, and dramatic poses reveal Michelangelo's influence on the next generation of artists. This painting was one of the most badly damaged victims of the 1966 flood, when it was submerged for 12 hours in polluted water. Restored in 2016, it now hangs on a pulley system so it can be quickly raised in case the waters surge again.

The refectory's entire far wall is frescoed with the impressive, 1,300-square-foot ⓯ *Tree of the Cross and Last Supper,* by Taddeo Gaddi. A crucifix sprouts branches blossoming with medieval symbolism, which dining monks ate up. Francis kneels at the base of the cross and makes sympathetic eye contact with Jesus. In one of the scenes that flank the cross (upper left), Francis has a vision in which he receives the stigmata—the same wounds in his hands, feet, and side that Christ suffered when he was crucified. Beneath the Tree of the Cross is the Last Supper, a scene that gave the monastery's residents the illusion that they were eating in the symbolic company of Jesus and the apostles.

The concept of decorating a monastery's refectory with a grand Last Supper scene started in Florence. For example, Leonardo da Vinci, a Florentine, painted this theme in the refectory of the Santa Maria delle Grazie monastery in Milan. And as we've seen from this tour, it's the genius of great Florentines—from Giotto to Brunelleschi to Michelangelo to Galileo—that helped create our modern world.

• *Our tour is finished. If you'd like to visit the leather school, exit the cloister, turn right, and circle around to the back of the church (see map at the beginning of this chapter). Enter the doorway at Via San Giuseppe 5 red (labeled* Leather School of Florence*). Follow* Scuola del Cuoio *signs through the small garden and humble parking lot to the low-key entrance.*

## ⓰ Leather School (Scuola del Cuoio)

After World War II, the Franciscan monks created a "Boys Town" here to give war orphans a trade: making leather products. It was the first shop in what is now a popular leather district. The Gori family of merchants helped found the school and the grandson still runs it today. Wander through the former dorms for monks, watch the leatherworking in action, and browse the finished products for sale. Angled mirrors let you look over the shoulders of the busy leatherworkers. At the start of the long hallway, see the photos of visiting celebrities, from popes, Jimmy Stewart, and "Miss" Barbara Bush to Ozzy Osbourne. If you're in the market for leather, be aware that this shop—while top-quality—has some of the highest prices in Florence (for leather-buying tips, see page 331).

SANTA CROCE

# OLTRARNO WALK

*From Ponte Vecchio to Ponte Santa Trinità*

Staying in the tourist zone leaves you with an incomplete impression of Florence. Most of its people live and work in outlying areas, which frankly are not on any traveler's list. But the best place to get a sense of old working-class Florence is in the Oltrarno neighborhood, south of the Arno River. While the essence of the Oltrarno is best enjoyed by simply wandering, this walk gives you a structure you can use to cover its highlights.

We'll start at Ponte Vecchio, gaze at the Pitti Palace, explore some colorful back streets, peruse the artisan shops along Via di Santo Spirito, and end with a classic Ponte Vecchio view from Ponte Santa Trinità. This walk is a helpful way to link some of the Oltrarno's best sights.

## Orientation

**Length of This Walk:** Allow about an hour, not including shopping or gelato stops.

**When to Go:** What you'll see varies with the time of day, but mornings and evenings are best. Midafternoon is sleepy, and many shops and churches are closed. Most of the artisan shops are closed on weekends. In the evening, cafés, restaurants, and strolling people—locals and tourists—leave the strongest impression, but most shops close by about 19:00.

**Getting There:** Start at Ponte Vecchio, which crosses the Arno River (a 10-minute walk south of the Duomo).

**Santo Spirito Church:** Church—free, Mon-Tue and Thu-Sat 10:00-13:00 & 15:00-18:00, Sun 11:30-13:30 & 15:00-18:00, closed Wed; Michelangelo crucifix—€2.

**Extra Credit:** The church of Santa Felicità, on the similarly named piazza near the start of this walk, is home to Mannerist master Jacopo Pontormo's *Deposition* altarpiece (first chapel on the right, free).

**Eating:** The Oltrarno is a great destination for dining, and this walk takes you past some of my recommended restaurants (see page 319).

**Starring:** Views of the Arno, Florence's medieval past, present-day artisans at work, and few tourists.

# The Walk Begins

• *Start in the middle of Ponte Vecchio.*

## ❶ Ponte Vecchio

The Arno River separates the city center from the Oltrarno—the neighborhood on the "other" *(altro)* side of the river. The two sides have historically been connected by this oldest bridge—Ponte Vecchio (current version built in 1345)—lined with its characteristic shops.

Florence was born on the north bank (founded by the Romans in the first century BC), and since the 1200s, the Oltrarno has been the city's poorer, working-class cousin. As the Oltrarno grew in medieval times, the wooden walls were replaced by stone, and two more bridges were added, connecting it with the city center. Looking upstream (east), you'll see the lone crenellated tower that marks the wall that once defined the medieval city. By Michelangelo's day, the Oltrarno had grown enough that Ponte Vecchio was located about mid-Florence.

Look above to see the **Vasari Cor-**

OLTRARNO

# Oltrarno Walk

To B #12

To Porta San Frediano

↖ PONTE ALLA CARRAIA

Piazza Nazaro Sauro

Piazza Scarlatti

BORGO S. FREDIANO

VIA DEL LEONE

Piazza del Carmine

BORGO STELLA

VIA SANTA MONACA

VIA DEI SERRAGLI

VIA MAFFIA

VIA DI SANTO SPIRITO

VIA DE' GEPPI

VIA DE' COVERELLI

O L T R A R N O

BRANCACCI CHAPEL

SANTA MARIA DEL CARMINE

SANTO SPIRITO

VIA S. AGOSTINO

VIA DE' S. MARTINO

N

200 Meters

200 Yards

Giardino Torrigiani

Piazza Santo Spirito

MICHELOZZI

TEGOLAIO

SDRUCCIOLO DE' PITTI

MARSILI

PAL. DE COSIMO RIDOLFI

VIA MAZZETTA

Piazza di San Felice

VIA

VIA DELLA CHIESA

BORGO

VIA DELLE CALDAIE

VIA ROMANA

TICKET OFFICE

VIA DEL CAMPUCCIO

VIA S. MARIA

Giardino di Annalena

BOBOLI GARDENS ENTRANCE

VIALE DELLA MERIDIANA

↙ To Porta Romana

1 Ponte Vecchio
2 Torre dei Barbadori, Torre dei Belfredelli & Photo Op
3 Borgo San Jacopo
4 Via Toscanella
5 View of Pitti Palace
6 Shops along Sdrucciolo de' Pitti
7 Piazza Santo Spirito
8 Via dei Serragli
9 Via di Santo Spirito & more Oltrarno Shopping
10 Ponte Santa Trinità

OLTRARNO

**ridor** (the yellow wall with the round windows), which was named for its architect, Giorgio Vasari. This was the personal passageway built for the Medici family to give them a private commute from the Palazzo Vecchio and Uffizi (center of city government) to the Pitti Palace, their palatial home (which we'll see a bit later). The corridor, built in five months in 1565, drilled straight through people's homes. The only detour is where it curves around the tower at the end of the bridge. (The family who owned that tower must have had a lot of clout.) With Medici princes prancing back and forth in their corridor, the smells of the traditional shops had to go. That's when Ponte Vecchio's original merchants—butchers and fishmongers—were replaced by today's gold- and silversmiths.

Ponte Vecchio has seen a lot of turmoil. The plaque above the crowds on the uphill side honors Gerhard Wolf, the German consul in Florence who is credited with saving the bridge (as well

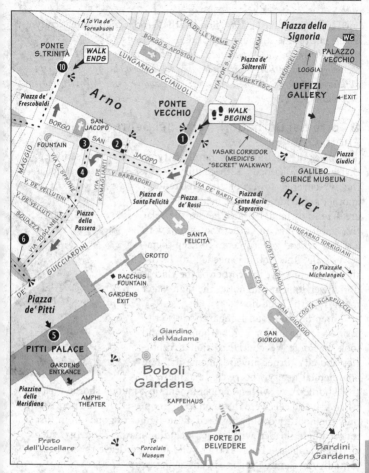

OLTRARNO

as other art treasures) from destruction during World War II. In August 1944, as Hitler's occupying troops fled the city, they were

ordered to destroy all of Florence's bridges to cover their retreat. Ponte Santa Trinità, where this walk ends, was demolished in 1944 (rebuilt in 1958)— and Ponte Vecchio was next in line. But thankfully, Wolf understood the bridge's historic value, and instead of destroying it, he had the buildings at either end blown up to render the bridge unusable. Later, Ponte Vecchio was threatened by the inundating 1966 flood of the Arno, which dramatically thrust entire trees through the bridge's buildings.

• *Cross the bridge, look up to notice the "detour" in the Vasari Corridor, then turn right on Borgo San Jacopo and walk one block. You'll pass ugly buildings from the 1950s, built after the damage from WWII bombs. Stop at the twin towers.*

## ❷ Torre dei Barbadori, Torre dei Belfredelli, and Photo Op

The tower of the **Barbadori** family is typical of countless towers that created Florence's 12th-century skyline. Across the street is the ivy-covered tower of the **Belfredelli,** another noble family. These medieval towers are a relic of feudal times, before the relative stability, law, and order that comes with a strong central government. To keep themselves safe, the nobility needed to fortify their mansions. At the corner of the Barbadori tower, look up and notice the high-water mark from the 1966 flood.

Step out to Hotel Lungarno's little riverside **viewpoint** for a good photo op and look at Ponte Vecchio. Envision a centuries-ago city turned inward, facing its main commercial artery, the river. Imagine it in the Middle Ages with no embankment, just muddy shores—back when fish and eels were the main source of protein for the poor and only the nobility could afford red meat. Barges of goods from Pisa moored here (loaded with cargo, including marble for artists such as Michelangelo). Today's strict building codes leave the view essentially the same as you see in engravings from 1700.

• *Continue down* ❸ *Borgo San Jacopo a half-block to the intersection (on the left) with the tiny street called Via Toscanella. On the corner, look up to find a little modern statue of a woman holding her nose—a dumpster is often left here. This is just one of countless bits of fun street art in the Oltrarno. Turn left into Via Toscanella, following the lane away from the river...and deeper into the Oltrarno.*

## ❹ Via Toscanella

You're on a quiet and characteristic lane typical of the Oltrarno. A high stone wall hides a private garden (common in this city). For a glimpse of the clothing styles of today's locals, look up at their laundry.

The little square ahead is Piazza della Passera. Also known as Canto ai Quattro Leoni, the piazza was officially renamed "Passera" (sparrow) in 2005. The legend goes that in 1348, the inhabitants of this neighborhood tried to help a sick little bird, which then brought the plague to the city. Some Florentines opt for a more titillating interpretation— the area around the square was occupied by brothels, and the word *passera* is slang for female genitalia.

The recommended **Trattoria 4 Leoni** dominates the square, and the classic little **Caffè degli Artigiani** (good for a light meal or drink) is a reminder of the earthy pride of this once rustic district, now gaining affluence as it becomes trendier. Demographically, the Oltrarno is an interesting melting pot of traditional craftspeople, immigrants, retired people, and artsy, alternative types.

This is a good time to pause and consider the impact of Airbnb-type rentals on traditional neighborhoods like this. You're surrounded by cheap little apartments rented to happy travelers. With landlords now able to make more money with short-term rentals, higher rents are driving locals from characteristic old centers like this and into the suburbs. The residents who once kept small everyday shops in business are gone; those shops are being replaced by cafés, restaurants, and gifty boutiques catering to tourists. On the corner, what had been my favorite little old-time grocery store is now just another bar selling cocktails to affluent people who don't live here.

Thankfully, for now, many of the artisans who are so integral to the charm of the Oltrarno are surviving. Continue down

Via Toscanella. You'll pass artisan shops on this and neighboring streets. Their doors are open to welcome browsers. Be comfortable stepping in and enjoying the proud work of the artisan. It's polite to say *"Buon giorno"* (in the morning and early afternoon) or *"Buona sera"* (in the late afternoon and evening). "Can I take a look?" is *"Posso guardare?"* (POH-soh gwahr-DAH-ray).

Long a working-class neighborhood, the Oltrarno is where artisans still ply the traditional trades of their forebears. You'll find handmade furniture, jewelry, leather items, shoes, pottery, and picture frames in a centuries-old style. Craftsmen bind books and make marbled paper. Antique pieces are refurbished by people

**OLTRARNO**

who've become curators of the rarefied techniques of gilding, engraving, etching, enameling, mosaics, and repoussé metal work. It was in artisan workshops like these that boys like Leonardo, Michelangelo, and little Sandy Botticelli apprenticed. (We'll hit a great artisan street—Via di Santo Spirito—later.)

• *We'll go shopping shortly. But first, continue to the end of Via Toscanella and turn left to see the stony facade of a huge palace.*

## ❺ View of Pitti Palace

The massive palace, with its rusticated stonework so pleasing to noble egos, sits conveniently in front of the quarry from where all

that stone was cut. (And what had been that quarry is now the delightful Boboli Gardens.) This behemoth facade shows the Renaissance aesthetics of symmetry and mathematical order on a giant scale.

Originally built for the Pitti family (15th century), the palace was later bought and enlarged by the Medici (16th century). In the 1860s, when Florence briefly ruled Italy as the interim capital, the palace was the "White House" for the ruling Savoy family. While stark on the outside, it is much warmer (and Baroque) on the inside, and its bulk hides the lush Boboli Gardens. It's been a museum since the early 1900s (for details on visiting, 📖 see the Pitti Palace Tour chapter).

• *Turn 180 degrees. With your back to the Pitti Palace, double back down the street called Sdrucciolo de' Pitti (enjoy wrapping your tongue around that "sdr"). Now let's do a little shopping.*

## ❻ Shops along Sdrucciolo de' Pitti

As you head down this lane, enjoy a cluster of fine little shops. **La Casa della Stampa** (at #11 red) is a cramped print shop cluttered with tattered antique papers, prints, and maps. Much of their inventory consists of colorful modern designs hand-painted on historic old printed pages. **Giulia Materia** (#13 red) is a hipster boutique with bright and creative clothes, cloth bags, and blank books. **Le Telerie Toscane** (#15 red) offers placemats, towels, table runners, and tablecloths with Tuscan designs. The jewelry and handbags at **Monnaluna** (#22 red) are inspired by Florence's Renaissance style. And **Tappezzeria Petrarchi** (#23 red) repairs and makes traditional cushions.

• *Continue west, toward busy Via Maggio—lined with more galleries, antique dealers, and palazzos. Crossing Via Maggio, walk straight for*

OLTRARNO

*another block. You'll pass a line of popular eateries before coming to a big church facing a square.*

## ❼ Piazza di Santo Spirito

Piazza di Santo Spirito, with its bald-faced church, is the community center, hosting a small but colorful produce and merchandise market in the morning. You can feel the friendly scene here. Later in the day, bohemians and winos move in to drink and strum guitars on the church steps.

Santo Spirito Church is worth a visit (see page 82) for its Brunelleschi-designed interior and crucifix by Michelangelo. As a teenager, Michelangelo was allowed to dissect bodies from the adjacent monastic mortuary in order to learn the secrets of anatomy—something he considered key to portraying bodies accurately. As thanks, he made the crucifix for this church.

The church's blank facade prompted the neighborhood to have a contest to design a fun finish: Caffè Ricchi, nearby on the square, displays the hundred or so entries on its walls. Choose your favorite while enjoying a gelato or a drink.

• *From the far end of Piazza di Santo Spirito (opposite the church), turn right on Via Sant'Agostino. Stroll a few blocks to Via dei Serragli.*

*At the intersection, your eye might be drawn to the trendy gelato place on the left, but be sure to notice and appreciate the tiny **Christian tabernacle** to the right, on the corner. Take a close look, and imagine 500 years ago how its candles might have marked this intersection after dark. Then head right. We'll stroll down Via dei Serragli to the end and turn right on Via Santo Spirito to cap our Oltrarno walk with a little cultural scavenger hunt and shopping stroll.*

## ❽ Via dei Serragli

Notice, at #19, the big **Palazzo Dati Baldovinetti.** Remember, Florence has a quirky address system where red numbers indicate businesses and black (or sometimes blue) numbers are homes. This is #19 blue and it marks a big home. Step back to appreciate the 16th-century palace facade. Notice how street-level windows could let in the welcome breeze but not unwelcome thieves. Step up close and look at the doorbell. Now far from the home of one noble family, such former palaces today house many tenants and generally come with a bank of bells.

Notice the tiny arched opening in the wall just to the right.

This is a little wine window (or *buchette del vino*). Noble families with a city palazzo would also have a country estate where they grew grapes and made wine. They used these wine windows to sell their product to thirsty locals, who would pass in a few coins and empty jugs to have them refilled. These are all over town.

Ahead on the left is **Duccio Banchi Bronzista** (#10 red) where a father-and-son team produces bronze and brass frames, door knockers, and other decorative items.

And if the door at #8 is open, peek into the elegant hidden **courtyard**—typical of Renaissance palaces throughout town. By the way, I can count three little wine windows between here and the next corner.

• *At Via di Santo Spirito (just a block in from the river), turn right.*

## ❾ Via di Santo Spirito and More Oltrarno Shopping

This is the traditional heart of artisan Oltrarno and is still home to a variety of workshops, small boutiques, and antique dealers. We'll stroll this until the next bridge. (Along the way, look for Clet art—street signs that have been slyly modified by the local street artist Clet Abraham. He has a small shop nearby, in the San Niccolò neighborhood; see page 322.)

Strolling down Via di Santo Spirito, along with furniture, antique, and clothing shops, you'll pass many old palazzos once owned by wealthy Florentine families such as the Machiavellis (#5, Niccolò himself is said to have lived here for a time) and the wine-making Frescobaldis (#11, they still reside here). Today, the ground floors of those buildings are filled with fine local shops, with some active artisans mixed in.

Be sure to peek into **Francesco da Firenze** (#62 red), the shop of an old-school shoemaker. Pick a style and a color you like, and they'll custom-make a surprisingly affordable pair of shoes for you.

In the next block (#58), **Angela Caputi,** designer of bold, chunky jewelry, has her flagship store.

Nearby, the art and antique restoration workshop **Ponziani** has been around since the late 1800s. It surrounds an old Renaissance palace courtyard down a hallway at #27. And at #29 you'll see a little wine door that actually works. Open it and see the string for ringing the bell when you want to buy a glass.

At **Castorina** (#15 red) a remarkable group of woodworkers carve delicate curlicue frames, mirrors, and other decorative objects, many of them gilded in Florentine style.

The florist and housewares shop **Fiorile** (#26 red) may just inspire you to pick up a bouquet for your hotel room. The cluttered, hole-in-the-wall **La Bottega di Mastro Geppetto** (#16 red) has Pinocchio-themed window displays up front, but a handmade wooden frame store in back. And **L'Ippogrifo** (at #5 red) offers Florentine-motif prints and an opportunity to see age-old copper-plate etching in action.

• *When you reach Via Maggio (30 yards beyond L'Ippogrifo), pause and appreciate the delightful little 16th-century fountain. It's a cute land-mark now. But 400 years ago it was the life-giving source of drinking water for this neighborhood. The medallion above reminded all that the water was thanks to the ruling Medici family. Now head left past a high school and a popular gelateria and onto the bridge.*

## ⓾ Ponte Santa Trinità

From this bridge, enjoy a great view of the cityscape flanking the Arno River and the venerable Ponte Vecchio, where this walk began. If the medley of shops on Via di Santo Spirito stoked your consumerism, then continue across the bridge to one of the most elegant shopping streets in Florence, Via de' Tornabuoni—where you'll find not a hint of the Oltrarno.

# BRANCACCI CHAPEL TOUR

*Capella Brancacci*

In the Brancacci (bran-KAH-chee) Chapel (rated ▲▲), Masaccio created a world in paint that looked like the world we inhabit. For the first time in a thousand years, Man and Nature were frozen for inspection. Masaccio's painting techniques were copied by many Renaissance artists, and his people—sturdy, intelligent, and dignified, with expressions of understated astonishment—helped shape Renaissance men and women's own self-images.

## Orientation

**Cost:** €10

**Hours:** Fri-Sat and Mon 10:00-17:00, Sun from 13:00, closed Tue-Thu.

**Information:** +39 055 284 361, www.musefirenze.it.

**Restoration:** The chapel may be undergoing restoration when you visit; if that's ongoing you may be able to climb the scaffolding and see the frescoes up close.

**Reservations Recommended:** Consider a reservation mandatory. Reservation times begin every 20 minutes, with a maximum of 30 visitors per time slot. But when it's not too busy, they generally let people stay longer.

    To reserve in advance, call or email the chapel (+39 055 276 8224 or +39 055 276 8558, English spoken, call center open Mon-Sat 9:30-13:00 & 14:00-17:00, Sun 9:30-12:30; cappellabrancacci@musefirenze.it).

**Dress Code:** Modest dress (covered shoulders and knees—a scarf will do) is requested when visiting the church and chapel (if it's very hot, they might be lenient—but better not to chance it).

**Getting There:** The Brancacci Chapel is in the Church of Santa Maria del Carmine, on Piazza del Carmine, in the Oltrarno neighborhood south of the Arno River. It's about a 10-minute walk from Ponte Vecchio.

**Getting In:** The chapel entrance is to the right of the church doors.

**Film:** Your ticket may include a 20-minute film (English subtitles) on the chapel, the frescoes, and Renaissance Florence (find it in the room next to the bookstore). The film takes liberties with the art, but it's visually interesting and the best way to see the frescoes up close.

**Tours:** A good videoguide describes the frescoes (€3, leave ID as deposit).

**Length of This Tour:** Allow 30 minutes (plus 30 minutes if you see the film or rent the videoguide).

**Starring:** Masaccio, Masolino, and Filippino Lippi.

## OVERVIEW

In 1424, Masolino da Panicale (1383-1435) was hired by the Brancacci family to decorate this chapel with the story of Peter (beginning with the Original Sin that Peter's "Good News" saves man from). Masolino, a 40-year-old contractor with too many other commitments, invited 23-year-old Masaccio (1401-1428) to help him. The two set up scaffolding and worked side by side—the older, workmanlike master and the younger, intuitive genius—in a harmonious collaboration. They divvied up the panels, never (or rarely) working together on the same scene.

Half of the chapel's frescoes are by Masaccio, and half by either Masolino or Filippino Lippi (the son of Filippo Lippi), who completed the chapel more than 50 years later. The panels are displayed roughly in the order they were painted, from upper left to lower right—the upper six by Masaccio and Masolino (1424-1425), the lower ones by Masaccio (1426-1427) and Lippi (1481-1485). Although Masaccio is the star (his works are sprinkled among the others, mostly on the left and center walls), the panels by his colleagues are interesting and provide a good contrast in styles.

It's best to read this chapter before you enter, because if the chapel is busy, you'll have only 20 minutes inside.

# The Tour Begins

· *Start with the left wall, the small panel in the upper left.*

### ❶ Masaccio, *Adam and Eve Banished from Eden*

Renaissance man and woman—as nude as they can be—turn their backs on the skinny, unrealistic, medieval Gate of Paradise and take their first step as mortal humans in the real world. For the first time in a thousand years of painting, these figures cast a realistic

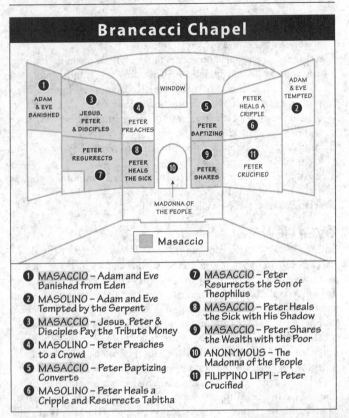

## Brancacci Chapel

WINDOW

1 ADAM & EVE BANISHED

3 JESUS, PETER & DISCIPLES

4 PETER PREACHES

5 PETER BAPTIZING

2 ADAM & EVE TEMPTED

PETER HEALS A CRIPPLE

6

7 PETER RESURRECTS

8 PETER HEALS THE SICK

10 MADONNA OF THE PEOPLE

9 PETER SHARES

11 PETER CRUCIFIED

☐ Masaccio

1 MASACCIO – Adam and Eve Banished from Eden
2 MASOLINO – Adam and Eve Tempted by the Serpent
3 MASACCIO – Jesus, Peter & Disciples Pay the Tribute Money
4 MASOLINO – Peter Preaches to a Crowd
5 MASACCIO – Peter Baptizing Converts
6 MASOLINO – Peter Heals a Cripple and Resurrects Tabitha
7 MASACCIO – Peter Resurrects the Son of Theophilus
8 MASACCIO – Peter Heals the Sick with His Shadow
9 MASACCIO – Peter Shares the Wealth with the Poor
10 ANONYMOUS – The Madonna of the People
11 FILIPPINO LIPPI – Peter Crucified

shadow, seemingly lit by the same light we are—the natural light through the Brancacci Chapel's window.

Eve wails from deep within. (The first time I saw her, I thought Eve's gaping mouth was way over the top, until I later saw the very same expression on someone dealing with a brother's death.) Adam buries his face in shame. These simple human gestures speak louder than the heavy-handed religious symbols of medieval art.

• Compare Masaccio's Adam and Eve *with the one on the opposite wall, by his colleague Masolino.*

### 2 Masolino, *Adam and Eve Tempted by the Serpent*

Masolino's elegant, innocent First Couple float in an ethereal Garden of Eden with no clear foreground or background (Eve hugs a tree or she'd float away). Their bodies are lit evenly by a pristine,

all-encompassing, morning-in-spring-time light that casts no shadows. Satan and Eve share the same face—a motif later Renaissance artists would copy.

• *Return to the left wall, upper level. From here, we'll work clockwise around the chapel. After* Adam and Eve, *the second panel is...*

### ❸ Masaccio, *Jesus, Peter, and the Disciples Pay the Tribute Money*

The tax collector (in red miniskirt, with his back to us) tells Jesus that he must pay a temple tax. Jesus gestures to say, "OK, but the money's over there." Peter, his right-hand man (gray hair and beard, brown robe), says, "Yeah, over there." Peter goes over there to the lake (left side of panel), takes off his robe, stoops down at an odd angle, and miraculously pulls a coin from the mouth of a fish. He puts his robe back on (right side of panel) and pays the man.

Some consider this (which dates from the 1420s) the first modern painting, placing real humans in a real setting, seen from a single viewpoint—ours. Earlier painters had done far more detailed landscapes than Masaccio's sketchy mountains, lake, trees, clouds, and buildings, but they never fixed where the viewer was in relation to these things.

Masaccio tells us exactly where we stand—near the crowd, farther from the trees, with the sun to our right casting late-afternoon shadows. We're no longer detached spectators, but an extension of the scene. Masaccio lets us stand in the presence of the human Jesus. While a good attempt at three-dimensionality, Masaccio's work is far from perfect. Later artists would perfect

mathematically what Masaccio eyeballed intuitively.

The disciples all have strong, broad-shouldered bodies, but each face is unique. Blond, curly-haired, clean-shaven John is as handsome as the head on a Roman coin (Masaccio had just returned from Rome). Thomas (far right, with a five-o'clock shadow) is intense. Their different reactions—with faces half in shadow, half in light—tell us that they're divided over paying the tax.

Masaccio's people have one thing in common—a faraway look

in the eye, as though hit with a spiritual two-by-four. They're deep in thought, reflective, and awestruck, aware they've just experienced something miraculous. But they're also dazzled, glazed over, and a bit disoriented, like tourists at the Brancacci Chapel.

• *Continuing clockwise, we move to the next panel on the center wall.*

## ❹ Masolino, *Peter Preaches to a Crowd*

Masolino and Masaccio were different in so many ways, but they were both fans of Giotto (c. 1266-1337), who told stories with

simple gestures and minimal acting, adding the human drama by showing the reaction of bystanders. Here, the miraculous power of the sermon is not evident in Peter (who just raises his hand) but in the faces of the crowd. The lady in the front row is riveted, while others close their eyes to meditate. The big nun (far right) is skeptical, but wants to hear more. The tonsured monk's mouth slips open in awe, while the gentleman to the left finds it interesting enough to come a little closer.

Masolino never mastered 3-D space like Masaccio. Peter's extreme profile is a cardboard cutout, his left leg stands too high to plant him realistically on flat ground, the people in the back have their gazes fixed somewhere above Peter, and the "Masacciesque" mountains in the background remain just that, background.

• *Continuing clockwise to the other side of the window, come to...*

## ❺ Masaccio, *Peter Baptizing Converts*

A muscular man kneels in the stream to join the cult of Jesus. On the bank (far right), another young man waits his turn, shiver-

ing in his jockstrap. Among the crowd, a just-baptized man wrestles with his robe, while the man in blue, his hair still dripping, buttons up.

The body language is eloquent: The strongman's humility, the shivering youth's uncertainty, and the bowed heads of the just-baptized communicate their reflection on the life-altering choice they've just made.

Masaccio builds these bodies with patches of color (an especially effective technique in fresco, where colors can bleed together). He knew that a kneeling man's body, when lit from the left (the direction of the chapel window), would look like a patchwork of bright hills (his pecs) and dark crevasses (his sternum). He assembles the pieces into a sculptural, 3-D figure, "modeled" by light and shade.

Again, Masaccio was the first artist to paint real humans—with 3-D bodies and individual faces, reflecting inner emotions—in a real-world setting.

• *Continue clockwise to the right wall.*

### ❻ Masolino, *Peter Heals a Cripple* (left side) and *Resurrects Tabitha* (right side)

Masolino takes a crack at the 3-D style of his young partner, setting two separate stories in a single Florentine square, defined by an arcade on the left and a porch on the right. Crude elements of the future Renaissance style abound: The receding buildings establish the viewer's point of reference; the rocks scattered through the square define 3-D space; there are secular details in the background (mother and child, laundry on a balcony, a monkey on a ledge); and the cripple (left) is shown at an odd angle (foreshortening). Masaccio may have helped on this panel.

But the stars of the work are the two sharply dressed gentlemen strolling across the square, who help to divide (and unite) the two stories of Peter. The patterned coat is a textbook example of the International Gothic style that was the rage in Florence—elegant, refined, graceful, with curvy lines creating a complex, pleasing pattern. The man walking is at a three-quarters angle, but Masolino shows the coat from the front to catch the full display. The picture is evenly lit, with only a hint of shadow, accentuating the colorful clothes and cheerful atmosphere.

In mid-project (1426), Masolino took another job in Hungary, leaving Masaccio to finish the lower half of the chapel. Masolino never again explored the Renaissance style, building a successful career with the eternal springtime of International Gothic.

• *Move to the lower level of the opposite side. Start on the left wall with the second panel and work clockwise.*

### ❼ Masaccio, *Peter Resurrects the Son of Theophilus*

Peter (in that same brown robe...like Masaccio, who was careless about his appearance) raises the boy from the world of bones, winning his freedom from stern Theophilus (seated in a niche to the left).

The courtyard setting is fully 3-D, Masaccio having recently learned a bit of the mathematics of perspective from his (older) friends Brunelleschi (with the long black hood) and Donatello. At the far right of the painting are three of the Quattrocento (1400s) giants who invented painting perspective (from right to left): Brunelleschi, who broke down reality mathematically;

Alberti, who popularized the math with his book, *On Painting;* and Masaccio himself (looking out at us), who opened everyone's eyes to the powerful psychological possibilities of perspective.

Little is known of Masaccio's short life. "Masaccio" is a nickname (often translated as "Sloppy Tom") describing his personality—stumbling through life with careless abandon, not worrying about money, clothes, or fame...a lovable doofus. Imagine the absent-minded professor, completely absorbed in his art.

Next to Masaccio's self-portrait is a painting within a painting of Peter on a throne. On a flat surface with a blank background, Masaccio has created a hovering hologram, a human more 3-D than even a statue made in medieval times.

"Wow," said Brother Philip, a 20-year-old Carmelite monk stationed here when Masaccio painted this. Fra Filippo ("Brother Philip") Lippi was inspired by these frescoes and went on to become a famous painter himself. At age 50, while painting in a convent, he fell in love with a young nun, and they eloped. Nine months later, "Little Philip" was born, and he too grew to be a famous painter—Filippino Lippi, who in 1481 was chosen to complete the Brancacci Chapel.

Filippino Lippi painted substantial portions of this fresco, including the group in the far left (five heads but only eight feet).

• *Moving clockwise to the center wall, you'll see...*

### ❽ Masaccio, *Peter Heals the Sick with His Shadow*

Peter is a powerful Donatello statue come to life, walking toward us along a Florentine street. Next to him, in the red cap, is bearded Donatello, Masaccio's friend and mentor.

Masaccio inspired more than painters. He gave ordinary people a new self-image of what it was to be human. Masaccio's people are individuals, not generic Greek gods, not always pretty (like the old bald guy) but still robust and handsome in their own way. They exude a seriousness that makes them very adult. Compare these street people with Masolino's two well-dressed dandies (above on the right), and you see the difference between Florence's working-class, urban, "democratic" spirit (Guelphs) and the courtly grace of Europe's landed gentry (Ghibellines).

• *The next panel, on the other side of the altar, is...*

### ❾ Masaccio, *Peter Shares the Wealth with the Poor*

Early Christians practiced a form of communal sharing. The wealthy Ananias lies about his contribution, and he drops dead at Peter's feet. Peter takes the missing share and gives it to a poor lady

who can't even afford baby pants. The shy baby, the grateful woman, and the admiring man on crutches show Masaccio's blue-collar sympathies.

The scene reflects an actual event in Florence—a tax-reform measure to make things equal for everyone. Florentines were championing a new form of government where, if we all contribute our fair share through taxes, we don't need kings and nobles.

• *The altar under the window holds an 11th-century icon that is not by Masaccio, Masolino, or Lippi.*

### ❿ Anonymous (possibly Coppo di Marcovaldo), *The Madonna of the People*

This medieval altarpiece replaces the now-destroyed fresco by Masaccio that was the centerpiece of the whole design—Peter's crucifixion.

With several panels still unfinished, Masaccio traveled to Rome to meet up with Masolino. Masaccio died there (possibly poisoned) in 1428, at age 27. After his death, the political and artistic climate changed, the chapel was left unfinished (the lower right wall), and some of his frescoes were scraped off whole (his *Crucifixion*

*of Peter*) or in part (in *Peter Resurrects the Son of Theophilus*, several exiled Brancaccis were erased from history, later to be replaced).

Finally, in 1481, new funding arrived and Filippino Lippi, the son of the monk-turned-painter, was hired to complete the blank panels and retouch some destroyed frescoes.

• *The right wall, lower section, contains two panels by Filippino Lippi. The first and biggest is…*

### ⓫ Filippino Lippi, *Peter Crucified*

Lippi completes the story of Peter with his upside-down crucifixion. Lippi tried to match the solemn style of Masaccio, but the compositions are busier, and his figures are less statuesque, more colorful and detailed.  Still, compared with Lippi's other, more hyperactive works found elsewhere, he's reined himself in admirably here to honor the great pioneer.

In fact, while Masaccio's perspective techniques were enormously influential and learned by every Tuscan artist, his sober style was not terribly popular. Another strain of Tuscan painting diverged from Masaccio. From Fra Filippo Lippi to Botticelli, Ghirlandaio, and Filippino Lippi, artists mixed in the bright colors, line patterns, and even lighting of International Gothic. But Masaccio was definitely a pioneer. His legacy remained strong, emerging in the grave, statuesque, harsh-shadow creations of two Florentine giants—Leonardo da Vinci and Michelangelo.

# PITTI PALACE TOUR

*Palazzo Pitti • Galleria Palatina*

The Pitti Palace, with its imposing exterior, offers one of the finest interiors in all of Europe with the second-best collection of paintings in Florence—as well as delightful gardens in a city where green space is particularly appreciated. While perhaps exhausting in an exhausting city, the Pitti Palace (rated ▲▲▲) is well worth the time and energy to experience.

First focus on the highlights of the Palatine Gallery, which has the painting collection, plus the sumptuous rooms of the Royal Apartments. The paintings pick up where the Uffizi leaves off, at the High Renaissance. Lovers of Raphael's Madonnas and Titian's portraits will find some of the world's best of each in the Pitti Palace.

While you're here, consider three other dimensions of the Pitti experience: the treasury, the costume and fashion museum, and the gardens.

## Orientation

**Cost:** The **Pitti Palace** ticket (the tour described here) costs €16 and covers the Palatine Gallery, Royal Apartments, Treasury of the Grand Dukes, Museum of Costume and Fashion, and Gallery of Modern Art. The **Boboli Gardens** ticket is €10 and admits you to the Boboli and Bardini Gardens as well as the Porcelain Museum (at the top of the Boboli Gardens). All sights are covered by the €38 Uffizi/Pitti/Boboli **"PassePartout"** combo-ticket (see later). Ticket prices are reduced off-season.

**Hours:** The **Pitti Palace** is open year-round Tue-Sun 8:15-18:50, closed Mon, last entry one hour before closing.

Hours for the **gardens** vary with the season: daily June-

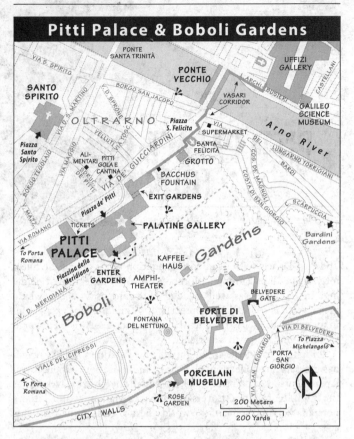

# Pitti Palace & Boboli Gardens

Aug 8:15-19:00, April-May and Sept-Oct until 18:30, Nov-March until 16:30; closed first and last Mon of each month, last entry one hour before closing.

**Information:** +39 055 238 8614, www.uffizi.it.

**Avoiding Lines:** Reservations are generally not necessary. But if there's a long line, get in the much shorter line for those with a reservation and buy a €3 reservation with your ticket (even if you'll ignore it).

**Uffizi/Pitti Palace/Boboli Gardens Combo-Ticket:** Valid for five consecutive days, this combo-ticket (called "PassePartout") offers a cost-saving skip-the-line admission to the Uffizi Gallery, Pitti Palace, and Boboli Gardens (€38 March-Oct, €18 Nov-Feb). Purchase in advance at www.b-ticket.com/b-Ticket/uffizi.

**Getting There:** The Pitti Palace is located several blocks southwest of Ponte Vecchio, in the Oltrarno neighborhood. Bus #C3 from the Santa Croce Church and bus #C4 from the train station stop right in front.

**Getting In:** The ticket office is at the far right of the massive facade. Once you have your ticket, enter through the main doorway in the center of the facade.

**Gardens Only:** To only see the gardens, there's a side entrance farther down Via Romano (see the map on page 80). The small ticket stand there has no lines (tickets for gardens only).

**Tours:** An €8 audioguide (€13/2 people) is available from the ticket office and covers the Palatine Gallery and the Gallery of Modern Art.

**Length of This Tour:** Allow one hour for the Palatine Gallery and Royal Apartments.

**Visitor Services:** WCs are in the basement corridor underneath the café and the Palatine Gallery/Royal Apartments staircase, next to the elevator. The bag check (cloakroom) is next to the elevator on the ground floor.

**Eating:** A basic café is in the palace courtyard. Several recommended Oltrarno restaurants are a few blocks away (see page 319). Across the piazza is the **$$ Pitti Gola e Cantina,** a cozy wine-by-the-glass *enoteca* that also serves a range of *antipasti* plates, homemade pastas, and other dishes (food served 12:00-23:00 but limited menu midday, closed Tue, Piazza Pitti 16, +39 055 212 704). For picnics, a tiny *alimentari* offers made-to-order sandwiches a half-block from the palace (Sdrucciolo de' Pitti 6). A drinking fountain is in front of the palace, at the base of the square, across the street from Banca Toscana.

**Starring:** Raphael, Titian, and the most ornate palace you can tour in Florence.

## The Tour Begins

The plain and brutal Pitti Palace facade is like other hide-your-wealth palace exteriors in Florence. The Pitti family (rivals of the Medici family) began building it in 1458 but ran out of money. It sat unfinished until the Medici bought it, expanded it, and moved in during the mid-1500s, choosing to keep the name. It's an imposing facade—more than two football fields long, made

of heavy blocks of unpolished stone, and set on a hill. For nearly

PITTI PALACE

two centuries (1549-1737), this palace was arguably Europe's cultural center, setting trends in the arts, sciences, and social mores.

• *Enter the palace through the central doorway and into the courtyard. From here, all of the sights are well marked: The Palatine Gallery entrance is to your right, the Boboli Gardens entrance is straight ahead, and the Treasury of the Grand Dukes is to the left. Climb several flights of stairs (or ride the elevator) to the Palatine Gallery (Galleria Palatina). The Museum of Costume and Fashion and the Gallery of Modern Art (skippable) are on the second floor.*

## PALATINE GALLERY

The collection is all on one floor. To see the highlights, walk straight down the spine through a dozen or so rooms. (Avoid the rooms that branch off to the side.) At the far end, make a U-turn left and double back. After the Palatine Gallery, the route flows naturally into the even-more-lavish rooms of the Royal Apartments.

You'll walk through one palatial room after another, with frescoed ceilings that celebrate the Medici family and give the rooms their names (the Venus Room, Apollo Room, and so on). The walls sag with floor-to-ceiling paintings in gilded frames, stacked three and four high, different artists and time periods all jumbled together. All along you'll notice secret doors and very wide walls, which hid a parallel world of servants (several hundred lived and worked here keeping the palace palatial). Use the information folders in each room to help find the featured paintings. Focus on my recommended highlights first, then let yourself browse.

Before actually entering the gallery (near the top of the stairs and elevator) check out the big white Sala Bianca (White Hall). This dates from Napoleonic times and is known for its fine stucco work. Imagine fine aristocratic balls here in the 19th century. Imagine also, in the 1960s, when this room hosted groundbreaking fashion shows—with models strutting in their Pucci-designed Lycra bodysuits and leggings.

### Rooms 1 and 2

• *Immediately to your right as you enter is the black...*

#### Bronze Bust of Cosimo I

Thank Cosimo I de' Medici (1519-1574, with beard and crown) for this palace. Cosimo I (not to be confused with Cosimo the Elder, the 15th-century founder of the Medici clan) was the first Grand Duke, and the man who revived the Medici family's dominance a generation after the death of Lorenzo the Magnificent. Cosimo I's wife, Eleonora, bought the palace from the Pittis and convinced him and their 11 children to move there from their home in the Palazzo Vecchio. They used their wealth to expand Pitti, building

# Pitti Palace—Palatine Gallery

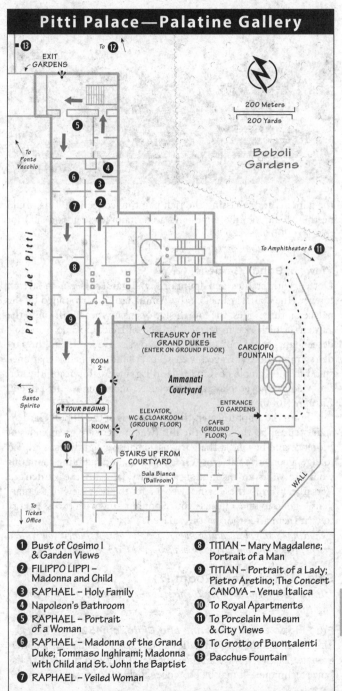

**200 Meters**
**200 Yards**

Boboli Gardens

To 12

13

EXIT GARDENS

To Ponte Vecchio

5

4

6

3

2

7

8

9

Piazza de' Pitti

To Santo Spirito

ROOM 2

1

TOUR BEGINS

ROOM 1

To 10

TREASURY OF THE GRAND DUKES (ENTER ON GROUND FLOOR)

Ammanati Courtyard

ELEVATOR, WC & CLOAKROOM (GROUND FLOOR)

STAIRS UP FROM COURTYARD

Sala Bianca (Ballroom)

CARCIOFO FOUNTAIN

ENTRANCE TO GARDENS

CAFE (GROUND FLOOR)

To Amphitheater & 11

WALL

To Ticket Office

---

① Bust of Cosimo I & Garden Views

② FILIPPO LIPPI – Madonna and Child

③ RAPHAEL – Holy Family

④ Napoleon's Bathroom

⑤ RAPHAEL – Portrait of a Woman

⑥ RAPHAEL – Madonna of the Grand Duke; Tommaso Inghirami; Madonna with Child and St. John the Baptist

⑦ RAPHAEL – Veiled Woman

⑧ TITIAN – Mary Magdalene; Portrait of a Man

⑨ TITIAN – Portrait of a Lady; Pietro Aretino; The Concert CANOVA – Venus Italica

⑩ To Royal Apartments

⑪ To Porcelain Museum & City Views

⑫ To Grotto of Buontalenti

⑬ Bacchus Fountain

**PITTI PALACE**

the gardens and amassing the rich painting collection. This would be the Medici family home (and a constant construction site) for the next 200 years.

• *Look out the windows to enjoy...*

## Views of Boboli Gardens

Dotted with statues and fountains, the gardens seem to stretch forever. The courtyard below (by Ammanati) is surrounded by the palace on three sides; the fourth side opens up theatrically onto the gardens, which rise in terraces up the hillside. Cosimo I and his descendants could look out their windows at eye level onto the garden's amphitheater, ringed with seats around an obelisk that once stood in the Temple of Ramses II in Egypt. At this amphitheater, the Medici enjoyed plays and spectacles, including the first opera, *Euridice* (1600).

From the amphitheater, the central axis of the Boboli Gardens stair-steps up to the top of the hill (where there are great views of Florence and beyond). The gardens' expansive sightlines, sculpted foliage, geometric patterns, Greek statues, and bubbling fountains would serve as an inspiration a century later for the gardens at Versailles. (From these windows you get the best view of the gardens—good to know in case you're not bursting with excess energy to visit them after touring the palace.)

• *Continue straight ahead through a handful of rooms until you reach a green-and-gold room virtually wallpapered with paintings.*

## Sala di Prometeo (Room 17)

• *Inside this room, look for the fireplace topped with a round-framed painting.*

### Fra Filippo Lippi, *Madonna and Child*, c. 1452

This pure, radiant Virgin cradles a playful Jesus as he eats a pomegranate. Lippi's work combines medieval piety with new Renaissance techniques. It may be Florence's first tondo (circular artwork),

PITTI PALACE

an innovative format that soon became a Renaissance staple. Seed-eating Jesus adds a human touch, but the pomegranate was also a medieval symbol for new life and the Resurrection. In medieval style, the background relates episodes from different places and times, including Mary's birth to Anne (in bed, at left) and the meeting of Mary's parents (distant background, right). But these stories are set

in rooms that are textbook Renaissance 3-D, with floor tiles and ceiling coffers that create the illusion of depth. The ladies bringing gifts to celebrate Mary's birth add another element of everyday Renaissance realism.

Compare Lippi's Madonna with two by Lippi's star pupil, **Botticelli** (one on the left wall, one on the right, both hung high). Botticelli borrowed much from Lippi, including the same facial features, pale skin, precise lines, and everyday details.

• *The next room is the...*

## Sala di Ulisse (Room 22)

This was the Grand Duke's bedroom. One of Cosimo I's favorite paintings hangs above the fireplace.

### Raphael, *Holy Family (Sacra Famiglia, a.k.a. Madonna dell'Impannata),* 1512-1514

This work introduces us to the range of this great artist. There's the creamy, rosy beauty of the Virgin alongside the gritty wrinkles of St. Anne/Elizabeth. At

first glance, it seems like a stately scene, until you notice that Jesus is getting tickled. Everyone is in motion—gazes pointed in all different directions— but they're also posed in a harmonious pyramid, with Jesus' crotch at the center. Little John the Baptist sticks a foot in our face and points to Jesus as The One. If Little John reminds you of a Leonardo painting, consider that Raphael lived and worked in Florence from 1504 to 1508, just a couple years after *Mona Lisa* was painted.

• *The next small room you pass by is known as...*

## Napoleon's Bathroom (Bagno di Napoleone)

The white-marble luxury and sarcophagus-shaped bathtub were intended for the great French conqueror, Napoleon Bonaparte, when he ruled Florence (1799-1814). Napoleon installed his little sister Ivanka as Grand Duchess, and she spent her years here redecorating the palace, awaiting her brother's return. But Napoleon was not destined to meet this water loo. After he was toppled from power, the palace returned to its previous owners.

Over the centuries, the palace hosted several rulers: 200 years of Medici (c. 1549-1737); 100 years of Austrians (the Habsburg-Lorraines, 1737-1860); 15 years of Napoleon (1799-1814); and 60 years under the Savoys, Italy's first royal family (1860-1919), who made Pitti their "White House" when Florence was briefly the capital of modern Italy.

• *Pass through the final rooms and exit out the far end into the stairwell (with some handy benches) and usually some open windows. Ahhh. Admire the views of the Duomo, the Palazzo Vecchio, and the green hills of Fiesole in the distance. The Medici could commute from here to downtown Florence by way of a private, covered passageway (Vasari Corridor) that goes from the Pitti Palace and across Ponte Vecchio to the Palazzo Vecchio. If you look down into the Boboli Gardens, you can see the melted-frosting entrance to the Buontalenti Grotto.*

*As you continue on through the second half of the collection, the first room you enter is the...*

## Sala dell' Iliade (Room 27)

This is the first of several former staterooms, used for grand public receptions. For centuries, Europe's nobles, ladies, and statesmen passed through these rooms as they visited the Medici. They wrote home with wonder about the ceiling frescoes and masterpiece-covered walls. The ceiling frescoes depict the Greek gods cavorting with Medici princes, developing the idea of rule by divine right—themes that decades later would influence the decoration of Versailles. Turn your attention to the painting by the entrance door.

### Raphael, *Portrait of a Woman (Ritratto di Donna, a.k.a. La Gravida)*, 1505-1506

This rather plain-looking woman has one hand on her stomach and a serious expression on her face. She's pregnant. Though she is no Madonna, and her eyes don't sparkle, the woman has presence. Raphael's sober realism cuts through the saccharine excesses of the surrounding paintings.

As one of Raphael's earliest portraits from his time in Florence, it shows the influence of Leonardo da Vinci. Like Mona Lisa, she's a human pyramid turned at a three-quarters angle, supporting her arm on an armrest that's almost at the level of the frame itself. It's as if she's sitting near the edge of an open window, looking out at us.

• *Enter the next room, straight ahead.*

## Sala di Saturno (Room 28)

This room boasts the second-biggest Raphael collection in the world—the Vatican beats it by one. A half-dozen Raphael paintings ring the room at eye level, ranging from dreamy, soft-focus Madonnas to down-to-earth, five-o'clock-shadow portraits.

• *Next to the door you just came through, find...*

### Raphael, *Madonna of the Grand Duke* *(Madonna del Granduca),* 1505

Raphael presents Mary in an unusually simple pose—standing, while she cradles Baby Jesus under his bum. With no background, the whole focus is on Mother, lost in thought, and Child, looking right at us. Mary's dreamy face and Jesus' golden body seem to emerge from the shadows. Try as you might, you can't quite discern the outlines of the figures, as they blend seamlessly into the dark background (Leonardo's sfumato technique).

The apparently simple pose is actually a skillful, geometric composition. Mary's head and flowing mantle form a triangle. The triangle's base is: first, the neckline of her dress, then her belt, then the horizontal line formed by her arm and Jesus' thighs. The geometric symmetry is enlivened by an off-kilter touch of reality: Mary's head tilts ever-so-slightly to the side.

This Madonna radiates tenderness and holiness, the divine embodied in human form. The iconic face, the pale colors, the simple pose, the geometric perfection—all are classic Raphael.

The famous self-portrait adjacent is Raphael in 1506 when he was just 23 years old and living here in Florence. This was before selfie sticks. Imagine the painter sitting in front of his easel looking into a mirror on his right.

• *Now survey a few more paintings, moving clockwise through the room. At the right end of the same wall as the* Madonna del Granduca *is...*

# Raphael (1483-1520)

Raphael (like most Renaissance greats, known by a single name) is considered the culmination of the High Renaissance. (Note that the museum uses his Italian name Raffaello, or Raffaello Sanzio.) He combined symmetry, grace, beauty, and emotion. With his debonair personality and lavish lifestyle, Raphael also epitomized the worldly spirit of the Renaissance.

Raphael lived a charmed life. Handsome and sophisticated, he quickly became a celebrity in the Medici family's high-living circle of bankers, princes, and popes. He painted masterpieces by day and partied by night. Both in his life and art, he exuded what his contemporaries called *sprezzatura*—an effortless, unpretentious elegance. In a different decade, he might have been thrown out of the Church as a great sinner, but his love affairs and devil-may-care personality were perfectly in keeping with the optimism of the times.

Raphael employed a wide range of styles and techniques, but there are some recurring elements. His paintings are bathed in an even light, with few shadows. His brushwork is smooth and blended, and colors are restrained. Works from the Florence years (1504-1508) show Leonardo's in-

## Raphael, *Portrait of Tommaso Inghirami,* c. 1510

Wearing his bright red Cardinal's suit, Tommaso was the friend and librarian of the Medici pope, Leo X. Raphael captures him during an unposed moment, as he pauses to think while writing. Without glossing over anything, Raphael shows us the man just as he was, complete with cleft chin, jowls, lazy eye, and all.

• *Immediately to the left of the door leading to the next room is...*

## Raphael, *Madonna with Child and St. John the Baptist (Madonna della Seggiola),* c. 1514-1516

This colorful, round painting (also known as the *Madonna of the Chair*) is one of Raphael's best-known and most-copied works. Mary hugs Baby Jesus, squeezing him along with little John the Baptist. This Mary is no distant Madonna; she wears a peasant's scarf and a colorful dress and looks directly out at us with a cheerful half-smile. The composition plays on the theme of circles and spheres. The whole

PITTI PALACE

fluence: Mona Lisa poses, sfumato brushwork (soft outlines), and lots of sweet Madonnas and Holy Families in a pyramid format. On the other hand, Raphael's portraits are never saccharine. The poses are natural, and individual quirks are never glossed over. He captures the personality without a hint of caricature.

In his later years, Raphael experimented with more complex compositions and stronger emotions. In group scenes, Raphael wants you to follow his subjects' gazes as they exchange glances or look off in different directions. This adds a sense of motion and psychological tension to otherwise well-balanced scenes. Raphael's compositions always have a strong geometric template. Figures are arranged into a pyramid or a circle. Human bodies are composed of oval faces, cylindrical arms, and arched shoulders. Subconsciously, this evokes the feeling that God's created world is geometrically perfect. But Raphael always lets a bit of messy reality spill over the lines so his scenes don't appear static. His work comes across as simple and unforced...*sprezzatura.*

When Raphael died in 1520, he was one of Europe's most celebrated painters (along with Michelangelo and Titian). His style went out of fashion with the twisted forms of Mannerism and the over-the-top drama of Baroque. The 1700s saw a revival, and today's museums are stuffed with sappy Madonnas by Raphael's many imitators. It's easy to dismiss his work and lump him in with his wannabes. Don't. This is the real deal.

canvas is patterned after round sculpture-relief tondi. Mary's halo is a circle, her scarf forms a half-circle, and her face is an oval. The pudgier-than-normal Bambino exaggerates the overall roundness of the scene. Mother and Child fit together like interlocking half-circles. As in a cameo, the figures seem to bulge out from the surface, suggesting roundness. Bathed in a golden glow, Mary enfolds her Child into the safe circle of motherly love.

• *Head into the next room. By the way, the next four rooms (each with a celestial theme) were designed to be seen coming from the opposite direction, as visitors progressed through the palace. Together these rooms weave a complicated and cohesive progression celebrating the half-divinity of the Medici princes.*

## Sala di Giove (Room 29)
Here in the throne room, the Grand Duke once saw visitors beneath a ceiling fresco showing Jupiter receiving legendary guests.
• *To the left of the door leading into the next room is...*

PITTI PALACE

### Raphael, *Veiled Woman (La Velata),* 1514-1515

The dark-haired beauty's dark eyes stare intently at the viewer. The elaborate folds of her shiny silk dress contrast with her creamy complexion. It's a study in varying shades of white and brown, bathed in a diffuse golden glow. A geometric perfection underlies this woman's soft, flesh-and-blood beauty: Her oval face, almond eyes, arch-shaped eyebrows, and circular necklace are all framed by a triangular veil. She is the very picture of perfection...except for that single wisp of loose hair that gives her the added charm of human imperfection.

Who is she? She may be the same woman Raphael depicted topless for a painting in Rome and as a Virgin (in Dresden). The biographer Vasari claims (and scholars debate) that La Velata is Raphael's beloved girlfriend Margherita Luti, known to history as La Fornarina, or the baker's daughter. Raphael became so obsessed with her that he had to have her near him to work. Vasari says that Raphael's sudden and premature death at age 37 came after a night of wild sex with her. Whoever La Velata is, she's one of the beauties of Western art.

• *Continue into the Mars Room (Sala di Marte, Room 30), which has paintings by Tintoretto, Rubens, Titian, and Van Dyke. Notice the ceiling: Here, the heroic Medici prince is spearing the bad guy. Look for the cupids holding the Medici balls (the coat-of-arms) in the center.*

*As you enter the next room, the Sala di Apollo, look up to see the prince surrounded by sexy muses, enjoying his education in classics. Two paintings by Titian flank the entrance door.*

## Sala di Apollo (Room 31)
### Titian, *Mary Magdalene (La Maddalena),* c. 1530-1535

According to medieval lore (but not the Bible), Mary Magdalene was a prostitute who repented when she heard the message of Jesus. Titian captures her right on the cusp between whore and saint. She's naked, though covered by her hair, which she pulls around her like a cloak as she gazes heavenward, lips parted. Her hair is a rainbow of red, gold, and brown, and her ample flesh radiates gold. The rippling locks (echoed by gathering clouds in the background) suggest the inner turmoil and spiritual awakening of this passionate soul.

Among the upper classes in Renaissance times, Mary Magdalene was a symbol of how sensual enjoyment (food, money, sex) could be a way of celebrating God's creation. The way this Mary Magdalene places her hand to her breast and gathers her hair around her is also the classic "Venus Pudica" pose of many ancient Greek statues. It's simultaneously a gesture of modesty and a way of drawing attention to her voluptuous nudity.

### Titian, *Portrait of a Man (Ritratto Virile)*, c. 1545

This unknown subject has so mesmerized viewers that his portrait has become known by various monikers, including *The Young Englishman*, *The Gray-Eyed Nobleman*, and *Hugh Jackman's Evil Twin*. The man is dressed in dark clothes and set against a dim background, so we only really see his face and hands, set off by a ruffled collar and sleeves. He nonchalantly places his hand on his hip while holding a glove, and stares out. The man is unforgettable, with a larger-than-life torso and those piercing blue-gray eyes that gaze right at us with extreme intensity. Scholars have speculated that the man could be a well-known lawyer...eternally cross-examining the museumgoers.

• *The next room, dedicated to Venus, has several more Titians. Notice this ceiling's theme, with the prince being pulled away from Venus' bed by Hercules. Sorry, it's time to grow up, get educated, learn war, and be a leader.*

## Sala di Venere (Room 32)

• *Survey the room in clockwise order. First up, turn around and face the door you just came through. Immediately to the right is...*

### Titian, *Portrait of a Lady (Ritratto di Donna, a.k.a. La Bella)*, c. 1536

Titian presents a beautiful *(bella)* woman in a beautiful dress to create a beautiful ensemble of colors: the aqua-and-brown dress, the gold necklace, pearl earrings, creamy complexion, auburn hair, and dark jewel-like eyes. She embodies the sensual, sophisticated, high-society world that Titian ran around in. The woman is likely Titian's Venus of Urbino, standing up and with her clothes on (see page 141). Scholars speculate on who she really was; perhaps she's Eleonora, the Duchess of Urbino, or the mistress of the previous Duke, or maybe she's just a paid model that Titian found to be...beautiful.

• *At the right end of the same wall is...*

### Titian, *Portrait of Pietro Aretino,* c. 1545

The most notorious and outrageous figure in Renaissance high society was the writer Pietro Aretino (1492-1556). In 1527, he fled Rome, having scandalized the city with a collection of erotic/pornographic sonnets known as the *Sixteen Ways* (or sex positions). He took refuge in luxury-loving Venice, where he befriended Titian, a fellow connoisseur of eroticism and the arts. Titian and Aretino were both commoners, but they moved easily in court circles: Titian the diplomat and Aretino the fiery satirist who tweaked the noses of arrogant princes. (In fact, Aretino was part of the Rat Pack of rowdy Medici that included the father of Cosimo I.)

This portrait captures the self-confidence that allowed Aretino to stand up to royalty. Titian portrays him with the bearded face of an ancient satyr (a lecherous, untamed crea-ture in Greek mythology). His torso is huge, like a smoldering volcano of irreverence that could erupt at any moment. Rather than the seamless brushstrokes and elaborate detail of Titian's earlier works, the figure of Aretino is composed of many rough strokes of gold and brown paint. Around age 60, Titian radically altered his style, adopting this "unfinished" look that the Impressionists would elaborate on centuries later. Aretino joked when he saw the portrait, "It breathes and moves as I do in the flesh. But perhaps [Titian] would have spent more time on my fine clothes— the robe, the silk, the gold chain—if I'd paid him more." Aretino gave the portrait to Cosimo I as a gift.

• *On the opposite wall, just over the small table, find...*

### Titian, *The Concert (Concerto),* 1510-1512

An organ-playing man leans back toward his fellow musician (a monk), who's put down his cello to tap him on the shoulder. A young dandy in fancy clothes and a feathered cap looks on. The meaning of the work is a puzzle, perhaps intentionally so. Titian may have collaborated on this early painting with his colleague

## Titian (c. 1490-1576)

Titian the Venetian (the museum uses his Italian name Tiziano or Tiziano Vecellio) captures the lusty spirit of his hometown. Titian was one of the most prolific painters ever, cranking out a painting a month for almost 80 years. He excelled in every subject: portraits of kings, racy nudes for bedrooms, creamy-faced Madonnas for churches, and pagan scenes from Greek mythology. He was cultured and witty, a fine musician and businessman—an all-around Renaissance kind of guy. Titian was famous and adored by high society, including Cosimo I and other Medici.

Titian's style changed over his long career. In his youth, he painted alongside Giorgione, even working on the same canvases (scholars still debate who did what). When he reached middle age, he found his voice: bright colors (particularly the famed "Titian red"), large-scale canvases, exuberant motion, and complex compositions, rebelling against the strict symmetry of the early Renaissance. In his 60s, his technique became more impressionistic. He applied the paint in rough, thick brushstrokes, even using his fingers. In these late works, his figures don't pop from the background; instead, they blend in, creating a moody atmosphere.

Throughout his life, his bread and butter were portraits of Europe's movers and shakers—kings, popes, countesses, mistresses, artists, and thinkers. Without ever making the people who sat for him more handsome or heroic than they were, he captured both their outer likeness and their inner essence. Their clothes and accessories tell us about their social circle, so collectively, his portraits are a chronicle of the Renaissance in all its sensual glory.

Giorgione, who specialized in enigmatic works used by cultured hosts as conversation starters.

Maybe it's just a slice-of-life snapshot of Venetian musicians briefly united in their common task. Or maybe it's a philosophical metaphor, in which a middle-aged man, blithely engaged in the gay music of his youth, is interrupted by a glimpse at his future—the bass notes and receding hairline of old age.

• *In the middle of the Sala di Venere stands...*

### Canova, *Venus Italica (Venere)*, 1810

This pure white marble statue of Venus looks like the Uffizi Gallery's *Venus de' Medici* with a sheet. Like the Medici Venus, she's nude, modestly crossing her hands in front of her (the "Venus Pudica" pose), while turning her head to the side. But Canova's Venus clutches a garment, which only highlights her naked vulnerability.

In 1796, a young French general named Napoleon Bonaparte toured the Uffizi and fell in love with the *Venus de' Medici*. A few years later, when he conquered Italy, he carried Venus off with him to Paris. To replace it, the great Venetian sculptor Canova was asked to make a copy. He refused to make an exact replica, but he agreed to do his own interpretation, combining motifs from many ancient Venuses of the Pudica (modest) and Callipigia (ample derriere) styles. Canova's *Venus Italica* stood in the Uffizi until Napoleon was conquered and *Venus de' Medici* returned.

• *From here, the rooms of the Palatine Gallery lead into the...*

## ROYAL APARTMENTS

These 14 rooms (of which only a few are open at any one time) are where Florence's aristocrats lived in the 18th and 19th centuries. The decor reflects both Italian and French styles. In the 16th century, the two countries cross-pollinated when Catherine de' Medici (Lorenzo the Magnificent's great-granddaughter) married the king of France. Soon power shifted northward, which is why many of these rooms mimic the Versailles style, rather than vice versa. You'll see rooms of different themes and color schemes. Each room features the style of a particular time period. Ogle the velvety wallpaper, heavy curtains, white-and-gold stucco ceilings, chandeliers, and Louis XIV-style chairs, canopied beds, clocks, and candelabras. Gazing over it all are portraits of some of the people who lived in these rooms. (The many Medici portraits have that inbred cousin look: the long noses and jutting chins of the Habsburgs, and bulging eyes.) Here, you get a real feel for the splendor of the dukes' world.

The attic is still filled with boxes of palace supplies—sets of silverware and a huge inventory of 200-year-old candles (which still stock the chandeliers).

## THE REST OF THE PITTI PALACE

If you've got the energy and interest, it'd be a Pitti not to consider some of the palace's other offerings:

## Museum of Costume and Fashion

This collection is accessed from the second floor of the Palatine Gallery (and included in your ticket). It contains mostly temporary exhibits with almost nothing historic. But don't miss the darkened room that displays the clothes that Cosimo I and Eleonora of Toledo were buried in (retrieved from their tombs and preserved in the 20th century—a rare chance to see original 16th-century garments).

## Treasury of the Grand Dukes

This Medici treasure chest fills the ground and mezzanine floors in what were the summer apartments. The first room celebrates Lorenzo the Magnificent as the great patron of arts and sciences. The walls were painted in the 17th century with 3-D effects, creating an architectural fantasy.

Cases and cases feature treasures and exquisite curiosities that dazzled wonderstruck guests. You'll see jeweled crucifixes, exotic porcelain, rock-crystal goblets, gadgets made of amber, and etched crystal. Upstairs you'll find cameos, jewelry cleverly made from odd-shaped pearls, ostrich eggs, and a silver bidet.

## Boboli and Bardini Gardens

For those eager to escape the halls upon halls of fancy apartments, two adjoining gardens are located behind the palace. Enter the Boboli Gardens directly from the Pitti Palace's courtyard. The less-visited Bardini Gardens are higher up and farther out behind the Boboli, rising in terraces toward Piazzale Michelangelo. Both gardens are similar, providing a pleasant and shady  refuge from the city heat, with statues, fountains, and scenic vistas down tree-lined avenues.

You can also stroll up the steep terraces directly behind the palace. From the top, you're greeted by a panoramic view of the palace and Oltrarno churches (but only peekaboo views of the old town center, the Palazzo Vecchio, and Duomo). On your way up, you'll pass the **amphitheater** (ringed with statues). At the top, just beyond the hillcrest, is a pleasant **rose garden** with bucolic views of the rolling Tuscan hills (punctuated by cypress trees). The small building adjoining the rose garden houses the **Porcelain Museum**, with a modest and sparsely described collection of ducal dinnerware. From here, you can follow signs around to the **Belvedere Fortress**, with even higher and better views, and the Belvedere Gate, which leads to the Bardini Gardens.

A few fun little sights are in the low-lying area to the far left as you enter the Boboli Gardens. First, near the end of the palace, is the much-photographed **Bacchus Fountain** (Fontana di Bacco,

1560), starring Cosimo I's fat dwarf jester straddling a turtle—a fitting metaphor for this heavyweight palace.

Just beyond Bacchus is the **Grotto of Buontalenti,** an artificial cave crusted with fake stalactites and copies of Michelangelo's *Prisoners,* which once stood here (and are now in the Accademia). Playful figures—a hunter with his dog, goats, a monster—seem to morph into existence from the cottage cheese-like walls.

The grotto provided an erotic escape for people of the court. Peering through the gates, imagine how sensuous this must have been in the 16th century: the earthy fertility and sexiness of the grotto's sounds and musty smells; the suggestive poses of the statues creating a kind of marble foreplay; and princes slipping into this grotto with their women. Occasionally, at the top of the hour, the grotto gates are opened to allow tourists a few minutes to frolic among the statues.

# GALILEO SCIENCE MUSEUM TOUR

*Museo Galilei e Istituto di Storia della Scienza*

Enough art, already! Forget the Madonnas and Venuses for a while to ponder weird contraptions from the birth of modern science. The same spirit of discovery that fueled the artistic Renaissance helped free the sciences from medieval mumbo jumbo. This museum (rated ▲▲) offers a historical overview of technical innovations from roughly AD 1000 to 1900, featuring early telescopes, clocks, experiments, and Galileo's fingers in a jar.

English majors will enjoy expanding their knowledge. Art lovers can admire the sheer beauty of functional devices. Engineers will be in hog heaven among endless arrays of gadgets. Families with little kids looking for a hands-on experience may be disappointed, but students of all ages will be amused by my feeble attempts to explain technical concepts. And admission to the museum gives you access to one of the marvels of modern science: air-conditioning.

## Orientation

**Cost:** €10, €24 family ticket covers two adults and two kids ages 18 and under, tickets good all day.

**Hours:** Daily 9:30-18:00 except Tue until 13:00.

**Information:** +39 055 265 311, www.museogalileo.it.

**Getting There:** The museum is located one block east of the Uffizi on the north bank of the Arno River at Piazza dei Giudici 1.

**Tours:** There's a free self-guided tour in English on their Museo Galileo app. They offer a 1.5-hour English-language guided tour of the collection plus behind-the-scenes areas, which includes demonstrations of some of the devices (€65 flat fee for 2-14 people, cash only, doesn't include museum entry, book at least a week in advance, great for kids, +39 055 265 3174, gruppi@museogalileo.it).

**Length of This Tour:** Allow one hour or more (especially for those interested in science).

**Starring:** Galileo's telescopes, experiment models, and fingers.

# The Tour Begins

The collection is on the first and second floors. Excellent descriptions are posted throughout, and engaging video screens in many rooms illustrate the inventions and scientific principles.

Take advantage of the helpful English-speaking docents. They're available to answer questions about how these scientific gadgets work. In fact, the staff is happy that you're there to see this museum and not just lost on your way to the Uffizi.

• *Buy your ticket and head up the stairs to the first floor, Room I.*

## Room I: The Medici Collections

In this room, you immediately get a sense of the variety of devices in the collection: everything from a big wooden quadrant and maps to

optical illusions and old science books. These belonged to that trendsetting family, the Medici, who always seemed at the forefront of Europe's arts and sciences. In their day, objects like these were more like curiosities to show off to party guests (like an optical illusion painting), but the Medici also funded actual

research. Many of the objects we'll see measured the world around us—the height of distant mountains, the length of a man's arm, the movement of the sun and stars across the sky. In fact, one of the bold first steps in science was to observe nature and measure it. What scientists found was that nature—seemingly ever-changing and chaotic—actually behaves in an orderly way, following rather simple mathematical formulas.

## Room II: Astronomy and Time

This room has (triangle-shaped) quadrants and (round) astrolabes. In medieval times, sailors used these to help find their way at sea. They mapped the constellations as a starting point. Next they had to figure out where they stood in relation to those stars.

**Quadrants:** A *quad*-rant is one-*fourth* of a 360-degree circle, or 90 degrees. You'd grab this wedge-shaped object by its curved edge, point it away from you, and sight along the top edge toward,

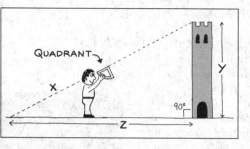

say, a distant tower or star. Then you'd read the scale etched along the curved edge to find how many degrees above the horizon the object was.

The quadrant *(quadrante)* measured the triangle formed by you, the horizon, and a distant object. Once you knew at least three of the triangle's six variables (three angles and three sides), you could calculate the others. (That's trigonometry.) Armed with this knowledge, you could use the quadrant to measure all kinds of things. On land, you could calculate how high or how far away a building was. At sea, you

could figure your position relative to the sun and stars.

**Astrolabes:** Astrolabes—invented by the ancient Greeks and pioneered by medieval Arab sailors—combined a quadrant with a

map of the sky (a star chart), allowing you to calculate your position against the stars without doing all the math. You'd hang the metal disk from your thumb and sight along the central crossbeam, locate a star, then read its altitude above the horizon on the measuring scale etched around the rim.

Next, you'd enter this information by turning a little handle on the astrolabe's face. This set the wheels-within-wheels into motion, and the constellations would spin across a backdrop of coordinates. You'd keep turning until the astrolabe mirrored the current heavens. With your known coordinates dialed in, the astrolabe calculated the unknowns, and you could read out your position along the rim.

In the center display case, find the celestial globe, the oldest object in the collection (AD 1085). Knowing the position of the stars and sun (using the astrolabe and celestial globe) also revealed the current time of day, which was especially useful for Arab traders (i.e., Muslims) in their daily prayers.

• *Continue to Room III, dominated by a big globe.*

## Room III: The Representation of the World

The big globe is an **armillary sphere,** a model of the universe as conceived by ancient Greeks and medieval Europeans. You'd turn a crank and watch the stars and planets orbit around the Earth in the center. This Earth-centered view of the universe—which matches our common-sense observations of the night sky—was codified by Ptolemy, a Greek-speaking Egyptian of the second century AD.

Ptolemy (silent P) summed up Aristotle's knowledge of the heavens and worked out the mathematics explaining their movements. His math was complex, especially when trying to explain the planets, which occasionally lag behind the stars in their paths across the night sky. (We now know it's because fast-orbiting Earth passes the outer planets in their longer, more time-consuming orbits around the sun.)

Ptolemy's system dominated Europe for 1,500 years. It worked most of the time and fit well with medieval Christianity's human-centered theology. But, finally, Nicolaus Copernicus (and Galileo) made the mental leap to a sun-centered system. This simplified the math, explained the movement of planets, and—most importantly—changed Earthlings' conception of themselves forever.

Thanks to Columbus' voyages, the Europeans' world suddenly got bigger and rounder. Increasingly, maps began to portray the spherical world on a flat surface.

• *Pass through **Room IV**, with more globes and a map from 1459. Notice that, by this time, Europe is pretty well mapped. But south is up, the Holy Land marks the center, and the Western Hemisphere is nowhere to be found. Now enter...*

## Room V: The Science of Navigation

This room has more quadrants and maps, plus a new navigational feature: clocks. By measuring time accurately, sailors could not only establish their latitude (north-south on the globe), but also their longitude (east-west).

In the 1700s, with overseas trade booming, there was a crying need for an accurate and durable clock to help in navigation. Sighting by the stars told you your latitude but was less certain on whether you were near Florence, Italy (latitude 44), or Portland, Maine (also latitude 44). You needed a way to time Earth's 24-

hour rotation, to know exactly where you were on that daily journey—that is, your longitude. Reward money was offered for a good clock that could be taken to sea, and scientists sprang into action.

The longitude problem was finally solved—and a £20,000 prize won—by John Harrison of England (1693-1776), who developed the "chronometer" (not in this museum), a spring-driven clock that was set in a suspension device to keep it horizontal. It was accurate within three seconds a day, far better than any clock displayed here.

• **Room VI** *(The Science of Warfare) displays not weapons but surveyors' tools, crucial for plotting the trajectory of, say, a cannonball. Next up is one of the museum's highlights.*

## Room VII: Galileo's New World

Galileo Galilei (1564-1642) is known as the father of modern science. His discoveries pioneered many scientific fields, and he was among the first to blend mathematics with hands-on observation of nature to find practical applications. Raised in Pisa, he achieved fame teaching at the University of Padua before working for the Grand Duke of Florence. The museum displays several of his possessions (lens, two telescopes, compass, and thermometer), models illustrating his early experiments, and his fingers, preserved in a jar.

• *Immediately to the right, look for the case containing...*

**Galileo's Telescopes:** Galileo was the first Earthling to see the moons of Jupiter. With a homemade telescope, he looked through the lens and saw three moons lined up next to Jupiter. This discovery also irked the Church, which insisted that all heavenly bodies orbited the Earth. You could see Jupiter's moons with your own eyes if you simply looked through the telescope, but few church scholars bothered to do so, content to believe what they'd read in ancient books.

Galileo built these telescopes based on reports he'd read from Holland. He was the first person to seriously study the heavens with telescopes. Though these only magnified the image about

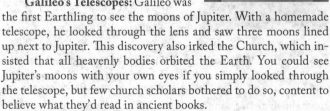

30 times ("30 power," which is less than today's binoculars), he saw Jupiter's four largest moons, Saturn's rings, the craters of the moon (which he named "seas"), and blemishes (sunspots) on the supposedly perfect sun.

• *In the same case is a...*

**Pendulum Clock Model:** Galileo's restless mind roamed to other subjects. It's said that during a church service in Pisa, Galileo looked up to see the cathedral's chandelier swaying slowly back and forth, like a pendulum. He noticed that a wide-but-fast arc took the same amount of time as a narrow-but-slow arc. "Hmmm. Maybe that regular pendulum motion could be used to time things..."

• *The last case on this wall contains a glass object called a...*

**Thermoscope:** Galileo also invented the thermometer (or thermoscope—similar to the museum's 19th-century replica), though his glass tube filled with air would later be replaced by thermometers filled with mercury.

• *Across the room is a giant model of an...*

**Inclined Plane:** The large wooden ramp figures in one of the most enduring of scientific legends. Legend has it that Galileo

dropped cannonballs from the Leaning Tower of Pisa to see whether heavier objects fall faster than lighter ones, as the ancient philosopher Aristotle (and most people) believed. In fact, Galileo probably didn't drop objects from the Leaning Tower, but likely rolled them down a wooden ramp like this reconstructed one. It slowed them down, making it easier to measure.

Rolling balls of different weights down the ramp, he timed them as they rang the bells posted along the way. (The bells are spaced increasingly far apart, but a ball—accelerating as it drops—will ring them at regular intervals.) What Galileo found is that—if you discount air resistance—all objects fall at the same rate, regardless of their weight. (It's the air resistance, not the weight, that makes a feather fall more slowly than a cannonball.)

He also found that falling objects accelerate at a regular rate (9.8 meters per second faster every second), summed up in a mathematical formula (distance is proportional to the time squared).

Galileo pioneered the art of experimentation. He built devices that could simulate nature on a small scale in a controlled laboratory setting, where natural forces could be duplicated and measured.
• *And last but not least, in the glass case perched on the column, look for...*

**Galileo's Finger:** Galileo is perhaps best known as a martyr for science. He popularized the belief (conceived by the Polish astronomer Nicolaus Copernicus in the early 1500s) that the Earth orbits around the sun. At the time, the Catholic Church (and most of Europe) preached an Earth-centered universe. At the age of 70, Galileo was hauled before the Inquisition in Rome and forced to kneel and publicly proclaim that the Earth did not move around the sun. As he walked away, legend has it, he whispered to his followers, "But it does move!"

A century after his death, Galileo's followers preserved his finger bone *(Dito Medio della Mano Destra di Galileo),* displayed on an alabaster pedestal, as a kind of sacred relic in this shrine to science. (This case also holds two other fingers and a tooth that were rediscovered a few years ago.) Galileo's beliefs eventually triumphed over the Inquisition, and, appropriately, we have his right middle finger raised upward for all those blind to science.
• ***Room VIII*** *has early glassware and thermometers. Continue on to the following rooms to see many of the experimental tools and techniques Galileo inspired.*

## Room IX: Exploring the Physical and Biological World

This room has both telescopes (for observing objects far away) and microscopes/magnifying glasses (to see the world up close).

A **telescope** is essentially an empty tube with a lens at the far end to gather light, and another lens at the near end to magnify the image. The farther apart the lenses, the greater the magnification, which is why telescopes have increased in size over time. The longest ever built was 160 feet, but the slightest movement would jiggle the image.

Galileo used a "refracting telescope," made with lenses that bend (refract) light. Later on, scientists started using "reflecting telescopes," which were often thick-barreled, with the eyepiece sticking out the side. These telescopes use mirrors (not lenses) to bounce light rays back and forth through several lenses, thereby increasing magnification without the long tubes and distortion of refractors.

• *Ascend to the second floor and enter…*

## Room X: The Lorraine Collections (Medical Science)

Look at the big table with all the drawers and jars in the glass case in the center of the room. Back when the same guy who cut your hair removed your appendix, medicine was crude. In the 1700s, there were no anesthetics beyond a bottle of wine, nor was there any knowledge of antiseptics. The best they could do was resort to the healing powers of herbs and plants. Consider what was thought to be therapeutic in the 1700s: cocaine, anise, poisonous plants like belladonna, tea, and ipecac.

The room also displays models detailing the varieties of complications that could arise during childbirth. Not a pretty sight, but crucial to finding ways to save lives.

## Room XI: The Spectacle of Science

This room is filled with odd-looking devices used by scientists to instruct and amaze. Chief among them, in the middle of the room, are the turn-the-crank machines dealing with electricity.

**Electromagnetism:** Lightning, magnets, and static cling mystified humans for millennia. Little did they know that these quite different phenomena are all generated by the same invisible force—electromagnetism.

In the 1700s, scientists began to study, harness, and play with electricity. As a popular party amusement, they devised big static electricity-generating machines. You turned a crank to spin a glass disk, which rubbed against silk cloth and generated static electricity. The electricity could then be stored in a glass Leyden jar (a jar coated with metal and filled with water). A metal rod sticking out of the top of the jar gave off a small charge when touched, enough to create a spark, shock a party guest, or tenderize a turkey (as Ben Franklin attempted one Thanksgiving). But such static generators could never produce enough electricity for practical use.

• *In the corner near where you entered, look for a...*
**Model for Demonstrating Newton's Mechanics:** Isaac Newton (1642-1727) explained all of the universe's motion ("mechanics")—from spinning planets to rolling rocks—in a few simple mathematical formulas.

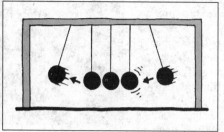

The museum's collision balls (the big wooden frame with hanging balls—labeled *Elastic and Inelastic Collisions Apparatus*), a popular desktop toy in the 1970s, demonstrate Newton's three famous laws.

1. Inertia: The balls just sit there unless something moves them, and once they're set in motion, they'll keep moving the same way until something stops them.
2. Force = Mass × Acceleration: The harder you strike the balls, the more they accelerate (change speeds). Strike with two balls to pack twice the punch.
3. For every action, there's an equal and opposite reaction: When one ball swings in and strikes the rest, the ball at the other end swings out, then returns and strikes back.

• *Room XII has more devices to teach the "new" physics (motion, gravity) of Newton. In the following room, there's another instructive model.*

## Room XIII: The Archimedes Screw Model
Back in third century BC Greece, Archimedes—the man who gave us the phrase "Eureka!" ("I've found it!")—invented a way to pump water that's still occasionally used today. It's a screw in a cylinder. Simply turn the handle and the screw spins, channeling the water up in a spiral path (as seen in the video in Room XII). Dutch windmills powered big Archimedes screws to push water over dikes, reclaiming land from the sea.

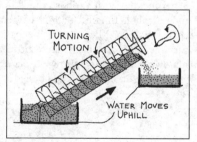

## Room XIV: Precision Instruments
This room shows the development of big reflecting **telescopes** and finer **microscopes**.

One day, a Dutchman picked something from his teeth, looked at it under his crude microscope, and discovered a mini universe, crawling with thousands of "very little animalcules, very prettily a-moving" (i.e., bacteria and protozoa). Antonie van Leeuwenhoek (1632-1723) popularized the microscope, finding that fleas have fleas, semen contains sperm, and one-celled creatures are our fellow animals.

Microscopes can be either simple or compound. A simple one is just a single convex lens—what we'd call a magnifying glass. A compound microscope contains two (or more) lenses in a tube, working like a telescope: One lens magnifies the object, and the eyepiece lens magnifies the magnified image. Van Leeuwenhoek opted for a simple microscope (not in this museum), since early compound ones often blurred and colored objects around the edges. His glass bead-size lens could make a flea look 275 times bigger.

## Room XV: Atmosphere and Light

Even nature's most changeable force—the weather—was analyzed by human reason, using thermometers and barometers.

**Thermometers:** You'll see many interesting thermometers—spiral ones, tall ones, and skinny ones on distinctive bases. All operate on the basic principle that heat expands things. So, liquid in a closed glass tube will expand and climb upward as the temperature rises.

Galileo's early thermoscope was not hermetically sealed, so it was too easily affected by changing air pressure. So scientists experimented with various liquids in a vacuum tube—first water, then alcohol. Finally, Gabriel Fahrenheit (1686-1736) tried mercury, the densest liquid, which expands evenly. He set his scale to the freezing point of a water/salt/ice mixture (zero degrees) and his own body temperature (96 degrees). With these parameters, water froze at 32 degrees and boiled at 212 degrees. Anders Celsius (1701-1744) used water as the standard, and called the freezing point 0 and the boiling point 100.

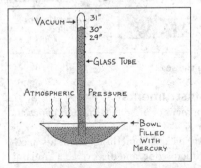

**Barometers:** To make a barometer, take a long, skinny glass tube (like the ones in the wood frames), fill it with liquid mercury, then turn it upside-down and put the open end into a bowlful of more mercury. The column of mercury does not drain out because the air in the room "pushes back," pressing down on the surface of the mercury in the bowl.

Changing air pressure signals a shift in the weather. Hot air expands, pressing down harder on the mercury's surface, thereby causing the mercury column to rise above 30 inches; this indicates the "pushing away" of clouds and points to good, dry weather. Low pressure lets the mercury drop, warning of rain. If you have a barometer at home, it probably has a round dial with a needle (or a digital readout), but it operates on a similar principle.

• *In the next room, you'll find (among magnets, generators, and small machines) a curious box-shaped object—an early battery.*

## Room XVI: Electricity

Alessandro Volta (1745-1827) built the first battery in Europe. (Although the museum does not have one of Volta's batteries, it does have a couple of similar devices made by Florence's own Leopoldo Nobili.) A battery generates electricity from a chemical reaction. Volta (and others) stacked metal disks of zinc and copper between disks of cardboard soaked with salt water. The zinc slowly

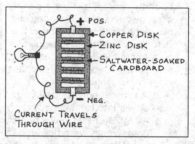

dissolves, releasing electrons into the liquid. Hook a wire to each end of the battery, and the current flows. When the zinc is gone, your battery is dead.

England's Michael Faraday (c. 1831) created the first true electric motor, which could generate electricity by moving a magnet through a coil of copper wire. Faraday shocked the world (and occasionally himself), and his invention soon led to the production of electricity on a large scale.

• *In the next room, find the chart on the wall.*

## Room XVII: Making Science Useful

**Chemistry:** Antoine Lavoisier (1743-1794) was the Galileo of chemistry, introducing sound methodology and transforming the mumbo jumbo of medieval alchemy into hard science. He created the precursor to our modern periodic table of the elements and used the standardized terminology of suffixes that describe the different forms a single element can take (sulfur, sulf-ide, sulf-ate, sulf-uric, etc.).

The large object with lenses nearby was used, I believe, by 18th-century dukes to burn bugs.

# Tick, Tock, Clocks

Pop into the museum's ground-floor **bookshop,** where some impressive clocks are on display.

In an ever-changing universe, what is constant enough to measure the passage of time? The sun and stars work for calendar time, but not for hours, minutes, or seconds. Sundials, or the steady flow of water or sand through an opening, were long used but these were approximate.

In medieval times, humans invented mechanical clocks that work similarly to the classic grandfather clock. The clock is powered by suspended weights that slowly "fall," producing enough energy to turn a series of cogwheels that methodically move the clock hands around the dial. The whole thing is regulated by a pendulum rocking back and forth, once a second. A clock has three essential components:

1. Power (falling weights).
2. An "escapement" (the cogs that transform the "falling" power into turning power).
3. A regulator that keeps gears turning evenly.

Later clocks were powered by a metal spring that slowly uncoiled (also used in most watches). The power was regulated by a pendulum—Galileo's contribution. Unfortunately, a rocking pendulum on a rocking ship wasn't going to work.

During the Age of Reason (1600s) and Age of Enlightenment (1700s), the clock was the perfect metaphor for the orderly workings of God's well-crafted universe. So, wondered the philosophers/scientists, would the universe eventually wind down like an old clock? In fact, in every energy exchange (as stated in the second law of thermodynamics), a certain amount of energy is transformed into nonrecyclable heat, meaning a perpetual motion machine is impossible. This principle of entropy (the trend toward dissipation of energy) has led philosophers to ponder the fate of the universe itself.

• *In the case to the left of this primitive bug zapper, look for the metal rod in a wooden box.*

**Standard Meter:** Much of the purpose of science is to use constants to measure an ever-changing universe. For centuries, one of these constants was the meter-long metal rod, established in 1790 as the fundamental unit by which all distances are measured.

The rod is exactly one meter. Or 39.37 inches. Or 1/1,000th of

the distance from the Galileo Science
Museum to *David*. Or 1/10,000,000th
of the distance from the equator to the
North Pole. Or, according to the updated definition from 1960, a meter
is the length of 1,650,763.73 wave-
lengths in a vacuum of the orange-red
radiation of krypton 86.

Ain't science wonderful?

• *On the way out, **Room XVIII** is filled
with novelty pieces—a barometer hidden
in a walking stick, a portable pharmacy
kit, and an early air-conditioner (ventila-
tor/fan). If the pocket watches catch your
fancy, there are more **clocks** downstairs (see the sidebar), as well as a
small kids' zone with interactive exhibits.*

# SLEEPING IN FLORENCE

Most of my recommended hotels are grouped in central Florence, to either side of the Arno River. Around the big sights you'll find tourist-friendly options. Across the Arno in the Oltrarno area— between the Pitti Palace and Ponte Vecchio—good budget alternatives dot an area with a neighborly vibe. If arriving by train, you can either walk (usually around 10-20 minutes) or take a taxi (roughly €7-10) to reach most of my recommended accommodations.

Outside the city, I list several rustic and serene hotels and *agriturismi*—rural farms offering accommodations in the Tuscan countryside south of Florence.

The accommodations listed here cluster around the €100-200 range, but include everything from €25 bunks to deluxe €400 doubles. Competition among hotels is stiff—when things slow down, fancy hotels drop their prices and become a much better value for travelers than the cheap, low-end places. For some travelers, short-term, Airbnb-type rentals can be a good alternative; search for places in my recommended hotel neighborhoods.

Book any accommodations well in advance, especially if you'll be traveling during peak season or if your trip coincides with a major holiday or festival (see "Holidays and Festivals" in the appendix). Note, though, that Florence can be busy any time of year.

I rank accommodations from **$** budget to **$$$$** splurge. For the best deal, contact my family-run places directly by phone or email. When you book direct, the owner avoids a steep commission and may be able to offer a discount. For more details on reservations, short-term rentals, and more, see the "Sleeping" section in the Practicalities chapter.

**Beware of Bugs:** Florence is notorious for its mosquitoes. If your hotel lacks air-conditioning, request a fan and don't open your windows, especially at night. Many hotels furnish a small plug-in bulb *(zanzariere)*—usually set in the ashtray—that helps keep the bloodsuckers at bay. If not, you can purchase one cheaply at any pharmacy.

## NEAR THE DUOMO

The following places are within a block of Florence's biggest church and main landmark. While touristy—and expensive—this location puts just about everything in town at your doorstep.

**$$$$ Palazzo Niccolini al Duomo,** one of five elite Historic Residence Hotels in Florence, is run by the Niccolini di Camugliano family. The lounge (where tea and pastries are offered every afternoon) is palatial, but the six rooms and seven suites, while splendid, vary in size and are only worth the splurge for an up-close Duomo view. If you have the money and want a Florentine palace to call home, this can be a good bet (RS%, family rooms, elevator, air-con, pay parking—reserve ahead, Via dei Servi 2, +39 055 282 412, www.niccolinidomepalace.com, info@niccolinidomepalace.com).

**$$$$ Hotel Duomo**'s 24 rooms are modern and comfortable enough, but you're paying for the location and the views—the Duomo looms like a monster outside the hotel's windows. If staying here, you might as well spring the extra €20 or so for a "classic" room with a view (RS%, air-con, historic elevator, Piazza del Duomo 1, fourth floor, +39 055 219 922, www.hotelduomofirenze.it, info@hotelduomofirenze.it, Paolo, Gilvaneide, and Federico).

**$$$ Soggiorno Battistero** rents seven simple yet pristine rooms, most with great views, overlooking the Baptistery and the Duomo square. Request a view or a quieter room in the back when you book, but keep in mind there's always some noise in the city center. It's a minimalist place with no public spaces or full-time reception, but the location is great (RS%—use code "Rick_Steves_Discount," air-con, elevator, Piazza San Giovanni 1, third floor, +39 055 295 143, www.soggiornobattistero.it, info@soggiornobattistero.it, Francesco).

**$$$ Residenza Giotto B&B** offers a well-priced chance to stay on Florence's upscale shopping drag, Via Roma. Occupying the top floor of a 19th-century building, this place has six bright rooms (three with Duomo views) and a terrace with knockout views of the Duomo's tower. Reception is generally open Mon-Sat 9:00-17:00 and Sun 9:00-13:00; let them know your arrival time in advance (RS%, air-con, elevator, Via Roma 6, +39 055 214 593, www.residenzagiotto.it, info@residenzagiotto.it).

**$$ La Residenza del Proconsolo B&B** has six older-feeling rooms a minute from the Duomo (three rooms have Duomo views). The place lacks public spaces, but the rooms are quite large and nice—perfect for eating breakfast, which is served in your room (extra cost for slightly larger "deluxe" with view, air-con, no elevator, Via del Proconsolo 18 black, +39 055 264 5657, www. proconsolo.com, info@proconsolo.com, Susie).

## NORTH OF THE DUOMO
### Near the Accademia

**$$$$ Hotel Morandi alla Crocetta,** a former convent, envelops you in a 16th-century cocoon. Located on a quiet street with 12 rooms, its period furnishings, squeaky clean parquet floors, and original frescoes (in the chapel bedroom) take you back a few centuries and up a few social classes. A few rooms come with lovely patios (family rooms, air-con, elevator, pay parking, a block off Piazza Santissima Annunziata at Via Laura 50, +39 055 234 4748, www. hotelmorandi.it, welcome@hotelmorandi.it, well-run by Rachele, Maurizio, Rolando, and Cristiano).

**$$$ Residenza dei Pucci** rents 13 pleasant rooms (each one different) spread over three floors (with no elevator). The appealing decor, a mix of traditional fabrics and aristocratic furniture, makes this place feel upscale for the price range (RS%—use code "RICK," family rooms, no breakfast or reception, air-con, Via dei Pucci 9, +39 350 074 7676, www.residenzadeipucci.com, info@ residenzadeipucci.com, Gaia and Pietro).

### North of Mercato Centrale

After dark, this neighborhood can feel a little deserted, but I've never heard of anyone running into harm here. It's a short walk from the train station and a stroll to all the sightseeing action. While workaday, it's practical, with plenty of good budget restaurants and markets nearby.

**$$$ Relais & Maison Grand Tour** has eight cozy, eclectic, and thoughtfully appointed rooms on a nondescript street between the train station and the Accademia. The spacious suites and one three-bedroom apartment come with a garden ambience. Friendly Ulrike, from Germany, takes good care of her guests (RS%, family suites; includes breakfast voucher for the corner bar, for "green" rate, ask to skip breakfast and cleanings; air-con, Via Santa Reparata 21, +39 055 399 5223, www.florencegrandtour.com, info@florencegrandtour.com).

**$$$ Galileo Hotel,** located on a busy street, is a comfortable, old-school business hotel with 31 rooms and dated bathrooms (RS%, family rooms, quadruple-paned windows shut out street noise, air-con, elevator, Via Nazionale 22a, +39 055 496 645, www.galileohotel.it, info@galileohotel.it).

**$$ Hotel Il Bargellino,** run by Bostonian Carmel and her Italian husband Pino, is a good-value place with an old-time convivial atmosphere. In a residential neighborhood within walking distance of the center, the 10 summery rooms are decorated with funky antiques and Pino's modern paintings. Guests enjoy relaxing and chatting on the big, breezy, momentum-slowing terrace adorned with plants and lemon shrubs (RS%, cheaper rooms with shared bath, no breakfast served but espresso machine available in rooms, some rooms have air-con, north of the train station at Via Guelfa 87, +39 055 238 2658, www.ilbargellino.com, carmel@ilbargellino.com).

**$ Casa Rabatti,** a great option for budget travelers, rents four simple and clean rooms (RS%, cheaper rooms with shared bath, family rooms, cash only but secure reservation with credit card, no breakfast, air-con, communal kitchen, 5 blocks from station at Via San Zanobi 48 black, +39 338 153 4159, www.casarabatti.it, info@casarabatti.it). Sergio also rents two modern **$$ apartments** with kitchenettes and access to a tranquil garden—ideal for longer stays.

## Near the Medici Chapels

This touristy zone has lots of budget and midrange hotels catering to an international clientele, stacks of basic trattorias, and easy access to major sights (just steps from the Medici Chapels, Basilica of San Lorenzo, and Mercato Centrale, and only a bit farther to the biggies). The mostly pedestrianized Via Faenza is the spine of this neighborhood, with lots of tourist services.

**$$$$ Hotel Centrale** is indeed central, just a short walk from the Duomo. The 35 spacious but overpriced rooms—with a tasteful mix of old and new decor—are over a businesslike conference center (air-con, elevator, Via dei Conti 3, check in at big front desk on ground floor, +39 055 215 761, www.hotelcentralefirenze.it, info@hotelcentralefirenze.it, Roberto).

**$$$$ Hotel Accademia** has 18 quiet rooms on a pedestrianized street in a convenient location. The modern, sizeable rooms cluster around a sunny courtyard (RS%, family rooms, air-con, no elevator, Via Faenza 7, +39 055 290 993, www.hotelaccademiafirenze.com, info@hotelaccademiafirenze.com, Tea and Francesca).

**$ Hotel Lorena,** just across from the Medici Chapels, has 19 simple, well-worn rooms (six with shared bathrooms) and a tiny

SLEEPING

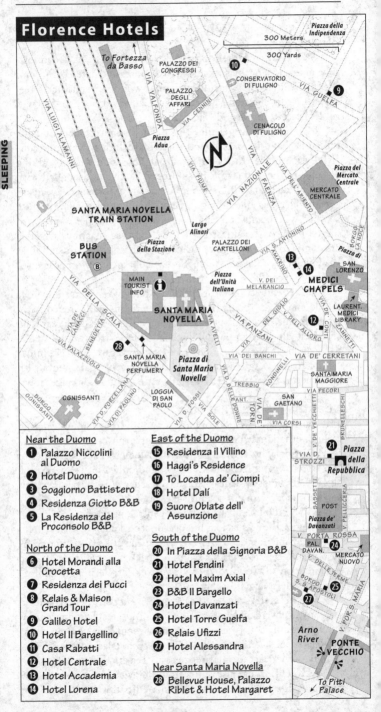

# Florence Hotels

300 Meters
300 Yards

### Near the Duomo
1. Palazzo Niccolini al Duomo
2. Hotel Duomo
3. Soggiorno Battistero
4. Residenza Giotto B&B
5. La Residenza del Proconsolo B&B

### North of the Duomo
6. Hotel Morandi alla Crocetta
7. Residenza dei Pucci
8. Relais & Maison Grand Tour
9. Galileo Hotel
10. Hotel Il Bargellino
11. Casa Rabatti
12. Hotel Centrale
13. Hotel Accademia
14. Hotel Lorena

### East of the Duomo
15. Residenza il Villino
16. Haggi's Residence
17. To Locanda de' Ciompi
18. Hotel Dalí
19. Suore Oblate dell' Assunzione

### South of the Duomo
20. In Piazza della Signoria B&B
21. Hotel Pendini
22. Hotel Maxim Axial
23. B&B Il Bargello
24. Hotel Davanzati
25. Hotel Torre Guelfa
26. Relais Ufizzi
27. Hotel Alessandra

### Near Santa Maria Novella
28. Bellevue House, Palazzo Riblet & Hotel Margaret

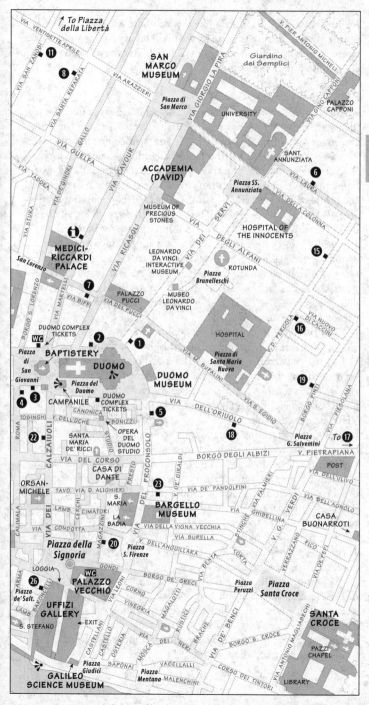

↑ To Piazza
della Libertà

**11**
**8**

SAN
MARCO
MUSEUM

Giardino
dei Semplici

V. PIER ANTONIO MICHELI

VIA VENTISETTE APRILE
VIA SAN ZANOBI
VIA SANTA REPARATA

VIA ARAZZIERI

VIA GIORGIO LA PIRA

VIA GINO CAPPONI

PALAZZO
CAPPONI

Piazza di
San Marco

UNIVERSITY

VIA GUELFA

VIA DEGLI NORI

VIA CAVOUR

VIA RICASOLI

ACCADEMIA
(DAVID)

SANT.
ANNUNZIATA

VIA DELLA COLONNA

VIA LAURA

**6**

VIA TADDEA

VIA STUFA

VIA GALLO

Piazza SS.
Annunziata

MUSEUM
OF PRECIOUS
STONES

VIA DEI
SERVI

HOSPITAL OF
THE INNOCENTS

**15**

San Lorenzo

**i**

MEDICI-
RICCARDI
PALACE

BORGO S. LORENZO

VIA MARTELLI

LEONARDO
DA VINCI
INTERACTIVE
MUSEUM

DEGLI ALFANI

ROTUNDA

Piazza
Brunelleschi

VIA NUOVO
DI CACCINI

**7**

VIA BIFFI

PALAZZO
DEL PUCCI

VIA DEL PUCCI

MUSEO
LEONARDO
DA VINCI

**16**

V. D. PERGOLA

DUOMO COMPLEX
TICKETS

**WC**

**2**

**1**

Piazza
di
San Giovanni

BAPTISTERY

DUOMO

Piazza del
Duomo

DUOMO
MUSEUM

HOSPITAL

Piazza di
Santa Maria
Nuova

VIA M. BUFALINI

VIA S. EGIDIO

BORGO PINTI

VIA FIESOLANA

**19**

**4**
**3**

CAMPANILE

DUOMO
COMPLEX
TICKETS

CANONICA

**5**

VIA DELL'ORIUOLO

TOSINGHI

V. DELL'OCHE

BONIZZI

**18**

ROMA

**22**

SANTA
MARIA
DE' RICCI

OPERA
DEL DUOMO
STUDIO

STUDIO

CALZAIUOLI

Piazza
G. Salvemini

To **17**

VIA DEL CORSO

CASA DEL
DANTE

VIA DE' PROCONSOLO

BORGO DEGLI ALBIZI

V. PIETRAPIANA

POST

VIA DELL'ULIVO

ORSAN-
MICHELE

TAVO. VIA D. ALIGHIERI

**23**

VIA DE' GIRALDI

VIA DE' PANDOLFINI

VIA DELL'AGNOLO

CASA
BUONARROTI

CALIMALA

VIA DEI

LAMB. CERCHI

CIMATORI

S. MARIA
LA BADIA

BARGELLO
MUSEUM

VIA STINCHE GHIBELLINA

VIA V. G. VERDI

VIA CONDOTTA

MAGAZZINI

VIA DELLA VIGNA VECCHIA

**20**

VIA BURELLA

VERRAZZANO

FICO

VIA DE' PEPI

Piazza della
Signoria

GONDI

Piazza
S. Firenze

VIA DELL'ANGUILLARA

VIA BENTA

TORTA

Piazza
Peruzzi

Piazza
Santa Croce

LOGGIA

**26**

**WC**

PALAZZO
VECCHIO

BARONCELLI

CORNO

BORGO DE' GRECI

MAGALOTTI

RUSTICI

VIA DE' BENCI

SANTA
CROCE

Piazza
de' Salt.

LAMB.

UFFIZI
GALLERY

VINEGRIA

VIA DEI NERI

BRACHE

BORGO S. CROCE

VIA ANTONIO MAGLIABECHI

S. STEFANO

← EXIT →

CASTELLANI

CASTELLO

OSTERIA

MOSCA

SAPONAI

Piazza
Giudici

VAGELLALLI

Piazza
Mentana

MALENCHINI

CORSO DEI TINTORI

PAZZI
CHAPEL

GALILEO
SCIENCE MUSEUM

LIBRARY

lobby. Though it feels a little like a youth hostel, it's well located, inexpensive, and run with care by the Galli family (air-con, elevator from first floor, Via Faenza 1, +39 055 282 785, www.hotellorena. com, info@hotellorena.com).

## EAST OF THE DUOMO

While convenient to the sights and offering a good value, these places are mostly along nondescript urban streets, lacking the grit, charm, or glitz of some of my other recommended neighborhoods.

$$$ **Residenza il Villino** has 10 charming rooms and a picturesque, peaceful little courtyard. As it's in a "little villa" (as the name implies) set back from the street, this is a quiet refuge from the bustle of Florence (RS%, family rooms, air-con, parking available, just north of Via degli Alfani at Via della Pergola 53, +39 055 200 1116, www.ilvillino.it, info@ilvillino.it, friendly Barbara).

$$$ **Haggi's Residence,** once a convent and today part of the owner's extensive home, is a classy B&B, with five chic, romantic, and spacious rooms, antique furnishings, and historic architectural touches (RS%, family room, air-con, closed Dec-Feb, Via della Pergola 42, +39 351 818 7488, www.pergola42.com, info@pergola42.com, suave Alex).

$$ **Locanda de' Ciompi,** overlooking the inviting Piazza dei Ciompi in a lively neighborhood, is just right for travelers who want to feel like a part of the town. Mira and Francesco have five attractive rooms that are tidy, lovingly maintained, and a good value (RS%, cheaper room with private bath across the hall, includes breakfast at nearby bar, air-con, 8 blocks behind the Duomo at Via Pietrapiana 28 black—see map on page 36, +39 055 263 8034, https://locandadeciompi.itmailto:, info@locandadeciompi.it).

$$ **Hotel Dalí** has 10 cheery, worn rooms in a nice location for a great price. Samanta and Marco, who run this guesthouse with a charming passion and idealism, are a delight to know (request one of the quiet and spacious rooms facing the courtyard when you book, cheaper rooms with shared bath available, nearby apartments sleep 2-6 people, no breakfast, fans but no air-con, elevator, free parking, 2 blocks behind the Duomo at Via dell'Oriuolo 17 on the second floor, +39 055 216 680, www.hoteldali.com, hoteldaliflorence@gmail.com).

$$ **Suore Oblate dell' Assunzione,** run by the Oblate Sisters of the Assumption, is an institutional 42-room hotel in a Renaissance building with a dreamy garden, great public spaces, appropriately simple rooms, and a quiet, prayerful ambience (family rooms, single beds only, air-con, elevator, Borgo Pinti 15, +39 055 234 6291, www.oblate.it, info@oblate.it).

## SOUTH OF THE DUOMO
### Between the Duomo and Piazza della Signoria

Buried in the narrow, characteristic lanes in the very heart of town, these are the most central of my accommodation recommendations (and therefore a little overpriced). While this location is worth the extra cost for many, nearly every hotel in this chapter can be considered central given Florence's walkable, essentially traffic-free core.

**$$$$ In Piazza della Signoria B&B,** in a stellar location overlooking Piazza della Signoria, is peaceful, refined, and homey. The service is friendly and efficient. The nine rooms are beautifully decorated; the priciest ones have genuine views of the square (from other rooms, views are peekaboo). Guests enjoy socializing at the big, shared breakfast table (RS%, 2 family apartments, air-con, tiny elevator, Via dei Magazzini 2, +39 055 239 9546, mobile +39 348 321 0565, www.inpiazzadellasignoria.com, info@inpiazzadellasignoria.com).

**$$$$ Hotel Pendini,** with three stars and 44 plush, flowery rooms, fills the top floor of a grand building overlooking Piazza della Repubblica. This place just feels classy; walking into the lobby is like stepping back in time. While pricey, this level of elegance makes it a good value for those looking to indulge (RS%, "deluxe" rooms come with square view and after-hours liveliness, family rooms, air-con, elevator, near the arch at Via Strozzi 2, +39 055 211 170, www.hotelpendini.it, info@hotelpendini.it).

**$$$ Hotel Maxim Axial,** well run by the Maoli family since 1981, has 39 straightforward rooms spread over three floors in a good location on the main pedestrian drag. Its painting-lined halls and cozy lounge have old Florentine charm. More expensive "comfort" and "deluxe" rooms are renovated and worth the splurge, but budget travelers can choose an "economy" room on the fourth floor—which is a walk-up from the third floor (RS%—use code "RICK," family rooms, reception on third floor, air-con, elevator, Via dei Calzaiuoli 11, +39 055 217 474, www.hotelmaximaxial.com, info@hotelmaximaxial.com, Chiara).

**$$ B&B Il Bargello** is a home away from home, run by friendly and helpful Canadian expat Gabriella. Hike up three long flights (no elevator) to reach six traditional rooms. Gabriella offers a cozy living room, a communal kitchenette, and an inviting rooftop terrace with close-up views of Florence's towers (RS%, fully equipped apartment across the hall sleeps up to six with one bathroom; air-con, 20 yards off Via Proconsolo at Via de' Pandolfini 33 black, +39 055 215 330, mobile +39 339 175 3110, www.firenze-bedandbreakfast.it, info@firenze-bedandbreakfast.it).

## Near Ponte Vecchio

This sleepy zone is handy to several sights and some fine shopping streets (from top-end boutiques to more characteristic hole-in-the-wall shops), though it's accordingly pricey and lacks a neighborhood feel of its own.

**$$$$ Hotel Davanzati,** bright and shiny with artistic touches, has 26 cheerful rooms with all the comforts. The place is a family affair, thoughtfully run by friendly Tommaso, Riccardo, and their father Fabrizio, who offer tea time, drinks, and snacks each evening at their intimate happy hour, plus lots of other extras (RS%, family rooms, free on-demand videos—including my travel shows about Italy—on your room TV, air-con, 20 steep steps to the elevator, handy room fridges, next to Piazza Davanzati at Via Porta Rossa 5—easy to miss so watch for low-profile sign above the door, +39 055 286 666, www.hoteldavanzati.it, info@hoteldavanzati.it).

**$$$$ Hotel Torre Guelfa** has grand public spaces and is topped by a fun medieval tower with a panoramic rooftop terrace (72 stairs take you up—and back 720 years). Its 31 pricey rooms vary wildly in size and furnishings, but most come with the noise of the city center. Room 315, with a private terrace, is worth reserving several months in advance (RS%, family rooms, air-con, elevator, a couple of blocks northwest of

Ponte Vecchio, Borgo SS. Apostoli 8, +39 055 239 6338, www.hoteltorreguelfa.com, info@hoteltorreguelfa.com, Niccolo).

**$$$$ Relais Uffizi** is a modern, upscale hotel offering 15 classy rooms tucked away down a tiny alley off Piazza della Signoria. The cocktail lounge has a huge window overlooking the action in the piazza—a unique view (family rooms, air-con, elevator; official address is Chiasso del Buco 16—from the square, go down tiny Chiasso de Baroncelli lane—right of the loggia—and after 50 yards turn right through the arch and look for entrance on your right; +39 055 267 6239, www.relaisuffizi.it, info@relaisuffizi.it).

**$$$ Hotel Alessandra** is a tranquil and sprawling place, occupying part of a 16th-century building with 30 big, old-school rooms with modern bathrooms and a tiny Arno-view terrace (family rooms, air-con, 30 steps to the elevator, Borgo SS. Apostoli 17, +39 055 283 438, www.hotelalessandra.com, info@hotelalessandra.com; Anna, son Andrea, and spunky Monti). Their annex across the street, **Residenza Alessandra,** is more contemporary and a good option for families or small groups (apartments sleep up to 4 people).

## NEAR SANTA MARIA NOVELLA

These fine, charming little budget options are around the corner from Santa Maria Novella, near the train station. The sweet-smelling Farmacia di Santa Maria Novella perfumery is just across the street.

**$$ Bellevue House** is a third-floor oasis of tranquility, with six spacious, old-fashioned rooms flanking a long, mellow-yellow lobby. It's a peaceful home away from home, thoughtfully run by the Michel family (RS%, family rooms, no breakfast, air-con, elevator, Via della Scala 21, +39 055 260 8932, www.bellevuehouse.it, info@bellevuehouse.it; Luciano, Susan, and Alessandro). On a lower floor, their other property, **$$ Palazzo Riblet,** offers three upscale rooms (one with a private terrace) with frescoes and elegant furnishings (+39 055 260 8932, www.palazzoriblet.it, info@palazzoriblet.it).

**$$ Hotel Margaret** offers seven tidy, simple rooms but no public lounge or breakfast (RS%, some cheaper rooms with shower but toilet down the hall, air-con, Via della Scala 25, +39 055 210 138, www.hotel-margaret.it, info@hotel-margaret.it; Francesco and Graziano).

## THE OLTRARNO

Across the river in the Oltrarno area, between the Pitti Palace and Ponte Vecchio, you'll find small, traditional crafts shops, neighborly piazzas, and family eateries. The following places are walkable from Ponte Vecchio.

**$$$$ Hotel Palazzo Guadagni,** perched high above Piazza Santo Spirito, is a romantic, Grand Tour retreat from modern Florence. The 15 refined rooms are spacious, with antique furnishings and frescoes. While the ample, chandeliered public spaces are pleasant, the highlight is the panoramic wrap-around loggia/terrace with comfy, stay-awhile seating and lovely views (family rooms, air-con, elevator, Piazza Santo Spirito 9, +39 055 265 8376, www.palazzoguadagni.com, info@palazzoguadagni.com).

**$$$$ Hotel la Scaletta** has 36 pricey, sleek rooms hiding in a convoluted floor plan. Their fabulous rooftop terrace overlooks the Boboli Gardens and is a nice place for a drink (RS% when you pay with cash, family rooms, breakfast extra, air-con, elevator, Via de' Guicciardini 13, +39 055 283 028, www.hotellascaletta.it, info@hotellascaletta.it, Sara).

**$$$ Hotel Silla** is a classic three-star hotel with 36 cheery rooms. Rooms with river views are modern and sleek, while rooms along the back are more spacious and classic. The breezy terrace faces the Arno River, overlooking a small park near the San Niccolò neighborhood. There's free coffee and tea for guests in the late afternoon. The surroundings can be a bit noisy (RS%—use promo

SLEEPING

# Oltrarno Hotels & Restaurants

**Accommodations**
1. Hotel Palazzo Guadagni
2. Hotel la Scaletta
3. Casa Santo Nome di Gesù
4. Soggiorno Alessandra
5. Foresteria Valdese di Firenze
6. Ostello Santa Monaca

**Eateries**
7. Signorvino
8. Golden View Firenze & La Forneria Firenze Wine Bar/Bakery
9. Osteria Ponte Vecchio
10. Tamerò
11. Trattoria Casalinga
12. Gusta Osteria

code "RICK," air-con, elevator, self-service washing machine, Via dei Renai 5, for location see map on page 80, +39 055 234 2888, www.hotelsilla.it, hotelsilla@hotelsilla.it; Laura, Chiara, Massimo, Ravin, Stefano, and Salvo).

**$$ Hotel Annalena,** on the third floor of a faded palazzo, is a bit tatty with small bathrooms, but it's in a quiet location near the Pitti Palace. Many of its 19 tidy rooms (some with terraces) overlook a private park next door (family rooms, bar/lounge, air-con, no elevator, laundry service, opposite the side entrance to the Boboli Gardens at Via Romana 34, for location see map on page 80, +39

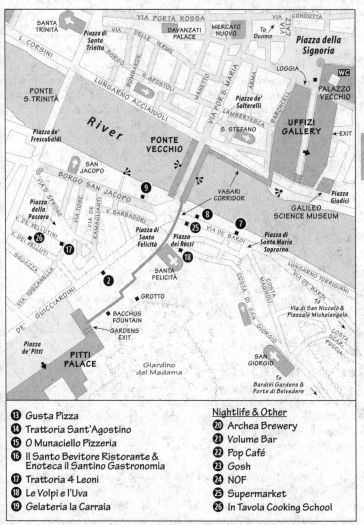

| | |
|---|---|
| ⑬ Gusta Pizza | <u>Nightlife & Other</u> |
| ⑭ Trattoria Sant'Agostino | ⑳ Archea Brewery |
| ⑮ O Munaciello Pizzeria | ㉑ Volume Bar |
| ⑯ Il Santo Bevitore Ristorante & Enoteca il Santino Gastronomia | ㉒ Pop Café |
| ⑰ Trattoria 4 Leoni | ㉓ Gosh |
| ⑱ Le Volpi e l'Uva | ㉔ NOF |
| ⑲ Gelateria la Carraia | ㉕ Supermarket |
| | ㉖ In Tavola Cooking School |

055 222 402, www.annalenahotel.com, reception@annalenahotel.com).

**$$ Casa Santo Nome di Gesù** is a grand convent whose sisters—Franciscan Missionaries of Mary—are thankful to rent 24 simple but spacious rooms to tourists. Staying in this 15th-century palace, you'll be immersed in the tranquil atmosphere created by a huge, peaceful garden, generous and prayerful public spaces, and smiling nuns. It's a good value and understandably popular—it's best to reserve a couple of months in advance (family rooms, aircon, elevator, memorable breakfast room, Piazza del Carmine 21, +39 055 213 856, www.fmmfirenze.it, info@fmmfirenze.it).

**$ Soggiorno Alessandra** has four bright and comfy rooms, all with en suite bathrooms. Because of its double-paned windows, you'll hardly notice the traffic noise (family rooms, includes basic breakfast in room, air-con, no elevator; there's no formal reception, so let them know what time you'll arrive; just past the Carraia Bridge at Via Borgo San Frediano 6, +39 055 290 424, www.soggiornoalessandra.it, info@soggiornoalessandra.it, Alessandra).

**$ Foresteria Valdese di Firenze,** with 40 clean and functional rooms, is located in a 17th-century palace overlooking a beautiful garden courtyard. The complex also houses the Instituto Gould, which helps socially disadvantaged kids, and proceeds raised from renting rooms help fund that important work (extra for quieter garden rooms, air-con, elevator reaches most rooms, family rooms, breakfast extra, Via dei Serragli 49, +39 055 212 576, www.firenzeforesteria.it, info@firenzeforesteria.it). The reception desk closes at lunchtime—confirm hours before you arrive. After-hours check-in is possible with advance notice.

**Hostel: ¢ Ostello Santa Monaca** is a well-run, institutional-feeling hostel a long block east of the Brancacci Chapel. As clean as its guests, it attracts a young backpacking crowd (2:00 in the morning curfew, air-con, bike rental, pay laundry, Via Santa Monaca 6, +39 055 268 338, www.ostellosantamonaca.com, info@ostellosantamonaca.com).

## RURAL *AGRITURISMI*

The Tuscan countryside south of Florence is loaded with countryside hotels and enticing rural farms offering accommodations, called *agriturismi* (for details, see the "Sleeping" section in the Practicalities chapter).

The following places are south of Florence and within 30 minutes of the city. The rustic and cozy **$$$$ Villa Salvadonica** has a gorgeous setting overlooking rolling Tuscan hills (Via Grevigiana 82, Mercatale Val di Pesa, +39 055 821 8039, www.salvadonica.com, info@salvadonica.it). **$$$$ Villa Il Poggiale** is a serene manor house with classy, spacious rooms and expansive countryside views (Via Empolese 69, San Casciano Val di Pesa, +39 055 828 311, www.villailpoggiale.it, villailpoggiale@villailpoggiale.it). The spa hotel **$$$$ Villa I Barronci** offers a relaxing respite from sightseeing (Via Sorripa 10, San Casciano Val di Pesa, +39 055 820 598, www.ibarronci.com, info@ibarronci.com).

Another option about 45 minutes south of Florence is in the Chianti region: **$$$ I Greppi di Silli** is a lovely, family-run *agriturismo* set among rolling hills. Owners Anna and Michele cultivate grapes and olive trees, and offer six carefully remodeled apartments, some with panoramic views and/or terraces; a seventh apartment is a mile away in an old country house (minimum stay required, breakfast and heating extra, pool, kids play area, Via Vallacchio 17/b, near San Casciano and just outside the village of Mercatale Val di Pesa, 45-minute drive to San Gimignano and 1 hour to Siena, +39 055 821 7956, www.igreppidisilli.it, igreppidisilli@gmail.com).

If you want to go farther afield, I've listed several good choices near Siena (see page 415) and throughout the Tuscan hill towns chapters.

# EATING IN FLORENCE

The old center of Florence is dominated by tourism. Locals still keep restaurants busy at lunch, but with the city's many Airbnb guests and city-center traffic restrictions, the hometown clientele tends to retreat away from downtown in the evening. This makes it tough to find a "nontouristy" place for dinner. Still, the competition is fierce, and you'll find plenty of fine options and good values even in the tourist zone. With an embattled middle class, Florence is in a race to the bottom—so you'll also see lots of pizza and sandwich joints catering to low-end eaters. For the best experience and better quality meals, hike to places further out and across the river in the Oltrarno.

## EATING TIPS

I rank eateries from **$** budget to **$$$$** splurge. For general advice on eating in Italy, including ordering, tipping, and Italian cuisine and beverages, see the "Eating" section of the Practicalities chapter.

**Restaurants:** You may have the best luck finding local ambience at lunch, when many restaurants in the center cater to office workers. Most restaurants close their kitchens between lunch and dinner, typically reopening around 19:00 or later. Before 21:00 or so, restaurants are usually filled with tourists; after that, locals trickle in. Even if a restaurant is fully booked at night, it may accommodate walk-in diners who are willing to eat early and quickly.

Restaurants serve what's fresh. Seasonal ingredients are most likely featured in the *piatti del giorno* (specials of the day) section on menus. For dessert, it's all about gelato (see sidebar on page 316). Rather than eat it at the restaurant, I'd enjoy a gelato-fueled evening stroll.

**Budget Eating:** The sightseer's reality is to eat a quick and simple lunch and spend more time and money at a well-chosen and more memorable res-

taurant for dinner. Keep lunch fast and simple at one of Florence's countless sandwich shops and stands, pizzerias, or self-service cafeterias. You'll find a unique range of sandwich options. In addition to the basic *panino* (usually on a baguette), crostini (open-faced, toasted baguette), and *semel* (big, puffy roll), you'll see places advertising *schiaccata* (sandwich made with a "squashed," focaccia-like bread). Florence is also peppered with carts selling tripe sandwiches—a prized local specialty (see the sidebar).

Picnicking is easy. You can picnic your way through Mercato Centrale, near the Basilica of San Lorenzo. You'll also find good *supermercati* throughout the city. I like the classy Sapori & Dintorni markets (run by Conad), with branches near the Duomo (Borgo San Lorenzo 15 red) and just over Ponte Vecchio in the Oltrarno (Via de Bardi 45). Carrefour Express is another handy grocery chain (there's one around the corner from the Duomo Museum at Via dell'Oriuolo 66).

**Reservations Recommended:** Florence is so crowded that reservations are smart for any serious dinner. Most restaurateurs speak English and are used to tourists. It's quick and easy to call ahead and book a table. Without reservations, have dinner early or very late.

**Cooking Classes:** To spend the morning cooking your lunch before eating it, see the sidebar on page 321.

EATING

EATING

# Florentine Food Carts
# for Those with Guts

While on a lunch break from chipping trapped statues out of blocks of marble, Michelange-lo would swing by the market and dig into a bun stuffed with stewed organs. Offal sand-wiches originated as an afford-able source of protein for working-class Florentines. While this longstanding tradi-tion nearly faded away a few years back, the recent world-wide foodie trend for "nose-to-tail" eating has kicked off a renaissance of food carts selling this local delicacy.

Tourists may find it hard to stomach, but Florentines' favorite quick lunch is a *panino* (sandwich) of *trippa* or *lam-predotto*—the second and fourth stomach of a cow, respec-tively—slow-boiled to tender perfection. Less common varia-tions include *poppo* (udder) and *nervetti* (tendons). While these are worth trying (be brave), most carts also offer *bollito* (stewed beef) and the always delicious—and easier to stom-ach—*porchetta* (roast pork with herbs). When you order, the food-cart proprietor pulls the lid from a gently simmering pot, forks out some tender meat, and—if you're lucky—dips the bun in the broth. The sandwich is topped with *salsa piccante* (spicy red sauce) and/or *salsa verde* (tangy parsley sauce).

As it's been for centuries, these food stands are most commonly found at or near markets. Good places include **Nerbone in the Market** at Mercato Centrale; **Da' Vinattieri,** a literal hole-in-the-wall tucked in the tight streets between the Duomo and the Palazzo Vecchio; the locally beloved *lam-predotto* **cart** at Mercato Nuovo; or anywhere else that locals are excited about. Come on, have some guts. It's offal.

## MERCATO CENTRALE AND NEARBY
## In Mercato Centrale

Florence's Industrial Age steel-and-glass Mercato Centrale (Cen-tral Market) is all about feeding people. The ground floor is a fun-to-explore edible wonderland of vendors selling meat, fish, produce, and other staples to a mostly local clientele, plus some lunch-only food counters. And the upstairs food court bustles until midnight.

**$ Ground Floor:** The market zone, with lots of raw ingredi-ents and a few humble food counters, is open only through lunch-time (Mon-Fri 7:00-14:00, Sat until 17:00, closed Sun). Buy a picnic of fresh mozzarella cheese, olives, fruit, and crunchy bread to munch on the steps of the nearby Basilica of San Lorenzo. Merchants are often happy to give samples. The fancy deli, **Perini,** is famous for its quality products and enticing displays. The adjacent **Pasta Perini** stand is good for a quick bowl of pasta. For a simple sit-down meal, head for the venerable **Nerbone in the Market.** It's generally mobbed by shoppers and workers who crowd up to the bar to grab inexpensive plates, then find a stool at cramped shared tables nearby (lunch menu served Mon-Sat 12:00-14:00, cash only, on the side closest to the Basilica of San Lorenzo). Its less-famous sisters, nearby, have better seating and fewer crowds.

**$$ Upstairs:** The upper floor is a touristy and jam-packed food court (daily 10:00-24:00) with counters selling pizza, pasta, fish, meat, *salumi, lampredotto,* wine, and so on. Buy what you like at any counter and grab a table (drinks will be brought to your table). Even if you're not eating, it's fun to explore the many options. While the food court can be a zoo at lunch, it's often more relaxed at dinnertime.

## Near Mercato Centrale

A huge array of eateries is within a couple of blocks of the market. Each has its own distinct vibe, so scout around to find your favorite.

**$ Casa del Vino,** Florence's oldest operating wine shop, is a crowded little bar offering an unforgettable stand-up lunch experience with a selection of wine by the glass from 20 different bottles (prices are chalked onto each opened bottle behind the cashier). Owner Gianni, a sommelier whose family has run the Casa for 70 years, is a class act. Pair a glass of wine with a sandwich, crostini, or €7 "Tuscany appetizer plate" of meat and cheese for a great little lunch. During busy times, it's a mob scene—you'll munch and sip standing outside amongst workers on a lunch break. But early or late you can actually connect with Gianni (Mon-Thu 10:00-15:30, Fri-Sat until 20:00; closed Sun year-round, Sat in summer, and Aug; Via dell'Ariento 16 red, +39 055 215 609).

**$$ Pepò,** a colorful and charmingly unpretentious space, is tucked just around the corner from the touristy glitz on Piazza del Mercato Centrale. The short menu offers simple but well-prepared Florentine classics such as *ribollita* and *pollo alla cacciatora*—chicken cacciatore (daily 12:00-14:30 & 19:00-22:30, Via Rosina 4 red, +39 055 283 259).

**$$$ Trattoria da Garibaldi** is a big, practical place serving traditional Tuscan dishes and pizzas with a sprawling interior and delightful tables on the square (daily 11:00-23:00, Piazza del Mercato Centrale 38 red, +39 055 212 267).

**$$ Trattoria Sergio Gozzi** is your classic neighborhood lunch-only place, serving hearty, traditional Florentine fare to

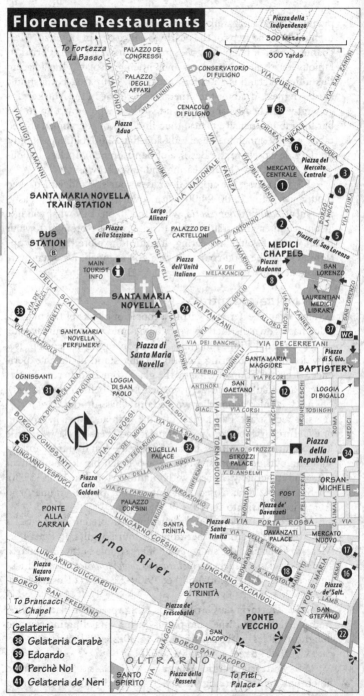

# Florence Restaurants

Piazza della Indipendenza

300 Meters
300 Yards

To Fortezza da Basso

PALAZZO DEI CONGRESSI

CONSERVATORIO DI FULIGNO

**10**

PALAZZO DEGLI AFFARI

VIA VALFONDA

VIA CENNINI

CENACOLO DI FULIGNO

VIA GUELFA

VIA SAN ZANOBI

*Piazza Adua*

VIA LUIGI ALAMANNI

VIA FIUME

VIA NAZIONALE

VIA FAENZA

VIA DELL'ARIENTO

V. CHIARA PANICALE

VIA TADDEA

**36**

**6**

*Piazza del Mercato Centrale*

MERCATO CENTRALE

**1**

**3**

**4**

VIA S. ANTONINO

BORGO LA NOCE

VIA STUFA

SANTA MARIA NOVELLA TRAIN STATION

*Largo Alinari*

PALAZZO DEI CARTELLONI

**2**

*Piazza di San Lorenzo*

**5**

BUS STATION
**B**

*Piazza della Stazione*

VIA DEGLI AVELLI

VIA S. ANTONINO

V. D'AMARINO

*Piazza dell'Unità Italiana*

V. DEI MELARANCIO

MEDICI CHAPELS

*Piazza Madonna*

**8**

SAN LORENZO

VIA DE' CONTI

VIA DE' ZANNETTI

LAURENTIAN MEDICI LIBRARY

B. SAN LORENZO

VIA DELLA SCALA

MAIN TOURIST INFO **i**

SANTA MARIA NOVELLA

VIA DEL GIGLIO

V. DELL'ALLORO

**37**

**WC**

VIA DE' CANACCI

VIA BENEDETTA

**33**

VIA PALAZZUOLO

SANTA MARIA NOVELLA PERFUMERY

*Piazza di Santa Maria Novella*

**24**

VIA PANZANI

VIA D. BELLE DONNE

VIA DEI BANCHI

VIA DE' CERRETANI

SANTA MARIA MAGGIORE

*Piazza di S. Gio.*

BAPTISTERY

TREBBIO

RONDINELLI

SAN GAETANO

VIA PECORI

**12**

BRUNELLESCHI

LOGGIA DI BIGALLO

MEDICI

OGNISSANTI

**31**

LOGGIA DI SAN PAOLO

VIA DI PORCELLANA

VIA DI PAOLINO

ANTINORI

GIAC.

VIA CORSI

VIA DE' VECCHIETTI

TOSINGHI

ROMA

BORGO OGNISSANTI

VIA DEL FOSSI

VIA DEL SOLE

VIA DELLA SPADA

VIA DEL MORO

VIA DE' FEDERIGHI

SAN GAETANO

VIA DE' TORNABUONI

V. D. PESCIONI

**14**

RUCELLAI PALACE

**32**

VIA DELLA VIGNA NUOVA

V. D. ANSELMI

STROZZI PALACE

V. D. STROZZI

*Piazza della Repubblica*

**34**

ORSAN-MICHELE

**35**

LUNGARNO VESPUCCI

*Piazza Carlo Goldoni*

VIA DEL PARIONE

PALAZZO CORSINI

PURGATORIO

INFERNO

PARIONCINO

MONALDA

SASSETTI

*Piazza de' Davanzati*

POST

VIA PELLICCERIA

CALIMALA

PONTE ALLA CARRAIA

LUNGARNO CORSINI

SANTA TRINITA

*Piazza di Santa Trinita*

VIA PORTA ROSSA

DAVANZATI PALACE

MERCATO NUOVO

**17**

*Arno River*

LUNGARNO GUICCIARDINI

*Piazza Nazaro Sauro*

BORGO SAN FREDIANO

*Piazza de' Frescobaldi*

PONTE S.TRINITA

VIA DELLE TERME

BORGO SS. APOSTOLI

LUNGARNO ACCIAIUOLI

BOMBARDE

**18**

VIA POR S. MARIA

PARMA

**16**

*Piazza de' Salt.*

LAMB

SAN STEFANO

**22**

To Brancacci Chapel

*Piazza di Frescobaldi*

SAN JACOPO

PONTE VECCHIO

To Pitti Palace

BORGO SAN JACOPO

VIA MAGGIO

O L T R A R N O

SANTO SPIRITO

*Piazza della Passera*

**Gelaterie**
**38** Gelateria Carabè
**39** Edoardo
**40** Perchè No!
**41** Gelateria de' Neri

EATING

1. Mercato Centrale Eateries
2. Casa del Vino
3. Pepò
4. Trattoria da Garibaldi
5. Trattoria Sergio Gozzi
6. Trattoria la Burrasca
7. Simbiosi Organic Pizza & Lovely Food
8. Trattoria lo Stracotto
9. Ristorante Cafaggi
10. Trattoria la Gratella
11. Enoteca Coquinarius
12. Self-Service Ristorante Leonardo
13. EATaly
14. Procacci
15. Rosalia Salad Gourmet
16. Ristorante Pizzeria Il Bargello
17. Rivoire Café
18. Ristorante Toto
19. Osteria Vini e Vecchi Sapori
20. Cantinetta dei Verrazzano
21. I Fratellini
22. 'Ino Sandwich Shop/Wine Bar
23. Da' Vinattieri
24. Shake Café (3)
25. La Mescita Fiaschetteria
26. Pasticceria Robiglio
27. To Trattoria Cucchietta & Antica Trattoria da Tito
28. Ristorante del Fagioli
29. Ristorante Boccadama
30. Via dei Neri Sandwich Mosh Pit
31. Trattoria Sostanza-Troia
32. Trattoria Marione
33. Trattoria "da Giorgio"
34. Caffè Tosca & Nino
35. Sesto Bar
36. Mostodolce Craft Brewery
37. Groceries (3)

EATING

market-goers since 1915—long before the tourist crush of today. The handwritten menu is limited and changes daily, and service can be hectic, but it's understandably a local favorite (Mon-Sat 12:00-15:00, closed Sun, Piazza di San Lorenzo 8, +39 055 281 941).

**$$ Trattoria la Burrasca** is a rustic time-warp, where a dozen rickety tables cluster under a single vault. Elio and his staff offer a traditional menu featuring fine steak and good-value seasonal specials—both Sicilian and Tuscan (Tue-Sat 12:00-15:00 & 19:00-22:30, closed Sun-Mon, Via Panicale 6, north corner of Mercato Centrale, +39 055 215 827).

**$ Simbiosi Organic Pizza and Lovely Food** is a happy little pizzeria under a medieval vault with a young crew, open fire, and healthy, organic energy (daily 18:30-23:00, good salads, craft beer, Via de' Ginori 56 red, +39 055 064 0115). Their similarly named pasta sister is next door at #58.

**$$ Trattoria lo Stracotto** is an inviting eatery with a modern interior and good outdoor seating, where you'll enjoy good-value, standard Tuscan dishes in the shadow of the Medici Chapels (daily 12:00-15:00 & 18:00-22:30, Piazza di Madonna degli Aldobrandini 17, +39 055 230 2062, Francesco).

**$$$ Ristorante Cafaggi** fills a bright yet low-energy space on a drab street between the Accademia and Mercato Centrale. With a vaguely 1950s vibe, the place emphasizes their generations-old passion for Florentine food, serving up *ribollita* (hearty Tuscan soup), osso buco, and tripe. It's been family-run since 1922 (Mon-Sat 12:30-15:00 & 19:00-22:00, closed Sun and several weeks in Aug, Via Guelfa 35 red, +39 055 294 989).

**$$$ Trattoria la Gratella,** near my recommended hotels north of the center, serves solid Tuscan cuisine to a mostly local crowd. The crowded front room gives way to a sprawling interior and an outdoor courtyard, full of diners grilling their own *bistecca alla fiorentina* on mini barbeques at the table (daily 12:00-15:00 & 19:00-23:00, Via Guelfa 81 red, +39 055 211 292).

## AROUND THE DUOMO

**$$ Enoteca Coquinarius** feels as welcoming as someone's cool and spacious living room or library. It's a relaxed, hip place with a slow-food ethic, tasty salads and pastas, and a nice selection of wines by the glass (daily 12:00-15:30 & 19:00-22:30, a few steps from the Duomo workshop at Via delle Oche 11 red, +39 055 230 2153).

**$$$ Ristorante Natalino** is worth the short walk for a memorable dinner. It's a family-run fixture in its neighborhood with outdoor seating on a characteristic corner. The place is known for its homemade pasta, *bistecca alla fiorentina*, and classic Tuscan dishes (daily 12:00-14:30 & 19:00-22:30, Borgo degli Albizi 17 red, for location see the "Florence" map on page 36, +39 055 289 404).

**$ Self-Service Ristorante Leonardo** is a quick, cheap, air-conditioned, and handy cafeteria just a block from the Duomo. While it's no-frills and stuck in the 1970s, the food is better than many table-service eateries in this part of town. Stefano and Luciano run the place with enthusiasm and free pitchers of tap water (lots of vegetables, daily 11:45-14:45 & 18:45-21:45, upstairs at Via Pecori 11, +39 055 284 446).

**$$ EATaly,** a slick, modern space a half-block from the Duomo, is an outpost of a chain of foodie mini malls located in big Italian cities (as well as in a few major US cities). Along with a grocery store for top-end Italian ingredients, plenty of edible gifts, and kitchen gadgets, it has a bright, modern dining area in the back serving pastas, pizzas, salads, and *secondi* to tourists (daily 10:00-22:30, Via de' Martelli 22 red, +39 055 015 3601).

**$$$ Procacci,** right on Florence's most genteel boutique-browsing street, is upscale and posh. This wine-and-cocktail bar, with a swanky, 1885 atmosphere, specializes in pungent truffle-scented ingredients: cheap mini panini and €20 sampler plates of *salumi* and cheeses. They have a small lunch menu of pasta, salads, and sandwiches. There's no dinner menu, but their tiny sandwiches are always available. Paired with an €8 glass of wine, a bite here makes an elegant light meal (daily 10:00-21:00, Via Tornabuoni 64 red, +39 055 211 656).

**$ Rosalia Salad Gourmet** is a quick, build-your-own-salad spot behind the Duomo. Eat in or take out a salad bowl, veggie wrap, smoothie, or fresh fruit juice (daily 8:00-20:00, Via dei Servi 37, +39 320 706 9331).

## ON OR NEAR PIAZZA DELLA SIGNORIA

Piazza della Signoria, the scenic square facing the Palazzo Vecchio, is ringed by beautifully situated yet touristy eateries serving overpriced, forgettable food with an unforgettable view.

**$$$ Ristorante Pizzeria il Bargello** is a good choice if you want to eat outdoors on Florence's main square with a view of the Palazzo Vecchio. It's a happy, family-run place with good salads, pastas, and pizzas (Tue-Sun 11:30-22:30, closed Mon, Piazza della Signoria 4 red, +39 055 214 071, Mimmo).

**$$$ Rivoire Café** is famous for its fancy desserts and thick hot chocolate (€7). A bowl of pasta or a salad—when enjoyed at the best view tables on the square—can be a worthwhile experience. Their delightful bar is perfectly affordable, and drinks often come with fine *aperitivo* munchies (daily 8:00-24:00, +39 055 214 412).

**$$ Ristorante Toto** is a simple, fun, traditional eatery with a spacious dining hall serving classic Tuscan plates at decent prices. The focus is on steak, homemade pasta, and pizza (Thu-Tue 12:00-15:00 & 19:00-22:00, closed Wed, indoor seating only, tucked away two blocks from the Ponte Vecchio at Borgo SS. Apostoli 6 red, +39 055 212 096).

**$$ Osteria Vini e Vecchi Sapori** is a colorful eatery—tight, tiny, and with attitude. They serve Tuscan food—like *pappardelle* with duck—from a fun, accessible menu of delicious pastas and *secondi*. For dessert, Tommaso promises a free Vin Santo and *cantucci* for readers with this book (Mon-Sat seatings at 12:30, 14:00, 19:30, and 21:30; closed Sun, call ahead to reserve; Via dei Magazzini 3 red, +39 055 293 045, run by Mario while wife Rosanna cooks and son Tommaso serves).

## Favorite Sandwiches near Piazza della Signoria

**$$ Cantinetta dei Verrazzano** is an elegant wine bar serving delightful sandwich plates. Their *selezione Verrazzano* is a plate of four little crostini featuring breads, cheeses, and meats from the Chianti region. The *tagliere di focacce*, a sampler of mini focaccia sandwiches, is also fun. Add a glass of Chianti to either of these dishes to make a fine, light meal. Office workers pop in for a quick lunch, and it's traditional to share tables. You can eat cheaper at the bar (or at the tiny stools facing it). Simply step to the back and point to a hot *focacce* sandwich, order a drink at the bar, and enjoy the action while you munch (Mon-Sat 8:00-15:30, closed Sun, no reservations, off Via dei Calzaiuoli, at Via dei Tavolini 18 red, +39 055 268 590).

**$ I Fratellini** is a literal hole-in-the-wall stand-up joint where the "little brothers" have served peasants two dozen types of sandwiches and a fine selection of wine at great prices (see list on wall) since 1875. Join the local crowd to order, then sit on a nearby curb to eat, placing your glass on the wall rack as you leave. Be adventurous with the menu (order by number: perhaps #22, cured lard aged in Carrara marble; or #19, spicy boar salami). It's worth ordering the most expensive wine they're selling by the glass (daily 12:00-18:00, open later on weekends, 20 yards in front of Orsanmichele Church on Via dei Cimatori, +39 055 239 6096).

**$ 'Ino Sandwich Shop/Wine Bar** is a mod little spot (on a back alley between the Uffizi and Ponte Vecchio) where Alessandro and his staff serve creative sandwiches and glasses of their house wine. You'll munch your meal while perched on a tiny, uncomfortable stool—and be glad you did. The sandwiches—arguably the best and among the most expensive in town—are easily splitable (daily 12:00-16:00, immediately behind Uffizi Gallery courtyard on Ponte Vecchio side, at Via dei Georgofili 7 red, +39 055 214 154).

$ **Tripe Sandwiches in Dante's Neighborhood:** Another literal hole-in-the-wall with a tiny bar next door, **Da' Vinattieri** sells traditional *schiaccata* sandwiches, plus *trippa* (tripe) and *lampredotto* (stomach). While it's a hit with locals, ordering here takes an adventurous spirit (daily 11:30-19:00, next to Casa di Dante at Via Santa Margherita 4 red, +39 392 734 5773). The best place to enjoy your sandwich while people-watching is nearby on Piazza della Signoria.

## NEAR THE ACCADEMIA

There are piles of cheap and practical eateries (serving pizza, sandwiches, and salads to eat in or take out) on the boring streets near *David*. Hungry tourists looking for a quick lunch can survey a line of economical options a block away on Piazza di San Marco and around the corner from that along Via Cavour. If picnicking, head over to the traffic-free Piazza Santissima Annunziata—the first Renaissance square in Florence, with a fountain for washing fruit and plenty of stony places to sit.

$ **Shake Café,** great for a quick and healthy lunch, is a modern salad bar on busy Via Cavour with spacious and inviting courtyard seating. Along with tasty salads, the menu includes veggie bowls, wraps, smoothies, and fancy juices (daily 7:00-19:00, Via Cavour 67 red). Other handy Shake locations are on Piazza Santa Maria Novella and between the Duomo and Bargello at Via del Corso 28.

$ **La Mescita Fiaschetteria** is a characteristic hole-in-the-wall where, since 1919, locals have been enjoying a simple menu of pastas, traditional Tuscan soups, and the daily *secondi* with tasty, cheap house wine. The place can either be mobbed by students or a peaceful time warp, depending on when you stop by. Mirco and Alessio are gregarious to the point of being a bit pushy...order carefully and check your bill. They serve a nice Vin Santo and *cantucci* dessert (daily 11:30-15:30, Via degli Alfani 70 red, +39 338 992 2640).

$$ **Pasticceria Robiglio** is a classy local fixture with a stately and calm dining area and a few shaded tables on the sidewalk. They have a small lunch-only menu of salads and daily pasta and *secondi* specials. It's good any time for a coffee and one of their pretty pastries—famous among Florentines (café open daily 7:30-20:00, lunch served 12:00-16:00, a block toward the Duomo off Piazza Santissima Annunziata at Via dei Servi 112 red, +39 055 212 784).

# Florentine and Tuscan Cuisine

In general, Tuscan cuisine is hearty, simple food: grilled meats, high-quality seasonal vegetables, fresh herbs, prized olive oil, and rustic bread. If a dish ends with *"alla toscana"* or *"alla fiorentina,"* it's cooked in the Tuscan or Florentine style—usually a preparation highlighting local products. In addition to specialty dishes, most restaurants also serve pasta and pizza, veal cutlets, and salad (for more on Italian cuisine, see page 682).

There's nothing wrong with your Tuscan bread—it's supposed to taste like that. *Pane alla toscana* is unsalted and nearly flavorless (from the days when salt's preservative powers made it more valuable than gold). Italians drench it in olive oil and sprinkle it with salt, or use it to scoop up sauce.

EATING

## *Antipasti* (Appetizers)

**Bruschetta:** Toasted bread brushed with olive oil and rubbed with garlic, topped with chopped tomato, mushrooms, or whatever else sounds good.

**Crostini:** Toasted bread rounds topped with meat or vegetable pastes. *Alla toscana* generally means with chicken liver pâté.

**Panzanella:** Simple summer salad, made of day-old bread, chopped tomatoes, onion, and basil, tossed in a light vinaigrette.

**Pecorino cheese:** Fresh *(fresco)* or aged *(stagionato)*, from ewe's milk.

**Porcini mushrooms:** Used as a topping on bruschetta; also served marinated or stewed.

**Salumi:** Cold cuts, usually air- or salt-dried pork. Popular kinds include prosciutto (air-cured ham hock), pancetta (cured pork belly), *lardo* (cured pork lard), and *finocchiona* (fennel salami). For a list of other *salumi*, see page 684.

**Tagliere:** Selection of cold cuts and/or cheeses served on a wooden platter.

## *Primo Piatto* (First Course)

**Carabaccia:** Onion soup.

**Pappa al pomodoro:** Thick stew of tomatoes, olive oil, and bread.

**Pappardelle al sugo di lepre:** Rich wild-hare sauce over long, broad noodles.

**Pici al ragù:** Fat, spaghetti-like, hand-rolled pasta served with a meat-tomato sauce.

**Ribollita:** "Reboiled" soup, traditionally made with leftovers including white beans *(fagioli)*, seasonal vegetables, and olive oil, with layers of day-old Tuscan bread.

**Zuppa alla volterrana:** Volterra-style soup, similar to *ribollita* but with fresh bread.

## *Secondo Piatto* (Second Course)

**Arrosto misto:** Assortment of roasted meats, sometimes served on a skewer *(spiedino)*.

**Bistecca alla fiorentina:** Thick T-bone steak, generally grilled very rare and lightly seasoned (often sold by weight—per *etto*, or 100 grams). The best—and most expensive—is from the white Chianina cattle you'll see grazing throughout Tuscany.

**Cinghiale:** Wild boar, served grilled; in soups, stews, and pasta; or made into many varieties of sausage and *salumi.*

**Fegatelli:** Liver meatballs.

**Game birds:** Squab *(piccione)*, pheasant *(fagiano)*, and guinea hen *(faraona)* are popular.

**Trippa alla fiorentina:** Tripe and vegetables sautéed in tomato sauce, sometimes baked with parmesan. *Trippa* (and the similar *lampredotto*) are popular in sandwiches; see page 304.

## Dolci (Desserts)

**Cantucci:** Florentines love to end a meal by dipping this crunchy almond cookie in Vin Santo wine (described below). These are commonly misnamed "biscotti" by Americans.

**Gelato:** The Florentines claim they invented Italian-style ice cream. Rather than order dessert in a restaurant, I like to stroll with a gelato. For more on gelato, see page 686; for tips on enjoying it here, see page 316.

**Panforte:** Dense, clove-and-cinnamon-spiced cake from Siena.

## Local Wines

Many Tuscan wines are made with sangiovese ("blood of Jupiter") grapes. But the characteristics of the soil, temperature, and exposure make each wine unique to its area.

**Brunello di Montalcino:** One of Italy's best reds, this full-bodied wine comes from the slopes of Montalcino, south of Siena. Smooth and dry, it pairs well with hearty, meaty food.

**Chianti:** This red hails from the Chianti region (20 miles south of Florence). Varieties range from cheap, acidic basket-bottles of table wine (called *fiaschi*) to the hearty Chianti Classico.

**Rosso di Montalcino:** This cheaper, younger "baby Brunello," also made in Montalcino, lacks Brunello's depth of flavor and complexity—but it's still a great wine at a bargain price.

**Super Tuscans:** This newer wine blends traditional grapes with locally grown non-Italian grapes (such as cabernet or merlot).

**Vernaccia di San Gimignano:** This medium-dry white goes well with pasta and salad. Trebbiano and vermentino are two other local white grapes.

**Vino Nobile di Montepulciano:** This high-quality, ruby red, dry wine pairs well with meat, especially chicken.

**Vin Santo:** Sweet and syrupy, this "holy" dessert wine is often served with a cookie for dipping.

## Memorable Dining North of the Center

These places are away from the tourists and offer perhaps the most authentic of all. The first is a 10-minute taxi ride north of the center, and the second is just a few blocks' walk from *David*.

**$$$ Trattoria Cucchietta** is your chance for a modern, totally local dining experience. It's a hard-working family affair with a youthful and passionate team and a small, enticing menu filled with creative Tuscan temptations. Venturing out here, you risk having the best meal of your trip (Mon-Sat 12:00-14:30 & 19:30-22:30, closed Sun, reservations strongly recommended, 10-minute taxi ride north of the center at Via Firenzuola 15 red, +39 055 578 889, http://cucchietta.it).

**$$$ Antica Trattoria da Tito,** a 10-minute hike from the Accademia along Via San Gallo, is a fun-loving food party. Come here for a memorable meal with a local crowd and smart-aleck service inspired by the lovable boss, Bobo. The food is hearty and rustic, the ingredients are fresh, and there's lots of wine and no pretense. It's a noisy playground of Tuscan cuisine. Their €18 *antipasti sampler plate* (cold cuts, cheeses, a few veggies, and bruschetta) is plenty for two. Dinner is served in four seatings: 19:30 (more sanity), 20:30, 21:30, and 22:15 (less sanity; daily 12:30-15:00 & 19:00-23:00, reservations recommended, Via San Gallo 112 red, +39 055 472 475, http//trattoriadatito.business.site).

## BETWEEN THE PALAZZO VECCHIO AND SANTA CROCE CHURCH

**$$ Ristorante del Fagioli** is an enthusiastically run eatery where you can sense the heritage, from the wood-paneled dining room to the daily specials chalked on a board. Maurizio commands the kitchen while family members Antonio and Simone keep the throngs of loyal customers returning. The cuisine: home-style bread-soups, hearty steaks, and other Florentine classics. Don't worry—while *fagioli* means "beans," that's the family name, not the extent of the menu (Mon-Fri 12:30-14:30 & 19:30-22:30, closed Sat-Sun, cash only, reserve for dinner, a block north of the Alle Grazie bridge at Corso dei Tintori 47 red, +39 055 244 285).

**$$$ Ristorante Boccadama** is a fun place with great tables on Piazza di Santa Croce. The menu focuses on meat and traditional dishes. For dessert, Giorgio and Marco offer a free Vin Santo and *cantucci* to readers with this book (daily 12:00-23:00 & 18:00-23:00, Piazza Santa Croce 25 red, +39 055 243 640).

**$ The Via dei Neri Sandwich Mosh Pit:** Via dei Neri has become a human traffic jam of people munching hearty and cheap sandwiches in the street. These low-end sandwich shops are the trend all over town, but the craze originated here at #65, **All'Antico**

**Vinaio.** Just walking down this street—a sandwich ghetto—is an experience.

## NEAR THE CHURCH OF SANTA MARIA NOVELLA

**$$$ Trattoria Sostanza-Troia,** characteristic and well established, is famous for its steaks and its *pollo al burro* (chicken in butter). Whirling ceiling fans and walls strewn with old photos evoke earlier times, while the artichoke pie *(tortino di carciofi)* and Max (who insists on no changes) remind locals of Grandma's cooking. Crowded, with just eight shared tables, a small menu, and grumpy service, the place feels like a simple bistro. Reservations are essential for their two dinner seatings: 19:30 and 21:00 (cash only, open Mon-Sat, closed Sun, lunch served 12:30-14:00, Via del Porcellana 25 red, +39 055 212 691).

**$$ Trattoria Marione** serves home-cooked-style meals to a mixed group of tourists and Florentines crowding very tight tables beneath hanging ham hocks. The ambience is happy and a bit frantic—no reservations, so arrive early. You come here for the character...not for fine cuisine (daily 12:00-16:00 & 19:00-23:00, Via della Spada 27 red, +39 055 214 756).

**$$ Trattoria "da Giorgio"** is a rustic family-style diner on a sketchy street serving up simple home cooking to happy locals and tourists alike. Their €15 three-course lunch fixed-price meal, including a drink, is a great value (€20 at dinner). This place is completely without pretense—head here for a taste of working-class Florence (no reservations, Mon-Sat 12:00-14:30 & 19:00-22:00, closed Sun, Via Palazzuolo 100 red, +39 055 284 302, Silvano).

**$ Shake Café,** another outpost of this handy chain, is a healthy salad bar with seating on Piazza Santa Maria Novella. It's good for a quick lunch, with a menu of veggie bowls, wraps, smoothies, and juices (daily 7:00-20:00, two blocks in front of the train station at Via degli Avelli 2 red).

## HIDDEN ROOFTOP CAFÉ TERRACES

If you're willing to pay extra to enjoy a drink surrounded by splendid Florentine views, head to one of these rooftop terraces:

**$$ Caffè Tosca & Nino** is on the rooftop of La Rinascente department store overlooking Piazza della Repubblica. While the place is a tight and plain little perch, its handful of tables come with commanding views of the Duomo, which looms gloriously on the horizon (daily 9:00-24:00; coffee drinks, pastas, salads, and light bites; +39 055 493 3468).

**$$$$ Sesto** is a dressy bar and restaurant designed for dressy people on a partially covered terrace atop the luxurious Westin Hotel. While their Mediterranean cuisine and cocktails are pricey, it all comes with amazing city views. To turn your spendy drink

EATING

## Gelato

Italy's ice cream is famed—and many believe the best is in Florence. But beware of scams at touristy joints on busy streets that turn a simple request for a cone into a €10 "tourist special" rip-off. To avoid this, survey the size options and specify what you want—for example, *un cono da tre euro* (a €3 cone). A rule of thumb: Stay away from places with heaping mounds of brightly (artificially) colored gelato. For more gelato tips, see the "Eating" section of the Practicalities chapter. The following places are a cut above the norm and open long hours daily.

**Near the Accademia:** A Sicilian choice on a tourist thoroughfare, **Gelateria Carabè** is particularly famous for its pistachio and its luscious *granite*—Italian ices made with fresh fruit. A *cremolata* is a *granita* with a dollop of gelato (almond and pistachio work well together). From the Accademia, it's a block toward the Duomo (at Via Ricasoli 60 red).

**Near the Duomo:** A favorite, **Edoardo** features organic ingredients and tasty handmade cones (facing the southwest corner of the Duomo at Piazza del Duomo 45 red).

**Near Orsanmichele Church:** This shop's name, **Perchè No!,** translates to "Why not!"—good advice when it comes to gelato. It feels touristy but serves one of the widest range of flavors around, and the quality's top notch (just off the busy main pedestrian drag, Via dei Calzaiuoli, at Via dei Tavolini 19).

**Near the Church of Santa Croce:** Florentines flock to **Gelateria de' Neri,** with an enticingly wide array of flavors (Via dei Neri 9 red).

**Just Across the Carraia Bridge:** On the Oltrarno side of the bridge, **Gelateria la Carraia** is a hit with locals (Piazza Nazario Sauro 25 red—see the map on page 299).

into a light dinner, come during their *aperitivo* happy hour (18:00-21:00) when, for €30, your drink includes a little gourmet buffet of six tapas, giving you something to nibble as you enjoy the sunset (daily 12:00-24:00, reservations required, Piazza Ognissanti 3, +39 055 27151, www.sestoonarno.com).

**$$ Caffè del Verone** is perched on the rooftop terrace of the Hospital of the Innocents on Piazza Santissima Annunziata. It offers a nice, peaceful atmosphere for a coffee break with rooftop view (no ticket required, just catch the elevator by the museum entrance, Wed-Mon 16:00-20:00, open later on weekends, closed Tue, Piazza Santissima Annunziata 13, for location see the "Florence" map on page 36, +39 345 167 8267).

## THE OLTRARNO

In general, dining in the Oltrarno, south of the Arno River, offers a more authentic experience. While it's just a few minutes' walk beyond Ponte Vecchio, this area sees far fewer tourists than the other side of the river. You may even find that Florentines outnumber tourists.

### Dining or Drinking with a Ponte Vecchio View

For locations, see the "Oltrarno Hotels and Restaurants" map on page 298.

**$$$ Signorvino** is a bright and modern *enoteca* (wine shop) with a simple restaurant that has a rare terrace literally over the Arno River, with Ponte Vecchio views. Though it lacks historic charm with its stark-white IKEA vibe, it's a fun-loving place with a passion for quality Italian ingredients. They serve regional dishes and plates of fine meats and cheeses to pair with a wonderful array of wines by the glass, allowing you to drink and eat your way merrily across Italy. If you're up for a full bottle, their huge selection is available—for the same fair prices—at both the restaurant and their wine store (food served 12:00-22:30, call to reserve for river-view seating, Via dei Bardi 46 red, +39 055 286 258, www. signorvino.com).

**$$$$ Golden View Firenze** is two-in-one: a classy restaurant and a simpler wine bar/bakery, both overlooking the Ponte Vecchio and Arno River. The restaurant's white, minimalist interior is a dramatic contrast to atmospheric old Florence. Reservations for window tables are essential. Mixing their fine wine and river views makes for a wonderful evening (long hours daily, 50 yards east of Ponte Vecchio at Via dei Bardi 58, +39 055 214 502, https:// goldenview.it, run by Paolo and Tommaso). Tommaso's new venture, **La Forneria Firenze** is a combo wine bar/bakery with gourmet focaccia. The philosophy here is that top quality fundamentals like bread, cheese, meat, and wine can amount to fine dining, especially if it comes with a view of the Ponte Vecchio.

**$ Osteria Ponte Vecchio** is a tiny place—little more than a bar—serving basic drinks, panini, pasta, and microwaved snacks with a couple of amazing tables on the river (daily 10:00-23:00, off-season until 20:00, a block downstream from Ponte Vecchio at Via Borgo San Jacopo 16 red, Giacomo).

### On or near Piazza di Santo Spirito

Piazza di Santo Spirito is a thriving neighborhood square in the heart of the Oltrarno, with a collection of fun **$$** eateries and rustic bars. Several bars offer *aperitivo* buffets with their drinks during happy hour (generally 18:00-20:00). For locations, see the map on page 298.

On balmy evenings, the tables of half a dozen simple restaurants spill onto the square and line up to compete for your attention. They serve standard Tuscan dishes and trendier bar food. After noting the plain facade of the Brunelleschi church facing the square, step inside Caffè Ricchi to see pictures of the many possible ways the church might be finished.

Later in the evening, the area becomes a club scene (see the Nightlife in Florence chapter), filled with foreign students and young locals.

**$$ Tamerò** is an artsy pasta bar—a kind of "ruin pub" in an old auto mechanic's shop—serving Sardinian-Tuscan dishes (daily 12:00-late, Piazza Santo Spirito 11 red, +39 055 282 596).

**$$ Trattoria Casalinga** was here long before any of the others. It's an inexpensive standby with bustling aproned waiters. Florentines (who enjoy the tripe and tongue) and tourists (who opt for *ribollita,* anything with ragu sauce, and easier to swallow Tuscan favorites) both pack the place and leave full and happy. Their streetside tables are fun, but the old-time trattoria action is inside (Mon-Sat 12:00-14:30 & 19:00-22:00, closed Sun and Aug, just off Piazza di Santo Spirito, near the church at Via de' Michelozzi 9 red, +39 055 218 624, www.trattorialacasalinga.it, Andrea and Paolo).

**$$ Gusta Osteria,** just around the corner from the piazza, serves big salads and predictable Tuscan fare at playful, cozy indoor seating or at outdoor tables (Tue-Sun 12:00-23:00, closed Mon, Via de' Michelozzi 13 red, +39 055 285 033).

**$ Gusta Pizza** is a jam-packed, touristy, cheap, sloppy, and fun neighborhood pizzeria (Tue-Sun 11:30-15:30 & 19:00-23:30, closed Mon, two blocks off Piazza di Santo Spirito at Via Maggio 46 red, +39 055 285 068).

**$$ Trattoria Sant'Agostino,** a block away from the Piazza di Santo Spirito action, is charming and more relaxed with comfortable seating. It's a good place for local favorites, soups, and the Roman noodle dish *pici cacio e pepe* (daily 12:00-23:00, Via Sant'Agostino 23 red, +39 055 281 995).

**$ O Munaciello Pizzeria** is where Italian kids dream of going on their birthday. Named after a ghost of Neapolitan folklore, it's a kitschy, sprawling, family-friendly festival of happy eating. The menu is fun, there's a youthful energy, and the Naples-style pizza is a hit (daily 12:30-15:00 & 19:00-24:00, Via Maffia 31 red, +39 055 287 198).

## Beyond Piazza del Carmine, away from Tourists

While Piazza di Santo Spirito is well known by tourists, a short walk beyond it gets you completely away from the tourist scene. These neighboring restaurants (on quiet Via dell'Orto, each with sidewalk tables) are worth the five-minute walk beyond Piazza del Carmine. For locations, see the "Oltrarno, South of the Arno River" map on page 80.

**$$$ Burro & Acciughe Fish Restaurant** ("butter and anchovies") is a minimalist place packed with locals enjoying fresh seafood. With just 35 seats in a long, narrow setting, it oozes quality (Tue-Sun 19:30-24:00, closed Mon, Via dell'Orto 35 red, +39 055 045 7286).

**$$ Trattoria dell'Orto** is a classic Florentine trattoria filled with Florentines enjoying steaks, grilled dishes, and quintessential local fare. It has a boisterous vibe and an inviting covered outdoor terrace in back (Wed-Mon 12:00-15:00 & 19:30-23:30, closed Tue, Via dell'Orto 35a, +39 055 224 148).

**$$$ Ristorante il Guscio** is another very local place with a more romantic feel, an enticing menu, and quality wine (Mon-Sat 12:00-15:00 & 19:30-23:00, closed Sun, Via dell'Orto 49, +39 055 224 421).

## Dining near the Oltrarno

These trendy spots are closer to the river and more formal. Reservations are a good idea in the evening. For locations see the map on page 298.

**$$$ Il Santo Bevitore Ristorante,** lit like a Rembrandt painting and unusually spacious, serves creative, modern Tuscan cuisine at dressy tables. They're enthusiastic about matching quality produce from the area with the right wine (daily 12:30-14:30 & 19:30-23:00, good wine list by the glass or bottle, acoustics can make it noisy inside, Via di Santo Spirito 64 red, +39 055 211 264, www.ilsantobevitore.com).

**$$ Enoteca il Santino Gastronomia,** Il Santo Bevitore's tiny wine bar next door, feels like the perfect after-work hangout for foodies who'd like a glass of wine and a light bite. Tight, cozy, and atmospheric, it can be impossibly intimidating if you're shy, so come early before the crowds. There's a prominent bar, where you can assemble an €8-12 *tagliere* of local cheeses and *salumi*. They also have a few affordable hot dishes. The food and the wine are locally sourced from small producers (daily 12:30-23:00, Via di Santo Spirito 60 red, no reservations, +39 055 230 2820).

**$$$ Trattoria 4 Leoni** creates the quintessential Oltrarno dinner scene, and is understandably popular with tourists. The Tuscan-style food is made with an innovative twist and an appreciation for vegetables. Their steak and *fiocchetti* pasta are big hits. You'll enjoy the fun energy and characteristic seating, both outside on the colorful square and inside (daily 12:00-24:00; midway between Ponte Vecchio and Piazza di Santo Spirito, on Piazza della Passera at Via de' Vellutini 1; +39 055 218 562, www.4leoni.com).

**$$$ Antico Ristoro di' Cambi** is thick with Tuscan traditions, rustic touches, T-bone steaks, and a bustling beer-hall energy. The glass case filled with red chunks of Chianina beef makes clear the house specialty (for the famous *bistecca alla fiorentina* it's €50/kilo). Before you order, they'll show you the cut and tell you the weight (1.2 kilos is the typical serving for two; 800 grams is the smallest two can split). Unless you insist otherwise, the steak comes nearly uncooked (as it's air-dried for 21 days, it's not really raw, just very tasty and tender). Sit inside the convivial woody interior or outside on the square (Mon-Sat 12:00-14:30 & 18:00-22:30, closed Sun, Via Sant'Onofrio 1 red, one block south of Ponte Amerigo Vespucci, see map on page 80, +39 055 217 134, www.anticoristorodicambi.it, run by Stefano).

## Casual Oltrarno Neighborhood Eateries

**$$ Le Volpi e l'Uva,** a wine bar just steps from Ponte Vecchio, has a limited menu of *affettati* (cold cuts), cheese, and *crostone* (hearty bruschetta)—a nice spot for a light lunch (for details, see the listing on page 344; for location see the map on page 298).

**$ Trattoria Sabatino,** the farthest away of my Oltrarno listings (and not touristy), is a spacious, brightly lit mess hall. It's changed little since it opened in 1956. It's disturbingly cheap, with family character and a simple menu—a super place to watch locals munch, especially since you'll likely be sharing a table. It's a 15-minute walk from Ponte Vecchio (Mon-Fri 12:00-14:30 & 19:15-22:00, closed Sat-Sun, no reservations, just outside Porta San Frediano, Via Pisana 2 red, see map on page 80, +39 055 225 955, little English spoken). Let eating here be your reward after following the stroll in my 📖 Oltrarno Walk chapter.

**$$ Santarosa Bistrot** is part of a city government project to redevelop the public gardens along the city wall and the river. It's a trendy, youthful, and family-friendly spot. The creative and modern menu has a dash of Naples. Offerings include salads, pastas, bar food, and cocktails (Tue-Sun 10:00-18:00, closed Mon, fills a garden just behind Trattoria Sabatino at Lungarno di Santa Rosa, see map on page 80, +39 055 230 9057).

## San Niccolò Neighborhood

The charming little Via San Niccolò—just over Ponte alle Gra-

# Cooking Classes

Florence is a natural place to learn a thing or two from this region's prodigious culinary tradition. Cooking classes range from multiday or multi-week courses for professional and semiprofessional chefs, to two- or three-hour crash courses for tourists. These are a great use of time: combining a unique Italian experience (learning to cook, say, pasta from scratch) with a satisfying meal, all in just a few hours.

In my experience, the best cooking classes are taught in a real kitchen environment (rather than a stuffy classroom or "show" kitchen) and have a spirit of fun and collaboration. Look for smaller groups (allowing more personal interaction with the instructor) and—perhaps most importantly—classes that are hands-on rather than demonstration-based.

You'll typically spend a couple of hours cooking, then sit down to a hard-earned (if not always flawlessly executed) meal. They'll send you on your way with the recipes you prepared that day. Some classes also include a shopping trip to the market. While this adds an engaging dimension to your cooking experience, it also adds time and expense, and (some think) draws the focus away from the actual cooking.

Below are a few of your many choices. Do some homework online and book well ahead.

**In Tavola:** This cooking school in the heart of the Oltrarno features trained, English-speaking Italian chefs who quickly demonstrate each step before setting you loose. You'll work in a functional kitchen, then sit down to eat in the cozy wine cellar (RS%, classes range from €55-129/person, ideally book well ahead but you can try calling last-minute, between the Pitti Palace and Brancacci Chapel at Via dei Velluti 20 red, +39 055 217 672, www.intavola.org, Fabrizio).

**Artviva:** The Artviva walking-tour company offers a wide range of hands-on cooking, pasta, and pastry classes, as well as unique foodie experiences such as truffle hunting (from €60/person, see listing on page 44).

**Florencetown:** This walking-tour company offers a five-hour experience that starts with a trip to Mercato Centrale, then settles in to their kitchen for a cooking lesson (from €99/person, also 3-hour pizza- and gelato-making class for €69/person, see listing on page 44).

EATING

zie—is the heart of the San Niccolò neighborhood and a fun place to get away from the tourist mobs (for locations, see the map on page 80).

This is groovy Italy, with a convivial neighborhood pizzeria, happening little restaurants, trendy cocktail bars, and a good *gelateria* (**Il Gelato di Filo,** at Via San Miniato 5 red). Street-art lovers enjoy popping into the gallery of **Clet Abraham,** the artist who stealthily and humorously alters street signs around town. You can buy stickers and T-shirts at his corner gallery (daily 10:30-19:30, 50 meters from my recommended eateries at Via dell'Olmo 8 red). For those looking to dine, several good eateries anchor the square:

**$$ Il Rifrullo,** creatively run by Filippo and his young and hard-working team, is a rollicking cocktail bar with a sprawling, breezy terrace out back. They serve a fun lunch menu and delightful gourmet platters of cold cuts *(tagliere)* any time of day (daily until late, Via San Niccolò 55 red, +39 055 234 2621).

**$$ Antica Mescita San Niccolò,** with traditional decor but a modern approach, feels like the grandkids took over Nonno's trattoria. Technically a wine bar, they also serve up Tuscan standbys (like soups and stews). There's delightful seating outside and in (daily 12:00-23:00, Via San Niccolò 60 red, +39 055 234 2836).

**$$ Boccadarno,** next door at #56 red, is run by brother-and-sister team Gerardo and Carlotta. The service is friendly, and the menu is all about fish. Eat in the light, bright interior or at an outdoor table (Tue-Sat 18:00-23:30, closed Sun, +39 055 386 0860).

**$$$ Zeb** is tight and mod, and Michelin rated for its gourmet plates. A minimalist wine-bar/deli, it's just one long counter with two dozen seats. Although the name stands for *zuppe e bolliti* ("soup and boiled meats"), they dish up all types of well-executed and elegantly presented Italian dishes. Portions are large and fun to share, served up by charming Mama Guiseppina and her son Alberto (Mon-Tue and Thu-Sat 12:00-15:30 & 19:30-22:30, closed Sun and Wed, reservations recommended, Via San Miniato 2 red, +39 055 234 2864, www.zebgastronomia.com).

# FLORENCE WITH CHILDREN

With relatively few kid-friendly activities, Florence may not be the ideal destination for a family vacation. But it does offer enough entertainment to keep kids occupied for a few days. Spend the morning hiking up to Piazzale Michelangelo or the top of the Duomo's dome. In the afternoons, wander the city's streets and squares looking for quirky sculptures or visit various interactive museums. Here are a few ideas for family fun in the art capital of Europe.

## Trip Tips

### EATING

Florence offers plenty of food options for children.

#### What to Eat (and Drink)

- Kid-friendly foods found everywhere include fresh bread *(pane)* and pasta (plain is *"pasta bianca"* and pasta with butter is *"pasta al burro"*; grated cheese will be served on the side). Pizza is another popular favorite—kids like margherita (tomato, basil, and cheese) and the slightly spicy Italian version of pepperoni *(diavola, salsiccia piccante, or salame piccante).*
- Popular drinks are *granitas* (slushies), *frullati* (smoothies), *frappés* (shakes), Orangina (orange soda), *limonata* (lemonade), *spremuta d'arancia* (fresh-squeezed orange juice), and *cioccolata calda* (hot chocolate).
- While the official drinking age in Italy is 18, teens 16 and over are sometimes offered wine or beer in restaurants, especially when accompanied by a parent. It's best to decide on a family policy beforehand.

## When to Eat
- Eat dinner early (at about 19:00) to dodge the romantic crowd. Restaurants are less kid-friendly after 21:00. Skip the famous places. Look instead for self-service cafeterias, bars (children are welcome), or fast-food restaurants where younger kids can move around without bothering others.

## Where to Eat

- For a refreshing respite from the mid-day heat, take a gelato break or go to a casual, air-conditioned place for lunch.
- Eating *al fresco* is fun; try places on squares where kids can run free while you dine. For ready-made picnics that can please everyone, try the *rosticcerie* (delis). *Pizza al taglio* shops sell cheap takeout pizza by the slice.
- For fast and kid-approved meals in the old center, there are plenty of hamburger and pizza joints. For a good cafeteria, try Self-Service Ristorante Leonardo (a block from the Duomo). *Gelaterie* such as Perchè No! (Via dei Tavolini 19) are brash and neon, providing some of the best high-calorie memories in town. These are described in the Eating in Florence chapter.

# SIGHTSEEING

The key to a successful Florence family vacation is to slow down. Tackle one or two key sights each day, mix in a healthy dose of pure fun at a park or square, and take extended breaks when needed.

One of my favorite suggestions is to buy your child a trip journal, where they can record observations, thoughts, and favorite sights and memories. This journal could end up being your child's favorite souvenir.

## Planning Your Time
- Incorporate your child's interests into each day's plans. Let your kids make some decisions, such as choosing lunch spots or deciding which stores or museums to visit. Deputize your child to lead you on my self-guided walks and museum tours.
- Older kids and teens can help plan the details of a museum visit, such as what to see, how to get there, and ticketing details.
- Italy's national museums and Florence's municipal museums generally offer free admission to children under 18—always ask before buying tickets for your kids.

CHILDREN

## Books and Films for Kids

Get your kids into the spirit of Florence with these books and movies:

*Florence: Just Add Water* (Monica Fintoni, Simone Frasca, and Andrea Paoletti, 2007). This guidebook, excellent for travelers ages 10 and up, makes history more accessible for kids. It's easy to find in the US or in Florence (see bookstores listed on page 38).

*If You Were Me and Lived In...Renaissance Italy* (Carole P. Roman and Silvia Brunetti, 2016). This award-winning book helps kids imagine life in 15th-century Florence.

*Kids Go Europe: Treasure Hunt Florence* (Ellen Mouchawar and Marvin Mouchawar, 2006). Pocket-size and spiral-bound, this handy little book encourages youngsters to journal and sketch.

*Michelangelo* (Diane Stanley, 2003). The great Renaissance artist comes to life through Stanley's vibrant narration and illustrations.

*Pinocchio* (1940). This classic Disney animation, based on the Carlo Collodi novel written in Florence in the late 1800s, features the misadventures of a wooden marionette in his quest to become a real boy.

*Stravaganza* series (Mary Hoffman, 2002-2012). This popular, imaginative adventure series follows individuals who time-travel to 16th-century Italy. The series' second book, *City of Stars*, is set in "Remora," an alternate-universe Siena, and the third book, *City of Flowers*, takes place in "Giglia," a.k.a. Florence.

*The Wizards Return: Alex vs. Alex* (2013). Alex Russo, from the Disney TV show *Wizards of Waverly Place*, accidentally creates an evil version of herself during a trip to Tuscany, leading to an epic battle atop the Leaning Tower of Pisa.

**CHILDREN**

- Use the tips in the Sights in Florence chapter to avoid lines whenever possible, especially at the Uffizi and Accademia.
- Public WCs are hard to find: Try museums, bars, gelato shops, and fast-food restaurants.

### Successful Sightseeing

- If you're visiting art museums with younger children, you could hit the gift shop first to buy postcards; then hold a scavenger hunt to find the pictured artwork.
- Museum audioguides help older children and teens get the most out of a sight.
- Bring a sketchbook to a museum and encourage kids to select

a painting or statue to draw. It's a great way for them to slow down and observe.

- Context Florence offers a children's tour program run by scholarly guides who make the city's great art and culture accessible to a younger audience (see page 44). Local guide Alessandra Marchetti also does kid-tailored tours (see page 45).
- If homesickness sets in, take your kid to see a movie—American movies are commonplace (often shown in English with Italian subtitles).

## MONEY, SAFETY, AND STAYING CONNECTED

Before setting them loose, talk to your kids about safety and money.

- Give your child a money belt and an expanded allowance; you are on vacation, after all. Let your kids budget their funds by comparing and contrasting the dollar and euro.
- If you allow older kids to explore a museum or neighborhood on their own, be sure to establish a clear meeting time and place.
- For kids of all ages, have a "what if" procedure in place in case something goes wrong. If your child has a mobile phone, enable the "Find My Phone" feature in case you get separated (and show them how to make calls in Italy). Give your kids your hotel's business card, your phone number, and emergency taxi fare. If they don't have a phone, let them know to ask to use the phone at a hotel if they are lost.
- Teens traveling with a mobile device can keep in touch with friends at home—and Europeans they meet—via apps such as WhatsApp (common in Europe), Snapchat, Google Chat, FaceTime, Facebook Messenger, or Skype. Readily available Wi-Fi helps keep online time affordable, or consider buying an international data plan (see page 692).

## TRANSPORTATION

Kids often travel cheaper or for free.

- Children under three feet tall ride free on public buses when accompanied by an adult.
- Families with kids can sometimes get price breaks on train tickets; see "Transportation" in the Practicalities chapter for details.

# Top Kids' Sights and Activities

Seek out kid-friendly sights, such as the Leonardo museums, the Galileo Science Museum, or the Palazzo Vecchio.

## MUSEUMS AND CHURCHES
### Leonardo Museums

After touring a bunch of hands-off museums, squirming kids will enjoy the hands-on activities at either the Museo Leonardo Da Vinci Firenze (on Via del Castel-laccio) or the Leonardo da Vinci Interactive Museum (on Via dei Servi). They can burn off some of that human energy while powering modern re-creations of the brilliant scientist's machines (see page 67).

### Palazzo Vecchio

With a number of activities and tours for kids, this palace can be a good place for the whole family to explore together. The palazzo sometimes offers free family kits filled with materials for helping kids learn about the Medici and uncover interesting details about the place. The palace's family program offers a variety of daily activities for kids as young as four all the way up to teenagers (€5/person, reservations recommended). Enjoy brief performances portraying Medici history, or help your kids paint their own frescoes. As the offerings are always changing, check online or drop by the info desk at the ticket office to find out what your options are and make reservations.

📖 See the Palazzo Vecchio Tour chapter.

### Galileo Science Museum

See several of Galileo's fingers on display, plus cool old telescopes and early chemical and science lab stuff. Engaging video screens illustrate scientific principles. Private tours and special child-friendly programs are available. Be warned that some parents find the museum's displays on childbirth too graphic for kids.

📖 See the Galileo Science Museum Tour chapter.

### Duomo Dome Climb

Climbing the dome of the cathedral is almost like climbing an urban mountain—you'll spiral up in a strange dome-within-a-dome space, see some musty old tools used in the construction, get a bird's-eye peek into the nave from way up, and then pop out to see the best city view in town (see page 55).

### Bargello Museum

While kids are likely to be more familiar with Michelangelo's *David*, they may prefer the works at the Bargello. This underappreciated sculpture museum in a former police-station-turned-prison hosts Florence's most interesting collection of statues—with many bizarre poses.

☐ See the Bargello Tour chapter.

### Uffizi Courtyard

This courtyard, filled with artists and souvenir stalls, is ringed by statues of all the famous Florentines (Amerigo Vespucci, Machiavelli, Leonardo, and so on)—great for putting faces to names on a sweep through history (see page 106 of the Renaissance Walk chapter).

### Museum of Precious Stones

Find 500 kinds of stones on display, demonstrating the fascinating techniques of inlay and mosaic work (see page 62).

## PARKS AND SQUARES

### Boboli and Bardini Gardens

These adjacent gardens outside the Pitti Palace are landscaped wonderlands. While designed to give adults a break from the city, they're kid-friendly, too.

☐ See the Pitti Palace Tour chapter.

### Parco delle Cascine

Originally constructed as a hunting ground and farm for the Medici family, Florence's sprawling public park has lots of grass, historic monuments, and a playground. For a fee, families can cool off in the park's outdoor swimming pool, the Pavoniere.

**Cost and Hours:** Park—free and open year-round; swimming pool—€7 for kids 4-12, €9 for adults, open daily May-Aug 10:00-19:00, until 18:30 on Sat-Sun, Via della Catena 2, +39 055 362 233.

**Getting There:** Head west of the old center along the north side of the river (25-minute walk from Ponte Vecchio) or take tram T1 from the Alamanni-Stazione stop (near the train station; direction: Villa Costanza) to the stop Cascine.

### Piazza d'Azeglio

This peaceful and breezy park, complete with playground, can be a welcome refuge from touring madness (open daily, dawn to dusk).

**Getting There:** It's a 15-minute walk east from the Duomo. Or take bus #6 from the train station or #31 or #32 the Piazza San Marco bus stop just north of the Duomo.

### Piazzale Michelangelo

Older children may enjoy hiking up to this panoramic piazza for the superb view of Florence and the Duomo. Or take a taxi or ride the bus up and then enjoy the easy downhill walk back into town. Bring a picnic and eat lunch on the somewhat hidden terrace, just off the west side of the piazza (see page 82).

### Piazza della Repubblica

For kids running on their gelato buzz well into the evening hours, this vibrant piazza has a sparkling carousel and lively street musicians.

## MORE EXPERIENCES

### Open-Air Markets

Florence's various markets are fun for kids (see the Shopping in Florence chapter). Remember to haggle.

### Artviva Art Classes

Local tour company Artviva offers cooking, painting, and sculpture classes that work well for older kids and teens (see page 44).

### Leaning Tower of Pisa

Of your day-trip options from Florence, this one is probably the most interesting for kids. Note that kids under age eight aren't allowed to climb the tower (see page 450 of the Pisa chapter).

# SHOPPING IN FLORENCE

Florence may be one of Europe's best shopping towns—it's been known for its sense of style since the Medici days. While some legacy businesses are as staid and stately as the city itself, a sampling of creative shops will help you appreciate the younger side of Florence.

**Hours:** Smaller stores are generally open about 9:00-13:00 and 15:30-19:30, usually closed on Sunday, often closed on Monday (or at least Monday morning), and sometimes closed for a couple of weeks around August 15. Bigger stores have similar hours, without the afternoon break.

**Information:** For shopping ideas, ads, and a list of markets, see *The Florentine* newspaper (www.theflorentine.net). For authentic, locally produced wares, look for shops displaying the *Esercizi Storici Fiorentini* seal, with a picture of the Palazzo Vecchio's tower. At these city-endorsed "Historical Florentine Ventures," you may pay a premium, but quality is assured (for a list of shops, see www.esercizistoricifiorentini.it).

**Tax Refunds:** For details on VAT refunds and customs regulations, see page 659.

**Department Stores:** Department store chains include the upscale **La Rinascente** (daily 10:00-20:30, on Piazza della Repubblica); and **OVS,** a discount clothing chain (daily 10:00-19:30, near train station at intersection of Via Panzani and Via del Giglio).

## What to Buy

### LEATHER
With its inimitable sense of style, richly perfumed leather shops, and persuasive salesclerks, Florence has a way of turning leather browsers into leather buyers. Florence's long leatherworking tradi-

tion was born at Santa Croce Church, where Franciscan monks perfected the art of binding gorgeously illustrated manuscripts. Over the centuries, the skill evolved into a more fashion-forward form of leatherworking—designer shoes, jackets, and handbags. You'll see leather for sale all over Florence.

## Leather-Buying Tips

If you're serious about buying a big-ticket leather item, do some homework before your trip. Visit importers and boutiques in your home city so that you can smartly comparison-shop when you get to Florence.

A good-quality, authentic Italian leather jacket starts at about €250-350. Top-quality and designer jackets can cost much more.

For a lower price range, you'll find plenty of merchants willing to help you part with your money, particularly at San Lorenzo Market. But if quality, craftsmanship, and durability are important to you, steer clear of San Lorenzo. Because any item that is even partially assembled in Italy can be legally labeled Italian, much of what is sold there has been made abroad, then brought home for a few final stitches and a "Made in Italy" label.

Here are a few things to look for when evaluating leather: It should smell woody and natural, not like chemicals, and it should feel soft and pliable, not stiff. Crumple the leather to see how well it rebounds. If it remains wadded or wrinkled, it's not top-notch. Examine the seams and stitching: They should be tight and regular. Consider the quality of the liner, and test the zippers.

Consider the fit. Italians prefer their jackets more fitted than Americans, and their idea of the "right size" may feel snug to you. Don't let a salesperson talk you into a jacket that doesn't fit. Better leather shops can alter your jacket (sometimes on the spot). They may even offer to custom-make a jacket for you and ship it— though, both for matters of fit and finances, this should only be considered at a shop that has a stellar reputation.

## Leather Jackets

When Italians want to shop for affordable leather, they go to suburban outlet malls (such as The Mall, with outlet stores for many top-name Italian designers, about 15 miles southeast of the Duomo, www.themall.it). Or they head for a leather factory (Piero Tucci is one of many with a good reputation, www.pierotucci.com). But this isn't practical for a carless tourist on a short visit. Most leather shops within walking distance of the historic core cater to tourists and well-heeled locals, so bargains are rare.

Here are a few shops in the center with good reputations (all selling jackets in the €250-500 range):

**La Pelle,** straight ahead from the Oltrarno end of Ponte Vecchio, stocks a fine variety of good-quality leather coats (Via Guicciardini 11 red, +39 055 292 031, www.lapellesrl.it).

**Atelier Classe** sits down a mostly neglected alley near Piazza Santa Croce. This boutique feels classier than its cut-rate neighbors—and its prices are higher too (on-site alterations possible, closed Sun and Mon until 14:00, Via Torta 16 red, +39 055 268 145, www.atelierclasse.com). They also have a shoe store two doors down.

**Davide Cerasi**—specializing in fine leather jackets, coats, and handbags—sits along the embankment on the north side of the Arno, just steps from Ponte Vecchio. You can buy a jacket off the rack or have one custom-made (Lungarno Acciaiuoli 32 red, +39 055 493 5346).

**Noi,** facing Piazza Davanzati, has jackets of reputable quality as well as a good selection of well-priced bags (Via Porta Rossa 65 red, +39 055 210 319).

**Michelangelo,** burrowed down a side street from the San Lorenzo Market chaos, has helpful staff and is a bit cheaper than the others (Via Giovan Battista Zannoni 9 red, +39 334 97 42 868, www.michelangeloflorentineleather.it).

**On Borgo La Noce:** To step down a notch, browse the aggressive shops that line Borgo La Noce between the Basilica of San Lorenzo and Mercato Centrale—including **Massimo Leather, Raffaello,** and **Pelletteria La Noce.**

## Handbags and Other Leather Accessories

Consider these places when shopping for leather handbags, wallets, gloves, and other items; some of the jacket shops listed earlier also sell accessories.

The venerable **Leather School** (Scuola del Cuoio) at **Santa Croce Church**—described on page 236—is the most famous place to buy leather in Florence. The quality is unsurpassed, and a splurge here will get you a top-end item that should last a lifetime (figure €70 for a simple wallet or €150 for a small purse; monogramming costs just a bit extra). But even for browsers, the school is worth a visit as the most accessible place to watch leather workers in action. The leather school produces handbags, briefcases, travel cases, wallets, belts, and jackets (daily 10:00-18:00, artisans at work Mon-Fri 11:00-14:30, enter around behind Santa Croce Church at Via San Giuseppe 5 red; 055-244-533, www.scuoladelcuoio.com).

Of Florence's many midrange shops specializing in bags, **Via de Ginori 23r** is well worth a look. This family-run shop, located a few blocks from the San Lorenzo Market, carries a collection of stylish bags—some of their own production, some from other local suppliers—and a line of eco-friendly bags made from recycled tires (Mon 15:00-19:00, Tue-Sat 10:00-14:00 & 15:00-19:00, closed Sun, may close Sat afternoon in summer, Via de Ginori 23 red, +39 055 239 8031).

Not far away, **Furò e Punteruolo** ("Flatknife and Awl") sells a small selection of wallets, purses, and handbags in a simple, classic style. Paulo makes everything by hand on the premises (closed Sun, between Santa Maria Novella and the Medici Chapels at Via del Giglio 29 red, mobile +39 348 437 0867).

**Benheart** has a casual style and a young owner, who makes finely crafted, hand-cut leather jackets, belts, and shoes (Via dei Calzaiuoli 78 red and in the "Shopping Triangle"—see later—at Via della Vigna Nuova 97 red, +39 055 199 35276).

Across the river in the Oltrarno, a block up from the Ponte Vecchio, **Madova** has been selling handmade leather gloves—and nothing else—for more than 100 years. Their expert salespeople can tell your glove size with just a glance at your hand (Via Guicciardini 1 red). Nearby, **Roberta** is another popular choice for fashionable but moderately priced handbags (Mon-Sat 10:00-19:00, closed Sun, also closed Mon Nov-Feb, Borgo San Jacopo 74 red, +39 055 284 017, www.robertafirenze.com).

## PERFUME AND COSMETICS

Long ago, as part of their service to the community, Dominican friars typically served as pharmacists (a.k.a. chemists or alchemists). And—back in an age when "medicine" meant potions and herbal remedies—the pharmacy at the Dominican church of Santa Maria Novella was a local trendsetter in the art of fragrance. In the centuries since, perfumes and colognes have taken off in a big way in other parts of this fashion-forward city. Below are two fragrance experiences—both elegant, but quite different: a big, staid, historic perfumery, and a smaller, more intimate alternative.

The **Farmacia di Santa Maria Novella** is as formal as it is historic, with dressy, no-nonsense clerks. Pick up the history sheet from the rack, and wander deep into the shop. The main sales room was a chapel in the 14th century. Now you can sample more than 60 perfumes here, including "Acqua della Regina," which

SHOPPING

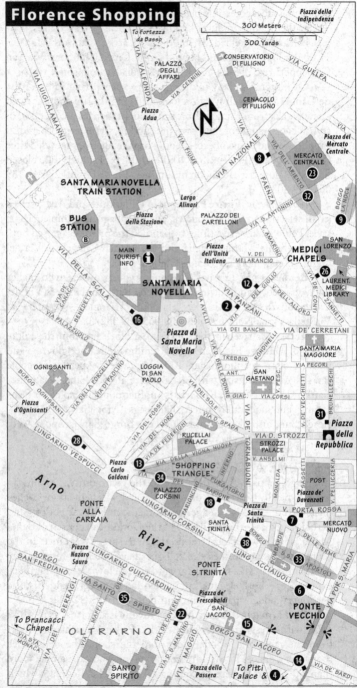

# Florence Shopping

300 Meters

300 Yards

To Fortezza
da Basso

Piazza della
Indipendenza

VIA VALFONDA

PALAZZO
DEGLI
AFFARI

VIA CENNINI

CONSERVATORIO
DI FULIGNO

VIA GUELFA

Piazza
Adua

VIA FIUME

VIA NAZIONALE

CENACOLO
DI FULIGNO

VIA DELL'ARIENTO

Piazza del
Mercato
Centrale

8

MERCATO
CENTRALE

23

SANTA MARIA NOVELLA
TRAIN STATION

Largo
Alinari

FAENZA

32

BORGO
LA NOCE

VIA S. ANTONINO

9

BUS
STATION

B

Piazza
della Stazione

PALAZZO DEI
CARTELLONI

VIA V. AMERIGO

VIA S. MARTINO

VIA DELLA SCALA

MAIN
TOURIST
INFO

i

Piazza
dell'Unità
Italiana

V. DEI
MELARANCIO

SAN
LORENZO

MEDICI
CHAPELS

LAURENT.
MEDICI
LIBRARY

VIA DE' GINORI

VIA DE' CONTI

VIA CANACCI

VIA PALAZZUOLO

SANTA MARIA
NOVELLA

16

VIA AVELLI

VIA PANZANI

12

VIA DEL GIGLIO

V. DELL'ALLORO

26

S. DI ZANNETTI

2

VIA DEI BANCHI

VIA DE' CERRETANI

OGNISSANTI

BORGO OGNISSANTI

VIA DELLA PORCELLANA

VIA D'PALOINO

Piazza di
Santa Maria
Novella

VIA DEL TREBBIO

VIA D. BELLE DONNE

RONDINELLI

SANTA MARIA
MAGGIORE

VIA PECORI

VIA DELLE BENEDETTA

LOGGIA
DI SAN
PAOLO

VIA ANT.
GIAC.

SAN
GAETANO

VIA CORSI

VIA DE' PESC.

BRUNELLESCHI

Piazza
d'Ognissanti

VIA DEL FOSSI

VIA DEL MORO

VIA DEL SOLE

VIA DE' TORNABUONI

V. DE' VECCHIETTI

31

Piazza
della
Repubblica

LUNGARNO VESPUCCI

28

VIA D. SPADA

RUCELLAI
PALACE

VIA DE FEDERIGHI

VIA DELLA VIGNA NUOVA

VIA D. STROZZI

STROZZI
PALACE

V. ANSELMI

SASSETTI

POST

Piazza de'
Davanzati

Arno

13

Piazza
Carlo
Goldoni

VIA

"SHOPPING
TRIANGLE"

34

DEL

VIA DELLA VIGNA NUOVA

PARIONE

INFERNO

PURGATORIO

MONALDA

V. PELLICCERIA

PONTE
ALLA
CARRAIA

PALAZZO
CORSINI

LUNGARNO CORSINI

18

PARIONE

SANTA
TRINITÀ

Piazza di
Santa
Trinità

7

V. PORTA ROSSA

MERCATO
NUOVO

River

Piazza
Nazaro
Sauro

BORGO
SAN FREDIANO

LUNGARNO GUICCIARDINI

PONTE
S. TRINITÀ

38

BORGO

LUNG. ACCIAIUOLI

BOMBARDE

S.S.

33

V. DELLE TERME

S. APOSTOLI

VIA POR S. MARIA

VIA SANTO SPIRITO

VIA GEPPI

35

Piazza de'
Frescobaldi

SAN
JACOPO

15

BORGO SAN JACOPO

6

PONTE
VECCHIO

To Brancacci
Chapel

VIA DEI SERRAGLI

VIA MAFFIA

VIA DE' COVERELLI

VIA S. MARTINO

22

VIA DE' BARDI

OLTRARNO

VIA STA.
MONACA

VIA D. S. MAGGIO

Piazza della
Passera

To Pitti
Palace &

4

14

SANTO
SPIRITO

**Department Stores**
1. La Rinascente
2. OVS

**Leather**
3. To The Mall Outlet Shop
4. To La Pelle
5. Atelier Classe
6. Davide Cerasi
7. Noi
8. Michelangelo
9. Borgo La Noce Shops
10. S. Croce Leather School
11. Via de Ginori 23r
12. Furò e Punteruolo
13. Benheart (2)
14. Madova
15. Roberta

**Perfume & Cosmetics**
16. Farmacia di S. Maria Novella
17. Aqua Flor

**Paper, Stationery & Prints**
18. Alberto Cozzi
19. Il Papiro (3)
20. Bottega d'Arte Eredi Paperone
21. Fabriano Boutique
22. L'Ippogrifo

**Food**
23. Mercato Centrale
24. EATaly
25. Migone Confetti

**Ceramics & Housewares**
26. Ceramica Ricceri
27. Sbigoli
28. La Bottega d'Arte Lastrucci
29. To Mesticheria Tucci
30. Civaiolo
31. Bialetti

**Shopping Areas**
32. San Lorenzo Market
33. Borgo Santi Apostoli
34. Via del Parione
35. Via di Santo Spirito
36. To Via Pietrapiana & Borgo La Croce

**Fashion Museums**
37. Gucci Garden Gallery
38. Ferragamo Museum

SHOPPING

Catherine de' Medici commissioned from the Dominicans in 1533, as well as face creams, body lotions, and talcum powders.

If serious about buying, clerks will load your selections onto a digital card. When you're ready to check out, bring it to the bunker-like perfume room to pick up your purchases (daily 10:00-19:00, a block from Piazza Santa Maria Novella, 100 yards down Via della Scala at #16, +39 055 216 276, www.smnovella.com).

**Aqua Flor** is a rare shop where the master perfumer sells his wares in the same space where he makes them. Hidden away on a side street between Piazza della Signoria and Piazza Santa Croce, Aqua Flor uses only natural extracts to pull out subtle but warmly pungent aromas. They're generous with samples, and the old-world space is enjoyable to simply be in. In one of the three cavernous rooms, you'll see Sileno's "organ"—the giant cabinet stocked with little jars and bottles—where, like a musician, he finds just the right combination of notes. They can create a custom fragrance just for you (daily 10:00-19:00, Borgo Santa Croce 6, +39 055 234 3471, www.aquaflor.com). After your visit, be sure to dip into the court-yard of the sprawling palazzo-turned-condominium complex that houses the shop.

## PAPER, STATIONERY, AND PRINTS

Long known as a literary center, Florence offers traditional mar-bled stationery (with its edge dipped carefully into a bath of swirl-ing pigments) and leatherbound journals, plus reproductions of old documents, prints, maps, and manuscripts.

**In the Historic Center:** Family-owned **Alberto Cozzi,** now in its fourth generation, specializes in marbled paper products as well as leather-bound journals (closed Sun, Via del Parione 35 red, +39 055 294 968). **Il Papiro** doesn't have a storied history (it's a chain), but their outlets are conveniently positioned around town, selling pretty marbled papers, stationery, and paper boxes (branch-es at Piazza Duomo 24 red, Via Cavour 49 red, and Borgo San Lorenzo 45 red, www.ilpapirofirenze.eu). **Bottega d'Arte Eredi Paperone** also sells high-end stationery and paper products, as well as fine table linens (near the Duomo at Via del Proconsolo 26 red, +39 055 268 296). **Fabriano Boutique,** tucked in the twisty streets between the Duomo and the river, is part of a top-end chain sell-ing leatherbound office tools and modern stationery (daily, Via del Corso 59 red, www.fabrianoboutique.com).

**In the Oltrarno: L'Ippogrifo** makes high-quality prints of mostly Florentine scenes—a notch above the mass-produced post-ers you'll see around town (closed Sun, at Via di Santo Spirito 5 red, +39 055 213 255, www.ippogrifostampedarte.com). **Legatoria il Torchio** (Via de Bardi 17, in the Oltrarno's San Niccolò neigh-borhood) is an old-fashioned book bindery that makes albums, frames, and other giftables from handmade marbled papers and Florentine leather.

## EDIBLE GOODIES

**Mercato Centrale** is a prime spot for stocking up on culinary souvenirs (closed Sun, a block north of the Basilica of San Lorenzo).

Classic purchases include olive oil and balsamic vinegar, unusually shaped and colored pasta, dried porcini mushrooms, spices, and jars of pestos and sauces (such as pesto *genovese* or *tartufo*—truffle).

**EATaly,** an outpost of the gourmet mini mall chain, is a convenient place to pick up pricey, premium consumable souvenirs (see listing on page 309).

**Migone Confetti** has a dazzling array of nougats, fudge, jellied fruit drops, and biscotti, available in beribboned Duomo, Baptistery, and Campanile boxes or wrapped in classic Florentine paper (daily, Via dei Calzaiuoli 85 red, +39 055 314 004).

## CERAMICS AND HOUSEHOLD GOODS

There are more famous ceramics destinations in Tuscany than Florence, but the city has several worthy shops for classic Italian pottery. If you don't want to lug it home, most shops will ship your purchases. **Ceramica Ricceri** has colorful hand-decorated majolica (near the Basilica of San Lorenzo at Via dei Conti 14 red, www.riccericeramica.com); **Sbigoli,** near the Duomo, has affordable, timeless pieces, some of which are hand-painted in a back workshop (closed Sun, Via Egidio 4 red). **La Bottega d'Arte Lastrucci** sells high-caliber Florentine souvenirs, particularly ceramics but also wooden trays and nativity sets (closed Sun, Borgo Ognissanti 11 red).

To get a sense of fine textile production in Florence, visit the friendly Oltrarno showroom of **Busatti.** This family of weavers has been operating since the 1840s, making beautiful (and expensive) bedding and table linens. But thrifty shoppers will find packable and affordable souvenirs such as towels and oven mitts (Via San Niccolò 48, www.busatti.com).

Italians have a knack for producing well-designed, functional housewares—which you can find at a *mesticheria*—basically a store that sells a little bit of everything at hardware store prices. Prowl the packed shelves of **Mesticheria Tucci** (Via dei Servi 76 red, near the Duomo) to find olive oil dispensers, cheap ceramics, cheese graters, and olive wood bowls. **Civaiolo** (Via Taddea 5 red, east of Mercato Centrale) is a store for *casalinghi* (household items)—besides a selection of cookware and utensils, this shop sells portable and packable spices, dried legumes, and mushrooms. The kitchen supply store **Bialetti** is more upscale (under the arcade at Piazza della Repubblica 25) and fun to browse for their comprehensive selection of the classic Italian Moka coffee maker.

# Best Shopping Areas

Many visitors never break out of Florence's heavily traveled tourist zones in the heart of town—and you can find some worthy shops there. But you'll find several pleasant streets and neighborhoods with a more authentic and innovative array of shops if you leave the historic center.

## SAN LORENZO MARKET

The market stalls between the Basilica of San Lorenzo and Mercato Centrale are no secret—this is ground zero for tourists seeking cheap, cut-rate souvenirs, lower-end leather, clothing, T-shirts, and handbags. It's a fun area to browse and bargain (just hang onto your wallet—this is pickpocket central). You'll find many of the stalls in the narrow streets around Mercato Centrale (daily 9:00-19:00, closed Mon in winter).

If you end up going overboard on Florentine finds, you can buy a cheap suitcase here and at the various open-air market stalls around town. A big suitcase with wheels costs about €25 and should last just long enough to haul your purchases home.

**Bargaining:** At Florence's street markets, the first price you're quoted is an opening volley; sometimes if you simply show small signs of reluctance, you'll be offered a better price. Feel free to push back with a much lower offer. Vendors may also sweeten the deal if you offer to pay cash or buy two or more of something.

## THE HISTORIC CENTER

**Borgo Santi Apostoli:** This narrow street, just one short block up from Ponte Vecchio, hosts boutiques, designer handbag shops, antique and art stores, and jewelers. Though near the tourist zone, you'll feel a bit removed from kitsch in the stretch between Via Por Santa Maria and Via de' Tornabuoni.

Among jewelry stores, watch for **Gatto Bianco,** selling big,

# Florence's Upscale Boutique Streets

Florence is a bastion of high fashion, where budget travelers can enjoy high-end window shopping. The entire area between

the river and the cathedral is busy with inviting boutiques that show off ritzy Italian fashions. The highest concentration of shops is along Via dei Calzaiuoli, Via de' Tornabuoni, and the streets in between (particularly around Piazza della Repubblica). In recent years, city officials have been pedestrianizing and sprucing up more and more streets in an

attempt to cement Florence's status as a high-fashion destination. (Many locals grouse that in so doing, they've forced out more characteristic, low-rent mom-and-pop shops that have thrived here for generations.)

**Via dei Calzaiuoli** mixes tourist-rip-off pizza and gelato joints with upscale chain boutiques.

**Via de' Tornabuoni** is a delightfully pedestrianized, flower-lined street where Prada and Gucci face each other, like bitter rivals, kicking off a string of Italian designers and international chains. The bottom half of the street features the big Italian "-i" designers (Gucci, Armani, Fendi, Tiffan-i).

**Piazza della Repubblica** has several fine shops, including the upscale La Rinascente department store, with its Duomo-view café terrace (see page 70).

If you head under that piazza's arch and down **Via degli Strozzi,** you'll pass big names—Dolce & Gabbana, Louis Vuitton, Cartier, and Bulgari—on the way to the fine Palazzo Strozzi (a good place for a coffee break; described on page 71) and the intersection with Via de' Tornabuoni.

Fashionistas will enjoy the **Ferragamo Museum** and flagship store near Ponte Santa Trinità and the **Gucci Garden Gallery,** with a prime address on Piazza della Signoria (both described on page 76).

chunky, modern-style pieces (#12 red); **T. Pestelli,** where silversmith Tommaso creates finely detailed jewelry and small sculptures (#20 red); and **Angela Caputi,** whose colorful, oversize pieces have earned her a loyal following (#42 red).

**Solo a Firenze** has a tasteful collection of cards, prints, and silverwork ("Only in Florence," #37 red). The stylish and upscale **Viajiyu** sells a selection of pricey, fashionable shoes and will custom-make a pair for you (#45 red). At the end of the street, filling a stately 800-year-old building, is the flagship store for the famous shoemaker **Ferragamo,** with its shoe museum in the basement (Via de' Tornabuoni 2; see description on page 76).

**Shopping Triangle:** For a fun and productive shopping stroll, trace a triangle from Via del Parione, Via della Vigna Nuova, and Via de' Tornabuoni. You'll get a good look at high fashion, one-of-a-kind boutiques, craft workshops, and collectibles.

From Piazza Santa Trinità (near the Ferragamo flagship store), angle up **Via del Parione.** This classically Florentine street mixes old artisanal workshops (**Alberto Cozzi**'s paper, stationery, and print shop at #35 red, closed Sun), fun surprises (**Letizia Fiorini**'s puppet store, #60 red, closed Sun-Mon), and contemporary bling (**Vertigo** jewelry store, #22 red, closed Sun-Mon).

At the end of the street, you'll pop out at a lively three-way intersection (take note of **Marioluca Giusti,** selling high-quality plastic tableware, at Via Lunga 133). From here, take a sharp right onto **Via della Vigna Nuova,** with many fine clothing stores for men and women. This is a great spot to shop for affordable, everyday apparel, with a few splurge boutiques mixed in. Right at the corner is the leather store **Benheart** (described under "Leather," earlier); **A. Bianda Coltelleria,** across the street, has been offering classy gentlemen's accessories, such as pocketknives and shaving gear, since 1820 (#86 red, closed Sun). And **Secret**, a small boutique, has plenty of unique finds (#16 red, daily but closed Mon morning).

You'll gradually work your way back toward the upscale **Via de' Tornabuoni,** arguably Florence's most inviting top-of-the-line boutique browsing street. This pedestrianized street is lined with oversize flowerpots, well-heeled shoppers, and international designers (Gucci, Prada, Pucci, Bulgari). Even if your wallet won't stretch far enough to shop here, the window-shopping is as good as it gets.

## THE OLTRARNO

Florence's artistic legacy endures most strongly in the Oltrarno neighborhood. Just a short walk across the river, past the tourist crowds, takes you to small artisan shops with handmade furniture, jewelry, leather shoes, and pottery. In unassuming workshops, craftsmen breathe new life into antique pieces and artworks using age-old techniques.

To experience this slice of Florence, take my Oltrarno Walk (see page 238), where I've highlighted shops that are easily accessible to browsers. Various tour operators also offer tours of Oltrarno workshops (see page 44).

## NEAR PIAZZA SANTA CROCE

The area around Santa Croce Church is a popular, if touristy, shopping zone.

**Shop with the Florentines** (Via Pietrapiana and Borgo La Croce): To get off the beaten path, walk about 10 minutes northeast of Santa Croce, to the axis formed by Via Pietrapiana, Borgo La Croce, and Via Gioberti. This authentic-feeling area isn't about artsy souvenirs, but about getting a glimpse at what Florentines buy for day-to-day life.

Short but bustling **Via Pietrapiana** is lined with shops and dominated by a big, Renaissance loggia that marks the entrance to a park. Inside the park is the quirky, grubby **Piazza dei Ciompi flea market,** which blurs the boundary between antiques and junk (daily 9:00-19:30, bigger the last Sun of each month). Also along this street is **Sotto Sotto** (#67 red), where local bargain hunters browse last year's deeply discounted designer fashions (closed Sun, www.sottosotto.it).

Heading east on Via Pietrapiana, you'll reach Piazza Sant'Ambrogio, with its namesake church. To the right of the church, **Borgo La Croce** teems with local shoppers. Stroll this mostly pedestrianized street two blocks to the big piazza, passing stores selling housewares, kitchen gadgets, linens, haircuts, clocks, everyday fashions, shoes, home decor, organic body products, ceramics, pets, candy, antiques, and bridal wear.

SHOPPING

# NIGHTLIFE IN FLORENCE

With so many American and international college students in town, Florence by night can have a frat-party atmosphere. For me, nighttime is for eating a late meal, catching a concert, strolling through the old-town pedestrian zone and piazzas with a gelato, or hitting one of the many pubs or wine bars.

The latest on nightlife and concerts is listed in several publications available free at the TI, such as *The Florentine* monthly (the online version is updated biweekly at www.theflorentine.net). The TI can give you a rundown of the day's musical events; also check www.feelflorence.it. *Firenze Spettacolo* (www.firenzespettacolo.it), is also a good resource for events and nightlife (mostly in Italian, but there's an English section).

## STROLLING AFTER DARK

The **historic center** has a floodlit ambience that's ideal for strolling. The entire pedestrian zone around the Duomo and along Via dei Calzaiuoli, between the Uffizi and the Duomo, is lively with people.

**Piazza della Repubblica,** lined with venerable 19th-century cafés, offers good people-watching. In the evening, it's a hub of activity, with opera singers, violinists, harpists, bizarre street performers, and a cover band that plays cheesy tunes for the seating area of one of the piazza's bars. A ride on the carousel is always fun, but more so at night.

**Ponte Vecchio** is a popular place to enjoy river views (and kiss), and often has a street musician after dark who encourages passersby to dance.

A few areas feel creepy after dark. Use good judgment. I'd skip the seedy area between Mercato Centrale and the train station.

## SUNSETS

For the perfect end to the day, watch the sun descend over the Arno River from any of the bridges, especially Ponte Vecchio. Piazzale Michelangelo, perched on a hilltop across the river, is also great for sunset-watching; it's packed with Romeos and Juliets on weekend evenings (for directions on how to get there, see page 82).

The nearby San Miniato Church (200 yards uphill) is quieter and comes with the same commanding view. If you're going after dark, it's more efficient to zip up by taxi (rather than take a one-hour round-trip hike; see page 83). While side-tripping out to Fiesole for the sunset is popular (see page 87), I'd stick with Piazzale Michelangelo.

## LIVE MUSIC

Frequent **live concerts** enhance Florence's beautiful setting. In the summertime, piazzas host a wide range of performers, including pop bands on temporary stages. The lovely sounds of classical music fill churches year-round for special performances. At the TI, ask about current musical events, and keep an eye open for posters as you wander around town.

**Orsanmichele Church** regularly holds concerts under its Gothic arches. Tickets are sold on the day of the concert from the door facing Via dei Calzaiuoli or, on Sunday, from the doorway opposite the church entrance.

**Orchestra della Toscana** presents classical concerts from November to May in Teatro Verdi (€13-20, check website for box office hours or to buy tickets online, near Bargello at Via Ghibellina 97, +39 055 212 320, www.orchestradellatoscana.it).

**Dinner Theater at Teatro del Sale** is a quirky place for dinner and theater. Every night (except Sun-Mon) at 19:30 they kick off a buffet with a fun array of tasty dishes for an hour and a half. Then they take away the tables for an hour-long show. Sometimes the show is great for non-Italian speakers (live music, for example)—and sometimes it's not (call or check their website). The old theater is not technically a restaurant, so you'll pay a €7 membership fee to "join" the association, plus €36 for the evening, including drinks (10 blocks behind the Duomo, northeast of Santa Croce at Via dei Macci 111 red, +39 055 200 1492, www.teatrodelsale.com).

**Boxoffice Toscana** sells tickets for rock concerts and theater productions in Italian (check website for box office hours or to pur-

---

## Sights Open Late

You can extend your sightseeing day into the night at several Florence sights. In peak season, the Uffizi, Accademia, and Pitti Palace typically stay open into the early evening every day but Monday.

Other sights with evening hours include the Duomo Museum, Duomo's dome (Mon-Fri), the Baptistery (Mon-Sat), the Campanile (daily), and in summer, Pitti Palace's Boboli and Bardini Gardens. The stalls at the San Lorenzo Market (closed Mon in winter) and Mercato Nuovo stay open late for shoppers every night.

---

chase tickets online, east of Santa Croce Church at Via delle Vecchie Carceri 1, +39 055 210 804, www.boxofficetoscana.it).

**Ponte Vecchio** often hosts a fine street musician late each evening in summer. He plugs in his amp while young people get comfortable on the curb. There's also generally a street musician nightly in the **Uffizi courtyard.**

## DRINKS

Grab a drink and enjoy the scene at one of the following places.

**Wine Bars:** An *enoteca* is fun for sampling regional wines and enjoying munchies, especially before dinnertime. Throughout the old town, *enoteche* serve fine Italian wines by the glass with memorable atmospheres. **Le Volpi e l'Uva,** specializing in small, often organic wine producers, has a cozy interior and romantic seating on a quiet little piazza. They have 40 open bottles to choose from and a short menu of appropriate dishes. For maximum tasting, they are happy to arrange a flight of half-glasses and make a little plate of mixed *affettati* (cold cuts) and cheeses (Mon-Sat 12:00-21:00, closed Sun, 65 yards south of Ponte Vecchio—walk through Piazza Santa Felicità to Piazza dei Rossi 1, see map on page 298, +39 055 239 8132, run by wine experts Riccardo, Ciro, and Emilio).

**Caffè del Verone,** a terrace bar on the top floor of the Hospital of the Innocents, keeps late hours in summer so you can enjoy a spritz while taking in rooftop views. They have jazz on some weekend nights—call for details (Wed-Mon 12:00-20:00, open later on weekends and summer, closed Tue, Piazza SS. Annunziata 13, see map on page 36, +39 392 498 2559).

**Pubs:** Irish and English pubs abound in Florence, attracting a mixed crowd of locals and tourists. Most are open late daily. Popular ones include **The Old Stove** (Via Pellicceria 2 red, south of Piazza della Repubblica), **Angie's Pub** (Via dei Neri 35 red, east of the Uffizi), **The Fiddlers Elbow** (Piazza Santa Maria Novella 7 red), and the **Dublin Pub** (Via Faenza 27, near Mercato Centrale).

**Microbreweries:** Italy is experiencing a craft beer fad, and Florence has several places where you can join in. Handy to many recommended hotels (and near Mercato Centrale) is **Mostodolce.** A *birrificio artigianale* (craft brewery), they serve nine original beers and basic pub grub to raucous, youthful patrons who pin their drawings to the walls and spill out onto the street (daily 11:00-24:00, Via Nazionale 114 red, see map on page 306, +39 055 230 2928). Or head across the river to **Archea Brewery,** a small pub that brews several of their own varieties, with a few other Italian-produced beers on tap (daily 18:00-24:00, Via de'Serragli 44 red, a 5-minute walk west of Piazza di Santo Spirito, see map on page 298, +39 055 219 671, Carmine).

## LATE-NIGHT LOCAL SCENES

American university students in Florence seem to do more drinking than studying during their semesters abroad. Despite the college party vibe, there is something for everyone in Florence after hours.

As elsewhere in Italy, many bars have a nightly *aperitivo,* a spread of snacks intended to tide you over until dinner. For the price of a drink, anyone can sample a dish, and the frugal can stretch it to a light meal.

**Piazza Santa Croce:** It's a hangout at night, often with concerts in front of the church. The epicenter of American student partying is around this square, where you'll find lots of bars and more foreigners than Italians. The neighboring Via de' Benci is busy with trendy night spots that jump daily until late: **Moyo,** a slick, gold-lit lounge (#23 red), is noisy and popular with a hip, young crowd (*aperitivo* buffet 18:30-20:00)—there are tables outside, if you want to hear yourself talk. The **Red Garter** next door (#35 red) is lively and loud, with karaoke and dancing. The casual **Soul Kitchen** (#34 red) has DJ sets and keeps its *aperitivo* buffet going nightly 19:00-22:00.

**Piazza Demidoff:** To rub elbows with the locals, head across the river toward tiny Piazza Demidoff (cross the bridge east of Ponte Vecchio and turn left, about a 10-minute walk). **Zoe** has outdoor seating (opens Mon-Sat at 9:00, Sun at 18:00, Via dei Renai 13 red—see map on page 81, +39 055 243 111).

**San Niccolò:** Just a few steps around the corner from Piazza Demidoff, Via di San Niccolò has a compact and enjoyable cluster of nighttime hangouts. The bar called **Il Rifrullo** is the center of attention, with a lively, friendly setting, a big, breezy and convivial terrace out back and delightful mixed cold cuts plates to go with your drinks (open daily until late, Via San Niccolò 55 red—see map on page 81, +39 055 234 2621).

**Piazza di Santo Spirito:** This square—long known for its riffraff and druggies—has become a more mainstream place to enjoy the evening. It's lined with popular bars and restaurants; for locations see the map on page 298. **Volume** caters to a younger crowd with a living-room atmosphere in an old woodshop. You'll see tools still on the walls amid modern art (daily 8:30-24:00, *aperitivo* 18:30-22:00, Piazza di Santo Spirito 5 red, +39 055 238 1460). On the opposite side of the square, **Pop Café** feels trendy, though it's plastic-plate simple, with students getting comfortable on the curbs and cobbles (daily 8:00-late, *aperitivo* 19:00-22:00, Piazza di Santo Spirito 18, +39 055 217 475). A bit farther from the square, **Gosh** bar, wallpapered in pink flamingoes, mixes up craft cocktails and herb-infused drinks with flair (daily until 24:00, Via Santo Spirito 46 red, +39 055 046 9048). **NOF** is a late-night hangout with drinks and live music ranging from rock to jazz (Mon-Sat 18:30-late, Borgo San Frediano 17 red, +39 333 614 5376).

## MOVIES

Find first-run films in their original languages—including English—at Odeon Cinema, a beautiful historic movie house right downtown, a half-block west of Piazza della Repubblica (Piazza Strozzi, +39 055 214 068, www.odeonfirenze.com; for schedule of original-language films, look under *"Original Sound"*).

NIGHTLIFE

# FLORENCE CONNECTIONS

Florence is Tuscany's transportation hub, with fine train, bus, and plane connections to virtually anywhere in Italy. The city has several train stations, a bus station (next to the main train station), and an airport (and Pisa's airport is nearby). Livorno, on the coast west of Florence, is a major cruise-ship port.

## By Train

Florence's main train station is called **Santa Maria Novella** (*Firenze S.M.N.* on schedules and signs). Florence also has two suburban train stations: **Firenze Rifredi** and **Firenze Campo di Marte.** Note that some trains don't stop at the main station—before boarding, confirm that you're heading for S.M.N., or you may overshoot the city. (If this happens, don't panic; the other stations are a short taxi ride from the center.)

For general information on train travel in Italy—including ticket-buying options—see the Practicalities chapter.

### SANTA MARIA NOVELLA STATION

Built in Mussolini's "Rationalism" style back between the world wars, in some ways the station seems to have changed little—notice the 1930s-era lettering and architecture. The signage still refers to long-gone services while the photographs and artwork also evoke an earlier era.

As at any busy train station, be on guard: Don't trust "porters" who want to help you find your train or carry your bags (they're not official), and politely decline offers of help using the ticket machines by anyone other than uniformed staff.

To orient yourself to the station, stand with your back to the tracks. Look left to see the green cross of a 24-hour pharmacy *(farmacia)* and the exit to the taxi queue. Baggage storage *(deposito bagagli)* is also to the left, halfway down track 16 (long hours daily, passport required). Fast-food outlets are along track 16. Directly ahead of you is the main hall *(salone biglietti)*, where you can buy train and bus tickets. Pay WCs are to the right, near the head of track 5.

To reach the **TI,** walk away from the tracks and exit the station; it's straight across the square, 100 yards away, by the stone church.

**Buying Tickets:** Be aware that there are two train companies: Trenitalia, with most connections (+39 06 6847 5475, www.trenitalia.it), and Italo, with high-speed routes between larger cities (no rail passes accepted, +39 06 8937 1892, www.italotreno.it).

For travel within Italy, it's quick and easy to buy tickets online; with the Trenitalia app, you can even purchase them minutes before the train departs. If you buy tickets at the station, take advantage of the ticket *(biglietti)* machines that display schedules and issue tickets.

For most international tickets, you'll need to either go to a Trenitalia ticket window (in the main hall) or a travel agency (ask at your hotel for the nearest one).

For Trenitalia information, use window #18 or #19 (take a number). For Italo tickets and information, use window #10 or #11, or visit their main office, opposite track 5, near the exit.

To buy city bus tickets, head to the bus station next door (and ask for a transit map while you're there).

**Eating:** **$ VyTA,** across from track 13, has good sandwiches, snacks, and pastries. **$ Tentazioni Café,** near track 5, offers drinks, salads, and other goodies. A Carrefour Express, next to the bus station, is the closest supermarket (daily until 21:00).

**Services: Feltrinelli** has English language books and magazines and a café (across from track 14) while a modern **shopping gallery** with clothing stores and another café is down the escalator, across from tracks 11-12.

## Getting to the Duomo and City Center

The Duomo and town center are to your left (with your back to the tracks). Out the doorway to the left, you'll find city buses and the taxi stand. **Taxis** cost about €8 to the Duomo, and the line moves fast. **Buses** generally don't cover the center well and probably aren't the best way to reach your hotel (walking could be faster), but if you need to take one, buy a ticket at the bus station next door or at tobacco shops *(tabacchi),* newsstands, or tram stops. Tickets may not be sold onboard.

To **walk** into town (10-15 minutes), exit the station straight ahead (with your back to the tracks), through the main hall and head straight across the square outside (toward the Church of Santa Maria Novella). On the far side of the square, keep left and head down the main Via dei Panzani, which leads directly to the Duomo.

## Train Connections

The following connections are for Trenitalia unless noted.

**From Florence by Train to: Pisa** (2/hour, 45-75 minutes), **Lucca** (2/hour, 1.5 hours), **Siena** (direct trains hourly, 1.5 hours; bus is better because Siena's train station is far from the center), **Camucia-Cortona** (hourly, 1.5 hours), **Livorno** (hourly, 1.5 hours, some change in Pisa), **La Spezia** (for the Cinque Terre, 5/day direct, 2.5 hours, otherwise nearly hourly with change in Pisa), **Milan** (hourly, 2 hours; Italo: 2/hour, 2 hours), **Venice** (hourly, 2-3 hours, may transfer in Bologna, often crowded—reserve ahead; Italo: 4/day, 2 hours, reservations required), **Assisi** (7/day direct, 2-3 hours), **Orvieto** (hourly, 2 hours, some with change in Campo di Marte or Rifredi Station), **Rome** (2-3/hour, 1.5 hours, most require seat reservations; Italo: 2/hour, 1.5 hours), **Naples** (at least hourly, 3 hours; Italo: hourly, 3 hours), **Brindisi** (8/day, 8 hours with change in Bologna or Rome), **Interlaken** (2/day, 5.5 hours, 2 changes), **Frankfurt** (6/day, 10-11.5 hours, 2 changes), **Paris** (5/day, 9-10.5 hours, 1-2 changes; 1 night train with change in Milan, 13 hours, important to reserve ahead at www.thello.com), **Vienna** (5/day, 10-11 hours, 1-2 changes).

# By Bus

The bus station, operated by **Autolinee Toscane**, is 50 yards southwest of the train station, near the T1 tram stop. Its hard-to-find entrance is located just off the main square, on Via Santa Caterina da Siena; you enter through the same portal the buses do. The station is little more than a big, old-school lot with numbered stalls, a ticket office, and a snack bar. Schedules for regional trips are posted, and monitors show imminent departures. It's best to buy tickets in the station or at machines, as they aren't always sold aboard the bus. Bus info: +39 800 373 760 (daily 6:30-20:00), www.at-bus.it.

**Getting to the Train Station and City Center:** Exit the station through the main door and turn left along the busy street. The train station is on your left, while downtown Florence is straight ahead and a bit to the right.

## Bus Connections

Note that bus service drops dramatically on Sunday. As some Tuscan towns (including Volterra and Montepulciano) have few connections, day-trippers could instead consider a guided tour (see page 42).

**From Florence by Bus to: San Gimignano** (hourly, fewer on Sun, 1.5-2 hours, change in Poggibonsi), **Siena** (roughly 2/hour—fewer off-season, 1.5-hour *rapida/via superstrada* buses are fastest, avoid the slower *ordinaria* buses, in Siena get off at Piazza Gramsci or Via Tozzi, www.tiemmespa.it), **Volterra** (4/day Mon-Sat, 1/day Sun, 2 hours, change in Colle di Val d'Elsa; or faster train to Pontedera-Casciana Terme and then transfer to bus #500 to Volterra, 7/day, fewer on Sun, 1.5 hours), **Montepulciano** (1-2/day, 2 hours, LFI bus, www.lfi.it; or train to Chiusi, then bus to Montepulciano).

## By Private Car

For small groups with more money than time, zipping to nearby towns by private car service can be a comfortable option. Florence-based **Transfer Chauffeur Service** has a fleet of modern vehicles with drivers who can whisk you between cities throughout Italy, to and from the cruise ship port at Livorno, and through the Tuscan countryside for around the same price as a cab (+39 338 862 3129, www.transfercs.com, welcome@transfercs.com, Marco). **Prestige Rent** also has friendly, English-speaking drivers and offers similar services (office at Via della Saggina 98, +39 055 286 059, www.prestigerent.com, usa@prestigerent.com, Saverio).

## By Car

For general information on car rental and driving in Italy, see the Practicalities chapter. For tips on driving in Tuscany, see page 707. Renting a car at the Florence airport, with easy access to the autostrada, is the best option. There's also a rental office located on the T1 tram line (Sansovino stop) that's far enough from the historic core to make driving out of the city doable.

### DRIVING IN FLORENCE

Don't even attempt driving into the city center. The autostrada has several exits for Florence. Get off at the Nord, Scandicci, Impruneta, or Sud exits and follow signs toward—but not into—the *Centro*. Park on the outskirts—see the next section—and take a bus, tram, or taxi in.

Florence has a traffic-reduction system that's complicated and confusing even to locals. Every car passing into the "limited traffic zone" (*Zona Traffico Limitato*, or *ZTL*) is photographed; those who haven't jumped through bureaucratic hoops to get a permit can expect a €100 ticket in the mail (and an "administra-

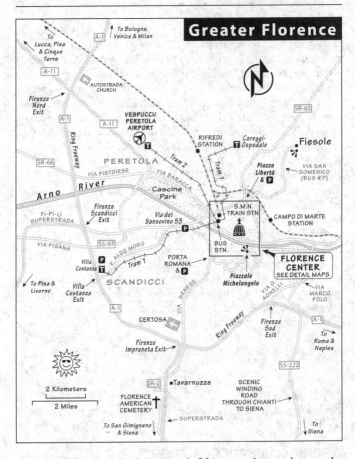

**Greater Florence**

To Lucca, Pisa & Cinque Terre

To Bologna, Venice & Milan

A-1

A-11

AUTOSTRADA CHURCH

Firenze Nord Exit

A-1

SR-65

VESPUCCI/ PERETOLA AIRPORT

RIFREDI STATION

Careggi-Ospedale

Fiesole

SR-66

Tram 2

VIA BARACCA

PERETOLA

VIA PISTOIESE

Piazza Libertà & P

VIA SAN DOMENICO (BUS #7)

Arno River

Cascine Park

Tram 1

S.M.N. TRAIN STN

CAMPO DI MARTE STATION

FI-PI-LI SUPERSTRADA

Firenze Scandicci Exit

Via del Sansovino 53

P

BUS STN.

**FLORENCE CENTER** SEE DETAIL MAPS

VIA PISANA

SS-67

V. ALDO MORO

PORTA ROMANA & P

Piazzale Michelangelo

VIA G. AGNELLI

VIA MARCO POLO

Villa Costanza

Tram 1

SCANDICCI

To Pisa & Livorno

Villa Costanza Exit

A-1

CERTOSA

VIA SENESE

Ring Freeway

Firenze Sud Exit

A-1

To Rome & Naples

SS-222

Firenze Impruneta Exit

2 Kilometers

2 Miles

FLORENCE AMERICAN CEMETERY

SR-2

Tavarnuzze

SCENIC WINDING ROAD THROUGH CHIANTI TO SIENA

SUPERSTRADA

To San Gimignano & Siena

To Siena

---

tive" fee from the rental company). If you get lost and cross the line several times...you get several fines. Since this is Italy, it can take as long as a year for your ticket to show up. If you have a reservation at a hotel within the ZTL area—and it has parking—ask in advance if they can get you permission to enter town.

The no-go zone (defined basically by the old medieval wall, now a boulevard circling the historic center of town—watch for *Zona Traffico Limitato* signs) is roughly the area between the river, main train station, Piazza della Libertà, Piazza Donatello, and Piazza Beccaria; across the river, in

zona traffico limitato

7,30 - 19,30

the Oltrarno, the area around the Pitti Palace and Santo Spirito is also a ZTL. Some streets are classified ZTL only at certain times of day; at the beginning of each block, watch for a stoplight with instructions (in Italian and English)—the green light means it's currently OK to drive there, while the red light means, well...

Another potentially expensive mistake drivers make in Florence is using the lanes designated for buses only (usually marked with yellow stripes). Driving in these lanes can also result in a ticket in the mail. Pay careful attention to signs.

## PARKING IN FLORENCE

The city center is ringed with big, efficient parking lots (signposted with a big *P*). From these, you can ride into the center (via taxi, bus, or possibly tram). Check www.fipark.com for details on parking lots, availability, and prices. From the freeway, follow the signs to *Centro*, then *Stadio*, then *P*.

The huge park-and-ride lot called Villa Costanza, just outside the town of Scandicci (south of Florence), is the smart answer to your parking challenges. It has its own dedicated freeway off-ramp (just north of Impruneta) and is the terminus for the T1 tram line that zips smart drivers downtown (€1.50, departing every five minutes). Just look for it as you approach Florence on the autostrada (see the "Greater Florence" map on previous page).

# By Plane

For information on Pisa's **Galileo Galilei Airport,** see the end of the Pisa chapter.

## AMERIGO VESPUCCI AIRPORT

Also called Peretola Airport, Florence's compact, manageable airport is about five miles northwest of the city (code: FLR, www.aeroporto.firenze.it).

On the ground floor, you'll find a TI, café, and ATMs, and a customs desk where you can get a stamp for your VAT refund (if you need to return it by mail, there's a red mailbox just outside the main arrivals door). Global Blue has a desk upstairs, facing the check-in area.

### Getting Between the Airport and City Center

**By Tram:** The **T2 tram** (to the left as you exit the arrivals hall) runs every five minutes from the airport to near the train station (Alamanni Stazione, across from the station) and Piazza dell'Unità (one stop beyond the station, slightly closer to downtown) in about 20 minutes (runs 5:00-24:00, €1.50, buy ticket from machine on platform, cash or credit card, validate on-board, good for 90 minutes and transferable to bus lines, www.gestramvia.com). For stop locations in town, see the map on page 58.

**Shuttle buses** (to the far right as you exit the arrivals hall) connect the airport with Florence's train and bus stations (2/hour until 22:00, 1/hour until 00:30, 30 minutes, runs 5:00-00:30, €6 one-way—buy ticket on board, €10 round-trip—buy ticket inside airport). If you're changing to a different intercity bus in Florence (for instance, one bound for Siena), stay on the bus through the first stop (at the train station); it will continue on to the bus station nearby.

Official **taxi** companies have fixed rates for the 20- to 30-minute ride between the airport and downtown: €22 during the day (6:00-22:00), €25.30 at night, and €24 on Sunday. They may tack on €1 per bag, and €2 if you call for a cab rather than hailing one. Be sure to use an official taxi (white, marked with *Taxi/Comune di Firenze* and a red fleur-de-lis).

The airport's **rental-car** offices share one big parking lot at Via Palagio degli Spini that's a three-minute drive away (shuttle bus departs directly outside the arrivals door). It can be tricky to find the place to drop off your car. One option is to drive to the airport, wait for the rental-car shuttle bus to show up, then follow that bus to the lot.

## By Cruise Ship

Cruise ships dock in the coastal town of **Livorno,** about 60 miles west of Florence. For more details, see my *Rick Steves Mediterranean Cruise Ports* guidebook.

**Getting to Florence:** To reach Florence, ride the cruise line's shuttle bus from the port to downtown Livorno's Piazza del Municipio. From there, catch a transfer-only shuttle-bus to Florence; they guarantee you'll make it back to your ship in plenty of time (+39 058 6188 8623, www.tuscanybus.com). On your own, you can take a local public bus from Piazza del Municipio to Livorno Centrale train station (10 minutes) and then a train to Florence (hourly, 1.5 hours). Taxis are pricey, but sharing a minibus taxi with other cruisers can bring the round-trip cost to Florence down.

**Getting to Pisa and Lucca:** The easiest way to get to Pisa is to take a TuscanyBus.com shuttle bus for cruisers. They also offer a combo Pisa-Lucca excursion (for contact info, see earlier). To get to Pisa on your own by train (2-3/hour, 20 minutes), follow the directions above to reach the Livorno train station.

To also visit the neighboring town of Lucca on your own, take the train there first to avoid the morning cruise-ship crowds in Pisa (trains depart Livorno about hourly, 1 hour, transfer at Pisa Centrale). A handy bus connects Lucca's Piazzale Giuseppe Verdi to Pisa's Field of Miracles, or take a train from Lucca to Pisa San Rossore Station, near the Field of Miracles.

# TUSCANY

## *Toscana*

# TUSCANY

*Toscana*

When travel dreams take people to Italy, Tuscany is often their first stop. Wedged between Florence and Rome, this region offers the quintessential Italian experience: well-preserved medieval cities, sun-soaked hill towns, green and rolling fields, romantic farms, and cypress trees marching single file up lonely ridges.

Connoisseurs of Italy find a blissful mix of scenic beauty and rich history in Tuscany's emblematic hill towns. Built for defensive purposes in ancient and medieval times, today their lofty perches protect them from the modern world.

Proud locals will remind you that their ancestors—the Etruscans (the word Tuscany comes from "Etruscan")—thrived here long before anyone had heard of Julius Caesar. Many Tuscan hill towns date back to the Etruscan era—well before ancient Rome. Others date to the last days of Rome: when Rome fell, chaos followed, and people naturally grabbed the high ground to escape marauding Dark Ages barbarians. Over time, these hilltop towns were fortified and eventually functioned as independent city-states.

The Middle Ages were formative, when warring factions divided towns between those loyal to the pope and those supporting the Holy Roman Emperor. Cities developed monumental defensive walls and built great towers. Then, in 1348, the Black Death—an epidemic of bubonic plague—swept through Tuscany, devastating the region. The plague, plus the increasing dominance of Florence, turned many bustling cities into docile hamlets. Ironically, what was bad news in the 14th century is good news today: Tuscany and its hill towns enjoy a tourist-fueled affluence and retain a unique, medieval charm.

Slow down and savor the delights that this region offers. Spend the night in a hill town to experience the quiet after the day-trippers go home. In Florence you experience the finesse of Italy,

# Hill Towns of Central Italy

but it's in Tuscany that you'll find the rustic-yet-elegant essence of "Italia."

## Visiting Tuscany

It's a joy to downshift to the more peaceful pace of Italy's small cities...and even smaller hill towns. I've covered my favorites in the following chapters.

Siena, Pisa, and Lucca are in a category of their own, with more artistic and historic sights. **Siena** is the ultimate (and biggest) hill town, with an unrivaled spirit any visitor can enjoy. Like a medieval stage set, its pedestrian-friendly old town is surrounded by its fortified wall. Siena's stunning main square—the gently tilted red-brick Campo—is the city's proud centerpiece. As Tuscany's hub, Siena is well connected by bus to Florence (also handy by train) and the surrounding hill towns. For drivers it's a convenient jumping-off point for my loop drive through the clay hills of the Crete Senesi.

**Pisa**'s iconic Leaning Tower draws flocks of tourists, but this midsize city also offers plenty of history and beautiful architecture, along with a thriving student scene. Lesser-known and smaller, charming **Lucca** is a "flat hill town" with winding streets ringed by a well-preserved Renaissance wall, perfect for circling on a bike. Both lie an hour or so west of Florence and are easily reached by train or bus.

But how in Dante's name does one choose from among Tuscany's hundreds of small hill towns? The one(s) you visit will depend on your interests, time, and mode of transportation.

**Volterra**—with its rustic vitality—is a beautifully preserved jewel. Its out-of-the-way location keeps this town from being trampled by tourist crowds, and its Etruscan history makes for compelling sightseeing. With 14 surviving medieval towers, walled **San Gimignano** is a classic. But because it's easy to visit from Florence—about 1.5 hours by bus—midday crowds can overwhelm its charms (it's an evocative delight early and late in the day). Both Volterra and San Gimignano work best for drivers but can be reached by public transportation.

South of Siena, in the region I call the "Heart of Tuscany," drivers have their pick of hill towns. Ridge-hugging **Montepulciano**'s medieval cityscape resembles a miniature Florence. With several historic wine cellars and easy access to wine country, it attracts wine aficionados, as does **Montalcino,** itself a happy gauntlet of wine shops and art galleries. Fans of architecture and urban design appreciate little **Pienza**'s well-planned streets and squares. All three towns are covered in the Heart of Tuscany chapter, which also includes driving routes tying together the sights, villages, *agriturismi,* and wineries in the countryside.

Those enamored with Frances Mayes' memoir, *Under the Tuscan Sun,* can make the pilgrimage to thriving **Cortona.** It soars high above a scenic landscape near the border of neighboring Umbria and is dotted with grand churches, Renaissance art, and Etruscan ruins. It's possible to reach by train but best by car.

Finally, if you're looking for a vacation from your vacation, the island of **Elba** is a three-hour drive-and-ferry combo away from Pisa, Lucca, Siena, or the Heart of Tuscany. Known mostly as the island where Napoleon spent his 10-month exile, Elba offers at least an overnight stay's worth of Italian relaxation.

## Getting Around Tuscany

**By Bus or Train:** Buses are often the only public-transportation choice to get between small hill towns. Train stations are likely to be in the valley below the town center, connected by a local bus.

**By Car:** Exploring Tuscany and its hill towns by car can be a great experience. Wait to pick up your car until the last sizable town you visit (or at the nearest airport to avoid big-city traffic), and carry a good, detailed road map in addition to a mapping app. Freeways (such as the toll autostrada and the non-toll *superstrada*) are the fastest way to connect two points, but smaller roads, including the super-scenic SS-222, connecting Florence and Siena, are more rewarding.

Some towns don't allow visitors to drive or park in the city center. Be alert for "ZTL" *(Zona Traffico Limitato)* signs, indicating no cars allowed. Leave your car outside the walls and walk into town. Lots are usually free and plentiful outside city walls (and sometimes linked to the town center by elevators or escalators). For more driving and parking tips, see the Practicalities chapter.

## Eating in Tuscany

One of the greatest Tuscan treats—the food—varies wildly depending on where you are. The areas around Florence and Siena are famed for serving hearty "farmer food," but as you move west, dishes become lighter, based more on seafood and grains. Each town proudly boasts local specialties—ask for the *specialità della città*. For an overview of Tuscan cuisine, see the sidebar on page 312. Wine is good throughout Tuscany, with pleasing selections for both amateurs and connoisseurs (see page 586).

## Sleeping in Rural Tuscany

For a relaxing break from big-city Italy, settle down in an *agriturismi*—a farmhouse that rents out rooms to travelers (usually for a minimum of a week in high season). These rural B&Bs—almost by definition in the middle of nowhere—provide a good home base from which to find the magic of Italy's hill towns. Many provide memorable meals from locally sourced ingredients. I've listed several good options throughout these chapters. For more information, see *"Agriturismi"* in the Practicalities chapter.

# SIENA

Siena was medieval Florence's archrival. And while Florence ultimately won the battle for political and economic superiority, Siena still competes for the tourists. Sure, Florence has the heavyweight sights. But Siena seems to be every Italy connoisseur's favorite town. In my office, whenever Siena is mentioned, someone moans, "Siena? I looove Siena!"

Situated atop three hills, Siena qualifies as Italy's ultimate "hill town." Its thriving historic center, with movie-set lanes cascading every which way, offers Italy's best medieval city experience. Most people visit Siena, just 35 miles south of Florence, as a day trip, but it's best experienced at twilight. While Florence has the blockbuster museums, Siena has an easy-to-enjoy soul: Courtyards sport flower-decked wells, alleys dead-end at rooftop views, and today, even with all the tourists, a strong local spirit pervades.

For those who dream of a Fiat-free Italy, Siena is a haven. Pedestrians rule in the old center of town, as the only drivers allowed are residents and cabbies. Nurse a drink on the stunning main square, Il Campo. Wander narrow streets, tether an imaginary horse to the old metal rings, be stirred by colorful flags. Take time to savor the first European city to eliminate automobile traffic from its main square (1966) and then, just to be silly, wonder what would happen if they did it in your hometown.

## PLANNING YOUR TIME

On a quick trip, consider spending two nights in Siena (or three nights with a whole-day side trip into Florence). Whatever you do, be sure to enjoy a sleepy medieval evening in Siena. The next morning, you can see the city's major sights in half a day. Or consider using Siena as your jet-lag pillow. With its lazy small-town ambience and impressive but user-friendly sights, this is a fine way to settle into Italian life.

Drivers home-basing in Siena can consider my scenic Crete Senesi Drive, a countryside loop tour described at the end of this chapter.

# Orientation to Siena

Siena lounges atop a ridge, stretching its three legs out from Il Campo. This pedestrianized main square is the historic meeting point of Siena's neighborhoods.

Just about everything is within a 10-minute walk of the square. Navigate by three major landmarks (Il Campo, Duomo, and Basilica of San Domenico), following the excellent system of street-corner signs. The typical visitor sticks to the Il Campo-San Domenico axis. But make it a point to stray from this main artery to find a corner of town to yourself. Sienese streets go in anything but a straight line, so it's easy to get lost—but equally easy to get found.

Siena's individual attractions come in two main clusters: Il Campo (Civic Museum and City Tower) and the cathedral (Duomo Museum, with its surprise viewpoint; and Santa Maria della Scala, a hospital-turned-museum, just across the street). Roughly between them is the Pinacoteca, for medieval art lovers. Check off some or all of these sights, and then you're free to wander.

## TOURIST INFORMATION

The TI is right on Il Campo (daily 9:00-18:00, Il Campo 7, +39 0577 292 222, www.terresiena.it). At busy times, there may be other TI outposts near the Duomo and at Piazza Gramsci, where some buses arrive.

## ARRIVAL IN SIENA
### By Train

Siena's small train station is at the base of the hill, on the edge of town. It has a bar/tobacco shop, an Autolinee Toscane intercity bus office (Mon-Fri 7:15-19:30, Sat until 17:45, Sun 9:00-12:15 & 14:30-18:30), and a newsstand (which sells tickets for other buses, including city buses—you can buy one now if you're taking the bus into town; closed Sun). There's no baggage check or lockers. A shopping mall with a supermarket is across the plaza facing the station. WCs are on track 1, past the pharmacy.

**Getting from the Train Station to the City Center:** To reach central Siena, you can ride a long series of escalators (free, slow); hop a city bus (cheap, somewhat faster); or take a taxi (fastest and most expensive). For two or more traveling together, unless you

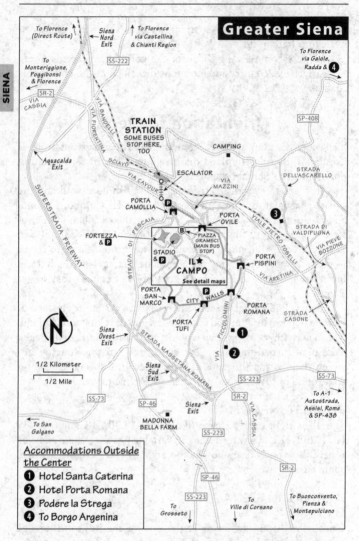

**Greater Siena**

To Florence (Direct Route)

Siena Nord Exit

To Florence via Castellina & Chianti Region

To Florence via Galole, Radda & ❹

SS-222

To Monteriggione, Poggibonsi & Florence

SR-2

VIA CASSIA

VIA FIORENTINA

VIA BANDELL

SP-408

Aquacalda Exit

SCIAVO

VIA CAVOUR

**TRAIN STATION**
SOME BUSES STOP HERE, TOO

CAMPING

ESCALATOR

VIA MAZZINI

STRADA DELL'ASCARELLO

PORTA CAMOLLIA

PORTA OVILE

VIALE PIETRO TOSELLI

❸

STRADA DI VALDIPUGNA

FORTEZZA & P

STRADA DI PESCAIA

PIAZZA GRAMSCI (MAIN BUS STOP)

VIA PIEVE BOZZONE

STADIO & P

IL ★ CAMPO
See detail maps

PORTA PISPINI

VIA ARETINA

PORTA SAN MARCO

CITY WALLS

P

PORTA ROMANA

STRADA CASONE

SUPERSTRADA FREEWAY

Siena Ovest Exit

STRADA MASSETANA ROMANA

PORTA TUFI

VIA PICCOLOMINI

❶

❷

1/2 Kilometer
1/2 Mile

Siena Sud Exit

SS-223

SS-73

To A-1 Autostrada, Assisi, Rome & SP-438

SS-73

SR-2

Siena Exit

SP-46

MADONNA BELLA FARM

SS-223

VIA CASSIA

SR-2

To San Galgano

SP-46

SS-223

To Grosseto

To Ville di Corsano

To Buonconvento, Pienza & Montepulciano

**Accommodations Outside the Center**
❶ Hotel Santa Caterina
❷ Hotel Porta Romana
❸ Podere la Strega
❹ To Borgo Argenina

have far more time than money, the **taxi** is your best value (€10 to the center, taxi stand just outside station, +39 0577 49222).

*By Escalator or City Bus:* To reach either the bus or the escala-tors, head for the shopping mall across the square (far left corner as you leave—look for the bull's-eye). The first of a series of **escala-tors** climbs through the mall up into the town. From the top of the escalators, it's a 20-minute walk to the town center: Turn left, walk about five minutes to the Porta Camollia gate, then walk through it and follow Via Camollia into town.

To ride the **city bus,** head to the dreary, concrete, cave-like bus stop below the mall (catch the down elevator from inside the mall's first glass door, on immediate right). All buses (big and small) go to Piazza del Sale or Piazza Gramsci (both at the edge of the action and within a block of each other—see "By Bus," below). Buy your €1.50 bus ticket from the train station newsstand or at the machines by the bus stop; before boarding, confirm that the bus is going to the center—ask *"Centro?"* (CHEHN-troh).

**Returning to the Train Station from the City Center:** Catch a small shuttle bus directly to the station from Piazza del Sale, or take a big city bus from Piazza Gramsci. Look for *Ferrovia* or *Stazione* on schedules and marked on the bus, and confirm with the driver that the bus is going to the *stazione* (staht-see-OH-nay).

## By Bus

Siena is a pleasant 90-minute express bus ride from Florence (for more on buses, see "Siena Connections," later). Most buses from Florence and other cities arrive in Siena at Piazza Gramsci (or the adjacent Via Tozzi), a few blocks north of the city center. (Some buses only go to the train station; others go first to the train station, then continue to Piazza Gramsci—to confirm, ask your driver, "pee-aht-sah GRAHM-shee?")

Downstairs, in the concrete underpass beneath Piazza Gramsci, you'll find ticket offices and pay WCs. If day-tripping, confirm your departure from timetables posted at the platform where you disembark or at the ticket counters downstairs. Late-afternoon buses back to Florence can fill up, so arrive at least 15 minutes early.

From Piazza Gramsci, it's an easy walk into the town center—just head in the opposite direction of the tree-filled park.

## By Florence-Siena Taxi

Taxis make the trip from Florence to Siena—hotel to hotel—in about an hour for around €140. (Prices can be soft. Ask a couple of cabbies for their best price. Clearly agree on a price from the start.) If debating the value of this splurge, consider that a couple will spend roughly €40 for two taxi transfers and two train tickets, and the luxury of a hotel-to-hotel cab ride saves you about an hour.

## By Car

Siena is not a good place to drive. Park in a big lot or garage and walk into town. For more on where to park legally—and how to avoid a big fine by driving into the restricted "ZTL" zone—see "Driving" in the Practicalities chapter.

Drivers coming from the autostrada take the *Siena Ovest* exit and follow signs for *Centro*, then *Stadio* (stadium). The soccer-ball signs take you to the **stadium lot** (Parcheggio Stadio, pay when you

## Siena's Big Plans and Slow Fade

Once upon a time (about 1260-1348), Siena was a major banking and trade center, and a military power in a class with Florence, Venice, and Genoa. With a population of about 50,000, it was even bigger than Paris and Rome. Situated on the north-south road to Rome (Via Francigena), Siena traded with all of Europe.

After rival republic Florence began its grand cathedral (1296), proud Siena planned to build one even bigger—the biggest church in all Christendom. Construction began in the 1330s on an extension off the right side of the existing Duomo (today's cathedral would have been used as a transept). The vision was grand, but it underestimated the complexity of constructing such a building without enough land for it to sit upon.

When the Black Death raged across Europe in 1348, Siena's population was cut by more than a third. Many Sienese saw the plague as a sign from God, punishing them for their pride. Plans for the cathedral expansion were cancelled, and the city began a slow fade into the background of Tuscan history.

In the 1550s, Florence, with the help of Philip II's Spanish army, conquered the flailing city-state, forever rendering Siena a nonthreatening backwater. Siena's loss became our sightseeing gain, as its political and economic irrelevance pickled the city in a purely medieval brine. Today, Siena's population is again at its medieval level of 50,000, although only 18,000 of those live within the walls.

leave) near Piazza Gramsci and the huge, bare-brick Basilica of San Domenico. The **Fortezza lot** is also nearby.

Another good option is the underground **Santa Caterina garage** (you'll see signs on the way to the stadium lot). From the garage, hike 150 yards uphill through a gate to an escalator on the right, which carries you up into the city. Take a left at the top onto Siena's main street.

If you're staying in the south end of town—or if you're arriving from the Val d'Orcia area or the Crete Senesi Drive—try the **Il Campo** lot, near Porta Tufi. From here, you can walk right up to the center of town in a few minutes.

Yet another option is the **Leonardo garage**, near the Porta Camollia; they offer a "valet" service where they'll meet you at the garage, drive you into town with your bags, then park your car for you (€25/day, arrange in advance, Via Bettino Ricasoli 29, +39 389 577 5886, www.parcheggiosiena.it).

You can park for **free** in the lot west of the Fortezza, in white-striped spots south of the Fortezza, and overnight in most city lots (20:00-8:00).

## HELPFUL HINTS

**Combo-Tickets:** Siena often experiments with different combo-tickets. The Opa Si Pass covers the Duomo-related sights (see "Duomo and Related Sights," later); the other pass offers various combinations of city sights, including the Civic Museum, City Tower, Santa Maria della Scala, and Pinacoteca (see listing for City Hall and Civic Museum, later).

**Market:** Every Wednesday morning a market of clothes, knick-knacks, and food sprawls between the Fortezza and Piazza Gramsci along Viale Cesare Maccari and the adjacent Viale XXV Aprile.

**Bookstores:** For books and magazines in English, try **Libreria Senese** (daily, Via di Città 62) and the **Feltrinelli** bookstore (closed Sun, Via Banchi di Sopra 52),

**Cooking Classes:** At **Fonte Giusta Cooking School,** you'll prepare a meal (pasta, meat, dessert) under the instruction of a local chef—and then eat it. Lessons last two to three hours and cost €80-120 (Via Camollia 78, call +39 0577 40506 or email info@trattoriafontegiusta.com for schedule and details, www.scuoladicucinafontegiusta.com).

**Laundry:** Try **Lavanderia San Pietro** (daily 8:00-21:00, not far from the Duomo at Via San Pietro 70) or **Lavanderia Waterland** (daily 7:00-21:00, north of Il Campo near Porta San Francesco at Via dei Rossi 94).

**Souvenirs:** For easy-to-pack souvenirs, consider one of the large, colorful scarves/flags that depict the symbols of Siena's 17 neighborhoods (such as the Wolf, the Turtle, the Porcupine, or the Snail).

# Tours in Siena

🎧 To sightsee on your own, download my free Siena City Walk audio tour.

## LOCAL GUIDES

**Federica Olla,** who leads walking tours of Siena, is a smart, friendly guide with a knack for creative teaching (€55/hour, minimum 2 hours, +39 338 133 9525, www.ollaeventi.com, info@ollaeventi.com).

**Anna Piperato,** fiercely proud of her adopted hometown of Siena and an expert on Palio culture, leads walking tours in Siena—including a visit to her *contrada*, Lupa—and environs (€60/

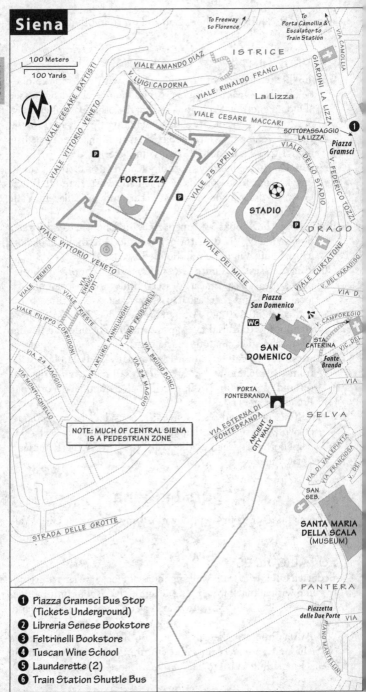

SIENA

# Siena

100 Meters
100 Yards

**1** Piazza Gramsci Bus Stop (Tickets Underground)
**2** Libreria Senese Bookstore
**3** Feltrinelli Bookstore
**4** Tuscan Wine School
**5** Launderette (2)
**6** Train Station Shuttle Bus

SIENA

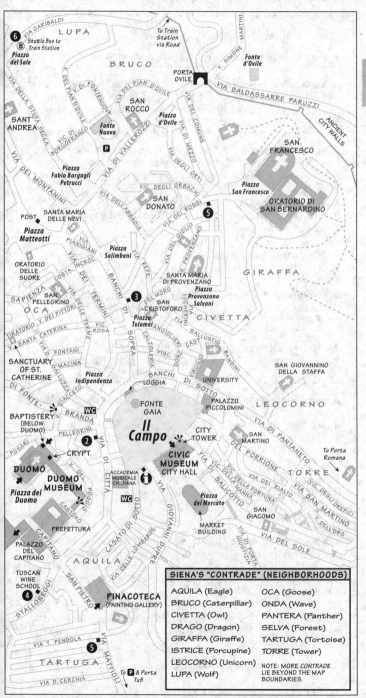

**SIENA'S "CONTRADE" (NEIGHBORHOODS)**

| | |
|---|---|
| AQUILA (Eagle) | OCA (Goose) |
| BRUCO (Caterpillar) | ONDA (Wave) |
| CIVETTA (Owl) | PANTERA (Panther) |
| DRAGO (Dragon) | SELVA (Forest) |
| GIRAFFA (Giraffe) | TARTUGA (Tortoise) |
| ISTRICE (Porcupine) | TORRE (Tower) |
| LEOCORNO (Unicorn) | NOTE: MORE *CONTRADE* |
| LUPA (Wolf) | LIE BEYOND THE MAP BOUNDARIES. |

SIENA

# Siena at a Glance

▲▲▲**Il Campo** Best square in Italy. See page 382.

▲▲▲**Duomo** Art-packed cathedral with mosaic floors and statues by Michelangelo and Bernini. **Hours:** Mon-Sat 10:00-19:00, Sun 13:30-17:30, Nov-March closes daily at 17:00. See page 391.

▲▲**Civic Museum** City museum in City Hall with Sienese frescoes, the *Effects of Good and Bad Government.* **Hours:** Daily 10:00-19:00, Nov-Feb until 18:00. See page 382.

▲▲**Duomo Museum** Siena's best museum, with cathedral art (Duccio's *Maestá*) and sweeping Tuscan views. **Hours:** Same hours as Duomo. See page 400.

▲**City Tower** Siena's 330-foot tower climb. **Hours:** Daily 10:00-19:00, Nov-Feb until 16:00. See page 388.

▲**Pinacoteca** Fine Sienese paintings. **Hours:** Mon and Fri-Sun 8:30-13:30, Tue-Thu 14:00-19:00, closed two Sun a month. See page 388.

▲**Baptistery of San Giovanni** Cave-like building with baptismal font decorated by Ghiberti and Donatello. **Hours:** Same hours as Duomo. See page 404.

▲**Santa Maria della Scala** Museum with much of the original Fountain of Joy, Byzantine reliquaries, and vibrant frescoes. **Hours:** Daily 10:00-19:00, Thu until 22:00; mid-Oct-mid-March Mon and Wed-Fri until 17:00, Sat-Sun until 19:00, closed Tue. See page 405.

▲**Sanctuary of St. Catherine** Home of St. Catherine. **Hours:** Daily 9:00-18:00, chapel closes 12:30-15:00. See page 408.

## Near Siena
▲▲▲**Abbey of Monte Oliveto Maggiore** Rural abbey buried in a cypress forest, with vivid Renaissance art in an untrampled setting (if old frescoes bore you, don't bother). **Hours:** Daily 9:30-12:30 & 14:30-18:00, Nov-March until 17:00. See page 427.

▲▲**Crete Senesi** Rugged region tucked between Siena and the "Heart of Tuscany," with breathtaking scenery and workaday towns. See page 423.

hour, special treat for Rick Steves readers, +39 333 682 9336, www. sienaitalytours.com, anna@sienaitalytours.com).

**Stefania Fabrizi** is another good Siena guide (+39 338 640 7796, stefaniafabriziguide@gmail.com).

## ON FOOT
### Walking Tours
A changing lineup of companies offer basic, affordable walking tours of the old town, often including the Duomo. A two-hour tour runs about €20 (€5 extra to enter the Duomo); some are only in English, while others are in both English and Italian. Some of these are operated by the TI (get details there), while others are offered by a private company called Siena Tourism (https:// sienatourism.com).

### Siena City Walks by Roberto
Roberto and his guides offer private three-hour Siena walking tours (€180 for up to 8 people, admissions extra) or joinable group tours (€45/person, admissions extra, minimum 4 people; book online or call +39 320 147 6590, www.toursbyroberto.com, toursbyroberto@ gmail.com).

## OTHER TOURS
### Tuscany Minibus Tours by Roberto
Roberto Bechi and his guides lead off-the-beaten-path, full-day minibus tours of the countryside surrounding Siena (€110/person, up to eight passengers, pickup at hotel). The first participants to book choose one of seven itineraries—then others join until the van fills. Roberto and his team share the same passion for Sienese culture, Tuscan history, and local cuisine (see website for tour options, RS%-10 percent discount, entry fees extra; also offers multiday tours, booking mobile +39 320 147 6590, Roberto's mobile +39 328 425 5648, www.toursbyroberto.com, toursbyroberto@gmail.com). See later listing for Roberto's farm tours; he also provides private van connections to Volterra—see the Volterra & San Gimignano chapter.

### Wine Tasting
The Tuscan Wine School offers two foodie experiences in English. The midday **food tour** focuses on local food culture with tastings (focaccia, cured meats, truffles, gelato) at vendors around town (€60); the afternoon **wine-appreciation classes**, held in a classroom, let you taste a variety of Tuscan wines paired with small bites (€45). For the latest times, and to book, check their website or stop by their office (RS%-20 percent discount, Via di Stalloreggi 26, 30 yards from Hotel Duomo, +39 0577 221 704, mobile +39 333

722 9716, www.tuscanwineschool.com, tuscanwineschool@gmail.com, Georgia and Milo).

## Farm Visit

Madonna Bella, a farm co-owned by local guide Roberto Bechi, sits just a few minutes outside Siena. Monica welcomes visitors to stop in, enjoy the views, visit the farm, take part in wine and olive-oil tastings, and learn how olive oil and pasta are made. It's best to book ahead if you want to enjoy a food/wine pairing that anyone would consider an abundant lunch. They also offer cooking classes and can arrange a taxi from and to central Siena for about €15 each way (Strada del Tesoro 25—just outside Siena on road SP-46, +39 393 858 2981, www.madonnabella.com).

# Siena City Walk

It's easy to get to know Siena on foot, and this short self-guided walk laces together its most important sights. You can do this walk as a quick orientation, or use it to tie together visits to the major sights (City Hall, the Duomo, the Duomo Museum, and Santa Maria della Scala—all described in more detail under "Sights in Siena"). If you do the walk without entering the sights, it works great at night when the city is peaceful.

🎧 This walk is also available as a free Rick Steves audio tour.

• *Start in the center of the main square, Il Campo, standing just below the fountain.*

## ❶ Il Campo

This square is the heart of Siena, both geographically and metaphorically—and it's worth ▲▲▲. First laid out in the 12th century, today Il Campo (officially the Piazza del Campo) is the only town square I've seen where people stretch out as if at the beach. However, if you start eating—well, now you're "picnicking," which is not allowed; you could be fined.) At the flat end of its clamshell

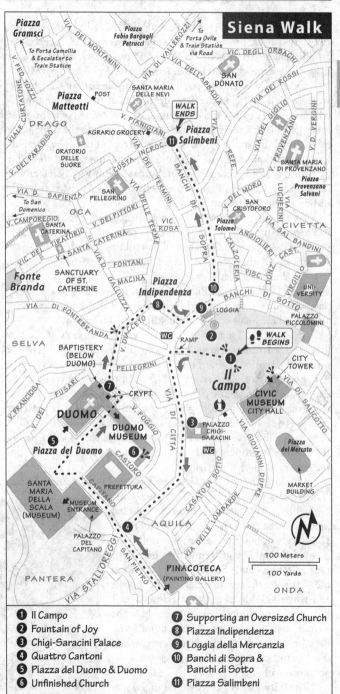

# Siena Walk

SIENA

1 Il Campo
2 Fountain of Joy
3 Chigi-Saracini Palace
4 Quattro Cantoni
5 Piazza del Duomo & Duomo
6 Unfinished Church
7 Supporting an Oversized Church
8 Piazza Indipendenza
9 Loggia della Mercanzia
10 Banchi di Sopra & Banchi di Sotto
11 Piazza Salimbeni

shape is City Hall, where you can tour the Civic Museum and climb the City Tower. From there the square fans out as if to create an amphitheater. All eyes are on Il Campo twice each summer, when it hosts the famous Palio horse races (see sidebar on page 374).

Originally, this area was just a field *(campo)* outside the city walls (which encircled the cathedral). Bits of those original walls, which curved against today's square, can be seen above the pharmacy (the black and white stones, third story up, to the right as you face City Hall). In the 1200s, with the advent of the Sienese republic, the city expanded. The small medieval town wrapped around its cathedral grew to become a larger, humanistic city gathered around its towering City Hall. And the focus of power shifted from the bishop to the secular city council.

As the city expanded, Il Campo became its marketplace and the historic junction of Siena's various competing *contrade* (neighborhood districts). The square and its buildings are the color of the soil on which they stand—a color known to artists and Crayola users as "burnt sienna."

**City Hall** (Palazzo Pubblico), with its looming tower, dominates the square. In medieval Siena, this was the center of the city, and the whole focus of Il Campo still flows down to it.

The building's facade features the various symbols of the city. The **stylized sun** hearkens back to St. Bernardino of Siena, who preached devotion to the Holy Name of Jesus. (The "IHS" inside is a shortening of Jesus' name in Greek.) Born in the year that St. Catherine of Siena died, Bernardino grew up here and went on to travel throughout Italy, giving spirited sermons that preached peace between warring political factions. His sermons often ended with reconciling parties exchanging a *bacio di pace* (kiss of peace). Bernardino, who personally designed the sun logo, later became the patron saint of advertising.

Flanking the sun logo, **she-wolf gargoyles** lean out and snarl, "Don't mess with Siena, Mister Pope!" This Ghibelline city prided itself on its political independence from the papacy; it embraced as a city symbol the pagan she-wolf who suckled Romulus and Remus (Remus' twin sons Aschius and Senius—"Siena"—were the city's legendary founders). The black-and-white **shields** over the windows recall the black-and-white horses that brought Remus' sons to the city. Near ground level, the iron rings are for tying your horse, while the fixtures above once held flags (and, on occasion, still do).

The **City Tower** (Torre del Mangia) was

built around 1340. At 330 feet, it's one of Italy's tallest secular towers. Medieval Siena was a proud republic, and this tower stands like an exclamation point—an architectural declaration of independence from papacy and empire. The tower's Italian nickname, Torre del Mangia, comes from a hedonistic bell ringer who consumed his earnings like a glutton consumes food. (His chewed-up statue is just inside City Hall's courtyard, to the left as you enter.)

The open **chapel** at the base of the tower was built as thanks to the Virgin Mary for ending the Black Death of 1348 (after it killed more than a third of the population). Siena rededicated itself to the Virgin in 2022, to implore her help in weathering another plague—Covid-19. The Sienese should also be thankful that the top-heavy tower still stands—it was plunked onto the building with no extra foundation and no iron reinforcement. These days, the chapel is where Palio contestants are blessed (and where EMTs stand by during the race).

You can visit the Civic Museum inside City Hall and climb the tower (see page 383 for a self-guided tour of the Civic Museum).

• *Now turn around and take a closer look at the fountain in the top center of the square.*

## ❷ Fountain of Joy (Fonte Gaia)

This fountain—a copy of an early 15th-century work by Jacopo della Quercia—marks the square's high point. The joy is all about

how the Sienese republic blessed its people with water. Find Lady Justice with her scales and sword (right of center), overseeing the free distribution of water to all. Imagine residents gathering here in the 1400s to fill their jugs. The Fountain of Joy still reminds locals that life in Siena is good. Notice the pigeons politely waiting their turn to tightrope gingerly down slippery spouts to slurp a drink from wolves' snouts.

The relief panel on the far left shows God creating Adam by helping him to his feet. It's said that this reclining Adam (carved a century before Michelangelo's day) influenced Michelangelo when he painted his Sistine Chapel ceiling. The fountain's original statuary is exhibited at Santa Maria della Scala (see page 405).

Siena and Florence have always been very competitive. In medieval times, a statue of Venus stood on Il Campo. After the plague hit Siena, the monks blamed the pagan statue. According to leg-

# Siena's *Contrade* and the Palio

Siena's 17 historic neighborhoods, or *contrade*—each with a parish church, well or fountain, and square—still play an active role in the life of the city. Each is represented by a mascot (porcupine, unicorn, wolf, etc.) and unique colors worn proudly by residents.

*Contrada* pride is evident year-round in Siena's parades and colorful banners, lamps, and wall plaques. If you hear the thunder of distant drumming, run to it for some medieval action—there's a good chance it'll feature flag throwers. Buy a scarf in *contrada* colors, and join in the merriment of these lively neighborhood festivals. (But be careful where you wear them...you don't want to stumble naively into a rival *contrada*'s celebration.)

*Contrade* rivalries are most visible twice a year—on July 2 and August 16—during the city's world-famous horse race, the **Palio di Siena.** Ten of the 17 neighborhoods compete (chosen by rotation and lot), hurling themselves with medieval abandon into several days of trial races and traditional revelry. Jockeys—usually from out of town—are considered hired guns, no better than mercenaries. Locals boast about which *contrada* will win...and lose. Betting on the outcome is strictly forbidden...officially. Despite the shady behind-the-scenes dealing, on the big day the horses are taken into their *contrada*'s church to be blessed. ("Go and return victorious," says the priest.) It's considered a sign of luck if a horse leaves droppings in the church.

On the evening of the race, Il Campo is stuffed to the brim with locals and tourists. Dirt is brought in and packed down to create the track's surface, while mattresses pad the walls of surrounding buildings. The most treacherous spots are the sharp corners, where many a rider has bitten the dust.

Picture the scene: Ten snorting horses and their nervous riders line up near the pharmacy (on the west side of the square) to

end, the people of Siena cut the statue to pieces and buried it along the walls of Florence.

• *Leave Il Campo uphill on the widest ramp (with your back to the tower, it's at 10 o'clock). After a few steps you reach Via di Città. Turn left and walk 100 yards uphill toward the imposing white palace with brick crenellations on top.*

Halfway to the palace, at the first corner, notice small plaques on the first level of the building facades—these mark the boundary of a neighborhood, or **contrada**. If the flags are flying, they rein-

await the starting signal. Then they race like crazy while spectators wave the scarves of their neighborhoods.

Every possible vantage point and perch is packed with people straining to see the action. One lap around the course is about a quarter of a mile; three laps make a full circuit. In this no-holds-barred race—which lasts just over a minute—a horse can win even without its rider (jockeys ride precariously without saddles and often fall off the horses' sweaty backs).

When the winner crosses the line, 1/17th of Siena—the prevailing neighborhood—goes berserk. Winners receive a *palio* (banner)—painted by a Sienese artist in July and an international artist in August, and always featuring the Virgin Mary (the race is dedicated to her). But the true prizes are proving that your *contrada* is *numero uno,* and mocking your losing rivals.

All over town, sketches and posters depict the Palio. This is not some folkloric event—it's a real medieval moment. If you're packed onto the square with 15,000 people, all hungry for victory, you may not see much, but you'll feel it. Bleacher and balcony seats are expensive, but it's free to join the masses in the square. Go with an empty bladder (as there are no WCs) and be prepared to surrender any sense of personal space.

While the actual Palio packs the city, you can more easily see the horse-race trials—called *prove*—on any of the three days before the main event (usually at 9:00 and after 19:00, bleacher seats may be available; the calmest, most accessible *prova* is the final one—9:00 on the morning of the race—since nobody wants to risk injury so close to the real thing). Good sources for more information include IlPalio.org and ComitatoAmiciDelPalio.it.

force the point. You are stepping from the *contrada* of the Forest (Selva) into the *contrada* of the Eagle (Aquila).

Notice also the once mighty and foreboding medieval **tower house** (on the Il Campo side). Towers once soared all around town, but they're now truncated and no longer add to the skyline—look for their bases as you walk the city.

As you stroll, consider the density of this city over the years. Siena had about 50,000 people living within its walls before the plague hit in 1348. Today, only 18,000 live within the walls.

• *On the left, you reach the big curving facade of the...*

# ❸ Chigi-Saracini Palace (Palazzo Chigi-Saracini)

This old fortified noble palace is today home to a prestigious music academy, the Accademia Musicale Chigiana. If open, step into the courtyard with its photogenic well (powerful medieval families enjoyed direct connections to the city's underground network of aqueducts). The walls of the loggia are decorated with the busts of Chigi-Saracini patriarchs, and the vaults are painted in the Grotesque style popular during the Renaissance. What

look like pigeonholes in the other walls are actually for scaffolding, for both construction and ongoing maintenance. (Notice the wire mesh to keep pigeons from nesting.) The palace, which dates back to the 13th century, was owned by a succession of Sienese families, including the Saracinis and then the Chigis. Its last owner, Guido Chigi-Saracini, established the music academy here, leaving his estate to house and fund it.

Head into the shop/café, which sprawls into a mild museum with old musical instruments, portraits of classical composers, pictures of old Siena, and a chance to watch classical concert videos. In July and August, students may be presenting concerts around town—ask (www.chigiana.it).

Head back outside, but before moving on, take a restful moment to sit on the **stone bench** embedded in the outer wall, and absorb the scene. Here in the old center, strict rules protect the building exteriors. Even though many families live in each building, all the shutters must be the same color. Inside, apartments can be modern, and expensive—some of the priciest in Italy. I think it's classy that the local government prohibits unlicensed vendors from selling their wares on the streets.

Watch the parade of people and imagine how Siena has changed in the last generation, as tourism has boomed and the population within the walls has dropped in half. Look up and consider the phenomenon of Airbnb travelers. They're pushing up the cost of living while driving locals away from the center. It's changing the character of the local economy—homegrown shops catering to residents are being replaced by tourist shops catering to you and me.

• *OK, your break's over. Continue your tour, walking uphill to the next major intersection. You'll pass a small* salumi *and cheese shop marked by a wild boar's head on the left.* **Antica Pizzicheria al Palazzo della Chigiana** *(a.k.a. Pizzicheria de Miccoli) may be the official name, but I bet locals just call it Antonio's. For most of his life, frenzied Antonio has* *carved salumi and cheese for the neighborhood. Locals line up here for their sandwiches (a pricey €5-7 for a big, splittable salami or prosciutto sandwich, plus €2 more to add cheese; be careful—he's a good salesperson; standing room only, Via di Città 95).*

*Now carry on up to...*

## ❹ Quattro Cantoni

The intersection known as Quattro Cantoni (Four Corners) offers a delightful perch from which to study the city. The modern column (from 1996) with a Carrara marble she-wolf marks one of the three hills on which the city is built. You are still in the Eagle district (see the fountain and the corner plaque)—but beware. Just one block up the street, a ready-to-pounce panther—from the rival neighboring district—awaits.

Only the very rich could afford stone residences. The fancy facades here hide their economical brick construction behind a stucco veneer. The stone tower on this corner had only one door—30 feet above street level and reached by ladder, which could be pulled up as necessary. Within a few doors, you'll find a classy bar, an elegant grocery store, and a *gelateria*.

Take a little side trip, venturing up Via San Pietro. Interesting stops (mostly on the left) include the window with Palio video clips playing (at #1), Simon and Paula's art shop with delightful Palio and *contrade* knickknacks (#5), a weaver's shop (#7), the recommended La Vecchia Latteria *gelateria* (on the right, at #10), an art gallery (#11), and four enticing little osterias (just a few of Siena's many great eateries). At the end of the block you'll reach the best medieval art collection in town, the **Pinacoteca** (for a self-guided tour of its interior, see page 388). If you continue on toward the former town gate (Porta all'Arco), a couple of short blocks ahead, the street becomes more workaday, with local shops and few tourists.

• *Return to the Four Corners and carry on straight up Via del Capitano, passing another massive Chigi family palace (on the left, at #1). The Chigi were a family of bankers serving both popes and Holy Roman Emperors (bankers expertly getting their hands on people's money is nothing new). Siena's 13th-century golden age was fueled by banking and resulted in grand building projects like this palazzo.*

*Up next, at the end of the street, find a shady seat on the stone bench against the wall of the old hospital opposite the church.*

## ❺ Piazza del Duomo and the Duomo

The pair of she-wolves atop columns flanking the cathedral's facade says it all: The church was built and paid for not by the pope but by the people and the republic of Siena.

This 13th-century Gothic cathedral, with its striped bell

tower—Siena's ultimate tribute to the Virgin Mary—is heaped with statues, plastered with frescoes, and paved with art. Take in this architectural festival of dark green, white, pink, and gold. Imagine pilgrims arriving at this church, its facade trumpeting the coming of Christ and the true path to salvation.

The current structure dates back to 1215, with the major decoration done during Siena's heyday (1250-1350). The lower story, by Giovanni Pisano (who worked from 1284 to 1297), features remnants of the fading Romanesque style (round arches over the doors), topped with the pointed arches of the new Gothic style that was seeping in from France. The upper half, in full-blown frilly Gothic, was designed and built a century later.

The six-story bell tower (c. 1315) looks even taller, thanks to an optical illusion: The white marble stripes get narrower toward the top, making the upper part seem farther away.

The she-wolf columns flanking the entrance honor Romulus and Remus, the mythical founders of Rome. Legend has it that Remus' sons Aschius and Senius rode north—one on a black horse and the other on a white one—to found the city of Siena.

The interior is a Renaissance riot of striped columns, remarkably intricate inlaid-marble floors, a Michelangelo statue, evocative Bernini sculptures, and the amazing Piccolomini Library. (If you want to enter now, you'll need a ticket—the ticket office moves around, but it's most likely around the left side of the Duomo's entrance; for a self-guided tour of the interior, see page 393.)

Facing the cathedral is **Santa Maria della Scala**, a huge building that housed pilgrims and, until the 1990s, was used as a hospital. Its labyrinthine 12th-century cellars—carved from sandstone and finished with brick—go down several floors and, during medieval times, stored supplies for the hospital upstairs. Today, the exhibit-filled hospital and cellars can be a welcome refuge from the hot streets (for more on this sight, see page 405).

• *Walk along the right side of the church toward its rear end. Look right and find the unfinished wall with see-through windows. This is part of what was once intended to be an extension of the Duomo.*

## ❻ Unfinished Church

Grand as Siena's cathedral is, it's actually the rump of a failed vision. After rival republic Florence began its grand cathedral (1296), proud Siena planned to build an even bigger one, the biggest in all Christendom. But Siena is so hilly that there wasn't enough

flat ground upon which to build a church of that size. What to do? Build a big church anyway, and prop up the overhanging edge with the Baptistery (which we'll pass shortly).

Look at the unfinished wall with see-through windows (circa 1330). Just imagine the audacity of this vision: Today's cathedral would have been just a transept. Worshippers would have entered the church through the unfinished wall. (Look way up at the highest part of the wall. That viewpoint is accessible from inside the Duomo Museum.) Some of the nave's dark-green-and-white-striped columns were built, but the space between them is now partially filled in with brick. White stones in the pavement mark where a row of pillars would have been.

But this grand vision underestimated the complexity of constructing such a building without enough land. That, coupled with the devastating effects of the 1348 plague, killed the city's ability and will to finish the project. Many Sienese saw the Black Death as a sign from God, punishing them for their pride. They canceled their plans and humbly faded into the background of Tuscan history.

• *On your left is the entrance to the* **Duomo Museum**, *housing the church's art (for a self-guided tour, see page 400).*

*To continue our walk, exit the piazza through the doorway in the wall abutting the back end of the church. After a few steps, pause at the top of the marble stairs leading down.*

## ❼ Supporting an Oversized Church

From here you can understand the problem with placing a too-big church on this tiny hilltop. See how the church sticks out, high above the lower street level? Because there wasn't enough flat ground, they propped up the overhanging edge with the church's subterranean features—the Crypt and Baptistery. Each is an integral part of the foundation for the oversized structure. (Both are worth entering and included in the Opa Si Pass; see page 391.)

• *Descend the stairs, nicknamed* **"The Steps of St. Catherine,"** *as she*

*would have climbed them each day on her walk from home to the Santa Maria della Scala hospital where she worked. Below the Baptistery, jog right, then immediately left, through a tunnel down Via di Diacceto. You're passing through what was a gate in the 13th-century city wall. The dark Vicolo delle Carrozze lane on your left would have been outside the wall. Just ahead, pause on the bridge (originally a drawbridge) to enjoy a beautiful view (to the left) of the towering brick Dominican church in the distance. Then continue straight up the lane until you reach the next big square.*

## ❽ Piazza Indipendenza

This square celebrates the creation of a unified Italy (1861) with a 19th-century loggia sporting busts of the first two Italian kings. Stacking history on history, the neo-Renaissance loggia is backed by a Gothic palace and an older medieval tower.

• *Head right, downhill one block (on Via delle Terme), back to the grand Via di Città, and take a few steps to the left to see another, fancier loggia.*

## ❾ Loggia della Mercanzia

This Gothic-Renaissance loggia was built about 1420 as a kind of headquarters for the union of merchants. Here businessmen would

display their goods in shaded comfort. It was perfectly located along Siena's main street, next to Il Campo, and right by the main intersection of town. Siena's nobility purchased the loggia, and eventually it became the clubhouse of the local elites. To this day, it's a private, ritzy, and notoriously out-of-step-with-the-times men's club. The "Gli Uniti" above the door is a "let's stick together" declaration.

• *Next to the loggia, steep steps lead down to Il Campo, but we'll go left and uphill on Via Banchi di Sopra. Pause at the fork in the road, which separates...*

## ❿ Banchi di Sopra and Banchi di Sotto

These main drags are named "upper row of banks" and "lower row of banks." They were once lined with market tables *(banchi)*, and vendors paid rent to the city for a table's position along the street. If the owner of a *banco* neglected to pay up, thugs came along and literally broke *(rotto)* his table. It is from this practice—*banco rotto*, broken table—that we get the English word "bankrupt."

In medieval times, these streets were part of the Via Francigena, the main thoroughfare (busy with pilgrims, merchants, and crusaders) linking Rome with northern Europe. The medieval Sienese traded wool with passing travelers, which required moneychangers, which led to banks. As Siena was a secular town, local Christians were allowed to loan money and work as bankers.

Today, strollers—out each evening for their *passeggiata*—fill Via Banchi di Sopra. Join the crowd, strolling past Siena's finest shops. You could nip into **Nannini** (halfway along, on the right), a venerable café and *pasticceria* famous for its local sweets. The traditional Sienese taste treats (*cantucci, ricciarelli*, and various kinds of fruity and nutty *panforte*) are around the far end of the counter in the back (sold by weight, small amounts are fine, a little slice of *panforte* costs about €3).

A block or so farther up the street, **Piazza Tolomei** faces the imposing Tolomei family palace (now an imposing bank). This is a center for the Owl *contrada*. The column in the square, topped by the she-wolf, marks another of Siena's three hills (called *terzi*, "thirds").

• *Continue on Banchi di Sopra to Piazza Salimbeni. This gets my vote for Siena's finest stretch of palaces.*

## ⓫ Piazza Salimbeni

Piazza Salimbeni is dominated by Monte dei Paschi, the head office of a bank founded in 1472. It's amazing to think this bank has

been in business on this square for over 500 years. Originally Monte dei Paschi was a kind of community bank for common people.

The statue in the center of the square honors Sallustio Antonio Bandini, a reformer who helped develop a system that let people secure firm title to their land. By the way, much of Siena was restored in the 19th century in a neo-Gothic style. When you see architecture that looks almost too good to be true (like some of the facades on this square), it's likely a romantic rebuild from the 1800s.

Directly across from Piazza Salimbeni, the steep little lane called Costa dell'Incrociata leads straight (down and then up) to the Basilica of San Domenico (it's worth the hike; see page 407). Also nearby (behind the cute green newsstand) is the most elegant

SIENA

grocery store in town, Consorzio Agrario di Siena. This farming consortium has been around since 1901, and today lets a group of local producers showcase their finest olive oils, pastas, wines, sweets, and various sauces and pastes. It's like a museum of local edibles (for more on this store, see page 421) and a great place for a quick lunch.

• *With this walk under your belt, you've got the lay of the land. The city is ready for further exploration—the sights associated with City Hall and the Duomo are all just a few minutes away. Enjoy delving deeper into Siena.*

# Sights in Siena

## IL CAMPO AND NEARBY

The gorgeous red-brick square known as Il Campo—worth ▲▲▲—is the best in Italy (for more on the square itself, see page 370). It's also home to City Hall (with the Civic Museum and City Tower) and other sights.

### ▲▲City Hall (Palazzo Pubblico) and Civic Museum (Museo Civico)

Siena's fine Gothic City Hall is still the seat of city government. With its proud tower, this building symbolizes a republic independent from the pope and the Holy Roman Emperor. It also represents a rising secular society, one that appeared first in Tuscany in late medieval times, then spread throughout Europe as humanism took hold during the Renaissance.

City Hall has a fine and manageable museum on its top floor. You'll see the large assembly hall where democracy was forged, adorned with some of Siena's most historic frescoes. There's memorabilia from the birth of the nation of Italy. The highlight is a room of medieval-era frescoes depicting fascinating examples of governance—good and bad. (Note that these frescoes are undergoing an extensive renovation and may be covered up.) Strolling the halls, you'll get a glimpse into the city-as-utopia, when this proud town understandably considered itself the vanguard of Western civilization.

## Siena's Civic Museum

*Piazza del Mercato*

SALA DELLA PACE
(SALA DEI NOVE)

SALA DEL MAPPAMONDO

GIFT SHOP

COURT-YARD

CHAPEL

SALA DI BALIA

SALA DEL RISORGI-MENTO

VIA SALICOTTO

TOUR BEGINS

VIA GIOVANNI DUPRÈ

WC

TORRE DEL MANGIA (TOWER)

*Il Campo*

20 Meters
20 Yards

1. Victor Emmanuel II at Battle of San Martino
2. King Shakes Hands with Garibaldi
3. King Receives Politicians
4. Funeral Procession
5. Sala di Balia
6. Chapel
7. MARTINI – Maestà
8. MARTINI – Guidoriccio da Fogliano
9. DUCCIO – The Surrender of the Castle of Giuncarico
10. St. Catherine
11. St. Bernardino
12. LORENZETTI – Good Government
13. LORENZETTI – City & Countryside
14. LORENZETTI – Bad Government
15. Stairs to View

**Cost and Hours:** Museum-€10 by itself (cheaper if frescoes are covered), or €15 with City Tower; also covered by other combo-tickets that include Santa Maria della Scala and/or the Pinacoteca (up to €25 for everything)—review options and decide which sights you want to see before buying; look for small ticket window straight ahead as you enter City Hall courtyard; open daily 10:00-19:00, Nov-Feb until 18:00, last entry 45 minutes before closing; +39 0577 292 232, www.comune.siena.it.

### ➔ Self-Guided Tour

• *Climb two flights of stairs (elevator on request—ask at ticket desk), pass through the gift shop, and on the left enter the Sala del Risorgimento (Room 7 on the museum-issued map).*

### Sala del Risorgimento (Hall of Italian Unification)

This hall has dramatic scenes of the 19th-century unification of Italy. On the left wall, find the leader of the movement, **1 Victor Emmanuel II** (on the white horse, with beard and pointy moustache), as he takes on the Austrian oppressors at the decisive Battle of San Martino (1859). Beneath that (in a display case), you'll see the very coat he's wearing in the painting. On the next wall, the ❷ **king shakes hands** with the dashing revolutionary Giuseppe Garibaldi, sealing their alliance. In this scene, Garibaldi famously says, "I obey," even as the king's white horse seems to honor him. The soldiers—Garibaldi's famed "Redshirts"—cheer. On display nearby you'll see the red uniform of a proud Sienese citizen who fought under both Victor Emmanuel and Garibaldi. In the next painting, the Italians have won the war, and the ❸ **king receives politicians**, who bow and present the election results that created modern Italy, with Victor Emmanuel II as a symbolic head. Finally, on the far wall, the beloved king has died (see his ❹ **funeral procession** passing through Rome's Pantheon portico), but he's left Italy well on the way to modern nationhood. The mythological grandeur on the ceiling seems designed to legitimize the Kingdom of Italy, a latecomer to the European family of nations. The figure of Italy in the center of the ceiling is surrounded by allegorical panels representing each of the regions making up the newly unified country.

• *Pass through a hallway and into the colorfully frescoed...*

### ❺ Sala di Balia

Here in the seat of government, this room housed one of the city councils, part of the checks and balances of the budding Sienese democracy. The council members presided from the inlaid-wood benches.

The frescoes (by Aretino, c. 1410) celebrate one of medieval Siena's proudest sons, Pope Alexander III. Above the door straight ahead, we see a chaotic naval battle, pitting Alexander's troops against the upstart Holy Roman Emperor (and king of Germany) Frederick Barbarossa (see the German eagle on the shields). The long ships stand side-by-side (or stacked top to bottom in this pre-Renaissance attempt at 3-D), as soldiers lock in intense hand-to-hand combat with spears, swords, and crossbows. Alexander won, so (in the scene high over the entrance door), "Red Beard" Barbarossa is forced to kneel before the pope. Finally (lower on the wall), Alexander parades triumphantly through Rome—celebrated as the great Sienese citizen who saved the papacy from foreign rivals.

• *In the next room, turn left and pass through the ironwork screen into the...*

### ❻ Chapel

This is where the city's governors and bureaucrats prayed. Back in the 14th century, Siena was overseen by a "revolving" government, with nine representatives serving for two-month terms. The system was designed to combat corruption by keeping any one politician from becoming too famous or powerful. "The Nine" were cloistered within this building, and therefore they needed their own chapel. The fine frescoes by Taddeo di Bartolo from the early 1400s show scenes from the life of the Virgin. Note also the inlaid choir chairs; some have carved scenes placed under arcades, as the artist struggled valiantly with perspective.

• *Continue into the large...*

## Sala del Mappamondo (Hall of the World Map)

Siena's main ruling body, the Grand Council, met in this room. The frescoes on its walls pumped citizens up with scenes of their

great military victories and of the Virgin Mary, protector of their city. On one end of the room is the beautiful ❼ *Maestà* (*Enthroned Virgin*, 1315), by Siena's great Simone Martini (c. 1280-1344). Mary sits on a throne under a red silk canopy, a model to Siena's city council of what a just ruler should be. Siena's black-and-white coat of arms is woven into the canopy. Mary is surrounded by saints and angels, clearly echoing the *Maestà* of Simone's teacher, Duccio (Duccio's *Maestà*, then in the Duomo, is now in the Duomo Museum.)

This is a groundbreaking work. It's Siena's first fresco showing a Madonna not in a faraway, gold-leaf heaven, but under the blue sky of a real space that we inhabit. As Mary delicately holds Baby Jesus, her concerned look anticipates the sacrifice of her son. A scraggly John the Baptist (on the right) looks out, connecting viewers with the scene. Mary holds a message from the Book of Solomon in her hand: "Love justice, those who rule the land."

The canopy creates a 3-D stage, with saints in front of, behind, and underneath it. Some saints' faces are actually blocked by the support poles. These saints are not a generic conga-line of Byzantine icons, but a milling crowd of 30 individuals with expressive faces. Some look straight out, some are in profile, and some turn at that difficult-to-draw three-quarter angle, grabbing onto the canopy poles.

This *Maestà* was ingeniously lighted in pre-Edison days. Look up at the roof beam nearest the painting and find two human-looking arms made of wood. These once held hanging lamps that kept Mary gloriously lit.

On the opposite end of the room is the famous ❽ *Equestrian Portrait of Guidoriccio da Fogliano* (1330; traditionally attributed to Simone Martini). The year is MCCCXXVIII (1328), and we see

Siena's renowned mercenary commander Guidoriccio da Fogliano. With unbeatable Florence to its north, Siena has been expanding south. Guido leaves his camp (on the right), rides across a barren landscape, and surveys the scene. After a six-month-long siege, the Sienese have finally captured the rich and fortified city of Montemassi (left). What looks like a castle (in the middle) is a siege fort the Sienese built just for that battle, flying their black-and-white flag and with the catapult that helped them win. Check out the commander's determined expression—this is one of Europe's first secular portraits. (Guido and his horse have the same tailor.)

On the same wall, just below the horse and rider, is ❾ *The Surrender of the Castle of Giuncarico* (1314), attributed to Duccio. A man in green is about to hand over his sword to the Sienese republic. In the background, on a rocky outcrop, is the man's castle and village. This painting may have inspired the 3-D landscape of *Guidoriccio da Fogliano*.

Also in the room (frescoed on pillars between the arches) are two of the city's best-known saints. ❿ **St. Catherine,** a mystic nun, influenced world events through her eloquent letters written from her humble Sienese home (see page 408). ⓫ **St. Bernardino** (holding a flaming sun in a frame) drew huge crowds to Il Campo with his charismatic sermons. At sunset, he'd announce that he would begin speaking again at sunrise...and people would actually come back. His words brought together sworn enemies to share a *bacio di pace*—kiss of peace.

• *Continue into the next room.*

## Sala della Pace, a.k.a. Sala dei Nove (Hall of Peace/Hall of the Nine)

The powerful Council of Nine, who ruled Siena from 1287 to 1355, met in this room, surrounded by images reminding them of their responsibility to rule wisely. It's a fascinating fresco series showing the *Effects of Good and Bad Government*, by Ambrogio Lorenzetti (1337-1340). (Unfortunately, these frescoes may be covered for restoration during your visit.)

The short wall opposite the window features the ⓬ *Allegory of Good Government,* which celebrates the Sienese social system:

"Siena," the stately, bearded man on the throne, is flanked by the six virtues. The greatest of the virtues, Peace (Pax), has been achieved by wise rule, so she can just kick back on a pile of discarded armor. Farther to the left, Lady Justice (in red, holding the scales) is hard at work punishing and forgiving, guided by angels. Below her, Concordia (balancing a carpenter's plane) assures that all citizens get a level playing field. Near her, a line of happy Sienese citizens file by, with no one's head above another's. But on the far right of the fresco, wrongdoers are rounded up by the authorities. And the symbolic foundation of it all (at "Siena's" feet) are Romulus and Remus, with the she-wolf, linking Siena's origins with the glory of ancient Rome.

On the long wall to the right, a well-preserved fresco depicts the beneficial effects of good government in both ⓫ **city and countryside.** The city is,

of course, Siena—note the Duomo in the upper left corner. The skyline is bright and fresh, and people go about their business with whistle-while-you-work happiness: Cobblers make boots, workers repair roofs, ladies dance in the streets to a tambourine, a professor teaches, and the conversation flows.

Study this intimate and rare look at 14th-century life. It shows Siena's proud, pointy towers before they were lopped off by the Florentines. And the buildings wear their original stucco veneer, which was lost over the years, resulting in today's exposed brickwork, so "typical" of Siena.

The blessings of a good government extend even to the countryside (right half of the wall). It's lush and green, with neatly planted fields. Bringing stability and safety to the land outside the city walls was a big accomplishment in the 14th century. The fields are tilled, the Via Francigena is busy with pilgrim traffic, and above the gate, the angel-like figure of Security (with a scroll) declares

that justice rules (and a gallows in her hand reminds all that laws are strictly enforced).

In this utopian community ruled by a utopian government, the city and countryside worked together—so their paintings are exactly the same size, 20 feet wide. The painter, a proud citizen of Siena, boldly signed his work—one of the earliest landscapes. And the caption is written not in Latin but in early Italian, another example of how progressive Siena was in its heyday.

On the opposite wall, it's a whole different story in the badly damaged ⓬ *Allegory of Bad Government.* A dictator, symbolized by a horned, fanged, wine-drinking devil-like tyrant, sets the vices loose ("Avarice," "Vainglory"). He's assisted by a dog-headed monster with a knife. Lady Justice slumps at the devil's feet, bound, too depressed to look up. The consequences are that, rather than dancing in the streets, people are being arrested. Arsonists torch homes and fields, soldiers rape and pillage, crime is rampant, and frescoes get damaged. A lady in red (center) is harassed by soldiers while her friend lies fallen in the street. The only person still working is making weapons. In the countryside (left) fields are barren, the landscape is dark and devastated, and no one leaves the city unarmed. The message: Without good government, there can be no prosperity.

• *An enlightened city government also provides convenient toilets for the public—which you'll find just off this room. Backtracking to the exit, just before the Sala del Risorgimento, the looooong* ⓯ *stairs lead to a grand view of the city and its surroundings. (For a less impressive view, you could skip the stairs and simply peek behind the curtains in the Sala della Pace.)*

## Other Sights on or near Il Campo
### ▲City Tower (Torre del Mangia)

The tower's nearly 400 steps get pretty skinny at the top, but the reward is a grand view. (If you're also visiting the Duomo Museum, note that the rooftop viewpoint from that location is arguably at least as good as this one.) For more on the tower, see page 372.

**Cost and Hours:** €10, €15 combo-ticket with Civic Museum, also included in various combo-tickets with Santa Maria della Scala and/or the Pinacoteca, daily 10:00-19:00, Nov-Feb until 16:00, closed in rain, last entry one hour before closing, free and mandatory bag check.

**Crowd Alert:** Admission is limited to 50 people at a time. Wait at the bottom of the stairs for the green *Avanti* light. Try to avoid midday crowds (up to an hour wait at peak times).

### ▲Pinacoteca

If you're into medieval art, you should enjoy this quiet, uncrowded, colorful museum. The museum (officially the Pinacoteca Nazionale di Siena) walks you through Siena's art chronologically, from the 12th through the 16th century, when a revolution in realism was percolating in Tuscany. If you're nearly museumed out, however, this may be one too many, without any spectacular highlights.

**Cost and Hours:** €8, Mon and Fri-Sun 8:30-13:30, Tue-Thu 14:00-19:00, closed two Sundays a month; from Il Campo, walk out Via di Città and go left on Via San Pietro to #29; +39 0577 281 161, www.pinacotecanazionale.siena.it.

❷ **Self-Guided Tour:** In general, the collection lets you follow the evolution of painting styles from Byzantine to Gothic, then to International Gothic, and finally to Renaissance. The medieval and early Renaissance core of the collection is on the second floor (Rooms 1-19). The also-impressive later art of the Cinquecento is downstairs, on the first floor.

· *Start your visit by climbing to the second floor and Room 1.*

Long after Florentine art went realistic, the Sienese embraced a timeless, otherworldly style glittering with lots of gold. But Sienese art features more than just paintings. In this city of proud craftsmen, the gilding and carpentry of the frames almost compete with the actual paintings. The exquisite attention to detail gives a glimpse into the wealth of the 13th and 14th centuries, Siena's golden age. As you walk through the museum, take time to trace the delicate features with your eyes. The woven silk and gold clothing you'll see was worn by the very people who once walked these halls, when this was a private mansion (appreciate the colonnaded courtyard).

**Room 1** mostly features early Sienese works of the 13th century, with the intense color, stylized compositions, and gold backgrounds of the Byzantine style. The altarpieces here emphasize the heavenly and otherworldly.

**Rooms 2-4** contain a number of works by Duccio di Buoninsegna, who revolutionized a more human realism in the Sienese approach to painting. His groundbreaking innovations are subtle: less gold-leaf background, fewer gold creases in robes, translucent garments, inlaid-marble thrones, and a more human Mary and Jesus. Notice that the Madonna-and-Bambino pose is eerily identical in each version. While artists had yet to master depth and perspective, they appreciated it—see how in the crucifixes, Jesus' head actually tilts out. (Duccio also created the *Maestà* in the Duomo Museum, the Duomo's big stained-glass window, and a fresco in the Civic Museum.)

In **Room 5** are works by Duccio's one-time assistant, Simone Martini, including his *Blessed Augustine of Siena*. Scenes from the saint's life appear in an attempt at realistic Sienese streets, buildings, and landscapes. In each

panel, the saint pops out at the oddest (difficult to draw) angles to save the day by performing one of his many miracles, to the obvious relief of those involved—notice the dramatic emotion on their faces. (Simone Martini also did the *Maestà* and possibly the Guidoriccio frescoes in the Civic Museum.)

**Room 7** includes religious works by the hometown Lorenzetti brothers (Ambrogio is best known for the secular masterpiece, the *Effects of Good and Bad Government*, in the Civic Museum). The rest of the rooms on this floor are a menagerie of gold-backed saints and Madonnas.

In **Room 11** (from the atrium, cut through Room 10), find the powerful *Crucifixion* (c. 1400) by Taddeo di Bartolo. In the dreamy, delicate *Annunciation* (also by Taddeo di Bartolo), follow the exciting action between the cast: God, Holy Spirit, Mary, and the angel Gabriel. The patron saints glance out—as if to say, "Are you seeing this?"—to connect us with the scene. The adjacent chapel is a reminder that this was formerly the home of a noble family.

In **Room 12,** on the right wall, are two famous small wooden panels: *Città sul Mare (City by the Sea)* and *Castello in Riva al Lago (Castle on the Lakeshore)*. These beautifully drawn pieces, done by an early 15th-century Sienese painter, feature a strange, medieval-landscape Cubism. Notice the weird, melancholic light that captures the sense of the Dark Ages.

• *Loop through Rooms 13 to 17 and notice how, even in the 15th century, Siena stays retro, clinging to its Gothic glory. Then descend one floor to view an entertaining collection of later Renaissance art.*

In **Room 20,** suddenly the gold is gone—Madonna is set on Earth. See works by the painter/biographer Giorgio Vasari **(Room 22),** a stunning view out the window **(Room 26),** and several colorful rooms **(27-30)** dedicated to Domenico Beccafumi (1486-1551). In the center of **Rooms 28 and 29** stand finely painted end panels (1540) for a stretcher used to carry the sick and dead. Beccafumi designed many of the Duomo's inlaid pavement panels, and his original cartoons are displayed in **Room 30.** With strong bodies, twisting poses, and dramatic gestures, Beccafumi's works epitomize the Mannerist style of the High Renaissance.

**Room 31** has the sympathetic *Christ on the Column* by Il Sodoma (Giovanni Antonio Bazzi—see page 432), and the long **Room 32** displays large-scale works by Il Sodoma, Beccafumi, and others. In **Room 34,** Bernardino Mei gives a Sienese take on the wrinkled saints and dark shadows of Caravaggio.

## DUOMO AND RELATED SIGHTS

Siena's monumental cathedral complex encompasses the Duomo, Duomo Museum (and its panoramic terrace), Baptistery, and Crypt.

### Ticket Options and Hours

The Duomo's various sights are covered by a confusing variety of tickets. Here are your basic choices:

**Duomo Interior** (including the Piccolomini Library): €5 most of the year; €8 when floor panels are uncovered (typically July and mid-Aug–mid-Oct.

**Opa Si Pass:** €13; €15 when floor panels are uncovered. Covers Duomo interior, Duomo Museum (with original Duomo art, plus a fantastic viewpoint over Siena), the Crypt (frescoes), and the Baptistery (with a fine baptismal font).

**Porta del Cielo ("Gate of Heaven") Pass:** €20, covers everything in the Opa Si Pass and adds an escorted visit up to the cathedral's dome and rooftop (described later). It's wise to reserve this pass—see "Crowd-Beating Tips," below.

**Hours:** The Duomo is open Mon-Sat 10:00-19:00, Sun 13:30-17:30; Nov-March daily until 17:00. The associated sights keep similar hours (but if arriving late in the day, confirm closing times to plan your visit strategically). The Porta del Cielo roof visits are offered daily, Nov-March on weekends only with some closures.

**Information:** +39 0577 286 300, www.operaduomo.siena.it.

**Getting Tickets:** As of this writing, the ticket office for Duomo sights is on the left side of the Duomo, as you face it. However, ticket options and sales points get reconfigured frequently. Expect changes, and when in doubt, ask uniformed staff for help.

**Crowd-Beating Tips:** Crowds peak midmorning in high season; early, late, or lunchtime visits can be less busy. If you anticipate crowds, you can prebook at www.operaduomo.siena.it (€2 booking fee/ticket; click "Booking Online" to be redirected to official ticket-booking site). Prebook Porta del Cielo cathedral roof visits; slots fill up.

### ▲▲▲Duomo (Duomo di Siena)

Siena's 13th-century cathedral and striped bell tower are one of the most illustrious examples of Romanesque-Gothic style in Italy. This ornate but surprisingly secular shrine to the Virgin Mary is slathered with colorful art inside and out, from inlaid-marble floors to stained-glass windows. The cathedral's interior showcases the work of the greatest sculptors of successive eras—Pisano, Donatello, Michelangelo, and Bernini—and the Piccolomini Library features a series of 15th-century frescoes chronicling the adventures of Siena's philanderer-turned-pope, Aeneas Piccolomini.

SIENA

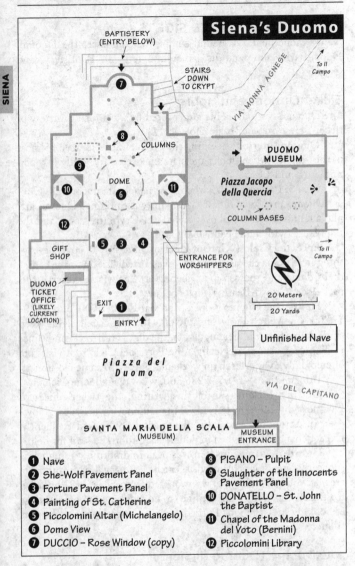

**Siena's Duomo**

BAPTISTERY (ENTRY BELOW)

STAIRS DOWN TO CRYPT

VIA MONNA AGNESE

To Il Campo

COLUMNS

DUOMO MUSEUM

Piazza Jacopo della Quercia

DOME

COLUMN BASES

To Il Campo

GIFT SHOP

ENTRANCE FOR WORSHIPPERS

DUOMO TICKET OFFICE (LIKELY CURRENT LOCATION)

EXIT

ENTRY

20 Meters
20 Yards

Piazza del Duomo

Unfinished Nave

VIA DEL CAPITANO

SANTA MARIA DELLA SCALA (MUSEUM)

MUSEUM ENTRANCE

❶ Nave
❷ She-Wolf Pavement Panel
❸ Fortune Pavement Panel
❹ Painting of St. Catherine
❺ Piccolomini Altar (Michelangelo)
❻ Dome View
❼ DUCCIO – Rose Window (copy)
❽ PISANO – Pulpit
❾ Slaughter of the Innocents Pavement Panel
❿ DONATELLO – St. John the Baptist
⓫ Chapel of the Madonna del Voto (Bernini)
⓬ Piccolomini Library

**Cost and Hours:** See "Ticket Options and Hours," earlier.

**Dress Code:** Modest dress is required, but stylish paper ponchos are provided for the inappropriately clothed.

**Church Services:** Worshippers attending Mass can enter the church free; use the entrance on the right side of the building, set farther back from the main one (Mon-Sat at 10:00; Sun at 8:00, 11:00, 12:15, and 18:30). At times of year when the fragile floor panels are uncovered (July and mid-Aug-mid-Oct), Mass is held elsewhere or in a side chapel.

**Tours:** There may be a downloadable app or a rentable audioguide (ask on-site)—but the information covered here is plenty for a casual visit.

### ❷ Self-Guided Tour

The Duomo sits atop Siena's highest point, with one of the most extravagant facades in all of Europe. Like a medieval altarpiece,

the facade is divided into sections, each frame filled with patriarchs and prophets, studded with roaring gargoyles, and topped with prickly pinnacles (for more about the facade, see page 377).

• *Step inside, putting yourself in the mindset of a pilgrim as you take in this trove of religious art.*

### ❶ Nave

The heads of 171 popes—who reigned from the time of St. Peter to the 12th century—peer down from above, looking over the fine inlaid art on the floor. With a forest of striped columns, a coffered dome, a large stained-glass window at the far end (it's a copy—the original is viewable up close in the Duomo Museum), and an art gallery's worth of early Renaissance art, this is one busy interior. If you look closely at the popes, you'll see the same four faces repeated over and over.

For almost two centuries (1373-1547), 40 artists paved the marble floor with scenes from the Old Testament, allegories, and intricate patterns. The series starts near the entrance with historical allegories; the larger, more elaborate scenes surrounding the altar are mostly stories from the Old Testament.

Many of the floor panels are roped off and covered to prevent further wear and tear. But typically in July and from mid-August through October, the cathedral uncovers them and holds Mass

elsewhere. The following two panels are always visible.

• *On the floor, find the second pavement panel from the entrance.*

### ❷ She-Wolf Pavement Panel

Depicted as a she-wolf, the proud city of Siena is the center of the Italian universe, orbited by such lesser lights as Roma, Florentia (Florence), and Pisa. This is pretty secular stuff for such prime church real estate. Five yards to the left and right are panels with pre-Christian imagery of the ancient Greek prophetesses known as the sibyls. The sibyls parade up both aisles to the front as the faithful process to redemption at the main altar. This church's mix of pre-Christian wisdom, secular humanism, and Christian piety gives an insight into the Sienese approach to religion.

• *The fourth pavement panel from the entrance is the...*

### ❸ Fortune Pavement Panel

Lady Luck (lower right) arrives on earth, where she teeters back and forth on a ball and a tipsy boat. The lesson? Fortune is an unstable foundation for life. Truth seekers wind their way up the precarious path to the top, where Socrates accompanies Lady Wisdom. Having attained wisdom, the world's richest man ("Crates," upper right) realizes that money doesn't buy happiness, and he dumps his jewels out. They fall to earth, and the cycle of Fortune begins again.

On the right wall hangs a dim ❹ **painting of St. Catherine** (fourth from entrance). Siena's homegrown saint (see page 408) had a vision in which she mystically married Christ. Here's the wedding ceremony in heaven. Jesus places the ring on Catherine's finger as her future mother-in-law, Mary, looks on.

• *On the opposite wall is a marble altarpiece decorated with statues (next to a doorway leading to a shop, snacks, and WC).*

### ❺ Piccolomini Altar

The Piccolomini Altar was commissioned by the Sienese-born Pope Pius III (born Francesco Piccolomini) as a memorial hon-

oring his uncle Pius II. As the cardinal of Siena at the time, Piccolomini also expected this fancy tomb to be his own final resting place, but because he later became pope he was buried in the Vatican instead. (A few feet to the right of the altar, a colorful fresco shows the coronation of Pope Pius—way up top—wearing a golden robe.)

The Piccolomini Altar is most interesting for its statues: one by Michelangelo and three by his students. Michelangelo was originally contracted to do 15 statues, but another sculptor had started the marble blocks, and Michelangelo's heart was never in the project. He personally finished the figure of St. Paul (lower right, clearly more interesting than the bland, bored saints above him).

Paul has the look of Michelangelo's *Moses,* the self-portrait of the sculptor himself, and the relaxed hand of his *David*. It was the chance to sculpt *David* in Florence that convinced Michelangelo to abandon the Siena project.

• *Now grab a seat under the dome to study the...*

## ❻ Dome and Surrounding Area

The dome sits on a 12-sided base, but its "coffered" ceiling is actually a painted illusion.

Closer to ground level, attached to columns (easy to miss) are two 60-foot-tall wooden poles that are dear to any Sienese heart. These **flagpoles**—bearing the Florentine flag—were captured during the pivotal Battle of Montaperti (1260, fought near Siena), when 20,000 Sienese squared off against 35,000 soldiers from their archrival city, Florence. The two armies battled back and forth all day, until one of the Florentine soldiers—actually, a Sienese spy under cover—attacked the Florentine standard-bearer from behind. Florence's flag fell to the ground, the army lost its bearings and confidence, and Siena seized the moment to counterattack and win. It was the city's finest hour, ushering in its 88-year golden age (it lasted from 1260 until the plague hit in 1348).

The church was intended to be much larger. Look into the right transept and mentally blow a hole in the wall. You'd be looking down the nave of the massive extension of the church—that is, if the original grandiose plan had been completed (see page 378).

• *At the far end of the church, high up above the altar, is a round stained-glass window.*

## ❼ Duccio's Stained-Glass Rose Window

The rose window is a kaleidoscope of colors and intricate designs. And if you zoomed in close, you'd see that the central panel depicts the Virgin Mary. She's dressed in blue and red, sitting in a holy bubble as winged angels carry her up to heaven. The window is dedicated to the Virgin Mary, as is the church and the city itself.

This is a copy of the original window made about 1287-1290 (and now in the Duomo Museum). For a fuller description, see page 395.

• *Closer to you, on the left side of the nave, is a stone podium sitting atop columns. This is...*

## ❽ Pisano's Pulpit

The octagonal Carrara marble pulpit (1268) rests on the backs of lions, symbols of Christianity triumphant. Like the lions, the Church eats its catch (devouring paganism) and nurses its cubs. The seven relief panels tell the life of Christ in rich detail. The pulpit is the work of Nicola Pisano (c. 1220-1278), the "Giotto of sculpture," whose revival of classical forms (columns, sarcophagus-like relief panels) signaled the coming Renaissance. His son Giovanni (c. 1240-1319) carved many of the panels, mixing his dad's classicism and realism with the decorative detail and curvy lines of French Gothic—a style that would influence Donatello and other Florentines.

The Crucifixion panel (facing the nave under the eagle) is proto-Renaissance. Christ's anatomy is realistic. Mary (bottom left) swoons into the arms of the other women, a very human outburst of emotion. And a Roman soldier (to the right, by Giovanni) turns to look back with an easy motion that breaks the stiff, frontal Gothic mold.

Look at the two panels facing the altar. It's Judgment Day, and Christ is flanked by the saved (on his right, almost hypnotized by the presence of their savior) and, on his left, the desperate damned.

If you visit Pisa, you'll see two similar Pisano pulpits there, in that city's Duomo and Baptistery.

• *A few steps to the left of the pulpit (in the left transept), find a panel in the floor, the...*

### ❾ Slaughter of the Innocents Pavement Panel

Herod (left), sitting enthroned amid Renaissance arches, orders the massacre of all babies to prevent the coming of the promised Messiah. It's a chaotic scene of angry soldiers, grieving mothers, and dead babies, reminding locals that a republic ruled by a tyrant will always experience misery. The work was designed by the Sienese Matteo di Giovanni (late 1400s) and inlaid with a colorful array of marble, including yellow marble, a Sienese specialty quarried nearby.

• *Nearby in the left transept is a small chapel with a well-known statue.*

### ❿ Donatello's St. John the Baptist

The rugged saint in his famous rags stands in a quiet chapel. Donatello, the aging Florentine sculptor, whose style was now considered passé in Florence, came here to build bronze doors for the church (similar to Ghiberti's in Florence). Donatello didn't complete the door project, but he did finish this bronze statue (1457). Appreciate John's expressive face and the realistic stance of his body—done before Michelangelo was even born. Notice the cherubs high above in the dome, playfully dangling their feet.

• *Cross the church. Directly opposite find the Chigi Chapel (with its ironwork entrance), also known as the...*

### ⓫ Chapel of the *Madonna del Voto*

To understand why Bernini is considered the greatest Baroque sculptor, step into this sumptuous chapel (designed in the early

1660s for Fabio Chigi, a.k.a. Pope Alexander VII). Move up to the altar and look back at the **two Bernini statues** that frame the doorway: Mary Magdalene in a state of spiritual ecstasy and St. Jerome playing the crucifix like a violinist lost in heavenly music.

The chapel is classic Baroque, combining statues, stained glass, a dome, marble in several different colors, and golden angels holding an icon-like framed painting, creating a multimedia extravaganza that offers a glimpse of heaven. It's enough to make even a Lutheran light a candle.

The painting over the altar is the *Madonna del Voto,* a Madonna and Child adorned with a real crown of gold and jewels (painted by a Sienese master in the mid-13th century). In typical medieval fashion, the scene is set in the golden light of heaven. Mary has the almond eyes, long fingers, and golden folds in her robe that are found in orthodox icons of the time. Still, this Mary tilts her head and looks out sympathetically, ready to listen to the prayers of the faithful. This is the Mary to whom the Palio is dedicated, dear to the hearts of the Sienese.

For untold generations, the Sienese have prayed to the *Madonna del Voto* for help. In thanks, they give **offerings** of silver hearts and medallions, many of which now hang on the walls to the right and left as you exit the chapel. On the other side of the chapel door, the glass display case on the wall looks like a jewelry store's front window—with rings, necklaces, and other precious items given by thankful worshippers. To leave an offering yourself, light a candle for a small donation.

• *Cross back to the other side of the church, toward the big Piccolomini Altar we saw earlier. Next to the altar, look for the door to the...*

## ⓬ Piccolomini Library

If crowds slow your way into this library, spend your waiting time reading ahead. Brilliantly frescoed, the library captures the exuberant, optimistic spirit of the 1400s, when humanism and the Renaissance were born. The never-restored frescoes look nearly as vivid now as the day they were finished 550 years ago. (With the bright window light, candles were unnecessary in this room—and didn't sully the art with soot.) The painter Pinturicchio (c. 1454-1513) was hired to celebrate the life of one of Siena's hometown boys—a man many call "the first humanist," Aeneas Piccolomini (1405-1464), who became Pope Pius II. (Pius II fans can visit his birthplace, Pienza—which was named for him—described in the Heart of Tuscany chapter.) Each of the 10 scenes is framed with an arch, as if Pinturicchio were opening a window onto the spacious 3-D world we inhabit. Start with the painting in the far right corner, then follow the frescoes clockwise:

**1. Leaving for Basel:** Twenty-seven-year-old Aeneas, riding a white horse and decked out in an outrageous hat, pauses to take

one last look back as he leaves Siena to charge off on the first of many adventures in his sometimes sunny, sometimes stormy life. Born poor but noble, he got all A's in his classics classes in Siena. Now, having soaked up all the secular knowledge available, he leaves home to crash a church council in Switzerland, where he would take sides against the pope.

**2. Meeting James II of Scotland:** Aeneas (with long brown hair) charmed King James and the well-dressed, educated, worldly crowd of Europe's courts. Among his many travels, he visited London (writing home about Westminster Abbey and St. Paul's), barely survived a storm at sea, negotiated peace between England and France, and fathered (at least) two illegitimate children.

**3. Crowned Poet by Frederick III:** Next we find Aeneas in Vienna, working as secretary to the German king. Aeneas kneels to ceremonially receive the laurel crown of a poet. Aeneas wrote love poetry, bawdy stories, and a play, and is best known for his candid autobiography. Everyone was talking about Aeneas—a writer, speaker, diplomat, and lover of the arts and pretty women, who was the very essence of the *uomo universale*, a.k.a. Renaissance Man.

**4. Submitting to Pope Eugene IV:** At age 40, after a serious illness, Aeneas changes his life. He journeys to Rome and kisses the pope's foot, apologizing for his heretical opposition. He repents for his wild youth and becomes a priest. (In his autobiography, he says it was time to change anyway, as women no longer aroused him...and he no longer attracted them.)

**5. Introducing Frederick III and Eleanora:** Quickly named bishop of Siena, Aeneas (in white pointed bishop's hat) makes his hometown a romantic getaway for his friend Frederick and his fiancée. Notice the Duomo's bell tower in the distance and the city walls (upper left). Aeneas always seemed to be present at Europe's most important political, religious, and social events.

**6. Made Cardinal:** Kneeling before the pope, with shaved head and praying hands, Aeneas receives the flat red hat of a cardinal. In many of these panels, the artist Pinturicchio uses all the latest 3-D effects—floor tiles and carpets, distant landscapes, receding lines—to suck you into the scene. He tears down palace walls and lets us peek inside, into the day's centers of power.

**7. Elected Pope:** In 1458, at age 53, Aeneas is elected to be Pope Pius II. Carried in triumph, he blesses the crowd. One of his first acts as pope is to declare as heresy the antipope doctrines he championed in his youth.

**8. Proclaims a Crusade:** He calls on all of Europe to liberate the Christian city of Constantinople, which had recently fallen (in 1453) to the Ottoman Turks. Europe is reluctant to follow his call, but Pius pushes the measure through.

**9. Canonizes St. Catherine:** From his papal throne, Pius looks down on the mortal remains of Catherine (clutching her symbol, the lily) and proclaims his fellow Sienese a saint. The well-dressed candle-holders in the foreground pose proudly.

**10. Arrival in Ancona:** Old and sick, the pope has to be carried everywhere on a litter because of rheumatic feet. He travels to Ancona, ready to board a ship to go fight the Turks. But only a handful of Venetian galleys arrive at the appointed time, the crusade peters out, and Pius, disheartened, dies. He wrote: "I do not deny my past. I have been a great wanderer, wandering away from the right path. But at least I know it, and hope the knowledge has not come too late."

Circle around a second time to appreciate the library's intricately decorated, illuminated music scores and a statue (a Roman copy of a Greek original) of the Three Graces, who almost seem to dance to the beat. The oddly huge sheepskin sheets of music are from the days before individual hymnals—they had to be big so that many singers could read the music from a distance. If the musical notation looks off, that's because 15th-century Italians used a movable C clef, not the fixed F and G clefs musicians commonly use today. This clef marked middle C, and the melodies could be chanted in relation to it. Appreciate the fine painted decorations on

the music—the gold-leaf highlights, the blue tones from expensive ultramarine (made from precious lapis lazuli), and the miniature figures. All of this exquisite detail was lovingly crafted by Benedictine monks for the glory of God. Find your favorite—I like the blue, totally wild god of wind with the big hair (in the fourth case from the right of the window).

• *Our tour is finished. But to truly appreciate the grandeur of the Duomo, exit the church and make a U-turn to the left, walking alongside the church to Piazza Jacopo della Quercia. Had the massive church Siena envisioned been built, the nave would be where the piazza is today. Look through the unfinished entrance facade, note blue sky where the stained-glass windows would have been, and ponder the struggles, triumphs, and failures of the human spirit. (For more on the unfinished church, see page 378.)*

## ▲▲Duomo Museum and Viewpoint (Museo dell'Opera e Panorama)

Siena's most enjoyable museum, housing the cathedral's art, is located in the skeleton of the Duomo's grand but unfinished extension (to the right as you face the cathedral's main facade). Stand eye-to-eye with the saints and angels who once languished, unknown, in the church's upper reaches (where copies are found today). The ground floor features the original Duccio stained-glass window that once hung over the high altar, along with an army of statues from the facade. Upstairs is Duccio's *Maestà* (*Enthroned Virgin*, 1311), a masterpiece of medieval art. The flip side of the *Maestà* (displayed on the opposite wall) has 26 panels—the medieval equivalent of pages—showing scenes from the Passion of Christ. And the museum's high point is one of the loftiest viewpoints in town, offering expansive views of the church and the city.

**Cost and Hours:** See "Ticket Options and Hours," earlier.

### ❯ Self-Guided Tour

• *Start on the ground floor, which houses the church's original statues, mainly from the facade and exterior. After descending a few steps, turn your back on the hall of statues and wrought-iron gate. You're now face-to-face with...*

### Donatello's *Madonna and Child,* c. 1458

In this round, carved relief, a slender and tender Mary gazes down at her chubby-cheeked baby. The thick folds of her headdress stream down around her smooth face. Her sad eyes say that she knows the eventual fate of her son. Mary's expressive hands are both strong and tender. Donatello creates the illusion of Mary's three-dimensional "lap" using only a few inches of depth cut into the creamy-rose stone. Move to the far right and look at Mary's face from an angle (try not to notice impish Jesus); think of the challenge involved in carving the illusion of such depth.

• *At the opposite end of the room is...*

### Duccio's Stained-Glass Rose Window, c. 1287-1290

This splendid original window was installed for centuries above and behind the Duomo's altar. Now the church has a copy, and art lovers can enjoy a close-up look at this masterpiece. The rose window—20 feet across—is dedicated (like the church and the city itself) to the Virgin Mary. In the window's bottom panel, Mary (in blue) lies stretched across a red coffin while a crowd of mourners looks on. Miraculously, Mary was spared the pain of death; instead, her mortal form simply fell asleep forever (the Assumption, central panel). Winged angels carry her up in a holy bubble to heaven (top panel), where Christ sets her on a throne beside him and crowns her.

The work is by Siena's most famous artist, Duccio di Buoninsegna (c. 1255-1319). Duccio combined elements from rigid Byzantine icons (Mary's almond-shaped bubble, called a *mandorla*, and the full-frontal saints that flank her) with a budding sense of 3-D realism (the throne turned at a three-quarter angle to simulate depth, with angels behind). Also notice how the angels in the central panel spread their wings out beyond the border of the window frame.

The Sienese believed it was the Virgin Mary who helped them defeat Florence in the bloody Battle of Montaperti, so for the next 80 years of prosperity, Sienese artists cranked out countless similar Madonnas as a way of saying *grazie*. Picture the original setting inside the Duomo: Duccio's window above the altar, bathing his *Maestà* altarpiece (which we'll see upstairs) in a golden-blue light.

• *Lining this main room are...*

### Pisano's Statues, 1285-1296

Giovanni Pisano—who helped his dad carve the Duomo's pulpit—spent a decade overseeing the cathedral's decoration. It included these statues of saints, prophets, sibyls, animals, and the original she-wolf with Romulus and Remus. These life-size, robed saints stand in a relaxed *contrapposto*, with open mouths and expressive gestures. Their heads jut out—Pisano's way of making them more visible from below. The most dramatic statue is Moses (*Mosè*, near the back on the left), with his "horns" of spiritual light. See how Moses turns. In his original place atop the church, he would appear to be conversing with his sister, Miriam (*Maria di Mosè*)—just as they do here in the museum.

Down a few steps, in Room 11, are the two lions that once

looked down from the church's main entrance, and Pisano's 12 apostles, who originally lined the nave. (See old photos on the wall.) Tastes changed over the centuries, and the apostles were later moved up to the roof, where they eroded. Pisano's relaxed realism and expressive gestures were a major influence on later Florentine sculptors like Donatello.

• *Retrace your steps and go up to the first floor. Turn left, through a glass door into the darkened Room 6, for a private audience with Duccio's Madonna.*

### Duccio's *Maestà* and Passion Panels, 1311

The panels in this room were once part of the Duomo's main altarpiece. Grab a seat and study one of the great pieces of medieval art. Although the former altarpiece was disassembled (and the frame was lost), most of the pieces are displayed here, with the front side (*Maestà*, with Mary and saints; pronounced my-STAH) at one end of the room and the back side (26 Passion panels) at the other.

Imagine these separate panels pieced together, set into their original gold, prickly, 15-by-15-foot wood frame and placed on the main altar in the Duomo.

*Maestà (Enthroned Virgin):* The main scene shows the Virgin and Child, surrounded by angels and saints. Mary is a melancholy queen on an inlaid-marble throne. Young angels lean their elbows on the back of the throne and sigh. We see the throne head-on, unnaturally splayed open (a Byzantine style popular at the time in Siena). Mary is massive, twice the size of the saints around her, and she clearly stands out from the golden background. Unlike traditional full-frontal Byzantine icons, she turns slightly sideways to touch her baby, who does not bless us.

The city of Siena is dedicated to this Lady, whom the faithful believe favored the Sienese against Florence in the bloody Battle of Montaperti in 1260. Here, she's triumphant, visited by Siena's four patron saints (kneeling in front), John the Baptist and other saints (the first choir row), more angels in a row (soprano section), and, chiming in from up in the balcony, James the Great and the 12 apostles.

The painting was revolutionary for the time in its sheer size and opulence, and in Duccio's budding realism, which broke standard conventions. Duccio, at the height of his powers, used every innovative arrow in his quiver. He replaced the standard gold-leaf background (symbolizing heaven) with a gold, intricately patterned curtain draped over the throne. Mary's blue robe opens to reveal her body, and the curve of her knee suggests real anatomy beneath the robe. Baby Jesus wears a delicately transparent garment. Their faces are modeled with light—a patchwork of bright flesh and shadowy valleys, as if lit from the left (a technique he likely learned from his contemporary Giotto during a visit to Florence).

Along the base of Mary's throne is an inscription (*"Mater sancta dei..."* or "Holy Mother of God...") asking Mary to bring peace to Siena *(Senis)* and long life to Duccio *(Ducio)*—quite a tribute in a time when painters were usually treated as anonymous craftsmen.

**The Passion of Christ:** The flip side of the altarpiece featured these 26 smaller panels showing colorful scenes from the Passion of Christ.

The panels showcase the budding Tuscan style that united realism and storytelling. It doesn't take a Bible scholar to "read" these panels, left to right. Christ on a donkey (lower left) makes his triumphal entry into the city gate of Jerusalem (or is it Siena?). Next, he washes his disciples' feet in a realistic, three-dimensional room. But Duccio hasn't fully mastered perspective—in the Last Supper, we see Christ eye-to-eye, but view the table from above. Next, Christ is arrested in Gethsemane, and so on, until the climactic Crucifixion. The Crucifixion is given the standard gold background, but the cross is set in a real-world location: on a terraced hillside, amid the crowd. Jesus' followers express human emotion rarely seen in earlier art.

The crowd scenes in the Passion panels aren't arranged in neat choir rows, but in more natural-looking groups. Duccio sets figures in motion, with individual faces expressing sorrow, anger, and agitation. Duccio's human realism would be taken to the next level by his Florentine counterpart Giotto, often called the proto-Renaissance painter.

Duccio and assistants (possibly including Simone Martini) spent three years on this massive altarpiece. It was a triumph, and at its dedication the satisfied Sienese marched it around the Campo and into the church in a public procession.

But by 1506, at the height of the Renaissance, Duccio's medieval altarpiece looked musty and old-fashioned, and was moved to a side altar. In 1771 it was disassembled and stored in the church offices (now the Duomo Museum). Today, scholars hail it as a quantum leap in the evolution of art, even while they debate how to reassemble it accurately.

• *Our museum tour is done, but the finale of your visit is yet to come. To go to the viewpoint at the top of the unfinished Duomo facade (included in your ticket), return to the stairs and continue up. Take a right at the first landing. At the landing just before the top floor, turn right and walk past the rooms, going through the small doorway to the stairwell. If the line is all the way to the middle of the room, you're facing a 40-minute wait. Eventually you'll climb up about 60 tight and claustrophobic spiral stairs to the first viewpoint. You can continue up another 70 steps of a similar spiral staircase to reach the very top.*

**Panorama del Facciatone:** Standing on the wall from this high point in the city, you're rewarded with a stunning view of Siena…and an interesting perspective.

Look toward the Duomo and remember this: To outdo Florence, Siena had planned to enlarge this cathedral by turning it into a transept and constructing an enormous nave. You're standing on top of what would have been the new entrance facade. Columns would have stood where you see the rows of white stones in the pavement below. Had the church been completed, you'd be looking straight down the nave toward the altar.

## ▲Baptistery of San Giovanni (Battistero di San Giovanni)

This richly adorned and quietly tucked-away cave of art is worth a look for its cool tranquility and exquisite art, including an ornately painted vaulted ceiling.

The highlight is the baptismal font created in the 1420s by a host of early Renaissance all-stars from marble, bronze, and enamel. The overall design was by Jacopo ("Fountain of Joy") della Quercia. On the base, the first bronze panel you encounter was done by Lorenzo ("Gates of Paradise") Ghiberti. It shows John the Baptist baptizing Jesus, done in the same simple but elegant style Ghiberti used on the famous doors of Florence's Baptistery. To the right, the tiny bronze statues of Lady Faith and (farther right) the Angel of Hope were done by the great Donatello. Also on the right side, Donatello made the bronze panel depicting John the Baptist's severed head being brought in on a platter, set in a 3-D banquet hall of receding arches. With this font, we're witnessing the start of the Renaissance.

**Cost and Hours:** See "Ticket Options and Hours," earlier; located at the back end of the Duomo, all the way down the stairs.

### Crypt (Cripta)

The cathedral "crypt" is archaeologically important. The site of a small 12th-century Romanesque church, it was filled in with dirt a century after its creation to provide a foundation for the huge church that sits atop it today. Recently excavated (with modern metal supports from the 1990s), the several rediscovered rooms show off what are likely the oldest frescoes in town (well described in English).

The best frescoes (in the main room) are by Duccio. Moving left to right, we see Christ crucified, brought down from the cross, buried, and finally descending into purgatory to rescue grateful souls, including the first man—long-haired and bearded Adam.

**Cost and Hours:** See "Ticket Options and Hours," earlier; located at the back end of the Duomo, partway down the stairs.

### Porto del Cielo ("Gate of Heaven") Cathedral Roof Visit

To make a 30-minute escorted (but not guided) visit to the dome's cupola and roof, buy the Porto del Cielo combo-ticket (reservation recommended; see "Ticket Options and Hours," earlier). For spectacular interior and exterior views, you'll climb 79 steps to see restored rooms with impressive inlaid floors and get a close-up look at the cupola, with its blue, star-decorated panels and 12 windows (representing the 12 apostles) by Ulisse De Matteis. You'll also walk briefly outside on the rooftop for a breathtaking view. While exciting for Duomo completists, this is one thing too many for casual visitors.

## Other Cathedral-Area Sights
### ▲Santa Maria della Scala

This museum, opposite the Duomo, operated for centuries as a hospital, foundling home (orphanage), and pilgrim lodging. Many of those activities are visible in the 15th-century frescoes of its main hall, the Pellegrinaio. Today, the hospital and its cellars are filled with fascinating exhibits (well described in English).

**Cost and Hours:** €9; various combo-tickets also include Civic Museum, City Tower, and/or Pinacoteca; daily 10:00-19:00, Thu until 22:00, mid-Oct-mid-March Mon and Wed-Fri 10:00-17:00, Sat-Sun until 19:00, closed Tue; on Piazza del Duomo opposite the cathedral, +39 0577 534 571, www.santamariadellascala.com.

**● Self-Guided Tour:** It's easy to get lost in this gigantic complex, so stay focused on the main attractions—the fancily frescoed Pellegrinaio Hall (ground floor) and the Fountain of Joy statues (one floor down). Then explore the lower floors, with some of the most ancient Byzantine reliquaries in existence (first basement), and the Etruscan collection in the Archaeological Museum (second basement, where the Sienese took refuge during WWII bombing).

• *Enter from inside the hall where tickets are sold. Passing through the turnstile, turn right. You're entering what was, until the 1970s, Siena's main hospital, serving citizens and pilgrims alike. Enter the first room on your right, the Sagrestia Veccia, or Old Sacristy.*

The **Sacristy** displays some powerful relics preserved in golden and silver reliquaries. You may see a drop of Jesus' blood in a vial *(sangue di Christo)*, a nail from Jesus' cross *(sacro chiodo)*, a piece of the Virgin's robe *(beata Vergine)*, and lots of saints' bones. They're encased in reliquaries that befit the preciousness of these sacred bits and saintly pieces. Some of the oldest are Byzantine reliquaries made of gold, silver, and precious stones. Legend has it that some were owned by Helen, Roman emperor Constantine's mother. They were donated (around 1350) to the hospital shortly after the plague that decimated the city (and the rest of Europe). The hospital then used them very effectively for fundraising from the many visiting pilgrims. An old document on display certifies that one of the hospital's major donors made his gift in 1359. One of the Sacristy's (faded) frescoes is a *Madonna and Child* by Domenico di Bartolo, an important Sienese painter, whose work we'll see next.

• *Continue down the hallway (browsing exhibits in side rooms) until you reach a long, colorfully painted room.*

The sumptuously frescoed **Pellegrinaio Hall** was a reception hall for visiting pilgrims before being converted into a hospital room, lined with beds for the sick. The frescoes (mostly by Domenico di Bartolo, c. 1440) show medieval Siena's innovative health care and social welfare system in action. Starting in the 11th century, the hospital nursed the sick and cared for abandoned children, as is vividly portrayed in these frescoes. The left wall is dedicated to scenes of donors who built the hospital. In the first painting, find the man in a green robe and white cap kneeling before a priest. This humble laborer had a heavenly vision to build this hospital. In the next painting (Domenico's masterpiece), others ride in to donate money, as brick workers expand the complex. Next, you'll see more scenes of wealthy donors.

On the right wall, scenes from inside the hospital depict public health care in those days: tending orphans, feeding and comforting the poor, distributing bread to the hungry (with stamps on it so it can't be resold), and tending to emergencies, such as a doctor treating a man with a horrible gash in his leg.

The good works inspired more charity, and bequests and donations poured in, creating the wealth that's evident throughout this building.

• *Backtrack one room and find a staircase heading down. Take the stairs, then continue straight, following signs to Fonte Gaia.*

In these vast cellars, you'll find the original statues from the **Fountain of Joy** (Fonte Gaia), Siena's landmark fountain on Il Campo. Jacopo della Quercia's early 15th-century masterpiece began crumbling, so in the 19th century, it was dismantled and plaster casts were made. (These casts formed the replica that graces Il Campo today.) Here you'll see the badly eroded original statues and relief panels, paired alongside their casts (labeled "*calco*"). In addition, there are modern artists' attempts to re-create what they imagine Quercia's original statues would have looked like.

• *Your essential tour of the place is over. But there's much more to explore on a lower floor, a confusing and somewhat spooky labyrinth of rooms.*

*If you're game, go down to the second basement, where you'll find the entrances to two adjoining exhibits.*

The exhibit called **"Siena: History of the City"** (Racconto della Città) charts the city's growth from ancient Roman times (stone fragments of lions) to the medieval (jars from the hospital's pharmacy).

Under the groin vaults of the **Archaeological Museum** (Museo Archeologico), you're alone with piles of ancient stuff, from Bronze Age axes to  Roman pottery. The highlight is a group of Etruscan artifacts excavated from tombs dating from the seventh to second century before Christ—the Etruscan heyday. (Remember, the Etruscans dominated this part of Italy before the Roman Empire arrived in the second century BC.) Wealthy Etruscans had their exquisite treasures buried with them, to take into the next life. You'll see their coins, figurines, and terra-cotta funeral urns for ashes (often designed with a standard body but a personalized head). The Etruscans' painted pottery looks Greek (because they traded with the Greeks), and their ultrarealistic portrait busts look Roman (their Latin neighbors to the south). The sarcophagi show the deceased reclining atop the lid, a reminder of their lofty social status.

## SAN DOMENICO AREA
### Basilica of San Domenico (Basilica di San Domenico)
This huge brick church is worth a quick look. Spacious and plain (except for the colorful flags of the city's 17 *contrade*), the Gothic interior fits the austere philosophy of the Dominicans and invites meditation on the thoughts and deeds of St. Catherine.

**Cost and Hours:** Free, daily 7:00-18:30, shorter hours off-season, www.basilicacateriniana.com.

**Visiting the Church:** Walk up the steps in the rear to see painted scenes from the saint's life. The vertical fresco on the far left (over the small altar) showing Catherine, wearing the black and white of the Dominican order and holding a lily symbolizing purity, is from her lifetime and therefore considered a true likeness.

Halfway up the nave on the right, find a copper bust of St. Catherine (for four centuries it contained her skull), a small case housing her thumb (on the left), and her little flagellation whip (on the right).

A few steps beyond is a chapel, surrounded with candles,

SIENA

## St. Catherine of Siena (1347-1380)

The youngest of 25 children born to a Sienese cloth dyer, Catherine began experiencing heavenly visions as a child. At 16 she became a member of the Dominican order, locking herself away for three years in a room in her family's house. She lived the life of an ascetic, which culminated in a vision wherein she married Christ. Catherine emerged from solitude to join her Dominican sisters, sharing her experiences, caring for the sick, and gathering both disciples and enemies. At age 23, she lapsed into a spiritual coma, waking with the heavenly command to spread her message to the world. She wrote essays and letters to kings, dukes, bishops, and popes, imploring them to find peace for a war-ravaged Italy. While visiting Pisa during Lent in 1375, she had a vision in which she received the stigmata, the wounds of Christ.

Still in her 20s, Catherine was invited to Avignon, France, where the pope had taken up residence. With her charm, sincerity, and reputation for holiness, she helped convince Pope Gregory XI to return the papacy to the city of Rome. Catherine also went to Rome, where she died young. She was canonized in the next generation (by a Sienese pope), and her relics were distributed to churches around Italy.

Because of her commitment to peace and unity, today Catherine is revered (along with St. Benedict) as the patron saint of Europe and remembered as a rare outspoken medieval woman still appreciated for her universal message: that this world is not a gift from our fathers, but a loan from our children.

where atop the altar you'll see Catherine's head (a clay mask around her skull with her actual teeth showing through). Through the door just beyond are the sacristy and the bookstore.

▲**Sanctuary of St. Catherine (Santuario di Santa Caterina)**
Step into the cool and peaceful site of Catherine's home. Siena remembers its favorite hometown gal, a simple, unschooled but mystically devout soul who helped convince the pope to return to Rome from France, where the papacy had moved in 1309 (see sidebar). Pilgrims have visited this place since 1464, and architects and artists have greatly embellished what was probably once a humble home (her family worked as wool dyers). You'll see paintings throughout showing scenes from her life.

**Cost and Hours:** Free, daily 9:00-18:00 but chapel closes

12:30-15:00, a few downhill blocks toward the center from San Domenico—follow signs to *Santuario di Santa Caterina*—at Costa di Sant'Antonio 6, +39 0577 288 175.

**Visiting the Sanctuary:** Enter through the courtyard and walk down the stairs at the far end. The chapel on your right contains the wooden crucifix upon which Catherine was meditating when she received the stigmata. Take a pew, and try to imagine the scene.

Back outside, the oratory across the courtyard stands where the kitchen once was. (Visible through a grate under the altar are the remains of the kitchen's hearth.) The room is ringed by 19th-century Romantic paintings depicting scenes from Catherine's life.

To reach the saint's room, from the entry courtyard, go down the stairs to the left of the gift shop. Catherine's bare cell is behind wrought-iron doors where, on the floor (under an iron grille), is the stone that served as her pillow.

## NEAR SIENA
You'll need a car to reach the **Abbey of Monte Oliveto Maggiore**, but for Renaissance art pilgrims it's well worth the 40-minute drive from town. You can combine a visit to the abbey with a loop drive through the scenic countryside. For details on the abbey and driving directions, see my "Crete Senesi Drive" on page 423.

# Sleeping in Siena

Finding a room in Siena is tough during Easter or the Palio (July 2 and Aug 16). Many hotels won't take reservations until the end of May for the Palio, and even then they might require a four-night stay. While day-tripping tour groups turn the town into a Gothic amusement park in midsummer, Siena is basically yours in the evenings and off-season.

Part of Siena's charm is its lively, festive character—this means that all hotels can be plagued with noise, even in the pedestrian-only zone. If tranquility is important to you, ask for a room that's off the street, or consider staying outside the center. If your hotel doesn't provide breakfast, eat at a bar on Il Campo or near your hotel.

## BIGGER HOTELS IN THE CENTER
These places are a 10-minute walk from Il Campo. If driving, get directions and parking instructions from your hotel in advance and make sure that you don't violate the *Zona Traffico Limitato (ZTL)* restrictions.

**$$$ Pensione Palazzo Ravizza** is elegant, friendly, and beautifully appointed, with 40 rooms and an aristocratic feel—fitting for what was once a noble's residence. Guests enjoy a peaceful garden set on a dramatic bluff (where the on-site restaurant sometimes serves sunset dinners), along with a Steinway in the upper lounge (RS%, family rooms, rooms in back overlook countryside, aircon, elevator, free parking makes this a good value for drivers, Via Piano dei Mantellini 34, +39 0577 280 462, www.palazzoravizza. it, bureau@palazzoravizza.it).

**$$$ Hotel Palazzetto Rosso** is a boutique hotel that fills a stunningly restored, 13th-century, red tower house down a side street from the main drag. The entrance and historic stairwell feel like a museum, and the French owners have adorned the nine rooms with modern, colorful, minimalist style—a quirky combination of new and old. If you want an air of luxury without "classic Siena" ambience, this is a good choice (lavish "design" suites, no air-con but innovative floor-cooling system, elevator, Via dei Rossi 38, +39 0577 236 197, www.palazzettorosso.com, info@palazzettorosso. com).

**$$$ Hotel Duomo** is dated but well located, with 20 spacious but overpriced rooms (many with Duomo views—request when booking), a picnic-friendly roof terrace, and a bizarre floor plan (family rooms, air-con, elevator with some stairs, expensive pay parking; Via di Stalloreggi 38, +39 0577 289 088, www. hotelduomo.it, booking@hotelduomo.it, Alessandro).

## B&BS IN THE CENTER

Siena specializes in small, characteristic B&Bs tucked in its narrow lanes. As these places typically lack a real reception desk, it's essential to clearly communicate your arrival time in advance.

**$$ Antica Residenza Cicogna** is a seven-room guesthouse with a homey elegance and an ideal location. It's warmly run by charming Elisa (who named this family property for her grandmother) and her friend Ilaria, who set out biscotti, Vin Santo, and tea for their guests in the afternoon. With artfully frescoed walls and ceilings, this is remarkably genteel for the price (aircon, no elevator, Via delle Terme 76, +39 0577 285 613, mobile +39 347 007 2888, www.anticaresidenzacicogna.it, info@ anticaresidenzacicogna.it).

**$$ Palazzo Masi B&B,** run by friendly Alizzardo and Daniela, is just below Il Campo. They rent six pleasant, spacious, antique-furnished rooms with shared common areas on the second and third floors of a restored 13th-century building (RS%—use code "RICK," cheaper rooms with shared bath, no elevator; breakfast provided on Il Campo; from City Hall, walk 50 yards down Casato di Sotto to #29; +39 349 600 9155, www.palazzomasi.com, info@palazzomasi.it).

**$$ Il Giardino di Pantaneto,** down a less-touristed street not far from Il Campo, rents 12 fresh, smartly designed rooms—many with views over a garden for slightly higher prices (family rooms, air-con, elevator, Via Pantaneto 77, +39 0577 574 910, mobile +39 335 630 6949, www.ilgiardinodipantaneto.com, info@ilgiardinodipantaneto.com).

**$$ B&B Palazzo Bruchi,** a bit farther down the same street, is another charming spot with four rooms overlooking a fine little courtyard, garden, and the countryside (air-con, Via Pantaneto 105, +39 351 927 7340, www.palazzobruchi.it, booking@palazzobruchi.it).

**$$ B&B Alle Due Porte** is a charming little establishment renting three big rooms with sweet furniture under medieval beams. The shared breakfast room is delightful (air-con, Via di Stalloreggi 51, +39 351 835 1819, www.sienatur.it, alledueportesiena@gmail.com, Mariangela).

**$$ Siena Gallery B&B,** run by kindhearted Elisabetta and Fabio, is tucked onto the fourth floor of a relatively modern building, offering four contemporary-yet-simple rooms (air-con, elevator, Via Banchi di Sopra 31, enter at Galleria Odeon—look for green pharmacy sign, +39 334 3997 8694, www.sienagallery.it, info@sienagallery.it).

**$$ I Terzi di Siena,** run by the same family as Siena Gallery B&B, houses six rooms in an 11th-century building. It's absent an elevator but full of humble charm and noteworthy views (air-con, Via dei Termini 13, +39 339 669 9143, www.terzidisiena.it, info@terzidisiena.it).

**$ Le Camerine di Silvia,** a romantic hideaway perched near a sweeping, grassy olive grove, rents five simple rooms in a converted 16th-century building. A small terrace with fruit trees and a private hedged garden lends itself to contemplation (cash only, view room on request, breakfast on request, fans, free parking nearby, Via Bastianini 1—ring bell marked "Conti," +39 338 761 5052 or +39 339 123 7687, www.lecamerinedisilvia.com, info@lecamerinedisilvia.com, Conti family).

## SIMPLE PLACES IN THE CENTER

These places are nothing fancy—basic, tired, dated rooms at an affordable price in a great location. The B&Bs listed above offer more charm and personality, but these places have more rooms and hotel anonymity.

**$$ Piccolo Hotel Etruria,** with 20 rooms, is well located, very close to Il Campo (RS%, family rooms, breakfast extra, air-con May-Oct only, elevator, at Via delle Donzelle 3, +39 0577 288 088, www.hoteletruria.com, info@hoteletruria.com, friendly Leopoldo and Lucrezia). They also rent apartments nearby.

**$ Albergo Tre Donzelle,** run by the same family as Piccolo

SIENA

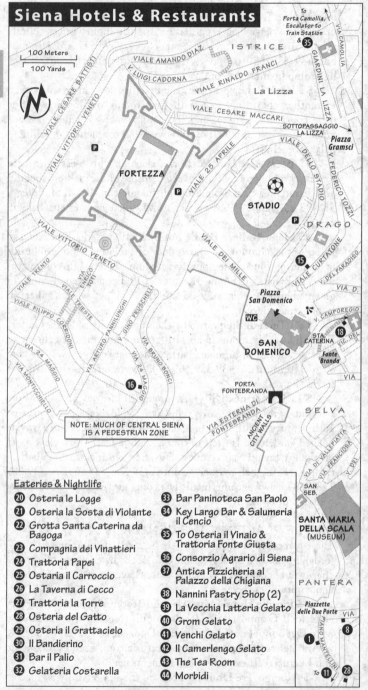

# Siena Hotels & Restaurants

100 Meters
100 Yards

To Porta Camollia, Escalator to Train Station & 35

ISTRICE

VIALE AMANDO DIAZ

V. LUIGI CADORNA

VIALE RINALDO FRANCI

La Lizza

VIALE CESARE MACCARI

VIA CAMOLLIA

GIARDINI LA LIZZA

SOTTOPASSAGGIO LA LIZZA

Piazza Gramsci

VIALE CESARE BATTISTI

VIALE VITTORIO VENETO

P

FORTEZZA

P

VIALE 25 APRILE

VIALE DELLO STADIO

V. FEDERICO TOZZI

VIALE VITTORIO VENETO

STADIO

P

DRAGO

VIALE DEI MILLE

15

VIALE CURTATONE

V. DEL PARADISO

VIA D

VIALE TRENTO

VIA ENRICO TOTI

VIALE TRIESTE

VIALE FILIPPO CORRIDONI

V. ARTURO FANIULUNGHI

V. GINO FRUSCHELLI

VIA BRUNO BONCI

Piazza San Domenico

WC

SAN DOMENICO

V. CAMPOREGIO

STA. CATERINA

18

Fonte Branda

VIA 24 MAGGIO

VIA MONTICCHIELLO

16

VIA 24 MAGGIO

PORTA FONTEBRANDA

VIA ESTERNA DI FONTEBRANDA

ANCIENT CITY WALLS

SELVA

NOTE: MUCH OF CENTRAL SIENA IS A PEDESTRIAN ZONE

SAN SEB.

SANTA MARIA DELLA SCALA (MUSEUM)

VIA DI VALLEPIATTA

VIA FRANCIOSA

V. DEL

PANTERA

Piazzetta delle Due Porte

VIA PIANO MANTELLINI

8

1

To 11

28

## Eateries & Nightlife

20 Osteria le Logge
21 Osteria la Sosta di Violante
22 Grotta Santa Caterina da Bagoga
23 Compagnia dei Vinattieri
24 Trattoria Papei
25 Ostaria il Carroccio
26 La Taverna di Cecco
27 Trattoria la Torre
28 Osteria del Gatto
29 Osteria il Grattacielo
30 Il Bandierino
31 Bar il Palio
32 Gelateria Costarella

33 Bar Paninoteca San Paolo
34 Key Largo Bar & Salumeria il Cencio
35 To Osteria il Vinaio & Trattoria Fonte Giusta
36 Consorzio Agrario di Siena
37 Antica Pizzicheria al Palazzo della Chigiana
38 Nannini Pastry Shop (2)
39 La Vecchia Latteria Gelato
40 Grom Gelato
41 Venchi Gelato
42 Il Camerlengo Gelato
43 The Tea Room
44 Morbidi

SIENA

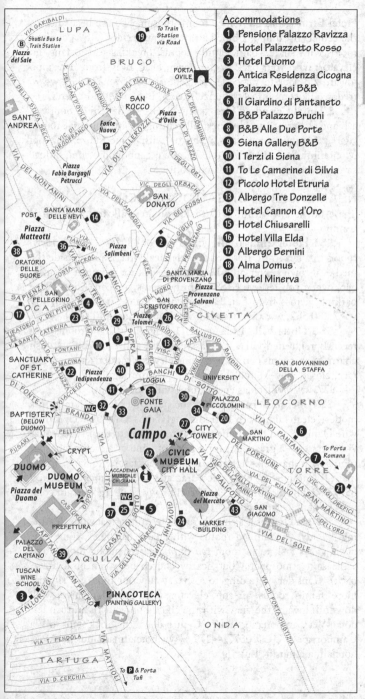

**Accommodations**

1. Pensione Palazzo Ravizza
2. Hotel Palazzetto Rosso
3. Hotel Duomo
4. Antica Residenza Cicogna
5. Palazzo Masi B&B
6. Il Giardino di Pantaneto
7. B&B Palazzo Bruchi
8. B&B Alle Due Porte
9. Siena Gallery B&B
10. I Terzi di Siena
11. To Le Camerine di Silvia
12. Piccolo Hotel Etruria
13. Albergo Tre Donzelle
14. Hotel Cannon d'Oro
15. Hotel Chiusarelli
16. Hotel Villa Elda
17. Albergo Bernini
18. Alma Domus
19. Hotel Minerva

Hotel Etruria, has 20 homey rooms that may be the best value in the center. Il Campo, a block away, is your terrace (RS%, cheaper rooms with shared bath, family rooms, breakfast extra, fans, no elevator; with your back to the tower, head away from Il Campo toward 2 o'clock to Via delle Donzelle 5; +39 0577 270 390, www. tredonzelle.com, info@tredonzelle.com, Leopoldo and Lucrezia).

**$ Hotel Cannon d'Oro,** a few blocks up Banchi di Sopra, is a bland, labyrinthine slumbermill renting 30 institutional rooms (RS%, family rooms, fans, elevator with some stairs, Via dei Montanini 28, +39 0577 44321, www.cannondoro.com, info@ cannondoro.com, Tommaso and Rodrigo).

## NEAR BASILICA OF SAN DOMENICO

These hotels are within a 10-to-15-minute walk northwest of Il Campo.

**$$$ Hotel Chiusarelli,** with a mix of 48 classic and modern rooms in a beautiful, frescoed Neoclassical villa, is just outside the medieval town center on a busy street—ask for a quieter room in back when you reserve (RS%, family rooms, air-con, limited free parking, across from San Domenico at Viale Curtatone 15, +39 0577 280 562, www.chiusarelli.com, info@chiusarelli.com).

**$$$ Hotel Villa Elda** rents 11 bright and light rooms in a recently renovated villa. It's classy, stately, and run with a stylish charm (view rooms extra, air-con, no elevator, garden and view terrace, closed Nov-March, Viale Ventiquattro Maggio 10, +39 0577 247 927, www.villaeldasiena.it, info@villaeldasiena.it).

**$$ Albergo Bernini** makes you part of a Sienese family in a modest, clean home with 10 traditional rooms. Giovanni, charming wife Daniela, and their daughters welcome you to their spectacular view terrace—a great spot for a glass of wine or a picnic (cheaper rooms with shared bath, family rooms, breakfast extra, fans, on the main Il Campo-San Domenico drag at Via della Sapienza 15, +39 0577 289 047, mobile +39 339 112 4113, www.albergobernini.com, info@albergobernini.com).

**$ Alma Domus** is a church-run hotel and a great value, featuring 49 tidy, streamlined rooms with quaint balconies, some fantastic views (ask for a room *con vista*), stately public rooms, and a pleasant atmosphere (but nearby church bells can be a drawback). Consider upgrading to a snazzy superior room for slightly more (family rooms, air-con, elevator; from San Domenico, walk downhill toward the view with the church on your right, turn left down Via Camporegio, make a U-turn down the brick steps to Via Camporegio 37; +39 0577 44177, www.hotelalmadomus.it, info@ hotelalmadomus.it, Luigi).

## FARTHER FROM THE CENTER

These options are convenient for drivers but only a 15-to-20-minute walk from the center. The first two are about 200 yards outside the Porta Romana (for locations, see the map on page 362).

**$$$ Hotel Santa Caterina** is a three-star, 18th-century place renting 22 rooms with a homey elegance. It's professionally run with real attention to quality. While it's on a busy street, it has a delightful garden terrace with views over the countryside (RS%, family rooms, garden side is quieter, air-con, elevator, pay parking—request when you reserve, Via E.S. Piccolomini 7, +39 0577 221 105, www.hotelsantacaterinasiena.com, info@hotelsantacaterinasiena.com, Lorenza).

**$$ Hotel Porta Romana,** on the same busy road, has simple rooms with cheap finishes. Request one of the 14 rooms that face the open countryside and the hotel's terraced footpaths into the valley. Breakfast is served in the scenic garden (RS%, air-con in half the rooms, free parking, inviting sun terrace, outdoor hot tub open April-Oct free to guests with this book, Via E.S. Piccolomini 35, +39 0577 42299, www.hotelportaromana.com, info@hotelportaromana.com).

**$$ Hotel Minerva** is your big, impersonal, plain, efficient option. It's got zero personality and mediocre views, but offers predictable business-class comfort in its 56 rooms. It works best for those with cars—its pay parking is reasonable, and it's a 15-minute walk from the action (RS%, view rooms extra, air-con, elevator, just inside Porta Ovile at the north end of town at Via Garibaldi 72, +39 0577 284 474, www.albergominerva.it, info@albergominerva.it).

## OUTSIDE SIENA

The following accommodations, set in the peaceful countryside surrounding Siena, are best for those traveling by car (see map on page 362). For options in the Crete Senesi, including one just six miles from the Porta Romana gate, see page 549.

**$$$$ Podere la Strega** sits a short drive (or €15 taxi ride) from central Siena, in a country-like setting. Run by Letizia with help from neighbor Cara, it has eight color-themed rooms, a cozy lounge, a breakfast terrace, and an infinity pool with spectacular views of Siena. Two of the rooms have that same view, which you can pay extra for (RS%, family rooms, air-con, Strada dell'Ascarello 6, +39 0577 43646, mobile +39 338 664 9721, www.ilpoderedellastrega.com, letizia@poderelastrega.it). They also rent out the entire villa next door, with classic antique furnishings (sleeps 12).

**$$$$ Borgo Argenina,** 20 minutes' drive north of Siena in the heart of the Chianti region, is an entire little hilltop village *(borgo)* set amidst vineyards. It's thoughtfully run by Stefania (who grew up here) and Gabriele, who mix a respect for tradition with welcome modern flourishes. The property has two parts: The B&B has eight rooms, an inviting breakfast room and terrace, a classic old kitchen where Elena teaches cooking classes, and a *piccola villa* (a small, stand-alone cottage). At the other end of the property are seven one- and two-bedroom apartments, with fully equipped kitchens. Everyone has access to the BBQ, pool, and hot tub (RS%, +39 0577 160 6120, www.borgoargenina.it, info@borgoargenina.it).

# Eating in Siena

Sienese restaurants are a great value by Florence, Venice, or Rome standards. You can enjoy ordering high on the menu here without going broke, especially in places farther from the touristic center. For pasta, a good option is *pici* (PEE-chee), a thick Sienese spaghetti that seems to be at the top of every menu; this is often served with *ragù* (meat sauce) but also comes with a simple tomato and garlic sauce *(all'aglione)* or even *cacio e pepe* (grated *pecorino romano* cheese and fresh-ground pepper). For the *secondo*, big honkin' steaks—served rare, *bistecca alla fiorentina*-style—are easy to find but hard to finish.

At any place, reservations are wise for dinner—especially as you approach the weekend.

## IN THE OLD TOWN
### Fine Dining
These places deliver an upscale ambience, interesting menus, and finer food than my more rustic recommendations.

$$$$ **Osteria le Logge** caters to a fancy crowd and offers pricey Tuscan favorites with a gourmet twist, made with seasonal local ingredients. Inside you'll enjoy a gorgeous living-room setting (books, wood, and wine bottles), and outside there's fine seating on a pedestrian street. I find dining inside on the ground floor most romantic (Mon-Sat 12:00-15:00 & 19:00-23:00, closed Sun, two blocks off Il Campo at Via del Porrione 33, +39 0577 48013, www.osterialelogge.it, Mirko).

$$ **Osteria la Sosta di Violante,** beyond the tourist zone, is the best fine-dining value of my listings. You'll share this dreamy little spot with smart locals. For over 20 years, chefs Duccio and Enrico have offered artfully executed food with no pretense—they make sure diners feel right at home. Order with a sense of adventure. Diners with this book cap their meal with complimentary Vin Santo and *contucci* (great indoor and outdoor seating, Mon-Sat 12:30-15:00 & 19:00-23:00, closed Sun, walk down Via Banchi di Sotto to Via Pantaneto 115, +39 0577 43774).

**$$$ Grotta Santa Caterina da Bagoga,** tucked down a less-touristed lane below Il Campo, offers an all-around memorable experience. The cook (whose nickname, Bagoga, means "apricot" in the dialect of his native Montalcino) cultivates a menu that's traditional yet creative, and fun to peruse. The shareable *misto Bagoga* mixed-appetizer plate kicks off the meal nicely. The cave-like interior, under brick vaults, is adorned with old photographs and other artifacts of Sienese life, and oozes with atmosphere; there are also some benches lining the stony lane outside. It's worth reserving ahead (Tue-Sat 12:00-15:00 & 19:00-22:00, Sun 12:00-15:00 only, closed Mon, Via della Galluzza 26, +39 0577 282 208, www. ristorantebagoga.it).

**$$$ Compagnia dei Vinattieri,** a good bet for wine lovers, serves Tuscan dishes with a creative touch. In this elegant space—which feels dressy and sedate—you can enjoy a romantic meal under graceful brick arches. The menu is small and accessible. Owner Marco is happy to take you down to the marvelous wine cellar (leave this book on the table for a complimentary *aperitivo* or *digestivo,* daily 12:30-15:00 & 19:30-23:00, Via delle Terme 79, +39 0577 236 568, www.vinattieri.net).

## Traditional and Rustic Places

**$$ Trattoria Papei** is a sprawling, crank-'em-out place with festive outdoor seating under a big tent and a high-energy interior. It has a casual, rollicking family atmosphere and friendly servers dishing out generous portions of rib-stickin' Tuscan specialties and grilled meats (daily 12:00-15:00 & 19:00-22:30, on the market square behind City Hall at Piazza del Mercato 6, +39 0577 280 894; Amedeo and Eduardo).

**$$ Osteria il Carroccio,** artsy and convivial, seats guests in a characteristic but tight dining room. The name means "war chariot"—the cart that brings the Palio flag to Il Campo on the day of the race. They serve traditional "slow food" with innovative flair at affordable prices. To maintain their quality, they have only 35 seats and don't turn the tables—reserve ahead. They give complimentary Vin Santo and *contucci* with this book (Thu-Tue 12:15-15:00 & 19:15-22:00, closed Wed, Casato di Sotto 32, +39 0577 41165).

**$$ La Taverna di Cecco** is a cozy, comfortable little eatery on a quiet back lane where grandma Olga cooks, and earnest Luca and Gianni serve. The place settings feel like nana's finest, and the few tables outside are inviting as well. They offer a simple menu of traditional Sienese favorites along with hearty salads (daily 12:00-16:00 & 19:00-23:00, Via Cecco Angiolieri 19, +39 0577 288 518).

**$$ Trattoria la Torre** is an unfussy family-run *casalinga* (home-cooking) place, popular for its homemade pasta. Its open kitchen and 10 tables are packed under one medieval brick arch.

## Gelato, Tea, and Cocktails in Siena

Evenings are a wonderful time to be out and about in Siena, after the tour groups have left for the day. Join the evening *passeggiata* (peak strolling time is 19:00) along Banchi di Sopra with gelato in hand. And remember: A great way to cap any meal or day in Siena is with a drink or dessert on Il Campo.

**Gelato:** There's always a good gelato place nearby (all open daily, generally until late). A good locally owned option is **La Vecchia Latteria** (a 5-minute walk from Il Campo at Via di San Pietro 10). Two chains—reliable, if overrated—have outposts in Siena: **Grom** (across from Nannini at Banchi di Sopra 13) and **Venchi** (across from the Loggia della Mercanzia at Via di Città 28). And, for gelato on Il Campo, drop by the *bar gelateria* **Il Camerlengo** (at #6, just to the right of City Hall, with a handy WC).

**Tea: The Tea Room** is an artful ensemble of stone vaults, cozy furniture, romantic lighting, lovingly presented pastries, and a long list of fine teas. Hiding out behind City Hall, it offers a tranquil and relaxing escape (Tue-Sun 17:00-24:00, closed Mon, 200 yards below Il Campo, from the car park banister at the far end of Piazza del Mercato, look down and to the left, at Porta Giustizia 11, +39 0577 222 753).

*Aperitivo* **Happy Hour:** As elsewhere in Italy, you'll find bars all over town attracting an early evening crowd by offering an *aperitivo*—a free buffet of snacks that's included with the purchase of a drink. For many, this happy-hour special (usually nightly 18:00-20:00) can make a light dinner. Four good ones to consider are: **Morbidi**, a trendy and youthful cocktail bar (closed Sun, Via Banchi di Sopra 75); the classic *caffè/pasticceria* **Nannini** (Via Banchi di Sopra 24, also a branch at Piazza Matteotti 15); and **Bar il Palio**, for cocktails and light bites on Il Campo (described later).

Service is brisk and casual—the only menu is posted outside because they like to explain your options individually—and the food is simple but good. Even though located just under the City Tower, it feels more like a local hangout than a tourist trap (Fri-Wed 12:00-15:00 & 19:00-22:00, closed Thu, steps below Il Campo at Via di Salicotto 7, +39 0577 287 548, Marco).

**$ Osteria del Gatto** is a classic neighborhood fixture thriving with townspeople and powered by a passion for good Sienese cuisine. Friendly Marco Coradeschi and his staff cook and serve daily specials with attitude. As it's so small and popular, it can get loud (Mon-Sat 12:30-15:00 & 19:30-22:00, closed Sun, 10-minute walk from Il Campo at Via San Marco 8, look for *La Vecchia Osteria* sign, +39 0577 287 133).

**$ Osteria il Grattacielo** is a funky hole-in-the-wall—the name, meaning "skyscraper," is sarcastic. It has an extremely tight yet homey interior and three big tables under a tunnel-like arch outside. Luca, who's clearly found his niche in life, has no menu and just one solid house wine. You'll eat what he's cooking. Lunch is a mixed plate from the bar (be bold and point) or pasta (€10, includes wine). Dinner is three courses—antipasto bar, pasta, and a *secondi*—€20 for Rick Steves readers; €3 extra adds a Vin Santo and cookies finale. At these prices, this place is ideal for a cheap, hearty, memorable, yet no-frills meal (Mon-Sat 12:00-15:00 & 19:30-21:30, Sun 12:00-15:00 only, Via dei Pontani 8, +39 331 742 2835).

## ON IL CAMPO

If you choose to dine on perhaps the finest town square in Italy, you'll pay a premium, meet waiters who don't need to hustle, and eat mediocre food. And yet, I recommend it. The clamshell-shaped Il Campo is lined with venerable cafés, bars, restaurants, and pizzerias. Survey the scene during your sightseeing day and reserve a table at the place that suits you. (All places listed are open daily for long hours.)

To experience Il Campo without paying for a full meal, do as the locals do and have drinks or breakfast on the square. For me, the best €6 you can spend in Siena is on a cocktail at Bar il Palio, overlooking Il Campo. If your hotel doesn't include breakfast or if you'd like something more memorable, Il Campo has plenty of options. A cappuccino and a *cornetto* (croissant) run about €5. Historically, frugal eaters could gather a picnic and join the crowds sitting on the bricks—but that's now illegal, and doing so can earn you a stiff fine.

### Dining and Drinks on the Square

$$$ **Il Bandierino,** with an angled view of City Hall, has solid food and no cover but a 20 percent service charge (Piazza del Campo 64, +39 0577 275 894).

$$$ **Bar il Palio** is the best bar on Il Campo for a before- or after-dinner drink: It has straightforward prices, no cover, and a fine view (Piazza del Campo 47, +39 0577 282 055).

### Drinks or Snacks Overlooking Il Campo

These places (all open daily until late) have skinny balconies with benches overlooking the main square for their customers. Sipping a coffee or nibbling a pastry here while marveling at the Il Campo scene is one of Europe's great experiences. And it's cheap. Survey these four places from Il Campo (with your back to the tower, they are at 10 o'clock, high noon, and 3 o'clock, respectively).

**$ Gelateria Costarella,** on the corner of Via di Città and Costarella dei Barbieri, is a modern cocktail/gelato bar with a great little balcony over Il Campo—which is open to anyone ordering off their pricier menu (Via di Città 33).

**$ Bar Paninoteca San Paolo** has a youthful English-pub ambience and a row of stools overlooking the square. They have dozens of hearty sandwiches, big salads, and several beers on tap—it's not traditional Italian, but it's quick, filling, and available all day (order and pay at the counter, under the arch on Vicolo di San Paolo, +39 0577 226 622).

**$ Key Largo Bar** has a nondescript interior, but two long, upper-story benches in the corner offer a wonderful secret perch. Buy your drink or snack at the bar, climb upstairs, and open the ancient door (no cover and no extra charge to sit on the balcony). Enjoy stretching out, and try to imagine how, during the Palio, three layers of spectators cram into this space—notice the iron railing used to plaster the top row of sardines up against the wall. Suddenly you're picturing Palio ponies zipping wildly around the square's notoriously dangerous corner (closed Mon, on the corner at Via Rinaldini 17, +39 0577 236 339).

**$ Salumeria il Cencio** is a simple rustic sandwich shop with a tiny balcony upstairs (enter through back), where, for the takeout price, you can munch your humble meal (daily, near Key Largo Bar at the corner of Il Campo and Via del Porrione, +39 0577 283 007).

## DINING WITH LOCALS, AWAY FROM THE CENTER

A pleasant 15-minute stroll north of Il Campo, Via Camollia—a continuation of the chic Via Banchi di Sopra and Via dei Montanini shopping streets—offers good eating options. This more residential part of town has become popular with locals seeking to get away from the tourist crowds.

**$$ Osteria il Vinaio**—also called **Bobbe e Davide** for its owners—is my favorite in this area, at #167. Festooned with neighborhood memorabilia on the walls, it's an informal place—bright and fun—offering simple dishes at good prices from an inviting menu (Mon-Sat 19:00-22:00, closed Sun, +39 0577 49615).

**$$ Trattoria Fonte Giusta,** at #102, is a big, family-friendly eatery known for its grilled meat dishes (plenty of streetside tables, daily 12:00-23:00, +39 0577 40506).

## EATING CHEAPLY IN THE CENTER

**Gourmet Tuscan Supermarkets/***Rosticceria:* **Consorzio Agrario di Siena** is a great place to assemble a cheap yet top-quality meal. Wander through the entire place (salad and smoothie bar at the front, bakery/pizzeria at the back) and enjoy a parade of artisanal Tuscan foods. Office workers pack the excellent pizza counter in the rear (Menchetti). Take a stool and enjoy some people-watching while you eat. Or, for a super-cheap, fast, and healthy option, go back to the entry and oversee the assembly of salad and cooked vegetables sold by weight, choose a smoothie, and then find a spot on the big comfy stone bench across the way on Piazza Salimbeni (Mon-Sat 8:00-20:00, Sun from 9:30, just off Piazza Matteotti, facing Piazza Salimbeni at Via Pianigiani 9).

**Pizza in the Center:** There seem to be pizza joints on every corner offering a basic, budget meal. The cheapest option is take-away pizza by the slice. But even more formal restaurants (and those on Il Campo) offer an array of pizzas for around €10.

## DESSERTS AND TREATS

Siena's claim to caloric fame is its panforte, a rich, chewy concoction of nuts, honey, and candied fruits that impresses even fruitcake haters. There are a few varieties: *Margherita,* dusted in powdered sugar, is fruitier, while *panpepato* has a spicy, peppery crust. Locals also enjoy chewy, super-sweet, white macaroon-and-almond cookies called *ricciarelli.*

**Nannini** is the top-end, classic café and pastry shop every grandmother has fond memories of. It's ideally located in the center of the evening strolling scene a few blocks off Il Campo. For a special dessert or a sweet treat any time of day, stop by. The local specialties are around back at the far end of the bar (Mon-Sat 7:30-21:00, Sun until 19:00, *aperitivo* happy hour 18:00 until closing, Banchi di Sopra 24). There's also a branch at Piazza Matteotti 15.

# Siena Connections

Siena has sparse train connections but is a handy hub for buses to the hill towns. For most, Florence is the gateway to Siena. The bus and train take about the same amount of time, but Siena's bus station is more convenient and central than its train station.

## BY TRAIN

Siena's train station is at the edge of town. For details on getting between the town center and the station, see page 361. Trains to and from Siena can be slow; because only one train line serves this area, you may even have to stop and wait a few minutes to let something else pass. (This is typically figured into schedules.)

**From Siena by Train to: Florence** (direct trains hourly, 1.5 hours), **Pisa** (2/hour, 1.5 hours, most change at Empoli), **Lucca** (approximately hourly, requires change either in Florence or in Pisa and Empoli, 2.5-3 hours), **Assisi** (10/day, about 4 hours, most involve 2 changes, bus is faster), **Rome** (1-2/hour, 3-4 hours, 1 change), **Orvieto** (12/day, 2.5 hours, change in Chiusi). Train info: Trenitalia.com.

## BY BUS

Siena's intercity buses are operated by two companies. For each one, buses may use the handy-to-downtown stop at Piazza Gramsci (sometimes labeled *Via Tozzi* on schedules), or they may stop at the more distant train station. Be clear on which stop(s) they use when booking your ticket, and if you have a choice, opt for Piazza Gramsci. And remember: On schedules, the fastest buses are marked *rapida*.

**Autolinee Toscane (AT) Buses:** This company serves destinations throughout Tuscany (for timetables, see www.at-bus.it). Buy tickets at an Autolinee Toscane office, either inside the train station or in the underground passageway beneath Piazza Gramsci—look for stairwells, or take the elevator near the bus stops. You can also buy tickets from machines. Destinations include **Florence** (roughly 2/hour—fewer off-season, take the 1.5-hour *rapida/via superstrada* bus—*ordinaria* buses take longer; tickets available at tobacco shops/*tabacchi;* generally leaves from Piazza Gramsci as well as train station), **San Gimignano** (8/day direct, on Sun must change in Poggibonsi, 1.5 hours, from Piazza Gramsci), **Volterra** (4/day Mon-Sat, no buses on Sun, 2 hours, change in Colle di Val d'Elsa, leaves from Piazza Gramsci), **Montepulciano** (6-7/day, none on Sun, 1.5 hours, from train station), **Pienza** (6/day, none on Sun, 1.5 hours, from train station), **Montalcino** (6/day Mon-Sat, 4/day Sun, 1.5 hours, from train station or Piazza del Sale).

**Flixbus Buses:** This company serves destinations beyond Tuscany. Tickets can only be booked on their website (https://global.flixbus.com; you'll be emailed a QR code that you'll show as you board). Destinations include **Rome** (13/day, 3 hours, arrives at Rome's Tiburtina station on Metro line B with easy connections to the central Termini train station), **Naples** (6/day direct, 5.5 hours, one overnight bus), **Milan** (6-8/day direct, 5-7 hours, arrives at Milan's Lampugnano Metro station for the red line 1), **Assisi** (3/day direct, 2 hours, departs from Siena train station. To reach the town center of **Pisa,** the train is better (described earlier).

## ROUTE TIPS FOR DRIVERS

Drivers heading south from Siena can follow a scenic back-roads route into the heart of Tuscany by modifying my "Crete Senesi Drive," next (see "Route Option Heading South" on the next page).

# Crete Senesi Drive

## SIENA BACK-ROADS LOOP

Between Siena and the Tuscan heartland is the hilly Crete Senesi area—the "Sienese Clay Hills" (rated ▲▲). The Crete Senesi (KRAY-teh seh-NAY-zee) begins at Siena's doorstep and tumbles south through eye-pleasing scenery. You'll see an endless parade of classic Tuscan scenes: rolling hills topped with medieval towns, olive groves, rustic stone farmhouses, expanses of windblown grass, and a skyline punctuated with cypress trees. During spring, the fields are painted yellow and green with fava beans and broom, and fringed by red poppies. Sunflowers bloom in June and July, and for much of the early spring and summer.

This driving route, designed for someone home-basing in Siena, takes you south from Siena to Buonconvento, where you'll track back to Siena on an even more remote—but visually stunning—road. The entire loop, without stops, takes about an hour and a half. Besides visits to some less-trampled hill towns, the tour includes the Abbey of Monte Oliveto Maggiore, the undisputed artistic treasure of this part of Tuscany. The stops on the tour are all described in more detail under "Crete Senesi Sights," later.

**Route Option Heading South:** If you'd rather continue south toward Montepulciano and Montalcino (covered in the Heart of Tuscany chapter in this book, including driving tours), break the loop at Buonconvento, where you'll meet the main SR-2 highway. Wine lovers can head directly south to **Montalcino,** then continue into Brunello wine country (the Buonconvento-Montalcino road passes the recommended Altesino winery). If you'd instead like to head for **Montepulciano** or **Pienza,** continue south on SR-2 toward San Quirico d'Orcia.

For a primer on this area's geology, see the sidebar on page 558. For rural accommodations in the Crete Senesi, see page 549.

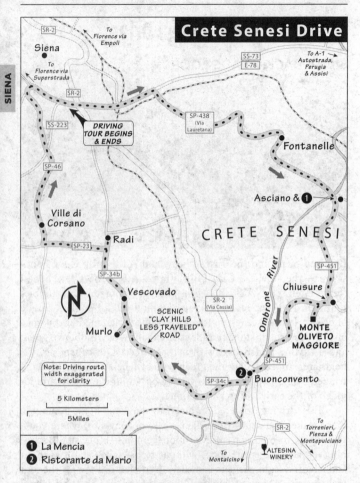

# Crete Senesi Drive

Siena

To Florence via Empoli

To Florence via Superstrada

SR-2

SS-73
E-78

To A-1 Autostrada, Perugia & Assisi

SS-223

**DRIVING TOUR BEGINS & ENDS**

SP-438 (Via Lauretana)

Fontanelle

SP-46

Asciano & ❶

Ville di Corsano

C R E T E    S E N E S I

SP-23

Radi

SP-451

SP-34b

Vescovado

Chiusure

SR-2 (Via Cassia)

Murlo

SCENIC "CLAY HILLS LESS TRAVELED" ROAD

**MONTE OLIVETO MAGGIORE**

Note: Driving route width exaggerated for clarity

SP-451

5 Kilometers

5 Miles

SP-34c

❷ Buonconvento

SR-2

To Torrenieri, Pienza & Montepulciano

❶ La Mencia
❷ Ristorante da Mario

To Montalcino

ALTESINA WINERY

## Siena to Buonconvento

Begin by leaving Siena, heading east on E-78/SS-73 (following green *Roma/A1* signs toward the expressway). After just three kilometers, take the Taverne d'Arbia (nord) exit. Once off the expressway, carefully track *Asciano* signs, which will put you on road SP-438—also called the **Via Lauretana.** Just sit back and enjoy the drive; it's about 20 kilometers to Asciano, through a stunning and very lush landscape. You'll come across plenty of turnouts for panoramic photo opportunities on this road. Eventually you'll drop down into the village of **Asciano,** with a humble but historic townscape and a good lunch restaurant.

At Asciano's main roundabout, follow signs for *Chiusure* and *Monte Oliveto Maggiore* and onto SP-451, which winds through beautiful hills for about eight kilometers to our next two stops.

What you do next depends on the time: If it's open, press on to the **Abbey of Monte Oliveto Maggiore,** with a remarkable inlaid-wood choir and a fascinating fresco cycle of the life of St. Benedict, painted by Renaissance masters Il Sodoma and Luca Signorelli (described later). The abbey is just a few kilometers beyond Chiusure.

If the abbey is closed for its midday break, you might as well first drop into the pleasant village of **Chiusure**—a charming, steep, relatively untouristy town that's a fun place to explore or grab lunch; at the roundabout just before Monte Oliveto Maggiore, take the left turn, marked for *S. Giovanni d'Asso, Pienza,* and—in brown—*Chiusure*). The Santa Giulia winery is a nice lunch option for those who plan ahead—see "Wineries near Montalcino," in the Heart of Tuscany chapter).

Carry on past the abbey on SP-451, following *Buonconvento* and *Roma* signs. This takes you (in about 9 kilometers) to **Buonconvento,** a workaday town with some good eating options.

## Scenic Return Route, Buonconvento to Siena

This remote, "Clay Hills Less Traveled" route (partly on gravel roads) culminates with a gorgeous approach to Siena. From the main parking lot next to Buonconvento's old town, head just a few short blocks south (toward *Roma*), and watch for the easy-to-miss turnoff on the right to *Murlo.* Drive 12 kilometers through beautiful countryside until you reach the sleepy hamlet of **Murlo,** where you could park your car and hike up through the main gate into the heart of town. While the Etruscans had a settlement here, the current fortifications were added by a bishop in the 13th century. His palace—at the very center of town—now hosts an Etruscan Museum.

Leaving Murlo, continue to Vescovado (the adjacent town), where you'll follow signs to *Grosetto.* Watch on the right for the turnoff to *Radi*—on a gravel road—and then on the left for *Ville di Corsano.* As you approach and go through **Ville di Corsano,** you'll start to notice sumptuous country-estate villas, built by aristocrats who wanted a grand view of Siena. In the village, turn right toward *Siena,* and head back to town.

## CRETE SENESI SIGHTS

These stops are linked by the Crete Senesi self-guided driving tour described above.

### Asciano

This quaint but not-quite-charming town offers a medieval core, a smattering of churches and museums, and a rare look at everyday Tuscan living. Asciano is known as a center for white truffles, pecorino cheese, and olive oil. There's not much to see here other than a normal Tuscan town going about its work and play. That's why I like it. Stroll Asciano's wide, traffic-free main road, which boasts a relaxed and real *passeggiata* scene. **Bar da Piero** is a popular hangout for gelato or coffee. On the main street, **$$ La Mencia** is an inviting restaurant with a charming garden terrace out back and not a tourist in sight (closed Mon, Corso Matteotti 85).

## Buonconvento

This valley-crossroads town—an important refueling stop for weary pilgrims on the Via Francigena—has a name that literally means "happy meeting place." Today it's humble but handy, with a large chunk of surviving town wall and some fine restaurants. Its economy has little to do with tourism, and it's an easy and accessible fortified town to explore.

Park in the big lot between the main road and the town wall (which hosts a farmers market every Saturday). As you face that wall, loop around the right side, passing the Sienese Sharecropping Museum (Museo della Mezzadria Senese) to reach the 13th-century **main gate** of Buonconvento, called Porta Senese. Buonconvento is 20 kilometers south of Siena—one day's trek for a pilgrim on the Via Francigena. Approaching this gate, they'd look up and be comforted to see two coats of arms, indicating that this town was sponsored and protected by the republic and the army of Siena.

Step inside the 17th-century doors (weathered by four centuries of thumbtacks) and venture to the right down a tight lane. This was the double-decker **guard path,** allowing town defenders to keep a close watch on approaching enemies. (Originally there was another gallery overhead.) Old houses lean up against the wall, like flying buttresses. Notice the slits—wide on the inside, but tapering to a very narrow opening—which allowed archers maximum range of motion but minimum exposure to enemy fire.

Head back to the main gate, then continue straight ahead down the main drag (Via Soccini) toward the courthouse and Town Hall (on the left). The **courthouse**'s facade is embedded with coats of arms—some dating from the 15th century—of the various regional aristocrats who served one-year terms here as the town judge. Next door is the Museum of Sacred Art (Museo d'Arte Sacra, with pieces from the 14th-19th century) and a sleepy TI (+39 0577 807 181). The **Town Hall** still sports a plaque celebrating the vote in 1860, when the people of Tuscany voted 386,571 to 14,923 to join the newly united country of Italy.

Farther along the street, you'll pass the outdoor tables at the recommended **$$ Ristorante da Mario** (daily, Via Soccini 60, +39 0577 806 157), after which the lane opens up into the town's main square. Nearby, don't miss the picture of the **Porta Romana** gate, which was destroyed by German soldiers in 1944. Turning left, you're back to the parking lot where you started.

## Chiusure

The charming, neatly preserved clay village of Chiusure (kyew-ZOO-reh), with a population of just 66, is a fine stop for those seeking "untouristy Tuscany." (Notice that, as this is clay country, the dominant building material is brick.) This steep town offers no sights other than its grand views and real-world village atmosphere.

Park at the entrance to town, then follow signs as you walk up a steep driveway to the *casa di riposo* (the castle-turned-nursing home) and *Gesù Redentore*. Greet the old folks (a good percentage of the town's entire population) sitting in the shade. Then belly up to the railing to enjoy a fine viewpoint over the Crete Senesi, including jagged *calanchi* cliffs and the Abbey of Monte Oliveto Maggiore. On a clear day, you can see all the way to Siena.

Now follow the lone, twisty street steeply downhill into the village, enjoying the solitude. As this town is famed for its artichokes (and hosts an artichoke festival in late April), you'll notice artichoke-themed flowerpots decorating the walls. You'll arrive at Chiusure's general store/*tabacchi*/sometimes-restaurant, the local hangout—where Ilio can make you a hearty sandwich to munch back up at the viewpoint. Continuing to loop around (and bearing right after the square), you'll wind up back at the main road and parking lot.

## ▲▲▲Abbey of Monte Oliveto Maggiore (Abbazia di Monte Oliveto Maggiore)

This Benedictine abbey features perhaps the best in-situ art you'll find in rural Tuscany. The order spared no expense in decorating their main church, import-ing the great artists of the day: Fra Giovanni da Verona, one of the most talented inlaid-wood artists who ever lived, and the skilled fresco artists Luca Signorelli and Il Sodoma. What you see today is very close to what a pilgrim would have seen during a 16th-century visit. It stars an astonishingly detailed inlaid choir, and a cloister frescoed with vivid, detail-and-symbolism-packed, sometimes outlandish scenes by Renaissance masters Il Sodoma and Luca Signorelli.

**Cost and Hours:** Free Mon-Thu, €5 Fri-Sun, modest dress required, daily 9:30-12:30 & 14:30-18:00, Nov-March until 17:00; Gregorian chanting Mon-Fri at 7:30, Sun at 11:00—call to confirm; +39 0577 707 258, www.monteolivetomaggiore.it. The historic cellar has similar hours (weekends only Nov-March) and is open for visits and tastings (reserve in advance).

**Getting There:** The abbey is well signed both from the SR-2 highway (turn off at Buonconvento) and from the scenic SP-451 road through the Crete Senesi. Park at the La Torre lot at the top of the monastery complex (pick up parking ticket and pay at meter near restaurant before returning to car). From the parking lot, it's a steep 10-minute wooded walk downhill to the monastery: Head across the drawbridge and through the fortress (fortified in the 14th century to protect against bandits; notice the fine ceramic Della Robbia sculptures over the doors of Mary and St. Benedict), pass the restaurant, and continue down the hill. (The big, artificial fishpond on the left made sure there was fish on Friday.) At the courtyard before the church, the shop and WCs are to the left; to reach the church entrance, circle around the right side.

**Background:** In the 14th century, Bernardo Tolomei (1272-1348), the middle son of a wealthy Sienese silver-mining family, moved to the hillsides south of Siena to become a hermit-monk. (That's his statue in the courtyard, holding the books of rules for this notoriously strict order.) One day he had a vision of a glorious staircase leading dramatically up into the heavens. He took this as a sign to build a church on that very spot, and founded the Olivetan order (a branch of the Benedictines, named for the Holy Mount of Olives). His original, humble church has since been turned into a brick monastery complex with a beautiful Baroque church interior and a Renaissance-frescoed cloister. (Tolomei was made a saint in 2009, and this complex is the now-global order's mother abbey.)

### ⊘ Self-Guided Tour
Your visit has two parts: The church interior, with its amazing choir, and the adjacent, fresco-slathered cloister.
• *First, follow the signs for the church and head for the main nave, filled with...*

### Fra Giovanni da Verona's Choir
This spectacularly detailed masterpiece is made entirely of inlaid wood—no paint or other foreign flourishes were used to enhance the remarkable detail and optical illusions. Fra Giovanni (1457-1525), from the city of Verona, used this painstaking method to achieve a mastery of three dimensions that eluded many of his contemporaries working in far more forgiving media. Even more

astonishing, this was completed in just two years (1503-1505). Fra Giovanni is deservedly called the "Michelangelo of Wood." Hopefully the choir isn't roped off, so you can linger on the details up close. Have a €2 coin ready to illuminate the work.

Start with the **left panel** (with your back to the main altar) and work clockwise. First you'll see a self-portrait of Fra Giovanni, then 3-D shutters that are left partway open, revealing olive branches, the symbol of the Olivetan order. The 3-D utopian city (showing off Fra Giovanni's mastery of perspective) is followed by a set of not two, but four shutters—as if upping the technical complexity of the first set. The fifth panel, showing Siena's City Hall and Il Campo, recalls that Olivetan monks—including their founder, Bernardo Tolomei—lost their lives helping plague victims in Siena in 1348. The next panel shows more shutters, decorated with a wafer for the Eucharist (symbolizing the sacrifice of Jesus—and suggesting Tolomei's own self-sacrifice). The seventh panel depicts a woodpecker, with this monastery on the right side. The terrain is accurate—showing the jagged *calanchi* (cliffs)—but is missing the now-familiar roads lined with cypresses planted in the 18th century to combat erosion. The next panel is another four-shutter composition. Examine the potted flower (representing fertility), where each petal is different. The ninth panel shows a utopian, geometrically flawless depiction of the artist's hometown of Verona. Finally, in the tenth panel, get lost in the perfectly executed, three-dimensional details of four shutters and two guitars. Notice the individual strings of the guitar, and the crumpled piece of sheet music with actual words.

Cross over to the **right side** and work your way back toward the front of the church, starting with the panel showing the skull—a common symbol for Adam, often shown at the base of Jesus' cross (reminding us that Jesus died to atone for the original sin of Adam). Next is Verona's arena (evoking the classical period that provided a foundation for the Renaissance), then tambourines that allow Fra Giovanni to experiment with the play of light and foreshortening. Next is another view of this monastery, followed by another four-shutter composition. In the top part, the universe rests on the Old and New Testaments; below that are the guild symbols of the monks (ax, compass, and so on) wrapped in a ribbon. This side finishes with another idealized Verona townscape; symbols of pharmacists and alchemists; another perfect town; the entire universe revolving around the earth (remember, this was a century before Galileo); and another self-portrait. Before moving on, pause and say *grazie* to Fra Giovanni.

• *Now check out a few more features worthy of note.*

## The Rest of the Church

In the side chapel to the left of the main altar, find the medieval **crucifix** that clashes with its Baroque surroundings. Supposedly, this crucifix would periodically—and miraculously—speak to Bernardo Tolomei. Behind the crucifix is a painting of Tolomei talking to Jesus (added in 1701). In the sacristy to the right of the altar, examine the huge **stand** created by Fra Raffaele, a student of Fra Giovanni. This originally sat in the center of the choir to display huge music pages so that all the assembled monks could read and chant together.

• *Now head back outside and then into the...*

## Great Cloister

Big personalities—and clashes between them—influenced the art you're about to see. In 1497, the abbot of this monastery commis-
sioned the famous artist Luca Signorelli to decorate the cloister with scenes from the life of St. Benedict. But Signorelli completed only a third of the frescoes before he got an even better gig in Orvieto. After Signorelli left, the abbot commissioned another artist: Il Sodoma. To test him before entrusting the cloister to
him, the abbot had him paint the **panel** to the immediate left of the door as you leave the church, showing Benedict giving books to the Olivetan monks. It was a hit, and Sodoma was hired.

A temperamental artist, Sodoma liked to work at his own pace. But after his frustrating experience with Signorelli, the abbot was short on patience and nudged Sodoma to work faster and faster (while not always paying him on time). To get back at the abbot, Sodoma included painted digs here and there in the panels (which I'll point out).

We'll head clockwise around the cloister. The primary story traces events from the life of St. Benedict (based on the sixth-century accounts of St. Gregory). But the fresco series also offers insight into both monastic and pilgrim life at the cusp of the Renaissance...as well as some fun peeks at the personality of the artist. Gothic art was for the glory of God. Renaissance art—including these frescoes—was designed for a viewer: in this case, pilgrims walking the Via Francigena. This art tells a story and serves a propagandistic agenda: recruitment of pilgrims to join the Olivetan order and become monks.

• *Head into the cloister and begin with the first panel, on your left. The panels are titled in Italian and aren't numbered—but to help you keep your place, I've numbered the descriptions below and organized them into sections: east, south, west, and north.*

## East Wall (Panels 1-11)

1. During the fifth century, Benedict (in blue tunic and orange sash) leaves his hometown and heads for Rome. He leans back on his horse toward his mother, suggesting his reluctance to set out on this journey. In the little townscape on the far-right horizon, notice the body of a man hanging on the gallows—suggesting the barbarism of the time. The servant in red leggings points ahead to Rome (the next panel, identified by the Tiber River and Castel Sant'Angelo). Just above and to the right, in the middle ground, notice the two donkeys that share six legs. According to Sodoma's diary, this intentional error was a message to the impatient abbot: "Working too fast causes mistakes."

2. Benedict (on the right) leaves the theology school in Rome (filled with fancy hedonists), which he has concluded is corrupt.

3. Angelic-looking Benedict (on the left) performs his first miracle: fixing a broken tray (shown before and after, on the ground in front of him). Sodoma has included a self-portrait in this scene, dead-center, with his pet badger and sarcastic smirk.

4. In the rounded panel, Benedict seeks a mentor (the hermit-monk Romano). He leaves his civilian clothes on the ground, taking on the white robe and beard of the monastic lifestyle, where individuality is irrelevant. By covering their bodies, monks are symbolically returning to the Garden of Eden.

5. A shaved-headed Benedict, now a hermit, goes into the wilderness to meditate. As he can't be seen by other people during this time, Romano must lower food to him with a basket on a rope. The devil spins in—Tasmanian-style—to throw a rock and break the bell on the food basket, so Benedict won't know it's chow time. The small snake peeking out to the right represents temptation.

6. After 40 days of isolation, it's Easter—the lamb is on the table (left of window). Inspired by a vision of Christ (far right, looking up toward a mysterious voice), a local priest brings some of the sacraments to Benedict, who realizes that it will be through community with others—not as a hermit—that he will find his calling.

7. Benedict begins his mission to convert shepherds, enumerating the points he's making on his fingers. (Notice the sheepdog at the far right. Why do dogs wear spiked collars? Because wolves would go after the sheepdogs first—clamping down on their necks—before attacking the sheep.) The two men whispering and giggling in the middle are interpreted by some as flirtatious, suggesting Sodoma's sexual orientation.

8. After being tempted by fantasies of a woman (at the top, with horns and see-through negligee, being chased away by the

## Il Sodoma (1477-1549)

Giovanni Antonio Bazzi was as irreverent as he was talented, a free spirit in every sense: He filled his house with exotic animals, he dressed in garish colors, and he was known to sing dirty little ditties to himself while he worked. During the time that he painted this cloister, the monks gave him the nickname Il Mattaccio ("the Madman").

A few years later, his contemporary Giorgio Vasari—an artist, academic, and vocal critic—gave him a different nickname, which stuck: Il Sodoma. Vasari wasn't a fan of Bazzi, and in those very primitive times, a homophobic slur ("The Sodomite") was one of the most withering insults possible. Ever iconoclastic, the artist embraced the nickname, and today it's how history remembers him.

But was Sodoma actually gay? Scholars are divided. Some art critics point to details in the frescoes that suggest a proclivity for the male form, or even suggestions of gay relationships between his figures. Others suggest that Sodoma was just being his usual provocative self, adhering to an artistic style and documenting events he observed. As with other were-they-or-weren't-they greats throughout history—from Michelangelo to Shakespeare to Abraham Lincoln—it's impossible to know for sure.

Archangel Michael), Benedict tries to regain his self-control by stripping and throwing himself into a patch of poison ivy.

9. Impressed by his devotion, other brothers come to Benedict and ask him to become their leader.

10. Benedict accepts their offer and presents them with an extremely strict set of rules. The regretful monks try to kill him with poisoned wine (left side). But miraculously, the glass shatters in the poisoner's hand. (The man with the long nose, holding the glass, is an unflattering caricature of the abbot.) On the right, the watchful little cat is a symbol of vigilance against sin and temptation.

11. The last panel shows that Benedict was also an architect, building 12 monasteries in his life.

### South Wall (Panels 12-19)

12. The first panel on the next wall is one of Sodoma's masterpieces. Benedict meets the two young boys Placido and Mauro, who will carry on his mission after his death. Sodoma has sprinkled some portraits of his contemporaries throughout this fresco, including

Leonardo, Michelangelo, Raphael, and Lorenzo the Magnificent. Growing weary of hearing praise for Signorelli, Sodoma also included a portrait of his predecessor (immediately to the right of Benedict)... with a sarcastic halo.

13. The devil possesses a monk, leading him away from the monastery. Benedict catches up to him and beats the hell out of him—literally (right)—while the devil escapes (top).

14. Eight monks who live on a mountain are tired of hauling up their own water, so Benedict instructs them where to find a spring. The ghostly outlines of a tree and birds showing through are a mistake: Sodoma painted over some frescoes he didn't like before they had dried—causing them to bleed through as a double exposure.

15. A monk loses the head of his shovel in a lake, but Benedict sticks the handle in to miraculously reattach it. The distant scene on the right, with the naked men wrestling, is quite unusual for church art (and has been taken as a speculation of Sodoma's sexuality).

16. Benedict's disciples Placido and Mauro are now teenagers. Placido is drowning, and Benedict—inspired by a divine vision—sends Mauro to walk across the water and save him.

17. This fresco has had a door unceremoniously cut into the middle of it. But that's OK—it's time for a break anyway.

• *Phew. That's a lot of frescoes. We're about halfway through. Let's take a break by ducking into the little side courtyard.*

Entering this **courtyard,** turn left and look to the far end of the hall to see a ghostly monk walking this way. Oops, it's not a monk—it's another Sodoma fresco, this one a well-executed practical joke.

Head into the **refectory,** the grand dining hall where monks gathered for meals (as they still do to this day). Monks ringed the outside of the long table, eating in silence, without distraction. Above the tables, notice the pulpit where holy words are read while the brothers dine. In the hall just outside the refectory, notice the big yellow marble trough, where monks washed their hands before eating.

• *Head back out into the main cloister to resume our tour.*

18. The monastery's custodian, Florenzo (top left), is overcome with jealousy—and the devil—so he gives poisoned bread to a ser-

vant to bring to Benedict. On the right, Benedict throws the bread on the ground for a crow.

19. In this racy-for-church scene, Florenzo (still under the devil's influence) opens the monastery gate to let prostitutes in. Sodoma's salacious sensibilities come through boldly here. Notice the two ladies dancing, with their fingers intertwined (on the right)—one of them sticking her index finger into a hole formed by the other's hand. Subtle. In the lower right is another scandalously charged detail: A prostitute with a dark-skinned son. Even the animals are symbolic: The fluffy dog is a prostitute, while the hardworking donkey is a monk.

### West Wall (Panels 20-29)

20. The first fresco in the next wing is the only one in the cloister *not* by Sodoma or Signorelli. It shows Placido and Mauro (wearing cowboy boots and spurs) receiving their mission from Benedict.

Now begins the stretch of frescoes by **Signorelli.** Pay attention to the differences between the two artists: Signorelli is more of an anatomist (like Michelangelo), while Sodoma is less literal, gravitating to a figurative lyricism—like Botticelli. For example, compare the hands of Sodoma's prostitutes with the veiny, muscled monk's hand in Signorelli's first fresco.

21. Fed up with his failure to do in Benedict, the frenzied devil decides to kill Florenzo by collapsing the room he's in. In the upper right, cartoonish devils carry off Florenzo's screaming soul while they beat him.

22. Benedict goes to Monte Cassino—then deep in the pagan and barbarian wilds—on an important mission. On arrival, his monks pull graven images down from an ancient temple (right), while the faint and ghostly devil escapes at the top. On the left, monks convert pagan worshippers. The hourglass hits you over the head with its message: It's time to convert.

23. The devil is busy tormenting the monks: In the center, he sits on a rock, making it impossible to move—until Benedict (far left) makes the sign of the cross. In the upper right, the devil sets a fire that the monks must scramble to extinguish.

24. The devil kills a monk who's building a church (upper left)—but other monks bring him to Benedict (lower left), who revives him (lower right). Notice the devil's fiery flatulence.

25. Two monks disobey the rules and eat in a restaurant in the company of fair maidens (left side). Returning to the monastery (tiny scene on right side), they lie about where they've been—so Benedict shames them by telling them exactly what they ordered. Like Sodoma earlier, Signorelli uses the fluffy dog (lower right) to suggest prostitution. Position yourself close to the wall and walk

back and forth, noticing that the table moves with you—an impressive optical illusion.

26. A youth (in blue) aspiring to become a monk—who's supposed to be fasting—bumps into a friend on the road (on the right, horns and legless pants), and they decide to eat after all (upper left). In the main scene (lower left), the monk returns home and is admonished by Benedict.

27. The Visigoths' leader sends a stand-in (center, in armor) to pretend he wants to be converted. The monks sense the trick, and go to find the real guy (the half-moon at the top represents the "mysterious West").

28. In Signorelli's final scene, Benedict meets and converts the real Visigoth leader. Notice the fine details on the faces of the soldiers.

29. Sodoma returns, with bright colors and exacting details (see the horse's face). In the upper right, the monastery in Monte Cassino is destroyed—just as Benedict had prophesied.

### North Wall (Panels 30-35)

30. In the first panel on the final wall of the cloister, the monks have dinner. One sneaky fellow (far right) steals his neighbor's bread. This thief looks suspiciously like the accountant who was responsible for paying Sodoma. Sodoma got tired of hearing how amazing Signorelli's moving-table illusion was (back in #25)—so he topped it. You can actually see the objects on Sodoma's table more clearly the farther away you stand: Head back up the hallway you just came down, then walk slowly toward the table. When you reach it, turn right with the hall...and just keep your eyes on that table. The table stretches and shimmies while the dog's back straightens out.

31. Two monks dream of Benedict showing off a new monastery (left)—so they build it (right). The monk holding the plumb line is Fra Giovanni da Verona, who created the inlaid choir inside the church.

32. In this funeral memorial scene, two dead nuns who were excommunicated are on the left; in the center, the family makes a deal to get the Church to intervene; and in the tiny scene on the far right, Benedict forgives the nuns posthumously.

33. The corpse of a deceased monk surfaces from its grave each night because he had sinned by lying to Benedict. They place a

communion host on top of the body, symbolizing the hope for re-birth, and his remains find peace.

• *Next, skip over two open arches.*

34. A monk (on the right) leaves the monastery and finds the devil. But he returns and begs forgiveness from Benedict (scene on the left). The monk's face radiates devotion—Sodoma has brilliantly captured his emotion. The message: The world outside the monastery is a dangerous place, where the devil will hijack your faith.

35. A farmer is captured by soldiers (right, middle ground). They demand his money, and he says Benedict has it. They bring him to Benedict (left), and miraculously, the rope binding him becomes untied.

The right side of this final scene is Sodoma's final kiss-off to the abbot: A horse's rear end is very prominent (symbolism obvious). Look at the house up above the horse, to the tiny upper-floor window where a shirt hangs in the breeze. During this era, a typical person owned seven shirts: six for workdays, and a seventh for Sunday, when they could rest (and do laundry). With this detail, Sodoma is saying to the abbot: "You made me work on Sunday—made me sweat through my seventh shirt. You horse's ass!"

• *With this, you've enjoyed all that's open to the public in this holy place. Go in peace.*

# PISA

Famous for its tipsy Tower, Pisa ("PEE-zah") is much more than its iconic landmark. This thriving midsize city has a wealth of history and architectural treasures, an unexpectedly fun-to-explore arcaded core, and a prestigious university. The Tower and its companion buildings at the Field of Miracles are undoubtedly a must-see. But beyond that tourist-clogged zone, Pisa feels like a real-world antidote to all that Tuscan cutesiness...a humbler version of Florence.

Centuries ago, Pisa was a major power—rivaling Venice and Genoa for control of the seas. City leaders erected an ensemble of Pisan Romanesque landmarks—the Duomo, Baptistery, and Tower—that float regally on the best lawn in Italy. It's no surprise that Piazza del Duomo is now better known as the Campo dei Miracoli (Field of Miracles), for the grandness of the undertaking.

After its port silted up, Pisa was left high and dry, and eventually entered a period of steady decline...leaving those grand landmarks as reminders of its past glory.

While Pisa is rewarding even on a short visit, lingering here and exploring the medieval city center helps you round out your Tuscan experience.

## PLANNING YOUR TIME

For most visitors, Pisa is a touristy quickie—seeing the Tower, visiting the square, and wandering through the Duomo are 90 percent of their Pisan thrills. But it's a shame to skip the rest of the city. Considering Pisa's historic importance and the ambience created by its rich architectural heritage and vibrant student population, the city deserves at least a half-day visit. For many, the lack of tourists outside the Field of Miracles is both a surprise and a relief.

To ascend the Tower, it's smartest to book a time in advance online at OPAPisa.it. Otherwise, go straight to the ticket office upon arrival to snag an appointment—usually for a couple of hours later, especially in summer. If you'll be seeing both the town and the Field of Miracles, plan on a six-hour stop. If just blitzing the Field of Miracles, three hours is the minimum.

Pisa is a good half-day side trip from Lucca. It's quick and easy to connect the two cities by bus or train: Buses stop at the Field of Miracles and trains stop at Pisa's San Rossore station a short walk away (see "Pisa Connections" at the end of this chapter). For a full day and a complete look at Pisa, try this plan: Take the train from Lucca to Pisa's Centrale station; follow my self-guided walk through the heart of town all the way to the Field of Miracles (stopping for lunch en route); see the Tower and surrounding sights; then walk to the Pisa San Rossore train station for a speedy return to Lucca.

You can also side-trip to Pisa from Florence, or even from the Cinque Terre. Even the fastest trains stop in Pisa, so you might change trains here whether you plan to visit the sights or not. If you have time between trains, you can drop your bags at the station, take a taxi or a bus to the Tower, and zip back within a couple of hours.

## Orientation to Pisa

Pisa is manageable, with about 100,000 people. The city is framed on the north by the Field of Miracles (with the Leaning Tower) and on the south by Pisa Cen-

trale train station. The Arno River flows east to west, bisecting the city. The two main streets for tourists and shoppers are Via Santa Maria (running south from the Tower) and Corso Italia/Borgo Stretto (running north from the station). A thousand years ago, the city was a fortified burg on the north side of the river between those two main streets.

### TOURIST INFORMATION

The main TI is located on the Field of Miracles, next to the Duomo's ticket office at the Museum of the Sinopias (daily 10:00-18:00, Nov-Feb until 16:00, Piazza Duomo 7, +39 050 550 100, www. turismo.pisa.it). It sells bus tickets and offers videoguide walking tours of the main sights and the city center (€5-8). For those doing Pisa as a stopover, the TI offers baggage storage (€4). In summer,

# A Brief History of Pisa

Pisa sits near the mouth of the Arno River (six miles from the coast—when the wind blows right, you can still smell the sea). This easy access to the Mediterranean, with the added protection of sitting a bit upstream, made it a highly strategic settlement. The Romans established a naval base here, and Pisa's 150-foot galleys cruised the Mediterranean—gaining control of the sea, establishing outposts on the islands of Corsica, Sardinia, and Sicily, and trading with other Europeans, Muslims, and Byzantine Christians as far south as North Africa and as far east as Syria. European Crusaders hired Pisan boats to carry them and their supplies as they headed off to crusade against the Muslims ruling the Holy Land.

The Pisan "Republic" prided itself on its independence from both popes and emperors. For nearly three centuries (1000-1300), Pisa was a sea-trading power on par with Venice and Genoa, and in medieval times the city was a major player. In 1200, Pisa's power peaked. The city used its sea-trading wealth to build the grand monuments of the Field of Miracles, including the iconic Tower.

But the Pisan fleet was routed in battle by Genoa (1284, at Meloria, off Livorno), and their overseas outposts were taken away. After the port silted up, only the Field of Miracles and the university kept Pisa on the map. In 1406, Pisa fell under the control of its former rival, the Medici family of Florence. Cosimo de' Medici favored Pisa for its mild climate (thanks to that sea breeze) and distance from his enemies. He built palaces here and raised a mighty army. But—as a subordinate to Florence—Pisa lacked the opportunities to flourish in its own right.

The city never regained its former glory, though its famous architectural sights give modern-day Pisa outsize name recognition and a thriving tourist economy.

there may be another TI in the town center, on Piazza XX Settembre (near the loggia, just south of the Arno).

## ARRIVAL IN PISA
### By Train

Most trains (and visitors) arrive at Pisa Centrale station, about a mile south of the Tower and Field of Miracles. Some trains, particularly those from Lucca or La Spezia, also stop at the smaller Pisa San Rossore station, an easy walk (less than 10 minutes) from the Tower. If you're making a targeted stop at the Field of Miracles, check if your train stops at San Rossore.

**Pisa Centrale Station:** This station has a baggage-check desk—look for *deposito bagagli*, at the far-right end of platform 1 (with the tracks at your back).

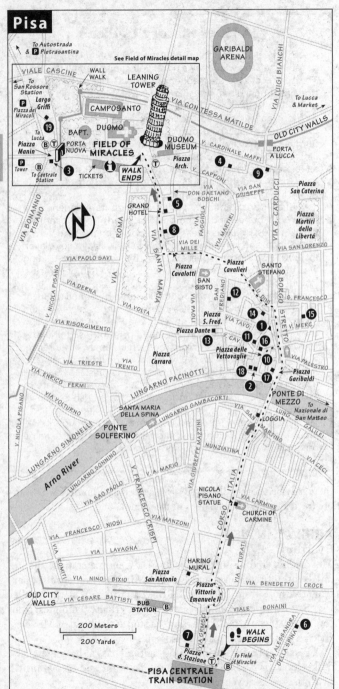

# Pisa

See Field of Miracles detail map

To Autostrada & P Pietrasantina

VIALE CASCINE

To San Rossore Station

Largo Griffi

Piazza dei Miracoli

To Lucca

Piazza Manin

PIAZZA

P Tower

To Centrale Station

**3**

TICKETS

WALK ENDS

WALL WALK

LEANING TOWER

CAMPOSANTO

DUOMO

BAPT.

PORTA NUOVA

**19**

FIELD OF MIRACLES

DUOMO MUSEUM

Piazza Arch.

GARIBALDI ARENA

VIA LUIGI BIANCHI

VIA CONTESSA MATILDE

To Lucca & Market

OLD CITY WALLS

V. CARDINALE MAFFI

PORTA A LUCCA

**4**

V. CAPPONI

**9**

Piazza San Caterina

VIA SAN GIUSEPPE

VIA G. CARDUCCI

Piazza Martiri della Libertà

VIA SAN LORENZO

VIA BONANNO PISANO

VIA ROMA

VIA SANTA MARIA

GRAND HOTEL

**5**

VIA DON GAETANO BOSCHI

**8**

VIA DEI MILLE

VIA FAGGIOLA

VIA MARTIRI

VIA PAOLO SAVI

Piazza Cavalotti

Piazza Cavalieri

SANTO STEFANO

S. FRANCESCO

VIA NICOLA PISANO

VIA DERNA

VIA VOLTA

SAN SISTO

SAN FREDIANO

**12**

VIA DINI

BORGO STRETTO

S. FRANCESCO

**15**

V. MERC.

VIA RISORGIMENTO

VIA PAOLI

Piazza S. Fred.

**14**

VIA TAVO.

**1**

**11**

VIA CAV.

**16**

Piazza Dante

**13**

Piazza delle Vettovaglie

**10**

VIA PALESTRO

V. NICOLA PISANO

VIA TRIESTE

VIA TRENTO

Piazza Carrara

**18**

**17**

Piazza Garibaldi

VIA ENRICO FERMI

VIA VOLTURNO

LUNGARNO PACINOTTI

**2**

PONTE DI MEZZO

To Nazionale di San Matteo

SANTA MARIA DELLA SPINA

LUNGARNO GAMBACORTI

LUNG. LOGGIA

VIA SAN MARTINO

GALILEI

V. CECI

PONTE SOLFERINO

LUNGARNO SONNINO

V. A. MARIO

VIA GIUSEPPE MAZZINI

NUNZIATINA

**Arno River**

LUNGARNO SIMONELLI

V. FRANCESCO CRISPI

VIA SAO PAOLO

VIA MANZONI

NICOLA PISANO STATUE

CORSO ITALIA

VIA CARMINE

CHURCH OF CARMINE

VIA FRANCESCO NIOSI

VIA LAVAGNA

VIA F. TURATI

VIA NINO BIXIO

HARING MURAL

Piazza San Antonio

Piazza Vittorio Emanuele II

VIA BENEDETTO CROCE

OLD CITY WALLS

VIA CESARE BATTISTI

BUS STATION

VIALE BONAINI

VIA ALESSANDRA DELLA SPINA

**6**

200 Meters

200 Yards

**7**

Piazza d. Stazione

WALK BEGINS

To Field of Miracles

VIA GRAMSCI

PISA CENTRALE TRAIN STATION

N

PISA

## Pisa Key

**Accommodations**
1. Relais dei Mercanti
2. Hotel Royal Victoria
3. Hotel Pisa Tower
4. Casa San Tommaso
5. Hotel Helvetia
6. Hotel Alessandro della Spina
7. Stazione22

**Eateries & Other**
8. Ristorante-Pizzeria La Torre
9. Pizzeria al Bagno di Nerone
10. La Vineria di Piazza & Produce Market
11. Antica Trattoria il Campano
12. Osteria dei Cavalieri
13. Caffetteria BetsaBea
14. Il Montino Pizzeria
15. Orzo Bruno Brewpub
16. La Mescita
17. La Bottega del Gelato
18. De' Coltelli Gelato & Caffè dell'Ussero
19. Supermarket

PISA

To get to the Field of Miracles, you can **walk** (30 minutes direct, one hour if you follow my self-guided walk), take a **taxi** (€10, +39 050 541 600, taxi stand at station), or go by **bus** (which can be plagued by pickpockets).

Bus **LAM Rossa** (also marked *L/R*) stops in front of the station (to the right when you exit; bus stop at the corner). It runs about every 10 minutes to Piazza Manin, in front of the Field of Miracles (15-minute ride, stop: Torre, buy €1.50 ticket at machine or from any tobacco shop before boarding).

If you need to return to the train station from the Tower, catch bus LAM Rossa across from the BNL bank, on the opposite side of the street from where you got off (buy your ticket from the ticket machine at the bus stop). You'll find taxi stands 30 yards from the Tower and in front of the BNL bank on Piazza Manin. Or see if your departing train also stops at San Rossore station (see next)—saving you the trip back to Pisa Centrale.

**Pisa San Rossore Station:** This little suburban train station is just a four-block walk (less than 10 minutes) to the Tower. On arrival, exit the underpass at platform 2L, and follow the exit signs to *Torre Pendente*. Once out of the station area, turn left and follow brown *Torre Pendente* signs on Via Andrea Pisano, heading for the Baptistery's dome.

## By Car

Driving in the city center is stressful, time-consuming, and costly, as Pisa has several restricted areas that are monitored by camera and marked by *"ZTL"* signs (you could get a ticket by mail).

For a quick visit, there are two pay lots just west of the tower (both around €2/hour): **Parcheggio di Piazza dei Miracoli** lot (enter from Via Giovanni Battista Niccolini); and **Tower Parking** (enter from Via Andrea Pisano). From either one, the Field of Miracles is practically across the street.

To save some money—or if the pay lots are full—try the free, big **Pietrasantina parking lot** (which you'll share with lots of tour buses). To find it, exit the autostrada at *Pisa Nord* and follow signs to *Pisa* (on the left), then *Bus Parking*. The parking lot has a cafeteria and WC. At the center of the lot is a high-roofed bus stop where you can catch the LAM Rossa **bus** to Piazza Manin at the gate of the Field of Miracles (€1.50 at the parking lot's cafeteria; bus continues to Pisa Centrale station if you'd like to follow my self-guided walk to the Field of Miracles). Or you can **walk** to the Tower in about 15 minutes: From the newspaper/souvenir kiosk at the east end of the lot, turn right onto the curving road. Follow the blue signs indicating a pedestrian path and brown signs pointing to the Leaning Tower. You'll cross train tracks on the left, then continue to the right.

## By Plane

For details on Pisa's Galileo Galilei Airport, see "Pisa Connections" at the end of this chapter.

## HELPFUL HINTS

**Markets:** An open-air produce market attracts picnickers to Piazza delle Vettovaglie, one block north of the Arno River near Ponte di Mezzo, and nearby Piazza Sant'Uomobuono (Mon-Sat 8:00-13:00, closed Sun). A street market—with more practical goods than food—bustles on Wednesday and Saturday mornings between Via del Brennero and Via Paparrelli (8:00-13:00, just outside of wall, about 6 blocks east of the Tower). A small flea market pops up in Via San Martino every Wednesday and Saturday morning.

**Supermarket:** Just to the northwest of the Field of Miracles entrance, **Carrefour Express** has everything you need. It sells quick lunch items and has a coffee bar and picnic area, Wi-Fi, and a clean WC free for customers (daily 10:00-18:00, Largo Cocco Griffi).

**Local Guides: Dottore Vincenzo Riolo** guides tours of the Field of Miracles, the city center, and other destinations in Tuscany such as Volterra (€150/3 hours, +39 338 211 2939, www. pisatour.it, info@pisatour.it). **Martina Manfredi** happily guides visitors through the Field of Miracles, but her real passion is helping them discover the other charms of Pisa and the surrounding countryside—from hidden gardens and piazzas to wine and truffle tastings and artisan visits. She also enjoys tailoring family-friendly itineraries (€140/3 hours, +39 328 898 2927, www.tuscanyatheart.it, info@tuscanyatheart.it).

# Pisa Walk

A leisurely one-hour self-guided stroll from Pisa Centrale train station to the Tower is a great way to get acquainted with the more subtle virtues of this fine city. Because the hordes that descend daily on the Tower rarely bother with the rest of the town, you'll find most of Pisa to be delightfully untouristy—a student-filled, classy, Old World town with an Arno-scape much like its upstream rival, Florence.

• *Exit Pisa Centrale and walk straight ahead (north, under the fascist marble arcade) up Viale Antonio Gramsci to the circular square called...*

## Piazza Vittorio Emanuele II

The Allies considered Pisa to be strategically important in World War II, and both the train station and its main bridge were targeted for bombing. Forty percent of this district was destroyed. The piazza has been rebuilt, and now this generous public space with grass and benches is actually a lid for an underground parking lot. The circular pink building in the middle of the square, on the right, is La Bottega del Parco, a shop that sells Tuscan products and offers light meals.

At the top of the square, on the left (by the modern gray tower with the Credito Artigiano bank), find the little piazza with a colorful bar/café that faces a mural, called  *Tuttomondo (Whole Wide World)*, painted by American artist **Keith Haring**. The mural, which decorates the back of a church that was bombed and rebuilt in the 1950s, is worth studying. It's a celebration of diversity, chaos, and the liveliness of our world, vibrating with energy. Enjoy the symbolism: the cross of people, three races connected like nesting dolls holding a heart. The message of tolerance is as timely today as it was when this mural was completed in 1989. Haring (who died of AIDS in 1990) brought New York City street art into the mainstream.

• *Head back to the middle of the big square and take the first left. This is Pisa's main drag.*

## Corso Italia

As you leave Piazza Vittorio Emanuele II, look to the right (on the wall of the bar on the corner, under the gallery) and orient yourself with the circa-1960 wall map of Pisa with a steam train. Then follow the pedestrianized Corso Italia straight north for several blocks, toward the river. This is Pisa's main shopping street for locals, not tourists. Students hang out and stroll here—you'll see plenty of cheap department stores and youthful fashions.

Stow your guidebook and enjoy the stroll. A few blocks up, in front of the Church of Santa Maria del Carmine (on the right, at #88), meet **Nicola Pisano.**
He and his son, Giovanni (who worked in the 13th century), represented the pinnacle of Gothic art and inspired Michelangelo. Although they were from the south, their work in their adopted town earned them the name "Pisano" (from Pisa).

Continuing on Corso Italia, just before the river, you run into a stately **loggia.** Like much of the city, this was built under Medici (Florentine) rule—and it resembles the markets you'll still find in Florence. But remember that before Florence ruled Pisa, this city was an independent and strong maritime republic.

This area (south of the river) was a marshland until the 11th century, and in the Middle Ages it was a crossroads of merchants from faraway lands: smelly, polluted, and a commotion of activity. Like the Oltrarno neighborhood in Florence and Trastevere neighborhood in Rome (and the "wrong side of the tracks" in many American towns), this was the most characteristic part of the city. Now we cross to the "high town."

• *At the Arno River, cross to the middle of the bridge.*

## Ponte di Mezzo

This modern bridge, the site of Pisa's first bridge and therefore its birthplace, marks the center of Pisa. In the Middle Ages, Ponte di Mezzo (like Florence's Ponte Vecchio) was lined with shops. It's been destroyed several times by floods...and in 1943 by British and American bombers. Enjoy the view from the center of the bridge of the elegant mansions that line the riverbank, recalling Pisa's days of trading glory—the cityscape feels a bit like Venice's Grand Canal. Back when the loggia area was stinky and crowded, nobles preferred to live in stately residences along the river.

Looking downstream (to the left), notice the red-brick building on the right bank (the former silk merchants' quarters) that looks like it's about to slide into the river. Pisa sits on shifting delta sand, making construction tricky. The entire town leans. Using innovative arches above ground and below, architects didn't stop the leaning—but they have made buildings that wobble without being threatened.

• *Cross the bridge to...*

## Piazza Garibaldi

This square is named for the charismatic leader of the Risorgimento, the unification movement that led to Italian independence in 1861. Knowing Pisa was strongly nationalist (and gave many of its sons to the national struggle), a wounded Garibaldi came here to be nursed back to health. Find his statue and study the left side of the bronze relief at the base of the statue to see him docking in Pisa and receiving a warm and caring welcome.

For a gelato break, stop by **La Bottega del Gelato,** right on this square and most Pisans' sentimental favorite. Or, for a fresh take on the same old gelato, head about 100 yards downstream (to the left on Lungarno Pacinotti as you come off the bridge) to **De' Coltelli** (at #23), which scoops up organic, artisanal gelato with unusual and vibrant flavors. Just beyond that, in the slouching red building (at #28), step into **Caffè dell'Ussero.** This venerable café has long been a hangout of both politicians...and the students bent on overthrowing them. Greet the proprietor and then browse its time-warp interior all the way to the back room—it's lined with portraits and documents from the struggle for Italian independence.

• *Back on Piazza Garibaldi, continue north up the elegantly arcaded street called...*

## Borgo Stretto

Welcome to Pisa's other main shopping street—this one higher-end. On the right, the Church of St. Michael, with its fine Pisan Romanesque facade, was likely built upon a Roman temple.

From here, look farther up the street and notice how it undulates like a flowing river. In the sixth century BC, Pisa was born when two parallel rivers were connected by canals. This street echoes the flow of one of those canals.

• *Just past the church, pause to appreciate the Renaissance arcades (loggias) in every direction. Then detour left onto Via delle Colonne, and walk one block down to...*

## Piazza delle Vettovaglie

Pisa's historic market square, Piazza delle Vettovaglie, is lively by day and sketchy by night. Its Renaissance loggia has hosted the fish-and-vegetable market for generations. Stalls are set up in this piazza in the morning and stay open later in the neighboring piazza to the west (Piazza Sant'Uomobuono). You could cobble together a picnic from the sandwich shops and fruit-and-veggie stalls ringing these squares, or enjoy lunch at the

recommended **La Vineria di Piazza** trattoria (under the arcades of Piazza delle Vettovaglie).

• *Return to Borgo Stretto and continue north another 100 yards, passing a modern apartment development on the right at Largo Ciro Menotti, an example of 1960s city design that followed WWII bombings. Standing out front is a statue of native son Galileo Galilei, erected in early 2020.*

*Carry on for a couple more short blocks, and turn left on nondescript Via Ulisse Dini (immediately at the arcade's end, just before the pharmacy). This leads in a few short blocks to Pisa's historic core, the square called...*

## Piazza dei Cavalieri (Knights' Square)

For Pisans, this square is a place of lost glory. It feels sad, nostalgic...the only piazza I've seen in Italy without a bar or café. The square (site of the market, or forum, in ancient Roman times) long hosted the head of a proud and independent Pisan government. A Palazzo Vecchio-like capitol stood here during Pisa's glory days when the city was a big maritime power in a league with Genoa and Amalfi.

Then came a couple of centuries of Florentine rule. Walk to the statue in front of the curved building. **Cosimo I,** a Medici who ruled the Grand Duchy of Tuscany (and Pisa), appears noble but reminds Pisans of those dark times. Pisa was the second city of his little state, and Cosimo asserted Florentine rule by turning this square into a Florentine military base.

The Pisan palace became the late-Renaissance Florentine military school you see here today. Cosimo's statue was a declaration that, as Grand Duke, he defended Christianity against the Turks, defended Florentine trade, and ruled the people of Pisa.

The adjacent Baroque **church,** with the Medici coat of arms, was a national church dedicated to the military/religious order of Saint Stephen (as indicated by the Maltese-like cross). Inside hang Turkish banners from the Battle of Lepanto (from 1571, when bickering Christian states united against a common enemy—the Ottoman Turks—and won). Napoleon came in 1812 and made the Florentine military school the Scuola Normale Superior (a place of higher education).

From here, take Via Corsica (to the left of the clock tower). The humble, stony, 11th-century **Church of San Sisto,** ahead on the left, is worth a quick look. This was the standard Romanesque style that predated the more lavish Pisan Romanesque style of the Field of Miracles structures: simple bricks, assorted reused columns—some of them ancient Roman, a delightful assortment of capitals, heavy walls, and tiny windows. Its 11th-century facade was once covered with plaster and colorfully painted. You can see the remains of the Eastern-flavored ceramic bowls across the top that once shined in the sun like gems.

• *Follow Via Corsica as it turns into Via dei Mille, then turn right after the little parklike square on Via Santa Maria, which leads north, becoming a touristy can-can of eateries, and finally ends at the Field of Miracles and the Tower. (Consider the Grand Hotel Duomo the border between tolerable touristy restaurants and terrible touristy restaurants nearer the Leaning Tower.)*

# Sights in Pisa

## THE BEST OF THE FIELD OF MIRACLES

Imagine arriving in Pisa as a sailor in the 12th century, when the river came to just outside the walls surrounding this square, the church here was one of the biggest in the world, and this ensemble in gleaming white marble was the most impressive space in Christendom. Calling it the Field of Miracles (Campo dei Miracoli) would not have been hyperbole.

Scattered across a golf-course-green lawn are five grand buildings: the cathedral (or Duomo), its bell tower (the Leaning Tower), the Baptistery, the hospital (today's Museum of the Sinopias), and the Camposanto Cemetery. The buildings are constructed from similar materials—bright white marble—and have comparable decoration. Each has a simple ground floor and rows of delicate columns and arches that form open-air arcades, giving the Campo a pleasant visual unity.

PISA

**Pisa's Field of Miracles**

To Autostrada
& P Pietrasantina

VIALE CASCINE
To San Rossore Station

VIA C. CAMMEO

VIA CONTESSA MATILDE

100 Meters
100 Yards

P Piazza dei Miracoli

Largo Cocco Griffi

WALL WALK
Jewish Cemetery

TACKY SOUVENIR STANDS

VIA S. NICOLA

BAPTISTERY

PORTA S. MARIA

VIA A. PISANO

Piazza Manin

VIA BONANNO PISANO

P Tower

CAMPOSANTO CEMETERY

WC

OLD CITY WALLS

LEANING TOWER

VIA C. P. MAFFI

DUOMO

Grassy Lawn

Piazza del Duomo

MUSEUM OF THE SINOPIAS

DUOMO MUSEUM

Piazza Archivescovado

VIA ROMA

VIA SANTA MARIA

To rest of town & Centrale Station

VIA TASSI

❶ Ticket Offices (2)
❷ Baggage Check
❸ Bus to Centrale Station
❹ Bus to Lucca
❺ Bus Ticket Machine

The style is called Pisan Romanesque. Unlike traditional Romanesque, with its heavy fortress-like feel—thick walls, barrel arches, few windows—Pisan Romanesque is light and elegant. At ground level, most of the structures have simple half-columns and arches. On the upper levels, you'll see a little of everything—tight rows of thin columns; pointed Gothic gables and prickly spires; Byzantine mosaics and horseshoe arches; and geometric designs (such as diamonds) and striped, colored marbles inspired by mosques in Muslim lands.

Architecturally, the Campo is unique and exotic. Traditionally, its buildings marked the main events of every Pisan's life: christened in the Baptistery, married in the Duomo, called to celebrate by the bells in the tower, healed in the hospital, and buried in the Camposanto Cemetery.

Lining this field of artistic pearls are dozens of people who have simultaneously had the same bright idea: posing for a photo as though they're propping up the Leaning Tower. Although the smooth green carpet looks like the ideal picnic spot—and many people are doing just that—officially, lounging on this lawn can result in a €25 fine. (The area around the Baptistery is typically more lenient.)

# Field of Miracles Tickets

Pisa's combo-ticket scheme is designed to get you into its neglected secondary sights: the Baptistery, Camposanto Cemetery, Duomo Museum, and Museum of the Sinopias (fresco patterns). Any of those sights costs €7 individually, but the €10 combo-ticket covers all the Field of Miracle sights (except the Tower climb).

It's free to enter the Duomo, but you either need a voucher with an appointed time, or you can get in anytime if you have any other ticket (the €7 or €10 version). The Tower by itself costs €20 (€27 includes the Tower plus all the other sights).

You can get the Duomo voucher and any of these tickets from either ticket office on the Field of Miracles: One is behind the Leaning Tower and the other is at the Museum of the Sinopias (near the TI, less crowded). It's also possible to buy tickets in advance online at OPAPisa.it (no sooner than 20 days ahead of your visit; Duomo voucher not available online).

So, which ticket to buy? This depends on your time and level of interest. The shortest visit doesn't cost a dime: Ogle the Tower and other buildings, and enter the Duomo (with the best interior) with the free timed voucher. If you're in a hurry, buy any €7 ticket and you can enter the Duomo right away.

When prioritizing your time, the interiors of the **Baptistery** and **Camposanto Cemetery** are easy to appreciate and the most rewarding. The **Duomo Museum,** while less thrilling, features a well-presented look at some original church art. The **Museum of the Sinopias** is "extra credit"; for most travelers, it's skippable.

And what about entering the **Tower?** Is it worth that hefty price tag—and a likely wait to enter? It's a minor thrill to clomp up those twisty stairs, and the view from the top is enjoyable. But Pisa isn't particularly scenic, and it's a lot of expense and hassle for a view. Unless climbing the Tower is what you came to do, the real thrill comes from seeing it from the outside.

As you consider your itinerary, remember that until the "cult of the Leaning Tower" was born around 1900, people came to Pisa not to see the Tower but to visit the historic (and, today, underrated) Camposanto Cemetery.

PISA

## ▲▲▲Leaning Tower

A 15-foot lean from the vertical makes the Leaning Tower one of Europe's most recognizable images. You can see it for free—it's always viewable, and worth ▲▲▲ simply to ogle from the outside—or you can pay to climb nearly 300 stairs to the top.

The off-kilter Tower parallels Pisa's history. It was started in the late 12th century, when Pisa was at its peak: one of the world's richest, most powerful, and most sophisticated cities. Pisans had built their huge cathedral to reflect their city's superpower status, and the cathedral's bell tower—the Leaning Tower—was the perfect complement. But as Pisa's power declined, the Tower reclined, and both have required a great deal of effort to prop up. Modern engineering has stabilized the Tower, so you can admire it in all its cockeyed glory and even climb up for a commanding view.

**Cost and Hours:** €20 (or €27 for combo-ticket covering all Field of Miracles sights), kids under age 8 not allowed, hours are variable (check ahead) but generally April-Sept daily 9:00-20:00, often until 22:00 during busy times (especially Fri-Sat), Oct and late March until 19:00, early March until 18:00, Nov-Feb 10:00-17:00, ticket office opens 30 minutes early, reservations necessary if you value your time, OPAPisa.it.

**Getting In:** Entry to the Tower is by a timed ticket good for a 30-minute visit. Every 15 minutes, 50 people can clamber up the 294 tilting steps to the top. Children ages 8-18 must be accompanied by—and stay at all times with—an adult.

**Reservations:** Reserve your timed entry online or in person at either ticket office. **Online bookings** are accepted no earlier than 20 days in advance (they can sell out, so don't wait). Choose your entry time and buy your ticket at OPAPisa.it.

To reserve in person, go to either **ticket office:** behind the Tower on the left (in the yellow building) or (less crowded) at the Museum of the Sinopias.

**Planning Your Time:** In summer, for same-day entry, you'll likely wait 2-3 hours before going up (see the rest of the monuments and grab lunch while waiting).

Arrive at least 15 minutes ahead of your entry time or you may not be allowed in. For your 30-minute time slot, figure about 10 minutes to climb, and 10 to descend. This leaves about 10 minutes for vertigo at the top.

It's busiest between 12:00 and 15:00. If you come after 18:00 there's generally no line at all...on my last visit, I was the only one climbing the Tower at 19:00.

**Baggage Check:** You can't take anything up the Tower other than your phone or camera. Day-bag-size lockers are available at the ticket office next to the Tower—show your ticket to check your

# Leaning Tower

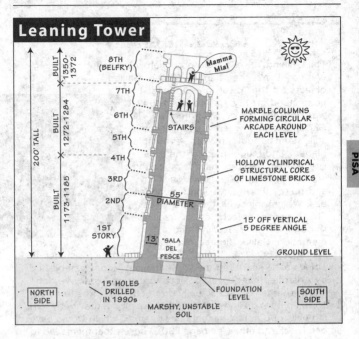

BUILT 1350-1372

BUILT 1272-1284

BUILT 1173-1185

200' TALL

8TH (BELFRY)

Mamma Mia!

7TH

6TH

STAIRS

5TH

4TH

3RD

2ND

1ST STORY

MARBLE COLUMNS FORMING CIRCULAR ARCADE AROUND EACH LEVEL

HOLLOW CYLINDRICAL STRUCTURAL CORE OF LIMESTONE BRICKS

55' DIAMETER

15' OFF VERTICAL 5 DEGREE ANGLE

13' "SALA DEL PESCE"

GROUND LEVEL

NORTH SIDE

15' HOLES DRILLED IN 1990s

FOUNDATION LEVEL

SOUTH SIDE

MARSHY, UNSTABLE SOIL

PISA

bag. You may check your bag 15 minutes before your reservation time and must pick it up immediately after your Tower visit.

**Caution:** The railings are skinny, the steps are slanted, there are no handrails, and rain makes the marble slippery—all in all, it's more dizzying than you might expect. Anyone with balance issues of any sort should think twice before ascending.

## The Tower and Its Story

Rising up alongside the cathedral, the Tower is nearly 200 feet tall and 55 feet wide, weighing 14,000 tons and currently leaning at a five-degree angle (15 feet off the vertical axis). It started to lean almost immediately after construction began (it would take two centuries to finish the structure). Count the eight stories—a simple base, six stories of columns (forming arcades), and a belfry on top. The inner structural core is a hollow cylinder built of limestone bricks, faced with white marble. The thin columns of the open-air arcades make the heavy Tower seem light and graceful.

**The Building of the Tower:** The Tower was built over two centuries by at least three architects. You can see

## Galileo and Gravity

The Leaning Tower figures prominently in scientific lore. Legend has it that the scientific pioneer Galileo Galilei dropped objects off the Tower in an attempt to understand gravity. Galileo (1564-1642) was born in Pisa, grew up here on Via Giuseppe Giusti (where the family home still stands, adorned with a humble plaque), and taught math at the university. Galileo is said to have climbed the Tower and dropped two balls: one heavy and metal, the other a lighter wooden ball. Which object hit the ground first? The heavier object, of course—but through further reasoning and experimentation, Galileo figured out that the

lighter object fell more slowly only because of air resistance. In doing so, he shattered the conventional wisdom, established by Aristotle, that heavier objects accelerate faster. We don't know whether Galileo actually dropped those orbs from this Tower, but we do know he tested this theory of gravity by rolling balls of different weights down ramps, which would have been easier to time (see page 280). These experiments led to Isaac Newton's formulation of the laws of gravity. Moreover, by forging theories through rigorous testing rather than through reasoning alone (as Aristotle had), Galileo helped reenvision science itself.

how the successive architects tried to correct the leaning problem—once halfway up (after the fourth story), once at the belfry on the top.

The first stones were laid in 1173, probably under the direction of the architect Bonanno Pisano (who also designed the Duomo's bronze back door). Five years later, just as the base and the first arcade were finished, someone said, "Is it just me, or does that look crooked?" The heavy Tower—resting on a very shallow 13-foot foundation—was sinking on the south side into the marshy, multilayered, unstable soil. (Actually, all of the Campo's buildings tilt somewhat.) The builders carried on anyway, until they'd finished four stories (the base, plus three arcade floors). Then, construction suddenly halted—no one knows why—and for a century the Tower sat half-finished and visibly leaning.

Around 1272, the next architect, Giovanni di Simone, tried to correct the problem by angling the next three stories backward, in the opposite direction of the lean. The project then again sat mysteriously idle for nearly another century. Finally, Tommaso Pisano put the belfry on the top (c. 1350-1372), also kinking it to overcome the leaning.

**Man Versus Gravity:** In an effort to stop the Tower's slow-motion fall, well-intentioned engineers in 1838 pumped out groundwater around it. But they only further destabilized the Tower, causing its lean rate to increase to a millimeter per year.

As well as gravity, erosion threatens the Tower. Since its construction, 135 of the Tower's 180 marble columns have had to be replaced. Stone decay, deposits of lime and calcium phosphate, accumulations of dirt and moss, cracking from the stress of the lean—all of these are factors in its decline.

It got so bad that in 1990 the Tower was closed for repairs, and $30 million was spent cleaning it and trying to stabilize it. Engineers dried the soil with pipes containing liquid nitrogen, anchored the Tower to the ground with steel cables, and buried 600 tons of lead on the north side as a counterweight (not visible)—all with little success. The breakthrough came when they drilled 15-foot-long holes in the ground on the north side and sucked out 60 tons of soil, allowing the Tower to sink on the north side and straighten out its lean by about six inches.

All the work to shore up, straighten, and clean the Tower has probably turned the clock back a few centuries.

**Climbing the Tower:** First, you'll enter the room at the bottom of the Tower known as the *Sala del Pesce* (for the Christian fish

symbol on the wall). Gape up through the hollow Tower to the oculus at the top, and marvel at the acoustics. Also check out the heavy metal braces stretching up to the top.

Wind your way up the outside along a spiraling ramp to the first level, where you can stroll the colonnaded arcade. Then, finding the tiny spiral staircase next to where you entered the first level, head to the belfry on the top, climbing a total of 294 stairs. At the top, you'll have fine views over the Duomo and the rest of the Field of Miracles, as well as over the rooftops of Pisa.

## ▲▲Duomo (Cathedral)

The huge Pisan Romanesque cathedral, with its carved pulpit by Giovanni Pisano, is artistically more important than its more famous bell tower. Budget some sightseeing time for the church's artistic and historic treasures.

**Cost and Hours:** Free. If you have a ticket for any Field of Miracles sight, you can walk right in; otherwise, pick up a voucher

# Pisa Duomo

*Not to Scale*

APSE

DOME

N A V E

EXIT

ENTRANCE

FIELD OF MIRACLES

To Leaning Tower

To Baptistery

To Tacky Souvenir Stands

1 Exterior View
2 Nave
3 Galileo's Lamp
4 Apse Mosaic
5 Dome
6 Giovanni Pisano's Pulpit
7 St. Ranieri's Body
8 Emperor Henry VII's Tomb
9 Bronze Doors of St. Ranieri (Outside)

PISA

with an entry time at either ticket office (voucher not available in advance online; see the "Field of Miracles Tickets" sidebar earlier). Hours vary (check ahead), but the interior always opens at 10:00, after morning Mass; it closes April-Sept at 20:00, Oct at 19:00, Nov-Feb at 17:00 (also 13:00-14:00), March at 18:00.

**Crowd-Beating Tips:** Because the Duomo is the only free interior at the Field of Miracles, it's on every tour itinerary and can be busy. Ideally, try to see the Duomo at lunchtime or late in the day.

**Dress Code:** Shorts are OK as long as they're not too short, and shoulders should be covered (although it's not really enforced).

**Baggage:** Big backpacks are not allowed, but you can leave your bags at the TI across the square.

## ◆ Self-Guided Tour

The Duomo is the centerpiece of the Field of Miracles' complex of religious buildings. Begun in 1063, it was financed by a galley-load of booty ransacked that year from the Muslim-held capital of Palermo, Sicily. The architect Buschetto created the frilly Pisan Romanesque style that set the tone for the Baptistery and Tower that followed. In the 1150s, the architect Rainaldo added the impressive main-entrance facade.

**① Exterior View:** The lower half of the church is simple Romanesque, with blind arches. The upper half has four rows of columns that form arcades. Stripes of black-and-white marble, mosaics, stone inlay, and even recycled Roman tombstones complete the decoration.

• *Enter the church at the west facade, opposite the Baptistery.*

**② Nave:** The 320-foot nave was designed to be the longest in Christendom when it was built. It's modeled on a traditional Roman basilica, with 68 Corinthian columns of granite (most shipped from Elba and Corsica in 1063) dividing the space into five aisles. But the striped marble and arches-on-columns give the nave an exotic, almost mosque-like feel. Dim light filters in from the small upper windows of the galleries. At the center of the gilded coffered ceiling is the shield of Florence's Medici family, with its round balls. With the arrival of the Florentine Renaissance, this powerful merchant and banking family took over Pisa after its glory days had passed. This ceiling was rebuilt after a 1595 fire with Medici funding (and 80 kilos of gold).

• *Walk up the nave, almost to the transept. Hanging from the ceiling of the central nave is...*

**③ Galileo's Lamp:** The bronze incense burner is said to be the one (actually, this is a replacement of the original) that caught the teenage Galileo's attention one day in church. According to legend, someone left a church door open, and a gust of wind set the lamp swinging. Galileo timed the swings and realized that the burner swung back and forth in the same amount of time regardless of how wide the arc. This pendulum motion was a constant that allowed Galileo to measure our ever-changing universe. For more on the famous Pisa native, see the "Galileo and Gravity" sidebar, earlier in this chapter.

· *High up in the apse (behind the altar) is the...*

**❹ Apse Mosaic:** The mosaic (c. 1300, partly done by the great artist Cimabue) shows Christ Pantocrator ("All Powerful") between Mary and St. John the Evangelist. The Pantocrator image of Christ is standard fare among Eastern Orthodox Christians—that is, the "Byzantine" people who were Pisa's partners in trade.

As King of the Universe, Christ sits on a throne, facing directly out, with penetrating eyes. Only Christ can wear this style of halo, divided with a cross. In his left hand is a Bible open to the verse *"Ego Lux Sum Mundi"*—"I am the light of the world." While his feet crush the devil in serpent form, Christ blesses us with his right hand. His fingers form the Greek letters *chi* and *rho*, the first two letters of "Christos." The thumb (almost) touches the fingers, symbolizing how Christ unites both his divinity and his humanity.

**❺ Dome:** Look up into the dome. Because this church is dedicated to Mary—the patron and protector of the city—you'll see the Assumption of Mary. As the heavens open, and rings of saints and angels spiral upward, a hazy God greets Mary (in red). Beneath the dome is an inlaid-marble, Cosmati-style mosaic floor. The modern (and therefore controversial) marble altar and pulpit were carved by a Florentine artist in 2002.

· *Next to Galileo's Lamp, you'll find...*

**❻ Giovanni Pisano's Pulpit** (1301-1311): The 15-foot-tall, octagonal pulpit by Giovanni Pisano (c. 1240-1319) is the last, big-

gest, and most complex of the four pulpits created by the Pisano father-and-son team. Giovanni's father, Nicola, started the family tradition four decades earlier, carving the pulpit in the Baptistery. Giovanni grew up working side-by-side with his dad on numerous projects. Now on his own, he crams everything he's learned into his crowning achievement.

Giovanni left no stone uncarved in his pursuit of beauty. Four hundred intricately sculpted figures smother the pulpit, blurring the architectural outlines. In addition, the relief panels are actually curved, making it look less like an octagon than a circle. The creamy-white Carrara marble has the look and feel of carved French ivories, which the Pisanos loved. Originally, this and the other pulpits were frosted with paint and gilding.

At the base, lions roar and crouch over their prey, symbolizing how Christ (the lion) triumphs over Satan (the horse, as in the Four Horsemen of the Apocalypse).

Four of the pulpit's support "columns" are statues. The central "column" features three graceful ladies representing Faith, Hope, and Charity. They in turn stand on the sturdy base of knowledge, representing the liberal arts taught at the University of Pisa. Another column is the pagan hero, Hercules, standing *contrapposto*, nude, holding his club and lion skin. To his right, Lady Church suckles the babies of the Old and New Testaments, while at her feet are the Four Virtues: Justice (with her scales), Moderation (modestly covering her nakedness), Courage (holding a lion), and Wisdom (with a horn of plenty).

Around the top of the pulpit, Christ's life unfolds in a series of panels saturated with carvings. The panels tilt out, so the viewer below has a better look, and they're bordered on top with a heavy cornice as a backdrop. Since the panels are curved and unframed, you "read" Christ's life less like a nine-frame comic strip and more like a continuous scroll.

The story unfolds from left to right, beginning at the back near the stairs:

**1. Story of the Virgin Mary:** Featuring Mary's birth, the Annunciation, and Mary meeting Elizabeth (John the Baptist's mother), among other events.

**2. Nativity:** Mary lounges across a bed, unfazed by labor and delivery. Her pose is clearly inspired by carved Roman sarcophagi (which you can see in the Camposanto Cemetery), showing the dearly departed relaxing for eternity atop their coffins. Mary and the babe are surrounded by angels (above) and shepherds (right).

**3. Adoration of the Magi:** The Wise Men ride in with horses and camels.

**4. Presentation in the Temple:** On the left side, Joseph and Mary hold Baby Jesus between them. On the right side of the panel, Giovanni adds the next scene in the story, when the nuclear family gets on a donkey and escapes into Egypt.

**5. Massacre of the Innocents:** Herod (at the top) turns and gestures dramatically, ordering the slaughter of all babies. A mother (bottom left corner) grabs her head in despair. Giovanni uses thick lips and big noses to let the faces speak the full range of human emotions. The soldiers in the tangled chaos are almost freestanding.

**6. Kiss of Judas:** Jesus is betrayed by a kiss (left side).

**7. Crucifixion:** An emaciated Christ is mourned by his followers, who turn every which way. A Roman horseman (bottom right corner) rides directly away from us—an example of Renaissance "foreshortening" a century before its time.

**8. and 9. Last Judgment:** Christ sits in the center, the dead rise from their graves, and he sends the good to heaven (left) and the bad to hell (right).

Giovanni was a better pure sculptor than his father. Armed with more sophisticated chisels, he could cut even deeper into the marble, freeing heads from the stone backdrop, creating almost freestanding, 3-D figures.

If the pulpit seems a bit cluttered and asymmetrical, blame Mussolini. Originally, Giovanni built the pulpit standing on the right side of the altar (the traditional location). But after a massive fire in 1595 (when the roof burned), the pulpit was disassembled and stored away for three centuries. In 1926, they pulled it out of storage, reassembled it on this spot...and ended up with pieces left over (now in other museums), leading scholars to debate the authenticity of the current look.

• *Find the following two sights in the right (south) transept. First, in an ornate, colonnaded, Baroque chapel at the end of the transept, you'll see...*

❼ **St. Ranieri's Body:** In a glass-lined casket on the altar lies the skeleton of Pisa's patron saint, encased in silver at his head, with his hair shirt covering his body. The silver, mask-like face dates from the year 2000 and is as realistic as possible—derived from an FBI-style computer scan of Ranieri's skull.

Ranieri Scacceri (1117-1161) was born into the city of Pisa at its peak, when the Field of Miracles was a construction zone. The son of a rich sea-trader, Ranieri chose the life of a partyer and musician. One day, he met a friar who inspired him to go seek deeper meaning in Jerusalem. Leaving his riches and the easy life, he joined a monastery and put on a hair shirt. When he finally returned to Pisa, he preached and performed miracles.

Ranieri, honored in grand style on June 16 and 17, is cause for Pisa's biggest local event—the Luminara—celebrated along the Arno with tens of thousands of candles lining the buildings and floating on the river. The next day, rowing teams play a game of capture-the-flag, racing to a boat in the Arno and shimmying up a long rope to claim the prize.

• *Look on the wall to the left to find...*

❽ **Emperor Henry VII's Tomb:** Pause at the tomb of Holy Roman Emperor Henry VII, whose untimely death plunged Pisa into its centuries-long decline. Henry lies sleeping, arms folded, his head turned to the side, resting on a soft pillow. This German king (c. 1275-1313) invaded Italy and was welcomed by Pisans as a non-partisan leader who could bring peace to Italy's warring Guelphs and Ghibellines. In 1312, he was crowned emperor by the pope in Rome. He was preparing to polish off the last opposition when he caught a fever and died. No longer enjoying its connection with the Holy Roman Empire, Pisa declined.

• *Exit the church, turn left, and walk around to its back end (facing the Tower), where you'll find (under a canopy) the...*

❾ **Bronze Doors of St. Ranieri** (Porta San Ranieri): Designed by Bonanno Pisano (c. 1186)—who is thought by some historians to have been the Tower's first architect—the doors have 24 panels that show Christ's story using the same simple, skinny figures found in Byzantine icons. (The doors are actually copies; the originals are housed in the Duomo Museum.) Cast using the lost-wax technique, these doors were an inspiration for Lorenzo Ghiberti's bronze doors in Florence.

The story begins in the lower right panel ("Magis"), as the three Wise Men ride up a hill, heading toward...the panel to the

left, where tiny Baby Jesus lies in a manger while angels and shepherds look down from above. Above the manger scene, King Herod ("Erodi") sits under a canopy (in Pisan Romanesque style) and orders a soldier to raise his sword to kill all potential Messiahs. The terrified mother pulls her hair out. In the panel to the right, John the Baptist stands under a swaying palm and baptizes the adult Jesus, who wears the rippling River Jordan like a blanket. There are 20 more scenes which, if you were here as a medieval pilgrim, you wouldn't need this book to interpret.

• *If you're planning to visit the **Duomo Museum**—described later—now's a good time. It's right across from where you're standing (on the far side of the Leaning Tower), and it makes sense to see it while all that church art is fresh in your mind.*

*Otherwise, you can circle back around to the Duomo's front door and find the entrances to the next two sights—the **Baptistery** and **Camposanto Cemetery**.*

## THE REST OF THE FIELD OF MIRACLES

The Leaning Tower nearly steals the show from the massive cathedral, which muscles out the other sights. But don't neglect the

rest of the Field of Miracles: the Baptistery, Camposanto Cemetery, Museum of the Sinopias, and Duomo Museum.

To do all of these sights takes about two hours. Start with the Baptistery, located in front of

the Duomo's facade, and then head for Camposanto Cemetery, on the north side of the Field of Miracles. With sufficient interest and time, you can visit the Museum of the Sinopias, across the street from the Baptistery entrance. The Duomo Museum, behind the Tower, makes a good segue from a visit to the Duomo.

**Cost and Hours:** €7 for one sight, €10 for all of the sights (see the "Field of Miracles Tickets" sidebar earlier in this chapter). All four sights share the same schedule: daily April-Sept 9:00-20:00, Oct 9:00-19:00, Nov-Feb 10:00-17:00, March 9:00-18:00.

## ▲Baptistery

Pisa's Baptistery is Italy's biggest. It's interesting for its pulpit and interior ambience, and especially great for its acoustics (which are demonstrated twice an hour).

**Visiting the Baptistery:** The building is 180 feet tall—John the Baptist on top is almost eye-to-eye with the tourists looking out from the nearly 200-foot Leaning Tower. Notice that the Baptistery leans about 1.5 feet to the north, toward the Tower (which leans 15 feet to the south). The building (begun in 1153) is modeled on the circular-domed Church of the Holy Sepulchre in Jerusalem, seen by Pisan Crusaders who occupied Jerusalem in 1099.

From the outside, you see three distinct sections, which reflect the changing tastes of the years spent building it: simple Romanesque blind arches at the base (1153) and ornate Gothic spires and pointed arches in the middle (1250). The roofing looks mismatched, but was intentionally designed with red clay tiles on the seaward side and lead tiles (more prestigious but prone to corrosion) on the sheltered east side. The statues of the midsection are by Nicola Pisano (c. 1220-1278, Giovanni's father), who sculpted the pulpit inside.

**Interior:** Inside, it's simple, spacious, and baptized with light. Tall arches atop thin columns once again echo the Campo's architectural theme of arches above blank spaces. The columns encircle just a few pieces of religious furniture.

In the center sits the beautiful marble **octagonal font** (1246). A statue of the first Baptist, John the Baptist, stretches out his hand and says, "Welcome to my Baptistery." The font contains plenty of space for baptizing adults by immersion (the medieval custom), plus four wells for dunking babies.

Baptismal fonts—where sinners symbolically die and are re-born—are traditionally octagons. The shape suggests a cross (sym-bolizing Christ's death), and the eight sides represent the eighth day of Christ's ordeal, when he was resurrected. The font's sides, carved with inlaid multicolored marble, feature circle-in-a-square patterns, indicating the interlocking of heaven and earth. The cir-cles are studded with interesting faces, both human and animal. Behind the font, the altar features similar inlaid-marble work.

**Nicola Pisano's Pulpit:** On your left is the pulpit created by Nicola Pisano. It's the first authenticated (signed) work by the

"Giotto of sculpture," working in what came to be called the Renaissance style. The freestanding sculpture has classical columns, realistic people and animals, and 3-D effects in the carved panels.

The 15-foot-tall, hexagonal pulpit is the earliest (1260) and simplest of the four pulpits by the Pisano father-and-son team. Nicola, born in southern Italy, settled in Pisa, where he found steady work. Ten-year-old Giovanni learned the art of pulpit-making here at the feet of his father.

The speaker's platform stands on columns that rest on the backs of animals, representing Christianity's triumph over pagan-ism. The white Carrara-marble panels are framed by dark rose-colored marble, making a pleasant contrast.

The relief panels, with scenes from the life of Christ, are more readable than the Duomo pulpit. They show bigger, simpler figures in dark marble "frames." Read left to right, starting from the back:

*1. Nativity:* Mary reclines across a bed like a Roman matron, a pose inspired by Roman sarcophagi, which had been found around Pisa in Nicola's day (on display in the Camposanto Cemetery, de-scribed later).

*2. Adoration of the Magi:* The Three Kings kneel before Baby Jesus in simple profile; but notice the strong 3-D of the horses' heads coming straight out of the panel. Just below and to the left of this relief, note the small statue of Hercules. Some art historians consider this the first Renaissance carving. Sculpted in 1260—200 years before Michelangelo—it's a nude depiction of a pagan charac-ter, with a realistic body standing in a believable *contrapposto* pose. This was clearly inspired by carvings found on ancient sarcophagi.

*3. Presentation in the Temple:* It lacks the star of the scene, the

Christ Child, who was broken off, but on the panel's right side, a powerful, bearded man in a voluminous robe epitomizes Nicola's solemn classical style.

**4. Crucifixion:** Everyone faces either straight out or in profile; the Roman in front actually has to look back over his shoulder to taunt Jesus.

**5. Last Judgment:** Christ reigns over crowded, barely controlled chaos. The pulpit's lectern is an eagle clutching its prey, echoing the "triumph of Christianity" theme of the base.

**Acoustics:** Make a sound in here and it echoes for a good 10 seconds. A priest standing at the baptismal font could sing three tones within those 10 seconds—"Ave Maria"—and make a chord, singing haunting harmonies with himself. Today, a security guard sings every 30 minutes (on the hour and half-hour), starting when the doors open in the morning.

**Gallery:** You can climb 75 steps to the interior gallery (midway up) for an impressive view back down on the baptismal font. Try to be here when the guard sings.

### ▲Camposanto Cemetery

Until people started getting excited about the Leaning Tower around 1900, the big attraction in Pisa was its dreamy and exquisite cemetery, the Camposanto. Lined with faint frescoes, this centuries-old cemetery on the north side of the Campo is famous for its "Holy Land" dirt, reputedly brought here from the Middle East in the 12th century. Until 1278, tombs littered the ground around the cathedral. Then things were cleaned up and

the tombs were gathered into the Camposanto (built from 1278 to 1465). Highlights are the building's cloistered interior courtyard, some ancient sarcophagi, and the large 14th-century fresco, *The Triumph of Death.*

**◐ Self-Guided Tour:** Even though the Camposanto was bombed in World War II, it remains a powerful (if currently underappreciated) visit.

• *Past the ticket-taker, head straight out the walkway to the middle of the grassy...*

**Courtyard:** The delightful open-air courtyard is surrounded by an arcade with intricately carved tracery in the arches. The courtyard's grass grows on special dirt (said to turn a body into bones in a single day) shipped here by returning Crusaders from Jerusalem's Mount Calvary, where Christ was crucified. If you

PISA

couldn't be buried in the Holy Land, you could be buried in dirt from the Holy Land. People believed that this technicality would fast-track you into heaven.

• *Now head back into the...*

**Arcade:** The arcade floor is paved with the **coats of arms** of some 600 dearly departed Pisans. In death all are equal—the most humble peasant (or tourist) can walk upon these VIP tombstones. Today much of the marble flooring is scarred, the result of lead melting from the roof during WWII bombing.

Displayed in the arcade are dozens of ancient Roman **sarcophagi.** These coffins, which originally held dead Romans, were reused by medieval big shots. In anticipation of death, a wealthy Pisan would shop around, choose a good sarcophagus, and chip his message into it. When he died, his marble box was placed with the others around the exterior of the cathedral. Great sculptors such as Nicola and Giovanni Pisano passed them daily, gaining inspiration.

• *Turn left from where you entered and circle the courtyard clockwise, noticing traces of fresco on the bare-brick walls. (We'll see some reconstructed frescoes later.)*

As you round the corner, the huge **chains** you see hanging on the west wall once stretched across the mouth of Pisa's harbor

as a defense. Then Genoa attacked, broke the chains, carried them off as a war trophy, and gave them to Pisa's archrival Florence. After unification (1861), the chains were returned to Pisa by the people of Florence as a token of friendship.

On the wall in the next corner, what looks like a big, faded **bull's-eye** is the politically correct 14th-century view of the universe—everything held by Christ, with the earth clearly in the center.

Below that is the cemetery's oldest object, an ochre-colored Greek tombstone. This **stele,** dating from the time of Alexander the Great (fourth century BC), shows a woman (seated) who's just died giving birth. As she's about to pull the veil of death over her face, she bids her child goodbye.

In the floor 10 yards away, by the corner of the courtyard, is a **pavement slab** dedicated to an American artist, Deane Keller. After serving in Italy during World War II as one of the "Monuments Men," he helped rebuild the Camposanto Cemetery and restore its frescoes.

PISA

• *Heading along the long north wall, you'll begin to see some...*

**Restored Frescoes:** After decorating these corridors for 600 years, the frescoes of Camposanto Cemetery were badly damaged in World War II. By the summer of 1944, Allied troops had secured much of southern Italy and pushed Nazi forces to the north bank of the Arno. German Field Marshal Kesselring dug in at Pisa, surrounded by the US Army's 91st Infantry. Germans and Americans lobbed artillery shells at each other. (The

Americans even considered blowing up the Leaning Tower—the "Tiltin' Hilton" was suspected to be the German lookout point.) Most of the Field of Miracles was miraculously unscathed, but the Camposanto took a direct hit from a Yankee incendiary grenade. It melted the lead-covered arcade roof and peeled historic frescoes from the walls—one of many tragic art losses of World War II. The Americans liberated the city on September 2 and rebuilt the Camposanto.

The frescoes have been under restoration ever since. Along these walls, you'll see the ones that have been returned to their original position.

• *At the far end of this corridor, turn right. Continuing along this short side of the courtyard, you come face-to-face with the masterpiece fresco called...*

**The Triumph of Death:** This 1,000-square-foot fresco (c. 1340, by a 14th-century master) captures late-medieval Europe's concern with death in a fascinating composition.

In the lower left, a parade of wealthy (finely dressed) and powerful (some with crowns) hedonists are riding gaily through the countryside when they come across a hermit-monk who blocks their path and shows them three corpses in coffins. Confronted with death, they each react differently—a woman puts her hand thoughtfully to her chin, a man holds his nose against the stench, while a horse leans in for a better whiff. Above them, a monk scours the Bible for the meaning of death.

The center features a pile of corpses—people both rich and poor—a reminder that all are equal in death. Nearby are miserable lepers. With stubs for arms, they call out to Lady Death to end their wretched lives. But Death has her eyes on the privileged youth in the next scene.

In the right half of the painting, young people gather in a garden to play music (symbolizing earthly pleasure), oblivious to the death around them. The sky is filled with winged demons fighting winged angels for the eternal destiny of souls (shown as babies).

This is just one of four big frescoes: Next to *The Triumph of Death* are *The Last Judgment*, the extremely graphic *Hell*, and *The Pious Life* (a handbook for avoiding hell). A posted information plaque near each fresco describes the intense scenes.

• *Having completed your circle, head back outside.*

**Piazza:** Stepping into the piazza, consider how this richly artistic but utilitarian square fit into the big picture of life. The ensemble around you includes the Baptistery, the cathedral, the bell tower, the hospital (present-day Museum of the Sinopias), and the cemetery you just visited.

## Museum of the Sinopias (Museo delle Sinopie)

Housed in a 13th-century hospital, this museum features the original preliminary sketches (sinopias) for the Camposanto's frescoes. If you loved *The Triumph of Death* and others in the Camposanto, or if you're interested in fresco technique, this museum is worthwhile. If not, you'll wonder why you're here.

**Visiting the Museum:** Whether or not you pay to go in, you can watch two free videos in the entry lobby that serve to orient you to the square: a 15-minute story of the Tower, its tilt, and its fix. Good students might want to come here first for this orientation.

Once inside the turnstile, the stars of this museum are the sinopias: sketches made in red paint directly on the wall, designed to guide the making of the final colored fresco. The master always did the sinopia himself. It was a way for him (and for those who paid for the work) to see exactly how the scene would look in its designated spot. If it wasn't quite right, the master changed a detail here and there. When satisfied with the design, the master and his team covered the sinopia with a thin layer of plaster and, while it was still wet, quickly filled in the color and details, producing the final frescoes (now on display at the Camposanto). These sinopias—never meant to be seen—were uncovered by the bombing and restoration of the Camposanto and brought here.

The museum presents several sinopias in a one-way route. Just past the ticket-taker, you'll see the multiringed, earth-centric, Ptolemaic universe of the *Theological Cosmography*. Continue to your right to find a faint *Crucifixion* and scenes from the Old Testament. At the end of the long hall, climb the stairs to the next floor to find more red-tinted sinopias: *The Triumph of Death*, *The Last Judgment*, and *Hell*. At the very top are colorful etchings of the frescoes.

## Duomo Museum (Museo dell'Opera del Duomo)

Near the Tower is the entrance to the Duomo Museum, which houses many of the original statues and much of the artwork that once adorned the Campo's buildings (where copies stand today), notably the statues by Nicola and Giovanni Pisano. You'll circle through a modern space with two manageable floors of well-presented artifacts, all described in English. While an interesting deep dive, this museum isn't a "must" on a casual visit.

**Visiting the Museum:** Starting on the ground floor, you'll see the Duomo's original 12th-century bronze doors of St. Ranieri, designed by Bonanno Pisano, with scenes from the life of Jesus (described at the end of the Duomo tour, earlier). Just beyond, items from Islamic artisans in today's Spain include a bronze griffin (sort of a medieval jackalope). You'll continue through rooms of weather-worn stone statues and busts (from the Pisanos), which once ringed the outside of the Baptistery, and a piece of the *gradule*—a row of carved human heads in boxes, which used to surround the base of the cathedral. The room dedicated to Giovanni Pisano features the beautiful stone *Madonna del Colloquio* (1280-85), in which an ethereal Mary solemnly exchanges gazes with Baby Jesus in her arms. You'll see more by Giovanni, then works by an entirely different sculptor, who became known as Andrea Pisano (no relation, but from the same city—Pisa). You may notice how these works (from the 1340s) begin to show more influence from France; the following rooms continue the chronological flow, bringing us up to the Renaissance. The giant, detailed model of the Leaning Tower was lovingly carved from alabaster by Volterra artisans in 2007.

Up on the first floor, the fine inlaid woodwork once graced the choir stalls of the sacristy. The "Cathedral Treasures" room features Giovanni Pisano's small, carved-ivory *Madonna and Child*. Mary leans back gracefully to admire Baby Jesus, her pose matching the original shape of what she's carved from—an elephant's tusk. From here, you'll pass through rooms of precious and delicate vestments; silver and gold liturgical aids (candelabras, platters, chalices, monstrances, and bishops' staves); two long scrolls with a special Easter hymn (one from the 11th century, the other from the 13th); and illuminated manuscripts. Be sure to step out to the upper gallery (with a fine, restful, and scenic café) for some fresh air and views of the Tower and the Duomo beyond.

## OTHER SIGHTS IN PISA
### City Wall Walk

Pisa is ringed by walls dating back to the 12th century. You can walk a two-mile stretch that connects the river and the Field of Miracles, where the wall walk begins in the corner northwest of the Baptistery. Buy your ticket and ascend, first heading straight ahead to enjoy the views of the Campo above the fray. Turning around, follow the walls as far as you like, passing residential areas and a quieter, greener side of Pisa. You can continue to the river and exit there, or return to the entry, where you'll be rewarded with some of the best, most uncrowded photo-ops of the Tower (€3, daily 9:00-19:00, shorter hours off-season, +39 050 098 7480).

### Museo Nazionale di San Matteo

In a former convent on the river, this art museum displays early-medieval to 15th-century works, including sculptures, illuminated manuscripts, and paintings on wood by pre- and early-Renaissance masters Martini, Masaccio, and others. It's a fine collection—especially its painted wood crucifixes—and gives you a chance to see Pisan innovation in 11th-to-13th-century art, before Florence took the lead.

**Cost and Hours:** €5, Tue-Sat 8:30-19:00, Sun until 13:00, closed Mon, near Piazza San Paolo at Lungarno Mediceo, a 5-minute walk upriver (east) from the main bridge, +39 050 541 865.

# Sleeping in Pisa

Pisa is an easy side trip from Florence or Lucca, either of which is a more all-around pleasant place to stay. But there's more to Pisa than the Tower, and if you want time to experience it, consider a night here. To locate these hotels, see the "Pisa" map, earlier.

## NORTH OF THE RIVER, NEAR THE TOWER

**$$$ Relais dei Mercanti** is tucked away in the historic core of the city, on a lively square that throbs on Friday and Saturday. The six rooms are bright, modern, and well appointed, with shiny marble floors and bathrooms (air-con, Piazza Sant'Omobono 16, +39 050 520 2135, www.relaisdeimercanti.it, relaisdeimercanti@gmail.com).

**$$ Hotel Royal Victoria** is like sleeping in a museum. Overlooking the Arno River, it's been run by the Piegaja family since 1837 (though it was a hotel long before that). Its tiled hallways and 38 creaky, antique-filled rooms with bygone plumbing and chipped plaster may not be for everybody. But with the elegant ambience of a long-gone era, it's ideal for romantics who missed out on the Grand Tour. The location—midway between the Tower and Pisa Centrale train station—is the most atmospheric of my listings (though it faces a busy riverfront road—river views come with rumbling traffic). The proud owner, Nicola Piegaja, sees your patronage as a contribution to save a piece of history (RS%, family rooms, air-con in most rooms, elevator, tight pay parking garage, lush communal terrace, Lungarno Pacinotti 12, +39 050 940 111, www.royalvictoria.it, post@royalvictoria.it).

**$$ Hotel Pisa Tower** has 12 rooms overlooking the noisy, souvenir-stand square just outside the gate to the Field of Miracles, along a busy street. But the prices are reasonable, and the proximity to the Tower is enticing (breakfast extra, family rooms, air-con, pay parking, Piazza Manin 9, +39 050 550 146, www.hotelpisatower. com, info@hotelpisatower.com).

**$ Casa San Tommaso** has 22 classic-feeling, homey rooms on a quiet back lane about a five-minute walk from the Tower (air-con, Via San Tommaso 13, +39 050 830 782, www.santommasopisa. com, info@santommasopisa.com, Giuliano).

**$ Hotel Helvetia,** a friendly, no-frills, clean, and quiet inn just 100 yards from the Tower, rents 29 economical rooms over four floors. Ask them to show you the "biggest cactus in Tuscany" in their garden courtyard...it really is (cheaper rooms with shared bath, family suites, no breakfast, ceiling fans, no elevator, Via Don G. Boschi 31, +39 050 553 084, www.pensionehelvetiapisa.com, helvetiapisatower@gmail.com, Micaele and Sandra).

## SOUTH OF THE RIVER, NEAR THE TRAIN STATION

This zone is far less atmospheric than the zone near the Tower—with a lot of concrete, congestion, and loitering. Stay here only if you value the convenience of proximity to the station.

**$$ Hotel Alessandro della Spina,** run by Pio and family, has 16 elegant and colorful rooms, each named after a flower (air-con, elevator, pay parking, an eight-minute walk from the train station at Via Alessandro della Spina 5, +39 050 502 777, www. hoteldellaspina.it, info@hoteldellaspina.it, Louisa).

**$ Stazione22** is a tidy B&B just across the piazza from the train station, perfect for a quick overnight or if your luggage is heavy. Friendly Alessandra tends her four budget rooms with a youthful warmth (some street noise, family room, breakfast extra at nearby bar, air-con, elevator, Piazza della Stazione 22, +39 327 857 5259, stazione22@gmail.com).

# Eating in Pisa

## A QUICK LUNCH CLOSE TO THE TOWER

The Via Santa Maria tourist strip is pedestrianized and lined with touristy eateries. From the Tower, walk past Grand Hotel Duomo to avoid the worst of the tourist traps. From there on you can find a decent (if overpriced) sandwich, pizza, or salad at any number of places. Of these, **$$ Ristorante-Pizzeria La Torre** (Via Santa Maria 86) has a good reputation.

**$$ Pizzeria al Bagno di Nerone,** a short walk from the Tower, is particularly popular with students. Belly up to the bar and grab a slice to go, or sit in their small dining room for a whole pie. Try the *cecina*, a crêpe-like chickpea flatbread (Wed-Mon 12:00-14:30 & 17:45-22:30, closed Tue, Largo Carlo Fedeli 26, +39 050 551 085).

## REAL MEALS DEEPER IN THE TOWN CENTER

These places are within about a 10-to-15-minute walk from the Tower, near the river, and several are within a few steps of the old Renaissance-style market loggia, Piazza delle Vettovaglie. For my money, unless you're in a huge rush, it's well worth the extra walk for a better-quality, better-value, more memorable meal in this area.

**$$ La Vineria di Piazza** is a quintessential little Tuscan trattoria tucked under the arcades of Piazza delle Vettovaglie. The menu changes with the seasons, and their wine selection is high quality. Sit in the elegantly simple interior or out at tables facing the market (lunch daily 12:00-15:00, dinner Wed-Sat 20:00-23:00, Piazza delle Vettovaglie 14, +39 050 520 7846).

**$$$ Antica Trattoria il Campano,** just off the market square, has a typically Tuscan menu and a candlelit, stay-awhile atmosphere. The ground floor, surrounded by wine bottles, is cozier, while the upstairs—with high wood-beam ceilings—is classier (nightly 19:30-22:45, open Sat-Sun for lunch in high season, Via Cavalca 19, +39 050 580 585, Giovanna).

**$$$ Osteria dei Cavalieri,** on a quiet back street just off Piazza dei Cavalieri (and a bit closer to the Tower than the other listings here), seems pleasantly oblivious to the tourists and students that abound in nearby streets. The ambience is classic yet relaxed and warm, and the short menu of artfully presented local dishes—some with modern flair—is fun to explore (Mon-Tue and Thu-Sat 12:00-15:30 & 19:30-22:20, Wed 19:30-22:20 only, closed Sun, Via San Frediano 16, +39 050 580 858).

**$ Caffetteria BetsaBea** is basic and handy for takeaway meals, has good seating on the square, whips up hearty and creative salads—which you design with their interactive menu—and is popular for its *aperitivo* happy hour (Mon-Sat 8:00-18:30, closed Sun, Piazza San Frediano 6).

**$ Il Montino** is a rambunctious favorite for tasty, no-frills pizza. Tucked behind a church in a grubby corner deep in the old center, it has a loyal following among students. Enjoy full pies in the *nuovo rustico* interior or out on the alley (Mon-Sat 11:30-15:00 & 17:30-22:30, closed Sun, Vicolo del Monte 1, +39 050 598 695).

**$$ Orzo Bruno**—*il birrifico artigiano* ("the artisan brew-pub")—is a lively, rollicking brew hall filled with Pisans of all ages enjoying rock, jazz, and blues, with seven different microbrews (including a rotating tap) and a simple menu of sandwiches and cold cuts (nightly 19:00-late, a block off Borgo Stretto at Via Case Dipinte 6, +39 050 578 802).

**$$ La Mescita,** just off the market square, serves up pasta and meat dishes in a jazz-inspired, artsy interior (daily 12:30-14:30 & 19:30-23:00, Via Domenico Cavalca 2, +39 050 314 4680).

## Pisa Connections

Pisa has excellent connections by train, bus, or car. The busy airport (popular with discount airlines) is practically downtown.

**Side-Tripping to (or from) Lucca:** Pisa and Lucca are well connected by train and by bus (both options are around €4), making a half-day side trip from one town to the other particularly easy.

The **train** takes about half as long as the bus (about 25 minutes compared to 45-55 minutes)—but getting between the Centrale train station and the Field of Miracles is time-consuming. Here's a time-saving tip: Check if your train also stops at the Pisa San Rossore station, less than a 10-minute walk from the Field of Miracles. From the tacky souvenir zone just outside the gate, cross the busy street and continue straight ahead along Via Andrea Pisano. After two blocks, you'll see the gray gateway to the train station on your right.

A handy **bus** connects the Field of Miracles with Lucca's Piazzale Giuseppe Verdi in about 45-55 minutes ("S.M. Guidice" is faster than "Ripafratta"; runs about hourly Mon-Sat, fewer on Sun, www.at-bus.it). To find the bus stops, from the Baptistery end of the Field of Miracles, walk straight out the gate to the edge of the souvenir-stand square. Along the busy road, the bus stop to Lucca is on the corner on your right (on the Tower side of the road, in front of the bakery). Buy tickets at the machine that's kitty-corner

across the street—straight ahead and a bit to the left (see "Pisa's Field of Miracles" map on page 448). You can also catch this bus at Pisa Centrale train station.

**From Pisa Centrale Station by Train to: Florence** (2/hour, 45-75 minutes), **Livorno** (2/hour, 20 minutes), **Rome** (1-2/hour, 3 hours, some change in Florence), **La Spezia** (about hourly, 1.5 hours), **Monterosso** (hourly, 1-1.5 hours), **Siena** (2/hour, 1.5 hours, some change at Empoli), **Lucca** (1-2/hour, 30 minutes, many also stop at Pisa San Rossore station).

**By Car:** The drive between Pisa and Florence is that rare case where the regular highway (free, more direct, and at least as fast) is a better deal than the autostrada.

**By Plane:** Pisa's handy **Galileo Galilei Airport**—just two miles from the train station—handles both international and domestic flights (code: PSA, +39 050 849 300, www.pisa-airport. com). The Pisa Mover train offers an easy connection to Pisa Centrale train station, where you can catch the LAM Rossa bus—see "Arrival in Pisa," earlier—to the Leaning Tower (€5, daily 6:00-24:00, 5-minute trip, www.pisa-mover.com). You can taxi into town for about €10.

Pisa's airport is handy for other towns as well: To reach **Lucca, Florence,** the **Cinque Terre,** or other destinations in Italy, take the Pisa Mover to Pisa Centrale train station and connect from there. There may be direct bus connections from Pisa Airport directly to Florence's Santa Maria Novella train station—check online or ask around.

# LUCCA

Surrounded by well-preserved ramparts, layered with history, alternately quaint and urbane, Lucca charms its visitors. The city is a paradox. Though it hasn't been involved in a war since 1430, it is Italy's most impressive fortress city, encircled by a perfectly intact wall. Most cities tear down their walls to make way for modern traffic, but Lucca's effectively keeps out both traffic and, it seems, the stress of the modern world. Locals are very protective of their wall, which they enjoy like a community roof garden.

Lucca has no single monumental sight to attract tourists—it's simply a uniquely human and undamaged, never-bombed city. Romanesque churches and shady piazzas filled with soccer-playing children seem to be around every corner. Perhaps it's a blessing that Lucca has no Uffizi or Leaning Tower—that lack of big-league sights keeps away the most obnoxious slice of tourism: people who just want to tick an item off their bucket list. Instead, refreshingly untrampled Lucca seems to attract travelers who want to melt into the local lifestyle for a few days.

Lucca is charming and well preserved, and even its touristic center—the mostly traffic-free old town—feels more local than touristy (aside from a few cruise excursions from nearby Livorno that pass through each day). Refreshingly, the city lacks dodgy vendors selling junk on every corner. While many cities throughout Tuscany are tagged by Florentine lions and Medici balls, Lucca is proudly free of those symbols of conquest. The city is big enough to have its own heritage and pride, yet small enough that it seems like the Lucchesi (loo-KAY-zee) all went to school together. Simply put, Lucca has elegance and plenty of reasons to be proud.

## PLANNING YOUR TIME

Lucca is easy to enjoy. With a day in town, start with my self-guided Lucca Walk and spend the afternoon biking (or strolling) atop the wall, popping in on whatever other sights interest you, and browsing. Music lovers enjoy the evening Puccini concert. The busy sightseer can consider visiting Pisa's Field of Miracles (with the Leaning Tower), an easy half-day side trip away by train (to Pisa San Rossore station in under 30 minutes) or bus (from downtown Lucca to the Leaning Tower in under an hour).

# Orientation to Lucca

Lucca (population 87,000, with roughly 10,000 living within the town walls) is big enough to be engaging but small enough to be manageable. Everything of interest to a visitor is within the 2.5-mile-long city wall; it takes just 20 minutes to walk from one end of the old town to the other. The train station sits south of the wall (just beyond the cathedral), and the bus to and from Pisa stops just inside the western tip. My self-guided walk traces the main thoroughfares through town; venturing beyond these streets, you realize Lucca is bigger than it first seems, but its back streets are very sleepy. While the core of the town is based on an old Roman grid street plan, the surrounding areas—especially near the circular footprint of the amphitheater—are more confusing. This, combined with tall houses and a lack of consistent signage, makes Lucca easy to get lost in. Pick up the town map at your hotel and use it.

## TOURIST INFORMATION

Lucca's helpful main TI is on Piazzale Giuseppe Verdi (daily 9:30-18:30, Nov-March until 16:30, WC, +39 0583 583 150, www.turismo.lucca.it). A smaller TI is close to the train station (to the right along the busy road, on Piazza Curtatone; Tue-Sat 9:30-13:30, Tue and Thu also 14:30-17:30, closed Sun-Mon, +39 0583 442 213).

## ARRIVAL IN LUCCA

**By Train:** Lucca's little station sits just outside its walls, to the south. Bag storage is available at the Tourist Center Lucca shop on the square in front of the station (see "Helpful Hints" for details). To reach the city center from the train station, walk toward the walls and head left, to the entry at Porta San Pietro. Or, if you don't mind steps, go straight ahead and follow the path through

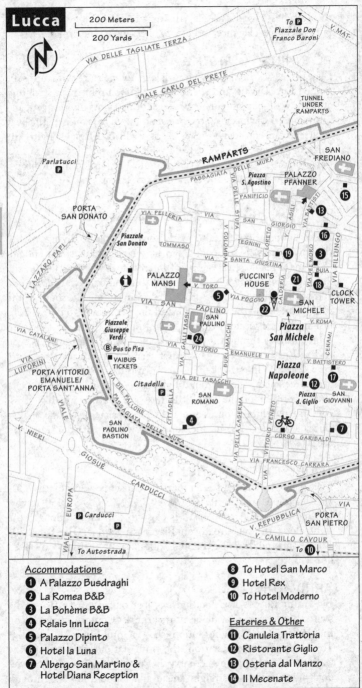

# Lucca

200 Meters
200 Yards

N

VIA DELLE TAGLIATE TERZA

VIALE CARLO DEL PRETE

To Piazzale Don Franco Baroni

V. MAT.

TUNNEL UNDER RAMPARTS

SAN FREDIANO

RAMPARTS

PASSAGIATA DELLE MURA

Parlatucci P

Piazza S. Agostino

PALAZZO PFANNER

15

PORTA SAN DONATO

VIA PELLERIA

VIA

PANIFICIO

VIA BATTISTI

13

VIA ASILI

Piazzale San Donato

TOMMASO

V. COLOMBANO

SAN GIORGIO

V. LORETO

16

VIA DEL MORO

3

V. LAZZARO PAPI

TEGNINI

VIA SANTA GIUSTINA

19

BUIA

VIA FILLUNGO

PALAZZO MANSI

V. TORO

PUCCINI'S HOUSE

CALDERIA

21

18

CLOCK TOWER

5

VIA POGGIO

22

SAN MICHELE

Piazzale Giuseppe Verdi

VIA SAN

PAOLINO

SAN PAULINO

24

Piazza San Michele

V. ROMA

CENAMI

B Bus to Pisa

VAIBUS TICKETS

VIA CATALANI

VIA LUPORINI

PORTA VITTORIO EMANUELE/ PORTA SANT'ANNA

Citadella

VIA CALLI TASSI

VIA BURLAMACCHI

VITTORIO EMANUELE II

VIA DEI TABACCHI

Piazza Napoleone

V. BATTISTERO

17

VIA DEL FALLONE

PASSAGIATA DELLE MURA

Piazza d. Giglio

12

SAN GIOVANNI

CITADELLA P

SAN ROMANO

VIALE

V. NIERI

SAN PAOLINO BASTION

4

VIA DELLA CASERMA

VIA VITTORIO VENETO

CORSO GARIBALDI

7

GIOSUE CARDUCCI

VIA FRANCESCO CARRARA

EUROPA

P Carducci

P

VIA

V. REPUBBLICA

PORTA SAN PIETRO

To Autostrada

V. CAMILLO CAVOUR

To 10

## Accommodations

1 A Palazzo Busdraghi

2 La Romea B&B

3 La Bohème B&B

4 Relais Inn Lucca

5 Palazzo Dipinto

6 Hotel la Luna

7 Albergo San Martino & Hotel Diana Reception

8 To Hotel San Marco

9 Hotel Rex

10 To Hotel Moderno

## Eateries & Other

11 Canuleia Trattoria

12 Ristorante Giglio

13 Osteria dal Manzo

14 Il Mecenate

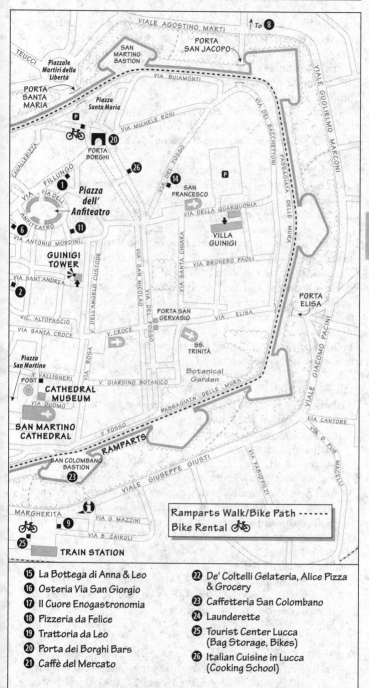

LUCCA

**Ramparts Walk/Bike Path** ------
**Bike Rental** &#x6274;

| | |
|---|---|
| ⑮ La Bottega di Anna & Leo | ㉒ De' Coltelli Gelateria, Alice Pizza & Grocery |
| ⑯ Osteria Via San Giorgio | ㉓ Caffetteria San Colombano |
| ⑰ Il Cuore Enogastronomia | ㉔ Launderette |
| ⑱ Pizzeria da Felice | ㉕ Tourist Center Lucca (Bag Storage, Bikes) |
| ⑲ Trattoria da Leo | |
| ⑳ Porta dei Borghi Bars | ㉖ Italian Cuisine in Lucca (Cooking School) |
| ㉑ Caffè del Mercato | |

the moat-like park to go up and over the wall. Taxis wait out front; otherwise, try calling +39 0583 1745 or +39 0583 164 6464; a ride from the station to Piazza dell'Anfiteatro costs about €8.

**By Bus:** Buses from Pisa, Viareggio, and nearby villages arrive just inside the walls, at the western end of town on Piazzale Giuseppe Verdi (near the TI).

**By Car:** Don't drive within the walls: Much of the center of Lucca is a limited traffic zone (€90 fine). You'll know when you're about to enter it when you see the letters "ZTL" painted on the road.

If you're making a quick, targeted visit to town and don't mind paying extra for proximity to the sights, consider **Parking Citadella**—a tree-lined lot just inside the walls (but outside the ZTL zone) in the southwestern part of town (€1.50/hour).

For longer stays, it's cheaper to park outside the city walls. Parking is always free in **Piazzale Don Franco Baroni,** a 10-minute walk north of the walls. Two pay lots are also nearby: **Parking Carducci,** southwest of town (this is the first lot you hit after leaving the autostrada) and **Parking Parlatucci,** to the northwest. Or park outside the gates near the train station or on the boulevard surrounding the city (pay and display). Overnight parking (20:00-8:00) on city streets and in city lots outside the walls is usually free; check with your hotelier to be sure. For more on parking in Lucca, see www.parcheggilucca.it.

## HELPFUL HINTS

**Markets:** Lucca's atmospheric markets are worth visiting. On the third weekend of the month, one of the largest **antique markets** in Italy sprawls in the blocks between Piazza Antelminelli and Piazza San Giovanni (8:00-19:00). The last weekend of the month, local artisans sell **arts and crafts** around town, mainly near the cathedral (8:00-19:00). At the **general market,** held Wednesdays and Saturdays on Piazza Don Franco Baroni, you'll find produce and household goods (8:30-13:00).

**Shops and Museums Alert:** City-run museums are often closed Sunday and/or Monday. Most shops close Sunday and Monday mornings.

**Puccini Concerts:** San Giovanni Church hosts themed one-hour concerts featuring a pianist and singers performing works by hometown composer Giacomo Puccini (€25 at the door, €20 in advance—buy tickets at the venue, the TI, or possibly your hotel; April-Oct nightly at 19:00, Thu-Sat off-season, www.puccinielasualucca.com).

**Festivals:** Lucca does festivals with gusto. The Lucca Classica festival offers lots of free concerts (four days in early May, www.luccaclassica.it). On September 13 and 14, the city celebrates

Volto Santo ("Holy Face"), with a procession of the treasured local crucifix and a fair in Piazza Antelminelli. The massive Comics & Games festival fills Lucca with crazy-for-comics characters over the last weekend in October.

**Baggage Storage:** Train travelers can store bags at **Tourist Center Lucca,** on the left side of the square at #203 as you exit the train station (€5/day, also rents bikes, daily 9:00-19:00, Nov-March until 18:00). If arriving by bus at the other end of town, ask at the TI if there are any options.

**Laundry:** The self-service **Lavanderia la Perfetta** is near the west end of town, between Piazza San Michele and the TI (daily 7:00-22:30, Via Galli Tassi 12).

**Bike Rental:** A one-hour rental (ID required) gives you time for two leisurely loops around the ramparts. Several places with identical prices cluster around Piazza Santa Maria (€4/first hour, then €2/hour, €16/all day, most shops also rent tandem bikes and bike carts, helmets available on request, daily about 9:00-19:00 or until sunset). Try these easygoing shops: **Antonio Poli** (Piazza Santa Maria 42, +39 0583 493 787, Cristiana) and, right next to it, **Cicli Bizzarri** (Piazza Santa Maria 32, +39 0583 496 682, Australian Dely). At the south end, at Porta San Pietro, you'll find **Chronò**  (Corso Garibaldi 93, +39 0583 490 591, www.chronobikes. com). At the train station, **Tourist Center Lucca** is good.

**Taxi:** A taxi from Lucca to Pisa's Leaning Tower costs €45. Drivers are also available for transfers (€80 to Pisa airport) or for half- and full-day unguided tours (up to 8 people, +39 0583 1745 or +39 0583 164 6464, www.luccataxi.it).

**Local Magazine:** For insights into American and British expat life and listings of concerts, markets, festivals, and other special events, pick up a copy of the *Grapevine* (€2.50), available at some newsstands.

**Cooking Class:** Gianluca Pardini runs a cooking school called **Italian Cuisine in Lucca,** where you can learn to prepare and then eat a four-course Tuscan meal. Depending on how many others attend, the price ranges from €70 to €100 per person. This is great for groups of four or more (3-hour lesson plus time to dine, includes wine, reserve at least 2 days in advance, Via della Zecca 37, +39 347 678 7447, www.italiancuisine.it, info@italiancuisine.it).

# Tours in Lucca

## Walking Tours

The **TI** offers two-hour guided city walks in English and Italian, departing from the office on Piazzale Giuseppe Verdi (€10, plus €3 to enter cathedral at the end, daily April-Oct at 14:00, weekends only in winter, +39 0583 583 150). On summer weekends, they run a slightly different tour in the mornings that includes the cathedral (€15, meet at Piazza San Michele). For either tour, confirm the latest schedule and book at the TI.

The **Andante...ma con Brio Music tour** celebrates Lucca's musical heritage with a music-loving local guide, visits to the Teatro del Giglio and the Puccini Museum, and musical clips along the way (€15 includes theater and museum entry, smart to book ahead, mid-April-Oct Sat at 11:00, 2.5 hours, in Italian and English, meet at Teatro del Giglio, turislucca@turislucca.com, +39 0583 342 404).

**Tuscany Like a Local** offers three-hour, casual, youthful, stream-of-consciousness rambles through town with stops in small bars or delis. These small-group tours are English-only and led by proud locals who love sharing Lucchese culture—past and present (basic food tour—€65, at 10:00; "bike and bites" tour—€85, at 14:00; *aperitivo* walk—€71, at 17:30; RS%—15 percent discount if you book direct by email, www.tuscanylocaltours.com, info@tuscanylocaltours.com, Chiara and Luca).

## Local Guide

**Gabriele Calabrese** knows and shares his hometown well. He was a big help in creating the Lucca Walk in this chapter, and with his guidance you'll go even deeper into the city (€130/3 hours, by foot or bike, +39 0583 342 404, mobile +39 347 788 0667, www.turislucca.com, turislucca@turislucca.com).

# Lucca Walk

This hour-long self-guided walk (not counting time at the sights) connects Lucca's main points of interest by way of its most entertaining streets.

• *Start right in the heart of things, at Lucca's main square. For the classic view of the circular square, stand at the east end of the oval at #29.*

## ❶ Piazza dell'Anfiteatro

The architectural ghost of a Roman amphitheater can be felt in the delightful Piazza dell'Anfiteatro. With the fall of Rome, the theater (which seated 10,000 and sat just outside the original rectangular city walls) was gradually cannibalized for its stones and inhabited by

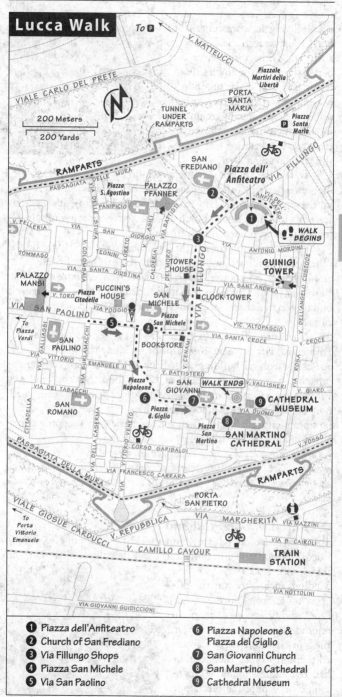

**LUCCA**

## Lucca Walk

- **1** Piazza dell'Anfiteatro
- **2** Church of San Frediano
- **3** Via Fillungo Shops
- **4** Piazza San Michele
- **5** Via San Paolino
- **6** Piazza Napoleone & Piazza del Giglio
- **7** San Giovanni Church
- **8** San Martino Cathedral
- **9** Cathedral Museum

people living in a mishmash of huts. The huts were cleared away at the end of the 19th century to better show off the town's illustrious past and make one purely secular square (every other square is dominated by a church) for the town market. The modern street level is nine feet above the original arena floor.

Today, the square is a circle of touristy shops, galleries, mediocre restaurants, and inviting al fresco cafés. For a cheap seat on the square, buy a gelato at **Gelateria Anfiteatro**—it's made by Lorenzo under an ancient arch at #18. You're welcome to nurse it for the takeout price at one of their tables.

Leave the amphitheater through the arch at #29. Once on the other side, turn back, look up to study the exterior of the Roman amphitheater, and notice how medieval scavengers transformed it. Barbarians didn't know how to make bricks. But they could recycle building material and stack stones in order to camp out in Roman ruins.

Now turn left and begin circling counterclockwise along Via Anfiteatro. For the next 100 yards or so, study the stonework and see how medieval buildings filled the ancient arches. As you approach the bigger cross street, at #2 on the left is the tempting Pizzicheria la Grotta *salumi* shop, with lots of gifty edibles—worth popping into for a peek at local specialties (like hay-covered pecorino from mountain farms). Then you reach the busy shopping street, Via Fillungo.

• *Turn left and walk a block down Via Fillungo. On the left, at #126, check out Zizzi (with a busy loom, weaving totally Italian scarves). Then go right and cross a little square to the big church with a fine mosaic facade.*

## ❷ Church of San Frediano

This impressive church was built in 1112 by the pope to one-up Lucca's bishop and his spiffy cathedral (which we'll see later on this walk). Lucca was the first Mediterranean stop on the pilgrim route from northern Europe, and the pope wanted to remind pilgrims that the action, the glory, and the papacy awaited them in Rome. Therefore, he had the church made "Romanesque." The pure marble facade

frames an early Christian Roman-style mosaic of Christ with his 12 apostles.

**Cost and Hours:** €3, daily 9:30-17:00, Piazza San Frediano.

**Visiting the Church:** Inside, stand at the back (under a fine 16th-century pipe organ) and survey the classic basilica plan. The arches lope rhythmically to the altar (reminding me of the victory animation when you win a computer solitaire game). The 40 powerful columns and lacy capitals (many of them recycled and ancient Roman) reminded pilgrims that, though this church may be impressive, the finale of their pilgrimage—in Rome—was worth the hike.

From here, circle the church interior counterclockwise, starting in the back-right corner with the 12th-century **baptistery.** Walk around it and follow the Old Testament stories about Moses (with the evil pharaoh played by Lucca's contemporary archenemy—the Holy Roman Emperor). Above is an exquisite 15th-century glazed terra-cotta of the Annunciation by Della Robbia.

Ten steps away—toward the main altar—is the **Chapel of St. Zita,** where St. Zita's actual body has been since 1278. Zita was a local Cinderella figure (abandoned by her parents when they were unable to care for her, she became a servant to a rich family and helped the poor). A painting on the left wall shows the famous episode: Her angry master thought he'd caught her disobediently distributing bread hidden in her apron to the poor—but when he opened the apron, the bread turned into flowers. (Hungary's St. Margaret has exactly the same story. Hmmm...)

Farther along (tucked along the back wall of a chapel on the right side, just past the pulpit, facing the main altar) is the *Assumption of the Virgin* (c. 1510). Ad-mire the painting on wood—enhanced with colorful carved 3D figures. The flat painting shows Doubting Thomas receiving Mary's red belt as she ascends so he'll doubt no more. The pinball-machine composition serves as a virtual catalog of the fine silk material produced in Lucca—a major industry in the 16th century.

Finally, across the nave, you'll find a **carved Virgin Mary.** It's in the corresponding chapel opposite the *Assumption* (high on the back wall, facing the stone-carved altar). This particularly serene Virgin Mary is depicted at the moment she gets the news that she'll bring the Messiah into the world (carved and painted by Lucchese artist Matteo

# The History of Lucca

Lucca began as a Roman settlement. In fact, the grid layout of the streets (and the shadow of an amphitheater) survives from Roman times. Trace the rectangular Roman wall—indicated by today's streets—on the map. As in typical Roman towns, two main roads quartered the fortified town, crossing at what was the forum (main market and religious/political center)—today's Piazza San Michele. The amphitheater sat just outside the original Roman walls.

Christianity came here early; it's said that the first bishop of Lucca was a disciple of St. Peter. While churches were built here as early as the fourth century, the majority of Lucca's elegant Romanesque churches date from about the 12th century.

Feisty Lucca, though never a real power, enjoyed a long period of independence (maintained by clever diplomacy). Aside from 30 years of being ruled from Pisa in the 14th century, Lucca was basically an independent city-state until Napoleon arrived.

In the Middle Ages, wealthy Lucca's economy was built on the silk industry, dominated by the Guinigi (gwee-NEE-jee) family. Paolo Guinigi (1372-1432)—whose name you'll see everywhere around town—was the lord of Lucca for the first three decades of the 15th century, during which time he spurred the town's growth and development. Without silk, Lucca would have been just another sleepy Italian town. By 1500, the town had 3,000 silk looms employing 25,000 workers. Banking was also big. Many pilgrims stopped here on their way to the Holy Land, deposited their money for safety...and never returned to pick it up.

In its heyday, Lucca packed 70 churches and 160 towers—one on nearly every corner—within its walls. Each tower was the home of a wealthy merchant family. Towers were many stories tall, with single rooms stacked atop each other: ground-floor shop, upstairs living room, and top-floor fire-safe kitchen, all connected by exterior wooden staircases. The rooftop was generally a vegetable garden, with trees providing shade. Later, the wealthy city folk moved into the countryside, trading away life in their city palazzos to establish farm estates complete with fancy villas. (You can visit some of these villas today—the TI has a brochure—but they're convenient only for drivers.)

In 1799, Napoleon stormed into Italy and took a liking to Lucca. He liked it so much that he gave it to his sister (who ruled 1805-1814). After Napoleon was toppled, Europe's ruling powers gave Lucca to Maria Luisa, the daughter of the king of Spain. Duchess Maria Luisa (who ruled 1817-1824) was partially responsible for turning the city's imposing (but no longer particularly useful) fortified wall into a fine city park that is much enjoyed today. Her statue stands on Piazza Napoleone, near Palazzo Ducale.

Civitali, c. 1460). Fittingly, she appears as if she's looking at a modern pregnancy test.

• *Leaving the church, head straight back through the little square, and turn right to peruse the many...*

## ❸ Via Fillungo Shops

Lucca's best street to stroll and main pedestrian drag connects the town's two busiest squares: Piazza dell'Anfiteatro (which we just left) and Piazza San Michele. Along the way, you'll get a taste of Lucca's rich past, including several elegant, century-old storefronts.

Head down the street. On the left, you'll pass Piazza degli Scapellini, with market stalls and another entrance into Piazza dell'Anfiteatro.

As you stroll, notice how many of the original storefront paintings, reliefs, and mosaics survive—even if today's shopkeeper sells something entirely different. Observe the warm and convivial small-town vibe on the street. Notice also the powerful heritage of shops named for the families that have run them for many generations, the creative new energy brought by small entrepreneurs, and the aggressive inroads big chain stores are making in this tender urban econo-system.

At #92 (left) a shop sells an array of beers from nearby microbreweries. Since 2007, vino-centric Italy has enjoyed a trendy and youthful microbrew industry. There are multiple breweries just in Lucca.

A few blocks farther, at #97 (right), is the classic old **Carli Jewelry Store.** Signore Carli is the 12th generation of jewelers from his family to work on this spot. (He still has a once-state-of-the-art 17th-century safe in the back.) The Carli storefront has kept its T-shaped arrangement, which lets it close up tight as a canned ham. After hours, all you see from the street is a wooden T in the wall, and during opening hours it unfolds with a fine old-time display. This design dates from when the merchant sold his goods in front, did his work in the back, and lived upstairs.

Judging from its historic sign, **"Intimo"** (#56, on the left) was once an underwear shop. It now sells truffles and generally offers samples of little treats with truffle oil.

At the corner with Via Buia, #67 is a surviving five-story **tower house**. At one time, nearly every corner in Lucca sported its own tower. The stubby stones that still stick out once supported wooden staircases (there were no interior connections between floors). So many towers cast shadows over this part of town that this cross street is called "Dark Street" (Via Buia).

Look left down Via Sant'Andrea for a peek at the town's tallest tower, Guinigi, in the distance—capped by its characteristic mini oak-tree forest. You can pay to climb up for the view (see "More Sights in Lucca," later).

The shop at #65 (right) sports a beautiful, Liberty-style *Profumaria Venus* sign. For over a century, its sexy reliefs (dating from the time of Puccini) have stirred Lucchesi menfolk to buy their woman a fragrant gift. Today the storefront is protected as a historic landmark—and, fittingly, a new perfume shop recently took up residence here.

Farther down, at #45, you'll see two more good examples of tower houses. On the left is the 14th-century **Clock Tower** (Torre delle Ore, #26), which has a hand-wound Swiss clock that clanged four times an hour from 1754 until it died for good a few years back (€4 to climb the 207 wooden steps for the view and to see the nonfunctioning mechanism; closed Nov-mid-March).

A bit farther along, on the left, is the striking 13th-century facade of a **Pisan Romanesque church.**

The intersection of Via Fillungo and Via Roma/Via Santa Croce marks the center of town, where the two original Roman roads crossed. The big old palace you're facing (on the right)—with the heavy grates on the windows and the benches built into its stony facade—is the **In Mondadori bookstore.** While the interior is worth a peek (for its speckled mosaic floors, columns, and stained-glass skylight), the benches out front are

even more interesting: They're the town hangout, where old-timers sit to swap gossip.

• *Turn right down Via Roma, studying the people warming those stone benches along the way. You'll pop out at...*

## ❹ Piazza San Michele

This square has been the center of town since Roman times, when it was the forum. It's dominated by the **Church of San Michele.** Circle around to the church's main door. Towering above the fancy Pisan Romanesque facade, the archangel Michael stands ready to flap his wings (which he actually did on special occasions with the help of crude but awe-inspiring-in-its-day mechanical assistance from behind).

The square is surrounded by an architectural hodgepodge. The circa-1495 loggia (to the right as you face the church) was the first Renaissance building in town. There's a late-19th-century interior in Buccellato Taddeucci, a 130-year-old pastry shop (#34, behind the church, next to its tower). The left section of the BNL bank

(#5, facing the church facade) sports an Art Nouveau facade that celebrates both Amerigo Vespucci and Cristoforo Colombo. This was the original facade of the Bertolli shipping company—famed among Italian Americans as the shipping company their grandparents sailed with to reach America. Bertolli is even better known as the first big-time Italian olive oil exporter. ("Bertolli" was even the generic term for olive oil coined by early Italian Americans.)

Perhaps you've noticed that those statues of big shots that decorate many an Italian piazza are mostly absent from Lucca's squares. That's because unlike Venice, Florence, and Milan—which were dominated by a few powerful dynasties—Lucca was traditionally run by an oligarchy of a hundred leading families, with no single central figure to commemorate in stone. (That's also why the town has so many tower houses, and why most of the sights—other than churches—are *palazzi*-turned-museums.) But after Italian unification—when leaders were fond of saying, "We have created Italy... now we need to create Italians"—stirring statues of national heroes popped up everywhere...even in Lucca. The statue on Piazza San Michele is a two-bit local guy, dredged up centuries after his death because he favored strong central government.

Look back at the church facade, which also has an element of patriotism—designed to give roots and legitimacy to Italian

statehood. Perched above many of the columns are the faces of a dozen or so heroes in the Italian independence and unification movement: Victor Emmanuel II (with a crown, above the short red column on the right, second level up), the Count of Cavour (next to Victor, above the column with black zigzags), and—hey, look—there's Giuseppe Mazzini (on the far left, fourth from the end).

If the church is open, pop **inside**. A fine 12th-century wooden crucifix hangs above the high altar. The altar shows off the body of St. Davino from the year 1050, sporting the scallop shells that identify him as a pilgrim. Immediately to its right is an exquisite painting, *The Four Saints*, by Filippino Lippi (a student of the Florentine master Sandro Botticelli). Painted in 1495, it exudes the spirit of the Renaissance (and Botticelli's influence) in the idealized beauty of the faces and the detailed glorification of nature (including the hardworking bugs at their feet). You may notice visitors shining their phone flashlights on the pillars. They're squinting at curious little doodles scratched into the marble back in the 12th century.

• *From here, continue out of the square (opposite from where you entered) to take a little detour down...*

## ❺ Via San Paolino

This bustling street—which eventually goes all the way to Piazzale Guiseppe Verdi (with the TI and bus to Pisa)—is another fine shopping drag. Along here, a wide variety of storefronts cater not just to tourists but also to locals. Appliance and electronics stores are mixed in with gifty Tuscan specialty boutiques. You'll also pass—after just a half-block, on the right—my vote for the best gelato in town (De' Coltelli, Sicilian-style gelato, at #10; described under "Eating in Lucca").

One block down this street, in the little square called **Piazza Citadella** (on the right), a statue of Giacomo Puccini (1858-1924) sits genteelly on a chair, holding court. The great composer of operas was born in the house down the little alley over his left shoulder (now the well-presented Puccini's House museum, worth a visit for music lovers—see "More Sights in Lucca," later). The ticket office for the museum—on the left side of the square, in front of Puccini—is also a well-stocked gift shop with all manner of Puccini-bilia (and a free WC; closed Tue). In the back of the shop a small theater loops a free five-minute video: home movies of Puccini from the 1920s. (If you'd like to hear some Puccini while you're in town, soon we'll be passing a church that hosts frequent concerts of his music—see "Helpful Hints," earlier).

Puccini had deep roots in Lucca. His musical family had served as choirmasters for the San Martino Cathedral for five generations. As a young man, Giacomo sang in the cathedral choir, served as the substitute organist, and attended the church school. Even when he left for Milan to pursue his opera career, he kept a villa near Lucca. The citizens of Lucca can be rightfully proud of their native son: Puccini is one of the most popular opera composers, and his *La Bohème, Madame Butterfly, Tosca,* and a half-dozen other works are regularly performed across the globe. His style, known as *verismo* (realism), is highly accessible and dramatic, making his works seem more like sung plays than merely a string of arias.

• *Feel free to browse your way as far down this street as you like, but eventually return to Piazza San Michele to continue the walk to Lucca's cathedral. Facing the church facade, turn right and go down Via Vittorio Veneto (with the loggia on your left) to the vast, café-lined pair of squares...*

## ❻ Piazza Napoleone and Piazza del Giglio

The first of these two squares is named for the French despot who was the first outsider to take over Lucca. The dominant building on the right was the seat of government for the independent Republic of Lucca from 1369 to 1799—the year Napoleon came and messed everything up. Caffè Ninci, on the left (with some nice tables for people-watching), has been caffeinating locals since 1925 and serves what's considered to be the best coffee in town.

Cross diagonally through this square into the smaller **Piazza del Giglio,** dominated by the Giglio Theater. Like a mini La Scala, this has long been the number-one theater (of seven) in the highly cultured city of Puccini.

*• Continue to the left, along the big orange building, up Via del Duomo. After a block, you'll see...*

## ❼ San Giovanni Church

This first cathedral of Lucca is interesting only for its archaeological finds. The entire floor of the 12th-century church has been

excavated in recent decades, revealing layers of Roman houses, ancient hot tubs that date back to the time of Christ, early churches, and theological graffiti. Sporadic English translations help you understand what you're looking at. As you climb under the church's present-day floor and wander the lanes of Roman Lucca, remember that the entire city sits on similar ruins. Ascend the 190 steps of the church's campanile (bell tower) for a panoramic view (but not quite as good as the one from the Guinigi Tower).

**Cost and Hours:** €4 includes tower climb, €10 combo-ticket also includes cathedral, its bell tower, and Cathedral Museum; daily 10:00-18:00, shorter hours Nov-Feb. For info on the Puccini concerts held at the church, see "Helpful Hints," earlier.

*• Continuing past San Giovanni, you'll be face-to-face with...*

## ❽ San Martino Cathedral

This cathedral—the main church of the Republic of Lucca and worth ▲—was begun in the 11th century and became an entertaining mix of architectural and artistic styles. It's also home to the

LUCCA

exquisite 15th-century tomb of Ilaria del Carretto, who married into the wealthy Guinigi family.

**Cost and Hours:** €3, tower climb-€3, €10 combo-ticket includes both plus Cathedral Museum and San Giovanni Church; Mon-Sat 10:00-18:00, Sun from 12:00, Nov-Feb until 17:00; Piazza San Martino, www.cattedralelucca.it. There's a WC under the bell tower.

**Visiting the Cathedral:** The cathedral's elaborate Pisan Romanesque **facade** features Christian teaching scenes, animals, and candy-cane-striped columns. The horseback figure (over the two right arches) is St. Martin, a Roman military officer from Hungary who, by offering his cloak to a beggar, came to more fully understand the beauty of Christian compassion. (The impressive original, a fine example of Romanesque sculpture, hides from pollution just inside, to the right of the main entrance.) Each of the columns on the facade is unique. Notice how the facade is asymmetrical: The 11th-century bell tower was already in place when the rest of the cathedral was built, so the builders fudged a bit while attempting to make it fit. Over the rightmost pillar (as if leaning against the older tower), the architect Guido from Como proudly holds a document declaring that he finished the facade in 1204.

Head under the **arcade** to see a few more details. On the right (at eye level on the pilaster), a labyrinth is set into the wall. The maze relates the struggle and challenge our souls face in finding salvation. (French pilgrims on their way to Rome could relate to this, as it's the same pattern they knew from the floor of the church at Chartres.) The Latin declaration carved into the marble just left of the main door is where moneychangers and spice traders met to seal deals (on the doorstep of the church—to underscore the reliability of their promises). Find the date: *An Dni MCXI* (AD 1111, second line from bottom, lower right).

The **interior**—bigger than it seems from outside—features brightly frescoed Gothic arches, Renaissance paintings, and stained glass from the 19th century.

On the left side of the nave, a small, elaborate, birdcage-like temple contains the wooden crucifix—much revered by locals—called **Volto Santo**. It's said to have been sculpted by Nicodemus in Jerusalem and set afloat in an unmanned boat that landed on the coast of Tuscany, from where wild oxen miraculously carried it to Lucca in 782. The sculpture (which is actually 12th-century Byzantine style) had quite a jewelry collection, which you can see in the Cathedral Museum. When locals look at Volto Santo they recall how, in 1096, the Christian forces of England and France met Pope Urban II right here in front of this crucifix. Those inglorious bastards were blessed and sent by the pope east on the First Crusade. As an example of Lucca's stature in 12th-century Europe, rather than say "I swear on a stack of bibles," people would say "I swear in front of the holy face of Christ of Lucca."

Circle around the birdcage. On the back side stands a sculpture of **St. Sebastian** (without his arrows) by Matteo Civitali. Carved in the late 1400s, this was the epitome of early-Renaissance beauty before the muscularity of Michelangelo's *David* came into vogue. Delicate and S-shaped, it's just as sensuous (though St. Sebastian is dressed in cute underpants in contrast to *David*'s powerful nudity).

In the center of the nave (five steps from St. Sebastian) is an inlaid marble **floor** depicting the Judgment of Solomon. Dating from around 1460, this first example of mathematically correct perspective in Lucca celebrates the new Renaissance aesthetic.

On the right side of the nave, just before the transept, the sacristy houses the enchanting **memorial tomb** of Ilaria del Carretto by Jacopo della Quercia (1407). This young bride of silk baron Paolo Guinigi is decked out in the latest, most expensive fashions, with the requisite little dog (symbolizing her loyalty) curled up at her feet in eternal sleep. She's so realistically realized that the statue was nicknamed "Sleeping Beauty." Her nose is partially worn off because of a long-standing tradition of lonely young ladies rubbing it for luck in finding a boyfriend.

As you head for the church's exit, stop by the third painting from the end (on the left)—*The Last Supper* by Jacopo Tintoretto. This is a typical Baroque spectacle, with the drama of the event emphasized as if it's theater. Notice the actors on the stage and how the mother, giving her child his "first supper" in the foreground, connects with us, inviting us to be present. Enjoy Tintoretto's perspective trick: As you walk by the painting, the foreshortened dinner table always faces you.

• *There's one more sight to consider, but it's extra credit—worthwhile only if you want to dig deeper into the history of the cathedral. As you face the cathedral facade, on the little square to the left is the entrance to the...*

## ❾ Cathedral Museum (Museo della Cattedrale)

This beautifully presented museum houses original paintings, sculptures, and vestments from the cathedral and other Lucca churches. Pass through a room with illuminated manuscripts on your way to the ticket desk, then follow the one-way route up and down through the collection. The first room displays jewelry made to dress up the Volto Santo crucifix (described earlier), including gigantic gilded silver shoes. Upstairs, notice the fine red brocaded silk—a reminder that this precious fabric is what brought riches and power to the city. You'll also see church paintings and sculptures, silver ecclesiastical gear, and a big cutaway model of the cathedral. The exhibits in this museum have basic labels and are meaningful only with the slow-talking audioguide—if you're not in the mood to listen, skip the place altogether.

**Cost and Hours:** €4, €10 combo-ticket includes cathedral, its bell tower, and San Giovanni Church; daily 10:00-18:00, shorter hours Nov-Feb; audioguide-€5, left of the cathedral on Piazza Antelminelli.

• *Our walk is finished. From here, it's just a short stroll south to the city wall—and a bike-rental office, if you want to take a spin. Otherwise, simply explore the city...lose yourself in Lucca.*

# More Sights in Lucca

## LUCCA RAMPARTS (AND BIKE RIDE)

Lucca's most remarkable feature, its Renaissance wall, is also its most enjoyable attraction, worth ▲▲—especially when circled on a rental bike. Stretching for 2.5 miles, this is an ideal place to come for an overview of the city by foot or bike.

Lucca has had a protective wall for 2,000 years. You can read three walls into today's map: the first rectangular Roman wall, the later medieval wall (nearly the size of today's), and the 16th-century Renaissance ramparts that still survive.

With the advent of cannons, thin medieval walls were suddenly vulnerable. A new design—the same one that stands today—was state-of-the-art when it was built (1550-1650). Much of the old medieval wall (look for the old stones) was incorporated into the Renaissance wall (with uniform bricks). The new wall was squat: a 100-foot-wide mound of dirt faced with bricks, engineered to absorb a cannonball pummeling. The townspeople cleared a wide no-man's-land around the town, exposing any attackers from a distance. Eleven heart-shaped bastions (now inviting picnic areas) were designed to minimize exposure to cannonballs and to maximize defense capabilities. The ramparts were armed with 130 cannons.

The town invested a third of its income for more than a century to construct the wall, and—since it kept away the Florentines and nasty Pisans—it was considered a fine investment. In fact, nobody ever bothered to try to attack the wall. Locals say that the only time it actually defended the city was during an 1812 flood of the Serchio River, when the gates were sandbagged and the ramparts kept out the high water.

If exploring the wall, you can venture into its tunnels and interior at either San Paolino Bastion or San Martino Bastion.

Today, the ramparts seem made to order for a leisurely bike ride (a wonderfully smooth 20-30-minute pedal, depending on

how fast you go and how crowded the wall-top park is). You can rent bikes cheaply and easily from one of several bike-rental places in town (listed earlier, under "Helpful Hints"; one hour buys you two slow loops, three fast ones, or one loop plus a refreshment break en route). There are also several handy places to get up on the wall. Note that the best people-watching—and slowest pedaling—is during *passeggiata* time, just before dinner, when it seems that all of Lucca is doing slow laps around its beloved wall.

**LUCCA**

## OTHER SIGHTS

Lucca has several small museums that stir local pride, but they're pretty dull on a pan-Italian scale (the Cathedral Museum is described earlier, on my "Lucca Walk"). Visit the following sights only if you have time to burn or a special interest.

### Guinigi Tower (Torre Guinigi)

Many Tuscan towns have towers, but none is quite like the Guinigi family's. Up 227 steps is a small garden with fragrant trees, surrounded by fine views over the city's rooftops. You'll head up wide stone stairs, then huff up twisty metal ones through the hollow brick tower.

**Cost and Hours:** €5, erratic hours but typically June-Sept daily 10:00-19:30, until later on weekends, mid-March-May until 18:30, winter until 16:00, Via Sant'Andrea 41.

**Visiting the Tower:** From the

top, orient yourself to the town. Lucca sits in a flat valley ringed by protective hills, so it's easy to see how the town managed to stay independent through so much of its history, despite its lack of a strategic hilltop position. From up here, pick out landmarks: the circular form of Piazza dell'Anfiteatro to the north, with the mosaic facade of the Church of San Frediano nearby; to the left (east), the open top of the Clock Tower, marking the Roman grid-planned streets of the oldest part of town; and to the south, the big, marble facade of San Martino Cathedral. The jagged cliffs to the distant northwest mark the Carrara marble quarries, frequented by Michelangelo (and countless home-improvement designers).

### Puccini's House

This modern, well-presented museum fills the home where Giacomo Puccini grew up. It's well worth a visit for opera enthusiasts... but mostly lost on anybody else.

**Cost and Hours:** €9; daily 9:30-19:30; April until 18:30; Oct Wed-Mon until 18:30, closed Tue; Nov-March shorter hours and closed Tue; Corte San Lorenzo 9, +39 0583 584 028, www.puccinimuseum.it.

**Visiting the Museum:** Buy your ticket at the shop/office on the square, then buzz to be let in. You'll huff two stories up the stairs and tour the composer's birthplace. In period-furnished apartments—including the room where he was born—you'll see lots of artifacts, including the Steinway piano where he did much of his composing, his personal belongings, and pull-out drawers with original compositions and manuscripts. Don't miss the small staircase up to the garret (storage room up above the house), where a stage set from *La Bohème* evokes the composer's greatest work. Throughout, costumes from his works are displayed; the most elaborate (in the small room near the reception desk) is from *Turandot*.

### Palazzo Pfanner

Garden enthusiasts (and anyone needing a break from churches) will enjoy this 18th-century palace built for a rich Austrian expat who came to Lucca to open a brewery. While far from the finest garden in Italy, it's a nice escape from the crowds and heat of the city.

**Cost and Hours:** €6.50 for garden and residence, daily 10:00-18:00, closed Dec-March, Via degli Asili 33, +39 0583 952 155, www.palazzopfanner.it.

**Visiting the Museum:** Up the stairs is the palace's lived-in interior, with Baroque furniture, elaborate frescoes, and a centuries-old kitchen. Those in the medical profession may be interested in the display of early 20th-century medical equipment and books. (Pfanner's son became a renowned doctor, and treated everyone from vagrants to Giacomo Puccini on the building's ground floor.)

The restful garden, with manicured lawns, rows of dynamic statues, potted citrus trees, and gurgling fountains, is tucked up against Lucca's imposing wall.

### Villa Guinigi

Built by Paolo Guinigi in 1413, the family villa is now a well-presented museum chronologically displaying a lot of art and artifacts that are meaningful to the Lucchesi.

**Cost and Hours:** €4, €6.50 combo-ticket includes Palazzo Mansi; Tue and Thu 9:00-19:30, Wed and Fri-Sat from 12:00, open just two Sun per month 9:00-19:30, closed Mon and other Sun, Via della Quarquonia, +39 0583 496 033, www.luccamuseinazionali.it.

**Visiting the Museum:** The exhibit starts with an archaeological section—Etruscan, Ligurian (a local pagan tribe), and Roman. Upstairs, you proceed chronologically through the Middle Ages, with lots of church art and altars, and the Renaissance. Highlights include a precious crucifix by Berlinghiero Berlinghieri (who also created the fine mosaic facade at the Church of San Frediano), two terra-cotta *Madonna-and-Bambino* sculptures attributed to Donatello, fine inlaid-wood panels from San Martino Cathedral, several works by the locally famous Lucchese sculptor Matteo Civitali, a *Sacra Conversazione* by Fra Bartolomeo, and a fine triptych by the multitalented Giorgio Vasari. In Vasari's vibrant altar painting, Adam and Eve clutch the tree of knowledge, while the devil (a snake with a woman's head) twists up the trunk toward the sky, flanked by biblical big shots (David, Solomon, Moses, and John the Baptist). But Mary floats triumphant on top, with one foot keeping down the devil's head. The collection wraps up with the Counter-Reformation and Neoclassicism (with works by more locally beloved artists, Paolo Guidotti and Pompeo Batoni).

### Palazzo Mansi

For a glimpse at a noble palace from centuries past, this is your best bet. Minor paintings by Tintoretto, Pontormo, Veronese, and others vie for attention, but the palace itself steals the show. This sumptuously furnished and decorated 17th-century confection gives you a chance to appreciate the wealth of Lucca's silk merchants.

**Cost and Hours:** €4, €6.50 combo-ticket includes Villa Guinigi, Tue and Thu 9:00-18:00, Wed and Fri-Sat from 12:00, open just two Sun per month 9:00-18:00, closed Mon and other Sun, English info posted in each room, Via Galli Tassi 43, +39 0583 55 570, www.luccamuseinazionali.it.

**Visiting the Museum:** Exploring rooms on one magnificent floor, you'll gape through several grand halls of both public and private apartments. Notice the emphasis on crests, portraits, and family trees—reminders of how important it was to marry smartly if you wanted to create a powerful family. In one wing, every surface is slathered in bubbly Baroque scenes; in another, each room is completely draped in tapestries, leading to one of the most impressive two-story canopy beds I've seen.

# Sleeping in Lucca

## BOUTIQUE B&BS
## WITHIN THE WALLS

$$ **A Palazzo Busdraghi** has eight comfortable, pastel-colored rooms with modern baths (some with whirlpool tubs) in a tastefully converted 13th-century palace tucked inside a courtyard. Sweet Marta (with help from Ingrid and Veronica) hustles to keep guests happy and bakes tasty cakes for breakfast. It's conveniently located on busy Via Fillungo, so it comes with some traffic rumbles and occasional weekend-revelry noise (family room, air-con, pay parking, Via Fillungo 170, +39 0583 950 856, www.apalazzobusdraghi.it, info@apalazzobusdraghi.it).

$$ **La Romea B&B,** in an air-conditioned, restored, 14th-century palazzo near Guinigi Tower, feels like a royal splurge. Its five rooms are lavishly decorated in handsome colors and surround a big, plush lounge with stately Venetian-style mosaic-linoleum floors (RS%, family rooms, Vicolo delle Ventaglie 2, +39 0583 464 175, www.laromea.com, info@laromea.com, Gaia and Giulio).

$$ **La Bohème B&B** has a cozy yet elegant ambience, offering seven large rooms, each named for a Puccini opera. Chandeliers, 1920s-vintage tile floors, and tasteful antiques add to the charm (RS%, family room, air-con, pay parking, one floor up at Via del Moro 2, +39 0583 462 404, www.boheme.it, info@boheme.it, Laura).

$$ **Relais Inn Lucca** takes up a stately palazzo near Piazza Napoleone. Their nine rooms are chic and modern, and run with youthful enthusiasm by Alessandra (air-con, elevator, pay parking, Corso Garibaldi 19, +39 0583 464 218, www.relaisinnlucca.it, info@relaisinnlucca.it).

## SLEEPING MORE FORGETTABLY
## WITHIN THE WALLS

$$$$ **Palazzo Dipinto** is your "design hotel with class" option, buried deep in the heart of the old town, just a few steps from Puccini's House. It has less character (and fewer quirks) than the B&Bs, but the stylish lobby and 22 rooms provide predictable comfort (family rooms, air-con, elevator, pay parking—book ahead, Piazza del Palazzo Dipinto 27, +39 0583 582 873, www. palazzodipinto.com, info@palazzodipinto.com).

$$$ **Hotel la Luna** has 29 rooms in a great location in the heart of the city. Rooms are split between two adjacent buildings

just off the main shopping street. Rooms in the main, historical building are larger and classier, with old wood-beam ceilings (and, in some, original frescoes), while the modern building feels newer and has an elevator but less personality (RS%, family rooms, air-con, pay parking, Via Fillungo at Corte Compagni 12, +39 0583 493 634, www.hotellaluna.it, info@hotellaluna.it).

**$$ Albergo San Martino** and **$ Hotel Diana** are two hotels run from the same reception—both friendly and conveniently located for train travelers. The main hotel has 12 art-adorned rooms, a nice lounge, and a cheery curbside breakfast terrace, plus six newer, slightly cheaper rooms in an annex. Hotel Diana is the budget choice, with nine fresh, affordable rooms with a colorful Italian-modern design flair (both hotels: skip breakfast to save a few euros, call ahead—reception not open 24 hours, family rooms, air-con, tight parking—free with this book if you book direct, bikes available, reception at Via della Dogana 9, +39 0583 469 181, www.albergosanmartino.it, info@albergosanmartino.it, Andrea and Fabrizio).

## OUTSIDE THE WALLS

**$$$ Hotel San Marco,** a 10-minute walk outside the Porta Santa Maria or Porta San Jacopo, is a postmodern place with a peaceful garden and pool. Its 42 rooms are sleek, with all the comforts, and its easy location makes it a good choice for drivers (air-con in summer, elevator, bike rental, free parking, taxi from station—€13, Via San Marco 368, +39 0583 495 010, www.hotelsanmarcolucca.it, info@hotelsanmarcolucca.com, proud Francesco).

**$$ Hotel Rex** rents 25 dated but lovingly maintained rooms in a practical contemporary building on the train station square. While in the modern world, this family-friendly place is just 200 yards away from the old town and offers a good value. Ask for a slightly quieter room at the back (family rooms, children's play area and toys, air-con, elevator, free parking, a few steps from the train station at Piazza Ricasoli 19, +39 0583 955 443, www.hotelrexlucca.com, info@hotelrexlucca.com, Elisabetta and Valentina).

**$ Hotel Moderno** is indeed modern, with 12 rooms tastefully decorated. Although it's in a strange location, backing up to the train tracks, the rooms are quiet, and it offers class unusual for this price range (RS%, family rooms, air-con, Via Vincenzo Civitali 38—turn left out of train station and go over stair-heavy bridge across tracks, +39 0583 570 819, www.albergomodernolucca.com, info@albergomodernolucca.com, Stefano).

# Eating in Lucca

## FINE AND ROMANTIC DINING

**$$ Canuleia Trattoria** is run by enthusiastic Matteo (the chef) and Eleonora (head waiter), who make everything fresh in their small kitchen. You can eat tasty Tuscan cuisine in a tight, dressy, and romantic little dining room or outside on the garden courtyard. As this place is justifiably popular, reserve for dinner (Tue-Sun 12:30-14:00 & 19:30-22:00, closed Mon, Via Canuleia 14, +39 0583 467 470, www.canuleiatrattoria.it).

**$$$$ Ristorante Giglio** is a venerable old dining hall where waiters are formal but not stuffy, and the spirit of Puccini lives on. This is where local families enjoy special occasions under a big chandelier. The short but thoughtful menu features a fusion of traditional Tuscan and creative international gastronomy concocted by three young chefs. Though pricier than most of my listings, this is a big step up in dining experience. Con-

sider their tasting menus (€80/six courses, €100/eight courses) to best appreciate how they've earned a Michelin star (reserve ahead, impressive wine list, Wed-Mon 12:15-14:30 & 19:15-22:15, closed Tue, Piazza del Giglio 2, +39 0583 494 058, www.ristorantegiglio.com).

**$$$ Osteria dal Manzo** feels both classy and inviting. Gentlemanly Antonio warmly welcomes diners with a concise and enticing menu of elegantly simple, seasonal cuisine. There are typically five items for each of three courses—two meat, two fish, and one vegetarian (Mon-Sat 19:30-23:00, Sun 12:30-14:30, Via Cesare Battisti 28, +39 0583 490 649).

**$$$ Il Mecenate** feels both rustic and refined—the kind of place where you want to book ahead and dress up a bit, to fit in with the Lucchese diners. It faces a tranquil, picturesque canal at the eastern edge of the tourist's Lucca, a five-minute walk beyond the main zone. The traditional dishes are beautifully executed; this is a good place to try meat-filled *tordelli* pasta, *garmugia* (vegetable soup), and *testaroli,* an ancient bread-like pasta tossed with pesto (Wed-Mon 12:00-14:30 & 19:30-22:30, closed Tue, Via del Fosso 94, +39 0583 511 861, www.ristorantemecenate.it).

## CHARMING AND RUSTIC DINING

**$$ La Bottega di Anna & Leo,** run by Claudio and Lidia (and named for their children), is a pastel and lovable little eatery with a simple menu and a passion for quality. They have tight seating inside and a few charming tables facing the side of the Church of San Frediano (erratic hours but typically Tue-Sat 12:00-14:30 & 19:00-22:30, Sun 12:00-14:30, closed Mon, reservations smart, Via San Frediano 16, +39 393 577 9910 or +39 393 530 2512, www. labottegadiannaeleo.it).

**$$ Osteria Via San Giorgio,** where Daniela cooks and her brother Piero serves, is a cheery family eatery that satisfies both fish and meat lovers. The indoor seating is tight and convivial, the outdoor courtyard is cheery in summer, and the house wine is high quality (Tue-Sun 12:00-16:00 & 18:30-23:00, closed Mon, Via San Giorgio 26, +39 0583 953 233).

**$$ Il Cuore Enogastronomia** is a cozy blend of restaurant and deli—if you like your meal you can buy more to take home. Browse their cases of prepared dishes and order some to take away, or sit in the dining room for homemade pasta, big salads, pizza, meats, and desserts (Tue-Sat 10:30-22:00, Sun lunch only, closed Mon, closed Jan-Feb, Via del Battistero 4, +39 0583 493 196, enthusiastic Anna takes good care of diners).

**$ Pizzeria da Felice** is a mom-and-pop hole-in-the-wall take-out pizza joint. Grab an *etto* of *cecina* (garbanzo-bean crepes) or a slice of freshly baked pizza and a short glass of wine. From September through April, they're known for their *castagnaccio,* a cake made with roasted chestnuts and ricotta (daily 10:00-20:30 except closed Sun Jan-Aug and closed 2 weeks in Aug, Via Buia 12, +39 0583 494 986).

**$$ Trattoria da Leo** packs in chatty locals for characteristic home cooking in a high-energy, diner-type atmosphere. Sit in the rollicking interior, or out on a tight, atmospheric lane (Mon-Sat 12:00-15:00 & 19:30-22:30, Sun 12:00-15:00, Via Tegrimi 1, +39 0583 492 236).

## SNACKS, GELATO, AND HAPPY-HOUR *APERITIVO* BARS

*Aperitivi* **near Porta dei Borghi:** This gate at the end of Via Fillungo (and the little square just beyond it) is a great area for characteristic bars serving free and tasty buffets with any drink during their *aperitivo* time. These places are popular with young locals and are a perfect spot to relax after cycling the wall (near Piazza Santa Maria bike rentals).

**Vinarkia,** a characteristic wine bar, is popular for its *aperitivo* buffet from 18:30 to 20:00 (closed Mon, Via Fillungo 188, +39 0583 152 5357, Alekos).

**De Cervesia** is a craft beer pub, with three microbrews on rotating taps (and one English-style pull) and dozens by the bottle

## Specialties in Lucca

Lucca has some tasty specialties worth seeking out. *Ceci* (CHEH-chee), also called *cecina* (cheh-CHEE-nah), makes an ideal cheap snack any time of day. This crepe-like garbanzo-bean flatbread is sold in pizza shops and is best accompanied by a nip of red wine. *Farro,* a grain (spelt) dating back to ancient Roman cuisine, shows up in restaurants in soups or as a creamy rice-like dish *(risotto di farro).*

*Tordelli,* the Lucchesi version of *tortelli,* is homemade ravioli. It's traditionally stuffed with meat and served with more meat sauce, but chefs creatively pair cheeses and vegetables, too.

*Lardo di Colonnata*—a specialty from the Carrara marble region—is *salumi* made with cured lard and rosemary, sliced thin, and served as an antipasto.

Lucca has excellent olive oil that appears in many dishes and soups, such as *garmugia* (a bounty of spring vegetables).

Meat, not fish, is the star at most restaurants, especially steak, which is listed on menus as *filetto di manzo* (filet), *tagliata di manzo* (thin slices of grilled tenderloin), or the king of steaks, *bistecca alla fiorentina.* Order *al sangue* (rare), *medio* (medium rare), *cotto* (medium), or *ben cotto* (well). Anything more than *al sangue* is considered a travesty for steak connoisseurs. *Ravellino* is a thin cut of beef that's deep-fried, then pan-fried again later to heat it up.

That said, you'll find more seafood on Lucca menus than in many other parts of Tuscany—after all, you're just a 30-minute drive from the sea.

Note that steaks (as well as fish) are often sold by weight, noted on menus as *s.q.* (according to quantity ordered) or *l'etto* (cost per 100 grams—250 grams is about an 8-ounce steak).

For something sweet, bakeries sell *buccellato,* bread dotted with raisins, lightly flavored with anise, and often shaped like a wreath. It's sold only in large quantities, but luckily it stays good for a few days (and it also pairs well with Vin Santo—fortified Tuscan dessert wine). An old proverb says, "Coming to Lucca without eating the *buccellato* is like not having come at all." *Buon appetito!*

(Tue-Sun 17:00-22:00, closed Mon, Via Michele Rosi 20—look for big *Italian Craft Beer* signs, +39 0583 492 620, Matteo).

**Ciclo DiVino,** across the street, is a wine bar with a bike-shop theme and enticing snacks (Mon-Fri 16:00-22:00, Sat-Sun from 11:00, Via Michele Rosi 7, +39 0583 471 869).

*Aperitivi* **on Piazza San Michele: Caffè del Mercato,** on the other side of the old town and catering to an older clientele, has good *aperitivo* snacks nightly from 18:00 to 20:00 (facing church at Piazza San Michele 17, +39 0583 494 127).

**Gelato:** Just off Piazza San Michele, **De' Coltelli** has some of my favorite gelato in Italy. It's proudly Sicilian-style (with Arab roots), and many of their flavors rotate with the season. Sample with a spirit of adventure and then have fun ordering: The salted caramel is a standout, and their granita takes the slushy to new heights (Sun-Thu 11:00-20:00, Fri-Sat until 21:00, Via San Paolino 10, Valentina).

**Pizza:** Two doors away from De' Coltelli, **Alice Pizza** offers good pizza by the slice (Tue-Sun 10:00-20:30, closed Mon, Via San Paolino 22, +39 0583 572 712).

**Refreshments on the Wall: Caffetteria San Colombano** is a handy pit stop for bikers and walkers on the city wall. This place is slick with bite-sized snacks and cappuccinos, perfect for a take-away meal on top of the wall (overpriced at the table). If you're not feeling too wobbly already from biking, try a *caffè corretto* (espresso with your choice of Sambuca, rum, or grappa) or a *Biadina*, a bittersweet liqueur served with pine nuts. The fancier sit-down restaurant serves pasta and big salads with a view (daily 9:00-late, near top of ramp at San Colombano Bastion, +39 0583 464 641).

**Groceries: Pam** is a small, central market just off Piazza San Michele (Mon-Sat 8:00-22:00, Sun 9:00-20:00, Via San Paolino 16).

# Lucca Connections

Even if you have a car, I'd opt for the much faster and cheaper train or bus to reach the Leaning Tower. For more on day-tripping to Pisa, see page 470.

**From Lucca by Train to: Florence** (2/hour, 1.5 hours), **Pisa** (1-2/hour, 30 minutes; if going directly to Leaning Tower, hop off at Pisa San Rossore station; to reach Pisa Airport, change to the tram at Centrale station), **Livorno** (about hourly, 1-1.5 hours, transfer at Pisa Centrale), **Milan** (2/hour except Sun, 4-5 hours, transfer in Florence), **Rome** (1/hour except Sun, 3-4 hours, change in Florence), **Cinque Terre** (hourly, about 2 hours, transfer in Viareggio and La Spezia).

**From Lucca by Bus:** Autolinee Toscane (AT) runs handy, direct routes from Lucca's Piazzale Giuseppe Verdi, at the west end of the old town (near the main TI). This is handiest to **Pisa**; the ones noted as going via "S.M. Guidice" (green on schedules) are about 10 minutes faster than the ones marked "Ripafratta" (black)—but both will take you right to the Field of Miracles and Leaning Tower (€3.50, continues to Centrale station, Mon-Sat about hourly, fewer on Sun, 45-55 minutes). Bus #DD runs to **Florence** (stops at Stazione Leopolda, west of the center; your bus ticket also covers the connecting tram to downtown); this bus can also drop you at **Florence Airport** (Peretola stop—request from driver; €7.60, Mon-Sat nearly hourly, less on Sun, 1.25 hours to airport, 1.5 hours total to downtown Florence). Before boarding, buy tickets at the bus ticket office on Piazzale Giuseppe Verdi (Mon-Sat 6:00-20:00, Sun 8:00-19:45; schedule info but no tickets at www.at-bus.it).

# VOLTERRA & SAN GIMIGNANO

*Volterra • San Gimignano • Moteriggioni*

This fine duo of hill towns—perhaps Italy's most underrated and most overrated, respectively—sits just a half-hour drive apart in the middle of the triangle formed by Florence, Siena, and Pisa. San Gimignano is the region's glamour girl, getting all the fawning attention from passing tour buses. And a quick stroll through its core, in the shadows of its 14 surviving medieval towers, is a delight. But once you've seen it, you've seen it...and that's when you head for Volterra. Volterra isn't as eye-catching as San Gimignano, but it has unmistakable authenticity and surprising depth, richly rewarding travelers adventurous enough to break out of the San Gimignano rut. With its many engaging museums, Volterra offers the best sightseeing of all of Italy's small hill towns.

To round things out with a look at a well-preserved hill-top fort, consider stopping off for a quick visit to Monteriggioni, perched above the highway south to Siena.

## GETTING THERE

These towns work best for drivers, who can easily reach both in one go. Volterra is farther off the main Florence-Siena road, but it's near the main coastal highway connecting the north (Pisa, Lucca, and Cinque Terre) and south (Montalcino/Montepulciano and Rome). It's a little more than an hour's drive from Pisa or Florence.

If you're relying on public transportation, both towns are reachable—to a point. Visiting either one by bus from Florence or Siena requires a longer-than-it-should-be trek, often with a change (in Colle di Val d'Elsa for Volterra, in Poggibonsi for San Gimignano). Volterra can also be reached by a train-and-bus combination from La Spezia, Pisa, or Florence (transfer to a bus in Pontedera). See each town's "Connections" section for details.

San Gimignano is better connected, but Volterra merits the

additional effort. Note that while these towns are only about a 30-minute drive apart, they're poorly connected to each other by public transit.

## PLANNING YOUR TIME

Volterra and San Gimignano are a handy yin-and-yang pair. Ideally, you'll overnight in one town and visit the other either as a side trip or en route. Sleeping in Volterra lets you really settle into a charming burg with good restaurants, but it forces you to visit San Gimignano during the day, when it's busiest. Sleeping in San Gimignano lets you enjoy that gorgeous town when it's relatively quiet, but some visitors find it *too* quiet. Ultimately I'd aim to sleep in Volterra, and try to visit San Gimignano as early or late in the day as is practical to avoid crowds. Those with a car may choose to stay in the countryside between the two, visiting Volterra during the day and dining in San Gimignano at night.

# Volterra

Encircled by impressive walls and topped with a grand fortress, Volterra perches high above the rich farmland surrounding it. More than 2,000 years ago, Volterra was an important Etruscan city, and much larger than we see today. Greek-trained Etruscan artists worked here, leaving a significant stash of art, particularly cinerary urns. Eventually Volterra was absorbed into the Roman Empire, and for centuries it was an independent city-state. Volterra fought bitterly against the Florentines, but like many Tuscan towns, it lost in the end and was given a Medici fortress atop the city to "protect" its citizens.

Unlike other famous towns in Tuscany, Volterra feels neither cutesy nor touristy...but real, vibrant, and almost oblivious to the allure of the tourist dollar. Millennia past its prime, Volterra seems to have settled into a well-worn groove; locals are resistant to change. At a town meeting about whether to run high-speed internet cable to the town, a local grumbled, "The Etruscans didn't need it—why do we?" This stubbornness helps make Volterra a refreshing change of pace from its more aggressively commercial neighbors. Volterra also boasts some interesting sights, from an ancient Roman theater, to a finely decorated Pisan Romanesque cathedral, to an excellent museum of Etruscan artifacts. And most evenings, charming Annie and Claudia give a delightful, one-hour guided town walk sure to help you appreciate their city (see "Tours in Volterra," later). All in all, Volterra is my favorite small town in Tuscany.

## Orientation to Volterra

Compact and walkable, Volterra (pop. 10,000—6,000 inside the old wall) stretches out from the pleasant Piazza dei Priori to the old city gates and beyond. Be ready for some steep walking: While the spine of the city from the main square to the Etruscan Museum is fairly level, nearly everything else involves a climb.

### TOURIST INFORMATION

The helpful TI is on the main square, at Piazza dei Priori 20 (daily 10:00-13:00 & 14:00-18:00, shorter hours off-season, +39 0588 87257, www.volterratur.it). They have bus schedules, a city map, and plenty of suggestions to keep you busy. Check the TI website for details on frequent summer festivals and concerts. Ignore the private travel agency, disguised as a TI, in the opposite corner of the piazza.

### ARRIVAL IN VOLTERRA

**By Public Transport:** Buses stop at Piazza Martiri della Libertà in the town center. Train travelers can reach the town with a short bus ride from Pontedera, which has the nearest train station.

VOLTERRA & SAN GIMIGNANO

**By Car:** From Pisa, take the highway known as FI-PI-LI (for "Firenze-Pisa-Livorno") in the direction of Florence, exiting at Pontedera to follow the scenic country road SR-439 toward Ponsacco and on to Volterra. From Florence, leave the city to the south to reach SR-2 toward Siena. Exit just past Poggibonsi onto SR-68 toward Colle di Val d'Elsa, passing the road to San Gimignano on the way to Volterra

Don't drive into the town center; it's prohibited except for locals (and you'll get a huge fine). It's easiest to simply wind to the top where the road ends at Piazza Martiri della Libertà. (Halfway up the hill, there's a confusing hard right—don't take it; keep going straight uphill under the wall.) Immediately before the Piazza Martiri bus roundabout is the entry to *Parcheggio La Dogana* **underground garage** (€2/hour, €15/day, keep ticket and pay as you leave) that's within a few blocks of nearly all my recommended hotels and sights.

If the main garage is full, the police may direct you to other pay **lots** that ring the town walls (try the handy-but-small lot facing the Roman Theater and Porta Fiorentina gate). You can also pay to park outside the walls in any street spot marked with blue lines. Behind town, a lot named Docciola is free, but it requires a steep climb from the Porta di Docciola gate up into town.

If you're staying in town, check with your hotel about the best parking options.

## HELPFUL HINTS

**Volterra Card:** This €15 card covers all the main sights—except for the Palazzo Viti (valid 72 hours, buy at TI or any covered sight). If traveling with kids, ask about the family card, an especially good deal (€24 for 1-2 adults and kids under 18).

**Market Day:** The market is on Saturday morning near the Roman Theater (8:00-13:00; Nov-March it moves to Piazza dei Priori). The TI hands out a list of other market days in the area.

**Laundry:** The handy self-service **Lavanderia Azzurra** is just off the main square (daily 7:00-22:00, Via Roma 7, +39 0588 80030). Their next-door dry-cleaning shop also provides wash-and-dry services that usually take about 24 hours (closed Sun).

# Tours in Volterra

### ▲▲Guided Volterra Walk

Annie Adair and her colleague Claudia Meucci offer a great one-hour, English-only introductory walking tour of Volterra for €10. The walk touches on Volterra's Etruscan, Roman, and medieval history, as well as the contemporary cultural scene (daily April-Oct, rain or shine Mon, Wed, and Fri at 12:30, Tue, Thu, Sat, and

Sun at 18:00; meet in front of alabaster shop on Piazza Martiri della Libertà, no need to reserve; www.volterrawalkingtour.com or www.tuscantour.com, info@volterrawalkingtour.com). There's no better way to spend €10 and one hour in this city. I mean it. Don't miss this beautiful experience.

### Local Guides

American **Annie Adair** is an excellent guide for private, in-depth tours of Volterra (€180/half-day). Her husband **Francesco,** an easy-going sommelier and wine critic, and his team lead a Wine Tasting 101 crash course in sampling Tuscan wines (€60/hour per group, plus cost of wine). Annie and Francesco also offer excursions to a honey farm, alabaster quarry, and winery, or a more wine-focused trip to Montalcino or the heart of Chianti (about €450/day for 2-4 people, larger groups possible, +39 347 143 5004, www.tuscantour.com, info@tuscantour.com).

# Sights in Volterra

I've linked these sights with handy walking directions.
• *Begin at the Etruscan Arch at the bottom of Via Porta all'Arco (about 4 blocks below the main square, Piazza dei Priori).*

### ▲Etruscan Arch (Porta all'Arco)

Volterra's renowned Etruscan arch was built of massive stones in the fourth century BC. The original city wall was four miles around—twice the size of today's wall. Imagine: This city had 20,000 people four centuries before Christ. Volterra was a key trading center and one of 12 leading towns in the confederation of Etruria. The three seriously eroded heads, dating from the first century BC, show what happens when you leave something outside for 2,000 years. The newer stones are part of the 13th-century city wall, which incorporated parts of the much older Etruscan wall.

A plaque just outside remembers June 30, 1944. That night, Nazi forces were planning to blow up the arch to slow the Allied advance. To save their treasured landmark, Volterrans ripped up the stones that pave Via Porta all'Arco, plugged up the gate, and managed to convince the Nazi commander that there was no need to blow up the arch. Today, all the paving stones are back in their places, and like silent heroes, they welcome you through the oldest standing gate into Volterra. Locals claim this as the oldest surviving rounded arch of the Etruscan age; some experts believe this is where the Romans got the idea for using a keystone in their arches.

• *Go through the arch and head up Via Porta all'Arco, which I like to call...*

### "Artisan Lane" (Via Porta all'Arco)

This steep and atmospheric lane is lined with interesting shops featuring the work of artisans and producers. Because of its alabaster heritage, Volterra developed a tradition of craftsmanship and artistry, and today you'll find a rich variety of handiwork (shops generally open Mon-Sat 10:00-13:00 & 16:00-19:00, closed Sun).

From the Etruscan Arch, browse your way up the hill, checking out these shops and items (listed from bottom to top): alabaster shop (#45); book bindery and papery (#26); jewelry (#25); etchings (#23); and bronze work (#6).

• *Reaching the top of Via Porta all'Arco, turn left and walk a few steps into Volterra's main square, Piazza dei Priori. It's dominated by the...*

### Palazzo dei Priori

Volterra's City Hall, built about 1200, claims to be the oldest of any Tuscan city-state. It clearly inspired the more famous Pala-

zzo Vecchio in Florence. Town halls like this are emblematic of the era of powerful city-states. They were architectural exclamation points declaring that, around here, no pope or emperor called the shots. Towns such as Volterra were truly city-states—proudly independent and relatively democratic. They had their own armies, taxes, and even weights and measures. Notice the horizontal "cane" cut into the City Hall wall (10 yards to the right of the door). For a thousand years, this square hosted a market, and the "cane" was the local yardstick. You can pay to see the council chambers and to climb to the top of the bell tower.

**Cost and Hours:** €8, includes council chambers and tower climb, daily 9:00-19:00, Nov-mid-March until 16:30, tower closed in bad weather.

**Visiting the Palazzo:** When not in use for meetings or weddings, the building's historic **High Council Hall**—fine arches lavishly frescoed and lit with fun dragon lamps, as they have been for centuries of town meetings—is open to visitors. The adjacent Sala della Giunta is a simpler, smaller meeting room with bare stone walls.

Climbing the 159 steps (they get pretty tight at the top) to the **tower** will earn you a fine view. Midway up is a modest exhibit about the history of the town, including a model of Volterra in the late 13th century (looking much as it does today) and a wooden cutaway model of the tower itself.

• *Back in the piazza, you can't miss the black-and-white striped wall near the TI. The little back door in that wall, a private entrance for the bishop for the last 1,000 years, leads into Volterra's cathedral. Circle the building clockwise to find the...*

## Duomo

This church is not as elaborate as its cousin in Pisa, but it is a beautiful example of the Pisan Romanesque style. The simple 13th-century facade conceals a more intricate interior (rebuilt in the late 16th and 19th centuries), with a central nave flanked by monolithic stucco columns painted to imitate pink granite and topped by a gilded, coffered ceiling.

**Cost and Hours:** €7 includes the Duomo, baptistery, and skippable old hospital where you buy your ticket, Mon-Sat 10:00-18:00, Sun from 13:30, shorter hours off-season.

**Visiting the Church:** The interior was decorated mostly in the late 16th century during Florentine rule under the Medici family. Their coat of arms, with its distinctive balls, is repeated multiple times throughout the building.

Head down into the nave to face the main altar. Up the stairs just to the right is a dreamy, painted, and gilded wooden sculptural group depicting the **Deposition of Christ** from the cross. Carved in 1228, a generation before Giotto, it shows emotion and motion way ahead of its time. Pop a euro into the box to buy some light and stand here as a 13th-century pilgrim would have (their eyes were better in the dark).

The glowing **windows** just to the left (in the transept and behind the altar) are sheets of alabaster that add to the church's worshipful ambience.

The 12th-century marble **pulpit,** partway down the nave, is also beautifully carved. In the relief panel of the Last Supper, all the apostles are together except Judas, who's under the table with the evil dragon (his name is the only one not carved into the relief). As with most medieval art, the artist remains anonymous.

Just past the pulpit on the right (at the Rosary Chapel), check out the *Annunciation,* painted in 1497 by Mariotto Albertinelli

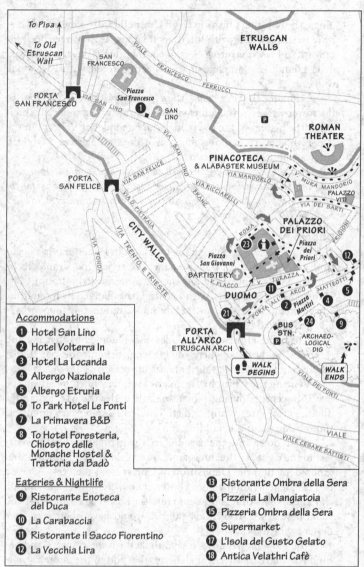

VOLTERRA & SAN GIMIGNANO

**Accommodations**
1 Hotel San Lino
2 Hotel Volterra In
3 Hotel La Locanda
4 Albergo Nazionale
5 Albergo Etruria
6 To Park Hotel Le Fonti
7 La Primavera B&B
8 To Hotel Foresteria, Chiostro delle Monache Hostel & Trattoria da Badò

**Eateries & Nightlife**
9 Ristorante Enoteca del Duca
10 La Carabaccia
11 Ristorante il Sacco Fiorentino
12 La Vecchia Lira
13 Ristorante Ombra della Sera
14 Pizzeria La Mangiatoia
15 Pizzeria Ombra della Sera
16 Supermarket
17 L'Isola del Gusto Gelato
18 Antica Velathri Cafè

and Fra Bartolomeo (both were students of Fra Angelico). The two, friends since childhood, delicately give worshippers a way to see Mary "conceived by the Holy Spirit." Note the vibrant colors, exaggerated perspective, and Mary's *contrapposto* pose—all attributes of the Renaissance.

**Visiting the Chapel**: Exit the church and enter the chapel through a separate entrance to see the painted terra-cotta statue groups of the Nativity and the Adoration of the Magi. One is by an

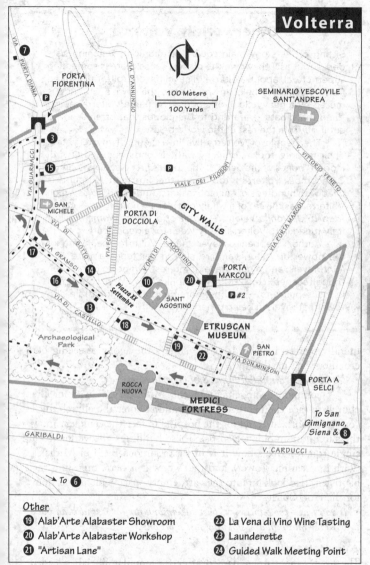

# Volterra

**Other**

19 Alab'Arte Alabaster Showroom

20 Alab'Arte Alabaster Workshop

21 "Artisan Lane"

22 La Vena di Vino Wine Tasting

23 Launderette

24 Guided Walk Meeting Point

anonymous local artist; the other is thought to be the work of master ceramist Andrea della Robbia. Remarkably, no one is certain who did which one—a testament to the skill of local craftsmen. Della Robbia's uncle, Luca, is credited with devising the glazing formula that makes Della Robbia's inventive sculptures shine even in poorly lit interiors. At the end of the chapel, ponder a poignant statue of the Mater Dolorosa ("sorrowful mother"), showing Mary

## Otherworldly Volterra

Sitting on its stony main square at midnight, watching bats dart about as if they own the place, I sense there is something supernatural about Volterra. The cliffs of Volterra inspired Dante's "cliffs of hell." In the winter, the town's vibrancy is muted by a heavy cloak of clouds. The name Volterra means "land that floats"—referring to the clouds that often seem to cut it off from the rest of the world below.

The people of Volterra live in a cloud of mystery, too. Their favorite cookie, crunchy with almonds, is called Ossi di Morto ("bones of the dead"). The town's first disco was named Catacombs. Volterra's top sight—the Etruscan Museum—is filled with hundreds of ancient caskets. And in the 1970s, when Volterra was the set of a wildly popular TV horror series called *Ritratto di Donna Velata (Portrait of a Veiled Woman)*, all of Italy tuned in to Volterra every week for a good scare.

Author Stephenie Meyer made Volterra the home of the powerful Volturi vampire clan in her teen-vampire *Twilight* novels, and a new wave of interest swept Volterra (even though scenes in the 2009 *Twilight* film *New Moon* were filmed in Montepulciano)—just one more chapter in a long tale of a town that revels in being otherworldly.

literally pierced by swords as she suffers the agony of seeing her crucified son's dead body.

• *Step outside again into Piazza San Giovanni.*

A common arrangement in the Middle Ages was for the church to face the baptistery (you couldn't enter the church until you were baptized)...and for the hospital to face the cemetery (now the site of an ambulance corps). These buildings all overlooked a single square. That's how it is in Pisa's famous Field of Miracles (with its Leaning Tower), and that's how it is here. Step into the baptistery and look up into the vast, empty space—plenty of room for the Holy Spirit.

• *As you leave the baptistery, pass the ambulance corps and head back toward the main square, stopping just short on...*

### ▲Via Matteotti

The town's main drag, named after the popular Socialist leader Giacomo Matteotti (killed by the fascists in 1924), provides a good cultural scavenger hunt.

At #1, on the left, is a typical **Italian bank security door.** (Step in and say, "Beam me up, Scotty.") Back outside, stand at the corner and look up and all around. Find the medieval griffin torch-holder—symbol of Volterra, looking down Via Matteotti—and imagine it holding a flaming torch. The pharmacy kitty-corner sports the symbol of its medieval guild. Across the street from the bank, #2 is the base of what was a San Gimignano-style **fortified Tuscan tower.** Look up and imagine heavy beams cantilevered out, supporting extra wooden rooms and balconies crowding out over the street. Throughout Tuscany, today's stark and stony old building fronts once supported a tangle of wooden extensions.

As you head down Via Matteotti, notice how the doors show centuries of refitting work. Doors that once led to these extra rooms are now partially bricked up to make windows. Contemplate urban density in the 14th century, before the plague thinned out the population. Be careful: A **wild boar** (a local delicacy) awaits you at #10.

At #12, on the right, notice the line of doorbells: This typical **palace,** once the home of a single rich family, is now occupied by many middle-class families. After the social revolution in the 18th century and the rise of the middle class, former palaces were condominium-ized. Even so, the original family still lives here—apartment #1 is the home of Count Guidi.

On the right at #16, pop into the **alabaster showroom.** Alabaster, quarried nearby, has long been a big industry here. Volterra alabaster—softer and more translucent than marble—was sliced thin to serve as windows for Italy's medieval churches.

At #19, the recommended **La Vecchia Lira** is a lively restaurant. The **Bar L'Incontro** across the street is a favorite for breakfast and pastries; in the summer, they sell homemade gelato, while in the winter they make chocolates. In the evening, it's a bustling local spot for a drink.

Across the way, side-trip 10 steps up Vicolo delle Prigioni to the fun **Panificio Rosetti** bakery. They're happy to sell small quantities if you want to try the local *cantuccini* (almond biscotti) or another treat.

Continue on Via Matteotti to the end of the block. Notice the bit of **Etruscan wall** artfully used to display more alabaster art (at #51).

By the way, you can only buy a package of cigarettes at the machine in the wall just to the right—labeled *"Vietato ai Minori"* (forbidden to minors)—by inserting an Italian national health care card to prove you're over 18.

Locals gather early each evening at **Osteria dei Poeti** (#57) for some of the best cocktails in town (served with free munchies). The cinema is across the street. Movies in Italy are rarely in their original language; Italians are used to getting their movies dubbed into Italian. To bring some culture to this little town, they also show live broadcasts of operas and concerts (advertised in the window).

Another **Tuscan tower** on the corner (#66) marks the end of the street. This noble house had a ground floor with no interior access to the safe upper floors. Rope ladders were used to get upstairs.

The tiny door was wide enough to let in your skinny friends...but definitely not anyone wearing armor and carrying big weapons.

Across the little square stands the ancient **Church of St. Michael.** After long years of barbarian chaos, the Germanic Langobards moved in from the north in the sixth century and asserted law and order in places like Volterra. That generally included building a Christian church over the old Roman forum to symbolically claim and tame the center of town. The church standing here today is Romanesque, dating from the 12th century.

Around the right side, find the crude little guy and the smiling octopus under its eaves—they've been making faces at the passing crowds for 800 years.

• *When you reach the little* piazzetta *with a Romanesque church, turn left down Via dei Sarti. Our next stop—Palazzo Viti—is halfway down the block. But if you want to linger on the square for a bit, drop in for a glass of wine at* **Enoteca Scali** *(at Via Guarnacci 3), where friendly Massimo and Patrizia sell a vast selection of wines and local delicacies in an inviting atmosphere.*

## ▲Palazzo Viti

Palazzo Viti takes you behind the rustic, heavy stone walls of the city to see how the wealthy lived—in this case, rich from the 19th-century alabaster trade. This time warp is popular with Italian movie directors. With 12 rooms on one floor open to the public, Palazzo Viti feels remarkably lived in—because it is. Behind the ropes you'll see intimate family photos. You may well find Signora Viti herself selling admission tickets.

**Cost and Hours:** €5, Mon-Fri 10:30-17:00, Sat-Sun 10:00-17:30, by appointment only Nov-March, ask for an English brochure, Via dei Sarti 41, +39 0588 84047, www.palazzoviti.it, info@palazzoviti.it.

**Visiting the Palazzo:** The elegant interior is compact and well described. You'll climb up a stately staircase, buy your ticket, and head into the grand ballroom. From here, you'll tour the blue-hued dining room (with slice-of-life Chinese scenes painted on rice paper); the salon of battles (with warfare paintings on the walls); and the long hall of temporary exhibits. Looping back, you'll see the porcelain hall (decorated with priceless plates) and the inviting library (notice the delicate lamp with a finely carved lampshade).

The Brachettone Salon is named for the local artist responsible for the small sketch of near-nudes hanging just left of the door into the next room. Brachettone (from *brache*, "pants") is the nickname for the hometown 16th-century artist Daniele da Volterra, who owns the dubious distinction of having painted all those wispy loincloths over the genitalia of Michelangelo's figures in the *Last Judgment* at the Sistine Chapel. (In this drawing, notice a similar aversion to showing the full monty...though everything-but is fair game.) On the table, notice the family wedding photo with Pope John Paul II presiding. In the red room, a portrait of Giuseppe Viti (looking like Pavarotti) hangs next to the exit door. He's the man who purchased the place in 1850. Your visit ends with bedrooms and a dressing room.

Your Palazzo Viti ticket sometimes gets you a fine little cheese, *salumi,* and wine tasting, typically in high season. As you leave the palace, climb down into the cool cellar (used as a disco on some weekends), where you can pop into a Roman cistern, marvel at an Etruscan well, and enjoy a friendly sit-down snack.

• *A block past Palazzo Viti, also on Via dei Sarti, is the...*

## Pinacoteca and Alabaster Museum (Pinacoteca e Ecomuseo dell'Alabastro)

The Pinacoteca fills a 15th-century palace with fine paintings that feel more Florentine than Sienese—a reminder of whose domain this town was in. You'll see a stunning altarpiece by Taddeo di Bartolo, once displayed in the original residence. You'll also find roomfuls of gilded altarpieces and saintly statues, as well as a trio of striking High Renaissance altar paintings by Signorelli, Fiorentino, and Ghirlandaio.

The adjoining Alabaster Museum gives a fascinating overview of the local alabaster industry, past and present.

**Cost and Hours:** €8, daily 9:00-19:00, Nov-mid-March until 16:30, Via dei Sarti 1, +39 0588 87580.

**Visiting the Museum:** Begin with the **Pinacoteca** and head upstairs to the first floor. Turn right at the landing and go directly into Room #11, with Luca Signorelli's beautifully lit *Annunciation* (1491), an example of classic High Renaissance from the town cathedral. To the right, find *Descent from the Cross* (a.k.a. *Deposition,* 1521), the groundbreaking Mannerist work by Rosso Fiorentino (note the elongated bodies and harsh emotional lighting and colors). In the adjacent room (#10), see Ghirlandaio's *Christ in Glory* (1492). The two devout-looking kneeling women are actually pagan, pre-Christian Etruscan demigoddesses, Attinea and Greciniana.

Rather than attempt to get locals to stop venerating them (as their images were all over town), the church simply sainted them. Upstairs, the second floor has three more rooms of similar art—huge frescoes and wood-panel paintings.

Back on the main floor, head through the fine, tranquil, cloister-like courtyard—with the remains of its original well—and enter the **Alabaster Museum.** With alabaster sculptures spread over three floors, this fun and easy little museum contains examples from Etruscan times until the present. Take the elevator to the top and work your way down. The top floor displays stone-working tools and offers fine views. Etruscan pieces are on the middle floor, and modern sculptures—including an intriguing alabaster fried egg—are on the lower floor.

• *Exiting the building, circle right along the side of the museum into the tunnel-like Passo del Gualduccio passage; then turn right and walk along the wall, enjoying views of the...*

VOLTERRA & SAN GIMIGNANO

## Roman Theater (Teatro Romano)

With the fine aerial view from the city wall promenade, there's no reason to pay to enter this well-preserved, first-century theater (although it is covered by the Volterra Card). The 13th-century wall that you're standing on divided the theater from the town center...so, naturally, the theater became the town dump. Over time, the theater was forgotten—covered in the garbage of Volterra. It was rediscovered in the 1950s and excavated.

The stage wall (immediately in front of the theater seats) was standard Roman design—with three levels from which actors would appear: one level for mortals, one for heroes, and the top one for gods. Parts of two levels still stand. Gods leaped out onto the third level for the last time around the third century AD, which is when the town began to use the theater stones to build fancy baths instead. You can see the scant remains of the baths behind the theater, including the little round sauna in the far corner with brick supports that raise the heated floor.

From this vantage point, you can trace Volterra's vast Etruscan wall. Find the church in the distance, on the left, and notice the stones just below. They are from the Etruscan wall that followed the ridge into the valley and defined Volterra in the fourth century BC.

• *From the theater viewpoint, continue along the wall downhill to the T-intersection (the old gate, Porta Fiorentina, with fine wooden medi-*

*eval doors, is on your left). Turn right, making your way uphill on Via Guarnacci which becomes Via Matteotti. A block up Via Matteotti, you can't miss the wide, pedestrianized shopping street called Via Gramsci. Follow this up to Piazza XX Settembre, walk through that leafy square, and continue uphill on Via Don Minzoni. At #18, you'll find an...*

## ▲Alabaster Showroom and Workshop

For a fun peek into the art of alabaster, visit the Alab'Arte showroom, featuring the work of Roberto Chiti and Giorgio Finazzo.

Lighting shows off the translucent quality of the stone and the expertise of these artists, who are delighted to share their work with visitors. If they're not in the showroom, the duo might be found at their nearby workshop (just down the narrow lane, Via Porta Marcoli, which runs next to the Etruscan Museum), where everything—including Roberto and Giorgio—is covered in a fine white dust. This is not a touristy guided visit, but something far more special: the chance to see busy artisans practicing their craft. For more such artisans in action, visit "Artisan Lane" (Via Porta all'Arco), described earlier on this walk, or ask the TI for a list of workshops open to the public.

**Cost and Hours:** Free, showroom—daily 10:00-13:00 & 15:00-19:00, closes at 17:30 in off-season, closed Nov-Feb, Via Don Minzoni 18; workshop—Mon-Sat 10:00-12:30 & 15:00-19:00, closed Sun, if showroom is closed ask in the workshop, Via Orti Sant'Agostino 28, www.alabarte.com.

• *Next pay a visit to the...*

## ▲▲Etruscan Museum (Museo Etrusco Guarnacci)

Filled top to bottom with rare Etruscan artifacts, this museum—founded in 1732 (one of Italy's first public museums and among the oldest in Europe)—makes it easy to appreciate how advanced this pre-Roman culture was.

**Cost and Hours:** €8, daily 9:00-19:00, Nov-mid-March 10:00-16:30, Via Don Minzoni 15, +39 0588 86347, www.volterratur.it/en/poi/guarnacci-etruscan-museum.

**Visiting the Museum:** To see the exhibits in chronological order, take the elevator or stairs to the top floor and make your way down. Otherwise, start on the ground floor with some beautiful Etruscan urns and an inviting public garden out back.

The ground-floor collection starts with an introduction to the Etruscans and the history of the excavations carried out in this area. Filling the rest of the ground floor is a vast collection of stone Etruscan **cinerary urns** (seventh-first century BC). Etruscan urns have two parts: The box on the bottom contained the cremated remains (with elaborately carved panels), while the lid was decorated with a sculpture of the deceased. The carved bas-relief scenes and motifs decorating the urns are a prized catalog of Etruscan life and activities.

First pay attention to the people on top. While contemporaries of the Greeks, the Etruscans were more libertine. Their religion was less demanding, and their women were a respected part of both the social and public spheres. Women and men alike are depicted lounging on Etruscan urns. While they seem to be just hanging out, the lounging dead were actually offering the gods a banquet—in order to gain the Etruscan equivalent of salvation. Etruscans really did lounge like this in front of a table, but this banquet had eternal consequences. The dearly departed are often depicted holding blank wax tablets (symbolizing blank new lives in the next world). Men hold containers that would generally be used at banquets, including libation cups for offering wine to the gods. The women are finely dressed, sometimes holding a pomegranate (symbolizing fertility) or a mirror. Look at the faces and imagine the lives they lived.

Now tune into the reliefs carved into the fronts of the boxes. The motifs vary widely, from floral patterns to mystical animals (such as a Starbucks-like mermaid) to parades of magistrates. Some show journeys on horseback—appropriate for someone leaving this world and entering the next. Some show the fabled horseback-and-carriage ride to the underworld, where the dead are greeted by Charun, an underworld demon, with his hammer and pointy ears.

While the finer urns are carved of alabaster, most are made of limestone. Originally they were colorfully painted. Many lids are mismatched—casualties of reckless 18th- and 19th-century archaeological digs.

Head upstairs to the **first floor.** You'll enter a room with a circular mosaic in the floor (a Roman original, found in Volterra and transplanted here). To the left of the stairs, explore more Etruscan treasures in a series of rooms filled with urns depicting Greek myths and the voyage of Ulysses. A large room displays statues and inscriptions from the city's Roman Theater.

To the right of the stairs, fans of Alberto Giacometti will be amazed at how the tall, skinny figure called *The Evening Shadow* (*L'Ombra della Sera,* third century BC) looks just like the modern Swiss sculptor's work—but 2,500 years older. This is an example of the ex-voto bronze statues that the Etruscans created in thanks to the gods. With his supremely lanky frame, distinctive wavy hairdo, and inscrutable smirk, this Etruscan lad captures the illusion of a shadow stretching long, late in the day. Admire the sheer artistry and modernity of the statue.

The museum's other top piece is the **Urn of the Spouses** (*Urna degli Sposi*, first century BC). It's unique for various reasons, in-

cluding its material (it's in terracotta—relatively rare for these urns) and its depiction of two people rather than one. Looking at this elderly couple, it's easy to imagine the long life they spent together and their desire to pass eternity lounging with each other at a banquet for the gods.

Other highlights include locally produced black-glazed pottery and painted kraters (vases with handles used for mixing water and wine), ex-voto water-bearer statues, bronze hand mirrors, exquisite golden jewelry that would still be fashionable today, a battle helmet ominously dented at the left temple, and hundreds of ancient coins.

The **top floor** features pieces from the Bronze Age and the early Etruscan period, including some impressive jewelry, the first examples of Etruscan writing, and the funeral dowry (artifacts that the dead would pack along and be buried with) of a warrior with his impressive helmet and remarkable double-spouted military flask for wine and water. Don't miss the re-created tomb, with several neatly aligned urns, a shattered eggshell, and more funeral dowries—including mirrors, coins, hardware for vases, votive statues, pots, pans, and jewelry.

• *After your museum visit, duck across the street to the...*

### ▲La Vena di Vino Wine Tasting

La Vena di Vino, just across from the Etruscan Museum, is a fun *enoteca* where Bruno and Lucio have devoted themselves to the

wonders of wine and share it with a fun-loving passion. Each day they open six or eight bottles, serve your choice by the glass, and pair it with characteristic munchies amid unusual decor (the place is strewn with bras). Hang out here with the local characters. According to Bruno, a Brunello is just right with wild boar and a Super Tuscan is perfect for meditation. Volterra can be quiet late at night, but this place is full of action (Wed-Mon 11:30-

# Under the Etruscan Sun
## (c. 900 BC-AD 1)

Around 550 BC—just before the golden age of Greece—the Etruscan people of central Italy had their own golden age. Though their origins are unclear, the Etruscans' mix of Greek-style art with Roman-style customs helped lay a civilized foundation for the rise of the Roman Empire. As you travel through Italy—particularly in Tuscany (from "Etruscan")—you'll find traces of this long-lost people.

Etruscan tombs and artifacts are still being discovered, often by farmers in the countryside. Museums in Volterra and Cortona house fine collections of urns, pottery, and devotional figures. You can visit several domed tombs outside Cortona, including some at the Baratti and Populonia Archaeological Park on the mainland facing the island of Elba (see page 638).

The Etruscans were established in central Italy by the early seventh century BC, when a number of settlements sprouted up in sparsely populated Tuscany and Umbria, including today's hill towns of Cortona, Chiusi, and Volterra. Possibly immigrants from Turkey, but more likely local farmers who moved to the city, they became sailors, traders, and craftsmen, and welcomed new ideas from Greece.

More technologically advanced than their neighbors, the Etruscans mined iron ore, smelting and exporting it around the Mediterranean. They drained and irrigated large tracts of land, creating the fertile farmland of central Italy's breadbasket. With their disciplined army, warships, merchant vessels, and (from the Greek perspective) pirate galleys, they ruled central Italy and the major ports along the Tyrrhenian Sea. For nearly two centuries (c. 700-500 BC), much of Italy lived in peace and prosperity under the Etruscan sun.

Judging from the frescoes and many luxury items that have survived, the Etruscans enjoyed the good life: They look healthy and vibrant as they play flutes, dance with birds, or play party games. Etruscan artists celebrated individual people, showing their wrinkles, crooked noses, silly smiles, and funny haircuts.

Thousands of surviving ceramic plates and cups attest to the importance of food and banqueting. Men and women celebrated together, propped on their elbows on dining couches, surrounded by colorful decor. The banqueters were entertained with music and dancing and were served by elegant slaves. According to contemporary accounts, the Etruscans—even their slaves—were Europe's best-dressed people.

Scholars today have deciphered the Etruscans' Greek-style alphabet and some individual words, but they have yet to fully understand their language, which is unlike any other in Europe. Much of what we know of the Etruscans comes from their tombs. The tomb was a home in the hereafter, complete with the deceased's belongings. The urn might have a statue on the lid of the deceased at a banquet—lying across a dining couch, spoon-

**The Etruscan Empire**

Bologna ■
Ravenna ●
*Adriatic Sea*

*Appenine Mountains*

La Spezia ●

Florence ● Fiesole ■
Arno R.
Pisa ●

*Ligurian Sea*

**ETRUSCAN**

ITALY

100 Miles

Volterra ■
(M)
Siena ●
Cortona ■
(M)
Murlo ■
(M)
Chiusi ■
(M)
Perugia ●
Lake Trasimeno

Populonia ●

**EMPIRE**

Vetulonia ■
Roselle ■

Orvieto ■
(M)
Bolsena ■
Lake Bolsena
Tiber R.

Elba

*Tyrrhenian Sea*

Vulci ■
Tarquinia ■

Veio ■
Cerveteri ■

● Rome
(M)

■ Etruscan Cities
● Modern Cities
(M) Etruscan Museum
— --- Border of Tuscany

**VOLTERRA & SAN GIMIGNANO**

ing with his wife, smiles on their faces, living the good life for all eternity.

Seven decades of wars with the Greeks (545-474 BC) disrupted their trade routes and drained the Etruscan League, just as a new Mediterranean power was emerging: Rome. In 509 BC, the Romans overthrew their Etruscan king, and Rome expanded, capturing Etruscan cities one by one (the last in 264 BC). Etruscan resisters were killed, the survivors intermarried with Romans, and their kids grew up speaking Latin. By Julius Caesar's time, the only remnants of Etruscan culture were its priests, who became Rome's professional soothsayers. Interestingly, the Etruscan prophets had foreseen their own demise, having predicted that Etruscan civilization would last 10 centuries.

But Etruscan culture lived on in Roman religion (pantheon of gods, household gods, and divination rituals), art (realism), lifestyle (the banquet), and in a taste for Greek styles—the mix that became our "Western civilization."

24:00, closed Tue, Nov-Feb open Fri-Sat only, Via Don Minzoni 30, +39 0588 81491, www.lavenadivino.com).

• *Volterra's final sight is perched atop the hill just above the wine bar. Climb up one of the lanes nearby, then walk (to the right) along the formidable wall to find the park.*

## Medici Fortress and Archaeological Park
## (Fortezza Medicea and Parco Archeologico)

The archaeological park marks what was the acropolis of Volterra from 1500 BC until AD 1472, when Florence conquered the pesky city. The Florentines burned Volterra's political and historic center, turning it into a grassy commons and building the adjacent Medici Fortress. The old fortress—a symbol of Florentine dominance—now keeps people in rather than out. It's a maximum-security prison housing only about 120 special prisoners.

Authorities prefer to keep organized crime figures locked up far away from their Sicilian family ties. (If you drive from Volterra to San Gimignano, you'll pass another big, modern prison—almost surreal in the midst of all the Tuscan wonder.)

The park sprawling next to the fortress (toward the town center) is a rare, grassy meadow at the top of a rustic hill town—a favorite place for locals to relax and picnic on a sunny day. Nearby are the scant remains of the acropolis, which can be viewed through the fence for free, or entered for a fee. Of more interest to antiquities enthusiasts is the acropolis' first-century Roman cistern. You can descend 40 tight spiral steps to stand in a chamber that once held about 250,000 gallons of water, enough to provide for more than a thousand people. While not huge, it provides a good look at Roman engineering and reminds you just how important a supply of water was to the survival of a hill town.

**Cost and Hours:** Park—free, open until 20:00 in peak of summer, shorter hours off-season; acropolis and cistern—€8, daily 10:30-17:30, shorter hours off-season.

## Countryside Strolls

If you have time for a stroll, Volterra—perched on a ridge overlooking pristine Tuscan hills—has countryside galore to explore. Get advice from the TI or consult www.valdicecinaoutdoor.it.

One popular walk is to head to the west end of town, out Porta San Francesco, into a workaday area (dubbed "Borghi," literally "neighborhoods") that sees few tourists. Continuing downhill from the gate, notice the bars and playgrounds filled with locals, before the imposing Church of San Giusto dramatically appears on your right. Soon after, you'll come to a cliff with a stretch of the original fourth-century-BC Etruscan wall. Peering over the cliff from here, you can see that Volterra sits upon orange sandy topsoil packed onto clay cliffs, called Le Balze. At various points in its history, the town has been threatened by landslides, and parts of its hilltop have simply disappeared. The big church you see in the distance was abandoned in the late 1800s for fear that it would be swallowed up by the land. The distinctive ridged hills surrounding Volterra, called *calanchi*, eroded by wind and rain and hardened by the sun, are Italy's version of badlands.

### Evening Scene

*Passeggiata:* As they have for generations, Volterrans young and old stroll during the cool of the early evening. The main cruising is along Via Gramsci and Via Matteotti to the main square, Piazza dei Priori.

*Aperitivo:* Each evening several bars put out little buffet spreads free with a drink to attract a crowd. Bars popular for their *aperitivo* include VolaTerra (Via Turazza 5, next to City Hall), L'Incontro (Via Matteotti 19), and Bar dei Poeti (across from the cinema, Via Matteotti 57). And the gang at La Vena di Vino (described under "Sights in Volterra") always seems ready for a good time.

**Antica Velathri Cafè:** Venture just a bit off the beaten path, between Piazza XX Settembre and the park, to Antica Velathri Cafè for a drink in the evening (or a light meal any time of the day). Pietro makes creative cocktails and good conversation while his mama makes the pastries (Tue-Sun 9:30-24:00, closed Mon, Via Ormanni 3, +39 0588 190 0121).

# Sleeping in Volterra

Volterra has plenty of places offering a good night's sleep at a fair price. Lodgings outside the old town are generally a bit cheaper (and easier for drivers). But keep in mind that some of these places involve not just walking, but steep walking.

## INSIDE THE OLD TOWN

**$$$ Hotel San Lino** fills a former convent with 40 modern rooms, all named for the nuns who lived in them. It's at the sleepy lower end of town—close to the Porta San Francesco gate, and about a five-minute uphill walk to the main drag. Although it's within the town walls, it doesn't feel like it: The hotel has a fine swimming pool and view terrace and is the only in-town option that's convenient for drivers, who can reserve pay parking in advance (RS%, family rooms, air-con, elevator, closed Nov-Feb, Via San Lino 26, +39 0588 85250, www.hotelsanlino.com, info@hotelsanlino.com).

**$$$ Hotel Volterra In** is fresh, tasteful, and in a central yet quiet location. Marco rents 10 bright and spacious rooms with thoughtful, upscale touches and a hearty buffet breakfast (RS%, air-con, elevator, Via Porta all'Arco 41, +39 0588 86820, www. hotelvolterrain.it, info@hotelvolterrain.it).

**$$ Hotel La Locanda** feels stately and old-fashioned. This well-located place (just inside Porta Fiorentina, near the Roman

Theater and parking lot) rents 18 rooms with flowery decor and modern comforts (RS%, family rooms, air-con, elevator, Via Guarnacci 24, +39 058 881 547, www.hotel-lalocanda.com, staff@hotel-lalocanda.com, Irina, Oksana, and Monica).

**$$ Albergo Nazionale,** with 36 big and overpriced rooms, is popular with school groups, and steps from the bus stop. It's a nicely located last resort if you have your heart set on sleeping in the old town (RS%, family rooms, elevator, Via dei Marchesi 11, +39 058 807 0681, www.allegroitalia.it, infonazionale@allegroitalia.it).

**$ Albergo Etruria** is a family-run hotel on Volterra's main drag. They offer a good location, a peaceful rooftop garden, and 19 frilly rooms (RS%, family rooms, air-con, Via Matteotti 32, +39 0588 87377, www.albergoetruria.it, info@albergoetruria.it, Paola, Daniele, and Sveva).

## JUST OUTSIDE THE OLD TOWN

These accommodations are within a 5- to 20-minute walk of the city walls.

**$$$ Park Hotel Le Fonti,** a dull and steep 15-minute walk downhill from Porta all'Arco, can't decide whether it's a business hotel or a resort. The spacious, imposing building, old and stately, has 64 modern, comfortable rooms, half with views. While generally overpriced, it can be a good value if you manage to snag a deal. In addition to the swimming pool, guests can use its small spa (pay more for a view or a balcony, elevator, on-site restaurant, wine bar, free parking, Via di Fontecorrenti 2, +39 0588 85219, www. parkhotellefonti.com, info@parkhotellefonti.com).

**$ La Primavera B&B** feels like a British B&B transplanted to Tuscany. It's a great value just a few minutes' walk outside Porta Fiorentina (near the Roman Theater). Silvia rents five charming, neat-as-a-pin rooms that share a cutesy-country lounge. The house is set back from the road in a pleasant courtyard and with a garden to lounge in. With free parking and a short walk to the old town, this is a handy option for drivers (RS%, fans but no air-con, closed Nov-Feb, Via Porta Diana 15, +39 0588 87295, mobile +39 328 865 0390, www.affittacamere-laprimavera.com, info@affittacamere-laprimavera.com).

**$ Hotel Foresteria,** near Chiostro delle Monache (see next) and run by the same organization, has 35 big, utilitarian, new-feeling rooms with decent prices but the same location woes as the hostel; it's worth considering for a family with a car and a tight budget (family rooms, air-con, elevator, restaurant, free parking, Borgo San Lazzaro, +39 0588 80050, www.foresteriavolterra.com, info@foresteriavolterra.com).

**¢ Chiostro delle Monache,** Volterra's youth hostel, fills a wing of the restored Convent of San Girolamo. It's modern, spacious, and very institutional, with lots of services and a tranquil cloister. Unfortunately, it's about a 20-minute hike from town, in a boring area near deserted hospital buildings (private rooms available and include breakfast, family rooms, reception closed 13:00-15:00 and after 19:00, elevator, restaurant, free parking, kids' playroom; Via dell Teatro 4, look for hospital sign from main Volterra-San Gimignano road; +39 0588 86613, www.chiostrodellemonache.com, info@chiostrodellemonache.it).

## IN THE COUNTRYSIDE NEAR VOLTERRA

Charming farmhouse accommodations dot the countryside surrounding Volterra, and for drivers, these can be a good value and a fun experience. Some properties offer swimming pools, cooking classes, and more. For locations, see the map on page 502.

**$$ Podere Marcampo** is an *agriturismo* set in the dramatic landscape surrounding Volterra. Run by Genuino (owner of the recommended Ristorante Enoteca del Duca), his wife Ivana, and their English-speaking daughter Claudia, this peaceful spot has three dark but well-appointed rooms and three apartments, plus a swimming pool with panoramic views. Genuino and Claudia produce their Sangiovese and award-winning Merlot on site; you can tour where the wine is made and then sample it in their view tasting room. Cooking classes are available for guests and non-guests (breakfast included for Rick Steves readers, air-con, free self-service laundry, about two miles north of Volterra on the road to Pisa, +39 0588 85393, Claudia's mobile +39 328 174 4605, www.poderemarcampo.com, info@agriturismo-marcampo.com).

**$$ Agriturismo il Mulinaccio** is a welcoming, family-friendly farm about a five-minute drive down a dirt road outside Volterra. Hardworking Alessio and his family rent four spacious apartments and four bed-and-breakfast rooms, all with a cozy style. They also offer dinner, truffle hunts, cooking classes, wine tastings, and a spa/wellness center (air-con, pool, Via Vicinale di Pretenzano 49, +39 338 149 8432, www.agriturismoilmulinaccio.it, info@ agriturismoilmulinaccio.it).

**$$ Agriturismo Santa Vittoria** sits on the top of a hill, with commanding views into the Volterra countryside. Their four bright apartments, decorated with funky art, have access to a cliffside pool. The popular restaurant serves up hearty dishes from their farm, served at view tables. Call ahead to confirm they are open (week-long stays preferred in summer, breakfast extra, Localita Molino d'Era, hotel +39 348 561 3670, restaurant +39 348 561 3670, www. agriturismosantavittoria.com, info@agriturismosantavittoria.com, Katuscia).

## Eating in Volterra

Menus feature a Volterran take on regional dishes. *Zuppa alla Volterrana* is a fresh vegetable-and-bread soup. *Torta di ceci*, also known as *cecina*, is a savory crêpe-like garbanzo-bean flatbread that's served at pizzerias. Those with more adventurous palates dive into *trippa* (tripe stew, the traditional breakfast of the alabaster carvers). *Fegatelli* are meatballs made with liver.

**$$$$ Ristorante Enoteca del Duca,** serving well-presented and creative Tuscan cuisine, offers the best elegant meal in town. You can dine under a medieval arch with walls lined with wine bottles, in a sedate, high-ceilinged dining room (with an Etruscan statuette at each table), in their little *enoteca* (wine cellar), or in their terraced garden in summer. The friendly staff take good care of diners. The fine wine list includes Genuino and Claudia's own highly regarded Merlot and Sangiovese. The spacious seating, dressy clientele, and calm atmosphere make this a good choice for a romantic splurge. Their €70 food-sampler fixed-price meal comes with a free glass of wine for diners with this book (Wed-Mon 12:30-14:45 & 19:30-21:45, closed Tue, reservations smart, near City Hall at Via di Castello 2, +39 0588 81510, www.enoteca-delduca-ristorante.it).

**$$ La Carabaccia** is unique: It feels like a local family invited you over for a dinner of classic Tuscan comfort food that's rarely seen on restaurant menus. They serve only two pastas and two *secondi* on any given day (listed on the chalkboard by the door), in addition to quality cheese and cold-cut plates. Committed to tradition, on Fridays they serve only fish. They also have fun, family-friendly outdoor seating on a traffic-free piazza (Tue-Sat 12:30-14:30 & 19:30-22:00, Sun 12:30-14:30, closed Mon, reservations smart, Piazza XX Settembre 4, +39 0588 86239, Patrizia and daughters Sara and Ilaria).

**$$ Ristorante il Sacco Fiorentino** is a family-run local favorite for traditional cuisine and seasonal specials. While mostly indoors, the restaurant has a few nice tables on a peaceful street (Thu-Tue 12:00-15:00 & 19:00-22:00, closed Wed, Via Giusto Turazza 13, +39 0588 88537, Cristina).

**$$ Trattoria da Badò,** a 10-minute hike out of town, is popular with a local crowd for its *cucina tipica Volterrana*. Giacomo and family offer a rustic atmosphere and serve food with no pretense—"the way you wish your mamma cooks." Reserve before you go, as it's often full, especially on weekends (Thu-Tue 12:30-14:30 & 19:30-22:00, closed Wed, Borgo San Lazzero 9—along the main road toward San Gimignano, near the turnoff for the old hospital, +39 0588 80402, www.trattoriadabado.com).

**$$ La Vecchia Lira,** bright and cheery, is a classy eatery that's a hit with locals looking for fresh fare and a focus on gluten-free and vegetarian options (Fri-Wed 12:00-14:30 & 19:00-22:00, closed Thu, Via Matteotti 19, +39 0588 86180, Massimo).

**$$ Ristorante Ombra della Sera** is another good fine-dining option for elegant Tuscan cuisine and truffle dishes. While they have a dressy interior, I'd eat here to be on the street and part of the *passeggiata* action (Tue-Sun 12:00-15:00 & 19:00-22:00, closed Mon and mid-Nov-mid-March, Via Gramsci 70, +39 0588 86663, Massimo and Cinzia).

**$$ Pizzeria La Mangiatoia** is a fun and convivial place with a Tuscan-cowboy interior and picnic tables outside amid a family-friendly street scene. Enjoy pizzas, huge salads, and kebabs at a table or to go (Thu-Tue 11:00-23:00, closed Wed, Via Gramsci 35, +39 0588 85695).

**$ Pizzeria Ombra della Sera** dishes out what local kids consider the best pizza in town (Tue-Sun 12:00-15:00 & 19:00-22:00, closed Mon and mid-Nov-mid-March, Via Guarnacci 16, +39 0588 85274).

**Picnic:** You can assemble a picnic at the few grocery stores around town and eat in the breezy archaeological park. The most convenient supermarket is **Punto Simply** at Via Gramsci 12 (Mon-Sat 7:30-13:00 & 16:00-20:00, Sun 8:30-13:00).

**Gelato:** Of the many ice-cream shops in the center, I've found **L'Isola del Gusto** to be reliably high quality, with flavors limited to what's in season (daily, closed Nov-Feb, Via Gramsci 3, cheery Giorgia will make you feel happy).

## Volterra Connections

**By Bus:** In Volterra, buses come and go from Piazza Martiri della Libertà (buy tickets at the tobacco shop right on the piazza or on board). Most connections are through Colle di Val d'Elsa ("koh-leh" for short), a workaday town in the valley (4/day Mon-Sat, 1/day Sun, 50 minutes); for Pisa, you'll change in Pontedera or Saline di Volterra. Ask at the TI for schedules or check www.at-bus.it.

From Volterra, you can ride the bus to these destinations: **Florence** (4/day Mon-Sat, 1/day Sun, 2 hours, change in Colle di Val d'Elsa), **Siena** (4/day Mon-Sat, no buses on Sun, 2 hours, change in Colle di Val d'Elsa), **San Gimignano** (4/day Mon-Sat, 1/day Sun, 2 hours, change in Colle di Val d'Elsa, one connection also requires change in Poggibonsi), **Pisa** (9/day, fewer on Sun, 2 hours, change in Pontedera).

**By Train:** The nearest train station is in Saline di Volterra, a 15-minute bus ride away (7/day, 2/day Sun); however, trains from Saline run only to the coast, not to the major bus destinations listed here. It's better to take a bus from Volterra to Pontedera (8/day, 1 on Sun, 1.5 hours), where you can catch a train to **Florence, Pisa,** or **La Spezia** (convenient for the Cinque Terre).

**By Private Transfer:** For those with more money than time, or for travel on tricky Sundays and holidays, a private transfer to or from Volterra is the most efficient option. **Roberto Bechi** and his drivers can take up to eight people in their comfortable vans (€165 to Siena, €185 to Florence, for reservations call +39 320 147 6590 or Roberto's mobile +39 328 425 5648, www.toursbyroberto.com, toursbyroberto@gmail.com.

# San Gimignano

The epitome of a Tuscan hill town, with 14 medieval towers still standing (out of an original 72), San Gimignano (sahn jee-meen-YAH-noh) is a perfectly preserved tourist trap. There are no important interiors to sightsee, and the town feels greedy and packed with crass commercialism. The locals seem spoiled by the easy money of tourism, and most of the rustic is faux. But San Gimignano is so easy to reach and so visually striking that it remains a good stop, especially if you can sidestep some of the hordes. The town is an ideal place to go against the touristic flow—arrive late in the day, enjoy it at twilight, then take off in the morning before

the deluge begins. (Or day-trip here from Volterra—a 30-minute drive away—and visit early or late.)

In the 13th century—back in the days of Romeo and Juliet—feuding noble families ran the hill towns. They'd periodically battle things out from the protection of their respective family towers. Pointy skylines like San Gimignano's were the norm in medieval Tuscany.

San Gimignano's cuisine is mostly what you might find in Siena—typical Tuscan home cooking. *Cinghiale* (cheen-gee-AH-lay, boar) is served in almost every way: stews, soups, cutlets, and, my favorite, *salumi*. The area is well known for producing some of the best saffron in Italy; you'll find the spice for sale in shops and as a flavoring in meals at finer restaurants. Although Tuscany is normally a red-wine region, the most famous Tuscan white wine comes from here: the inexpensive, light, and fruity Vernaccia di San Gimignano.

## Orientation to San Gimignano

While the basic ▲▲▲ sight here is the town of San Gimignano itself (pop. 7,800, just 2,000 of whom live within the walls), there are a few worthwhile stops. The wall circles an amazingly preserved stony town, once on the Via Francigena pilgrimage route to Rome. The road, which cuts through the middle of San Gimignano, is named for St. Matthew in the north of town (Via San Matteo) and St. John in the south (Via San Giovanni). The town is centered on two delightful squares—Piazza del Duomo and Piazza della Cisterna—where you find the town well, City Hall, and cathedral (along with most of the tourists).

### TOURIST INFORMATION

The helpful TI, in the old center on Piazza del Duomo, sells bus tickets to Siena and Florence (daily 10:00-13:00 & 15:00-19:00, Nov-Feb 10:00-13:00 & 14:00-18:00, +39 0577 940 008,

VOLTERRA & SAN GIMIGNANO

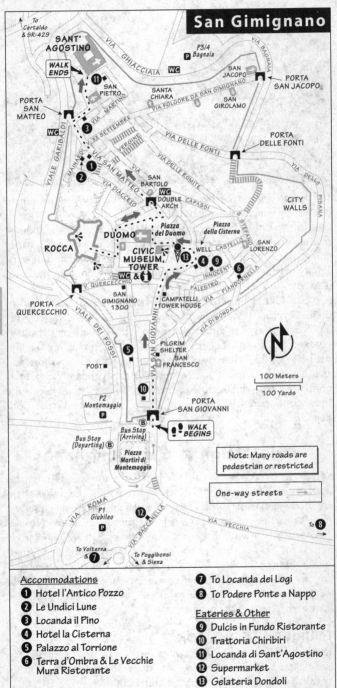

# San Gimignano

**Note:** Many roads are pedestrian or restricted

One-way streets

## Accommodations

1. Hotel l'Antico Pozzo
2. Le Undici Lune
3. Locanda il Pino
4. Hotel la Cisterna
5. Palazzo al Torrione
6. Terra d'Ombra & Le Vecchie Mura Ristorante
7. To Locanda dei Logi
8. To Podere Ponte a Nappo

## Eateries & Other

9. Dulcis in Fundo Ristorante
10. Trattoria Chiribiri
11. Locanda di Sant'Agostino
12. Supermarket
13. Gelateria Dondoli

www.sangimignano.com). They offer occasional countryside tours and a guided city tour (€15, April-Oct Mon, Wed, Fri-Sat at 11:00 and 16:00, Sun at 11:00).

## ARRIVAL IN SAN GIMIGNANO

The **bus** stops at the main town gate, Porta San Giovanni. There's no baggage storage in town.

You can't **drive** within the walled town; drive past the *"ZTL"* red circle and you'll get socked with a big fine. Three numbered pay lots are a short walk outside the walls (and connected to town by a shuttle bus in summer; see below): The handiest is Parcheggio Montemaggio (P2), at the bottom of town near the bus stop, just outside Porta San Giovanni (€2/hour, €15/day). Least expensive but a steeper walk into town is the lot below the roundabout and Co-op supermarket, Parcheggio Giubileo (P1; €1.50/hour, €6/day). And at the north end of town, by Porta San Jacopo, is Parcheggio Bagnaia (P3/P4, €2/hour, €15/day). Note that some lots—including the one directly in front of Co-op and the one just outside Porta San Matteo—are designated for locals and have a one-hour limit for tourists.

## HELPFUL HINTS

**Market Day:** Thursday is market day on Piazza del Duomo and Piazza delle Erbe (8:00-13:00), but for local merchants, every day is a sales frenzy.

**Services:** A public WC is just off Piazza della Cisterna; you'll also find WCs at the Rocca fortress, near San Bartolo church, just outside Porta San Matteo, and at the Parcheggio Bagnaia parking lot.

**Shuttle Bus:** A little electric shuttle bus does its laps about hourly all day from Porta San Giovanni to Piazza della Cisterna to Porta San Matteo. Route #1 runs back and forth through town; route #2—which runs only in summer—connects the parking lots to the town center (€1.20 one-way). When pedestrian congestion in the town center is greatest (Sat afternoons, all day Sun, and May-Sept), the bus runs along the road skirting the outside of town.

# San Gimignano Walk

This quick self-guided walking tour takes you across town, from the bus stop at Porta San Giovanni through the town's main squares to the Duomo, and on to the Sant'Agostino Church.

• *Start at the Porta San Giovanni gate at the bottom (south) end of town.*

## Porta San Giovanni

San Gimignano lies about 25 miles from both Siena and Florence, a day's trek for pilgrims en route to those cities, and on a naturally fortified hilltop that encouraged settlement. The town's walls were built in the 13th century, and gates like this helped regulate who came and went. Today, modern posts keep out all but service and emergency vehicles. The small square just outside the gate features a memorial to the town's WWII dead. Follow the pilgrims' route (and flood of modern tourists) through the gate and up the main drag.

About 100 yards up, where the street widens, look right to see a pilgrims' shelter (12th century, Pisan Romanesque). The eight-pointed Maltese cross on the facade of the church indicates that it was built by the Knights of Malta, whose early mission (before they became Crusaders) was to provide care for sick and poor pilgrims. It was one of 11 such shelters in town. Today, only the wall of the shelter remains, and the surviving interior of the church houses yet one more shop selling gifty edibles.

• *Carry on past all manner of shops, up to the top of Via San Giovanni. Look up at the formidable inner wall, built 200 years before today's outer wall. Just beyond that is the central Piazza della Cisterna. Sit on the steps of the well.*

## Piazza della Cisterna

The piazza is named for the cistern that is served by the old well standing in the center of this square. A clever system of pipes drained rainwater from the nearby rooftops into the underground cistern. This square has been the center of the town since the ninth century. Turn in a slow circle and observe the commotion of rustic yet proud facades crowding in a tight huddle around the well. Imagine this square in pilgrimage times,  lined by inns and taverns for the town's guests. Now finger the grooves in the lip of the well and imagine generations of women and children fetching water. Each Thursday morning, the square fills with a market—as it has for more than a thousand years.

• *Notice San Gimignano's famous towers.*

## The Towers

Of the original 72 towers, only 14 survive (and one can be climbed—at the City Hall). Some of the original towers were just empty, chimney-like structures built to boost noble egos, while others were actually the forts of wealthy families.

Before effective city walls were developed, rich people needed to fortify and protect their homes themselves. These towers pro-

vided a handy refuge when ruffians and rival city-states were sacking the town. If under attack, tower owners would set fire to the external wooden staircase, leaving the sole entrance unreachable a story up; inside, fleeing nobles pulled up behind them the ladders that connected each level, leaving invaders no way to reach the stronghold at the tower's top. These towers became a standard part of medieval skylines. Even after town walls were built, the towers continued to rise—now to fortify noble families feuding within a town (Montague and Capulet-style).

In the 14th century, San Gimignano's good times turned very bad. At the start of that century, about 13,000 people lived within the walls. But in 1348, a six-month plague decimated the population, leaving the once-mighty town with barely 4,000 survivors. Once fiercely independent, now crushed and demoralized, San Gimignano came under Florence's control and was forced to tear down most of its towers. (The Banca CR Firenze building occupies the remains of one such toppled tower.) And, to add insult to injury, Florence redirected the vital trade route away from San Gimignano. The town never recovered, and poverty left it in an architectural time warp. That well-preserved 14th-century cityscape, ironically, is responsible for the town's prosperity today.

• *From the well, walk 30 yards uphill to the adjoining square with the cathedral.*

## Piazza del Duomo

Stand at the base of the stairs in front of the church. Since before there was gelato, people have lounged on these steps. Take a 360-de-

gree spin clockwise: The cathedral's 12th-century facade is plain-Jane Romanesque—finished even though it doesn't look it. To the right, the two Salvucci Towers date from the 13th century. (Locals claim that the architect who designed New York

*Running sidebar (right margin):* VOLTERRA & SAN GIMIGNANO

City's Twin Towers was inspired by these). The towers are empty shells, built by the wealthy Salvucci family simply to show off. At that time, no one was allowed a vanity tower higher than the City Hall's 170 feet. So the Salvuccis built two 130-foot towers—totaling 260 feet of stony ego trip.

The stubby tower next to the Salvucci Towers is the Merchant's Tower. Imagine this in use: ground-floor shop, warehouse upstairs (see the functional shipping door), living quarters, and finally the kitchen on the top (for fire-safety reasons). The holes in the walls held beams that supported wooden balconies and exterior staircases. The tower has heavy stone on the first floor, then cheaper and lighter brick for the upper stories.

Opposite the church stands the first City Hall, with its 170-foot tower, nicknamed "the bad news tower." While the church got to ring its bells in good times, these bells were for battles and fires. The tower's arched public space hosted a textile market back when cloth was the foundation of San Gimignano's booming economy.

Next is the super-size "new" City Hall with its 200-foot tower (the only one in town open to the public; for visiting info, see the Civic Museum and Tower listing, later). The climbing lion is the symbol of the city. The coats of arms of the city's leading families have been ripped down or disfigured. In medieval times locals would have blamed witches or ghosts. For the last two centuries, they've blamed Napoleon instead.

Between the City Hall and the cathedral, a statue of St. Gimignano presides over all the hubbub. The fourth-century bishop protected the village from rampaging barbarians—and is now the city's patron saint. (To enter the cathedral, walk under that statue.)
• You'll also see the...

## Duomo (Duomo di San Gimignano/La Collegiata)

The nave of San Gimignano's Romanesque cathedral is lined with frescoes that tell the stories of the Bible—Old Testament on the left and New Testament on the right. Painted by masters of the 14th-century Sienese school, the frescoes are a classic use of teaching through art, with parallel themes aligned: Creation faces the Annunciation, the birth of Adam is opposite the Nativity, and—farther forward—the suffering of Job faces the agony of Jesus. Many scenes are portrayed with a 14th-century "slice of life" setting to help lay townspeople relate to Jesus.

To the right of the altar, the St. Fina Chapel honors the devout, 13th-century local girl who brought forth many miracles on her death. Her tomb is beautifully frescoed with scenes from her life by Domenico Ghirlandaio (famed as Michelangelo's teacher). The altar sits atop Fina's skeleton, and its centerpiece is a reliquary that contains her skull (€5, includes dry audioguide; April-Oct

Mon-Fri 10:00-19:30, Sat until 17:00, Sun 12:30-19:30; shorter hours off-season; buy ticket and enter from courtyard around left side, www.duomosangimignano.it).

• *From the church, hike uphill (passing the church on your left) following signs to* Rocca e Parco di Montestaffoli. *Keep walking until you enter a peaceful hilltop park and olive grove, set within the shell of a 14th-century fortress the Medici of Florence built to protect this town from Siena.*

## Hilltop Views at the Rocca

On the far side, 33 steps take you to the top of a little tower (free) for the best views of San Gimignano's skyline; the far end of town and the Sant'Agostino Church (where this walk ends); and a commanding 360-degree view of the Tuscan countryside. San Gimignano is surrounded by olives, grapes, cypress trees, and—in the Middle Ages—lots of wild dangers. Back then, farmers lived inside the walls and were thankful for the protection.

• *Return to the bottom of Piazza del Duomo, turn left, and continue your walk, cutting under the double arch (from the town's first wall).*

In around 1200, this wall defined the end of town. The **Church of San Bartolo** stood just outside the wall (on the right). The Maltese cross over the door indicates that it likely served as a hostel for pilgrims. As you continue down Via San Matteo, notice that the crowds have dropped by at least half. Enjoy the breathing room as you pass a fascinating array of stone facades from the 13th and 14th centuries—now a happy cancan of wine shops and galleries.

• *Reaching the gateway at the end of town, follow signs to the right to find...*

## Sant'Agostino Church

This tranquil church, at the far end of town (built by the Augustinians who arrived in 1260), has fewer crowds and more soul. Behind the altar, a lovely fresco cycle by Benozzo Gozzoli (who painted the exquisite Chapel of the Magi in the Medici-Riccardi Palace in Florence) tells of the life of St. Augustine, a North African monk who preached simplicity (pay a few coins for light). The kind, English-speaking friars (often from Britain and the US) are happy to tell you about the frescoes and their way of life. Pace the peaceful cloister before heading back into the tourist mobs (free, April-Oct daily 10:00-12:00 & 15:00-19:00, shorter hours off-season; Sunday Mass in English at 11:00).

# Sights in San Gimignano

### ▲Civic Museum and Tower (Musei Civici and Torre Grossa)

This small, entertaining museum, consisting of three unfurnished rooms, is inside the City Hall (Palazzo Comunale). The main reason to visit is to scale the tower, which offers sweeping views over San Gimignano and the countryside.

**Cost and Hours:** €9 includes museum and tower; daily 10:00-19:30, Oct-March 11:00-17:30, Piazza del Duomo, +39 0577 990 312, www.sangimignanomusei.it.

**Visiting the Museum:** You'll enter the complex through a delightful stony courtyard (to the left as you face the Duomo). Climb up to the loggia to buy your ticket.

The main room (across from the ticket desk), called the **Sala del Consiglio** (a.k.a. Dante Hall, recalling his visit in 1300), is covered in festive frescoes, including the *Maestà* by Lippo Memmi (from 1317). This virtual copy of Simone Martini's *Maestà* in Siena proves that Memmi didn't have quite the same talent as his famous brother-in-law. The art gives you a peek at how people dressed, lived, worked, and warred back in the 14th century.

Upstairs, the **Pinacoteca** displays a classy little painting collection of mostly altarpieces. The highlight is a 1422 altarpiece by Taddeo di Bartolo honoring St. Gimignano (far end of last room). You can see the saint, with the town—bristling with towers—in his hands, surrounded by events from his life.

Before going back downstairs, be sure to stop by the **Mayor's Room** (Camera del Podestà, across the stairwell from the Pinacoteca). Frescoed in 1310, it offers an intimate and candid peek into the 14th century. As you enter, look right up in the corner to find a young man ready to experience the world. He hits his parents up for a bag of money and is on his way. Suddenly (above the window), he's in trouble, entrapped by two prostitutes, who lead him into a tent where he loses his money, is turned out, and is beaten. Above the door, from left to right, you see a parade of better choices: marriage, the cradle of love, the bride led to the groom's house, and newlyweds bathing together and retiring happily to their bed.

The highlight for most visitors is a chance to climb the **Tower** (entrance halfway down the stairs from the Pinacoteca). The city's tallest tower, 200 feet and 218 steps up, rewards those who climb it with a commanding view. See if you can count the town's 14 towers. It's a sturdy, modern staircase most of the way, but the last stretch is a steep, ladder-like climb.

### ▲Campatelli Tower House (Torre e Casa Campatelli)

The Campatelli family, wealthy landowners from Florence, bought an age-old tower and adjacent properties in the 19th century and turned them into a palatial residence. They lived here until 2005, when the last of the family donated it to a nonprofit organization that protects heritage buildings and gardens, which opened it to the public. The house contains family belongings and tells the story of upper-class life in Tuscany, but the highlights are an audiovisual presentation on the history of the city and the chance to peer up through the tower, with a cutaway staircase and floor, to see how the towers in San Gimignano were built.

**Cost and Hours:** €7, Tue-Sun 10:30-19:00, closed Mon, shorter hours Oct-Feb, Via San Giovanni 15, +39 0577 941 419, www.fondoambiente.it/luoghi/beni-fai.

### San Gimignano 1300

Artists and brothers Michelangelo and Raffaello Rubino share an interesting attraction in their workshop: a painstakingly rendered 1:100 scale clay model of San Gimignano at the turn of the 14th century. Step through a shop selling their art to enjoy the model. You can see the 72 original "tower houses," and marvel at how unchanged the street plan remains today. You'll peek into cross-sections of buildings, view scenes of medieval life both within and outside the city walls, and watch a video about the making of the model.

**Cost and Hours:** Free, donations appreciated, daily 10:00-18:00, Dec-April until 17:00, on a quiet street a block over from the main square at Via Costarella 3, +39 327 439 5965, www.sangimignano1300.com.

# Sleeping in San Gimignano

Although the town is a zoo during the daytime, locals outnumber tourists when evening comes, and San Gimignano becomes mellow and enjoyable.

## NEAR PORTA SAN MATTEO, AT THE QUIET END OF TOWN

If arriving by bus, save yourself a crosstown walk to these accommodations by asking for the Porta San Matteo stop. Drivers can park at the less-crowded Bagnaia lots (P3 and P4), and walk around to Porta San Matteo.

**$$$ Hotel l'Antico Pozzo** is an elegantly restored, 15th-century townhouse with 18 tranquil, comfortable rooms, a peaceful interior courtyard terrace, and an elite air (RS%—use code RICK, family rooms, air-con, elevator, Via San Matteo 87, +39 0577 942 014, www.anticopozzo.com, info@anticopozzo.com; Emanuele, Elisabetta, and Mariangela).

**$$ Le Undici Lune** ("The 11 Moons") is situated in a tight but characteristic circa-1300 townhouse with steep stairs at the tranquil end of town. Its seven rooms are colorfully decorated (air-con, Via Mainardi 9, +39 328 053 5922, https://leundicilunesangimignano. it, info@leundicilune.it, Vincenzo).

**$ Locanda il Pino** has just seven rooms and a big living room. It's plain but clean and quiet. Run by English-speaking Elena and her family, it sits above their elegant restaurant just inside Porta San Matteo (fans, Via Cellolese 4, +39 0577 907 003, www. locandailpino.it, locandailpino@gmail.com).

## NEAR THE MAIN SQUARE, AT THE BUSY END OF TOWN

**$$ Hotel la Cisterna,** right on Piazza della Cisterna, feels old and stately. Its 48 rooms range from old-fashioned to more modern. It's worth paying extra for the contemporary rooms with panoramic views (RS%, family rooms, air-con, elevator, good restaurant with great view, closed Jan-Feb, Piazza della Cisterna 23, +39 0577 940 328, www.hotelcisterna.it, info@hotelcisterna.it, Alessio and Paola).

**$$ Palazzo al Torrione,** on an untrampled side street just inside Porta San Giovanni, is quiet and handy. Their 10 modern rooms, some with countryside views and terraces, are spacious and tastefully appointed (RS%, family rooms, breakfast extra, air-con, inside and left of gate at Via Berignano 76; +39 0577 940 375, www. palazzoaltorrione.com, info@palazzoaltorrione.com, Vanna).

**$ Terra d'Ombra** offers three good rooms above the recommended Le Vecchie Mura Ristorante, along a rustic lane just below the main square (no breakfast, air-con, Via Piandornella 15, +39 366 106 0631, www.terradombra.net, terradombra2022@gmail. com, Bagnai family).

## IN THE COUNTRYSIDE

**$$$$ Locanda dei Logi,** in the tiny *borgo* of San Donato—eight minutes from San Gimignano—houses six ultramodern luxury rooms within a cluster of medieval buildings. Each room is elegantly designed, and all look out over the property's vineyard. Wine lovers can combine an overnight and a tasting of their top-notch wines in their cantina (wine tastings available by appointment, lunch and dinner on request, air-con, plunge pool, Localita San Donato 1, +39 392 506 8229, www.locandadeilogi.it, info@ locandadeilogi.it).

VOLTERRA & SAN GIMIGNANO

**$$ Podere Ponte a Nappo,** run by enterprising Carla Rossi and her English-speaking sons Francesco and Andrea, has six basic rooms and two apartments in a kid-friendly farmhouse boasting fine San Gimignano views. Located a mile below town, it can be reached by foot in about 20 minutes if you don't have a car. A picnic dinner lounging on their comfy garden furniture next to the big swimming pool as the sun sets is good Tuscan living (RS%—use code "RickSteves," onsite restaurant and cooking classes, air-con, free parking, +39 0577 907 282, mobile +39 349 882 1565, www. accommodation-sangimignano.com, info@rossicarla.it). About 100 yards below the monument square at Porta San Giovanni, find tiny Via Baccanella/Via Vecchia and drive downhill. They also rent a dozen rooms and apartments on the main square in town.

## Eating in San Gimignano

My first two listings cling to quiet, rustic lanes overlooking the Tuscan hills; the rest are buried deep in the old center.

**$$$ Dulcis in Fundo Ristorante,** small and family-run, proudly serves modest portions of "revisited" Tuscan cuisine (with a modern twist and gourmet presentation) in a jazzy ambience. This enlightened place uses top-quality ingredients, many of which come from their own farm (Thu-Tue 12:30-14:30 & 19:15-21:45, closed Wed and Nov-Feb, Vicolo degli Innocenti 21, +39 0577 941 919, Cristina).

**$$ Le Vecchie Mura Ristorante** is welcoming, with good service, great prices, tasty if unexceptional home cooking, and the ultimate view. It's romantic indoors or out. They have a dressy, modern interior where you can dine with a view of the busy stainless-steel kitchen under rustic vaults, but the main reason to come is for the incredible cliffside garden terrace. To reserve a cliffside table, call or drop by: Ask for "front view" (open only for dinner 18:00-22:00 and lunch some weekends, closed Tue, reservations smart, Via Piandornella 15, +39 0577 940 270, Bagnai family).

**$ Trattoria Chiribiri,** just inside Porta San Giovanni, serves homemade pastas and desserts at good prices. While its petite size and tight seating make it hot in the summer, it's a good budget option—and as such, it's in all the guidebooks (daily 11:00-23:00, Piazza della Madonna 1, +39 0577 941 948, Roberto and Maurizio).

**$ Locanda di Sant'Agostino** spills out onto the peaceful square, facing Sant'Agostino Church. It's homey and cheerful, serving lunch and dinner daily—big portions of basic food in a restful setting. Dripping with wheat stalks and atmosphere on the inside, it has shady on-the-square seating outside (Thu-Tue 11:00-16:00 & 18:30-23:00, closed Wed, closed Jan-Feb, Piazza Sant'Agostino 15, +39 0577 943 141, Genziana and sons).

**Near Porta San Matteo:** Just inside Porta San Matteo is a variety of handy and inviting good-value restaurants, bars, cafés, and gelato shops.

**Picnics:** The big, modern **Co-op supermarket** sells all you need for a nice spread (Mon-Sat 8:00-20:00, closed Sun, at parking lot below Porta San Giovanni). Or browse the little shops guarded by boar heads within the town walls; they sell pricey boar meat *(cinghiale)*. Pick up 100 grams (about a quarter pound) of boar, cheese, bread, and wine and enjoy a picnic in the garden at the Rocca or the park outside Porta San Giovanni.

**Gelato:** To cap the evening and sweeten your late-night city stroll, stop by **Gelateria Dondoli** on Piazza della Cisterna (at #4). Gelatomaker Sergio was a member of the Italian team that won the official Gelato World Cup—and his gelato really is a cut above. He's usually near the front door greeting customers—ask what flavors he's invented recently (daily 9:00-23:00, until 19:00 in winter, +39 0577 942 244, Dondoli family). Charismatic Sergio also offers hands-on gelato-making classes in his kitchen down the street (www.gelateriadondoli.com).

## San Gimignano Connections

Bus tickets are sold at the bar just inside the town gate or at the TI. Many connections require a change at Poggibonsi (poh-jee-BOHN-see), which has the nearest train station. Note that the bus connection to Volterra is four times as long as the drive; if you're desperate to get there faster, you can pay about €70 for a taxi.

**From San Gimignano by Bus to: Florence** (hourly, fewer on Sun, 1.5-2 hours, change in Poggibonsi), **Siena** (8/day direct, on Sun must change in Poggibonsi, 1.5 hours), **Volterra** (4/day Mon-Sat; 1/day Sun—in the late afternoon and usually crowded—with no return to San Gimignano; 2 hours, change in Colle di Val d'Elsa, one connection also requires change in Poggibonsi).

**By Car:** San Gimignano is an easy 45-minute drive from Florence (take the A-1 exit marked *Firenze Imprugneta,* then a right past tollbooth following *Siena per 4 corsie* sign; exit the freeway at *Poggibonsi Nord*). From San Gimignano, it's a scenic and windy half-hour drive to Volterra.

# Monteriggioni

The perfectly preserved ring fort of Monteriggioni (mohn-teh-rih-jee-OH-nee) proudly caps its hill high above the main highway,

running from the Volterra/San Gimignano area south to Siena. Although it's a mostly empty shell today—and a tourist-bus magnet on par with San Gimignano—it's worth a quick stop if you're ready for a stretch-your-legs break. Visitors enjoy strolling its tidy square and climbing parts of its walls. Unless you linger over a meal, Monteriggioni works best as a half-hour to hour-long stop.

**Getting There:** Monteriggioni is well signed and only a mile off the main SR-2 highway, just north of Siena. Try parking in the lot at the top of the hill, below the main gate. If that's full, head to the large gravel lot closer to the base of the hill.

**Visiting the Town:** Monteriggioni's stout fortifications vividly illustrate two major historical trends in medieval Tuscany. Siena built the fortress around 1213 to protect its lands from the threatening expansion of its rival city-state, Florence. But Monteriggioni also protected religious pilgrims treading the Via Francigena route from northern Europe to Rome (who were, not coincidentally, a major source of Sienese wealth). Dante wrote poetically about Monteriggioni's might in his *Divine Comedy*. It finally surrendered to the Medici in 1554, becoming part of Florence and remaining in remarkably good repair.

Today, Monteriggioni feels like a historical theme park. English information plaques posted around the village explain its history. Entering its main gate (Porta Romana), you emerge onto its pleasant piazza, ringed with souvenir shops and al fresco eateries. On the right side of the square, tucked back in a little courtyard, is the **TI** and **Armor Museum,** with historical exhibits and models of the fortress, an explanation of siege warfare, and modern re-creations of weapons and armor that you can try on (€3 combo-ticket with walls, TI/museum open daily 10:00-13:30 & 14:00-19:00, shorter hours mid-Sept-March, audioguide-€1.50, Piazza Roma 23, +39 0577 304 834, www.monteriggioniturismo.it).

If you poke into the little courtyard beyond the TI, you'll find a **pilgrim's** *ospitalità,* a rustic refuge offering basic accommodations for present-day pilgrims following the Via Francigena. Like the more famous Camino de Santiago across northern Spain, this medieval pilgrim route is again in vogue—as, for the first time in centuries, people are walking its entire length, through Tuscan splendor to Rome. (For more on the Via Francigena, see page 595.)

The other main sight in Monteriggioni is the town's impressively intact **walls.** The blocky, angular towers—designed to shed incoming arrows—indicate the walls were built before the advent of cannons (when round towers became the norm). From Roman times through the Middle Ages, towers like these were built 50 yards apart—the distance an arrow could fly with accuracy. While the walls are about a third of a mile around, you can ascend them only for a stroll on two short stretches: above the town's main Porta Romana entrance gate, and at the opposite end, near the Porta Fiorentina gate. The same ticket—sold at the entry points or the TI—covers both sections (€3 combo-ticket with Armor Museum, same hours). Once up top, appreciate the strategic location, with 360-degree views over Tuscan hills. The busy highway below follows the route of the Via Cassia, the Roman-built road that connects Rome to Florence and points north, making it popular among ancient traders, medieval pilgrims...and contemporary tourists.

# THE HEART OF TUSCANY

*Montepulciano • Pienza •
Montalcino • Heart of Tuscany
Drive • Brunello Wine
Country Drive*

If your Tuscan dreams feature vibrant neon-green fields rolling to infinity, punctuated by snaking, cypress-lined driveways; humble but beautiful (and steep) hill towns; and world-class wines to make a connoisseur weep, set your sights on the heart of this region.

An hour south of Siena, this slice of splendor—which specializes in views and wine—is a highlight, particularly for drivers. With an astonishing diversity of towns, villages, abbeys, wineries, countryside restaurants, and accommodations—all set within jaw-dropping scenery—this subregion of Tuscany is a fine place to abandon your itinerary and just slow down.

Even though the area's towns sometimes seem little more than a rack upon which to hang the vine-draped hills, each one has its own endearing personality. The biggest and most interesting, Montepulciano, boasts a medieval cityscape wearing a Renaissance coat, wine cellars that plunge deep into the cliffs it sits upon, and a classic town square. Pienza is a sure-of-itself, planned Renaissance town that gave the world a pope. And mellow Montalcino is (even more than most towns around here) all about its wine: the famous Brunello di Montalcino.

Outside these three centers are some low-key sights: the pleasant spa town of Bagno Vignoni, the perfectly manicured gardens of La Foce, and the historic Sant'Antimo Abbey. (Just to the north, closer to Siena, is the Abbey of Monte Oliveto Maggiore, one of Tuscany's top art treasures—described in the Siena chapter.) And at the core of this region is the stunning landscape of the Val d'Orcia, with its famous tree-lined lanes and hill-capping farmhouses.

This area also enjoys a rich history: During the Middle Ages, the Via Francigena pilgrimage route ran from northern Italy—and northern Europe—right through here to Rome, blessing it with a

HEART OF TUSCANY

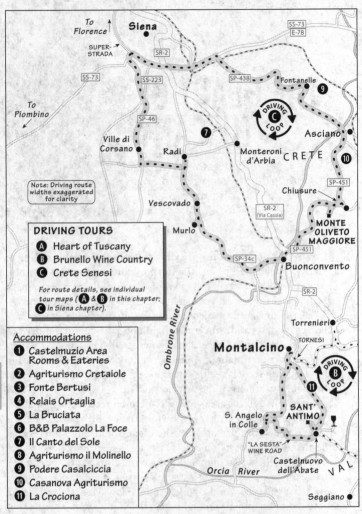

To Florence

Siena

To Piombino

SUPER-STRADA

SS-73

SS-223

SR-2

SP-46

SP-438

Fontanelle

9

DRIVING LOOP C

Asciano

10

Ville di Corsano

Radi

Monteroni d'Arbia

7

CRETE

SP-451

Vescovado

Chiusure

SR-2 (Via Cassia)

MONTE OLIVETO MAGGIORE

Murlo

Note: Driving route widths exaggerated for clarity

SP-34c

SP-451

Buonconvento

SR-2

**DRIVING TOURS**

Ⓐ Heart of Tuscany
Ⓑ Brunello Wine Country
Ⓒ Crete Senesi

*For route details, see individual tour maps (Ⓐ & Ⓑ in this chapter; Ⓒ in Siena chapter).*

Ombrone River

Torrenieri

TORNESI

Montalcino

DRIVING LOOP B

11

SANT' ANTIMO

S. Angelo in Colle

"LA SESTA" WINE ROAD

Orcia River

Castelnuovo dell'Abate

VAL

Seggiano

**Accommodations**

1 Castelmuzio Area Rooms & Eateries
2 Agriturismo Cretaiole
3 Fonte Bertusi
4 Relais Ortaglia
5 La Bruciata
6 B&B Palazzolo La Foce
7 Il Canto del Sole
8 Agriturismo il Molinello
9 Podere Casalciccia
10 Casanova Agriturismo
11 La Crociona

series of stout fortresses (including the one at Rocca d'Orcia) and welcoming pilgrim churches (including Sant'Antimo Abbey).

Don't be overly focused on ticking off a list of sights here. This region's attractions—while substantial—are best seen as an excuse for a countryside drive. I've narrated two ideal routes in this chapter (and a third in the Siena chapter). As you explore, every few minutes you'll want to pull over and marvel at the plush mix of man-made and natural beauty. And each time you frame a photograph—filling your lens with rolling fields, wispy lines of cypress trees, and stony hill towns, all reaching up toward a wide azure sky—you can only think one word: Tuscany.

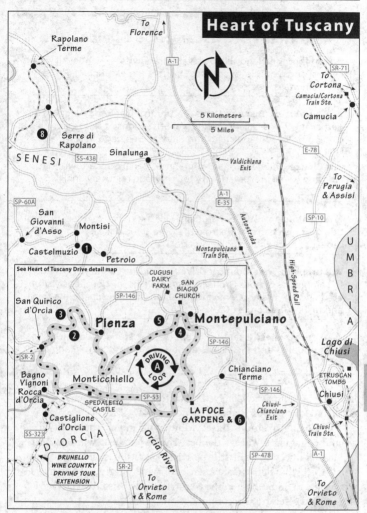

## PLANNING YOUR TIME

This region richly rewards whatever time you're willing to give it. At a minimum, splice this area into your drive between destinations to the north (Siena, Florence) and to the south (Orvieto, Rome). As this compact region is hemmed in by Italy's two main north-south thoroughfares—the A-1 expressway and SR-2 highway—even those with a few hours to spare can get an enticing taste. But ideally, spend two nights and three full days (see my three-day plan later). Many travelers enjoy home-basing here for up to a week, appreciating not only the area's many attractions, but also its strategic position for day trips to Siena and Cortona (each

## Heart of Tuscany at a Glance

**▲▲▲Montepulciano** Hill town with grand vistas, wonderful wine cellars, and a medieval soul that corrals the essence of Tuscany within its walls. See page 551.

**▲▲▲Heart of Tuscany Drive** An unforgettable day lacing together the views, villages, and rural attractions of this region (including both Montepulciano and Pienza). See page 591.

**▲▲Pienza** Unique, pint-sized planned Renaissance town that's amazingly well preserved, very touristy, and relatively unhilly. See page 568.

**▲▲Montalcino** Touristy "Brunello-ville" wine capital that still exudes a stony charm; aside from the wine, it feels like a second-rate repeat of Montepulciano. See page 578.

**▲▲Brunello Wine Country Drive** My favorite countryside places to sample the famous Brunello di Montalcino, all gorgeously situated among hills and vineyards. Call or email to schedule a tour and tasting. See page 603.

**▲▲Crete Senesi** Beautiful scenery—the stuff of coffee-table photo books—and the **▲▲▲** Abbey of Monte Oliveto Maggiore,

less than an hour away), or even to Volterra, San Gimignano, Florence, and Orvieto (each about 1.5 hours away).

**Choosing a Home Base:** Montepulciano is the most all-around engaging town; it's the best choice for those without a car (though connections can still be tricky). With easy access to the vineyards, Montalcino makes sense for wine pilgrims. For drivers who'd like to home-base in the countryside, I've listed several *agriturismi* and other rural accommodations, later.

**Navigating This Region:** With so much to see scattered across a wide area, this region can be challenging to organize from a touring point of view. Many travelers just lace together two or three of the main towns, with a few stopovers en route. The "Heart of Tuscany at a Glance" sidebar will help you narrow down your options. But with more time, consider one of my self-guided driving tours:

From Montepulciano or Pienza, my circular **Heart of Tuscany Drive** laces together a scenic string of minor sights, giving you the essence of the area.

From Montalcino, the capital of **Brunello Wine Country,** I've recommended several fine countryside wineries, as well as a driv-

best seen on a driving tour between Siena and the "Heart of Tuscany." See the Siena chapter.

▲▲**Sleeping at an *Agriturismo* or Countryside B&B** The best way to experience rural Tuscany: rustic, rural accommodations ranging from fragrant working farms to luxurious retreats. Most are run by families dedicated to making sure their cows and their guests are both well-fed. See page 547.

▲**La Foce Gardens** Delightful, unique gardens with gorgeous plantings, engaging history, and fine panoramas. See page 596.

▲**Bagno Vignoni** Quirky little spa town that's simply fun to check out, whether you take a dip or not. See page 597.

▲**Sant'Antimo Abbey** Historic church—stranded, holy and pristine, in the thick of wine country—and worth a quick, easy visit for those touring the wineries. See page 606.

▲**Stony Hill Towns (Rocca d'Orcia, Monticchiello)** Two fortified hilltop hamlets with cozy restaurants, rocky lanes, and vast vistas. See page 599.

ing tour that ties some of them together, along with Sant'Antimo Abbey.

If you're connecting to or from Siena, the prettiest back-roads route takes you through the **Crete Senesi,** with one major sight: the Abbey of Monte Oliveto Maggiore (drive and abbey covered at the end of the Siena chapter).

## The Heart of Tuscany in Three Days

Three days is enough to get a good look at the area's many highlights. Here's a smart plan, assuming you're coming from Siena. (If coming from the south, do it in reverse.)

**Day 1:** On your way south from Siena, enjoy the rugged landscape of the Crete Senesi (see the Siena chapter), then make a winery stop north of Montalcino before settling into Montepulciano (or your countryside accommodation).

**Day 2:** Follow my Heart of Tuscany Drive, including a sightseeing-and-gelato stop in Pienza. Have dinner in Montepulciano, or in the nearby countryside.

**Day 3:** Your day is free to enjoy and sightsee Montepulciano, or drive to countryside attractions (confirm tour availability at

La Foce Gardens in advance). You could head to your next destination this afternoon, or spend a third night.

## GETTING AROUND THE HEART OF TUSCANY

**By Car:** This area is ideal by car, and I've designed this chapter primarily with drivers in mind, including two self-guided driving tours that link the best stops with the most picturesque routes. Distances are short, and it's easy to mix-and-match sights.

Navigate by town names and use a good map (some local hotels and TIs hand out a fine free one) or—better yet—a mapping app with GPS to keep you on track. Be aware that GPS will usually take you on the most direct route—not always the most scenic. Look at the routes it suggests before choosing one, keeping in mind that some roads are not paved. Some sights and wineries are on tiny back lanes, marked only with easy-to-miss, low-profile signs. I've given distances in kilometers to match up with your rental car's odometer.

Many of the small towns in this area are designated as "ZTL" (limited-traffic zone)—off-limits to nonlocal traffic. While village ZTLs aren't monitored by cameras (as in big cities), you can still be ticketed if you're found crossing that line. In small hill towns, make it a habit to park at the lot just outside town and walk in. White lines indicate free parking; blue lines indicate paid parking (pay and display the ticket on your windshield); and yellow lines are only for locals. Parking machines typically don't accept bills or give change; have plenty of coins on hand. (Some may accept credit cards.)

**By Public Transportation:** While you can reach many of this chapter's sights by public buses, connections are slow, infrequent, and often require a transfer. Taxis can help connect the dots more efficiently. Montepulciano is the best home base for those without a car (though it's still not entirely convenient). See the map on page 703 for an overview.

## TOURS IN TUSCANY

A good local guide can help you take full advantage of everything this area has to offer. One with a car can save you lots of time and stress.

**Antonella Piredda,** who lives in the village of Montisi (just north of Pienza), is smart, well organized, and enjoyably opinionated (from €60/hour, 3-hour minimum, she can join you in your car or hire a driver for extra, mobile +39 347 456 5150, www. antonellapiredda.com, antonella.piredda@live.it).

**Roberto Bechi,** a great guide who lives in the Crete Senesi, runs all-day minibus tours with a passion for local culture, hands-on experiences, and offbeat sights. The price is reasonable, since he assembles groups of up to eight people to share the experience...and the cost (see website for tour options, RS%-10 percent discount, full-day minibus tours-€100/person, mobile +39 320 147 6590, www.toursbyroberto.com, toursbyroberto@gmail.com). For more on Roberto's tours, see page 369.

**Giovanni Adreani,** an energetic Cortona-based guide, is a good choice if you're home-basing in Cortona and want to hit Montepulciano, Pienza, and Montalcino in one efficient day (€220 for up to 5 people, €15-20/person extra for optional wine-tasting stop—must reserve in advance, mobile +39 347 176 2830, www. adreanigiovanni.com, adreanigiovanni@libero.it). For more on Giovanni, see page 611.

## COUNTRYSIDE ACCOMMODATIONS

While I've listed fine accommodations in Siena, Montepulciano, and Montalcino, a beautiful way to more fully experience this area is to sleep in a farmhouse B&B. Here I list favorites near Pienza, near Montepulciano, in the Crete Senesi (closer to Siena), and near Montalcino. For locations, see the "Heart of Tuscany" map, earlier in this chapter. Many of these are working farms (a prerequisite to be officially called an *agriturismo*) and give a great sense of rural family life. Others are just lovely homes in the countryside. The beautiful common denominator about these listings is the wonderful people you'll meet as your hosts. (A few countryside accommodations closer to Siena are listed in the Siena chapter, on page 415.)

### Near Pienza

On the outskirts of untouristy Castelmuzio (five miles north of Pienza), **$$$$ La Moscadella** (a.k.a. The Isabella Experience), is a luxurious countryside oasis run by Isabella and her team. It comes with 12 impeccably decorated rooms and a two-bedroom cottage, plus a gourmet-quality restaurant (also open to non-guests—see page 577). Isabella excels at creating vivid cultural experiences, from pasta-rolling classes to olive oil tastings. She and her concierge team pride themselves on helping each guest tailor their ideal getaway. This is an excellent value for those seeking a beautifully curated Tuscan experience (weeklong stays preferred but may be flexible, air-con, elevator, swimming pool, +39 0577 665 516, mobile +39 338 740 9245, www.theisabellaexperience.com, info@ theisabellaexperience.com).

Isabella rents two other properties nearby, in the village of Castelmuzio: **$$$ Le Casine di Castello,** a townhouse with two units, and **$$$$ Casa Moricciani,** a swanky villa with dreamy views and a garden terrace. She also works closely with Agriturismo Cretaiole (see below). For Isabella's help navigating your options, call or email her.

**$$$ Agriturismo Cretaiole** is rustic yet comfortable and idyllically set, perched on a ledge in an olive grove just outside of Pienza. Three generations of the farming Moricciani family—Luciano, Carlo, and Nicco—enjoy hosting travelers here. They even let their guests pick from the vegetable garden. The one-week minimum stay (Sat to Sat) facilitates a community feeling among the 20 or so guests and includes a variety of

hands-on activities, from farm tours to olive oil tastings to pasta-making classes (some coordinated via the Isabella Experience, described earlier; no air-con, swimming pool, or breakfast; shorter stays may be possible off-season, +39 0577 665 516 or +39 338 740 9245, www.cretaiole.it, info@cretaiole.it).

**$$$ Fonte Bertusi,** a classy and artistic guesthouse between Pienza and Cretaiole, is nicely run by young couple Manuela and Andrea, Andrea's artist-father Edoardo, and their attention-starved cats. The eight apartments mix rustic decor with avant-garde creations, and the cozy library/lounge/art gallery hosts installations and occasional music events. The setting is sublime, with a grand sunset-view terrace, a communal barbecue and outdoor kitchen, and a swimming pool (laundry service, outside Pienza toward San Quirico d'Orcia on the right—just after the turnoff for "Il Fonte," +39 0578 748 077, Manuela's mobile +39 339 655 5648, www.fontebertusi.it, info@fontebertusi.it).

## Near Montepulciano

**$$$$ Relais Ortaglia,** run by Americans Sandy, Phil (who was a Disney animator), and dog Cooper, rents five pricey rooms in a converted 17th-century farmhouse on the outskirts of Montepulciano. While preserving a rustic ambience, they offer modern amenities such as an infinity pool, activities (cooking classes), and a free bottle of prosecco for my readers. Well-organized Sandy keeps guests busy with her favorite experiences in the area (includes breakfast, 2-night minimum, air-con, mobile +39 391 163 9887, www.relaisortaglia.com, tuscany@ortaglia.it). Leaving Montepulciano on the main road toward Pienza, watch for the easy-to-miss brown *Ortaglia* sign on the left, just a half-mile past the San Biagio church turnoff.

**$$ La Bruciata** is a family-friendly *agriturismo* charmingly tucked into the countryside a five-minute drive outside Montepulciano (on the way to Pienza). Can-do Laura and several generations of her family produce wine and olive oil and rent several tasteful, modern rooms that share a peaceful yard with a swimming pool. From April through October, they prefer one-week stays (pay air-con, authentic farm-fresh meals and cooking classes, Via del Termine 9, +39 0578 757 704, mobile +39 339 781 5106, www.agriturismolabruciata.it, info@agriturismolabruciata.it). Leaving Montepulciano toward Pienza, turn off on the left for *Poggiano*, then carefully track brown *La Bruciata* signs (on gravel roads).

**$$$ B&B Palazzolo La Foce** lets you sleep aristocratically in a small villa just below the La Foce Gardens, south of Montepulciano. Its seven colorful rooms share a welcoming lounge and breakfast area with a giant fireplace, and an outdoor swimming pool with glorious Tuscan views. All the rooms bask in fine panoramas (air-con, Strada della Vittoria 61—but check in at gardens' main entrance to get specific directions to your room, villas also available, +39 0578 69101, www.lafoce.com, info@lafoce.com, Origo family).

## In the Crete Senesi

If pastoral landscapes are your goal, you can't do much better than sleeping in the Crete Senesi. These countryside options line up on (or just off) the scenic roads (SP-438 and SP-451) south of Siena.

**$$ Il Canto del Sole** is a restored 18th-century farmhouse turned family-friendly B&B located just six miles from Siena's Porta Romana city gate. The genial Lorenzetti family (Laura, Luciano, and son Marco) greet guests with a welcome drink and a helpful orientation. They have 10 bright and airy rooms, a plush lawn surrounding a saltwater swimming pool, a game room, a piano, and free loaner bikes. Their two apartments with antique furnishings fit six to eight people (RS%, air-con, free pickup/drop-off at train/bus station, affordable shuttle into town on request, dinner available some nights, Val di Villa Canina 1292, 53014 Loc. Cuna, +39 0577 375 127, mobile +39 392 811 0364, www.ilcantodelsole.com, info@ilcantodelsole.com).

**$ Agriturismo il Molinello** ("Little Mill") rents three rooms and six apartments (two built over a medieval mill) on the grounds of a working farm with organic produce, olives, and a truffle patch. Hardworking Alessandro and Elisa share their organic produce and offer wine and olive-oil tastings as well as bike and wine tours. More rustic than romantic, and lacking dramatic views, this is a family-friendly farm—complete with children, dogs, toys, and a relaxing swimming pool. Ask Alessandro about his true passion: cycling, including his collection of vintage bikes (breakfast extra, one-week Sat-Sat stay required July-Aug, discounts and no minimum stay off-season, between Asciano and Serre di Rapolano—on the road toward Rapolano, +39 0577 704 791, mobile +39 335 692 5720, www.molinello.com, info@molinello.com).

**$ Podere Casalciccia,** run by recommended local guide Roberto Bechi and his American wife Patti, is a spacious, modern home perched on a remote ridge immersed in 360 degrees of gorgeous Crete Senesi scenery. The four rooms and two-bedroom apartment offer stunning Tuscan countryside vistas. They've designed their entirely "green" house to be self-sufficient, with a zero-carbon footprint. Roberto happily plans tours for guests looking for an in-depth understanding of his homeland (RS%, includes self-service breakfast, communal kitchen, 2-night minimum, Patti's mobile +39 328 727 3186, Roberto's mobile +39 328 425 5648, www.casalciccia.com, poderecasalciccia@gmail.com). It's just off road SP-438: Turn down the rough gravel road next to the sign for *Fontanelle,* and follow it straight ahead for about five minutes.

**$ Casanova Agriturismo** is for people who *really* want to stay on an authentic working farm surrounded by spectacular scenery. This rustic place comes with tractors, plenty of farm noises, and a barn full of priceless Chianina cows. If the two simple rooms and three apartments take a backseat to the farm workings, the lodgings are accordingly inexpensive, and you'll appreciate the results of their hard work when you dig into one of their excellent farm-fresh dinners (€28/person, available by request). Wiebke (from Germany, speaks great English and runs the accommodations and kitchen), her Tuscan husband Bartolo (who works the fields), and the rest of the Conte clan make this a true *agriturismo* experience (breakfast extra, air-con, swimming pool with a view, just outside Asciano on road SP-451 toward Chiusure, +39 0577 718 324, mobile +39 346 792 0859, www.agriturismo-casanova.it, info@agriturismo-casanova.it).

## Near Montalcino

**$$ La Crociona,** an *agriturismo* farm and working vineyard, rents seven fully equipped and simple apartments with dated furnishings. Fiorella Vannoni and Roberto and Barbara Nannetti offer cooking classes and tastes of the Brunello wine grown and bottled on the premises (reception open 9:00-13:00 & 14:30-19:30, no air-con, breakfast extra, laundry service, pool, hot tub, fitness room, La Croce 15, +39 0577 847 133, www.lacrociona.com, info@lacrociona.com). The farm is about two miles south of Montalcino on the road to the Sant'Antimo Abbey; don't turn off at the first entrance to the village of La Croce—wait for the second one, following signs to *Tenuta Crocedimezzo e Crociona.* A good restaurant is next door.

# Montepulciano

Curving its way along a ridge, Montepulciano (mohn-teh-puhl-CHAH-noh) delights visitors with *vino*, views, and—perhaps more than any other large town in this area—a sense of being a real, bustling community rather than just a tourist depot.

Alternately under Sienese and Florentine rule, the city still retains its medieval *contrade* (districts), each with a mascot and flag. The neighborhoods compete the last Sunday of August in the Bravio delle Botti, where teams of men push large wine casks uphill from Piazza Marzocco to Piazza Grande, all hoping to win a banner and bragging rights. The entire last week of August is a festival: Each *contrada* arranges musical entertainment and serves food at outdoor eateries, along with generous tastings of the local *vino*.

The city is a collage of architectural styles, but the elegant San Biagio Church, just outside the city walls at the base of the hill, is its best Renaissance building. Most visitors ignore the architecture and focus more on the city's other creative accomplishment, the tasty Vino Nobile di Montepulciano red wine.

Montepulciano is a great starting and ending point for my scenic loop drive through the Heart of Tuscany, described later in this chapter.

## Orientation to Montepulciano

Commercial action in Montepulciano centers in the lower town, mostly along Via di Gracciano nel Corso (nicknamed "Corso"). This stretch begins at the town gate called Porta al Prato (near the TI, bus station, and some parking) and winds slowly up, up, up through town—narrated by my self-guided walk. Strolling here, you'll find eateries, gift shops, and tourist traps. The back streets are worth exploring. The main square, at the top of town (up a steep switchback lane from the Corso), is Piazza Grande. Standing proudly above all the touristy sales energy, the square has a noble, Florentine feel.

## TOURIST INFORMATION

The helpful TI is hidden below the Porta al Prato city gate, in the small P1 parking lot (Mon-Sat 9:00-13:00 & 14:00-19:00, Sun 9:00-13:00, sells train tickets, Piazza Don Minzoni, +39 0578 757 341, www.prolocomontepulciano.it). A TI branch inside the Palazzo Comunale sells tickets to climb its tower and has a good map of wine producers in the Vino Nobile di Montepulciano area (daily 10:00-18:00).

The office on the main square that looks like a TI, near the well, is actually the privately run Valdichiana Living tour agency. They provide wine-road maps, wine tours in the city, minibus winery tours farther afield, and cooking classes and other culinary experiences (Mon-Fri 10:00-13:30 & 14:30-18:00, shorter Sat hours, Sun 10:00-13:00, Piazza Grande 7, +39 0578 717 484, www.valdichianaliving.it).

## ARRIVAL IN MONTEPULCIANO

Whether you arrive by car or bus, ease your climb to the top of town by riding the shuttle bus. For details, see "Helpful Hints," later.

**By Car:** Well-signed pay-and-display parking lots ring the city center (marked with blue lines). Some free street parking is mixed in (marked with white lines)—look around before you park, and keep an eye out for time limits.

To start your visit by following my self-guided walk (up the length of the Corso to the main square), park at the north end of town, near the Porta al Prato gate. Around here, the handiest lots are P1 (in front of the TI, with some free spaces) and the unnumbered lot just above, directly in front of the stone gate. If these are full, try lots P2, P4, or P5 (all near the bus station).

For quicker access to the main square up top, use one of the parking lots at the top end of town: Approaching Montepulciano, follow signs for *centro storico, duomo,* and *Piazza Grande,* and use the Fortezza or San Donato lots (flanking the fortress).

Avoid "ZTL" no-traffic zone (signs marked with a red circle). If you're sleeping in town, your hotelier can give you a permit to park within the walls; be sure to get very specific instructions before you arrive.

**By Bus:** Buses leave passengers at the bus station on Piazza Nenni, downhill from the Poggiofanti Gardens. From the station, cross the street and head inside the gritty orange-brick structure burrowed into the hillside, where there's an elevator. Ride to level 1, walk straight down the corridor (following signs for *centro stori-*

# Montepulciano

## Accommodations

1. La Locanda di San Francesco & E Lucevan le Stelle Wine Bar
2. Palazzo del Mercante
3. Mueblè il Riccio
4. Albergo Duomo
5. Vicolo dell'Oste B&B
6. Camere Bellavista

## Eateries

7. Ost. dell'Acquacheta
8. Osteria del Conte
9. Le Pentolaccia
10. Ai Quattro Venti
11. La Schiaccia dell'Opio
12. Sgarbi Gelato Natura
13. To La Grotta

## Other

14. Copper Shop
15. Copper Workshop
16. Contucci Cantina
17. De' Ricci Cantine
18. Cantina della Talosa
19. Launderette
20. Valdichiana Living Tours

Ⓑ Local Shuttle Bus

To Siena via Sinalunga & A-1 Autostrada Freeway

To Chiusi

SANT' AGNESE

VIA E. DEENABEI

VIA CAL.

P #3

P #4

Piazza Don Minzoni

Poggio-fanti Gardens

BUS STN.

ELEVATOR

SANGALLO

Ⓑ

P #1

Porta al Prato

ℹ

WC

PORTA AL PRATO

Piazza Nenni

Ⓑ

P

VIA DELLE LETERE

P #5

P #2

VIALE 1 MAGGIO

WALK BEGINS

PALAZZO BUCELLI

12

COLONA DEL MARZOCCO

VIA GRACCIANO NEL CORSO

SANT' AGOSTINO

WC

SANTA LUCIA

VIA DI VOLTAIA NEL CORSO

CLOCK TOWER

PORTA DI GOZZANO

POST

VIA PIANA

VIA POGGIOLO

ARCHI

LOGGIA

CASEIFICIO CUGUSI

V. COSTE

SAN FRANCESCO

Piazza San Francesco

WALK ENDS

VIA

CAFFÈ POLIZIANO

VICOLO SDRUCC

VIA DI VOLTAIA NEL CORSO

GESÙ

1

5

19

2

6

18

9

17

20

3

PORTA DI GRASSI

VIA RICCI

VIA TALOSA

16

ℹ

Piazza Grande

WC

VIA D. ORIOLO

PALAZZO COMUNALE

10

Ⓑ

DUOMO

VIA FIORENZUOLA VECCHIA

15

14

COPPER SHOP

P #7

To San Biagio Church Cugusi Dairy Farm & 13

VIA DI SAN BIAGIO

VIA DEL POGGIO CORSO

VIA TEATRO

VIA D. SPIAGGE

11

PORTA DI FARINE

4

VIA SAN DONATO

VIA COLLAZZI

8

P

San Donato

Forteza

FORTEZZA

P #8

V. POLIZIANO

SANTA MARIA

V. DEL FILOSOFI

VIA DI CIRCONVALLAZIONE

VIA DI SAN PIETRO

To Pienza, Montalcino

200 Meters

200 Yards

HEART OF TUSCANY

*co*), and ride a second elevator (to a different level 1 and the Poggiofanti Gardens); walk to the end of this park and hook left to find the Porta al Prato gate (the starting point of my self-guided walk up the Corso to the main square). If the elevator isn't working, take the stairs, or hop on the shuttle bus (see "Helpful Hints," next).

## HELPFUL HINTS

**Market Day:** It's on Thursday morning (8:00-13:00), near the bus station.

**Services:** There's no official **baggage storage,** but the TI below the Porta al Prato gate might let you leave bags with them if they have space. Public **WCs** are located at the TI, to the left of Palazzo Comunale, and at the Sant'Agostino Church.

**Shuttle Buses:** To avoid the hike up through town to Piazza Grande, hop on the orange shuttle bus. It departs about every 30 minutes from the parking lot near the bus station and from the lane leading to the Porta al Prato gate, just above the TI (€1.20, buy tickets at bus station or tobacco shop). Some buses also go to San Biagio Church—confirm with the driver.

**Laundry:** An elegant self-service launderette, **Lavabenincasa,** is at the top of town at Via del Paolino 2, just around the corner from the recommended Camere Bellavista (daily 8:00-22:00, +39 0578 717 544).

**Taxis:** Two English-speaking taxi drivers operate in Montepulciano. Call +39 330 732 723 for short trips within town (€10 for rides up or down hill); to reach other towns, call +39 348 733 5343.

# Montepulciano Walk

This two-part self-guided walk traces the spine of the town from its main entrance up to its hilltop seat of power. Part 1 begins at the big gate at the bottom of town, Porta al Prato (near the TI and several parking lots); Part 2 focuses on the square at the very top of town and the nearby streets. Part 1 is steeply uphill; to skip straight to the more level part of town (and Part 2), ride the shuttle bus up, or park at one of the lots near the Fortezza. (When you're done there, you can still do Part 1—backwards—on the way back down.)

## PART 1: UP THE CORSO

This guided stroll takes you up through Montepulciano's commercial (and touristy) gamut from the bottom of town to the top. While the street is lined mostly with gift shops, you'll pass a few relics of an earlier age.

Begin in front of the imposing **Porta al Prato,** one of the many stout city gates that once fortified this highly strategic town. Walk directly through the Porta al Prato, looking up to see the slot where the portcullis (heavily fortified gate) could slide down to seal things off. Notice that there are two gates, enabling defenders to trap would-be invaders in a no-man's-land where they could be doused with hot tar. Besides having a drop-down portcullis, each gate also had a hinged door—effectively putting four barriers between the town and its enemies.

Pass through the gate and head a block uphill to reach the **Colonna del Marzocco.** This column, topped with a lion holding the Medici shield, is a reminder that Montepulciano existed under the auspices of Florence—but only for part of its history. Originally the column was crowned by a she-wolf suckling human twins, the civic symbol of Siena. At a strategic crossroads of mighty regional powers (Florence, Siena, and the Papal States), Montepulciano often switched allegiances—and this column became a flagpole where the overlords du jour could tout their influence.

The column is also the starting point for Montepulciano's masochistic tradition, the **Bravio delle Botti,** held on the last

Sunday of August, in which each local *contrada* (neighborhood) selects its two stoutest young men to roll a 180-pound barrel up the hill through town. If the vertical climb through town wears you out, be glad you're only toting a daypack. Do you see colorful flags lining the street? If so, you'll notice you're in the Gracciano *contrada*, symbolized by the green, black, and yellow lion. Notice how the flags change with the neighborhood as you continue through town. Speaking of wine barrels: As you head up the hill, you'll see lots of wine bars and other tasting opportunities. Hold off for now: Three characteristic cellars, burrowed deep into the rock, await near the end of this walk.

A few steps up, on the right (at #91, with stylized lion heads), is one of the many fine noble palaces that front Montepulciano's main strip. The town is fortunate to be graced with so many bold and noble *palazzi*—Florentine nobility favored Montepulciano as a breezy and relaxed place for a secondary residence. Grand as this palace is, it's small potatoes—the higher you go in Montepulciano, the closer you are to the town center...and the fancier the mansions.

Farther up on the right, at #73 (Palazzo Bucelli), take a moment to examine the **Etruscan and Roman fragments** embedded in the wall, left here by a 19th-century antiques dealer. You can quickly distinguish which pieces came from the Romans and those belonging to the earlier Etruscans by their alphabets: The "backwards" Etruscan letters (they read from right to left) resemble Greek. Many of the fragments show a circle flanked by a pair of inward-facing semi-circular designs. This symbol represents the libation cup used for drinking at an Etruscan banquet.

At the top of the block, just after the recommended Sgarbi Gelato Natura shop, is the **Church of Sant'Agostino.** Its late-Gothic facade features a terra-cotta sculpture group by the architect Michelozzo, a favorite of the Medicis in Florence. Throughout Montepulciano, Florentine touches like this underline that city's influence. The interior is a clean, serene, white-and-beige space.

Hike up a few more steps, then take a breather to look back and see the **clock tower** in the middle of the street. The bell ringer at the top takes the form of the character Pulcinella, one of the wild and carefree revelers familiar from Italy's commedia dell'arte theatrical tradition.

Continuing up, **Caseificio Cugusi** (at #29) has been selling pecorino cheese in Montepulciano for 50 years. Drop into their shop for some picnic supplies, and consider a trip to their dairy farm just outside of town (see "On the Outskirts," later in this chapter). At the *alimentari* on the right (at #23), notice the classic old sign advertising milk, butter, margarine, and olive and canola oil. Keep on going (imagine pushing a barrel now), and bear right with the street under another sturdy **gateway**—indicating that this city grew in concentric circles. Passing through the gate, you'll run into a loggia (with the Florentine Medici seal—a shield with balls). If the *contrada* flags are out, notice that you're at the boundary of two neighborhoods: To the left is the red-and-black castle flag of Voltaia, while to the right is the blue-and-white flag of Poggiolo.

Facing the loggia, veer left and keep on going. As you huff and puff, notice (on your right, and later on both sides) the steep, narrow, often-covered lanes called *vicolo* ("little street"). You're getting a peek at the higgledy-piggledy medieval Montepulciano. Only when the rationality of Renaissance aesthetics took hold was the main street realigned, becoming symmetrical and pretty. Beneath its fancy suit, though, Montepulciano remains a rugged Gothic city.

Again, notice the fine and ever-bulkier palaces. On the left, a tiny courtyard makes it easier to appreciate the grandiosity of the next palace. By the way, the stone scrolls under the window are a design element called a "kneeling window"—created by Michelangelo and a popular decorative element in High Renaissance and Mannerist architecture. You'll see kneeling windows all over town.

Just after is a fine spot for a coffee break (on the left, at #27): **Caffè Poliziano,** the town's most venerable watering hole (from 1868). Step inside to soak in the genteel atmosphere, with a busy espresso machine, loaner newspapers on long sticks, and a little terrace with spectacular views. It's named for a famous Montepulciano-born 15th-century poet who was a protégé of Lorenzo the Magnificent de Medici and tutored his two sons. So important is he to civic pride that townspeople are nicknamed *poliziani.*

A bit farther up, on the right, notice the precipitous **Vicolo dello Sdrucciolo**—literally "slippery lane." Any *vicolo* on the right can be used as a steep shortcut to the upper part of town, while those on the left generally lead to fine vistas. Many of these side lanes are spanned by brick arches, allowing centuries-old buildings to lean on each other for support rather than toppling over—a fitting metaphor for the tight-knit communities that vitalize small Italian towns.

Continuing up, notice more kneeling windows. The next church on the left, the Jesuit **Church of Gesù,** is worth a look. Its interior is elliptical in shape and full of 3-D illusions (the side chapels and the cupola are all painted on flat surfaces).

Soon the street levels out—enjoy this nice, lazy, easy stretch, with interesting shops and artisan workshops (such as the mosaics studio at #14, on the right). A few short blocks farther, across from #64, a lane leads to a charming terrace with a commanding view of the Tuscan countryside.

The Mazzetti **copper shop** (#64, marked *Rameria Mazzetti*) is crammed full of decorative and practical items. Because of copper's unmatched heat conductivity, it's a favored material in premium kitchens. The production of hand-hammered copper vessels like these is a dying art. This shop displays pieces by Cesare, who makes them in his **workshop** just up the street. To reach the workshop, go up the tiny covered lane just after the copper shop (Vicolo Benci, on the right). When you emerge, turn right and head uphill steeply; #4 (on the left), marked *Ramaio,* is Cesare's workshop and museum.

With your back to the trees, continue steeply uphill to the main square. At the bend just before the square, the Contucci family loves to introduce travelers to Montepulciano's fine wines at the **Contucci Cantina.** (See "Sights and Experiences in Montepulciano," later in this chapter, for details.) Visit Contucci now, or head up to the square for Part 2 of this walk.

Either way, Montepulciano's main square is just ahead. You made it!

## The Beauty of Tuscany's Geology (and Vice Versa)

While tourists have romanticized notions of the "Tuscan" landscape, there are a surprisingly wide variety of land forms in the region. Never having been crushed by a glacier, Tuscany is anything but flat. Its hills and mountains are made up of different substances, each suited to very different types of cultivation.

The Chianti region (between Florence and Siena) is rough and rocky, with an inhospitable soil that challenges grape vines to survive while coaxing them to produce excellent wine grapes.

Farther south, the soil switches from rock to clay, silt, and sand. The region called the Crete Senesi is the perfectly described "Sienese Clay Hills." Looking out from a breezy viewpoint, you can easily visualize how these clay hills were once at the bottom of the sea floor. The soil here is perfect for truffles and for vast fields of wheat, sun-yellow rapeseed (for canola oil), and periodically fava beans (to add nitrogen to the soil). In the spring and summer, the Crete Senesi is blanketed with brightly colorful crops and flowers, but by the fall, after the harvest, it's brown, dusty, and desolate. Within the Crete Senesi, you can distinguish two types of hills shaped by erosion: smooth, rounded *biancane* and pointy, jagged *calanchi.*

The sharecropping system—an almost feudal economic model, where a few super-elite aristocrats owned all the arable farmland and rented it out to peasant farmers—flourished here until soon after the birth of the Italian Republic in 1948. This prompted a population shift, as many Tuscans moved north to more lucrative industrial jobs in cities. The land they vacated be-

## PART 2: PIAZZA GRANDE AND NEARBY

This pleasant, lively piazza is surrounded by a grab bag of architectural sights. The medieval **Palazzo Comunale,** or Town Hall, re-

sembles Florence's Palazzo Vecchio—yet another reminder that Florence dominated Montepulciano in the 15th and 16th centuries. The crenellations along the roof were never intended to hide soldiers—they just symbolize power. The big, square central tower makes it clear that the city is keeping an eye out in all directions. It's made of locally quarried travertine stone, the same material ancient Romans used for their great buildings. (If you head up the street to the left of the facade and look back, you'll see

came dirt-cheap, and investors moved in, including many Sardinians—who brought their sheep and recipes for the pecorino cheese that now abounds here. (Many Sardinians—with names typically ending in "u"—still live here.)

The area around Montepulciano and Montalcino is more varied, with rocky protuberances that break up the undulating clay hills and provide a suitable home for wine grapes. Even farther south is the Val d'Orcia. This valley of the Orcia River is similar to the Crete Senesi, but has fewer rocks and jagged *calanchi*. Montepulciano sits in a unique position between the Val d'Orcia and the much flatter Val di Chiana (through which Italy's main north-south expressway runs).

You'll see many hot springs in this part of Tuscany, as well as town names with the word Terme (for "spa" or "hot spring") or Bagno ("bath"). These generally occur where clay meets rock: Water moving through the clay encounters a barrier and gets trapped. A byproduct of these mineral springs is the limestone called travertine, explaining the quarries you may see around spa towns.

that it's just that: a facade, pasted onto the front of a rough brick building.)

Take a moment to survey the square, where the town's four great powers stare each other down. Face the Palazzo Comunale, and keep turning to the right. You'll see the one-time building of the courts, behind the well (Palazzo del Capitano); the noble Palazzo Tarugi, a Renaissance-arcaded confection (with a public loggia at ground level and a private loggia—now enclosed—directly above); and the aristocratic Palazzo Contucci, with its 16th-century Renaissance facade. (The Contucci family still lives in their palace, producing and selling their own wine.) Continuing your spin, you see the unfinished Duomo looking glumly on, wishing the city hadn't run out of money for its facade. (Find a description of its interior under "Sights and Experiences in Montepulciano," later.)

A cistern system fed by rainwater draining from the roofs of surrounding palaces supplied the fine **well** in the corner. Check out its 19th-century pulleys, the grilles to keep animals from contaminating the water supply, and its decorative top: the Medici coat of arms flanked by lions (representing Florence) dwarfing griffins (representing Montepulciano).

Climbing the Town Hall's **tower** rewards you with a wind-blown but commanding panorama from the terrace below the clock (tower open daily May-Oct 10:00-18:00, closed in winter). To ascend, enter the Palazzo Comunale and buy your ticket at the TI on the main floor. You can pay to go just as far as the terrace, at the base of the tower (€2.50, 71 stairs, or ride the elevator halfway up); or pay more to go all the way to the top, twisting up extremely narrow brick steps past the antiquated bell-ringing mechanism (€5, 76 additional stairs). If you don't mind the claustrophobic climb, it's worth paying extra to reach the very top, from where you can see all the way to Pienza (look just to the right of San Biagio Church).

The street to the left as you face the tower leads to the **Fortezza.** While you might expect the town to be huddled protectively around its fortress, in Montepulciano's case, it's built on a distant ledge at the very edge of town. That's because this fort wasn't meant to protect the townspeople, but to safeguard the rulers keeping an eye on their townspeople.

**To the Church of San Francesco and Views:** From the main square, a short, mostly level walk leads to a fine viewpoint. You could head straight down the wide street to the right as you face the tower. But for a more interesting look at Montepulciano behind its pretty Renaissance facades, go down **Via Talosa,** the narrow lane between the two palaces in the far-left corner of the square. Within just a few steps, you'll be surrounded not by tidy columns and triangles, but by a mishmash of brick and stone. Pause at the recommended Mueblè il Riccio B&B (with a fine courtyard—peek inside) and look high up across the street to see how centuries of structures have been stitched together, sometimes gracelessly. Across the street is the recommended Cantina della Talosa wine cellar—imagine the wine caves below your feet.

Follow this lane as it bends left, and eventually you'll pop out just below the main square, a few doors from the recommended De' Ricci Cantine wine cellar. Turn right and head down toward the church. Just before #21 (on the left), look for a red-and-gold symbol over a door with the name *Talosa*. This marks the home of one of Montepulciano's *contrade*, or neighborhoods; birth and death announcements for the *contrada* are posted on the board next to the door.

Across the street and a few steps farther (on the right), you hit a **viewpoint.** From here, it's easy to appreciate Montepulciano's highly strategic position. The ancient town sitting on this high ridge was surrounded by powerful forces—everything you see in this direction was part of the Papal States, ruled from Rome. In the distance is Lake Trasimeno, once a notorious swampland that made it even harder to invade this town.

Continue a few steps downhill, then uphill, into the big parking lot in front of the **Church of San Francesco.** Head out to the overlook for a totally different view: the rolling hills that belonged to Siena. And keep in mind that Montepulciano itself belonged to Florence. For the first half of the 16th century, those three formidable powers—Florence, Siena, and Rome (the papacy)—vied to control this small area. You can also see Montepulciano's most impressive church, San Biagio—well worth a visit for drivers or hikers (described later).

From here, you can head back up to the main square, or drop into one of my recommended cantinas to spelunk their wine cellars.

# Sights and Experiences in Montepulciano

For me, Montepulciano's best "experiences" have long been personal: dropping in on Adamo, the winemaker at Contucci Cantina, and Cesare, the coppersmith at Ramaio Cesare. Adamo has now retired, and Cesare will likely retire soon. But today a new generation of winemakers, craftspeople, and cheesemongers are keeping Montepulciano's artisan traditions alive. Take some time to seek them out and make your own connections.

If you're visiting a wine cellar, study up on the local Vino Nobile di Montepulciano by reading the "Wines in the Region" sidebar later in this chapter.

### ▲▲Contucci Cantina

Montepulciano's most popular attraction isn't made of stone—it's the famous wine, Vino Nobile. This robust red can be tasted in any of the cantinas lining Via Ricci and Via di Gracciano nel Corso, but the cantina in the basement of Palazzo Contucci is both historic and fun. The palace's enoteca faces the square, but I prefer the actual cellars, down the lane on the right, where you'll meet the Contucci family and their staff. Andrea and Ginevra Contucci, whose family has lived here since the 11th century, love to share their family's products with the public. They usually have a few bottles open for you to sample. If you're lucky, you may even meet the famous Adamo, who recently retired after making wine here for almost 60 years.

After sipping a little wine, explore the palace basement, with its 13th-century vaults. Originally part of the town's wall, these chambers have been filled since the 1500s with huge barrels of wine. Dozens of barrels of Croatian and French oak (1,000-2,500 liters each) cradle the wine through a two-year in-the-barrel aging process, during which the wine picks up the personality of the wood. After about 35 years, an exhausted barrel has nothing left to offer its wine, so it's retired. The French oak gives the wine "pure elegance," and the Croatian is more masculine. Each barrel is labeled with the size in liters, the year the wine was barreled, and the percentage of alcohol (determined by how much sun shone in that year). To be "Nobile," wine needs a minimum of 13 percent alcohol.

**Cost and Hours:** Free drop-in tasting, free cellar tour upon request, daily 11:00-18:00, shorter hours off-season, Piazza Grande 13, +39 0578 757 006, www.contucci.it.

### ▲Ramaio Cesare

Cesare the coppersmith is an institution in Montepulciano, carrying on his father's and grandfather's trade by hammering into

existence an immense selection of copper objects in his cavernous **workshop.** Cesare (CHEH-zah-ray) greets guests with a torrent of cheerful Italian and photos of his work—including the copper top of the Duomo in Siena and the piece he designed and personally delivered to Pope Benedict. Just smile and nod, pick up what you can from gestures, and appreciate this rare opportunity to meet a true local character.

Peruse his tools: a giant Road Runner-style anvil, wooden hammers, and stencils dating from 1857 that have been passed down from his grandfather and father. Next door, he has assembled a fine museum with items he and his relatives have made, as well as pieces from his personal collection. Cesare is evangelical about copper, and if he's not too busy, he'll create personalized mementoes for visitors—he loves meeting people from around the world who appreciate his handiwork (as his brimming photo album demonstrates). Cesare's justifiable pride in his vocation evokes the hardworking, highly skilled craft guilds that once dominated small-town Italy's commercial and civic life.

**Cost and Hours:** Demonstration and museum are free, Cesare is generally in his workshop Mon-Sat 9:00-12:30 & 14:30-18:30, closed Sun, 50 yards steeply downhill from the Contucci

Cantina at Via del Teatro 4, +39 0578 758 753, www.rameria.com. If Cesare's not there, stop by his delightful **shop** on the main drag and ask about his availability, a block below at Corso #64—look for *Rameria Mazzetti*, open long hours daily.

## Duomo

This church's unfinished facade—rough stonework left waiting for the final marble veneer—is not that unusual. Many Tuscan churches

were built just to the point where they had a functional interior, and then, for various practical reasons, the facades were left unfinished. But step inside, where, amid the fairly austere interior, you'll be rewarded with some fine art. A beautiful blue-and-white, glazed-terra-cotta *Altar of the Lilies* by Andrea della Robbia is behind the baptismal font (on the left as you enter). The high altar, with a top like a pine forest, features a luminous, late-Gothic Assumption triptych by the Sienese artist Taddeo di Bartolo. Showing Mary in her dreamy eternal sleep as she ascends to be crowned by Jesus, it illustrates how Siena clung to the Gothic aesthetic—elaborate gold leaf and lacy pointed arches—to show heavenly grandeur.

**Cost and Hours:** Free, daily 8:30-18:30.

## ▲De' Ricci Cantine

The most impressive wine cellars in Montepulciano sit below the Palazzo Ricci, just a few steps off the main square (toward the Church of San Francesco). Enter through the unassuming door and find your way down, down, down a spiral staircase—with rounded steps designed to go easy on fragile noble feet, and lined with rings held in place by tiny, finely crafted wrought-iron goat heads. You'll wind up in the dramatic cellars, with gigantic barrels under even more gigantic vaults—several stories high. As you go deeper and deeper into the cellars, high up, natural stone seems to take over the brick. At the deepest point, you can peer into the atmospheric Etruscan cave, where a warren of corridors spins off from a filled-in well. Finally you emerge in the shop, where you're welcome to taste a few wines (with some local cheese). Don't miss their delightful dessert wine, vin santo.

**Cost and Hours:** First three tastings-free, two additional premium tastes-€5, €12-35 bottles, affordable shipping, daily 10:30-18:30, enter Palazzo Ricci at Via Ricci 11—look for signs for *Cantine de' Ricci*, +39 0578 757 166, www.cantinadericci.it, Enrico.

### Cantina della Talosa

This historic cellar, which goes down and down to an Etruscan tomb at the bottom, ages a well-respected wine. With a passion and love of their craft, Andrea and Cristian Pepi give enthusiastic tours and tastings. While you can drop by for a free sample, it's also possible to call ahead to book a complete tour and tasting (€20, including five wines to taste and light food).

**Cost and Hours:** Free tasting, daily March-Oct 10:30-19:00, shorter hours off-season, a block off Piazza Grande at Via Talosa 8, +39 0578 757 929, www.talosa.it.

## ON THE OUTSKIRTS

### ▲San Biagio Church (Chiesa de San Biagio)

Often called the "Temple of San Biagio" because of its Greek-cross style, this church—designed by Antonio da Sangallo the Elder and built of locally quarried travertine—feels like Renaissance perfection.

**Cost and Hours:** €3.50, includes 20-minute audioguide; Mon-Sat 10:00-18:00, Sun from 11:30, shorter hours in winter; www.tempiosanbiagio.it.

**Getting There:** The church is just west of town, at the base of Montepulciano's hill, down a picturesque cypress-lined drive-way.

**Visiting the Church:** Before entering, appreciate the **exterior** (the original front door is on the right side of today's entrance). The lone tower was supposed to have a twin, but it was never built. Walk around the building to study the freestanding towers—made that way so as not to interrupt the Greek cross.

Then step **inside.** The soaring interior (described by the au-dioguide), with a high dome and lantern, creates a quintessential Renaissance space. The proportions of the Greek-cross floor plan give the building a pleasing rhythmic quality. Stand on the center stone and do a slow 360-degree spin, enjoying the harmony and mathematical perfection in the design (and ignoring the bit of 18th-century, late-Baroque decor above the altar—which seems as appropriate as putting whipped cream on a nice steak). If the church is empty, experiment worshipfully with the marvelous acoustics.

Consider a picnic or snooze on the grass in back, with fine vis-tas over the Chiana Valley. The recommended La Grotta restaurant is across the street from the church.

#### Cugusi Dairy Farm (Caseificio Cugusi)
Perched scenically in the hills outside Montepulciano, this family-run dairy farm has been crafting fine pecorino cheeses for more than 50 years. Sisters Giovanna and Silvana welcome picnickers to assemble a custom basket of cheeses, meats, and wines before settling in under a shaded pergola with views over the countryside (April-Oct daily 8:00-19:30, shorter hours off-season; at Via della Boccia 8, look for signed turn-off from SP-146, a 10-minute drive from Montepulciano—for location, see the "Heart of Tuscany Drive" map on page 592; +39 0578 757 558, www.caseificiocugusi.it).

# Sleeping in Montepulciano

**$$$$ La Locanda di San Francesco** is overpriced but luxurious, with four stylish view rooms over a classy wine bar on a quiet square at Montepulciano's summit (air-con, free parking nearby, Piazza San Francesco 5, +39 0578 758 725, www.locandasanfrancesco.it, info@locandasanfrancesco.it, Luca).

**$$$ Palazzo del Mercante,** steps away from the Piazza Grande, offers six updated and neatly-appointed rooms with modern bathrooms (Via Ricci 14, +39 057 844 0591, www.palazzodelmercante.it, info@palazzodelmercante.it).

**$$ Mueblè il Riccio** ("The Hedgehog") is medieval-elegant, with 10 spotless rooms and an inviting roof terrace. Five are newer "superior" rooms with grand views across the Tuscan valleys (family rooms with lofts, breakfast extra, air-con, limited free parking—request when you reserve, a block below the main square at Via Talosa 21, +39 0578 757 713, www.ilriccio.net, info@ilriccio.net, friendly Gió and Ivana speak English). In summer, charming Gió and his son Iacopo give tours of the countryside in one of their classic Italian cars (€80/hour).

**$$ Albergo Duomo** is big, with 13 tattered rooms (with small bathrooms) and a comfortable lounge downstairs. Though the place lacks personality, it's in a handy location just a few steps from the main square at the very top of town, with free private parking nearby (RS%, elevator, air-con in some rooms, Via di San Donato 14, +39 0578 757 473, www.albergoduomo.it, info@albergoduomo.it, Simone).

**$$ Vicolo dell'Oste B&B,** just off the main drag halfway up through town, has five family-friendly modern rooms. Some are like tiny apartments (RS%, includes breakfast at nearby café, on Via dell'Oste 1—an alley leading right off the main drag just after Caffè Poliziano and opposite the *farmacia* at #47, +39 0578 758 393, www.vicolodelloste.it, info@vicolodelloste.it, Luisa and Giuseppe).

**$ Camere Bellavista,** owned by the same people who run Palazzo del Mercante across the street, has 10 tidy rooms that make you feel like you're at grandma's. True to its name, the rooms have fine views—though some are better than others. Room 6 has a view terrace worth reserving; there's also one economy room without a view (small breakfast delivered to room, lots of stairs with no elevator, reception not always staffed—call before arriving, Via Ricci 25, +39 338 229 1964, mobile +39 347 823 2314, www.camerebellavista.it, info@camerebellavista.it, Gabriella and Alessio speak just enough English).

## Eating in Montepulciano

Unless otherwise noted, these places are all open for lunch (about 12:30-14:30) and again for dinner (about 19:30-22:00).

**$$$ Osteria dell'Acquacheta** is a carnivore's dream come true, beloved among locals for its beef steaks. Its long, narrow room is jammed with shared tables and tight, family-style seating, with an open fire in back and a big hunk of red beef lying on the counter like a corpse on a gurney. Giulio and his wife, Chiara, run a fun-loving but tight ship—posing with slabs of red meat yet embracing decades of trattoria tradition (you'll get one glass to

use alternately for wine and water). Giulio—think George Carlin with a meat cleaver and a pen tucked into his ponytail—whacks off slabs of beef, confirms the weight and price with the diner, and tosses the meat on the grill, seven minutes per side. (You won't be asked how you like your steak.) Steaks are sold by weight. Typically, two people split a 1.6-kilo steak (that's 3.5 pounds; the smallest they'll cook is 1.2 kilos). They also serve hearty pastas and salads, other meaty plates, and a fine house wine (possible to bring your own wine for a tiny corkage fee, reservations required by phone; seatings generally at 12:30, 14:30, 19:30, and 21:30 only; closed Tue and unpredictably on other days; Via del Teatro 22, +39 0578 717 086, www.acquacheta.eu).

**$$ Osteria del Conte,** an attractive but humble family-run bistro, offers cooking like your Italian mom's. While the interior is very simple, they also have outdoor tables on a stony street at the top of the historic center (closed Mon, Via San Donato 19, +39 0578 756 062).

**$$ Le Pentolaccia** is a small, family-run restaurant about two-thirds of the way up the main drag. With both indoor and outdoor seating, they make tasty traditional Tuscan dishes as well as daily fish specials. Cristiana serves, and husband-and-wife team Jacobo and Alessia stir up a storm in the kitchen (Fri-Wed 12:00-15:00 & 19:00-22:00, closed Thu, Corso 86, +39 0578 757 582).

**$$ Ai Quattro Venti** is right on Piazza Grande, with a simple dining room and outdoor tables on the square. It offers reasonable portions of unfussy Tuscan food in an unpretentious setting. Try the organic house olive oil and wine (closed Thu, next to City Hall on Piazza Grande, +39 0578 717 231, Chiara).

**Wine Bar/Bistro:** With a terrace on a tranquil square in front of the Church of San Francesco, **$$ E Lucevan le Stelle** (part of La Locanda di San Francesco) is a fine place to nurse a glass of local wine (also pastas, salads, and soups; daily 12:00-24:00, closed Nov-Easter, may close when things are quiet, Piazza San Francesco 5, +39 0578 758 725, Luca).

**Sandwiches to Go: $ La Schiaccia dell'Opio,** at one of the hairpin turns near the top of town, is a takeout shop offering pricey but delicious made-to-order sandwiches on *schiaccia*—crispy, savory flatbread hot out of the oven (daily 11:00-15:00 & 16:30-21:00, lunch only off-season, Via dell'Opio nel Corso 45, +39 0578 778 861).

**Gelato:** For the best gelato in town, look for **Sgarbi Gelato Natura,** near the bottom of the main drag. Owner Nicola makes his gelato fresh every morning, using locally sourced ingredients from producers he knows personally (daily 11:00-20:00, open later in summer, Corso 50; also runs Buon Gusto in Pienza).

**Just Outside Montepulciano:** Facing San Biagio Church (at the base of Montepulciano's hill, and described earlier), **$$$ La Grotta** has an excellent reputation for elevated Tuscan cuisine in a sophisticated, dressy setting. Reservations are recommended (Thu-Tue 12:30-14:15 & 19:30-22:00, closed Wed, Via di San Biagio 15, +39 0578 757 479, www.lagrottamontepulciano.it).

**Near Montepulciano:** In addition to the places listed here, small-town and countryside dining options abound within a 20-minute drive. Skim this chapter for recommendations, and consider combining dinner with a scenic joyride. Good choices include **Ristorante Daria** in Monticchiello (page 602) and **The Isabella Experience**'s dinners near Castelmuzio (page 577).

# Montepulciano Connections

Get bus schedules at the TI or the bus station on Piazza Pietro Nenni, which seems to double as the town hangout, with a lively bar and locals chatting inside. In fact, there's no real ticket window—buy your tickets at the bar. Check www.at-bus.it for schedules.

HEART OF TUSCANY

**By Bus to: Florence** (1/day departs in the wee hours, 2/week additional departures a bit later in the morning, 2 hours, LFI bus, www.lfi.it; or take a bus to Chiusi to catch a train—see below), **Siena** (6-7/day, none on Sun, 1.5 hours, also possible to change here for Florence express bus), **Pienza** (8/day, 30 minutes), **Montalcino** (3-4/day, none Sun, change in Torrenieri, 1 hour; or consider a taxi—see below).

**By Train:** Trains are impractical here; the Montepulciano train station is served only by milk-run trains and a 15-minute taxi/bus ride to town. Instead consider connecting through the town of **Chiusi.** Its convenient train station is on the main Florence-Rome rail line and linked to Montepulciano by an hourly 50-minute bus ride.

**Taxi Alternatives:** As the **Montalcino** bus connection is infrequent and complicated, consider hiring a taxi (about €70; see contact info under "Helpful Hints," earlier). **Cortona** is another awkward public-transit connection where a taxi may be worth the expense (about €60; otherwise it's a bus to Chiusi, then a 30-minute train ride to the Camuccia-Cortona train station, four miles below town with poorly timed bus connections to Cortona itself).

# Pienza

Set on a crest and surrounded by green, rolling hills, the small town of Pienza packs a lot of Renaissance punch. In the 1400s, locally born Pope Pius II of the Piccolomini family decided to remodel his birthplace into a city fit for a pope, in the style that was all the rage: Renaissance. Propelled by papal clout, the town of Corsignano was transformed—in only five years' time—into a jewel of Renaissance architecture. It was renamed Pienza, after Pope Pius.

Pienza's architectural focal point is its main square, Piazza Pio II, surrounded by the Duomo and the pope's family residence, Palazzo Piccolomini. While Piazza Pio II is Pienza's pride and joy,

HEART OF TUSCANY

the entire town—a mix of old stonework, potted plants, and grand views—is fun to explore, especially with a camera or sketchpad in hand. You can walk every lane in the tiny town in well under an hour. Pienza is situated on a relatively flat plateau rather than the steep pinnacle of more dramatic towns like Montepulciano and Montalcino. (This is a plus for visitors with limited mobility, who find basically level Pienza easy to explore.)

Tidy, tranquil, and tame, Pienza feels like the idealized Renaissance burg it was designed to be. But along with that civic pride comes more than its share of pretense. (I guess constantly being reminded of your "Renaissance perfection" tends to stoke the ego.) And it's far from undiscovered; tourists flood Pienza on weekends and in peak season, and authentic local shops are outnumbered by boutiques selling gifty packages of pecorino cheese and local wine. Restaurants here tend to be more expensive and less reliable than alternatives in the nearby countryside. For these reasons, Pienza is made to order as a stretch-your-legs break to enjoy the townscape and panoramas, but it's not ideal for lingering overnight (though some excellent options exist just outside town; see "Countryside Accommodations" earlier in this chapter). For the best experience, visit late in the day, after the day-trippers have dispersed.

Nearly every shop sells the town's specialty: pecorino, a pungent sheep's cheese (you'll smell it before you see it) that's sometimes infused with other ingredients, such as truffles or cayenne pepper. Look on menus for warm pecorino (al forno or alla griglia), often topped with honey and pine nuts or pears and served with bread. Along with a glass of local wine, this just might lead you to a new understanding of la dolce vita.

## Orientation to Pienza

**Tourist Information:** The TI is 10 yards up the street from Piazza Pio II, inside the skippable Diocesan Museum (Wed-Mon 10:00-18:30, shorter hours off-season, closed Tue year-round, Corso il Rossellino 30, +39 0578 749 905). Ignore the Informaturista kiosk just outside the gate—it's a private travel agency.

**Arrival in Pienza:** If **driving**, read signs carefully—some parking spots are reserved for locals, others require the use of a cardboard clock, and others are pay-and-display. Parking is tight, so if you don't see anything quickly, head for the large pay lot at Piazza del Mercato near Largo Roma outside the old town: As you approach town and reach the "ZTL" cul-de-sac (marked with a red circle) in front of the town gate, head up the left side of town and look for the parking turnoff on the left (closed Fri morning during market). **Buses** drop you just a couple of blocks from the town's main entrance.

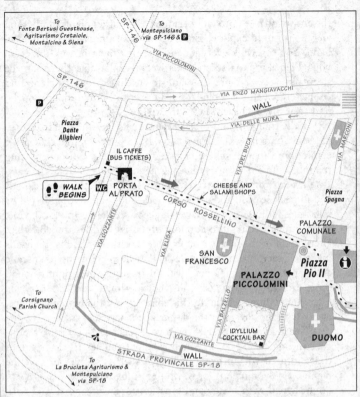

**Helpful Hints:** The TI and most sights are **closed on Tuesdays.** On Friday mornings, a **market** fills Piazza del Mercato, the main parking lot just outside the town walls. A public **WC,** marked *gabinetti pubblici,* is on the right as you face the town gate from outside on Piazza Dante Alighieri (down the lane next to the faux TI).

## Sights in Pienza

I've connected Pienza's main sights with walking directions, which can serve as a handy little orientation to the town. You could do this stroll in 30 minutes; entering some of the sights could extend your visit to a few hours.

• *Begin in the little park just in front of the town (near the main round-about and bus stop), called Piazza Dante Alighieri. Facing the town, go through the big, ornamental gateway on the right (which was destroyed in World War II, and rebuilt in 1955) and head up the main street...*

### Corso il Rossellino

This main drag—named for Bernardo Rossellino (1409-1464), the Renaissance architect who redesigned Pienza according to Pius'

**Pienza**

To
Plaza
del Mercato
Parking

SP-18

100 Meters

100 Yards

VIA PIA

Largo
Roma

BUON
GUSTO
GELATERIA

"NEW HOUSES"

VIA CASA NUOVE

SP-18

VIA DOGALI

WALK
ENDS

SAN
CARLO

VIA DELL'APPARITA

VIA DELLA VOLPE

SAN ANDREA

VIA SAN CARLO

LA BANDITA
TOWNHOUSE
CAFFÈ

PORCHETTA
SHOP

CORSO

VIA FORTUNA

VIA
DELL'AMORE

VIA

VIA BUIA

ROSSELLINO

TRATTORIA
LATTE DI LUNA

BISHOP'S
PALACE
& DIOCESAN
MUSEUM

PORTA
AL CIGLIO

VIEW TERRACE

WALL

SP-18

PORTA
AL SANTO

Note: No cars allowed
in town center

**HEART OF TUSCANY**

orders—is jammed with touristy boutiques. While you won't find great values, these shops are (like Pienza) cute and convenient.

As you stroll this street, step into one of the many **cheese-and-salami shops.** Take a deep whiff and survey the racks of pecorino cheese, made from sheep's milk. There are three broad categories of pecorino: *fresco* (young, soft, and mild), *medio* (medium), and *stagionato* (hard, crumbly, and pungent). Consider stocking up at one of these shops for a pricey but memorable picnic; some shops may be willing to give you a free sample. *Finocchiona* is salami with fennel seeds. This was first popularized by wine traders, because fennel seeds make wine taste better. To this day, Italians use the word *infinocchiare* ("fennel-ize") to mean "to trick."

Farther along, watch for the **Church of San Francesco** on the right. It's the only important building in town that dates from before the Pius II extreme makeover. Its humble facade, simple nave, wood-beamed ceiling, bits of 14th-century frescoes, and tranquil adjacent cloister have a charm that's particularly peaceful in the 21st century. But this gloomy medieval style was exactly what Pius wanted to get away from.

• *Continuing one more block, you'll pop out at Pienza's showcase square...*

## ▲Piazza Pio II

Pienza's small main piazza gets high marks from architecture high-brows for its elegance and artistic unity. One day, Pope Pius II

(who was born here) was travel-ing nearby with Leon Battista Alberti, one of the great archi-tectural pioneers of the Renais-sance. Proud to show off his hometown, Pius brought Alberti here...but, seeing it through the eyes of his esteemed compan-ion, he was filled with embar-rassment rather than pride at its primitive architectural style. Pius decided this just wouldn't do, and commissioned Alberti's student Bernardo Rossellino to remake the town into a Renaissance masterpiece.

Rossellino designed the piazza and surrounding buildings to form an "outdoor room." Everything is perfectly planned and plot-ted. Do a clockwise spin to check out the buildings that face the square, starting with the **Duomo** (which we'll visit soon). High up on the facade is one of many examples you'll spot around town of the Piccolomini family crest: five half-moons, advertising the number of crusades that his family funded.

To the right of the Duomo is the **Piccolomini family palace,** now a tourable museum (described later). Notice that the grid lines in the square's pavement continue all the way up the sides of this building, creating a Renaissance cube. Upon closer inspection, you can see that the windows at the far end of the building are a bit nar-rower—creating an optical illusion that the palace is longer than it actually is.

Looking farther right, you'll see **City Hall** (Palazzo Co-munale), with a Renaissance facade and a fine loggia (to match the square) but a 13th-century bell tower that's shorter than the church's tower. That's unusual here in civic-minded Tuscany, where municipal towers usually trumpet the importance of town over Church. It's also unusual that a pope would invest in beefing up a City Hall—another indication of Pius' deep Renaissance human-ism.

Looking up the lane to the left of City Hall, notice the can-tilevered upper floors of the characteristic old houses—a reminder that, while Pienza appears Renaissance on the surface, much of that sheen was added later to fit Pius' vision. Turning right again, see the **Bishop's Palace,** also called the Borgia Palace (now hous-ing the TI and the skippable Diocesan Museum). Pius envisioned

## Pope Pius II

Pope Pius II (Enea Silvio Bartolomeo Piccolomini, 1405-1464) was born into one of the most powerful families in Siena. He had an illustrious career as a diplomat, traveled far and wide (fathering two illegitimate children, in Switzerland and Scotland), and gained a reputation for his erotic writings *(The Tale of Two Lovers)*. Upon donning the frock, Piccolomini went from ordination to the papacy in just 11 years—a stunning pace spurred, no doubt, by his esteemed lineage. Owing to his educated and worldly upbringing, upon ascending to the papacy Piccolomini chose a name that was not religious, but literary: the ancient poet Virgil first used the term "pious" to describe his hero, Aeneus. One of the most enlightened popes of his time, Pius embraced the burgeoning Renaissance and set out to remake his hometown in pure Renaissance style. At the time, Christian Europe was facing the prospect of an Ottoman invasion, and Pius rallied Europeans around their common heritage and shared goals. In that respect, Pius was the first prominent figure to suggest the bold notion of a united Europe. (For more on the pope's dramatic life—depicted by a famous painter—see page 397.)

his remade hometown as a sort of "summer Vatican," where an entourage of VIPs would spend time—and each one needed their own palace. The Borgia clan, who built this palace, produced one of the most controversial popes of that age, Alexander VI, who ascended to the papacy a few decades after Pius II. The Borgia were notorious for their shrewd manipulation of power politics. By the way, our word "nepotism" dates from this era. Pius II's nephew *(nipote)* succeeded Alexander VI as Pius III—and died less than a month into his papacy.

Finally, between the Bishop's Palace and the Duomo, a lane leads to the best **view terrace** in town.

• *Before going there, now's the time to tour whichever of the square's sights interest you:*

### Duomo

The cathedral's classic, symmetrical Renaissance facade (1462) dominates Piazza Pio II. The interior, bathed in light, is an illuminating encapsulation of Pius II's architectural philosophy.

**Cost and Hours:** Free, generally daily 8:00-13:00 & 14:30-19:00.

**Visiting the Church:** Step inside...and into the light. Pius envisioned this church as an antidote to dark, claustrophobic medieval churches, like the Church of San Francesco we saw earlier. Instead, this was to be a "house of glass," representing the cul-

tural enlightenment that came
with the Renaissance. It also
has a Gothic feel—partly because Pius was a great admirer
of the German-born philosopher Nicola Cusano, and wanted
the church to feel like a German
Gothic church. This complicated concept clashed with the architect's plans for the building,

but Pius insisted on his way—creating this unusual (and unstable)
space. Although an east-west footprint would have better suited
this location, Pius demanded that the nave's tall Gothic windows
face south to capture maximum light (and, symbolically, to face
Monte Amiata—evoking Calvary Hill, where Jesus was crucified).
Atop the columns, notice the boxy risers. Pius was into astronomy:
He had the cathedral made tall enough so that on the spring equi-
nox, the shadow cast by the facade would just reach the pavement
grid line defining the far end of the square.

All of this caused structural problems. As you walk to the end
of the church, notice the cracks in the apse walls and floor, and get
seasick behind the main altar. The church's cliff-hanging position
bathes the interior in light, but the building also feels as though it
could break in half if you jumped up and down.

The church decoration is also unusual. Rather than Jesus and
Mary, the emphasis is on the pope and his family (find the cres-
cent-moon crest of Pius II on the windows). Instead of the colorful
frescoes you'd expect, the church has clean, white walls to reflect
the light. And with this "modern" interior, the Sienese Gothic altarpieces and painted arches with gold leaf seem out of place.

### ▲Palazzo Piccolomini

This palace, the home of Pius II and the Piccolomini family (until
1962), is not quite the interesting slice of 15th-century aristocratic
life that it could be (I'd like to know more about the pope's toilet).
But this is still the best small-town palace experience I've found
in Tuscany. (It famously starred as the Capulets' home in Franco
Zeffirelli's 1968 Academy Award-winning *Romeo and Juliet*.) You
can peek inside the door for free to check out the well-preserved
courtyard. In Renaissance times, most buildings were covered with
elaborate paintings like those you'll see here.

**Cost and Hours:** €7; Wed-Mon 10:00-12:30 & 14:00-18:00,
until 16:00 off-season, closed Tue year-round; Piazza Pio II 2, +39
0577 286 300, www.palazzopiccolominipienza.it.

**Visiting the Palazzo:** You'll see six rooms (dining room, ar-
mory, bedroom, library, and so on), three art-strewn galleries, and

a panoramic loggia before being allowed to linger in the beautiful hanging gardens. The palace's drab interiors, faded paintings, coffered ceilings, and scuffed furniture have a mothballed elegance that makes historians wish they'd seen it in its heyday, when this small-town palace hosted a big-name player in European politics.

• *When you're done sightseeing, head up the little lane to the left of the church facade. This takes you out to a grand pedestrian-only...*

### View Terrace

Stroll this panoramic promenade to the end, taking in views over the Tuscan countryside and, in the distance, Monte Amiata, the largest mountain in southern Tuscany. Retrace your steps and exit the viewpoint down the first alley, Via del'Amore—the original Lover's Lane—which leads back to the main drag, Corso il Rossellino.

• *Turn right and stroll along this street one block, then turn left up Via Sant' Andrea. Soon you'll run into **Via delle Case Nuove**, a charming row of homes with staggered doorways. These "new houses" (as the street's name means) were built by the pope to house the poor. Just to the left (as you face these houses) is Pienza's "destination" gelateria, the recommended **Buon Gusto**.*

*Ice-cream cone in hand, just wander—poke around your choice of Pienza's lovely, flower-bedecked lanes.*

## JUST OUTSIDE PIENZA

A short drive or a longish walk from Pienza, you can step into one of this region's many well-preserved Romanesque churches.

### Corsignano Parish Church (Pieve di Corsignano)

This classic Romanesque parish church *(pieve)*, hugging the slope just below Pienza, is a reminder of a much earlier, rougher, simpler time (before Pope Pius II).  This was one of the medieval pilgrimage stops on the Via Francigena (see the sidebar later in this chapter).

**Getting There:** On foot from Pienza, it's a steep 10-minute downhill walk (as you exit Pienza into the main park, look to your left for *pieve di Corsignano* signs). Drivers loop around the far end of town (as described on my Heart of Tuscany drive, later); just before the road bends sharply left and twists downhill, watch for the *pieve di Corsignano* signs on the right (free parking).

**Visiting the Church:** The round, eighth-century watchtower guards the squat, 11th-century church, whose unusual exterior iconography is from an age when the pagan roots of early Christianity were vivid and unmistakable—especially here, deep in the countryside. The church is decorated not with saints and angels, but with geometric and flowery motifs as well as mysterious creatures. In the stone lintel immediately above the front door, find the mermaid-like creature holding the two halves of her split tail—a warm

and fertile invitation to enter and find life. Locals enjoy the (quite plausible) idea that Starbucks appropriated its logo from this common pagan symbol. She's flanked by other figures fighting off demons, including (on the left) a snake that represents the sins of humanity. The mermaid tails and wavy water-

like lines suggest the springs that spout near here. The figure high above seems like both a Greek and an Etruscan fertility goddess.

For more mysterious medieval art, walk around the right side of the church and study the 13th-century carving above the doorway, showing the three kings journeying to Bethlehem, where the Baby Jesus lies under a star and an angel. (This area may be blocked off for renovation.)

If the church is open, step inside and let your eyes adjust to the dim surroundings. Better yet, drop a coin in the box to turn on the lights. This gloomy, cave-like interior—with just slits for windows—is a far cry from later, brighter architectural styles. Near the entrance on the right, look for the font that was used to baptize the infant who would grow up to be Pope Pius II.

## Eating in and near Pienza

### IN PIENZA

$$$ **La Bandita Townhouse Caffè** offers a break from Tuscan rusticity, focusing instead on tempting modern Italian cuisine (such as spring pea soup or spicy Chianina beef tartare). Diners watch the chef work in his open kitchen (dinner nightly 19:30-22:00, lunch Tue-Sun 12:30-15:00, indoor/outdoor seating, Corso il Rossellino 111, easier to enter around the corner on Via Sant'Andrea, +39 0578 749 005).

$$ **Trattoria Latte di Luna,** with outdoor tables filling a delightful little square, is the more traditional choice. While the food can be hit or miss, locals swear by their specialty, roast suckling pig *(maialino da latte arrosto).* Run by friendly Roberto with Delfina in the kitchen, the dining room features an ancient well and sits on

top of Etruscan tunnels (Wed-Mon 10:30-17:00, closed Tue, at the far end of town at Via San Carlo 2, +39 0578 748 606).

**Quick Lunch:** For something cheap, characteristic, and fast, just grab a tasty **$** *porchetta* **sandwich** at the little no-name shop 30 yards off the main square (at Corso il Rossellino 81) and munch it under the loggia or at the viewpoint (daily 8:00-20:00).

**Gelato:** Quality ingredients are on the menu at **Buon Gusto.** Nicola creates fun original flavors, such as carrot-ginger, creamy basil, or kiwi-spinach. They also do fresh-pressed juices and smoothies (daily 12:00-19:00, open later in summer, closed Nov-March, Via delle Case Nuove 26, +39 335 704 9165). Nicola also runs Sgarbi Gelato Natura in Montepulciano.

**Cocktails with Nibbles:** Pienza isn't much for nightlife, but for a cocktail in a local-feeling setting, drop in at **Idyllium**—a hip cocktail bar serving creative herb-infused drinks, light food, and outdoor seating facing grand Tuscan splendor (daily 11:00-late, shorter hours off-season; from the main square, go down the little lane to the right of the church to Via Gozzante 67; +39 0578 748 176).

## NEAR PIENZA

Despite having more than its share of tourists, Pienza suffers from a lack of quality restaurants. These options are all within about a 15-minute drive and offer a more memorable meal you'll find in town. To locate Castelmuzio, see the "Heart of Tuscany" map on page 542.

**Just Outside Castelmuzio:** For an excellent meal—perhaps combined with a memorable activity—consider dinner at the fine **$$$** restaurant at **La Moscadella,** run by The Isabella Experience (recommended in "Countryside Accommodations," earlier in this chapter). A limited number of tables are available to nonguests who book ahead. Chef Giancarlo prepares classic, always-delicious Tuscan meals, occasionally with a modern spin. You can dine in the rustic yet elegant glassed-in veranda or out on the pebbly terrace—both have views. Call or email ahead to check the schedule of activities (such as pasta-making and wine/olive oil tasting) or to reserve one of the limited tables (reservations required, restaurant open Fri-Wed, closed Thu, veggie and gluten-free options available, +39 0577 665 516, mobile +39 338 740 9245).

**In Castelmuzio:** To escape Pienza's tourist crowds, drive about 15 minutes to the remote village of Castelmuzio. The hamlet's lone restaurant, **$$ Locanda di Casalmustia,** is a cozy and typically uncrowded spot serving good local cuisine. Choose between sitting out on the stony lane or in a cute fresco-ceilinged dining room. While not quite a destination restaurant, it's a good excuse to explore an untrampled hill town and enjoy sweeping views of the countryside (Tue-Sun 8:00-22:00, closed Mon, in the heart of the town at Piazza della Pieve 3, +39 0577 665 166).

**In Monticchiello:** In the opposite direction but about the same distance away is the excellent **Ristorante Daria** (see "Eating in Monticchiello," later in this chapter; for location see the "Heart of Tuscany Drive" map on page 592).

## Pienza Connections

Bus tickets are sold at the bar/café (marked *Il Caffè*, closed Tue) just outside Pienza's town gate (or pay a little extra and buy tickets from the driver). Buses leave from a few blocks up the street, directly in front of the town entrance. Montepulciano is the nearest transportation hub.

**From Pienza by Bus to: Siena** (6/day, none on Sun, 1.5 hours), **Montepulciano** (8/day, 30 minutes), **Montalcino** (3-4/day, none Sun, change in Torrenieri, 1 hour). Bus info: www.at-bus.it.

# Montalcino

On a hill overlooking vineyards and valleys, Montalcino is famous for its delicious and pricey Brunello di Montalcino red wines. It's a pleasant, low-impact town crawling with wine-loving tourists and has a smattering of classy shops, but little sightseeing. Everyone touring this area seems to be relaxed and in an easy groove...as if enjoying a little wine buzz.

While today it's all about the wine, Montalcino (mohn-tahl-CHEE-noh) has an incredibly long history: Human settlement here dates back to the Etruscan period. It's possible that Neolithic humans were here long before that. That's because Montalcino has a unique setting, with protective caves and a freshwater spring high atop a rocky pinnacle—a highly desirable position for early settlers. For much of its long history, Montalcino was a veritable fortress, perched high overlooking the valley below and its Via Francigena pilgrim route.

Flash forward to the Middle Ages, when Montalcino was considered Siena's biggest ally. Originally aligned with Florence, the town switched sides after the Sienese beat up Florence in the Battle of Montaperti in 1260. The Sienese persuaded the Montalcinesi to join their side by forcing them to collect corpses and sleep one night in the bloody, Florentine-strewn battlefield. Later, the Montalcinesi took in Sienese refugees. To this day, in gratitude for their support, the Sienese invite the Montalcinesi to lead the parade that kicks off Siena's Palio celebrations.

Montalcino prospered under Siena, but like its ally, it waned after the Medici family took control of the region. The village became a humble place. Then, in the late 19th century, the Biondi Santi family created a fine, dark red wine, calling it "the brunette" (Brunello). Today's affluence is due to the town's much-sought-after wine. (For more on this wine, see the "Wines in the Region" sidebar later in this chapter). Montalcino provides a handy springboard for exploring the surrounding wine region. "Montalcino" literally means "Mountain of Oaks"—and sure enough, its surrounding hills are generously forested. For a self-guided driving tour connecting some of the most enjoyable wineries and views, see the "Brunello Wine Country Drive," later in this chapter.

If you're not a wine lover, you may find Montalcino (a.k.a. Brunello-ville) a bit dull. It's a bit humbler, mellower, and less touristy than Montepulciano or Pienza—less commercialized, but also a little less spectacular.

## Orientation to Montalcino

Sitting atop a hill amidst a sea of vineyards, Montalcino is surrounded by walls and dominated by its Fortezza (a.k.a. "La Rocca").

From here, roads lead down into the two main squares: Piazza Garibaldi and Piazza del Popolo.

**Tourist Information:** The TI, just off Piazza Garibaldi in the Old City Hall, is good for a map, but not much else (daily 10:00-13:30 & 14:00-18:30, +39 337 142 2762).

**Arrival in Montalcino:** For a short visit here by **car**, drivers should head to the pay lot in Piazzale Fortezza. Skirt around the fortress, take the first right (just past a little park), and follow signs to *parking* and *Fortezza* (€1.50/hour, free 20:00-8:00). Or, if you don't mind a short climb, park for free below the fortress: At the roundabout with the ugly statue, take the small downhill lane into the big lower parking lot (blue lines mean that you have to pay, but the lower-level unmarked spots are always free). If these lots are full, follow the town's western wall toward the Madonna del Soccorso church and a long pay lot.

The **bus** stop is on Piazza Cavour, a little park about 300 yards from the town center. From here, simply follow the main drag, Via Mazzini, straight up into town. While Montalcino has no official baggage storage, a few shops may be willing to hold on to one or two bags on a short-term basis; ask at the TI.

**Helpful Hints:** Friday is **market** day (7:00-13:00) on Viale della Libertà, near the Fortezza.

# Sights and Experiences in Montalcino

### Piazza del Popolo

All roads in tiny Montalcino lead to the main square, Piazza del Popolo ("People's Square").

The **Old City Hall** was the fortified seat of government. It's decorated by the coats of arms of judges who, in the interest of fairness, were from outside of town. Like Siena, Montalcino was a republic in the Middle Ages. When Florentines took Siena in 1555, Siena's ruling class retreated here and held out for four more years. The Medici coat of arms (with the six balls, or pills) dominates the others. This, and the much-reviled statue of Cosimo de' Medici in the small loggia under the clock, are reminders that Florence finally took Montalcino in 1559. The one-handed **clock** was the norm until 200 years ago.

For five centuries, the large arcaded **loggia** (on your left as you face the clock tower) hosted the town market. Under the loggia, notice the bulky stone monuments at either end, honoring Montalcinesi who died fighting in various wars.

For some wine-centric whimsy, go up around the right side of the Old City Hall and find a series of **plaques** (each designed by a different artist), which show off the annual rating of the Brunello harvest from two to five stars—important, as wine is the lifeblood of the local economy. And, of course, it's fun to simply observe the *passeggiata*—these days mostly a parade of tourists here for the wine.

Back on the square, in front of the clock tower, notice the grand café. Since 1888, **Caffè Fiaschetteria Italiana** has been *the* elegant place to enjoy a drink. Its founder, inspired by Caffè Florian in Venice, brought fine coffee to this humble town of woodcutters. It's now both a café and a wine bar.

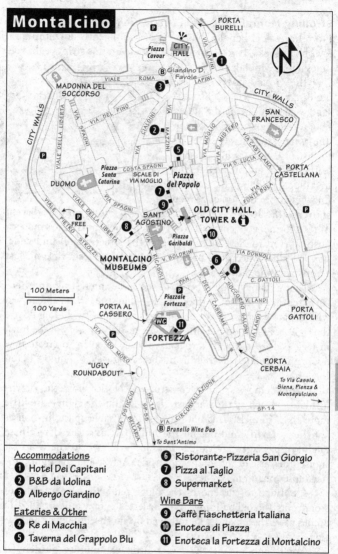

# Montalcino

PORTA BURELLI

P Piazza Cavour

CITY HALL

Giardino D. Favole

B

VIA LAPINI

VIALE ROMA

MADONNA DEL SOCCORSO

CITY WALLS

SAN FRANCESCO

VIA DEL FINO

VIA CALPINI

VIA MAZZINI

VIA P. MISTERO

VIA CASTELLANA

PORTA CASTELLANA

CITY WALLS

VIALE DELLA LIBERTA

VIA SPAGNI

Piazza Santa Catarina

COSTA SPAGNI

SCALE DI VIA MOGLIO

Piazza del Popolo

VIA S. LUCIA

VIA FONTE BULA

DUOMO

VIA SPAGNI

VIALE DELLA LIBERTA

SANT' AGOSTINO

OLD CITY HALL, TOWER & i

VIA PIETRO STROZZI

FREE

Piazza Garibaldi

VIA DONNOLI

MONTALCINO MUSEUMS

V. BOLDRINI

VIA FAN...

C. GATTOLI

100 Meters

100 Yards

Piazzale Fortezza

P

VIA DELLE CASERME

VIA SOCCORSO SALONI

V. LANDI

PORTA GATTOLI

PORTA AL CASSERO

WC

FORTEZZA

VIA LANDI

PORTA CERBAIA

"UGLY ROUNDABOUT"

VIA ALDO MORO

VIA OSTICCIO

VIA BELLARIA

SP-14

SP-55

VIA CIRCONVALLAZIONE

To Via Cassia, Siena, Pienza & Montepulciano

SP-14

B Brunello Wine Bus

To Sant'Antimo

---

<u>Accommodations</u>
1. Hotel Dei Capitani
2. B&B da Idolina
3. Albergo Giardino

<u>Eateries & Other</u>
4. Re di Macchia
5. Taverna del Grappolo Blu

6. Ristorante-Pizzeria San Giorgio
7. Pizza al Taglio
8. Supermarket

<u>Wine Bars</u>
9. Caffè Fiaschetteria Italiana
10. Enoteca di Piazza
11. Enoteca la Fortezza di Montalcino

---

Immediately across the street, **Farmacia Salvioni** has been in the same family since 1905. You can step into the historic interior, then walk to the back to peek out their window; it enjoys a spectacular view over Tuscan splendor.

From here, you're just a few minutes' walk from the Montalcino Museums and the old fortress (with its popular wine bar)—both described later. Or, with your back to the clock tower, head a few blocks downhill on the main drag to see a bit more of town.

### Strolling Montalcino's Main Drag (Via Mazzini)

From Piazza del Popolo, follow Via Mazzini gently downhill for a few short blocks. If you know what to look for, this strip speaks volumes about Montalcino's past.

The ground floors of these buildings are (at least) a thousand years old, with the upper floors added or modified later. The first stretch of shops is tourist-oriented: wine, foods, leather, and so on. After the first block, on the right, there's a fine view from the top of a **steep staircase** (Scale di Via Moglio). The big building on the adjacent hill is a former convent, and now the home of Montalcino's modern hospital. On the left (uphill) side of the street, you'll find wide, stepped lanes once used by donkeys (such as Costa Spagni, just across from the staircase).

Farther along, you'll begin to see some interesting **architectural features,** including doors made of chestnut wood and carved with ornate door knockers and other decorations (including #8, on the right, and #17, on the left). You can read the history of the town in its facades—old arches that have been filled in to create new doors and windows, such as in the houses at #15, #17, and #19 (on the left).

Montalcino is stoutly constructed. Notice how the downhill lanes—such as the one just after #22, on the right—are little more than tunnels. This both maximizes usable space for houses and helps fortify and defend the hilltop against invaders. These **enclosed passages** are called *"chiassino"*—related to the word for "noise," because of the loud echo inside. At #26 (on the right), notice more "phantom" arches.

Continue to the end of the block, enjoying the pastiche of storefronts and old buildings. On the left is a crazy quilt of filled-in arches at #31, #33, and #35, followed by another fine door decoration at #37.

You'll pop out at the sweet little community **garden** (Il Giardino delle Favole)—a welcome green oasis in this very stony town. Directly on the other side of the garden is the big, blocky, ochre-colored **City Hall** building (Comune di Montalcino). It's open to the public and hides some surprising details. Step through the door at #15. Just to the right, pause at the grilled window and press the button below to illuminate some beautiful 16th-century frescoes. From here, turn left, then follow the corridor to the end, where you'll turn right to a terrace with stunning views over the Tuscan countryside.

From here, return to the little garden. Find a bench to relax, as locals do, or nurse a drink at the little café, then head five minutes back up the main drag to Piazza del Popolo.

## Montalcino Museums (Musei di Montalcino)

While technically several museums in one, and surprisingly big and modern for this little town, Montalcino's **L'Oro di Montalcino** ranks only as a decent bad-weather activity. The cellar features two exhibits: one on prehistoric times, and a multimedia experience on the famed Brunello di Montalcino and its winemakers. The ground, first, and second floors hold medieval and modern art collections, with an emphasis on Gothic sacred art (with works from Montalcino's heyday, the 13th to 16th century). The ground floor is best, with a large collection of crucifixes and the museum's highlights, a glazed terra-cotta altarpiece and a statue of St. Sebastian, both by Andrea della Robbia.

**Cost and Hours:** €10, includes entry to Sant'Agostino Church, daily 10:30-19:00, Via Ricasoli 31, to the right of Sant'Agostino Church, +39 0577 286 300, www.orodimontalcino.it.

## Fortezza

This 14th-century fort, built under Sienese rule, is now little more than an empty shell (with a popular wine bar—see below). It was
built to defend against catapults and arrows, but the cannon was invented shortly thereafter. You can still see pockmarks from cannonballs fired here in 1553 on the outer wall (facing away from the town), but the fort withstood the attack. You're
welcome to enter the big, open courtyard (with WCs out the far end), or just enjoy a picnic in the park surrounding the fort, but if you want to climb the ramparts for a panoramic view, you'll have to pay.

**Cost and Hours:** €4, enter though wine bar, daily 9:00-20:00, off-season 10:00-18:00.

## Wine Bars in Town

If you're short on time and won't make it to the wineries outside Montalcino, simply visit a wine bar in town, where you can comfortably taste a variety of vintages before stumbling safely back to your hotel. This is also a great strategy for Sundays, when many countryside wineries are closed. Each of these places serves light food, and each has a different style—choose the one that suits your mood.

**Caffè Fiaschetteria Italiana,** a touristy café/wine bar, was founded by Ferruccio Biondi Santi, the creator of the famous Brunello wine. The wine library in the back of the café boasts many local choices. A meeting place since 1888, this grand café also serves light lunches. Come here for the venerable ambience and sidewalk seating—but don't expect good prices. You can taste wine more affordably elsewhere (Brunellos by the glass, light snacks and plates; same prices inside, outside, or in back room; daily 7:30-23:00, shorter hours off-season; Piazza del Popolo 6, +39 0577 849 043).

**Enoteca di Piazza**—part of a chain of wine shops with mechanical dispensers—is a fun way to efficiently taste a variety of different wines in a forgettable setting. Here's how it works: A "drink card" (like a debit card) keeps track of the samples you take, for which you'll pay from €1 to €9 apiece. They stock 100 different wines, including some whites—rare in this town. This is a good spot to assemble a box of wine from different local producers to ship home (free shipping if you buy pricier Brunellos). Their small restaurant across the street lets you enjoy your new purchase with local dishes (daily 9:00-20:00, near Piazza del Popolo at Via Matteotti 43, +39 0577 848 104, www.enotecadipiazza.com).

**Enoteca la Fortezza di Montalcino** offers a chance to taste top-end wines by the glass, each with an English explanation. While the prices are a bit higher than other *enoteche* in town, the medieval setting inside Montalcino's fort is popular with tourists. Spoil yourself with Brunello in the cozy *enoteca* or at an outdoor table in the fortress courtyard (tastings start at €18 for 3 wines and go up from there; small menu and sampler plates of cheeses and *salumi*; daily 9:00-20:00, until 18:00 Nov-March; inside the Fortezza, +39 0577 849 211).

## WINERIES NEAR MONTALCINO

The countryside around Montalcino is littered with wineries, some of which offer tastings. As Brunello is the poshest of Italian wines, these wineries feel a bit upscale, and most require an advance reservation. It's a simple process (just call or email to arrange a time), and they'll delight in showing you around. Tours generally last 45-60 minutes, cost at least €15 per person, and conclude with a tasting of three or four wines. The Montalcino TI can give you a list of more than 150 regional wineries. Or check with the vintners' consortium (+39 0577 848 246, www.consorziobrunellodimontalcino.it). Many wineries are closed on Sunday, so check before heading out.

If you lack a car (or don't want to drive), you can take a tour on the **Brunello Wine Bus,** which laces together visits to four wineries, with a lunch break in the middle, either on your own in Montalcino or at a farmhouse for an extra fee (€190, RS% with this book; tours run March-Nov Tue and Thu only; departs at 10:00, returns at 19:00; tours leave from their office, or they will pick you up within 3 miles of Montalcino; half-day tours available Tue and Thu-Sat for €95; Via Circonvallazione 3, +39 0577 846 021, www.winetravelsforyou.com, info@winetravelsforyou.com).

If you're paying for a wine tasting, you aren't obligated to buy. But if a winery is doing a small tasting just for you, they're hoping you'll buy a bottle or two. Italian vintners understand that North Americans can't take much wine with them, and they don't expect to make a big sale, but they do hope you'll look for their wines in the US. Some shops and wineries can arrange shipping.

## South of Montalcino

Some of these options are linked by my Brunello Wine Country Drive, later in this chapter. For locations, see the "Brunello Wine Country Drive" map on page 604.

### Tornesi

This charmingly low-key, family-run winery is a short drive outside of Montalcino, perched on a grand view terrace overlooking the famous Biondi Santi winery (where Brunello was invented). Maurizio, Elisa, and Valentina offer tours and tastings in this scenic setting. They enjoy explaining how their logo—the cuckoo *(kukula)* bird—was inspired by their chatty grandfather (€18 for 3 tastes plus tour, €40 tasting includes lunch, €20-40 bottles; closed Sun, reserve ahead, mobile +39 349 093 2167, www.brunellotornesi.it, degustazionicasatornesi@gmail.com). Leaving Montalcino, at the main roundabout, go uphill toward *Grosetto,* then watch for the brown *Benducce* sign on the left (just before the road bends right). Tornesi is a short drive down this gravel road, on the left.

### Mastrojanni

Perched high above the Sant'Antimo Abbey, overlooking sprawling vineyards, this winery (owned by the Illy coffee company) is big and glitzy—yet doesn't feel as corporate or soulless as some of the bigger players (€30-50 for tour and tasting, €17-36 bottles; daily 10:00-16:30, reserve ahead; Podere Loreto e San Pio, +39 0577 835 681, www.mastrojanni.com, visite@mastrojanni.com). To reach it, head up into the town of Castelnuovo dell'Abate (just above Sant'Antimo Abbey), bear left at the Bassomondo restaurant, and

# Wines in the Region

This region has two well-respected red wines, each centered on a specific town: Montepulciano is known for its Vino Nobile, while Montalcino is famous for its Brunello. In each wine, the predominant grape is a clone of sangiovese (Tuscany's main red wine grape).

**Vino Nobile di Montepulciano** ("noble wine of Montepulcia-no") is a high-quality, dry ruby red, made mostly with the Prugno-

lo Gentile variety of sangiovese (70 percent), plus other varieties including Mammolo (30 percent). Aged two years (or three for a *riserva*)—one year of which must be in oak casks—it's more full-bodied than a typical Chianti and less tannic than a Brunello. It pairs well with meat, especially roasted lamb with rosemary, rabbit or boar ragù over pasta, grilled portobello mushrooms, and local cheeses like pecorino. Several large wineries produce and age their Vino Nobile in the sprawling cellars beneath the town of Montepulciano. Three of these are fun and easy to tour (see "Sights and Experiences in Montepulciano" on page 580). The oldest red wine in Tuscany, Vino Nobile has been produced since the late 1500s. (Don't mistake this wine for lesser-quality wines from the Le Marche or Abruzzo regions that use a grape confusingly named Montepulciano.)

**Brunello di Montalcino** ("the little brown one of Montalcino"—named for the color of the grapes before harvest) is even more highly regarded and ranks among Italy's finest and most expensive wines. Made from 100 percent Sangiovese Grosso (a.k.a. Brunello) grapes, it's smooth, dry, and aged for a minimum of two years in wood casks, plus an additional four months in the bottle. *Riserva* wines are aged an additional year. Brunello is designed to cellar for 10 years or longer—but who can wait? It pairs well with the local cuisine, but the perfect match is the fine Chianina beef. *Buon appetito!*

First created by the Biondi Santi clan in the late 19th century, this wine quickly achieved a sterling reputation. Today, there are around 240 mostly small producers of Brunello in the Montalcino region; I've recommended just a few, which I find fun and accessible (see the "Brunello Wine Country Drive" in this chapter). A simpler option—and one that avoids having the taster be behind the wheel—is to sample a few different wines at one of the good wine bars in Montalcino (see page 583).

You'll also see Rosso di Montalcino (a younger version of Brunello), which is aged for one year. This "poor man's Brunello" is very good, at half the price. Note that in lesser-quality harvest years, only Rosso di Montalcino is produced.

Montalcino's climate is drier and warmer than Chianti or Montepulciano. Diverse soils and slopes create many microclimates that affect the wine. Locals explain that, due to overall temperature increases resulting from climate change, wineries on the higher ground reap benefits from slightly cooler temperatures (grapes love hot days and cool nights). Elevation is a bonus for wine-loving tourists, who enjoy stellar views while sampling the best wines.

Touring a winery, you'll see that many winemakers age Brunello in giant oak casks. This means that less liquid is in contact with the wood surface, so the wine picks up less of the harsh wood (tannic) taste and vanilla-like flavors, while still absorbing the desired leathery and peppery notes.

You'll also notice glass jars poking up from the tops of those casks, which allow expansion of the liquid during fermentation, and—by providing a small overflow reservoir—ensure that the wine reaches the very top of the cask. Before placing the wine in casks, modern wineries ferment it in temperature-controlled cement or stainless-steel tanks, which are easier to maintain than wood and preserve a more fruity bouquet.

Strolling through vineyards, you may notice "sentinel" roses at the ends of some of the rows of vines. These aren't just decorative; because disease affects roses before grapes, historically the flowers acted as a kind of canary in a coal mine, giving vintners advance notice if a phylloxera epidemic was imminent. Today the roses can warn of mildew.

But disease isn't the only pest: Locals say that wild boars make the best winemakers—they wait to raid the vineyards until the grapes are perfectly sweet. At that magic moment, it becomes a race between the boars and the human harvesters. But humans have the last laugh (or bite)—boar is found on many Tuscan menus and is considered the perfect accompaniment to the local wines.

**HEART OF TUSCANY**

continue up along the gravel road (enjoying vineyard and abbey views).

## Ciacci Piccolomini d'Aragona

Easier to remember by just its first name (pronounced like Chachi in *Happy Days*), this well-respected, family-run vineyard has

a classy tasting room/*enoteca* and an outdoor view terrace. If you're just dropping in, belly up to the wine bar for a few free tastes. Or reserve ahead for a more formal tasting of top-quality wines (€15 tasting, €40 tasting plus tour of cellar, €10-25 bottles; April-Oct Mon-Sat 10:00-18:00, closed Nov-March and Sun year-round; down a back lane near Sant'Antimo Abbey—for directions, see page 603, +39 0577 835 616, www.ciaccipiccolomini. com, visite@ciaccipiccolomini.com). They have a special passion for bikers, with a gallery of historic bikes and a shower for anyone who cycles in.

## Castello Banfi-Poggio alle Mura

Much bigger and glossier than the other recommended wineries, Banfi is one of the largest producers in the area. Despite its size, the estate is charming, set in a castle located in a picturesque corner southwest of Sant'Antimo. Although touristy, this is a good option for Sundays, when other places are closed, or for a spontaneous drop-in tasting at the winery's *enoteca* (tastings start at €24; daily 10:00-19:30, shorter hours off-season; expensive tours available on request, +39 055 877 500, www.castellobanfiilborgo.com, hospitality@banfi.it). You'll find Banfi about 20 minutes south of Montalcino; follow SP-14 to Borgo Santa Rita and cut back north, following signs to *Poggio alle Mura*.

## North of Montalcino

These more remote wineries are most convenient if you're linking Montalcino to the Siena area. But either one is also worth a special trip—Altesino feels like a classy California winery, with stunning views, while Santa Giulia feels like you're dropping in on friends who run a cool farm.

### Altesino

Elegant and stately, Altesino owns perhaps the most stunning location of all, just off the back road connecting Montalcino north to Buonconvento. You'll twist up on cypress-lined gravel lanes to this perch, which looks out over an expanse of vineyards with Montalcino hovering on the horizon (€15 for tour and basic tasting; daily 10:00-17:00, shorter hours off-season; reserve ahead, Loc. Altesino 54, +39 0577 806 208, www.altesino.it, info@altesino.it). You'll find the turnoff for Altesino along the back road (SP-45) between Montalcino and Buonconvento.

### Santa Giulia

On the outskirts of Torrenieri, this is a quintessential family-run winery, with an emphasis on quality over quantity (only 30,000 bottles a year). They also produce excellent olive oil, prosciutto, and sala-mi. Less picturesque and much more rustic than the other wineries listed here, a tour at Santa Giulia is a Back Door experience. The son, Gianluca, and his wife, Kae, enjoy showing  off their entire working farm—ham hocks, cheese, and winery— before giving you a chance to taste their products. Call or email in advance to reserve a "Zero Kilometer" lunchtime tasting, with farm-fresh cold cuts, cheese, and bruschetta for €25; add pasta and dessert for €20 more (€15 for 3 tastes and tour, 2-person minimum, €15-34 bottles; Mon-Sat 10:00-17:00, closed Sun; Loc. Santa Giulia 48, +39 0577 834 270, www.santagiuliamontalcino.it, info@ santagiuliamontalcino.it). From Torrenieri's main intersection, fol-low the brown *Via Francigena* signs. After crossing the train tracks and a bridge, watch on the left and follow signs for *Sta. Giulia;* you'll take gravel roads through farm fields to the winery.

## Sleeping in Montalcino

**$$$ Hotel Dei Capitani,** at the end of town near the bus station, has plush public spaces, an inviting summertime pool, and a cliff-side terrace offering plenty of reasons to lounge. About half of the 29 basic rooms come with vast Tuscan views and are worth pay-ing a bit extra for (no balconies, request a view room when you reserve); the nonview rooms are bigger but face a somewhat noisy street (RS%, air-con, elevator, limited free parking—first come, first served, Via Lapini 6, +39 0577 847 227, www.deicapitani.it, info@deicapitani.it).

**$ B&B da Idolina** has four good rooms above an antique shop on the main street (check-in 15:00-19:00—call if arriving later, parking available, Via Mazzini 65, check in at the antique shop,

+39 0577 849 212, www.idolina1946.com, fulvia.soda@gmail.com, Fulvia).

**$ Albergo Giardino** has nine big, modern-minimalist rooms in a convenient location near the bus stop (RS%, air-con, free parking, Piazza Cavour 4, +39 0577 848 257, mobile +39 371 426 1838, www.albergoilgiardino.it, info@albergoilgiardino.it.

# Eating in Montalcino

**$$ Re di Macchia** is an invitingly intimate restaurant where Antonio serves up the big, hearty portions of Tuscan fare that Roberta cooks. Look for their seasonal menu and a fine Montalcino wine list (reservations strongly recommended, Fri-Wed 12:00-14:00 & 19:00-21:00, closed Thu, Via Soccorso Saloni 21, +39 0577 846 116).

**$$ Taverna del Grappolo Blu,** tucked in a cellar down a picturesque staircase off the main drag, is serious about its wine, game, homemade pasta, and vegetarian options (reservations smart, daily 12:00-15:00 & 19:00-22:00, a few steps off Via Mazzini at Scale di Via Moglio 1, +39 0577 847 150, www.grappoloblu.it, friendly Luciano).

**$$ Ristorante-Pizzeria San Giorgio** is a homey trattoria/pizzeria with traditional decor and reasonable prices. It's great for families and a reliable choice for a simple meal (daily 12:00-15:00 & 19:00-22:30, Via Soccorso Saloni 10, +39 0577 848 507, Mara).

**Quick Bite:** The **$** *pizza al taglio* shop, right on Piazza del Popolo at #11, has both pizza slices and sandwiches that they can heat up for you—ask for *scalda* (daily 10:30-21:30).

**Picnic:** Gather ingredients at the **Co-op supermarket** on Via Sant'Agostino (Mon-Sat 8:30-13:00 & 16:00-20:00, closed Sun, near Sant'Agostino Church), then enjoy your feast up at the Madonna del Soccorso Church, with vast territorial views.

# Montalcino Connections

Montalcino is well connected to Siena; other bus connections are inconvenient but generally workable. Montalcino's bus stop is on Piazza Cavour, within the town walls. Bus tickets are sold at the bar on Piazza Cavour, at the TI, and at some tobacco shops, but not on board (except for the bus to Sant'Antimo). Check schedules at the TI, at the bus station, or online (at www.at-bus.it). The nearest train station is a 30-minute bus ride away, in Buonconvento.

**From Montalcino by Bus:** For long-distance journeys, you'll always start out on bus #114, which goes to **Siena** (6/day Mon-Sat,

4/day Sun, 1.5 hours). En route, this bus goes through Torrenieri (change for **Pienza** or **Montepulciano**, 3-4/day, none on Sun); from Torrenieri it's 25 minutes to Pienza, 45 minutes to Montepulciano, then **Buonconvento** (where you can catch a train to **Florence**). You can also reach Florence by riding the bus to Siena, then taking the train. Since the Montepulciano bus connection is sporadic, consider hiring a taxi (about €70 one-way). A local bus runs to **Sant'Antimo** (3/day Mon-Fri, 2/day Sat, none on Sun, 15 minutes, buy tickets on board).

# Heart of Tuscany Drive

## VAL D'ORCIA LOOP

If you have just one day to connect the ultimate Tuscan towns and views, this is the loop I'd stitch together with a driving tour. In addition to larger towns (Montepulciano, Pienza) and smaller ones (Bagno Vignoni, Rocca d'Orcia), this loop drive, worth ▲▲▲, gives you a good look at the area called the Val d'Orcia (val DOR-chah), boasting some of the best scenery in Italy.

While the nearby Crete Senesi, just to the north (described in the Siena chapter), is rugged, the Val d'Orcia is manicured and feels manmade—shaped by generations of hardworking farmers. Most of this journey is through velvety, gentle, rolling hillsides generously draped with vivid-green crops in the springtime, and a parched moonscape in the late summer and fall. Hilltop villas and hill towns big and small recede to the horizon. This almost otherworldly smoothness constitutes many travelers' notions of Tuscan perfection.

**Planning Your Drive:** If you're in a rush and don't linger in any of the towns, you could do this drive in a couple of hours. To hit the sights, explore the towns, and linger over a meal or a glass of wine, spread it out over an entire day. (You could even splice in a side trip to a Brunello winery for a tasting.) I've started and ended the clockwise loop in Montepulciano, but you could just as easily start and end in Pienza. If gardens are your thing, do this loop when La Foce Gardens are open.

HEART OF TUSCANY

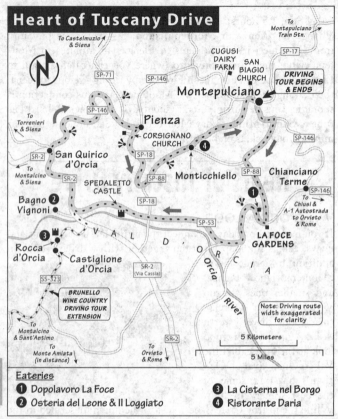

# Heart of Tuscany Drive

To Castelmuzio & Siena

To Montepulciano Train Stn.

SP-17

CUGUSI DAIRY FARM

SAN BIAGIO CHURCH

DRIVING TOUR BEGINS & ENDS

SP-71

SP-146

**Montepulciano**

SP-146

SP-146

**Pienza**

CORSIGNANO CHURCH

To Torrenieri & Siena

SP-18

❹

SR-2

**San Quirico d'Orcia**

To Montalcino & Siena

SR-2

SPEDALETTO CASTLE

SP-88

**Monticchiello**

SP-88

**Chianciano Terme**

SP-146

❶

To Chiusi & A-1 Autostrada to Orvieto & Rome

SP-18

**Bagno** ❷ **Vignoni**

SP-18

SP-53

**LA FOCE GARDENS**

V A L

❸

D '

O R C I A

**Rocca d'Orcia**

**Castiglione d'Orcia**

SR-2 (Via Cassia)

Orcia River

SS-323

BRUNELLO WINE COUNTRY DRIVING TOUR EXTENSION

Note: Driving route width exaggerated for clarity

To Montalcino & Sant'Antimo

To Monte Amiata (in distance)

To Orvieto & Rome

SR-2

5 Kilometers

5 Miles

## Eateries
❶ Dopolavoro La Foce
❷ Osteria del Leone & Il Loggiato
❸ La Cisterna nel Borgo
❹ Ristorante Daria

HEART OF TUSCANY

## From Montepulciano to Bagno Vignoni (via La Foce)

Before leaving Montepulciano, consider dropping by the showpiece Renaissance **San Biagio Church,** which sits at the base of the town (watch for its long, level, tree-lined driveway exactly where you leave Montepulciano on the road toward Pienza—see "Sights and Experiences in Montepulciano," earlier in this chapter).

To begin our loop, drive south, at first following signs to *Chianciano Terme* and *Chiusi*. Just 1 kilometer south of Montepulciano, watch on the right for the turnoff to *Castelluccio* and *Monticchiello*. Turn off here and zip along a pastoral back road for 5 kilometers. Pass the turnoff for Monticchiello on your right, and carry on straight ahead as the road continues uphill and becomes gravel. Grinding your way up, watch on your right for the jagged Tuscan cliffs called *calanchi*. You'll pop out at the T-intersection in front of the entrance to the **La Foce Gardens** (from this intersection, parking and reception are 50 yards to the left—look for *Loc. La Foce*; learn more about the gardens later in this chapter).

From La Foce, head downhill tracking signs toward *Siena* and *Roma*. After a few hundred yards, watch on the left for the big gravel parking lot of the recommended **Dopolavoro La Foce** restaurant (across the street). From this lot, you have a fine view of one of the iconic cypress-lined driveways of Tuscany.

Continue downhill along this road for about 5 kilometers, through pristine farm fields, until you reach a major intersection, where you'll turn right toward *Pienza* and *Siena* (on SP-53). Immersed in spectacular scenery, you'll twist between giant cypresses for about 10 kilometers. This road parallels the region's namesake **Orcia River** ("Val d'Orcia" means "Orcia River Valley").

Take a moment to simply appreciate your surroundings. The famous Chianti region to the north (right) and the Brunello region to the west (straight ahead) are each a short drive away; in those places, the rocky soil is perfect for grapes. But here, instead of rocks, you're surrounded by clay hills—once the floor of a prehistoric sea—that are ideal for cereal crops. Grains alternate every few years with a crop of fava beans, which help reintroduce nitrogen to the soil. It seems that every grassy hilltop is capped with a family farmhouse. Partway along this road, you'll pass a turnoff (on the right) offering a speedy shortcut to Pienza, just 8 stunning kilometers away. But there's so much more to see; I'd rather carry on with our loop.

The tower looming on the hill ahead of you is Rocca d'Orcia's Tentennano Castle (described later). Nearing the end of the road, you'll pass (on the left) the front door of an old farmhouse with oddly formidable crenellated towers, like a little castle in the field. This is **Spedaletto Castle,** built during the 12th century as a hospice for pilgrims walking the Via Francigena to Rome. Today it serves a similar purpose, as an *agriturismi*, housing wayfarers like you.

When you reach a T-intersection with the main SR-2 highway, turn left (toward *Roma*), then immediately take the exit for **Bagno Vignoni.** To explore this fascinating medieval spa town—with its main square filled with a thermal-spring-fed pool—see "Heart of Tuscany Sights," in the next section. To see the empty fortress at **Rocca d'Orcia,** stay on the SR-2 highway just 1 kilometer past Bagno Vignoni, then watch for the next turnoff.

## From Bagno Vignoni to Pienza (with Detours to Brunello Wineries and Tuscan Views)

From Bagno Vignoni, head north on SR-2 (toward *San Quirico d'Orcia* and *Siena*). After just 4 kilometers, in San Quirico d'Orcia, turn off onto the SP-146 road to Pienza, also marked for *Chiusi, Chianciano Terme,* and *Montepulciano.*

But before heading down that road, consider a few potential detours: First, if you won't have time to delve deeply into Brunello wine country, now is a good time to side-trip to your choice of **Brunello wineries;** those I've recommended on page 603 are all within about a 20- to 25-minute drive of San Quirico. Read the descriptions, take your pick, and call ahead to reserve a tour and tasting. Most of the places I list don't allow drop-ins. Another option is to zip into the town of **Montalcino** itself—an easy and well-signed 15-minute drive from San Quirico—and taste some local vintages at a wine bar there. And if you're collecting **views,** you could continue straight on SR-2 past San Quirico—toward *Siena*— for 4 kilometers and pull over next to the circle of cypress trees in a field called the Rondò (see the "Top Tuscan Views" sidebar).

Back on the SP-146 road from San Quirico to Pienza, you enjoy one of the region's most postcard-worthy stretches—with grand panoramas in both directions, including two more quintessential Tuscan scenes: the **Chapel of Madonna di Vitaleta** (after 2 kilometers, on the right); and a classic **farmhouse with trees,** just before Pienza (about 9 kilometers after San Quirico, on the left— both also described in the "Top Tuscan Views" sidebar).

Finally you'll pull into **Pienza,** where you can park and tour the town using the information earlier in this chapter.

## From Pienza to Montepulciano (via Monticchiello)

If you're in a hurry or losing sunlight, just hop back on the main SP-146 road for the 12-kilometer straight shot back to Montepulciano (enjoying some pullouts on the left with fine views of the town). But I prefer this longer, even more dramatic route, via the fortified village of Monticchiello.

From the traffic circle at the entry to Pienza's town center, instead of heading for Montepulciano, follow the road that runs along the left side of town (marked *Amiata* and *Monticchiello*—as you face Pienza, you'll continue straight when the main road bends left). This road loops around behind and below the far end of the village, where you can consider a brief detour to see Pienza's oldest church: Turn off on the right at the brown sign for *Pieve di Corsigiano* and drive a few hundred yards to **Corsignano Parish Church** (described on page 575).

Continuing on the main road past that turnoff, you'll drop steeply down into the valley, feeling as if you're sinking into a lavish painting. Dead ahead is **Monte Amiata,** the tallest mountain in Tuscany. This looming behemoth blocks bad weather, creating a mild microclimate that makes the Val d'Orcia a particularly pleas-

## The Via Francigena

Many of the sights in this region—and others in this book (including Siena, Lucca, and San Gimignano)—line up along the route of the Via Francigena (VEE-ah frahn-CHEE-jeh-nah). During the Middle Ages, when devout Christians undertook a once-in-a-lifetime pilgrimage to Rome, this route was heavily trod by the footsore faithful flowing in from northern Europe (hence the name, "Road of the Franks"—referring to the Germanic tribes who lived in present-day Germany and France). The main Via Francigena followed more or less the route of today's SR-2 highway, from Florence to Siena, then through the Val d'Orcia south to Rome. Without even realizing it, many modern-day tourists follow this millennium-old route as they travel through this part of Italy.

The first documented pilgrimages along here took place around AD 725, and the trend continued for many centuries. In 990, Archbishop Sigeric of Canterbury undertook the entire 1,100-mile round-trip from England. Upon his return, he documented tips for fellow pilgrims about where to sleep, where to eat, what to see, and how to pack light in a carry-on-size rucksack...arguably the world's first guidebook.

The history of Tuscany is inextricably tied to the Via Francigena. Pilgrim traffic provided an injection of wealth into communities along the Via Francigena, and fortresses popped up—or were repurposed—to keep the route safe. Abbeys and churches were built to cater to the masses. And many shrewd communities leveraged the passing pilgrim trade into enormous prosperity; for example, Siena boomed both as a financial center and a trading outpost for Via Francigena pilgrims.

Like the Camino de Santiago in northern Spain, this medieval pilgrim route—forgotten for centuries—has recently enjoyed renewed interest. Though the numbers are still small—and the path lacks the well-orchestrated conveniences of the Camino de Santiago—a handful of modern-day pilgrims are, once again, walking through Tuscany south to Rome.

**HEART OF TUSCANY**

ant place to farm...or to vacation. Meanwhile, don't forget to savor the similarly stellar views of Pienza in your rearview mirror. After 5 kilometers, look on the left for the turnoff to Monticchiello (brown sign). From here, carry on for 4 kilometers—watching on the left for fine vistas of Pienza and for another classic twisty cypress-lined road—to the pleasant town of **Monticchiello.** This town, with an excellent recommended restaurant (Daria) and a compact, fortified townscape worth exploring, is a good place to stretch your legs; see more in the next section.

From Monticchiello, there are two routes back to Montepulciano: For the shorter route (6 kilometers), partly on gravel roads, drive all the way to the base of the Monticchiello old town, then turn right. For the longer route (10 kilometers), which stays on paved roads but circles back the way our loop started, turn off for Montepulciano at the main intersection, in the flat part of town that's lower down.

## HEART OF TUSCANY SIGHTS

Below are the main sights you'll pass on my Heart of Tuscany driving route. Two of the main stops—the towns of Montepulciano and Pienza—are covered earlier in this chapter.

### ▲La Foce Gardens

One of the finest gardens in Tuscany, La Foce (lah FOH-cheh) caps a hill with geometrical Italian gardens and rugged English gardens that flow seamlessly into the Tuscan countryside. The gardens were a labor of love for Iris Origo, an English-born, Italian-bred aristocrat who left her mark on this area and wrote evocatively about her time here. The gardens—which are worth a pilgrimage for garden lovers—can be visited only with a guided tour, and only three days a week (Wed, Thu, Sun) and some holidays.

**Cost and Hours:** €10; 45-minute tours offered April-Oct Wed at 15:00, 16:00, 17:00, and 18:00; Thu, Sun, and holidays at 11:30, 15:00, and 16:30—can be closed for private events, so check online in advance; private tours available, no tours in winter, ticket office opens 15 minutes before tour time, +39 0578 69101, www.lafoce.com.

**Getting There:** La Foce sits in the hills above the busy town of Chianciano Terme. You can avoid SP-146 from Montepulciano through Chianciano (heavy traffic, poor signage) by following a more scenic route through the countryside (described at the start of my Heart of Tuscany Drive).

**Background:** In 1924, the British aristocrat Iris Cutting—who had grown up amidst wealth and privilege in Fiesole, overlooking Florence—married Antonio Origo, the son of the marquis of the Val d'Orcia. They took over a dilapidated country home high in the hills above Chianciano Terme and set about converting it into a luxurious estate of manor homes and gardens, importing British landscape architect Cecil Pinsent to bring their vision to life. The Origo clan also revived the Renaissance ideal of landowners supporting the local peasants, and built a school and other institutions for the public good. During World War II, the Origos took in refugee children and hid partisans—all recounted in Iris Origo's memoir, *War in Val d'Orcia*. The Origo family still owns and manages the property today.

**Visiting the Gardens:** From the entrance, your tour guide leads you first into the tidy Renaissance garden nearest the main house, with angular hedges, wisteria-draped walls, and potted citrus trees on pedestals. As you move away from the house, the garden's style changes to a more rugged, English-style design that bridges the tidy villa and the pristine Tuscan wilderness all around. From the garden, you'll have a perfect view of a classic Tuscan road—a cypress-lined lane zigzagging up an adjacent hill. If this road seems a little too perfect, that's because it is: It was built by the grandfather of Antonio Origo, who had a similar appreciation for aesthetics, and made sure even this utilitarian road was beautiful. He based the road's design on scenes in Renaissance-era frescoes in Florence's Medici-Riccardi Palace.

**Eating and Sleeping near La Foce:** Near the gardens, the Origo family runs a memorably charming roadside restaurant, **$$ Dopolavoro La Foce** ("After Work"). Once the quitting-time hangout for local farmers, today its interior is country-chic. The menu offers basic sandwiches or pasta and meat (featuring elegant hamburgers). The garden terrace out back is a chirpy delight, and the parking lot across the busy road offers one of the best vantage points on that perfect Tuscan road (Tue-Sun 12:30-21:30, closed Mon and Nov-March, Strada della Vittoria 90, +39 0578 754 025, run with flair by Asia). Also nearby is their remote, restful B&B (described on page 549).

## ▲Bagno Vignoni

Thanks to the unique geology of this part of Tuscany (see sidebar earlier in this chapter), several natural hot springs bubble up

between the wineries and hill towns. And the town of Bagno Vignoni (BAHN-yoh veen-YOH-nee)—with a quirky history, a pleasant-to-stroll street plan punctuated with steamy canals, and various places to take a dip—is the most accessible and enjoyable to explore. If you'd like to recuperate from your sightseeing and wine tasting by soaking in the thermal baths, bring your swimsuit.

**Getting There:** Bagno Vignoni is well signed, just off the main SR-2 highway linking Siena to Rome (5 kilometers south of

San Quirico d'Orcia). Park in the free lot (just past the Adler Spa Resort Thermae) or in the pay lot by the big roundabout and walk into town, taking the left fork (in front of Hotel Le Terme).

**Bagno Vignoni Town Walk:** Emerging into the main square, walk under the covered loggia and look out over the aptly named **Piazza delle Sorgenti** ("Square of the Sources"), filled with a vast pool. Natural spring water bubbles up at the far end at temperatures around 125 degrees Fahrenheit. Known since Roman times, these hot springs were harnessed for their medicinal properties in the Middle Ages, when footsore pilgrims could stop for a soothing soak midway through their long walk from northern Europe to Rome along the Via Francigena. St. Catherine of Siena also came here to convalesce, but—in true ascetic style—threw herself into the hottest part of the spring as a form of self-flagellation. (Under the loggia, notice the little chapel to St. Catherine, with pottery vases decorated with her symbolic goose.) Other Tuscan big shots—from Lorenzo the Magnificent (the Medici paterfamilias) to Pope Pius II (who remade Pienza in his own image)—also came here seeking cures for arthritis and other ailments.

You're not allowed to wade or swim in this main pool today, but an easy stroll through town shows you other facets of these healing waters. Turn right and circle the pool, then turn left down Via delle Sorgenti (passing the recommended Il Loggiato restaurant, then Piazza del Moretto and the recommended Osteria del Leone restaurant). Listen for the water that gushes under your feet, as it leaves the pool and heads for its big plunge over the cliff. Continuing straight, notice the stairs (on your right) down to Hotel Posta Marcucci, with the Piscina Val di Sole—the most accessible place in town for a dip (details below).

But continuing straight ahead for now, you'll emerge at an open zone with the cliff-capping **ruins** of medieval mills and cisterns that once made full use of Bagno Vignoni's main resource. Here you'll also have a chance to dip your toes or fingers into streams of now-tepid water. At the canals' end, the water plunges down into the gorge carved by the Orcia River. Looking deep into the valley, notice the pond with white mud, where locals enjoy going for a free soak. Then peek into the giant basin at the edge of the cliff, where natural showers once poured—back when this was a bathing complex. On the adjacent hillside is the castle-crowned **Rocca d'Orcia**, a heavily fortified near-ghost-town that's just a short drive away.

**Taking the Waters:** The modern **Piscina Val di Sole** bath complex, inside Hotel Posta Marcucci, is simple but sophisticated. It's a serene spot to soak (in water ranging from 80 to 105 degrees Fahrenheit) while taking in soaring views of Rocca d'Orcia across the valley (€33, towel rental and lockers available; daily 9:30-18:00,

Fri-Sat also 21:00-24:00; +39 0577 887 112, www.postamarcucci.it).

**Eating in Bagno Vignoni:** The town's class act is **$$$ Osteria del Leone,** on the cheery little *piazzetta* just behind the loggia, with charming tables out on the square. Inside it's dull and modern, with a fine interior garden (closed Mon, Via dei Mulini 3, +39 0577 887 300, www.osteriadelleone.it). For something a bit more affordable and casual, drop by the nearby **$$ Il Loggiato,** with stony indoor seating or outdoor tables (closed Thu, Via delle Sorgenti 36, +39 0577 139 0723).

## Rocca d'Orcia

The fortress looming over Rocca d'Orcia (ROH-kah DOR-chah) perches high above the main SR-2 highway. Likely inhabited and fortified since Etruscan times, this strategic hilltop was a seat of great regional power in the 12th century. During this time, Rocca d'Orcia was one of a chain of forts that watched over pilgrims walking the Via Francigena to Rome. Supposedly, St. Catherine  of Siena miraculously learned to read and write overnight while staying here.

Today the **Rocca di Tentennano** fortress—an empty shell of a castle with modern steel stairs and a grand 360-degree panorama at its top—looks stark and abandoned. It seems to dare you to pay €3 to take the very steep hike up from the parking lots below (May-Sept daily 10:30-13:30 & 16:30-18:30, shorter hours off-season; mobile +39 392 003 3028 or +39 333 986 0788).

The pleasant village of Rocca d'Orcia, just below the castle, is a sleepy community that's nice for a stroll, but without much to see. The village focuses on its stone cistern, in the aptly named Piazza della Cisterna. The bigger town just behind Rocca, Castiglione d'Orcia, also has a fortified hilltop town center.

**Eating in Rocca d'Orcia:** It's worth the effort to reach rustic **$$ La Cisterna nel Borgo.** Marta and Fede serve up simple but beautifully prepared dishes that mingle big Tuscan flavors and flourishes gathered from Marta's travels. The cavelike interior has character, but try to get an outdoor table, facing the namesake cistern on an enchanting, ivy-draped piazza where old ladies chat and stray dogs and cats beg for scraps (Tue-Fri 12:00-14:00 & 19:00-22:00, Sat-Sun 19:00-22:00 only, closed Mon and unpredictably at other times—call ahead; Borgo Mestro 37, tel. 0577-887-280,

# Top Tuscan Views

Tuscany is a land of splendid vistas, and many of the best—and most famous—viewpoints are in or near the Val d'Orcia. Shutterbugs who want to make their own custom calendar of iconic Tuscan scenes (rolling fields, cypress trees, serpentine driveways) should prioritize fitting these stops into their itineraries.

**Cypress-Lined Driveways:** You'll find dozens upon dozens of these in your Tuscan travels. But two in this area are classics. The first is the perfectly twisty road near La Foce gardens; the most accessible and unobstructed angle on this is from the parking lot across the street from the recommended Dopolavoro La Foce restaurant (see page 597)—but if you're

touring the gardens, the views from inside are even better. Another postcard-ready driveway crests a hill adjacent to Monticchiello (you'll spot it on the main road from Pienza).

**Circle of Cypresses (Rondò):** This ring of cypress trees stands dramatically alone on a gently sloping hillside of brilliant-green-in-springtime crops. Planted as a shelter for shepherds caught out in the elements, today it's one of Tuscany's top photo ops. You'll find it along the main SR-2

road north of San Quirico d'Orcia (about 4 kilometers north of the main San Quirico exit; it's just 1 kilometer south of the Montalcino exit, and 2 kilometers south of the Torrenieri exit). Pullouts on both sides of the road—next to a long bridge—can get crowded. Avid photographers walk partway across the bridge for fine views back on the Rondò.

**Chapel and Trees:** The super-scenic road between San Quirico d'Orcia and Pienza (SP-146) has several fine viewpoints, but the best-known is the tidy little chapel (Cappella della Madonna di Vitaleta) on a ridge, flanked by pudgy cypress trees. Keep an eye out for this (distant) church on the south side of the road, about 2 kilometers north of San Quirico d'Orcia (near Agriturismo Poderino). On the same road, closer to Pienza, is a classic "farmhouse with trees" scene (north side of road, a kilometer from Pienza).

**Farmhouse with Twisty Driveway:** Another time-less tableau is easy to spot if you're visiting Pienza: From anywhere along the panoramic terrace, just gaze off to the south, to the rolling hills of the Val d'Orcia. In the foreground, you'll see a perfect little farmhouse with a meandering drive-

way (Agriturismo Podere Terrapille). If this looks familiar, you may remember it as Russell Crowe's dreamy home-sweet-home in *Gladiator*.

**Abbey in Pasture and Olive Grove:** The Sant'Antimo Abbey, which is well worth a visit and described later in this chapter, sits

in a picturesque mead-ow. An adjacent cypress tree towers toward the heavens, seemingly in a contest with the church's bell tower to see who will get there first. Views of the abbey from the road above, or from the abbey to the surrounding landscape, are equally thrilling.

**Honorable Mention—Winery Views:** Several wineries—clinging to the high ground to pull the maximum sweetness out of their vines—have spectacular territorial vistas overlooking rolling vineyards, with other landmarks lingering on the horizon. Two of the best are Altesino (10 kilometers north of Montalcino, on the road to Buonconvento; see page 588) and Mastrojanni (11 kilometers south of Montalcino, on a ridge high above Sant'Antimo Abbey).

www.cisternanelborgo.com). Dining here comes with a hike: Park at the lot below Rocca di Tentennano, hike up past the castle entrance, then keep going as the road crests the hill and twists downhill into the village.

## ▲Monticchiello

This 200-person fortified village clings to the high ground in the countryside just south of Pienza and Montepulciano. As it's not along a main road, it feels more remote (for tips on getting here from Pienza, see page 594; from Montepulciano, see page 592). While not quite "undiscovered," Monticchiello is relatively untrampled, and feels like a real place where you can get in touch with authentic Tuscan village life. It's also a fine place for a meal.

Ignore the flat, modern lower town, and head up to the circular, fortified upper town huddled against the hillside. Park for free at the base of the village and hike up through the main gate, and just explore. The town is dominated by the late-13th-century Church of Sts. Leonardo and Christopher, with a Gothic exterior and Renaissance interior along with a few surviving 14th-century frescoes. Tucked in a square nearby is the TI (with gifty local products) and Piazza del Teatro, where townspeople periodically enact a summer al fresco theatrical show—called Teatro Povero ("Theater of the Poor")—about the town's past and present (www.teatropovero.it). Continuing up through town, you'll find a large park sprawling at the base of a leaning tower, which keeps watch over valley views.

**Eating in Monticchiello:** At the warm and classy **$$$ Ristorante Daria,** you'll enjoy seasonal, traditional Tuscan dishes presented with flair in a modern setting. It's in the heart of the stony hill town amid sumptuous scenery. Reservations are wise (Thu-Tue 12:15-14:30 & 19:15-22:00, closed Wed, Via San Luigi 3, +39 0578 755 170, www.ristorantedaria.it). Arriving in Monticchiello, walk through the town's gate, head about 50 yards straight up the hill, and bear right.

# Brunello Wine Country Drive

## BRUNELLO WINE LOOP

The rocky hillsides immediately surrounding Montalcino produce some of the best wine in Italy: Brunello di Montalcino (and the less pricey, nearly-as-good Rosso di Montalcino). This loop drive, worth ▲▲, takes you through a wooded and jagged terrain, where sangiovese grapes struggle for survival on their way to becoming fine wine and remote rural wineries give you the opportunity to sample the prized local vintages. (For a primer, see the "Wines in the Region" sidebar earlier in this chapter.) And tucked between the wineries, you'll also find time-passed villages and an evocative abbey in a secluded valley (Sant'Antimo).

**Planning Your Drive:** This loop drive starts in Montalcino and heads southwest through the hills before cutting the corner on a dramatic but challenging gravel road called "La Sesta." You'll be rewarded with the chance to visit three wineries and a fine old Romanesque abbey before either returning to Montalcino (on easier roads) or twisting over the hills to the Heart of Tuscany zone.

An **easier alternative** is to skip the gravel La Sesta stretch and simply drive from Montalcino down to Castelnuovo dell'Abate. After visiting the abbey, you're about a five-minute drive from two scenic wineries (in opposite directions): Ciacci Piccolomini d'Aragona and Mastrojanni.

## From Montalcino to Sant'Antimo Abbey and Back

At the south end of Montalcino, when you reach the roundabout circling a famously ugly statue, head for *Grosetto* and *S. Angelo*. This road will take you all the way to Sant'Angelo in Colle (9 kilometers south). Just a few minutes out of town, watch on the left for the turnoff to the recommended **Tornesi** winery (see page 585).

Back to the main road, continue south toward *Grosseto*. Just 1 kilometer before the town of **Sant'Angelo in Colle** (worth visiting for its restaurants—see page 606), watch carefully on the left for *Strada Sesta* signs, indicating the small turnoff onto the gravel road **La Sesta** ("The Sixth"). This dramatic road—7 gravelly kilometers—comes with spectacular views. Near the end of La Sesta, on the right, watch carefully for the snazzy **Ciacci Piccolomini d'Aragona** winery. This is effectively the only one in the area with a Napa Valley-style "drop in anytime you like for a taste" approach... just head to the wine bar inside and ask for a pour (for details, see page 588).

From Ciacci, it's 2 kilometers to the **Sant'Antimo Abbey:** Curl up a gravel road around the bottom of the town of Castelnuovo dell'Abate ("New Castle of the Abbot"), watching for the abbey

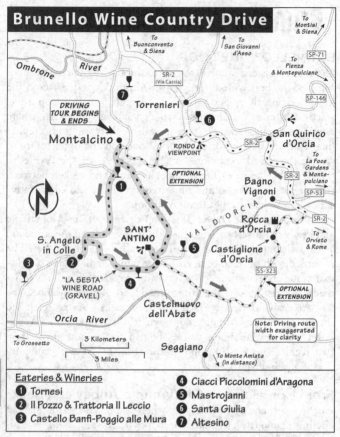

# Brunello Wine Country Drive

To Montisi & Siena

To Buonconvento & Siena

To San Giovanni d'Asso

To Pienza & Montepulciano

SP-71

Ombrone    River

SR-2 (Via Cassia)

SP-146

DRIVING TOUR BEGINS & ENDS

Torrenieri

6

San Quirico d'Orcia

SR-2

Montalcino

RONDO VIEWPOINT

To La Foce Gardens & Montepulciano

SR-2

OPTIONAL EXTENSION

Bagno Vignoni

SP-53

1

N

VAL D'ORCIA

Rocca d'Orcia

SR-2

SANT' ANTIMO

To Orvieto & Rome

S. Angelo in Colle

5

Castiglione d'Orcia

3

2

SS-323

4

OPTIONAL EXTENSION

"LA SESTA" WINE ROAD (GRAVEL)

Orcia    River

Castelnuovo dell'Abate

Note: Driving route width exaggerated for clarity

To Grossetto

3 Kilometers

3 Miles

Seggiano

To Monte Amiata (in distance)

**Eateries & Wineries**
1. Tornesi
2. Il Pozzo & Trattoria Il Leccio
3. Castello Banfi-Poggio alle Mura
4. Ciacci Piccolomini d'Aragona
5. Mastrojanni
6. Santa Giulia
7. Altesino

below you in a field. Drive down toward the abbey, park in the large lot, and head inside to step back to the Romanesque period (abbey described in "Brunello Wine Country Sights," later).

After visiting Sant'Antimo Abbey, consider driving up into the hills above Castelnuovo dell'Abate to the **Mastrojanni** winery, worth a visit for its vintages and views (see page 585). To get there, coming up the hill from the abbey, take the road around the left side of the Bassomondo restaurant. The road turns to gravel and climbs up, up, and up along the ridge. You'll enjoy spectacular panoramas back down over the pasture and olive groves surrounding Sant'Antimo. After 2.5 stunning kilometers, you'll reach Mastrojanni. Don't continue on the road past the winery; it quickly becomes a rocky trail.

Now head back down to the main road at Castelnuovo dell'Abate. It's easy to cut this loop short by taking the main (paved) road back up to Montalcino. Or consider an...

## Optional Extension to the Heart of Tuscany Drive

For a back-roads route from Brunello wine country to the Heart of Tuscany Drive described earlier (about a 35-minute drive away), do this: From the main road in front of Castelnuovo dell'Abate, head south on the uphill road, following signs for *Seggiano* (brown) and *Castiglione d'Orcia* (blue). This twisty road—with few worthwhile stops, but ample vistas—twists 19 kilometers over the mountains to the main valley road.

Leaving Castelnuovo, you'll crest a hill, then pass the dramatic **Castello di Velona,** a medieval castle-turned-luxury hotel. Locals explain that Silvio Berlusconi (Italy's repeatedly disgraced former prime minister) considered buying this property a few years back. But when he came to Montalcino—in the famously liberal region of Tuscany—locals threw rocks at the conservative politician.

The road drops down steeply to the valley village of Monte Amiata, where you'll cross the train tracks, then the Orcia River, then wind your way back up the other side. From here, enjoy the remote farmscapes as you follow signs: At the T-intersection, turn left, toward *Castiglione d'Orcia*. You'll pass through the hamlet of Poggio Rosa, and then, at the next T-intersection, bear left again, for *Siena, San Quirico d'Orcia,* and *Castiglione d'Orcia*.

In about 4 kilometers, you'll reach **Castiglione d'Orcia,** with a fortified hilltop old town; just past that, you'll see the dramatic hill-capping Tentennano Castle, with the village of **Rocca d'Orcia** at its base (described earlier). The easiest way to reach the top of Rocca is to drive through the town of Castiglione, and then—on the twisty road past Castiglione heading down toward the main valley road—watch for the turnoff on the left for *Rocca d'Orcia*. Drive up that road, park in the free lot at the base of the rock, and hike the rest of the way up into town and to the castle.

About 3 kilometers farther along, you'll reach the intersection with the main SR-2 Siena-to-Rome highway. Head north (toward Siena), then immediately turn off (on the left) for **Bagno Vignoni,** a fascinating old thermal spa town (described earlier).

Back on SR-2, head north (toward Siena) to reach the cross-roads at San Quirico d'Orcia. From here you can turn off for **Pienza** (10 kilometers away) and **Montepulciano** (24 kilometers). Or you can continue straight, to pass the dramatic **Rondò** viewpoint. Soon after the Rondò, you can turn off on the left to return to **Montalcino.** Or stay on SR-2 northbound a bit farther to reach the two recommended wineries north of Montalcino: For **Santa Giulia,** turn off to the right soon after the Rondò toward San Giovanni d'Asso (and follow the directions on page 589); for **Altesino,** stay on SR-2 all the way to Buonconvento, then turn off on the back road (SP-45) to Montalcino, and watch for the Altesino turnoff (see page 588).

## BRUNELLO WINE COUNTRY SIGHTS

These sights are linked by my driving tour, earlier.

### Sant'Angelo in Colle

This nondescript hill town, about 9 kilometers south of Montalcino, is worth visiting for a convenient lunch break with some high-altitude views. Twist up to the top of the hill and park by the square; both restaurants are just steps away. **$$ Il Pozzo,** run by the friendly Binerelli family, sits just a few steps below the square, serving simple homemade pasta dishes to guests on an outdoor patio or in a pleasant interior space with views overlooking the hillsides (free glass of Vin Santo for dessert with this book, closed Tue, +39 0577 844 015, www.trattoriailpozzo.com). **$$$ Trattoria Il Leccio** is the pricier and less friendly option, with a stone interior and seating out on the square (fried vegetables and beef, closed Wed off-season, Costa Castellare 1, +39 0577 844 175, www.trattoriailleccio.com).

### ▲Sant'Antimo Abbey

Set amidst postcard-perfect olive groves and pastures ringed by cypress-prickled hills, this Romanesque abbey—adorned with mysterious, pagan-seeming carvings—is one of the region's most rewarding to visit.

**Cost and Hours:** €4, includes multimedia guide and upstairs access, open to tourists daily 10:00-18:00, Nov-March 10:30-17:00, 11:00 Mass for worshippers only, shorter hours off-season, +39 0577 286 300, www.antimo.it.

**Getting There:** From Montalcino, **drivers** should head south toward Castelnuovo dell'Abate. Keep an eye out for the abbey—below you in the fields—as you approach. Large parking lots are in the field near the abbey. A **bus** runs from Montalcino (see "Montalcino Connections," earlier).

**Background:** Legends suggest that Sant'Antimo was founded by Charlemagne, who passed through here around the year 781, following the Via Francigena pilgrim route on his way back north from Rome. His army, suffering from illness, convalesced near here, and in appreciation Charlemagne presented the local religious community with relics of St. Anthimus (Sant'Antimo). Most of the abbey's current structure dates from the 11th and 12th centuries, when Sant'Antimo became a highly important center both for local aristocrats and for pilgrims walking the Via Francigena. But after Pope Pius II moved the diocese from Montalcino to Pienza in 1462, the abbey sat neglected for centuries, even becoming a stable for a time. Finally, starting in the late 19th century, it was restored, and in 1992 a small number of Augustinian monks moved in, reconnecting Sant'Antimo with its medieval importance. And today, once again, Sant'Antimo is a functioning abbey.

**Visiting the Abbey:** Before going inside, circle the building to see its faded but evocative decorations. At the back end of the church is the Charlemagne-era round apse (dwarfed by the Romanesque apse). Examine the varied carvings at the tops of the pillars under the roofline: geometrical patterns, heads of monsters, and pagan symbols. The stout rectangular bell tower is echoed by a strategically planted cypress tree. On the back side of the tower (next to the big tree), look up to find the sphinx, the small Madonna and Bambino, and the Four Evangelists.

Head back around to the main entrance. Ignore the modern doors and pick out the faint outline of the four original arches; at its peak, this church had two doors—an entrance and an exit—to handle the massive number of Via Francigena pilgrims who passed through. Just to the right, peek into the tranquil garden that fills the ruins of the original cloister.

Step inside the church and let your eyes adjust to the low light. Being Romanesque, this was as bright and as high as a church could be. (Gothic would soon come along, allowing churches to be brighter and loftier.) Looking up, see the windows of a gallery that once kept the female worshippers separate from the men (You may be allowed upstairs with your entrance fee). The carved capital of each pillar lining the nave is different. The second one on the right side—Daniel and the lions—is a favorite. On one side, a fearless Daniel prays despite being surrounded by lions; on the other side, those lions attack his enemies.

In the apse, notice that part of the altar platform is made of giant chunks of prized translucent alabaster. The many small chapels around the apse are a French architectural feature that made its way to Sant'Antimo. These chapels—and the overall height of the building—suggest a French influence...which seems fitting, here along the Via Francigena.

**HEART OF TUSCANY**

# CORTONA

Cortona blankets a 1,700-foot hill surrounded by dramatic Tuscan and Umbrian views. Frances Mayes' book *Under the Tuscan Sun* placed this town in the touristic limelight, but long before the book, Cortona was popular with 19th-century Romantics and considered one of the classic Tuscan hill towns. Although it's unquestionably touristy and has long welcomed expatriates besotted by Tuscan charm, Cortona, unlike San Gimignano, maintains a rustic and gritty personality.

The city began as one of the largest Etruscan settlements, the remains of which can be seen at the base of the city walls as well as in nearby tomb sites. It grew to its present size from the 13th to 16th century, when it was a colorful and crowded city, eventually allied with (or dominated by) Florence. The farmland that fills almost every view from the city was marshy and uninhabitable until about 200 years ago, when it was drained and turned into some of Tuscany's most fertile land.

Art lovers know little Cortona as the home of Renaissance painter Luca Signorelli, Baroque master Pietro da Cortona (Berretini), and the 20th-century Futurist artist Gino Severini. The city's museums and churches reveal many of the works of these native sons.

## Orientation to Cortona

Most of the main sights, shops, and restaurants cluster around the level streets on the Piazza Garibaldi-Piazza del Duomo axis, but Cortona will have you huffing and puffing up some steep hills. From Piazza Garibaldi, it's a level five-minute walk down bustling shop-lined Via Nazionale to Piazza della Repubblica, the heart of the town, which is dominated by City Hall (Palazzo del Comune).

From this square, a two-minute stroll leads you past the TI, the interesting Etruscan Museum, and the theater to Piazza del Duomo, where you'll find the recommended Diocesan Museum. These sights are along the more-or-less level spine that runs through the bottom of town; from here, Cortona sprawls upward. Steep streets, many of them stepped, go from Piazza della Repubblica up to the San Niccolò and Santa Margherita churches and the Medici Fortress (a 30-minute climb from Piazza della Repubblica). In this residential area, you'll see fewer tourists and get a better sense of the "real" Cortona.

In the flat valley below Cortona sprawls the modern, workaday town of Camucia (kah-MOO-cha), with the train station and other services (such as launderettes) that you won't find in the hill town itself.

## TOURIST INFORMATION

The TI, near Piazza Signorelli in the courtyard of the Etruscan Museum, is not particularly helpful, but can provide simple sightseeing and transit information (generally daily 10:00-19:00, shorter hours off-season, +39 0575 637 274, www.comunedicortona.it).

## ARRIVAL IN CORTONA

Cortona is challenging to reach by public transportation. Your best bet is by train (connecting by bus or taxi) or by car. Schedules for Cortona-area buses are available via www.at-bus.it. Schedules change frequently and buses are not a reliable option late or on Sundays.

**By Train:** Most trains arrive at the unstaffed Camucia station, in the valley four miles below Cortona. A shuttle **minibus** connects the train station and Piazza Garibaldi in Cortona in about 10 minutes (bus stop to left of station, schedule posted—not coordinated with train arrival, about hourly but only twice on Sun, buy €1.30 ticket from driver or from Bar La Stazione, to the right as you exit the train station; departures marked *S* don't run during school vacations, and those marked with *N* run *only* during school vacations). Regular city buses also connect the station with the less convenient Piazza del Mercato (just outside the city walls near Porta Santa Maria, departures about hourly), requiring a 10-minute uphill walk to Piazza Signorelli. For about €12, you can hop a **taxi** from the station (or call for Dejan and his 8-seater cab, +39 348 402 3501; see listing under "Tours in Cortona," later).

To return to the train station from Cortona, take a taxi or hop on the shuttle or a city bus (buy tickets at a newsstand or tobacco shop, or from driver). Confirm the schedule with the TI or your hotel.

The high-speed trains that link Rome, Florence, and Assisi nearly hourly arrive 10 miles away at **Terontola,** where you can catch a bus to Cortona (see "Cortona Connections" for details).

**By Car:** Piazza Garibaldi is the convenient entry to the city. While there's no parking here, it's a handy place to drop people. You'll find parking along streets and in lots outside the walls; some are free (no lines or white lines), others require payment (blue lines), and still others are for local residents only (yellow lines). The best option is to find something on the street a couple of blocks below Piazza Garibaldi or use the large, free Santo Spirito lot on Viale Cesare Battisti, just after the big Santo Spirito Church. From here, a series of stairs and escalators take you steeply up to Piazza Garibaldi. The small town is actually very long, and it can be smart to drive to the top for sightseeing up there (free parking and WC at Santa Margherita Basilica).

## HELPFUL HINTS

**Market Day:** The market is on Saturday on Piazza Signorelli (early morning until about 14:00). The most colorful produce section stretches to the cathedral square.

**Services:** The town has no baggage storage. The public WC is in Piazza del Duomo, under Santa Margherita's statue.

**Tuscan Cooking Classes:** Reserve at least 30 days in advance for a hands-on class with **Romano Magi**, who also offers cheese-making classes and custom tastings (see website for details; offered at Vicolo Cattani 1, near Ristorante La Bucaccia da Romano, +39 0575 606 039, www.labucaccia.it, info@labucaccia.it).

# Tours in Cortona

### Tuscan Day Trips with Driver/Guide Giovanni Adreani

High-energy Giovanni is a great guide for anyone home-basing in Cortona with limited time and an interest in Tuscany's highlights. Giovanni takes up to five people in his car to Montepulciano, Pienza, Montalcino, and a winery for a tour and tasting (winery visit optional and about €15-20/person extra; must reserve in advance). He also offers tours in and around Cortona (€120/half-day, €220/day with his car, +39 347 176 2830, www.adreanigiovanni.com, adreanigiovanni@libero.it).

### Tuscan Day Trips and Transfers with Driver Dejan Pruvlovic

Reliable, English-speaking taxi driver Dejan (DAY-zhan) and his brother Micky can take you on full-day tours from Cortona (€300 for up to 8 people). Most popular are Montepulciano, Pienza, Montalcino, and a winery tour. They also do Siena/San Gimignano and Assisi day tours and airport transfers (up to 8 people, to or from Florence's airport—€180, Rome—€290, +39 348 402 3501, dejanprvi70@yahoo.it).

# Cortona Walk

This introductory self-guided walk takes you from Piazza Garibaldi up the main strip to the town center, its piazzas, and the Duomo. (If your bus drops you at Piazzale del Mercato, use the "Cortona" map, later, to locate Piazza Garibaldi.)
• *Start at the bus stop in...*

## Piazza Garibaldi

Many visits start and finish in this square, thanks to its bus stop. While the piazza, bulging out from the town fortifications like a big turret, looks like part of an old rampart, it's really a souvenir of those early French and English Romantics—the ones who first created the notion of a dreamy, idyllic Tuscany in the early 19th century. During the Napoleonic Age, the occupying French built this balcony (and the scenic little park behind the adjacent San Do-

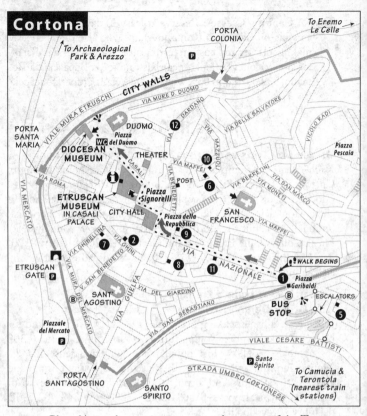

# Cortona

To Eremo
Le Celle

PORTA
COLONIA

To Archaeological
Park & Arezzo

CITY WALLS

VIA MURE D. DUOMO

VIA DELLE SALVATORE

VICOLO RADI

VIA DARDANO

Piazza
Pescaia

PORTA
SANTA
MARIA

VIALE MURA ETRUSCHI

DUOMO ⑫

Piazza
del Duomo WC

DIOCESAN
MUSEUM

VIA MAZZINI

THEATER

VIA MAFFEI ⑩

VIA BERRETTINI

VIA SAN MARCO

VIA MONETI

VIA ROMA

ETRUSCAN
MUSEUM
IN CASALI
PALACE

CITY HALL

VIA MERCATO

Piazza
Signorelli

VIA BENEDETTI

VIA CASALI

POST ⑥

SAN
FRANCESCO

VIA MAFFEI

Piazza della
Repubblica

⑨

⑦

VIA GHIBELLINA

VIA GHINI

② ①

VIA MURA DEL MERCATO

V. SAN BENEDETTO

SANT'
AGOSTINO

⑧

VIA

NAZIONALE

⑪

WALK BEGINS

① Piazza
Garibaldi

ETRUSCAN
GATE Ⓟ

VIA GUELFA

VIA DEL GIARDINO

VIA SAN SEBASTIANO

BUS
STOP Ⓑ

ESCALATORS

⑤

Piazzale
del Mercato Ⓟ

VIALE CESARE BATTISTI

PORTA
SANT'AGOSTINO

SANTO
SPIRITO

STRADA UMBRO CORTONESE

Ⓟ Santo
Spirito

To Camucia &
Terontola
(nearest train
stations)

---

menico Church) simply to enjoy a commanding view of the Tuscan countryside.

With Umbria about a mile away, Cortona marks the end of Tuscany. This is a major cultural divide, as Cortona was the last town in Charlemagne's empire and the last under Medici rule. Umbria, just to the south, was papal territory for centuries. These deep-seated cultural disparities were a great challenge for the visionaries who unified the fractured region to create the modern nation of Italy during the 1860s. An obelisk in the center of this square honors one of the heroes of the struggle for Italian unification—the brilliant revolutionary general Giuseppe Garibaldi.

Enjoy the impressive view from here. Assisi is just over the ridge on the left. Lake Trasimeno peeks from behind the hill, looking quite normal today. But, according to legend, it was blood-red

**Accommodations**

1 Hotel San Luca
2 Dolce Maria B&B & Locanda al Pozzo Antico
3 Hotel Villa Marsili
4 Villa Santa Margherita
5 Casa Kita

**Eateries**

6 Osteria del Teatro
7 Ristorante La Bucaccia da Romano
8 Trattoria la Grotta
9 Ristorante La Loggetta & Molesini Market
10 Fiaschetteria Fett'Unta
11 Caffè la Saletta
12 Via Dardano Eateries

after Hannibal defeated the Romans here in 217 BC, when 15,000 died in the battle. The only sizable town you can see (just to the right of the volcanic mountain) is Montepulciano. Cortona is still defined by its Etruscan walls—remnants of these walls, with stones laid 2,500 years ago, stretch from here in both directions.

Frances Mayes put Cortona on the map for many Americans with her book (and later movie) *Under the Tuscan Sun.* The book describes her real-life experience buying, fixing up, and living in a run-down villa in Cortona with her husband, Ed. Mayes' villa isn't "under the Tuscan sun" very often; it's named "Bramasole"— literally, "craving sun." On the wrong side of the hill, it's in the shade after 15:00. She and her husband still live in their adopted community for part of each year (Bramasole is outside the walls, behind the hill on the left—a 20-minute walk away; ask at the TI for directions if you'd like to see it up close). By the way, if you are moved to sing, Signor Franco Migliacci—who wrote the lyrics to the popular Italian song "Che sarà"—claims the words came to him as he stood right here and enjoyed this view.

• *From this square, head into town along...*

## Via Nazionale

The only level road in town, locals have nicknamed Via Nazionale the *ruga piana* (flat wrinkle). This is the main commercial street in this town of 2,500, and it's been that way for a long time. Every shop seems to have a medieval cellar or an Etruscan well. Notice the crumbling sandstone doorframes. The entire town is constructed from this grainy, eroding rock.

• *Via Nazionale leads to...*

## Piazza della Repubblica

City Hall faces Cortona's main square. The building is a clever hodgepodge: twin medieval towers with a bell tower added to connect them, and a grand staircase to lend some gravitas. Notice the fine wood balcony on the left. In the Middle Ages, wooden extensions like this one rebuilt in the 19th century were common features on the region's stone buildings, adding a pleasant outdoor living space to the dark, cold *palazzo*.

This spot has been the town center since Etruscan times. Four centuries before Christ, an important street led from here up to the hill-capping temple. Later, the square became the Roman forum. Opposite City Hall is the handy, recommended Molesini market, good for cheap sandwiches and grocery staples. Above that is the loggia—once a fish market, now the recommended Ristorante La Loggetta. Most of the buildings lining this square originally stood atop similar arched arcades, of which you can still see traces.

• *Walk down the lane to the right of City Hall to reach...*

## Piazza Signorelli

Dominated by Casali Palace, this square was the headquarters of the Florentine captains who used to control the city. Peek into the palace entrance (under the *MAEC* sign) for a look at the coats of arms. Every six months, Florence would send a new captain to Cortona, who would help establish his rule by inserting his family coat of arms into the palace's wall. These date from the 15th to the 17th century and were once painted with bright colors. Cortona's fine Etruscan Museum (described later) is in the Casali Palace courtyard, which is lined with many more of these family coats of arms. To the left of the palace, in the side wall of the City Hall, you can see a door leading to a long-gone wooden balcony—all that's left is the holes for the beams. On the right side of the Casali Palace, the charming 19th-century Teatro Signorelli, named for the town's most famous artist, Luca Signorelli, is *the* place in town for a movie or concert. Its inviting loggia offers a delightful all-weather perch.

• *Head down the street, just to the right of the museum, to...*

## Piazza del Duomo

Here you'll find the Diocesan Museum (described later), the cathedral, a fine view, and (closer to the top of the square) a statue of Santa Margherita (above a public WC). The cathedral's facade, though recently renovated, still seems a little underwhelming and tucked away. Cortona so loves its hometown saint, Margherita, that it put the energy it would otherwise have invested in its cathedral into the Santa Margherita Basilica at the top of the hill. Margherita was a 13th-century rich girl who took good care of the poor and was an early follower of St. Francis and St. Clare. Many locals believe that Margherita protected Cortona from bombs in World War II.

The Piazza del Duomo terrace comes with a commanding view of the Tuscan countryside. Notice Cortona's cemetery in the foreground. If you were standing here before the time of Napoleon, you'd be surrounded by tombstones. But Cortona's graveyards—like other urban graveyards throughout Napoleon's realm—were cleaned out in the early 1800s to reclaim land and improve hygiene.

Ready for a melody switch? The parents of Dino Paul Crocetti were born in this valley. Their son made many schmaltzy Italiano songs popular in the US...as Dean Martin.

• *Next, everybody loves a cathedral sometime, so* Mambo Italiano *to your left and enter the...*

## Duomo

The Cortona cathedral is not, strictly speaking, a cathedral, because it no longer has a bishop. The clean and elegant arches and columns defining its nave are pure Renaissance, inspired by the Basilica of San Lorenzo in Florence. While the once-pristine interior has been mucked up with lots of Baroque chapels filling the side niches, the cathedral still has the same heating system it had during the Renaissance (daily 8:00-19:30, shorter hours in winter).

• *From here, you can visit the nearby Diocesan Museum, or head back toward Piazza della Repubblica, where you can visit the Etruscan Museum in Piazza Signorelli or get a bite to eat.*

# Sights in Cortona

## ▲Etruscan Museum
### (Museo dell'Accademia Etrusca e della Città di Cortona)

Located in the 13th-century Casali Palace and called MAEC for short, this fine gallery established in 1727 was one of the first dedicated to artifacts from the Etruscan civilization. (In the logo, notice the E is backwards—in homage to the Etruscan alphabet.) The sprawling collection is nicely installed on four big floors.

**Cost and Hours:** €10; daily 10:00-19:00; Nov-March Tue-Sun until 17:00, closed Mon; Casali Palace on Piazza Signorelli, +39 0575 637 235, www.cortonamaec. org.

**Visiting the Museum:** The bottom two floors (underground) are officially the "Museum of the Etruscan and Roman City of Cortona." You'll see an exhibit on the Roman settlement and take a virtual tour of the Etruscan "Il Sodo" tombs (in the nearby countryside, possible to visit—see "Archaeological Park" listing later). The Cortona Tablet (*Tabula Cortonensis,* second century BC), a 200-word contract inscribed in bronze, contains dozens of Etruscan words archaeologists had never seen before its discovery in 1992. Along with lots of gold and jewelry, you'll find a seventh-century BC grater (for some *very* aged Parmesan cheese). The top two floors, called the "Accademia," are a maze displaying an even more eclectic collection, including more Etruscania, Egyptian artifacts, fine Roman mosaics, and a room dedicated to 20th-century abstract works by Severini, all lovingly described in English. A highlight is the magnificent fourth-century BC bronze oil lamp chandelier with 16 spouts. On the top floor, peek into the classic old library of the Etruscan Academy, founded in 1727 to promote an understanding of the city through the study of archaeology.

## ▲Diocesan Museum (Museo Diocesano)

This small collection contains some very choice artworks from the town's many churches, including works by Fra Angelico and Pietro Lorenzetti, and masterpieces by hometown hero and Renaissance master Luca Signorelli.

**Cost and Hours:** €6; daily 10:00-19:00; Nov-March Tue-Sun 10:00-17:00, closed Mon; free audioguide, Piazza del Duomo 1, +39 057 553 1256, www.cortonatuseibellezza.it.

**Visiting the Museum:** The L-shaped first room contains masterpieces by **Luca Signorelli,** Cortona's most famous son.

Signorelli worked during the height of the Renaissance, around 1500, often painting in fresco. A generation ahead of Michelangelo, Signorelli's passion for new painting ideas, his techniques of foreshortening and perspective, and his jewel-like colors strongly influenced the younger artist. Signorelli's San Brizio Chapel in Orvieto inspired Michelangelo's Sistine Chapel frescoes (to see more Signorelli works, visit the San Niccolò Church near the top of town). Take a slow stroll past his very colorful canvases, mostly relocated here from local churches. Among the most striking is *Lamentation over the Dead Christ* (1502). Everything in Signorelli's painting has a meaning: The skull of Adam sits under the sacrifice of Jesus; the hammer represents the Passion (the Crucifixion leading to the Resurrection); the lake is blood; and so on.

Across the top of the stairwell, the next room was the nave when this was the Gesù Church (look up at the beautiful wood-carved ceiling). Above a sweet 14th-century carved marble baptismal font is an early Renaissance master-piece: In **Fra Angelico**'s sumptuous *Annunciation* (c. 1430), Mary says "Yes," consenting to bear God's son. The angel's words are top and bottom, while Mary's answer is upside down (logically, since it's directed to God, who would be reading while looking down from heaven). Mary's  house sits on a pillow of flowers...the new Eden. The old Eden, featuring the expulsion of Adam and Eve from Paradise, is in the upper left. On the bottom edge, comic strip-like scenes narrate Mary's life. Compare the style in Fra Angelico's work to the Signorelli you just saw. Where Fra Angelico's figures are light and often out of scale—like paper dolls—Signorelli's are more realistic, with heft, and show his understanding of human anatomy. In only a few decades, painters had made huge leaps in their skills.

On the wall to the right, the crucifix (by Pietro Lorenzetti, c. 1325) is striking in its severity. Notice the gripping realism—even the tendons in Jesus' arms are pulled tight. (Speaking of realism, as this church is now deconsecrated, notice how the relic has been taken from the altar table below this painting and replaced by a wooden plug.)

Now head back to the stairwell, which is lined with colorful Stations of the Cross scenes by another local but much later artist, the 20th century's **Gino Severini.** These are actually "cartoons," models used to create permanent mosaics that line the approach up to the Santa Margherita Basilica today.

Downstairs, the lower refectory has a vault with dramatic

CORTONA

frescoes (1545) by the workshop of **Giorgio Vasari,** the architect and painter who designed the Uffizi in Florence (he did the ceiling here). Take a close look at the exquisitely painted circa-1500 terra-cotta pietà decorating the altar.

Back near the entrance, another staircase leads down to a collection of vestments and ecclesiastical gear.

### San Francesco Church (Chiesa di San Francesco)

Established by St. Francis' best friend, Brother Elias, this church dates from the 13th century. The wooden beams of the ceiling are original. While the place was redecorated in the Baroque age, some of its original frescoes peek through the whitewash in the second chapel on the left. Francis fans visit for its precious Franciscan relics. To the left of the altar, you'll find one of Francis' tunics, his pillow (inside a fancy cover), and his gospel book. Notice how the entire high altar seems designed to frame its precious relic—a piece of the cross Elias brought back from his visit to the patriarch in Constantinople. You're welcome to climb the altar for a close-up look. In the humble choir area behind the main altar is Elias' very simple tomb (see the *Frate Elia da Cortona* plaque).

**Cost and Hours:** Free, daily 9:00-17:30, often until 19:00 in summer.

### Santa Margherita Basilica (Basilica di Santa Margherita)

Capping the hill high above Cortona, this basilica houses the remains of Margherita, the town's favorite saint (her actual mummy is behind glass at the altar). The red-and-white-striped interior boasts some colorfully painted vaults. Santa Margherita, an unwed mother from Montepulciano, found her calling in the mid-1200s with the new Franciscan order in Cortona, tending to the sick and poor. The well-preserved and remarkably emotional 13th-century crucifix (made in Germany, painted on wood) on the right is the cross that, according to legend, talked to Margherita.

**Cost and Hours:** Free, daily 7:00-19:30, open later in summer, fine WC outside.

**Nearby:** Need more altitude and expansive views? Continue uphill five more minutes to the 13th-century **Medici Fortezza Girifalco,** today a parklike shell with a café, viewpoint, and special exhibits (confirm hours at TI). When Cosimo I de' Medici made a tour of all his fortresses in 1540 to assess their strategic value, he decided this one should be strengthened and modernized (and that Cortona's citizens should pay for it). **San Niccolò Church,** a few streets below, is a humble church with impressive views. It houses Luca Signorelli's workshop and a few of his paintings, the most famous being *The Deposition of Christ.*

## NEAR CORTONA

For locations of the sights below, see the "Cortona Area" map.

### ▲Eremo Le Celle

Hiding out in the fold of the neighboring hills, above a little river and buried in a forest, is an evocative hermitage founded in the early 1200s by St. Francis'

best friend, Brother Elias. Even today, 800 years later, you can feel the calm of this retreat. Francis visited three times (you can visit his cell—*celle* means cells). Today, the monastery is still alive, run by the Capuchin order, an

offshoot of the Franciscans that focuses on living with nature in solitude. The friars are on call—to meet one, just pull the cord outside the main chapel. Visitors are welcome to wander through two chapels and a couple of stark pilgrim's rooms, as well as the beautiful grounds. It's a five-minute drive from the top of Cortona (free, always open, follow signs to *Le Celle*, easy parking, Strada dei Cappuccini 1, www.lecelledicortona.it).

### Archaeological Park (Parco Archeologico) Il Sodo

The area around Cortona is rich with Etruscan tombs dating to the sixth century BC. Visitors are welcome to enter this active archaeological site, and bits of the ruins can be seen even from outside the fence. The two main tombs, called the Tumuli del Sodo, are connected by a footpath (€5; for the latest information and directions to the site, stop by the Etruscan Museum in town, which acts as an orientation center for the archaeological park; Tumulus II usually open daily 10:00-14:00 & 15:00-18:00, Nov-March Fri-Sun 10:00-14:00, closed Mon-Thu; Tumulus I open by reservation; +39 0575 637 235, www.cortonamaec.org, prenotazioni@cortonamaec.org). The tombs are in Sodo, just off the Arezzo road—SR-71—at the foot of the Cortona hill (ask anyone for "Il Sodo," parking available at entrance and at Tumulus I).

## Sleeping in Cortona

### WITHIN THE OLD TOWN

**$$$ Hotel San Luca,** perched on the side of a cliff, has 54 impersonal business-class rooms, half with stunning views of Lago Trasimeno. While the hotel feels tired and the rooms have seen better days, it has a beautiful outdoor terrace, friendly staff, and a convenient location right on Piazza Garibaldi at the entrance to the old town (request a view room when you reserve, family rooms, popular with Americans and groups, air-con, elevator, Piazza Garibaldi 2, +39 0575 630 460, www.sanlucacortona.com, info@sanlucacortona.com). If driving, you can unload bags in front of the hotel in Piazza Garibaldi, then park at the big, free Santo Spirito lot below and ride up the escalator.

**$ Dolce Maria B&B** is centrally located in a 16th-century building with high-beamed ceilings. The six rooms are a good value, luminous and spacious, with tasteful period furnishings and modern bathrooms. The B&B is efficiently run by Paola, who also runs the Pozzo Antico restaurant next door—the two businesses share a patio (family rooms, air-con, Via Ghini 12, +39 0575 601 577, www.cortonastorica.com, info@cortonastorica.com).

## OUTSIDE THE OLD TOWN

These accommodations line up along the road that angles downhill from Piazza Garibaldi, with easy parking on the street or at the large lot on Viale Battisti. All are just a five-minute uphill walk from the entrance to the old town.

**$$$$ Hotel Villa Marsili,** a comfortable splurge, pampers its visitors with thoughtful service. Originally a 15th-century church, and then an elegant 18th-century home, the hotel has 25 artfully decorated, romantic rooms (many with views) and inviting public areas. They offer an over-the-top breakfast buffet and a sweet goodnight treat after dinner (air-con, elevator, limited free street parking nearby, Viale Cesare Battisti 13, +39 0575 605 252, www.villamarsili.net, info@villamarsili.net, friendly Marina).

**$ Villa Santa Margherita** rents 22 nicely renovated rooms in a former convent with tall ceilings and lots of communal gathering space (family rooms, some rooms with air-con and views, elevator, free parking, Viale Cesare Battisti 17, +39 0575 082 440, www.villasantamargheritacortona.it, cortonaaccoglienza@gmail.com, Beatrice).

**$ Casa Kita,** renting five quirky, boldly decorated rooms at great prices, is a homey place with fine views from its terrace. It's a good option for budget travelers with lots of luggage, just 100 yards from the bus stop in Piazza Garibaldi. You'll really feel like you're staying in someone's home (closed Jan-Feb, below the piazza at Vicolo degli Orti 7, +39 389 557 9893, www.casakita.com, casakita@gmail.com, Lorenzini family).

# Eating in Cortona

## FINER DINING

**$$$ Osteria del Teatro** tries hard to create a romantic Old World atmosphere and does it well. The dining rooms, each decorated differently, are part of an old palace, and there's good outdoor seating, too. Chef/owner Emiliano serves nicely presented and tasty local cuisine that changes to match the season. Ask for the chef's version of tiramisu—*charlotte al mascarpone* (Thu-Tue 12:30-14:30 & 19:30-21:30, closed Wed, reservations smart, 2 blocks uphill from the main square at Via Maffei 2, +39 0575 630 556, www.osteria-del-teatro.it).

**$$$ Ristorante La Bucaccia da Romano,** dressy and romantic, is set in a rustic medieval wine cellar. Romano takes an evangelical pride in his Chianina beef dishes and homemade pastas, and presides over the dining room with humor and charm—he will sit down at your table to advise you on your meal choices. Try one of the signature truffle dishes or *pici in crosta di pecorino* (homemade pasta in the crust of a cheese wheel). Reservations are required for dinner (daily 12:30-14:30 & 19:00-22:30, closed Mon in winter; show this book for a welcome snack; Via Ghibellina 17, +39 0575 606 039, www.labucaccia.it). Romano also runs Tuscan cooking classes (see "Helpful Hints," earlier).

## TRADITIONAL RESTAURANTS, TRATTORIAS, AND OTHER EATERIES

**$$ Trattoria la Grotta,** just off Piazza della Repubblica, is a traditional family place, with Giancarlo and his daughters serving daily specials to an enthusiastic clientele under grotto-like vaults. The family owns the *enoteca* across the lane and will let you bring wine from their shop into the restaurant (good wine by the glass, Wed-Mon 12:00-15:00 & 19:00-22:00, closed Tue, Piazza Baldelli 3, +39 0575 630 271).

**$ Locanda al Pozzo Antico** offers an affordable menu of traditional Cortona fare (like *pici al fumo,* pasta with a creamy bacon sauce), with a focus on fresh, quality produce and local olive oil. Eat in a homey dining room or tucked away in a tranquil secret courtyard. Paola is a charming hostess (Fri-Wed 12:00-14:30 & 19:00-22:30, closed Thu, Via Ghini 14, +39 057 562 091 or +39 0575 601 577; Paola, husband Franco, and son Gianni).

**$$ Ristorante La Loggetta** serves up big portions of well-presented seasonal Tuscan cuisine on the loggia overlooking Piazza della Repubblica. While they have fine indoor seating under clamorous stone vaults, I'd eat on their loggia for the chance to gaze at the square while dining (Thu-Tue 12:00-15:00 & 19:00-23:00, closed Wed, Piazza Pescheria 3, +39 0575 630 575).

**$ Fiaschetteria Fett'Unta** is small and rustic. It serves traditional plates driven by the season—*bruschette,* soups, pastas, salads, and good wine by the glass (Thu-Tue 11:00-22:30, closed Wed, across from Osteria del Teatro at Via Maffei 5, +39 0575 630 582).

**$ Caffè la Saletta,** a dark and classy coffee bar with a nice,

CORTONA

mellow vibe, is good for fine wine and a light meal. You can sit inside surrounded by wine bottles or outside to people-watch on the town's main drag (daily 7:00-20:00, meals served 11:00-19:00, Via Nazionale 26, +39 0575 603 366).

**$ Restaurants along Via Dardano:** A handful of eateries line this street. **Pizzeria Croce del Travaglio** is good for pizza and **Trattoria Dardano** is a favorite for locally sourced meat. **Taverna Pane e Vino** offers good-value dishes and a great setting on Piazza Signorelli.

**Picnic:** On the main square, the chic little **Molesini** market makes tasty sandwiches, served with a smile (see list on counter), and sells whatever else you might want for a picnic (daily 7:00-13:30 & 16:30-20:00, shorter hours off-season, Piazza della Repubblica 23). Munch your picnic across the square on the steps of City Hall or just past Piazza Garibaldi in the public gardens behind San Domenico Church.

# Cortona Connections

Cortona has decent train connections with the rest of Italy through its Camucia-Cortona station at the foot of the hill. It's usually unstaffed, but has two ticket machines (one in front of the station, and one on platform 1; both take credit cards and cash). Bar Stazione, the café to the right as you exit the station, also sells tickets.

**From Camucia-Cortona by Train to: Rome** (7/day direct, 2.5 hours), **Florence** (hourly, 1.5 hours), **Assisi** (hourly, 1.5 hours), **Montepulciano** (9/day, 1-2 hours, change in Chiusi; because few buses serve Montepulciano's town center from its distant train station, it's better to go by train to Chiusi, then by hourly 40-minute bus to Montepulciano, or easier still to take a taxi for about €60), **Chiusi** (hourly, 25 minutes).

**From Terontola by Train:** Nearly hourly high-speed trains to/from **Rome, Florence,** and **Assisi** stop at Terontola, 10 miles away (linked to Cortona's Piazzale del Mercato or Camucia station by hourly buses, 20-30 minutes, check schedule at bus stop or at www.at-bus.it).

# ELBA
*Isola d'Elba*

Pebbly beaches, boat-speckled harbors, and seafood feasts...in Tuscany? While most people come to this region for great art, rolling farmland, and picturesque hill towns, Tuscany also has 140 miles of coastline. Most of the mainland coast is a mix of industrial towns and beach resorts that attract an Italians-only crowd, but a one-hour ferry ride takes you to the enticing isle of Elba.

The island is synonymous with Napoleon, who lived in exile here for about 10 months in 1814-15. But Elba is much more than its most famous short(-term) resident. Even though relatively small (about 18 miles long by about 11 miles wide), Elba packs in a variety of landscapes—from jagged coastline to sandy beaches to forested mountains—and it offers several fine little towns.

It's made to order for getting a taste of the Italian seaside and a relaxed island experience.

Elba's main town, Portoferraio, has a pleasant historic harbor and old town, good restaurants, and a handy ferry connection to the mainland. It's a fine home base and a suitable springboard for exploring the island's beaches, historic sites, charming towns, and scenic gondola.

## PLANNING YOUR TIME
On a trip focusing on Tuscany, travelers seeking some variety and a seaside break enjoy having two nights and a day on Elba. Spend your evenings in Portoferraio, and during the day, joyride around

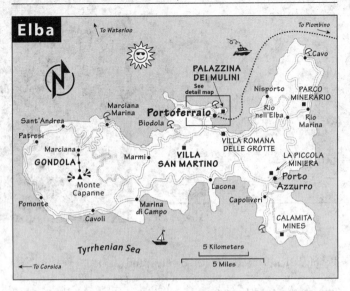

the island—including a trip on a rickety gondola to the island's peak.

Speaking of "peak," in late June, July, and especially August, Elba is miserably crowded with vacationers, hot, and expensive. But in May, early June, September, and early October, Elba is just the thing. Most sights and tourist services hibernate in winter.

On the way to or from Elba, aficionados of ancient sites might enjoy a quick detour to the Baratti and Populonia Archaeological Park (described at the end of this chapter).

## GETTING THERE

This chapter assumes you have a car—Elba isn't worth the effort without one (for a seaside fix by train, it's easier to visit the Cinque Terre and nearby towns, relatively close to Pisa and Lucca). But if you're determined, it is possible by public transportation.

**By Car Ferry:** The main ferry connection to Elba is from the mainland port city of Piombino, roughly a two-hour drive from most of the Tuscan heartland.

Moby Lines (www.mobylines. com) and Toremar (www. toremar.it) run Piombino-Portoferraio car ferries year-round. Two other companies operate seasonally: BluNavy from about Easter through October (www. blunavytraghetti.com), and Elba Ferries in July and August (part

of Corsica Ferries, www.corsica-ferries.co.uk). The crossing takes about an hour (fares vary by season: €30-50/car, €15-20/passenger, one-way).

Ferries run about hourly in spring and fall, with frequency increasing closer to summer; by July and August, there's typically a ferry every 30 minutes. Off-season, it can be two to three hours between ferries. In July, August, and on weekends in May-June and Sept-Oct, it's essential to book ahead; otherwise you can just show up and take whichever ferry is departing next. A single handy website lists the schedules for all ferry companies and lets you book online: www.traghetti-elbareservation.it. You'll see a dizzying number of private ticket sellers advertise on the roads near the ferry terminals, all of them with access to the same tickets—take your pick.

**By Public Transportation:** From other parts of Italy, trains get you as far as Campiglia Marittima, from which regional train and bus connections bring you the rest of the way into "Piombino Marittima" (the name of the bus/train junction near the mainland port). In peak season, there may also be a handy direct bus from Florence to Piombino Marittima (2.5 hours, run by Tiemme, www.tiemmespa.it). There are also fast passenger-only catamarans to other ports on Elba (listed at www.traghetti-elbareservation.it).

# Portoferraio

Elba's main entry point, and its biggest and most interesting town, Portoferraio is a good home base. Its historic harbor—ringed by stout Medici-built fortresses—is charming and colorful, luring visitors for a lazy stroll past sailboats, mega-yachts, and humble fishing dinghies. And just behind the harbor is an easygoing, local-feeling neighborhood that's equally fun to explore.

Broad stone staircases lead up, up, up to the 16th-century fortifications that feel too big for this little town.

Portoferraio has a few lightweight sights, most of them related either to those fortifications or its brief status as the home of Napoleon. Both Napoleonic residences—Palazzina dei Mulini, in the heart of Portoferraio; and Villa San Martino, a few minutes' drive outside town, hold some interest for history buffs but will underwhelm casual tourists (they're in pretty shabby repair, with only faint echoes of the island's most famous resident).

ELBA

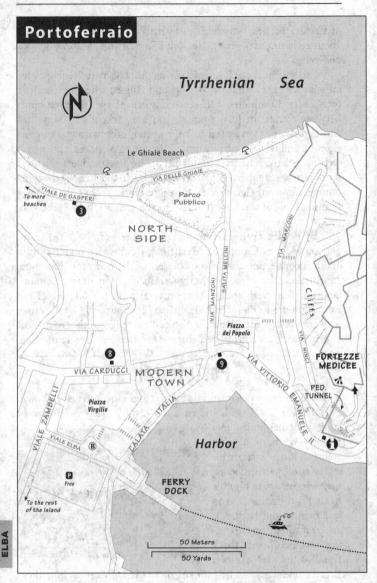

Portoferraio

*Tyrrhenian Sea*

Le Ghiaie Beach

VIA DELLE GHIAIE

VIALE DE GASPERI
To more
beaches
**3**

Parco
Pubblico

NORTH
SIDE

VIA MANZONI

SALITA MELLINI

VIA MARCONI

*Piazza
dei Popolo*

Cliffs

VIA NINCI

**8**
VIA CARDUCCI

MODERN
TOWN

**9**

VIA VITTORIO EMANUELE II

FORTEZZE
MEDICEE

PED.
TUNNEL

*Piazza
Virgilio*

VIALE ZAMBELLI

VIALE ELBA

**B**

CALATA ITALIA

*Harbor*

**i**

**P**
Free

To the rest
of the Island

FERRY
DOCK

50 Meters

50 Yards

ELBA

# Orientation to Portoferraio

Portoferraio, with about 12,000 residents, fills a peninsula dangling off the northern coast of Elba. There are three main zones to the city: the somewhat gritty modern town, radiating out from the ferry port; the sleepier back (north) side of town, facing the pebbly beach called Le Ghiaie; and—most attractive—the historic town

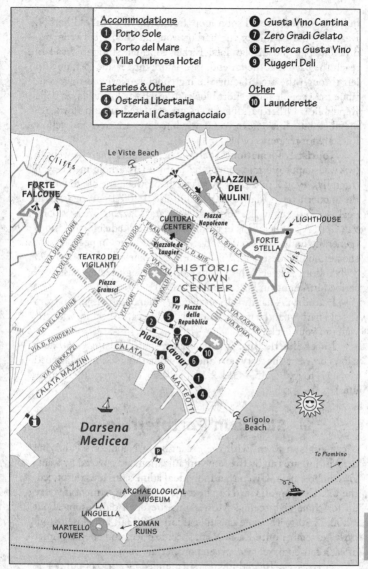

**Accommodations**
1. Porto Sole
2. Porto del Mare
3. Villa Ombrosa Hotel

**Eateries & Other**
4. Osteria Libertaria
5. Pizzeria il Castagnacciaio

6. Gusta Vino Cantina
7. Zero Gradi Gelato
8. Enoteca Gusta Vino
9. Ruggeri Deli

**Other**
10. Launderette

center, surrounding the postcard harbor called Darsena Medicea. From the harbor, streets climb steeply in three directions; each side of the U-shaped harbor is capped by fortresses.

**Arrival in Portoferraio:** The ferry arrives at the modern part of town, along Calata Italia. There's a relatively large free parking lot one block inland from the ferry dock (on Viale Zambelli)—a 15-minute walk from the old town. To park closer to the sights, turn right off the ferry and follow the waterfront road below the

ELBA

hulking fortress. You'll soon loop around the colorful old harbor. Reaching the middle of the harbor, you can choose between two different pay-and-display lots: Either continue straight ahead to reach the pay lot at the far end, just before the seaside fort; or turn left through the arch (facing the big concrete pier) and then continue for a couple more short blocks to reach the lot at Piazza della Repubblica. Other parking spaces are scattered around town; remember, blue lines mean you pay, white lines are free, and yellow lines are for residents only.

**Tourist Information:** The two helpful TIs share a website (www.visitaportoferraio.com). The main TI is a hole-in-the-wall (literally)—you'll pass right by as you go between the old town and the modern town (daily 9:30-12:30, also 15:00-18:30 or later in peak season, below the fortress at Calata Mazzini 37, +39 0565 914 121). A smaller TI is in the bowels of the Medici fortifications (generally daily 9:30-16:00, longer weekend hours in peak season, shorter hours off-season; Via Vittorio Emanuele II, +39 0565 193 3589). Both TIs sell the Cosmopoli Card sightseeing pass (described in "Sights in Portoferraio," below).

**Laundry:** A handy self-service 24/7 launderette is just in from the old harbor (at the right end of Via di Mercato Vecchio, with the water to your back).

**Local Shuttle Bus:** A little orange shuttle bus *(navetta)* does a loop between the ferry port and the old harbor's Calata Matteotti stop (€1, roughly 7:15-14:00 & 15:40-20:00, runs every 10-20 minutes).

## Sights in Portoferraio

Most sights in town (with the exception of Napoleon's Palazzina dei Mulini) are run by the same organization and covered by a single combo-ticket. Given that individual admissions are overpriced, the €15 **Cosmopoli Card** can be a worthwhile investment if you're up for some sightseeing. Most sights are open daily from about 10:00-18:30, with some closures 12:30-14:30 (all are closed from early November until Easter). For specific prices and opening times of each museum, see www.visitaportoferraio.com.

**Fortresses:** The old town is surrounded by a trio of bulky fortresses, which were built in the mid-16th century by the Medici—Florence's influential banking family—to defend the island against Barbary pirates. The sprawling Fortezze Medicee caps the high western ridge over the port (and surrounds the older Forte Falcone); Forte Stella crowns the top of town (not open to the public); and La Linguella is along the eastern waterline, with the bulbous Martello tower.

The **Medicee and Falcone fortress complex** requires a steep climb to visit, but it rewards with stunning views and three modest museums—about the Medici forts, World War II, and modern art. To reach it from the harbor, go up the stairs in the park to the left of the TI, take the second tunnel on the right, and wind your way up to the ticket desk. There's a beautiful panoramic view from the bar at the Falcone fortress.

**La Linguella,** across the port and along the water, is not much more than its landmark tower. Besides the Medici fortifications, it encompasses some Roman and Etruscan ruins and a skippable archaeological museum (basically two big rooms filled with old amphora jugs and other waterlogged artifacts).

**Napoleonic Villa:** On the saddle of land between the two high forts (Medicee/Falcone and Stella)—in a surprisingly nondescript, boxy yellow house—is the ▲ **Palazzina dei Mulini,** one of Napoleon's two residences on the island. This was  the deposed emperor's primary residence for about 10 months. The entire sight is a bit underwhelming—perhaps appropriate for the home of a deposed tyrant.

When Napoleon arrived, the mansion was spiffed up to suit the tastes of Elba's new ruler, with delicate ceiling frescoes, Empire-style furniture, and imperial eagles and N-for-Napoleon insignias. You'll tour the ground-floor rooms (with posted English descriptions) and the grander upstairs, which includes the Banqueting Hall, adorned with a grand mahogany bed with  bronze accents, and the apartments of Napoleon's sister, Pauline. Finally, you'll step out to the now-scruffy gardens, on a terrace overlooking the sea. As you linger in the gardens, imagine Napoleon looking out to sea, smelling the jasmine and salt air, and brooding...planning what he was sure would be his ultimate triumph at a place called Waterloo (€5, €8 combo-ticket with countryside Villa San Martino, not covered by Cosmopoli Card, Mon and Wed-Sat 8:30-19:30, Sun until 13:00, closed Tue, mornings only off-season, on—where else?—Piazza Napoleone, +39 0565 915 846).

ELBA

# Napoleon on Elba

Napoleon Bonaparte, emperor of France, was forced to abdicate in April 1814 after a string of stinging military defeats—most notably his disastrous invasion of Russia. European leaders exiled him to the little island of Elba as its sovereign ruler—all 85 square miles of it—a location comfortingly far from the trappings of power.

The disgraced Napoleon arrived in Portoferraio on May 3, 1814, and greeted his new subjects by saying, "I will be a good father to you; you try to be good children to me." Locals scrambled to improvise residences that would appeal to his imperial tastes and accommodate his entourage of military leaders, diplomats, and aides—not to mention thousands of books, and a herd of 70 horses. Ever the micromanager, Napoleon quickly set about remaking Elba into a proper little mini-empire—building roads and irrigation systems, and instituting educational and legal reforms. He even gave the island its first flag (to which he added three golden bees from his imperial seal). He exploited Elba's lucrative mines to grow his own personal wealth. And he invited his mother and his sister Pauline to come visit.

When Napoleon learned that European leaders were considering further punishment—or possibly even execution—he grew nervous, huddled with his aides, and decided to give emperorship one last go. On February 26, 1815, Napoleon escaped Elba with a small fleet of ships, and soon was back in France. That June, he was defeated at Waterloo and exiled to the even more remote island of Saint Helena in the south Atlantic, where he died in 1821.

Only a few tangible sights survive from Napoleon's 300-day stay on Elba: his mansion in Portoferraio (Palazzina dei Mulini), his country residence nearby (Villa San Martino), the theater built for his enjoyment (Teatro dei Vigilanti)...and the bees that the Elbans never bothered to remove from their flag.

Italians enjoy pointing out that Napoleon's stay in Italy was not as random as it seemed. Napoleon was born on the island of Corsica—which you can see from Elba—to a low-level aristocratic family from Liguria (the Italian Riviera). Until just a few months before Napoleon was born, Corsica was Italian (Genovese); the treaty ceding it to France meant that the future emperor was only just barely born as a French citizen. Even the name "Bonaparte" is more Italian than French (*buona parte* means "good part"). That's right: The most (in)famous Frenchman of all time...was Italian.

**Other Sights:** Also high up—on the Medicee/Falcone side of town—is the **Teatro dei Vigilanti,** a surprisingly fine and well-preserved little 19th-century theater. A disused Carmelite church was converted into a performance space during Napoleon's time here. Its cozy interior is ringed with three tiers of theater boxes under frescoed ceilings (it hosts occasional performances—check the schedule at www.elba-music.it).

A bit lower down, roughly between the Palazzina dei Mulini and the theater, is the Piazzale De Laugier cultural center. This houses a variety of special exhibits, the town cinema, and (probably) a multimedia exhibit called **Napoleone Bonaparte: L'Esilio dell'Aquila** ("Exile of the Eagle"). Given that there's no real Napoleon "museum" on the island, this exhibit's dramatized videos can help you get your historical bearings.

**Beaches and Water Activities:** If you're tempted to hit the beach but don't want to venture too far, head for **Le Ghiaie** (literally, "The Gravel")—the pebbly beach that stretches along the back of Portoferraio's peninsula. The beach is narrow and rocky, but enticing on a sunny day, with the typical array of beach bars and restaurants, rental chairs and umbrellas. About a 15-minute walk west are two additional, similar beaches, Padulella and Capo Bianco. But drivers will find better beaches elsewhere on the island (ask for tips at the TI, or see a few suggestions under "More Sights on Elba," later).

In good weather, Portoferraio and neighboring communities offer a wide range of outdoor activities and ways to enjoy the water—such as **sightseeing cruises, fishing trips,** and **kayak rentals.** Ask for details at the TI, or look for private agencies offering activities around town.

ELBA

## Sleeping in Portoferraio

While Portoferraio is a solid home base, accommodations right in town are limited. The coastline around the island is dotted with resort hotels, a few of which I've recommended elsewhere in this chapter (and others are easy to find online). The price rankings below are based on rates from May through June and September through October—rates can go way up in July and August.

The only accommodations worth considering right in the old town are a pair of small B&Bs (both with lots of stairs and

some street noise—earplugs
recommended): **$$ Porto Sole**
feels posh and modern, with
four big, bright, minimalist
rooms overlooking the pictur-
esque harbor (air-con, enter
one block behind harbor at Via
delle Galeazze 30, +39 388 743
3736, www.elbaportosole.com,
Anna). **$$ Porto del Mare** is

old-school, with just three rooms (one with a view, and one with a
bathroom down the hall). The location is central, overlooking the
bustling Piazza Cavour a block inland from the harbor (breakfast
at nearby café, no air-con and thin windows, open year-round, up
four floors with no elevator at Piazza Cavour 34, +39 328 826 1441,
www.bebportadelmarelba.com, Rosella, a.k.a. Scarlett).

A few hotels are on the quieter back end of town, overlooking Le Ghiaie beach—within a 10- to 15-minute walk of the busy
modern harbor or the atmospheric old harbor. The best choice is
**$$$ Villa Ombrosa Hotel,** a tidy, well-run beach hotel with 38
rooms—about half with sea views—and private beach access in
summer (air-con, elevator, free parking, Viale De Gasperi 9, +39
0565 914 363, www.villaombrosa.it).

## Eating in Portoferraio

The old harbor area is a picturesque place to browse for a meal.
Along the waterfront are several tempting restaurants with views
and seafood menus. Of these, **$$$ Osteria Libertaria** is a solid
bet, with a fish-forward menu and a welcome lack of pretense. The
outdoor tables facing the harbor are tops, and the nautical-min-
imalist interior is cozy; skip the less-inviting back terrace (daily,
Calata Giacomo Matteotti 12, +39 0565 914 978).

A block inland from the harbor is the buzzing Piazza Cavour—which feels like the town's main social hub. The popular
**$ Pizzeria il Castagnacciaio** is a neighborhood hangout, buzzing
with a local crowd. It's simply good pizza—crispy, hot, and fresh.
While there's not much else on the menu, they are proud of their
*torta de ceci*—chickpea crêpe (closed Wed, tucked off the top of
Piazza Cavour at Via del Mercato Vecchio 5, +39 0565 915 845).
Right on Piazza Cavour, **$$ Gusta Vino Cantina** is a wine bar and
restaurant with a chalkboard menu of local dishes (daily, Piazza
Cavour 51). Nearby is a branch of **Zero Gradi,** a good Elba gelat-
eria chain (daily, Piazza Matteotti 15).

The modern part of town, near the ferry port, is less appealing
for lingering over a meal. **$$ Enoteca Gusta Vino** is located right

on the main street, with *piccola cucina* (small dishes) designed to complement the local *elbani* wines (closed Sun, no full meals, Via Carducci 70, +39 0565 183 5211). **$ Ruggeri,** a high-end deli, is a fine place to stock up on quality local products for a picnic, as well as local wines and craft beers. They can also make you a sandwich from the deli case (by request) and heat up a small selection of ready-made meals (daily, Piazza Marinai d'Italia 4, +39 0565 915 497).

# More Sights on Elba

Vacationers spend days on Elba, simply joyriding around the island, exploring, dropping into pleasant harbor towns and hill towns, hiking, hitting the beach, sampling local wine, and eating well. For those on a quick visit, I've prioritized the most important sights close to Portoferraio; nothing here is more than about a 45-minute drive from the ferry dock. You could see virtually everything listed here in one busy, well-organized day (for general locations, see the "Elba" map earlier in this chapter). I've also listed a few restaurants and accommodations outside Portoferraio.

Drivers will find that Elba is slow going; the roads are quite twisty, and it's easy to get caught behind slow-moving cars and trucks. Parking is usually intuitive—just follow the *P* signs as you enter a town. Parking at beaches is notoriously tight and expensive in high season—expect to pay dearly and/or walk a bit.

## JUST OUTSIDE PORTOFERRAIO

These places are within a few minutes' drive from Portoferraio. Determined nondrivers can ask at the TI for public bus or taxi options.

### ▲Villa San Martino

Napoleon's summer home is situated in the countryside about three miles southwest of Portoferraio, with distant views of the town.

Like Palazzina dei Mulini in town, it's rough around the edges and feels a far cry from its peak. The two sights are similar and, for some, redundant (on a quick visit, Mulini is plenty). But San Martino adds a lush garden setting and a grand columned hall purpose-built to give Napoleon a (fleeting) reminder of his ornate palaces in France and throughout Europe.

**Cost and Hours:** €5, €8 combo-ticket with Palazzina dei Mu-

**ELBA**

lini; Tue, Thu, and Sat-Sun 8:30-13:30, Wed and Fri 14:00-19:30, closed Mon; pay parking, +39 0565 9140 688. Bus #1 runs between Portoferraio's port and the villa almost hourly (with a few gaps)—get schedule and details at the TI.

**Visiting the Villa:** From the parking lot, hike up the driveway and enter the gate—adorned with imperial eagles and N-for-Napoleon insignias. Circle around the left side of the colonnade (which you'll visit last) to buy tickets, then climb up behind the main building to the surprisingly humble house where Napoleon lived **(Casa di Napoleone).** A farmhouse was hastily adapted to accommodate the great ruler and his favorite generals, all of whom lived upstairs (you'll see their apartments). In the center of the building are the Knot of Love Room, with ceiling frescoes showing two doves tying a knot in a ribbon (supposedly representing Napoleon's forced separation from his wife), and the Egyptian Room, a grand dining hall elaborately frescoed with Egyptian motifs. Downstairs are humble functional rooms—kitchen, office, cloakroom, frescoed bathroom.

Back outside, you can explore the ragged gardens and peek in the greenhouse. Then head down to the estate's centerpiece, the **Galleria Demidoff**—named for the Russian architect who designed this space specifically to invoke Napoleon's many ornate palaces in Europe. The temple-like interior—a long hall with columns, ornate ceilings, and geometric designs on the floors—feels somber, stately, almost tomb-like...perhaps fittingly, given that here on Elba, Napoleon found himself at what many believed was the bitter end of his military career.

### Villa Romana delle Grotte

Covered by the Cosmopoli Card and heavily promoted, these scant ruins are not essential to see. Aficionados of Roman villas might find something to get excited about at these foundations, situated on a grassy bluff three miles from the town center. For others, they're mostly worth a visit for the sweeping views back on Portoferraio across the bay (stunning in the late afternoon light).

## WEST OF PORTOFERRAIO

These sights line up to the west of Portoferraio—an entertaining but winding drive away. The gondola—the farthest point I've mentioned—is about a 45-minute drive from town.

If you have more time, locals recommend driving all the way around the west coast of the island, on a winding seaside road that passes through charming, remote villages—Sant'Andrea, Patresi, Pomonte, Cavoli, and Marina di Campo (allow an extra 1.5 hours, at least, not including stops—or getting stuck behind slow-moving vehicles).

## Biodola Beach (Spiaggia della Biodola)

Many beaches hug Elba's coastline, but this is a particularly fine choice—since it's sandy and close to Portoferraio (about a 15-min-ute drive, most of which follows a vertiginously serpentine, scenic road down to the beach). The beach is small and squeezed between the cliff and the sea, so parking can be tricky—watch for pay lots as you approach.

**Sleeping at Biodola Beach: $$$$ Hermitage Hotel** is your elegant beachfront splurge, with 130 cheery, colorfully tiled rooms filling several buildings over a private beach at the south end of Biodola. Its exclusive grounds and amenities—gardens, three swimming pools, restaurants, tennis courts, golf, and direct beach access—make it an appealing place for a high-end vacation (look for off-season deals, air-con, elevator, free parking, +39 0565 9740, www.hotelhermitage.it).

## ▲Marciana Marina

This tidy, untrampled little beach town, less than a 30-minute drive from Portoferraio, is a lovely spot for a stroll. Set upon rocks and a narrow pebbly beach, it has a fine seafront prom-enade and a genteel, peb-ble-paved main square tucked between the main road and the coastline.

**Sleeping in Marciana Marina: $$$ Marina Garden Hotel** is a charming, well-kept property with 42 rooms, wedged between the town's main square and main road. It's a nice choice for a small-town overnight (air-con, elevator, small swimming pool, short walk to beach, closed early-Oct-mid-May, Viale Giuseppe Cerboni 1, +39 0565 99010, www.marinagardenhotel.it).

**Eating in Marciana Marina:** Several good restaurants cluster at the east end of the promenade (to the right, as you face the water); among these, the classy **$$$ Salegrosso Ristorante** serves modern *elbani* cuisine with a focus on seafood (reservations recommended, closed Mon, Piazza della Vittoria 14, +39 0565 996 862). Just up the street is a destination ice-cream shop—**Gelateria La**

ELBA

**Svolta,** where the owner whips up fresh gelato in creative flavors (daily, Via Cairoli 6).

### ▲▲Monte Capanne Gondola (Cabinovia Monte Capanne)

Elba's most memorable experience is riding an open-air gondola up to the very top of the island, where a steep 10-minute hike up chunky rocks leads to the summit of Monte Capanne (at more than 3,300 feet). Here you'll enjoy 360-degree views over all of Elba, and to neighboring islands (including Corsica) and the mainland. It's worth ▲▲▲ in good weather (or negative-▲▲▲ for those scared of heights).

**Cost and Hours:** €18, €12 one-way if you want to hike down (about 1.5 hours if you and your knees are in excellent shape); Easter-October daily 10:00-13:00 & 14:20-17:00, until 17:30 July-Sept, last descent is 30 minutes later, closed Nov-Easter. From Marciana Marina, drive up the very twisty road to the hill town of Marciana. Watch for the *"Cabinovia P"* parking lot just before you enter town, and from there, hike up along the little waterfall to the lower gondola station.

**Riding the Gondola:** The gondola *(cabinovia)* itself is unusual in that it's not enclosed: you stand up in a two-person, bright-yellow metal cage, holding on for dear life as you slowly trundle 20 minutes over steep terrain, which changes from palm trees to alpine-like pine forests to jagged rock above the tree line. You'll feel like a terrified parakeet going for the ride of its life. The views from the top are smashing, but for even better

panoramas, good hikers can tackle the steep climb (over very uneven terrain—wear good shoes and bring hiking poles if you have them) even higher to the island's summit, at the base of a radio installation. From here, jagged mountain spines—like the backs of giant dinosaurs—spin off in every direction. At your feet are the hill town of Marciana and its port of Marciana Marina, in the distance is Portoferraio, and Corsica looms to the west. On your way down, tiptoe (c-a-r-e-f-u-l-l-y) to the edge of a forgotten helipad to understand the meaning of "vertigo."

**Nearby:** The gondola is at the edge of the hill town of **Marciana.** Historically, the "real" town was up in the hills—for safety's

ELBA

sake—with an outpost down on the water (in this case, Marciana Marina). Before or after your gondola ride, consider a stroll through this steep little village. **$$ Osteria del Noce** is a well-regarded, quality restaurant in the heart of town (daily for lunch and dinner, Viale della Madonna 14, +39 0565 901 284, www.osteriadelnoce. com); there are also basic **$ cafés** at both the top and the bottom of the gondola.

## SOUTHEAST OF PORTOFERRAIO

Another cluster of fine towns is within an easy, less winding 30-minute drive southeast of Portoferraio.

### ▲Porto Azzurro

This pleasant town—scenically set under jagged cliffs, its harbor bobbing with sailboats and fancy yachts—feels like a poor-man's Portofino. Porto Azzur-

ro's elegant main square, which faces the harbor, is both genteel and welcoming, with benches under classy trellises. The beach is narrow and less appealing, but some visitors are lured for a meal at the big restaurants on piers jutting out into the harbor. Classy without being too ritzy, Porto Azzurro is an enjoyable place to simply join the *passeggiata* in the late afternoon and wind down from a busy day of sightseeing (drivers turn left just before entering town to find the pay-and-display parking lot).

### Capoliveri

Spreading across the top of its mountain just above Porto Azzurro, Capoliveri is one of Elba's biggest and finest hill towns—worth a stroll if you're curious to wander through a nonseaside town.

**ELBA**

### Mines on the East Coast

From Etruscan times all the way through Napoleon, Elba has been important for its rich deposits of ore. For those interested in this geological heritage, the communities in the eastern part of the island offer exhibits and visits to old mines. Consider these: **Calamita Mines,** near Capoliveri, includes a look at a historic workshop and the option to visit an old mine (www.minieredicalamita.it); **Parco Minerario** includes a tourist train ride into a mine (museum in Rio Nell'Elba, tourist train above Rio Marina, www.parcominelba.it); and **La Piccola Miniera** is a replica mine at a precious stones shop just outside Porto Azzurro (www.lapiccolaminiera.it). Booking ahead for any of these is recommended.

# On the Mainland

### Baratti and Populonia Archaeological Park
### (Parco Archeologico di Baratti e Populonia)

The curving bay of Baratti was once home to a thriving Etruscan civilization called Populonia, which was founded in the late ninth

century BC, peaked around the third to sixth century BC, was overtaken by Rome, and faded with the fall of Rome. Down along the bay was the settlement's port, necropolis (tombs), and industrial area where rich deposits of iron ore (and resources shipped over from Elba) were smelted into metal tools and weapons. Some of the hills you see are actually millennia-old slag heaps, where unused material was dumped by Etruscan metallurgists. Up high on the hill was the walled acropolis, with the main residential and commercial zone. This entire area was forgotten for centuries until the 20th century, when excavations for iron ore—those same deposits that originally gave birth to Populonia—uncovered artifacts of this great civilization. While there's less to see than at many ancient sites, it's a rare opportunity to explore buildings dating back to Etruscan times (and the Roman structures that were built on top of them).

Along the bay—overlooking the sea—you can tour the **San Cerbone Necropolis,** a gathering of domed tombs built into the ground, of various sizes and

states of repair. The largest—the Tomb of the Chariot (dei Carri)—is a domed structure 90 feet in diameter. These can be seen in an easy short walk from the main visitors center. A few more minutes takes you to the ruined foundations of some Etruscan industrial buildings.

# Elba, the Island of Metals

While most visitors focus only on Napoleon, Elba is really all about its metals.

In fact, one of the most important innovations in early Italian civilization took place on this island. In the 10th century BC, Etruscans here smelted iron from the island's rich iron ore deposits, using the island's abundant trees for fuel (having been taught by passing Phoenician and Greek traders). This marked the end of the Bronze Age and the inception of the Iron Age. Iron blades could be sharpened again and again, revolutionizing farming, military strategy, and much more. (The Greek name for the island was Aethalia—meaning "fume," for its many metal furnaces.)

Elba's precious deposits and metallurgy know-how made it powerful and desirable throughout history. That's why possession of it frequently passed between various mainland city-states (including Florence, whose Medici built Portoferraio's stout fortifications), and even among European powers (including France and Great Britain). With its rich resources, the island was a not entirely undesirable consolation prize for Napoleon. As recently as World War II, Elba was a heavily industrialized island (though traces of that industry are blessedly invisible today). The name of the island's main town—Portoferraio—means "port of iron." And the mainland town facing Elba—Piombino—is named for lead (whose periodic symbol is "Pb").

With more time, you can hike through the woods to the **Grotto Necropolis**—an evocative quarry carved into the rock, with additional tombs (40-minute walk each way).

Finally, you'll drive up to the **Acropolis of Populonia,** where you'll find mostly Roman-era structures built on the site of the original Etruscan town. Near the entrance are the ruins of various temples (including one partly reconstructed temple base). Just uphill are the remains of a Roman-era loggia (once part of a sprawling sanctuary and bath complex) and some intact  mosaic floors. Higher still, you eventually reach the original fifth-century-BC Etruscan wall. Near the ancient acropolis (and dominating the hilltop) is the walled, castle-like medieval Populonia—a town that's striking from afar, but humble up close, with a few touristy shops and not much to see.

ELBA

**Cost and Hours:** Each site charges a different admission—€10 each for the two necropoli, €12 for the acropolis, €17 for any two sights, €20 for all three, cheaper off-season. All three sites are open July-Aug daily 9:00-20:00; June and Sept Tue-Sun 10:00-19:00, closed Mon; March and May Tue-Sun 10:00-18:00, closed Mon; Oct Tue-Sun 10:00-17:00, closed Mon; Nov-Feb open limited hours, +39 0565 226 445, www.parchivaldicornia.it.

**Getting There:** The site is just north of Piombino, a 15-minute drive from the ferry dock. From the main road, you'll drive first to the lower necropolis sites. Park in the designated lot and hike across the field to the visitors' center (the building marked *Parco Archeologico*) to buy tickets and enter the sites (and to get your parking validated). Pick up the free, essential map, and then drive on to the hilltop pay lot between the acropolis and medieval Populonia (it's a five-minute walk to either).

# FLORENTINE & TUSCAN HISTORY

This chapter presents Florence and Tuscany's history in a nutshell, divided into major historical periods. For each era, I've given a list of sights you can see during your travels that bring that period to life.

## ETRUSCANS, ROMANS, AND "BARBARIANS" (550 BC-AD 1000)

In prehistoric times, much of what we today call "Tuscany" was part of the Etruscan Empire. This mysterious early civilization built hilltop forts (such as at Fiesole), traded metals with other Mediterranean peoples (including the golden age Greeks), established agriculture in central Italy, and buried their dead in distinctive caskets that show the deceased lounging at an eter-

nal banquet. Having lived their day in the sun, the Etruscans faded as Rome rose. (For more on the Etruscans, see page 518.)

In 59 BC, Julius Caesar founded Florentia (meaning "flowering" or "flourishing") at an easy-to-cross point on the Arno River. By AD 200, it had become a thriving provincial capital (population 10,000). The rectangular-grid street plan—aligned by compass points, rather than the river—is still evident in today's layout.

When the Empire converted to Christianity, Bishop (and Saint) Zenobius built a church where the Duomo stands today. Even as Rome fell and Italy was overrun by barbarians, Florence stood strong. Proud medieval Florentines traced their roots back to civilized Rome, and the city remained a Tuscan commercial center during the Dark Ages.

Many of Tuscany's medieval hill towns date from this era. Some were founded by the Etruscans, who appreciated a safe, sky-high location. Others date from after the fall of Rome, when terrified locals fled to hilltop forts. Some of those forts were constructed to protect the Via Francigena, the pilgrimage route from northern Europe to Rome that passed through the heart of today's Tuscany (for more on the Via Francigena, see page 595).

### Sights

- Roman and Etruscan fragments in Florence's Duomo Museum
- Etruscan wall in cellar of Church of San Francesco and artifacts in Archaeological Area, Fiesole
- Etruscan gate, museum, and other artifacts in Volterra
- Etruscan museums in Cortona, Chiusi, and many other towns
- Florence's Piazza della Repubblica—the old Roman Forum
- Baratti and Populonia Archaeological Park (just north of Piombino, near the ferry to Elba)

## FLORENCE'S FLOURISHING, PISA'S PEAK, AND SIENA'S SUMMIT (1000-1400)

Through the Middle Ages, Tuscany remained (relative to the rest of Europe) prosperous. Florence hummed along on trade. It became a regional capital in Charlemagne's Europe-wide empire (c. 800-1100). In 990, Archbishop Sigeric of Canterbury passed through Florence along the Via Francigena and was impressed enough to write it up in history's first travel guidebook. ("Verily," he supposedly wrote, "makest thou Uffizi reserva-

tions.") Around 1050, the Baptistery was built, likely on the site of an ancient Roman temple. Around 1100 (under Countess Matilda of Tuscany), Florence broke from its German-based Holy Roman Empire, gaining its independence. Florence was growing rich making wool cloth and trading it abroad. Traders became bankers, moneylenders, and investors. The merchant class, organized into guilds, was growing more powerful than the rural, feudal nobles. Florence emerged as Europe's first urban-based, capitalist economy.

Meanwhile, the maritime republic of Pisa (at the mouth of the Arno River) was also prospering, through sea trade with the

## Guelphs vs. Ghibellines

In medieval times, Italy was divided between two competing political factions, the Guelphs and the Ghibellines. Their conflict had more to do with power than ideology. (It wasn't what you believed, but who your allies were.) The faction names could mean something different depending on the particular place and time, but here's the gist:

| Guelphs | Ghibellines |
|---|---|
| Supported pope | Supported emperor |
| Middle-class merchants and craftsmen | Aristocrats of feudal order |
| Favored urban, new economy | Favored rural, traditional economy |
| Wanted independent city-states under local Italian leaders | Wanted unified small states under traditional dukes and kings |

Far East. They funneled their wealth into a glorious ensemble of buildings in the "Pisan Romanesque" style: a church, a baptistery, and a curious bell tower that began to lean before it had even been completed.

Siena, Florence's archrival, was also on the rise. Unlike Florence, Siena sat right along the bustling Via Francigena, which kept it wealthy. In all of these thriving merchant towns, aristocratic families erected tall, fortified tower houses, showing off their wealth and might (San Gimignano had 72).

By the 1200s, Florence was beginning to surpass its neighbors through shrewd diplomacy, military conquest, and sheer economic might. The Florentine currency, the gold florin, became Europe's strongest. There was a budding democracy. In 1266, the city's nobles were ousted, establishing the *primo popolo*, or "rule by the people." (This was part of a larger ongoing power struggle between merchant-class Guelphs and noble-class Ghibellines—see the sidebar.) Bursting with civic pride, Florence's guilds financed major construction projects: the Duomo (begun in 1296), Santa Croce, and Santa Maria Novella. Giotto was pioneering realistic painting, and the poet Dante (a prominent Guelph) wrote his epic poem, *The Divine Comedy*. By 1347, Florence (population 90,000) had become one of Europe's biggest cities, and the Renaissance seemed right around the corner. But then...

The Black Death (bubonic plague) arrived in 1348. Suddenly, Florence's population was cut nearly in half. Recovery was slowed by more plagues, bank failures, and political rivalries. But eventually a new leading family emerged: the Medici.

HISTORY

## Florence Almanac

**Population:** Approximately 380,000 people

**Currency:** Euro

**City Layout:** Florence is the capital of Tuscany and lies on the Arno River. It's divided into five administrative wards: the Historic Center, Campo di Marte, Gavinana, Isolotto, and Rifredi.

**Best Viewpoints:** Piazzale Michelangelo (and San Miniato Church, above it) overlooks the city and the Duomo from across the river, as does the top of the Boboli Gardens. For other panoramic views of Florence, climb the Campanile or the Duomo's dome (next to each other) or the tower at the Palazzo Vecchio. If you like your beverage with a view, try a rooftop café (see page 315).

**Sweetest Festival:** In spring, the city hosts an annual gelato festival, featuring tastings and demonstrations by gelato makers from all over Italy (www.gelatofestival.it).

**Tourist Tracks:** Tourism in Florence and Tuscany is booming. Each year, more than two million tourists flock to the Uffizi Gallery to gaze at Botticelli's *Birth of Venus*.

**Culture Count:** A little over 90 percent of Florence's population is indigenously Italian and Roman Catholic. Immigrant groups are mostly European (3.5 percent) and East Asian (2 percent), with small percentages of North and South Americans and Northern Africans.

**Famous Florentines:** Florence, birthplace of the Renaissance, bred many great minds, including Michelangelo, Leonardo, Donatello, Brunelleschi, Machiavelli, Dante, and...Florence Nightingale, whose English parents named her after the city in which she was born.

## Sights

- Baptistery and interior mosaics
- Pisa's Field of Miracles (Duomo, Baptistery, Cemetery, and Leaning Tower)
- San Gimignano's 14 surviving tower houses
- Bargello (Florence's first City Hall)
- Palazzo Vecchio (the next City Hall)
- Orsanmichele Church (originally a bustling granary)
- Duomo and Campanile (and original decorations in Duomo Museum)

- Santa Croce, Santa Maria Novella, and Giotto's bell-tower design (Campanile) and his paintings in the Uffizi

## THE QUATTROCENTO: A RENAISSANCE CITY UNDER MEDICI PRINCES (1400s)

There was just something dynamic about the Florentines. Pope Boniface VIII said there were five elements: earth, air, fire, water... and Florentines. For 200 years, starting in the early 1300s, their city was a cultural hub.

While 1500 marks Europe's Re-
naissance, in Florence—where the whole revival of classical culture got its start—the Renaissance began and ended in the 1400s (the Quattrocento). In fact, some say the Renaissance "began" precisely in the year 1401. That's when a competition to create new Baptistery doors caught the public's imagination, energizing the city. That was followed by a plan to top the medieval Duomo with Brunelleschi's Renaissance dome (dedicated in 1436).

The city was rich—from the wool trade, silk factories, and banking. There was a large middle class and strong guilds (trade associations for skilled craftsmen). Success was a matter of civic pride, and Florentines showed that pride by beautifying the city.

Florence's golden age coincided with the rise of the Medici family, whose wealth gave them political leverage around Europe. The Medici had grown wealthy as textile traders, then became bankers. The Medici bank had branches in 10 European cities, including London, Geneva, Bruges, and Lyon. The pope kept his checking account in the Rome branch. With money came power. In 1434, Cosimo the Elder took control of Florence. Although out-
wardly he honored the Florentine tradition of popular rule, in real-
ity he used his great wealth to rule as a tyrant, buying popularity with lavish patronage of public art. Cosimo was succeeded by his son Piero the Gouty, who ruled stiffly but ably. It was under the next Medici ruler that Florence reached its peak.

**Lorenzo de' Medici** (1449-1492)—inheritor of the family's wealth and power, and his grandfather Cosimo's love of art—was young (20 when he took power), athletic, and intelligent, in addi-
tion to being a poet, horseman, musician, and leader. He wrote love songs and humorous ditties to be performed loudly and badly at carnival time. His marathon drinking bouts and illicit love affairs were legendary. He learned Greek and Latin and read the clas-

sics, yet his great passion was hunting. He was the original Renaissance Man—a man of knowledge and action, a patron of the arts, a scholar and a man of the world. He was Lorenzo the Magnificent.

Lorenzo epitomized the Florentine spirit of optimism. Born on New Year's Day and raised in the lap of luxury (Donatello's *David* stood in the family courtyard) by loving parents, he grew up feeling that there was nothing he couldn't do. Florentines saw themselves as part of a "new age," a great undertaking of discovery and progress in man's history. They boasted that within the city walls, there were more "nobly gifted souls than the world has seen in the entire thousand years before." These people invented the term "Dark Ages" for the era that preceded theirs.

Lorenzo surrounded himself with Florence's best and brightest. They created an informal "Platonic Academy," based on that of ancient Greece, to meet over a glass of wine under the stars at the Medici villa and discuss literature, art, music, and politics—witty conversation was considered an art in itself.

Their neo-Platonic philosophy stressed the goodness of man and the created world; they believed in a common truth behind all religion. The Academy was more than just an excuse to go out with the guys: The members were convinced that their discussions were changing the world and improving their souls.

**Sandro Botticelli** (1445-1510) was a member of the Platonic Academy. He painted scenes from the classical myths that the group read, weaving contemporary figures and events into the ancient subjects. He gloried in the nude body, which he considered God's greatest creation.

Artists such as Botticelli thrived on the patronage of wealthy individuals, the government, the Church, and guilds. Botticelli commanded as much as 100 florins for one work, enough to live on for a year in high style, which he did for many years. In Botticelli's art we see the lightness, gaiety, and optimism of Lorenzo's court.

Another of Lorenzo's protégés was the young **Michelangelo Buonarroti** (1475-1564). Impressed with his work, Lorenzo took the poor, unlearned 13-year-old boy into the Medici household and treated him like a son.

Michelangelo's playmates were the Medici children, later to become Popes Leo X and Clement VII, who would give him important commissions. For all the encouragement, education, and contacts Michelangelo received, his most important gift from Lorenzo was simply a place at the dinner table, where he could absorb the words of the great men of the time and their love of art for art's sake.

But there was another side to Florence. Even with all the art and philosophy of the Renaissance, violence, disease, and warfare were still present in medieval proportions. For the lower classes, life was as harsh as ever. Florence's streets were filled with tough-talking, hardened, illiterate merchants who strode about singing verses from Dante's *Divine Comedy*. Though Florence was technically a republic with some upward mobility, most power was in the hands of a few wealthy banking families. This was the time of the ruthless tactics of the Borgias (known for murdering their political enemies) as they battled for power. Lorenzo himself barely escaped assassination in the Duomo during Easter Mass; his brother died in the attack. Many artists and scholars wore swords and daggers as part of everyday dress.

Florence's contributions to Western culture are immense: the revival of the arts, humanism, and science after centuries of medieval superstition and oppression; the seeds of democracy; the modern Italian language (which grew out of the popular Florentine dialect); the art of Botticelli, Leonardo, and Michelangelo; the writings of Machiavelli, Boccaccio, and Dante; and the explorations of Amerigo Vespucci, who gave his name to a newly discovered continent.

Florence dominated Italy economically and culturally. Meanwhile, 1400s Rome was a dirty, decaying, crime-infested place. Italy itself was a gaggle of squabbling city-states. (When someone suggested to the Renaissance Florentine Niccolò Machiavelli that the Italian city-states might unite against their common enemy, France, he wrote back, "Don't make me laugh.")

In 1492, Lorenzo the Magnificent died suddenly, many Medici banks went bankrupt, France invaded, and Florentine politics were thrown into disarray. In this political vacuum, the monk Girolamo Savonarola appeared on the scene as a voice of moral authority. He reestablished the Florentine constitution, sent the Medici into exile, and ruled with stern dictates. Condemning Renaissance excesses, he organized bonfires on Piazza della Signoria, where citizens burned their "vanities"—rich clothes, secular books, and paintings. In 1498, Savonarola was arrested, hanged, and burned by political enemies and a citizenry tired of his morally strict rule.

After a decade of chaos, Florence would never fully recover, and the Florentine Renaissance headed south.

## Sights

- Brunelleschi's Duomo dome and Pazzi Chapel
- Donatello's statues (Bargello, Duomo Museum, and Orsanmichele)

- Ghiberti's bronze Baptistery doors (originals in Duomo Museum)
- Botticelli's paintings in Uffizi
- Uffizi (painting's history from medieval to Michelangelo)
- Bargello (sculpture's history)
- Masaccio frescoes in Santa Maria Novella and Brancacci Chapel
- Fra Angelico paintings (and Savonarola history) in Museum of San Marco

## DECLINE, MEDICI DUKES, RENAISSANCE GOES SOUTH (1500-1800)

The center of the Renaissance gradually shifted to Rome, but its artists were mostly Florentine. When Rome began a beautification campaign (under popes that included Lorenzo's son and nephew), they hired Michelangelo, Raphael, and others. When the king of France wanted Renaissance culture, he hired Florence's Leonardo da Vinci to move north. The Florentine Renaissance was over, but Florentine culture lived on.

After Savonarola, the Medici returned. They'd spent their exile in Rome, where they married into royalty, and they returned as even less democratic nobles. Florence's long tradition as a self-governing republic ended for good in 1530, when—after a long siege— their last-gasp rebellion was snuffed out by a Medici pope backed by foreign powers. In succeeding centuries, the Medici dukes ruled an economically and politically declining city.

But as a city of culture, Florence still had that certain cachet that all of Europe wanted. The Medici married off their refined daughters (Catherine de' Medici, and later, Marie de' Medici) to the kings of Europe's new superpower, France. In Florence, Cosimo I and his sophisticated wife, Eleonora of Toledo, ruled as enlightened despots, beautifying the city with the Uffizi, a renovated Palazzo Vecchio, and a rebuilt Pitti Palace. The Medici supported Galileo in his scientific studies.

But by the late 1500s, Florence was increasingly a minor player in world affairs—a small dukedom with a stagnant economy, ruled by a series of forgettable Francescos, Ferdinandos, and Cosimos. In 1587, the Duomo's medieval facade was torn down in hopes of being rebuilt in a glorious new style. It remained bare brick for the next 200 years, a fitting metaphor for Florence's stalled dreams. In 1737, the last of the Medici line died, and in 1799 Florence

# Typical Church Architecture

History comes to life when you visit a centuries-old church. Even if you wouldn't know your apse from a hole in the ground, learning a few simple terms will enrich your experience. Note that not every church has every feature, and a "cathedral" isn't a type of church architecture, but rather a designation for a church that's a governing center for a local bishop.

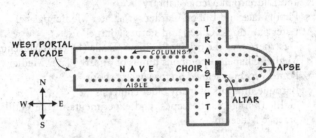

**Aisles:** Long, generally low-ceilinged arcades that flank the nave

**Altar:** Raised area with a ceremonial table (often adorned with candles or a crucifix), where the priest prepares and serves the bread and wine for Communion

**Apse:** Space behind the altar, sometimes bordered with small chapels

**Barrel Vault:** Continuous round-arched ceiling that resembles an extended upside-down U

**Choir:** Intimate space reserved for clergy and choir, located within the nave near the high altar and often screened off

**Cloister:** Covered hallways bordering a square or rectangular open-air courtyard, traditionally where monks and nuns got fresh air

**Facade:** Exterior of the church's main (west) entrance, usually highly decorated

**Groin Vault:** Arched ceiling formed where two equal barrel vaults meet at right angles

**Narthex:** Area (portico or foyer) between the main entry and the nave

**Nave:** Long central section of the church (running west to east, from the entrance to the altar) where the congregation sits or stands during the service

**Transept:** One of the two parts forming the "arms" of the cross in a traditional cross-shaped floor plan; runs north-south, perpendicularly crossing the east-west nave

**West Portal:** Main entry to the church (on the west end, opposite the main altar)

was conquered by French revolutionary forces under Napoleon, who briefly installed his sister as duchess. With Napoleon's fall, the once-proud city-state of Florence came under the rule of Austrian Habsburg nobles.

### Sights
- Michelangelo's Florentine works—*David*, Medici Chapels, and Laurentian Medici Library
- Pitti Palace and Boboli Gardens (the later Medici palace)
- Later paintings (Uffizi) and statues (Bargello)
- Destruction of the original Duomo facade (Duomo Museum)
- Medici Chapels—pompous tombs of (mostly) later Medici
- Ponte Vecchio cleaned up for jewelry shops
- Baroque interiors of many older churches
- Galileo's fingers, telescopes, and experiments in the Galileo Science Museum

## ITALIAN UNIFICATION, URBANIZATION, AND URBAN RENEWAL (1800s to Today)

After years of rule by Austrian nobles, Florence peacefully booted out the *Ausländer*s and joined the Italian unification movement. The city even served briefly as modern Italy's capital (1865-1870). It enjoyed an artistic revival of both medieval (Neo-Gothic) and Renaissance (Neoclassical) styles. The Duomo finally got its long-wished-for facade.

The 20th century was turbulent, with rapid population growth and rapid industrialization. During World War II, Florence was under Nazi occupation. As the Allies closed in, all the Arno bridges except Ponte Vecchio were blown up. In 1966, a disastrous flood, up to nearly 20 feet high, covered the city's buildings and artistic treasures in mud. The city was a cultural, economic, and touristic mess. An international effort of volunteer "mud angels" slowly brought the city's cultural heritage back into view.

More recently, the city's traffic-choked streets have been gradually pedestrianized. Today, the city of Florence—with a thriving university, plentiful cafés, and revamped museums, has become a model cultural destination. Now if they could just do something about those Vespas...

## Sights

- Duomo's current Neo-Gothic facade
- Piazza della Repubblica (commemorating unification), with fine 19th-century cafés
- Upscale designer boutiques on Via dei Calzaiuoli, Via degli Strozzi, and Via de' Tornabuoni
- Ever-growing pedestrian zones in the city center

*For more on Florentine and Tuscan history, consider* Europe 101: History and Art for the Traveler, *by Rick Steves and Gene Openshaw (available at RickSteves.com).*

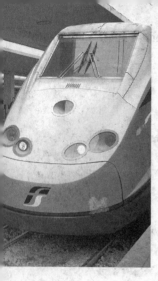

# PRACTICALITIES

This chapter covers the practical skills of European travel: how to get tourist information, pay for things, sightsee efficiently, find good-value accommodations, eat affordably but well, use technology wisely, and get between destinations smoothly. For more information on these topics, see RickSteves.com/travel-tips.

## Travel Tips

**Travel Advisories:** Before traveling, check updated health and safety conditions, including restrictions for your destination, on the travel pages of the US State Department (www.travel.state.gov) and Centers for Disease Control and Prevention (www.cdc.gov/travel). The US embassy website for Italy is another good source of information (see page 653).

**Covid Vaccine/Test Requirements:** It's possible you'll need to present proof of vaccination against the coronavirus and/or a negative Covid-19 test result to board a plane to Europe or back to the US. Carefully check requirements for each country you'll visit well before you depart, and again a few days before your trip. See the websites listed above for current requirements.

**ETIAS Registration:** The European Union may soon require US and Canadian citizens to register online with the European Travel Information and Authorization System (ETIAS) before entering Italy and other Schengen Zone countries (quick and easy process). For the latest, check www.etiasvisa.com.

**Tourist Information:** Before your trip, scan the website of the Italian national tourist office (www.italia.it) for a wealth of travel information. If you have a specific question, try contacting one of their US offices (New York: +1 212 245 5618, newyork@enit.it; Los Angeles: +1 310 820 1898, losangeles@enit.it).

**In Italy,** a good first stop in every town is generally the tourist information office (abbreviated **TI** in this book). TIs are in business to help you spend money in their town—which can color their advice—but I still swing by to pick up a city map and get info on public transit, walking tours, special events, and nightlife. While Italian TIs are about half as helpful as those in other countries, their information is twice as important. Some TIs have information on the entire country or at least the region, so you can pick up maps and other info for destinations you'll be visiting later in your trip.

**Emergency and Medical Help:** For any emergency service—ambulance, police, or fire—call **112** from a mobile phone or landline (operators typically speak English). If you get sick, do as the locals do and go to a pharmacist for advice. Or ask at your hotel for help—they'll know the nearest medical and emergency services. For English-speaking doctors in Florence, see page 35.

**Theft or Loss:** To replace a passport, you'll need to go in person to an embassy (see next). If your credit and debit cards disappear, cancel and replace them (see "Damage Control for Lost Cards" on page 658). File a police report, either on the spot or within a day or two; you'll need it to submit an insurance claim for lost or stolen items, and it can help with replacing your passport or credit and debit cards. For more information, see RickSteves.com/help.

**US Embassies and Consulates:** Embassy in Rome—+39 06 46741, passport and nonemergency consular services, by appointment only (Via Vittorio Veneto 121). Consulates in Milan—+39 02 290 351 (Via Principe Amedeo 2/10); Florence—+39 055 266 951 (Lungarno Vespucci 38); and Naples—+39 081 583 8111 (Piazza della Repubblica). For all, see http://it.usembassy.gov.

**Canadian Embassies:** Rome—+39 06 854 442 911 (Via Zara 30); Milan—+39 02 626 94238 (Piazza Cavour 3). For both, see www.italy.gc.ca. After-hours emergency in Ottawa +1 613 996 8885.

**Time Zones:** Italy, like most of continental Europe, is generally six/nine hours ahead of the East/West Coasts of the US. The exceptions are the beginning and end of Daylight Saving Time: Europe "springs forward" the last Sunday in March (two weeks after most of North America), and "falls back" the last Sunday in October (one week before North America). For a handy time converter, use the world clock app on your phone or download one (see www.timeanddate.com).

**Business Hours:** Traditionally, Italy used the siesta plan, with people generally working from about 9:00 to 13:00 and from 15:30-16:00 to 19:00-19:30, Monday through Saturday. Siesta hours are no longer required by law, so offices and many shops stay open through lunch or later into the evening, especially larger stores in tourist areas. Shops in small towns and villages are more likely to close during lunch. Stores are usually closed on Sunday, and often on Monday. Many shops close for a couple of weeks around August 15.

**Watt's Up?** Europe's electrical system is 220 volts, instead of North America's 110 volts. Most electronics (laptops, phones, cameras) and appliances (newer hair dryers, CPAP machines) convert automatically, so you won't need a converter, but you will need an adapter plug with two round prongs, sold inexpensively at travel stores in the US.

**Rip up this book!** Turn chapters into mini guidebooks: Break the book's spine and use a utility knife to slice apart chapters, keeping gummy edges intact. Reinforce the chapter spines with clear wide tape; use a heavy-duty stapler; or make or buy a cheap cover (see the Travel Store at RickSteves.com), swapping out chapters as you travel.

**Discounts:** Discounts for sights are generally not listed in this book. However, youths under 18 and students and teachers with proper identification cards (obtain from www.isic.org) can get discounts at many sights—always ask. Italy's national museums generally offer free admission to children under 18, but some discounts are available only for citizens of the European Union (EU).

**Online Translation Tips:** Google's Chrome browser instantly translates websites; Translate.google.com and DeepL.com are also handy. The Google Translate app converts spoken or typed English into most European languages (and vice versa) and can also translate text it "reads" with your smartphone's camera.

**Going Green:** There's plenty you can do to reduce your environmental footprint when traveling. When practical, take a train instead of a flight within Europe, and use public transportation within cities. In hotels, use the "Do Not Disturb" sign to avoid daily linen and towel changes (or hang up your towels to signal you'll reuse them). Bring a reusable shopping tote and refillable water bottle (Europe's tap water is safe to drink). Skip printed brochures, maps, or other materials that you don't plan to keep—get your info online instead. To find out how Rick Steves' Europe is offsetting carbon emissions with a self-imposed carbon tax, see RickSteves.com/about-us/climate-smart.

# Money

Here's my basic strategy for using money wisely in Europe. I pack the following and keep it all safe in my money belt.

**Credit Card:** You'll use your credit card for purchases both big (hotels, advance tickets) and small (little shops, food stands). Some European businesses have gone cashless, making a card your only payment option. A "tap-to-pay" or "contactless" card is widely accepted and simple to use.

**Debit Card:** Use this at ATMs to withdraw a small amount of local cash. Wait until you arrive to get euros (European airports have plenty of ATMs); if you buy euros before your trip, you'll pay bad stateside exchange rates. While most transactions are by card these days, cash can help you out of a jam if your card randomly doesn't work, and can be useful to pay for things like tips and local guides.

**Backup Card:** Some travelers carry a third card (debit or credit; ideally from a different bank) in case one gets lost or simply doesn't work.

**Stash of Cash:** I carry $100-200 in US dollars as a cash backup, which comes in handy in an emergency (for example, if your debit card gets eaten by the machine).

## BEFORE YOU GO

**Know your cards.** For credit cards, Visa and MasterCard are universal while American Express and Discover are less common. US debit cards with a Visa or MasterCard logo will work in any European ATM.

**Go "contactless."** Get comfortable using contactless pay options. Check to see if you already have—or can get—a tap-to-pay version of your credit card (look on the card for the tap-to-pay symbol—four curvy lines), and consider setting up your smartphone for contactless payment (see next section for details). Both options are widely used in Europe and are more secure than a physical credit card: Instead of recording your credit card number, a one-time encrypted "token" enables the purchase and expires shortly afterward.

**Know your PIN.** Make sure you know the numeric, four-digit PIN for each of your cards, both debit and credit. Request it if you

## Exchange Rate

**1 euro (€) = about $1.10**

To convert prices in euros to dollars, add about 10 percent: €20=about $22, €50=about $55. Like the dollar, one euro is broken into 100 cents. Coins range from €0.01 to €2, and bills from €5 to €200 (bills over €50 are rarely used).

Check www.oanda.com for the latest exchange rates.

don't have one, as it may be required for some purchases. Allow time to receive the information by mail—it's not always possible to obtain your PIN online or by phone.

**Report your travel dates.** Let your bank know that you'll be using your debit and credit cards in Europe, and when and where you're headed.

**Adjust your ATM withdrawal limit.** Find out how much you can withdraw daily and ask for a higher daily limit if you want to get more cash at once. Note that European ATMs will withdraw funds only from checking accounts, not savings accounts.

**Find out about fees.** For any purchase or withdrawal made with a card, you may be charged a currency conversion fee (1-3 percent) and/or a Visa or MasterCard international transaction fee (less than 1 percent). If you're getting a bad deal, consider getting a new card. Reputable no-fee cards include those from Capital One, as well as Charles Schwab debit cards. Most credit unions and some airline loyalty cards have low or no international transaction fees.

## IN EUROPE
### Using Credit Cards and Payment Apps

**Tap-to-Pay** or **Contactless Cards:** These cards have the usual chip and/or magnetic stripe, but with the addition of a contactless symbol. Simply tap your card against a contactless reader to complete a transaction—no PIN or signature is required. This is by far the easiest way to pay and has become the standard in much of Europe.

**Payment Apps:** Just like at home, you can pay with your smartphone or smartwatch by linking a credit card to an app such as Apple Pay or Google Pay. To pay, hold your phone near a contactless reader; you may need to verify the transaction with a face scan, fingerprint scan, or passcode. If you've arrived in Europe without a tap-to-pay card, you can easily set up your phone to work in this way.

**Other Card Types: Chip-and-PIN** cards have a visible chip embedded in them; rather than swiping, you insert the card into the payment machine, then enter your PIN on a keypad. In Europe, these cards have largely been supplanted by tap-to-pay cards, but you may be asked to use chip-and-pin for certain purchases. **Swipe-and-sign** credit cards—with a swipeable magnetic stripe, and a receipt you have to sign—are increasingly rare.

**Will My US Card Work?** Usually, yes. On rare occasions, at self-service payment machines (such as transit-ticket kiosks, toll-booths, or fuel pumps), some US cards may not work. Usually a tap-to-pay card does the trick in these situations. Just in case, carry cash as a backup and look for a cashier who can process your payment if your card is rejected. Drivers should be prepared to move on to the next gas station if necessary. (In some countries, gas stations sell prepaid gas cards, which you can purchase with any US card). When approaching a toll plaza or ferry ticket line, use the "cash" lane.

## Using Cash

**Cash Machines:** European cash machines work just like they do at home—except they spit out local currency instead of dollars, calculated at the day's standard bank-to-bank rate. In most places, ATMs are easy to locate—in Italy ask for a *bancomat*. When possible, withdraw cash from a bank-run ATM located just outside that bank.

If your debit card doesn't work, try a lower amount—your request may have exceeded your withdrawal limit or the ATM's limit. If you still have a problem, try a different ATM or come back later.

Avoid "independent" ATMs, such as Travelex, Euronet, Moneybox, Your Cash, Cardpoint, and Cashzone. These have high fees, can be less secure, and may try to trick users with "dynamic currency conversion" (see next).

**Dynamic Currency Conversion:** When withdrawing cash at an ATM or paying with a credit card, you'll often be asked whether you want the transaction processed in dollars or in the local currency. Always refuse the conversion and *choose the local currency*. While DCC offers the illusion of convenience, it comes with a poor exchange rate, and you'll wind up losing money.

**Exchanging Cash:** Minimize exchanging money in Europe; it's expensive (you'll generally lose 5 to 10 percent). In a pinch you can find exchange desks at major train stations or airports. Banks generally do not exchange money unless you have an account with them.

## Security Tips

Pickpockets target tourists. Keep your cash, credit cards, and passport secure in your money belt, and carry only a day's spending money in your front pocket or wallet.

Before inserting your card into an ATM, inspect the front. If

PRACTICALITIES

PRACTICALITIES

anything looks crooked, loose, or damaged, it could be a sign of a card-skimming device. When entering your PIN, carefully block other people's view of the keypad.

Avoid using a debit card for purchases. Because a debit card pulls funds directly from your bank account, potential charges incurred by a thief will stay on your account while your bank investigates.

To access your accounts online while traveling, be sure to use a secure connection (see the "Tips on Internet Security" sidebar, later).

## Damage Control for Lost Cards

If you lose your credit or debit card, report the loss immediately to the respective global customer-assistance centers. With a mobile phone, call these 24-hour US numbers: Visa (+1 303 967 1096), MasterCard (+1 636 722 7111), and American Express (+1 336 393 1111). From a landline, you can call these US numbers collect by going through a local operator.

You'll need to provide the primary cardholder's identification-verification details (such as birth date, mother's maiden name, or Social Security number). You can generally receive a temporary card within two or three business days in Europe (see RickSteves.com/help for more).

If you report your loss within two days, you typically won't be responsible for unauthorized transactions on your account, although many banks charge a liability fee.

## TIPPING

Tipping in Italy isn't as automatic and generous as it is in the US. For special service, tips are appreciated, but not expected. As in the US, the proper amount depends on your resources, tipping philosophy, and the circumstances, but some general guidelines apply.

**Restaurants:** In Italy, a service charge *(servizio)* is usually built into your check (look at the bill carefully). If it is included, there's no need to leave an extra tip. If it's not included, it's common to leave about €1 per person (a bit more at finer restaurants) or to round up the bill. If paying with a credit card, be prepared to tip separately with cash or coins; credit card receipts don't often have a tip line. For more details on restaurant tipping, see page 676.

**Taxis:** For a typical ride, round up your fare a bit (for instance, if the fare is €4.50, pay €5). If the cabbie hauls your bags and zips you to the airport to help you catch your flight, you might want to toss in a little more.

**Services:** In general, if someone in the tourism or service industry does a super job for you, a small tip of a euro or two is appropriate...but not required. If you're not sure whether (or how much) to tip, ask a local for advice.

## GETTING A VAT REFUND

Wrapped into the purchase price of your Italian souvenirs is a Value-Added Tax (VAT) of about 22 percent. You're entitled to get most of that tax back if you purchase more than €155 worth of goods at a store that participates in the VAT-refund scheme. Typically, you must ring up the minimum at a single retailer—you can't add up your purchases from various shops to reach the required amount. (If the store ships the goods to your US home, VAT is not assessed on your purchase.)

Getting your refund is straightforward...and worthwhile if you spend a significant amount.

**At the Merchant:** Have the merchant completely fill out the refund document (they'll ask for your passport; a photo of your passport usually works). Keep track of the paperwork and your original sales receipt. Note that you're not supposed to use your purchased goods before you leave Europe.

**At the Border or Airport:** Process your VAT document at your last stop in the European Union (such as at the airport) with the customs agent who deals with VAT refunds (allow plenty of extra time to deal with this process). At some airports, you'll have to go to a customs office to get your documents stamped and then to a separate VAT refund service (such as Global Blue or Planet) to process the refund. At other airports, a single VAT desk handles the whole thing. (Note that refund services typically extract a 4 percent fee, but you're paying for the convenience of receiving your money in cash immediately or as a credit to your card.) Otherwise, you'll need to mail the stamped refund documents to the address given by the merchant.

## CUSTOMS FOR AMERICAN SHOPPERS

You can take home $800 worth of items per person duty-free, once every 31 days. Many processed and packaged foods are allowed, including cheeses, dried herbs, jams, baked goods, candy, chocolate, oil, vinegar, condiments, and honey. Fresh fruits and vegetables and most meats are not allowed, with exceptions for some canned items. As for alcohol, you can bring in one liter duty-free (it can be packed securely in your checked luggage, along with any other liquid-containing items).

To bring alcohol (or liquid-packed foods) in your carry-on bag on your flight home, buy it at a duty-free shop at the airport. You'll increase your odds of getting it onto a connecting flight if it's packaged in a "STEB"—a secure, tamper-evident bag. But stay away from liquids in opaque, ceramic, or metallic containers, which usually cannot be successfully screened (STEB or no STEB).

For details on allowable goods, customs rules, and duty rates, visit http://help.cbp.gov.

# Sightseeing

Sightseeing can be hard work. Use these tips to make your visits to Florence's finest sights meaningful, fun, efficient, and painless.

## MAPS AND NAVIGATION TOOLS

A good map is essential for efficient navigation while sightseeing. The maps in this book are concise and simple, designed to help you locate recommended destinations, sights, hotels, and restaurants. In Europe, simple maps are generally free at TIs and hotels.

You can also use a mapping app on your mobile device, which provides turn-by-turn directions for walking, driving, and taking public transit. Google Maps, Apple Maps, and CityMaps2Go allow you to download maps for offline use; ideally, download the areas you'll need before your trip. For certain features, you'll need to be online—either using Wi-Fi or an international data plan.

## PLAN AHEAD

Set up an itinerary that allows you to fit in all your must-see sights. For a one-stop look at opening hours, see "Florence At a Glance" on page 48 (also see the "Daily Reminder" on page 40). You'll find "Siena at a Glance" on page 368. Most sights keep stable hours, but you can easily confirm the latest by checking at the TI or on museum websites. Or call sights in the morning and ask: "Are you open today?" (*"Aperto oggi?"*; ah-PER-toh OH-jee) and "What time do you close?" (*"A che ora chiude?"*; ah kay OH-rah kee-OO-day).

Don't put off visiting a must-see sight—you never know when a place will close unexpectedly for a holiday, strike, or restoration. Many museums are closed or have reduced hours at least a few days a year, especially on holidays such as Christmas, New Year's *(Capodanno)*, Italian Liberation Day (April 25), Labor Day (May 1), and Ferragosto (Feast of the Assumption, Aug 15). A list of holidays is in the appendix; check for possible closures during your trip. In summer, some sights may stay open late. Off-season hours may be shorter.

Going at the right time helps avoid crowds. This book offers tips on the best times to see specific sights. Try visiting popular sights very early or very late. Evening visits (when possible) are usually more peaceful, with fewer crowds. Late morning is usually the worst time to visit a popular sight.

# Covid Changes: What to Expect Post-Pandemic

The Covid-19 pandemic caused many disruptions and changes to the way museums and other sights operate—some of which were temporary, others of which may turn out to be permanent. Depending on what's happening during your visit, hours may be modified; reservations may be required (or strongly recommended) to control crowd flow; and paper maps and audioguides may have been replaced by apps.

For any must-see sight on your list, check in advance on its official website (listed throughout this book) or the TI's website to fully understand the current situation. You may learn that it's required to prebook, for example, or you may be able to download an app so you'll have an up-to-date museum map and audioguide on your phone when you arrive.

If you plan to hire a local guide, reserve ahead by email. Popular guides can get booked up.

Study up. To get the most out of the self-guided tours and sight descriptions in this book, read them before you visit.

## RESERVATIONS, ADVANCE TICKETS, AND PASSES

Many popular sights in Europe come with long lines—not to get in, but to buy a ticket. Visitors who buy tickets online in advance (or who have a museum pass covering these key sights) can skip the line and waltz right in. Advance tickets are generally timed-entry, meaning you're guaranteed admission on a certain date and time.

For some sights, buying ahead is required (tickets aren't sold at the sight and it's the only way to get in). At other sights, buying ahead is recommended to skip the line and save time. And for many sights, advance tickets are available but unnecessary: At these uncrowded sights you can simply arrive, buy a ticket, and go in.

Don't confuse the reservation options: available, recommended, and required. Use my advice in this book as a guide. Note any must-see sights that sell out long in advance and be prepared to buy tickets early. If you do your research, you'll know the smart strategy.

Given how precious your vacation time is, I'd book in advance both where it's required (as soon as your dates are firm) and where it will save time in a long line (in some cases, you can do this even on the day you plan to visit). If you plan to visit Florence's Uffizi Gallery or Accademia (Michelangelo's *David*), make reservations well in advance (see the Sights in Florence chapter). Reservations are also required to climb the dome of Florence's Duomo (see page 55) and smart for climbing Pisa's Leaning Tower (see page 450).

You'll generally be emailed an eticket with a QR or bar code that you'll store on your phone to scan at the entrance (if you prefer, you can print it out). At the sight, look for the ticket-holders line rather than the ticket-buying line; you may still have to wait in a security line.

Passes and combo-tickets that cover admission to several sights can save time and money (e.g., Florence's Duomo complex passes and the Uffizi/Pitti Palace/Boboli Gardens combo-ticket), though sometimes reservations to included sights are still required or recommended (such as the Duomo's dome and the Uffizi).

Booking a guided tour can help you avoid lines at many popular sights. So can knowing what days to avoid. State museums in Italy are free to enter (and more crowded) once or twice a month, usually on a Sunday. In peak season, check museum websites for specifics and avoid free entry days when possible.

## AT SIGHTS

Here's what you can typically expect:

**Entering:** You may not be allowed to enter if you arrive too close to closing time. And guards start ushering people out well before the actual closing time, so don't save the best for last.

Many sights have a security check. Allow extra time for these lines. Some sights require you to check day packs and coats. (If you'd rather not check your day pack, try carrying it tucked under your arm like a purse as you enter.) Pocketknives may not be allowed.

**Photography:** If the museum's photo policy isn't clearly posted, ask a guard. Generally, taking photos without a flash or tripod is allowed. Some sights ban selfie sticks; others ban photos altogether.

**Audioguides and Apps:** I've produced free, downloadable audio tours for my Florence Renaissance and Siena city walks, as well as my tours of Florence's Accademia, Uffizi, Bargello, and Museum of San Marco; look for the 🎧 in this book. For more on my audio tours, see page 24.

Some sights offer audioguides with excellent recorded descriptions in English. In some cases, you'll rent a device to carry around (if you bring your own plug-in earbuds, you'll enjoy better sound). Increasingly, museums and sights instead offer an app you can download with their audioguide (often free; check websites from home and considering downloading in advance as not all sights offer free Wi-Fi hotspots).

**Temporary Exhibits:** Museums may show special exhibits in addition to their permanent collection. Some exhibits are included in the entry price, while others come at an extra cost (which you may have to pay even if you don't want to see the exhibit).

**Expect Changes:** Artwork can be on tour, on loan, out sick, or shifted at the whim of the curator. Pick up a floor plan as you enter, and ask the museum staff if you can't find a particular item. Say the title or artist's name, or point to the photograph in this book and ask, *"Dov'è?"* (doh-VEH, meaning "Where is?").

**Dates for Artwork:** Art historians and Italians refer to the great Florentine centuries by dropping a thousand years. The Trecento (300s), Quattrocento (400s), and Cinquecento (500s) were the 1300s, 1400s, and 1500s. The Novecento (900s) means modern art (the 1900s). In Italian museums, art is dated with *sec* for *secolo* (century, often indicated with Roman numerals), AC (*avanti Cristo,* or BC), and DC (*dopo Cristo,* or AD). OK?

**Services:** Important sights usually have a reasonably priced on-site café or cafeteria (handy air-conditioned places to rejuvenate during a long visit). The WCs at sights are free and generally clean.

**Before Leaving:** At the gift shop, scan the postcard rack or thumb through a guidebook to be sure you haven't overlooked something that you'd like to see. Every sight or museum offers more than what is covered in this book. Use the information I provide as an introduction—not the final word.

## FIND RELIGION

Churches offer some amazing art (usually free), a cool respite from heat, and a welcome seat.

A modest dress code—no bare shoulders or shorts for anyone, even kids—is enforced at larger churches—such as the Duomo in both Florence and Siena—but is often overlooked elsewhere. If you're caught by surprise, you can sometimes improvise, using maps to cover your shoulders and a jacket for your knees. A few major churches let you borrow or buy disposable ponchos to cover up in a pinch. (I wear a super-lightweight pair of long pants rather than shorts for my hot and muggy Italian sightseeing.) If your heart's set on seeing a certain church, err on the side of caution and dress appropriately.

Some churches have coin-operated boxes that trigger lights to illuminate works of art. I pop in a coin whenever I can, to improve my experience (and photos), as a small contribution to that church, and as a courtesy to other visitors enjoying this great art. Whenever possible, let there be light.

# Sleeping

Extensive and opinionated listings of good-value rooms are a major feature of this book's Sleeping sections. Rather than list accommodations scattered throughout a town, I choose hotels in my favorite neighborhoods that are convenient to your sightseeing.

My recommendations run the gamut, from dorm beds to luxurious rooms with all of the comforts. I like places that are clean, central, relatively quiet at night, reasonably priced, friendly, small enough to have a hands-on owner or manager, and run with a respect for Italian traditions. I'm more impressed by a handy location and a fun-loving philosophy than oversized TVs and a fancy gym. Most of my recommendations fall short of perfection. But if I can find a place with most of these features, it's a keeper.

Book your accommodations as soon as your itinerary is set, especially if you want to stay at one of my top listings or if you'll be traveling during busy times. See the appendix for a list of major holidays and festivals in Italy.

Some people make reservations a few days ahead as they travel. This approach fosters spontaneity, and booking sites make it easy to find available rooms, but—especially during busy times—you run the risk of settling for lesser-value accommodations.

## RATES AND DEALS

I've categorized my recommended accommodations based on price, indicated with a dollar-sign rating (see sidebar). Room prices can fluctuate significantly with demand and amenities (size, views, room class, and so on), but relative price categories remain constant.

Taxes vary from place to place (in Florence, figure between €2-5 per person, per night).

**Booking Direct:** Once your dates are set, compare prices at several hotels. You can do this by checking hotel websites and booking sites such as Hotels.com or Booking.com. After you've zeroed in on your choice, book directly with the hotel itself. This increases the chances that the hotelier will be able to accommodate special needs or requests (such as shifting your reservation). And when you book on the hotel's website, by email, or by phone, the owner avoids the commission paid to booking sites, giving them wiggle room to offer you a discount, a nicer room, or a free breakfast (if it's not already included).

**Getting a Discount:** Some hotels extend a discount to those who pay cash or stay longer than three nights. And some accommodations offer a special discount for Rick Steves readers, indicated in this guidebook by the abbreviation **"RS%."** Discounts vary: Ask for details when you reserve. Generally, to qualify for

# Sleep Code

Hotels in this book are categorized according to the average price of a standard double room with breakfast in high season.

| | | |
|---|---|---|
| **$$$$** | **Splurge:** | Most rooms over €170 |
| **$$$** | **Pricier:** | €130-170 |
| **$$** | **Moderate:** | €90-130 |
| **$** | **Budget:** | €50-90 |
| **¢** | **Backpacker:** | Under €50 |
| **RS%** | **Rick Steves discount** | |

Unless otherwise noted, credit cards are accepted, hotel staff speak basic English, and free Wi-Fi is available. Comparison-shop by checking prices at several hotels (on each hotel's own website, on a booking site, or by email). For the best deal, *book directly with the hotel.* Ask for a discount if paying in cash; if the listing includes **RS%,** request a Rick Steves discount.

this discount, you must book direct (not through a booking site), mention this book when you reserve, show this book upon arrival, and sometimes pay cash or stay a certain number of nights. In some cases, you may need to enter a discount code (which I've provided in the listing) in the booking form on the hotel's website. Rick Steves discounts apply to readers with either print or digital books. Understandably, discounts do not apply to promotional rates.

## TYPES OF ACCOMMODATIONS
### Hotels

In Florence, you can snare a spartan, clean, and comfortable double with breakfast and a private bath for about €100. You get near-elegance in peak season for €170.

Some hotels can add an extra bed (for a small charge) to turn a double into a triple; some offer larger rooms for four or more people (I call these "family rooms" in the listings). If there's space for an extra cot, they'll cram it in for you. In general, a triple room is cheaper than the cost of a double and a single. Three or four people can economize by requesting one big room.

**Arrival and Check-In:** Hotels and B&Bs are sometimes located on the higher floors of a multipurpose building with a secured door. In that case, look for your hotel's name on the buttons by the main entrance. When you ring the bell, you'll be buzzed in.

Hotel elevators are common, though small, and some older buildings still lack them. You may have to climb a flight of stairs to reach the elevator (if so, you can ask the front desk for help carrying your bags up).

The EU requires hotels to collect your name, nationality, and ID number. At check-in, the receptionist will normally ask for your

# Using Online Services to Your Advantage

From booking services to user reviews, online businesses play a greater role in travelers' planning than ever before. Take advantage of their pluses—and be wise to their downsides.

## Booking Sites

Booking websites such as Booking.com and Hotels.com offer one-stop shopping for hotels. While convenient for travelers, they're both a blessing and a curse for small, independent, family-run hotels. Without a presence on these sites, small hotels become almost invisible. But to be listed, a hotel must pay a sizable commission...and promise that its own website won't undercut the price on the booking-service site.

Here's the work-around: Use the big sites to research what's out there, then book directly with the hotel by email or phone, in which case hotel owners are free to give you whatever price they like. Ask for a room without the commission markup (or ask for a free breakfast if not included, or a free upgrade). If you do book online, be sure to use the hotel's own website. The price will likely be the same as via a booking site, but your money goes to the hotel, not agency commissions.

As a savvy consumer, remember: When you book with an online service, you're adding a middleman who takes a cut. To support small, family-run hotels whose world is more difficult than ever, book direct.

## Short-Term Rental Sites

Rental juggernaut Airbnb (along with other short-term rental sites) allows travelers to rent rooms and apartments, often providing more value, space, and amenities than a cookie-cutter hotel. Airbnb fans appreciate feeling part of a real neighborhood and getting into a daily routine as "temporary Europeans." Some places are run by thoughtful hosts, allowing you to get to know a local and keep the money in the community; but beware: others are impersonally managed by large, absentee agencies.

passport and may keep it for several hours. If you're not comfortable leaving your passport at the desk, bring a copy to give them instead.

If you're arriving in the morning, your room probably won't be ready. Check your bag safely at the hotel and dive right into sightseeing.

**In Your Room:** Most hotel rooms have a TV and free Wi-Fi, which can vary in strength and quality. Simpler places rarely have a room phone. Pricier hotels usually come with a small fridge stocked with beverages, called a *frigo bar* (FREE-goh bar; pay for what you use).

Nearly all places offer private bathrooms, which have a tub or shower, a toilet, and a bidet (which Italians use for quick sponge

Critics of Airbnb see it as a threat to "traditional Europe." Landlords can make more money renting to short-stay travelers, driving rents up—and local residents out. Traditional businesses are replaced by ones that cater to tourists. And the character and charm that made those neighborhoods desirable to the tourists in the first place goes too. Some cities have cracked down, requiring owners to obtain a license and to occupy rental properties part of the year (and staging disruptive "inspections" that inconvenience guests).

As a lover of Europe, I share the worry of those who see residents nudged aside by tourists. But as an advocate for travelers, I appreciate the value Airbnb can provide in offering the chance to stay in a local building or neighborhood with potentially fewer tourists.

## User Reviews

User-generated review sites and apps such as Yelp and TripAdvisor can give you a consensus of opinions about everything from hotels and restaurants to sights and nightlife. If you scan reviews of a restaurant or hotel and see several complaints about noise or a rotten location, you've gained insight that can help in your decision-making.

As a guidebook writer, my sense is that there is a big difference between the uncurated information on a review site and the vetted listings in a guidebook. A user review is based on the limited experience of one person, who stayed at just one hotel in a given city and ate at a few restaurants there. A guidebook is the work of a trained researcher who forms a well-developed basis for comparison by visiting many restaurants and hotels year after year.

Both types of information have their place, and in many ways, they're complementary. If something is well reviewed in a guidebook and it also gets good online reviews, it's likely a winner.

baths). The cord over the tub or shower is not a clothesline. You pull it when you've fallen and can't get up.

Double beds are called *matrimoniale*, even though hotels aren't interested in your marital status. Twins are *due letti singoli*. Convents offer cheap accommodation but have more *letti singoli* than *matrimoniali*.

**Breakfast and Meals:** Italian hotels typically include breakfast in their room prices. If breakfast is optional, you may want to skip it. While convenient, it's usually pricey for what you get: a simple continental buffet with (at its most generous) bread, croissants, ham, cheese, yogurt, and unlimited *caffè latte*. It's cheaper—and much more Italian—to head to the corner café for a sweet roll

## Keep Cool

If you're visiting Italy in the summer, you'll want an air-conditioned room. Most hotel air-conditioners come with a remote control that generally has similar symbols and features: fan icon (click to toggle through wind power, from light to gale); temperature (20 degrees Celsius is comfortable); louver icon (choose steady airflow or waves); snowflake and sunshine icons (cold air or heat); and clock ("O" setting: run X hours before turning off; "I" setting: wait X hours to start). When you leave your room for the day, do as the environmentally conscious Europeans do, and turn off the air-conditioning.

and coffee and stand at the counter. If you need a bigger breakfast, have a little picnic in your room before heading out.

**Checking Out:** While it's customary to pay for your room upon departure, it can be a good idea to settle your bill the day before, when you're not in a hurry and while the manager's in.

**Hotelier Help:** Hoteliers can be a good source of advice. Most know their city well and can assist you with everything from public transit and airport connections to finding a good restaurant, the nearest launderette, or a late-night pharmacy.

**Hotel Hassles:** Even at the best places, mechanical breakdowns occur: Sinks leak, hot water turns cold, toilets may gurgle or smell, the Wi-Fi goes out, or the air-conditioning dies when you need it most. Report your concerns clearly and calmly at the front desk.

If you find that night noise is a problem (if, for instance, your room is over a nightclub or facing a busy street), ask for a quieter room in the back or on an upper floor.

To guard against theft in your room, keep valuables out of sight. Some rooms come with a safe, and other hotels have safes at the front desk. I've never bothered using one and, in a lifetime of travel, I've never had anything stolen out of my room.

For more complicated problems, don't expect instant results. Above all, keep a positive attitude. Remember, you're on vacation. If your hotel is a disappointment, spend more time out enjoying the place you came to see.

## Bed-and-Breakfasts

B&Bs can offer good-value accommodations in excellent locations. Usually converted family homes or apartments, they can range from humble rooms with communal kitchens to high-end boutique accommodations with extra amenities. Boutique B&Bs can be an especially good option, as they are typically less expensive than a big hotel, but often newer and nicer, with more personal service.

Because the B&B scene is constantly changing, it's smart to supplement this book's recommendations with your own research.

## Short-Term Rentals

A short-term rental—whether an apartment, a house, or a room in a private residence—is a popular alternative, especially if you plan to settle in one location for several nights. For stays longer than a few days, you can usually find a rental that's comparable to—and even cheaper than—a hotel room with similar amenities. Plus, you'll get a behind-the-scenes peek into how locals live.

Many places require a minimum-night stay and have strict cancellation policies. And you're generally on your own: There's no reception desk, breakfast, or daily cleaning service.

**Finding Accommodations:** Websites such as Airbnb, FlipKey, Booking.com, and VRBO let you browse a wide range of properties. Alternatively, rental agencies such as InterhomeUSA.com or RentaVilla.com can provide a more personalized service (their curated listings are also more expensive). Or try Cross-Pollinate, a booking service for private rooms and apartments in the old centers of Florence, Rome, and Venice; rates start at €35 per person (www.cross-pollinate.com).

Before you commit, be clear on the location. I like to virtually "explore" the neighborhood using Google Street View. Also consider the proximity to public transportation, and how well connected the property is with the rest of the city. Ask about amenities (elevator, air-conditioning, laundry, Wi-Fi, parking, etc.). Reviews from previous guests can help identify trouble spots.

Think about the kind of experience you want: Just a key and an affordable bed...or a chance to get to know a local? Some hosts offer self check-in and minimal contact; others enjoy interacting with you. Read the description and reviews to help shape your decision.

**Confirming and Paying:** Many places require payment in full before your trip, usually through the listing site. Be wary of owners who want to take your transaction offline; this gives you no recourse if things go awry. Never agree to wire money (a key indicator of a fraudulent transaction).

**Apartments or Houses:** If you're staying in one place several nights, it's worth considering an apartment or rental house (shorter stays aren't worth the hassle of arranging key pickup, buying groceries, etc.). Apartment or house rentals can be especially cost-effective for groups and families. European apartments, like hotel rooms, tend to be small by US standards. But they often come with laundry facilities and small, equipped kitchens *(cucinetta)*, making it easier and cheaper to dine in.

**Rooms in Private Homes:** In small towns, there may be few hotels or apartments, but an abundance of Airbnb rentals and

# Making Hotel Reservations

Reserve your rooms as soon as you've pinned down your travel dates. For busy national holidays, it's wise to reserve far in advance (see the appendix).

**Requesting a Reservation:** For family-run hotels, it's generally best to book your room directly via email or phone. For business-class and chain hotels, or if you'd rather book online, reserve directly through the hotel's official website (not a booking website). Almost all of my recommended hotels take reservations in English.

Here's what the hotelier wants to know:

- Type(s) of room(s) you want and number of guests
- Number of nights you'll stay
- Arrival and departure dates, written European-style as day/month/year (for example, 18/06/24 or 18 June 2024)
- Special requests (en suite bathroom, cheapest room, twin beds vs. double bed, quiet room)
- Applicable discounts (such as a Rick Steves discount, cash discount, or promotional rate)

**Confirming a Reservation:** Most places will request a credit-card number to hold your room. If the hotel's website doesn't have a secure form where you can enter the number directly, share this info via a phone call.

**Canceling a Reservation:** If you must cancel, it's courteous—and smart—to do so with as much notice as possible, especially for

---

some *affittacamere* (rental rooms). These can be anything from a set of keys and a basic bed to a cozy B&B with your own Tuscan grandmother. Renting a room in someone's home is a good option for those traveling alone, as you're more likely to find true single rooms—with just one single bed, and a price to match. Beds range from air-mattress-in-living-room basic to plush-B&B-suite posh. While you can't expect your host to also be your tour guide—or even to provide you with much info—some are interested in getting to know the travelers who pass through their home.

**Other Options:** Swapping homes with a local works for people with an appealing place to offer (don't assume where you live is not interesting to Europeans). Good places to start are HomeExchange.com and LoveHomeSwap.com. To sleep for free, Couchsurfing.com is a vagabond's alternative to Airbnb. It lists millions of outgoing members who host fellow "surfers" in their homes.

## Agriturismi

*Agriturismi*—working farms that double as countryside B&Bs—

| From: | rick@ricksteves.com |
|---|---|
| Sent: | Today |
| To: | info@hotelcentral.com |
| Subject: | Reservation request for 19-22 July |

Dear Hotel Central,

I would like to stay at your hotel. Please let me know if you have a room available and the price for:
• 2 people
• Double bed and en suite bathroom in a quiet room
• Arriving 19 July, departing 22 July (3 nights)

Thank you!
Rick Steves

smaller family-run places. Cancellation policies can be strict; read the fine print before you book. Many discount deals require pre-payment and can be expensive to change or cancel.

**Reconfirming a Reservation:** Always call or email to reconfirm your room reservation a few days in advance. For B&Bs or very small hotels, I call again on my arrival day to tell my host what time to expect me (especially important if arriving late—after 17:00).

**Phoning:** For tips on calling hotels overseas, see page 692.

began cropping up in the 1980s to allow small family farms to survive (as in the US, many have been squeezed out by giant agribusinesses). By renting rooms to travelers, farmers receive generous tax breaks that allow them to remain on their land and continue to grow food crops. These B&Bs make a peaceful home base for those exploring rural Italy, and are ideal for those traveling by car—especially families.

It's wise to book several months in advance for high season (late May-mid-Oct). July and August are jammed with Italians and other European vacationers; in spring and fall, it's mostly Americans. Weeklong stays (typically Saturday to Saturday) are preferred at busy times, but shorter stays are possible off-season. To sleep cheaper, try early spring and late fall. Most places are closed in winter (about Nov-Easter).

As the name implies, *agriturismi* are in the countryside, although some are located on the outskirts of a large town or city. Most are family-run. *Agriturismi* vary dramatically in quality—some properties are rustic, while others are downright luxurious, offering amenities such as swimming pools and riding stables. The

## Tips for Enjoying an *Agriturismo* Farmhouse Stay

- To sleep cheap, avoid peak season. Rental prices follow the old rule of supply and demand. Prices that are sky-high in summer can drop dramatically in early spring and late fall.

- Make sure your trip fits their requirements. Many properties rent on a traditional Saturday-to-Saturday time period. You might be unable to rent for a different or shorter time, especially during peak season.
- If you want amenities, be willing to pay more. A swimming pool can add substantially to the cost, but at the height of summer, could be worth every extra euro, particularly if you're bringing kids.
- Consider renting a rural apartment rather than an entire villa or farmhouse. Often the owners have renovated an original rambling farmhouse or medieval estate into a series of well-constructed apartments with private kitchens, bathrooms, living areas, and outdoor terraces. They usually share a common pool.
- You will need a rental car to fully enjoy—or even reach—your accommodations.
- To make the most of your time, ask an expert—the owner—for suggestions on restaurants, sights, and activities. Make sure you know how to operate the appliances.
- Slow down. One of the joys of staying for at least a week in one location is that you can develop a true *dolce far niente* (sweetness of doing nothing) attitude. If it rains, grab a book from the in-house library and curl up on the sofa.
- While your time in the countryside may not be action-packed, staying put in one spot leaves you open to the unexpected pleasures that come when you just let the days unwind without a plan.

rooms are usually clean and comfortable. Breakfast is often included, and *mezza pensione* (half-pension, which in this case means a home-cooked dinner) might be built into the price whether you want it or not. Most places serve tasty homegrown food; some are vegetarian or organic, others are gourmet. Kitchenettes are often available to cook up your own feast.

To qualify officially as an *agriturismo*, the farm must still generate more money from its farm activities, thereby ensuring that the land is worked and preserved. Some farmhouse B&Bs aren't working farms, but are still fine places to stay. Some travelers who are enticed by romanticized dreams of *agriturismi* are turned off when they arrive to actual farm smells and sounds. These folks would be more comfortable with a countryside B&B or villa that offers a bit more upscale comfort. In this book, I've listed both types of rural accommodations; if you want the real thing, make sure the owners call their place an *agriturismo*.

In addition to my listings, local TIs can give you a list of places in their area. For a sampling, visit www.agriturismoitaly.it or search online for *agriturismo*. One booking agency among many is Farm Holidays in Tuscany (closed Sat-Sun, tel. 0564-417-418, www.byfarmholidays.com, info@byfarmholidays.com).

## Hostels

A hostel provides cheap beds in dorms where you sleep alongside strangers for about €25-30 per night. Travelers of any age are welcome if they don't mind dorm-style accommodations and meeting other travelers. Most hostels offer kitchen facilities, guest computers, Wi-Fi, and a self-service laundry. Hostels almost always provide bedding, but the towel's up to you (though you can usually rent one). Family and private rooms are often available.

**Independent hostels** tend to be easygoing, colorful, and informal (no membership required; www.hostelworld.com). You may pay slightly less by booking directly with the hostel. **Official hostels** are part of Hostelling International (HI) and share a booking site (www.hihostels.com). HI hostels typically require that you be a member or else pay a bit more per night.

# Eating

The Italians are masters of the art of fine living. That means eating long and well. Lengthy, multicourse meals and endless hours sitting in outdoor cafés are the norm. Americans eat on their way to an evening event and complain if the check is slow in coming. For Italians, the meal is an end in itself, and only rude servers rush you.

I've written an entire book (with co-author Fred Plotkin) on the subject: *Rick Steves Italy for Food Lovers*, a region-by-region handbook on how to appreciate Italian cuisine like an Italian. This section condenses that book's most valuable tips and insights.

A highlight of your Italian adventure will be this country's cafés, cuisine, and wines. Trust me: This is sightseeing for your palate. Even if you liked dorm food and are sleeping in cheap hotels, your taste buds will relish an occasional first-class splurge. You can eat well without going broke. But be careful: You're just as likely

## Restaurant Code

Eateries in this book are categorized according to the average cost of a higher-end pasta or typical main course. Drinks, desserts, and splurge items can raise the price considerably.

**$$$$**   **Splurge:** Most main courses over €25
**$$$**   **Pricier:** €20-25
**$$**   **Moderate:** €15-20
**$**   **Budget:** Under €15

Pizza by the slice and other takeaway food is **$**; a basic trattoria or sit-down pizzeria is **$$**; a casual but more upscale restaurant is **$$$**; and a swanky splurge is **$$$$**.

to blow a small fortune on a disappointing meal as you are to dine wonderfully for €25. Your euros typically will go much further, and will net you far better food, in smaller Tuscan towns than in Florence. Rely on my recommendations in the Eating in Florence chapter and under the "Eating" sections in other destinations.

In general, Italians start their day with a light breakfast (*prima colazione*; coffee—usually cappuccino or espresso—and a pastry, often eaten while standing at a counter). Lunch (*pranzo*) was traditionally the largest meal of the day, eaten at home between 13:00 and 15:00 (earlier in northern Italy, later in the south). Dinner (*cena*) was a lighter affair, often just soup with cold cuts, eaten around 20:00 or 21:00 (maybe earlier in winter).

However, as times have changed, so have eating habits. So, while some Italian families still have a big lunch and a small dinner, others do the reverse. Many Italian urbanites grab a quick lunch in a *tavola calda* bar (cafeteria) or buy a *panino* or *tramezzino* (sandwich). To bridge the gap until dinner, people drop into a bar in the late afternoon for a cocktail (*aperitivo*), often served with snacks.

## RESTAURANT PRICING

I've categorized my recommended eateries based on the average price of a typical main course, indicated with a dollar-sign rating (see sidebar). Obviously, expensive specialties, fine wine, appetizers, and dessert can significantly increase your final bill.

The categories also indicate the personality of a place: **Budget** eateries include street food, takeaway, order-at-the-counter shops, basic cafeterias, and bakeries selling sandwiches. **Moderate** eateries are nice (but not fancy) sit-down restaurants, ideal for a pleasant meal with good-quality food. Most of my listings fall in this category—great for a taste of the local cuisine at a reasonable price.

**Pricier** eateries are a notch up, with more attention paid to the setting, presentation, and (often inventive) cuisine. **Splurge** eateries are dress-up-for-a-special-occasion swanky—typically with an elegant setting, polished service, and pricey and refined cuisine.

## BREAKFAST

Italian breakfasts, like Italian bath towels, can be small: The basic, traditional version is coffee and a roll with butter and marmalade. Many places have yogurt and juice (in season, look for *spremuta d'arancia rossa*—fresh-squeezed juice from Sicilian blood oranges), and possibly also cereal, cold cuts and sliced cheese, and eggs (typically hard-boiled; scrambled or fried eggs are less common). Small budget hotels may leave a basic breakfast in your room (stale croissant, roll, jam, yogurt, coffee).

If you want to skip your hotel breakfast, consider browsing for a morning picnic at a local open-air market. Or do as the Italians do: Step into a bar or café to drink a cappuccino and munch a *cornetto* (croissant) while standing at the counter. While the *cornetto* is the most common pastry, you'll find a range of *pasticcini* (pastries, sometimes called *dolci*—sweets). Look for *otto* (an 8-shaped pastry, often filled with custard, jam, or chocolate), *sfoglia* (filo-dough crust that's fruit-filled, like a turnover), or *ciambella* (doughnut filled with custard or chocolate)—or ask about local specialties.

## ITALIAN RESTAURANTS

In Italy, *ristorante* typically means a high-end, sit-down restaurant. A *trattoria* is a notch below a *ristorante* in price, but the food is often just as good, if not better. An *osteria*, which originated as a place to drink wine accompanied by food, is similar. *Trattorie* and *osterie* are generally family-owned and serve home-cooked meals at moderate prices. A *locanda* is an inn, a *cantina* is a wine cellar, and a *birreria* is a brewpub. *Pizzerie, rosticcerie* (delis), *enoteche* (wine bars), and other alternatives are explained later.

I look for restaurants that are convenient to your hotel and sightseeing. When restaurant-hunting, choose a spot filled with locals, not the place with the big neon signs boasting, "We speak English and accept credit cards." Restaurants parked on famous squares generally serve bad food at high prices to tourists. Venturing even a block or two off the main drag leads to higher-quality food for a better price. Locals eat better at lower-rent locales. Family-run places operate without hired help and can offer cheaper meals.

Most restaurant kitchens close between their lunch and dinner service. Good restaurants don't reopen for dinner before 19:00. If you arrive at opening time, most restaurants will be empty and available—the main push of customers arrives later. Small restaurants with a full slate of reservations for 20:30 or 21:00 often will accommodate walk-in diners willing to eat a quick, early meal, but you aren't expected to linger.

When you want the bill, mime-scribble on your raised palm or request it: *"Il conto, per favore."* You may have to ask more than once. If you're in a hurry, request the check when you receive the last item you order.

## Cover and Tipping

Avoid surprises when eating out by familiarizing yourself with two common Italian restaurant charges: *coperto* and *servizio*. You won't encounter them in all restaurants, but both charges, if assessed, by law must be listed on the menu.

The *coperto* (cover) is a minor fee (€1.50-3/person) covering the cost of the linens, cutlery, and typical basket of bread found on your table. (It's sometimes called *pane e coperto*—"bread and cover.") It's not negotiable, even if you don't eat the bread. And it's not a tip. Think of it as a fee paid to the owner entitling you to use the table for as long as you like.

The *servizio* is a 10- to 15-percent "service" charge that goes to the server (similar to the mandatory gratuity that American restaurants often add for groups of six or more). These days, most Italian restaurants don't charge this separately; rather, they include service in their prices—you'll see *servizio compreso* or *servizio incluso* on the menu. (At places that do levy a separate *servizio* charge, you don't need to leave an additional tip.)

Italian servers are well paid and are not as reliant on additional **tips** as servers are back home. Even so, if you're pleased with the service, it's polite to add a small tip *(una mancia)*. This is much smaller than the standard 20 percent in the US. A common tip at a simple restaurant or pizzeria is €1 per person (or simply round up the bill); at a finer restaurant, leave a few euros per person. While you could leave coins on the table, it's classier to simply round up the bill when paying. (For instance, if the bill is €46, hand the server €50 and tell them to keep the change.) If paying with a credit card, be prepared to tip separately with cash or coins; credit card receipts don't have a tip line.

## Italian Menu Courses

A full Italian meal consists of multiple courses.

**Antipasto:** An appetizer such as *salumi* (cured meats including salami and prosciutto), cheeses, bruschetta, grilled veggies, or deep-fried tasties. To get a sampler plate of *salumi* and cheeses in a restaurant, look for *affettato misto* (mixed *salumi*), *antipasto misto* (*salumi*, cheeses, and marinated vegetables), or *tagliere* (a sampler "board"). This could make a light meal in itself.

**Primo piatto:** A "first dish" generally consisting of pasta, soup, rice (usually risotto), or polenta. If you think of pasta when you think of Italian food, you can dine well here without ever going beyond the *primo*.

**Secondo piatto:** A "second dish" of meat or fish/seafood. Italians freely admit the *secondo* is the least interesting part of their cuisine.

**Contorno:** A vegetable side dish may come with the *secondo* but more often must be ordered separately. Typical *contorni* are *insalata mista* (mixed salad), spinach, roasted potatoes, or grilled veggies. This can be an interesting, if overlooked, part of the menu. Vegetarians can skip the *secondo* and order several *contorni* to make a meal.

**Dolce:** No meal is complete without a sweet. On most menus, you'll find typical Italian desserts such as tiramisu and *panna cotta*, or other local favorites. Servers are accustomed to diners splitting a single dessert—just ask for extra forks. Fruit *(frutta)* is often eaten as a dessert, often in the form of *macedonia* (a mixed-fruit salad). A shot of espresso *(un caffè)* is typically served after dessert. (Or skip the restaurant dessert and wander around licking a cone of gelato.)

## Ordering Tips

For most travelers, a complete, multicourse meal is simply too much food—and the euros can add up in a hurry. To avoid overeating (and to stretch your budget), share dishes. A good rule of thumb is for each person to order two courses. For example, a couple can order and share one *antipasto*, one *primo*, one *secondo*, and one dessert; or two *antipasti* and two *primi*; or whatever combination appeals. Small groups can mix *antipasti* and *primi* family-style (skipping *secondi*).

It can be worth paying a little more for an inventive fixed-price meal that shows off the chef's creativity. A *menù turistico* is a made-for-tourists plate of Italian food clichés for one fixed price. But locals have their own, typically more interesting version, usually called a *prezzo fisso* or sometimes *menù del giorno* (menu of the day). For a smaller appetite, some restaurants serve a *piatto unico*, with smaller portions of each course on one plate (for instance, a meat, starch, and vegetable).

Seafood and steak may be sold by weight and priced by the *etto* (100 grams, 3.5 ounces) or the kilo (1,000 grams, 2.2 pounds). The abbreviation *s.q. (secondo quantità)* indicates an item is priced by weight (often used at antipasto buffets). Unless the menu indicates a fillet *(filetto)*, fish is usually served whole with the head and tail. You can always ask your server to select a small fish and fillet it for you. Sometimes, especially for steak, restaurants require a minimum order of four or five *etti* (which diners can share). Make sure you're clear on the price before ordering.

Some dishes come in larger quantities meant to be shared by two people. The shorthand way of showing this on a menu is "X2" (for two), but the price listed could indicate the cost per person.

If you order only a pasta and a salad, the server may bring them in that order, which is the opposite of what you might expect; astute severs ask if you want it *insieme* (een-see-EH-meh; together).

Because pasta and bread are both starches, Italians consider them redundant. If you order only a pasta dish, bread may not come with it; you can request it, but you may be charged extra. On the other hand, if you order a vegetable antipasto or a meat *secondo,* bread is often provided to balance the ingredients.

At places with counter service—such as at a bar or a freeway rest-stop diner—you'll first order and pay at the *cassa* (cashier). Then take your receipt to the counter to claim your food.

When going to an especially good restaurant with an approachable staff, I like to find out what they're eager to serve. Sometimes I'll simply say "Make me happy"...and set a price limit.

## BUDGET EATING

Italy offers many budget options for hungry travelers. Self-service cafeterias offer the basics without add-on charges. Travelers on a hard-core budget equip their room with a pantry stocked at the market (fruits and veggies are remarkably cheap), or pick up a sandwich or *döner kebab,* then dine in at picnic prices. Bars and cafés are also good places to grab a meal on the go.

### Pizzerias

Italians head to a pizzeria at dinnertime to order a one-person pie. Some shops sell *pizza rustica* (also called *pizza al taglio* or *pizza al trancio*)—thick pizza baked in a large rectangular pan and sold by weight. This, rather than floppy New York-style slices, is the standard option for Italians on the go. If you simply ask for a piece, you may wind up with a gigantic slab and be charged top euro. Instead, clearly indicate how much you want: *un etto*— 100 grams—is a hot and cheap snack; *due etti*—200 grams—

makes a light meal. Or show the size with your hands: *tanto così* (TAHN-toh koh-ZEE; this much). They may ask if you want it *riscaldata* (ree-skahl-DAH-tah; heated up). The correct answer is *sì*. For a rundown of common types of pizza, see that section, later. Pizzerias also sell *cecina,* a savory crêpe-like garbanzo-bean flatbread—a cheap snack that pairs well with a glass of red wine.

## Bars/Cafés

An Italian bar isn't so much a tavern as an inexpensive café. These neighborhood hangouts serve coffee, light food, and drinks from the cooler. This is where locals go for a breakfast of cappuccino and *cornetto* (croissant). Throughout the day, bars are the place to drop in for a coffee or another drink.

Many bars are small—if you can't find a table, you'll need to stand or find a ledge to sit on outside. Most charge extra for table service. To get food to go, say, *"da portar via"* (for the road). All bars have a WC *(toilette, bagno)* in the back, available to customers...and the discreet public.

**Food:** For quick meals, bars usually have trays of cheap, pre-made sandwiches (*panini,* on a baguette; *piadine,* on flatbread; *tramezzini,* on crustless white bread; or *toasts,* on, well, toast)—some are delightful grilled. (Others have too much mayo.) In bigger cities, they'll have a variety of salads ready to serve up from under the glass counter. To save time for sightseeing and room for dinner, stop by a bar for a light lunch, such as a ham-and-cheese sandwich—ideally thrown on the grill to heat up.

**Ordering:** If the bar isn't busy, you can probably just order and pay when you leave. Otherwise, there's a particular procedure: First look around to decide what you want, then go to cashier *(la cassa)* to order and pay. Often, a list with two sets of prices is posted near the cashier: *al banco* (standing at the bar) or *al tavolo* (seated). Unless you really plan to settle in and watch the world go by, have your drink at the bar. If you're not sure, you can ask, "Same price if I sit or stand?": *"Costa uguale al tavolo o al banco?"* (KOH-stah oo-GWAH-lay ahl TAH-voh-loh oh ahl BAHN-koh).

Upon paying, you're handed a receipt *(scontrino).* Take that to the bartender (whose clean fingers handle no dirty euros) and tell them what you want. It's customary to set a small coin or two on the bar, as a tip, when you place your order. Throughout Italy, you can get cheap coffee at the bar of any establishment, no matter how fancy, and pay the same low, government-regulated price (generally about a euro if you stand).

## Rosticcerie

For a fast and cheap lunch, find an Italian variation on the corner deli: a *rosticceria* ("roasting place," specializing in roasted meats and accompanying sides, such as roasted potatoes or sautéed greens). For a healthy light meal, ask for a mixed plate of vegetables with a hunk of mozzarella (*piatto misto di verdure con mozzarella;* pee-AH-toh MEE-stoh dee vehr-DOO-ray). Don't be limited by what's displayed. If you'd like a salad with a slice of cantaloupe and some cheese, they'll whip that up for you in a snap. Belly up to the bar; with a pointing finger, you can assemble a fine meal. If something's a mystery, ask for *un assaggio* (oon ah-SAH-joh) to get a little taste. To have your choices warmed up, ask for them to be heated (*riscaldata;* ree-skahl-DAH-tah).

## Wine Bars

Wine bars *(enoteche)* are a popular, fast, and generally inexpensive option for lunch. Meaning "wine library," an *enoteca* is usually a bar highlighting local wines, accompanied with well-paired light food (such as *salumi* and cheese, a salad, or simple seasonal dishes). A good *enoteca* aims to impress visitors with its wine—look for a blackboard listing today's selection and price per glass. The food prices can add up—be careful with your ordering to keep this a budget choice). For more on Italian cocktails and wines, see page 688.

## Aperitivo Snacks ("Apericena")

The Italian term *aperitivo* means a predinner drink, but it's also used to describe their version of what we might call happy hour: a light buffet of snacks that many bars serve to customers during the predinner hours (typically around 18:00 or 19:00 until 21:00). The drink itself may not be cheap (typically around €8-12), but some bars lay out an enticing array of *salumi,* cheeses, grilled vegetables, and other *antipasti*-type dishes. (Really good spreads earn the nickname "*apericena*"—a pun combining *aperitivo* and *cena,* dinner.) You're welcome to nibble while you nurse your drink.

The *apericena* is intended as an appetizer course before heading out for dinner: You're invited to have a couple of hearty snacks with each drink you pay for. For light eaters who've had a too-big lunch, this could wind up being enough to skip dinner. Drop by a few bars around this time to scope out their buffets before choosing. Or opt for a place with a big view and simpler snacks—either way, you'll get your money's worth.

## Markets, Groceries, and Delis: Assembling a Picnic

Picnicking saves lots of euros and is a great way to sample regional specialties. A picnic can even be an adventure in high cuisine. Be daring. Try the fresh ricotta, *presto* pesto, shriveled olives, and any regional specialties the locals are excited about.

**Markets:** For the most colorful experience, gather your ingredients in the morning at a produce market. Towns big and small have markets selling everything imaginable for a fantastic picnic, including cheese, meat, bread, sweets, and prepared foods. You'll often find street-food stalls tucked into the mar-

ketplace as well (note that many stalls close in the early afternoon).

**Groceries and Delis:** Another budget option is to visit a supermarket (look for the Conad, Carrefour, Esselunga, and Co-op chains), *alimentari* (neighborhood grocery), or *salumeria* (delicatessen) to pick up *salumi*, cheeses, and other picnic supplies. Some grocery stores, *salumerie,* and any *paninoteca* or *focacceria* (sandwich shop) can make a sandwich to order. Just point to what you want, and they'll stuff it into a *panino*. Almost every grocery store has a deli case with prepared items like stuffed peppers, marinated olives, lasagna, and chicken, all usually sold by weight; if you want it reheated, remember the word *riscaldata* (ree-skahl-DAH-tah). And *rosticcerie* sell cheap food to go—you'll find options such as lasagna, rotisserie chicken, and sides including roasted potatoes and spinach. For more on *salumi* and cheeses, see those sections, later.

**Ordering:** A typical picnic for two might be fresh rolls, *un etto* (3.5 ounces) of cheese, and *un etto* of meat (sometimes ordered

by the slice—*fetta*—or piece—*pezzo*). For two people, I might get *un etto* of prosciutto and *due pezzi* of bread. Add two tomatoes, three carrots, two apples, yogurt, and a liter box of juice. Total: about €10.

If ordering *antipasti* (such as grilled or marinated veggies) at a deli counter, you can ask for *una porzione* in a takeaway container *(contenitore)*. Use gestures to show exactly how much you want. To set a price limit of 5 or 10 euros on what you order, say *"Da [cinque/dieci] euro, per favore."* The word *basta* (BAH-stah; enough) works as a question or as a statement.

Shopkeepers are happy to sell small quantities of produce, but it's customary to let the merchant choose for you. Say *"per oggi"* (pehr OH-jee; for today) and he or she will grab you something ready to eat. To avoid being overcharged, know the cost per kilo,

## Eating with the Seasons Across Italy

Italian cooks love to serve fresh produce and seafood at its tastiest. Each region in Italy has its seasonal specialties, which you'll see displayed in open-air markets. To get a plate of the freshest veggies at a fine restaurant, request *"Un piatto di verdure della stagione, per favore."* ("A plate of seasonal vegetables, please.") Italians take fresh, seasonal ingredients so seriously that a restaurant cooking with frozen ingredients *(congelato)* must note it on the menu. Here are a few examples of what's fresh when:

**April-May: Calamari (Venice),** romanesco (similar to cauliflower), fava beans (Rome), green beans, artichokes

**April-May and Sept-Oct:** Black truffles

**April-June:** Asparagus, zucchini flowers, zucchini

**May-June:** Mussels, cantaloupe, loquats, strawberries

**May-Aug:** Eggplant, clams

**July-Sept:** Figs, cherries, peaches, apricots, plums

**Oct-Nov:** Mushrooms, white truffles, persimmons, chestnuts

**Nov-Feb: Radicchio (Venice),** cardoon (wild artichoke), *puntarelle* (chicory shoots; Rome)

study the weighing procedure, and do the math. Remember that a kilo is 2.2 pounds.

## ITALIAN CUISINE STAPLES

Much of your Italian eating experience will likely involve the big five: pizza, pasta, *salumi,* cheese, and gelato. For a look at cuisine specific to Florence and Tuscany, see the sidebar on page 312. For more food help, try a menu translator, such as the *Rick Steves Italian Phrase Book & Dictionary,* which has a menu decoder and plenty of useful phrases for navigating the culinary scene.

### Pizza

Here are some of the pizzas you might see at restaurants or at a pizzeria. Note that if you ask for pepperoni on your pizza, you'll get *peperoni* (green or red peppers); instead, try requesting *salsiccia piccante* (spicy sausage) or *salame piccante* (spicy salami).

*Bianca:* White pizza with no tomatoes

*Capricciosa:* Prosciutto, mushrooms, olives, and artichokes—literally the chef's "caprice"

*Carciofi:* Artichokes
*Diavola:* Spicy hot
*Funghi:* Mushrooms
*Margherita:* Tomato sauce, mozzarella, and basil—the red, white, and green of the Italian flag
*Marinara:* Tomato sauce, oregano, garlic, no cheese
*Ortolana* or *vegetariana:* "Greengrocer-style," with vegetables
*Quattro formaggi:* Four different cheeses
*Quattro stagioni:* "Four seasons," with tomato, mozzarella, and usually one-quarter each of ham, mushrooms, artichokes, and olives
*Salsiccia:* Sausage
*Siciliana:* Capers, olives, and often anchovies

## Pasta

While we think of pasta as a main dish, in Italy it's considered a *primo piatto*—first course. There are hundreds of varieties of Italian pasta, each one specifically used to highlight a certain sauce, meat, or regional ingredient. *Pastasciutta* is dry-stored pasta, which is boiled until *al dente* (chewy, "to the tooth") and tossed with a sauce. *Pasta fresca* is fresh pasta cut into noodles and served with sauce, or cut into sheets *(sfoglie)*, filled with different ingredients, folded, cooked, and then covered lightly with butter, cream, or broth.

Don't mistakenly assume that dry pasta is inferior to fresh. If prepared well, it can be just as satisfying. There are two general types of dry pasta:

*Pasta lunga*, also called strand pasta, are noodles long enough to twist around a fork. Spaghetti is the most famous, but *pasta lunga* can be round, such as *capellini* (thin "little hairs"), *vermicelli* ("little worms"), and *bucatini* (long and hollow); or it can be flat, such as *linguine* (narrow "little tongues"), *fettuccine* (wider "small ribbons"), *tagliatelle* (even wider), and *pappardelle* (very wide, best with meat sauces).

*Pasta corta* ("short pasta") are smaller, designed to be scooped or speared with a fork. They go well with creamy sauces and chunkier meat sauces. The most common are dried tubular pastas called *maccheroni;* these come in endless forms, such as *penne* ("quills") and *maccheroncini* (tiny macaroni). Tubular pastas come either *lisce* (smooth) or *rigate* (grooved—so sauce clings better). Many short pastas are named for their shapes, such as *conchiglie* (shells), *farfalle* (butterflies), or *cavatappi* (corkscrews).

Here's a list of common pasta toppings and sauces. On a menu, these terms are usually preceded by *alla* (in the style of) or *in* (in):
*Aglio e olio:* Garlic and olive oil
*Alfredo:* Sweet butter and heaps of Parmigiano-Reggiano cheese

*Amatriciana:* *Guanciale* (pork cheek), tomatoes, *pecorino romano* cheese, and chili peppers

*Arrabbiata:* "Angry," spicy tomato sauce with chili peppers

*Bolognese:* "Bologna-style" meat and tomato sauce

*Boscaiola:* "Woodsman-style," with mushrooms and sausage or ham

*Brodo:* Broth (typical for filled pastas)

*Burro e salvia:* Butter and sage

*Cacio e pepe:* *Pecorino romano* cheese and fresh-ground pepper

*Carbonara:* Raw egg, *guanciale* (pork cheek), *pecorino romano* cheese, and fresh-ground pepper

*Carrettiera:* Spicy and garlicky, with olive oil and little tomatoes

*Diavola:* "Devil-style," spicy hot

*Frutti di mare:* Seafood

*Genovese:* Basil ground with Parmigiano-Reggiano cheese, garlic, pine nuts, and olive oil; a.k.a. pesto

*Gricia:* Cured pork cheek and *pecorino romano* cheese

*Marinara:* Usually tomato, often with garlic and onions, but can also be a seafood sauce ("sailor's style")

*Mollicata:* Simple sauce of tomato, onion, red wine, breadcrumbs, and sometimes anchovy

*Norma:* Tomato, eggplant, basil, and *ricotta salata* (Sicily)

*Pajata:* Calf intestines (also called *pagliata*)

*Pescatora:* Seafood ("fisherman style")

*Pomodoro:* Tomato only

*Puttanesca:* Tomato sauce with anchovies and/or tuna, olives, capers, and garlic

*Ragù:* Meaty tomato sauce (more meat in the north; more tomato in the south)

*Scoglio:* Mussels, clams, and tomatoes

*Sorrentina:* "Sorrento-style," with tomatoes, basil, and mozzarella (usually over gnocchi)

*Sugo di lepre:* Rich sauce made of wild hare

*Tartufi:* Truffles (also called *tartufate*)

*Vongole:* Clams and spices

## Salumi

*Salumi* (cured meats)—sometimes called *affettati* (sliced meats)—are an Italian staple. While most American cold cuts are cooked, in Italy they're far more commonly cured by air-drying, salting, and smoking. (While called "raw"—*crudo*—these are perfectly safe to eat.)

The two most familiar types of *salumi* are *salame* and *prosciutto*. *Salame* is an air-dried, sometimes-spicy sausage that comes in many varieties. When Italians say *"prosciutto,"* they usually mean *prosciutto crudo*—the raw ham that air-cures on the hock and is then thinly sliced. Produced mainly in the north of Italy, *prosciutto* can be either *dolce* (sweet) or *salato* (salty). Purists say the best is *prosciutto di Parma*.

Other *salumi* may be less familiar, but no less worth trying:

**Bresaola:** Air-cured beef

**Capocollo:** Peppery pork shoulder (also called *coppa*)

**Culatello:** High-quality, slow-cured prosciutto

**Finocchiona:** *Salame* with fennel seeds

**Guanciale:** Tender pork cheek

**Lardo:** Pork lard made fragrant with herbs and spices; the best is *lardo di Colonnata*

**Lonzino:** Cured pork loin

**Mortadella:** A finely ground pork loaf, similar to our bologna

**'Nduja:** Super-spicy, smoky, soft, spreadable pork sausage with a texture like bright-red pâté

**Pancetta:** Salt-cured, peppery pork-belly meat, similar to bacon

**Salame di Sant'Olcese:** What we'd call "Genoa salami"

**Salame piccante:** Spicy hot, similar to pepperoni

**Soppressata:** A simple dry *salame* that has some kick, common in the south

**Speck:** Smoked pork shoulder

Squeamish eaters should avoid *testa in cassetta* (headcheese—organs in aspic) and *lampredotto* (cow stomach).

## Cheese

When it comes to cheese (*formaggio* or *cacio*), you're probably already familiar with most of these Italian favorites:

**Asiago:** Hard cow cheese that comes either *mezzano* (young, firm, and creamy) or *stravecchio* (aged, pungent, and granular)

**Burrata:** Ball of mozzarella wrapped around a buttery, almost liquid center

**Caciocavallo:** This misnamed "horse cheese" is a cow's-milk cheese that's pear-shaped so it can be lashed at the top and hung to dry, like a saddlebag

**Fontina** and **Montasio:** Semihard, nutty, Gruyère-style mountain cheeses

**Gorgonzola:** Pungent, blue-veined cheese, either *dolce* (creamy) or *piccante* (aged and sharp)

**Grana:** Generic term for grating cheeses; most common is *grana padano* ("*grana* of the Po")

**Mascarpone:** Sweet, buttery, spreadable dessert cheese

**Mozzarella di bufala:** Made from the milk of water buffaloes

**Parmigiano-Reggiano:** Hard, crumbly, sharp, aged cow cheese with more nuanced flavor than American parmesan

**Pecorino:** Sheep's cheese, either *fresco* (fresh, soft, and mild) or *sta-*

*gionato* (aged and sharp, sometimes called *pecorino romano*—a popular grating cheese)

**Provolone:** Rich, firm, aged cow cheese

**Ricotta:** Soft, airy cheese made by "recooking" leftover whey

## Gelato

American and Italian ice cream are similar but decidedly not the same. Italy's gelato is denser and creamier (even though it has less butterfat than ice cream) than American versions, and connoisseurs swear it's more flavorful.

A key to gelato appreciation is sampling liberally and choosing flavors that go well together. At a *gelateria*, ask, as Italians do, for a taste: *"Un assaggio, per favore?"* (oon ah-SAH-joh pehr fah-VOH-ray). You can also ask what flavors go well together: *"Quali gusti stanno bene insieme?"* (KWAH-lee GOO-stee STAH-noh BEH-nay een-see-EH-may).

Most *gelaterie* clearly display prices and sizes. But in the textbook *gelateria* scam, the tourist orders two or three flavors—and the clerk selects a fancy, expensive chocolate-coated waffle cone, piles it high with huge scoops, and cheerfully charges the tourist €10. To avoid rip-offs, point to the price or say what you want—for instance, a €3 cup: *"Una coppetta da tre euro"* (OO-nah koh-PEH-tah dah tray eh-OO-roh).

The best *gelaterie* display signs reading *artigianale, nostra produzione,* or *produzione propria,* indicating that the gelato is made on the premises. Seasonal flavors are also a good sign, as are mellow hues (avoid colors that don't appear in nature). Gelato stored in covered metal tins (rather than white plastic) is more likely to be homemade. The chain called Grom is the Starbucks of Italian gelato: It's an acceptable choice, but try to find something more local.

Other Italian frozen treats include *sorbetto* (sorbet—made with fruit, but no milk or eggs); *granita* or *grattachecca* (a cup of slushy ice with flavored syrup); and *cremolata* (a gelato-*granita* float). *Caffè affogato* is a scoop of gelato "drowned" in a shot of hot espresso.

Classic gelato flavors include:

**After Eight:** Chocolate and mint

**Bacio:** Chocolate hazelnut, named for Italy's popular "kiss" candies

**Cassata:** With dried fruits

**Cioccolato:** Chocolate

**Crema:** Plain (similar to vanilla)

**Croccantino:** "Crunchy," with toasted peanut bits

**Fior di latte:** Sweet milk

**Fragola:** Strawberry

**Frutti di bosco:** Mixed berries

**Gianduia (or gianduja):** Chocolate-hazelnut

**Lampone:** Raspberry

*Macedonia:* Mixed fruits
*Malaga:* Similar to rum raisin
*Nocciola:* Hazelnut
*Noce:* Walnut
*Riso:* With actual bits of rice mixed in
*Stracciatella:* Vanilla with chocolate shreds
*Tartufo:* Super chocolate
*Zabaione:* Named for the egg yolk-and-Marsala wine dessert
*Zuppa inglese:* Sponge cake, custard, chocolate, and cream

## BEVERAGES

Italian bars serve great drinks—hot, cold, sweet, caffeinated, or alcoholic.

### Water, Juice, and Cold Drinks

Italians are notorious water snobs. At restaurants, your server just can't understand why you wouldn't want good water to go with your good food. It's customary and never expensive to order a *litro* or *mezzo litro* (half-liter) of bottled water. Simply ask for *con gas* if you want fizzy water and *senza gas* if you prefer still water. You can ask for *acqua del rubinetto* (tap water) in restaurants, but your server may give you a funny look.

Chilled bottled water—still *(naturale)* or carbonated *(frizzante)*—is sold cheap in stores. Half-liter bottles of mineral water are available everywhere for about €1. (I refill my water bottle with tap water.)

Juice is *succo,* and *spremuta* means freshly squeezed. Order *una spremuta* (don't confuse it with *spumante,* sparkling wine)—it's usually orange juice *(arancia),* and from February through April it can be made from Sicilian blood oranges *(arance rosse).*

In grocery stores, you can get a liter of OJ for the price of a Coke or coffee. Look for *100% succo* or *senza zucchero* (without sugar) on the label—or be surprised by something diluted and sugary sweet. Hang on to your water bottles. Buy juice in cheap liter boxes, then drink some and store the extra in your water bottle.

*Tè freddo* (iced tea) is usually from a can—sweetened and flavored with lemon or peach. Lemonade is *limonata.*

### Coffee and Other Hot Drinks

The espresso-based style of coffee so popular in the US was born in Italy. If you ask for *"un caffè,"* you'll get a shot of espresso in a little cup. Most Italian coffee drinks begin with espresso, to which they add varying amounts of hot water and/or steamed or foamed milk. The closest thing to American-style drip coffee is a *caffè americano*—a shot of espresso diluted with hot water. Milky drinks, like cappuccino or *caffè latte,* are served to locals before noon and to tourists any time of day. To an Italian, cappuccino is a morning drink; they believe having milk after a big meal impairs digestion. If they add any milk after lunch, it's just a splash, in a *caffè macchiato*.

Italians like their coffee only warm—to get it very hot, request *"Molto caldo, per favore"* (MOHL-toh KAHL-doh pehr fah-VOH-ray). Any coffee drink is available decaffeinated—ask for it *decaffeinato* (deh-kah-feh-NAH-toh).

If you want a hot drink other than coffee, *cioccolato* is hot chocolate, and *tè* is hot tea.

**Cappuccino:** Espresso with foamed milk on top (*cappuccino freddo* is iced cappuccino)

**Caffè latte:** Espresso mixed with hot milk, no foam, in a tall glass (ordering just a "latte" gets you only milk)

**Caffè macchiato:** Espresso "stained" with a splash of milk, in a small cup

**Latte macchiato:** Layers of hot milk and foam, "stained" by an espresso shot, in a tall glass. Note that if you order simply a *"macchiato,"* you'll probably get a *caffè macchiato* (see above).

**Caffè corto/lungo:** Concentrated espresso diluted with a tiny bit of hot water, in a small cup

**Caffè americano:** Espresso diluted with even more hot water, in a larger cup

**Caffè corretto:** Espresso "corrected" with a shot of liqueur (normally grappa, *amaro,* or *sambuca*)

**Marocchino:** "Moroccan" coffee with espresso, foamed milk, and cocoa powder; the similar *mocaccino* has chocolate instead of cocoa

**Caffè freddo:** Sweet and iced espresso

**Caffè hag:** Instant decaf

## Alcoholic Beverages

**Beer:** While Italy is traditionally considered wine country, in recent years there's been a huge and passionate growth in the production of craft beer *(birra artigianale)*. Even in small towns, you'll see microbreweries slinging their own brews. What's on tap is often inspired by the same trends you'll find stateside—IPAs, ambers, stouts, saisons, sours, seasonal beers, and so on. You'll also find local brews (Peroni and Moretti), as well as imports such as Heineken. Italians drink mainly lager beers. Beer on tap is *alla spina*. Get it *piccola* (33 cl, 11 oz), *media* (50 cl, about a pint), or *grande* (a liter). A *lattina* (lah-TEE-nah) is a can and a *bottiglia* (boh-TEEL-yah) is a bottle.

**Cocktails and Spirits:** Italians appreciate both *aperitivi* (palate-stimulating cocktails) and *digestivi* (after-dinner drinks designed to aid digestion).

# Ordering Wine

To order a glass of red or white wine, say, *"Un bicchiere di vino rosso/bianco."* House wine comes in a carafe; choose from a quarter-liter pitcher (8.5 oz, *un quarto*), half-liter pitcher (17 oz, *un mezzo*), or one-liter pitcher (34 oz, *un litro*). When ordering, have some fun, gesture like a local, and you'll have no problems speaking the language of the *enoteca. Salute!*

| English | Italian |
|---|---|
| Wine | *vino* (VEE-noh) |
| house wine | *vino della casa* (VEE-noh DEH-lah KAH-zah) |
| Glass | *bicchiere/calice* (bee-kee-EH-ray/KAH-lee-chay) |
| bottle | *bottiglia* (boh-TEEL-yah) |
| carafe | *caraffa* (kah-RAH-fah) |
| red | *rosso* (ROH-soh) |
| white | *bianco* (bee-AHN-koh) |
| rosé | *rosato* (roh-ZAH-toh) |
| sparkling | *spumante/frizzante* (spoo-MAHN-tay/freed-ZAHN-tay) |
| dry | *secco* (SEH-koh) |
| fruity | *fruttato* (froo-TAH-toh) |
| full-bodied | *corposo/pieno* (kor-POH-zoh/pee-EH-noh) |
| sweet | *dolce* (DOHL-chay) |

The classic *aperitivo* is the *spritz:* Prosecco (or white wine) and soda livened up with either Campari (carmine-red bitters with a secret blend of herbs and orange peel) or Aperol (sweeter, softer, bright-orange bitters with herbal, citrusy undertones). Vermouths (both red and white) from Carpano, Cinzano, Martini, or Riccadonna can be served straight, on the rocks, with a splash of soda, or as part of drinks like Punt e Mes (sweet red vermouth and red wine). Other choices include Americano (vermouth with bitters, brandy, and lemon peel); Garibaldi (also known as Campari-Orange, a mixture of Campari and orange juice); and Cynar (bitters flavored with artichoke).

*Digestivo* choices fall into three categories. First is the bittersweet, syrupy herbal drink called *amaro* (many restaurants have their own brew; popular commercial brands are Fernet Branca and Montenegro). For something sweeter, try *limoncello* (lemon-flavored), *amaretto* (almond), Frangelico (hazelnut), *sambuca* (anise), or Marsala wine. And grappa is a brandy distilled from grape skins and stems; *stravecchio* is an aged, mellower variation. *Acquavite* ("water of life") is similar to grappa, but distilled from fruit such as apples, berries, or plums.

PRACTICALITIES

**Wine:** The ancient Greeks who colonized Italy more than 2,000 years ago called it Oenotria—land of the grape. Centuries later, Galileo wrote, "Wine is light held together by water." Wine *(vino)* is certainly a part of the Italian culinary trinity—grape, olive, and wheat. (I'd add gelato.) Ideal conditions

for grapes (warm climate, well-draining soil, and an abundance of hillsides) make the Italian peninsula a paradise for grape growers, winemakers, and wine drinkers. For regional wines produced in Tuscany, see the sidebar on page 312.

In most years, Italian winemakers produce more wine than any other country—more than 4 million liters annually. Production is mainly red *(rosso)* and white *(bianco)* wines. Rosé *(rosato)* is less traditional—though as it's become trendy stateside and elsewhere, more Italian vintners are experimenting with it. A sparkling wine is *frizzante* or *spumante;* Prosecco is a bubbly white wine from northeastern Italy (though that word is sometimes, incorrectly, used to refer to any Italian sparkling white).

Even if you're clueless about wine, the information on an Italian wine label can help you choose something decent. Terms you may see on the bottle include *classico* (from a defined, select area), *annata* (year of harvest), *vendemmia* (harvest), and *imbottigliato dal produttore all'origine* (bottled by producers).

In general, Italy designates its wines by one of four official categories:

*Vino da Tavola* (VDT) is table wine, the lowest grade, made from grapes grown anywhere in Italy. It's often inexpensive, but Italy's wines are so good that, for many people, a basic *vino da tavola* is just fine with a meal. And, because it's grown in the same area as the other ingredients you're enjoying, it pairs perfectly with the food. Many restaurants, even modest ones, take pride in their house wine *(vino della casa),* bottling their own or working with wineries.

*Denominazione di Origine Controllata* (DOC) meets national standards for high-quality wine, produced in a legally controlled geographical area. It's usually good and still quite affordable.

*Denominazione di Origine Controllata e Guarantita* (DOCG), the highest grade, meets national standards for the highest-quality wine (made with grapes from a defined area whose quality is "guaranteed"). These wines can be identified by the pink or green label on the neck...and the high price. They're a good bet if you want a

## Hurdling the Language Barrier

Many Italians—especially those in the tourist trade and in big cities—speak English. Still, you'll get better treatment if you learn and use Italian pleasantries. In smaller, nontouristy towns, Italian is the norm. Italians have an endearing habit of talking to you even if they know you don't speak their language—and yet, thanks to gestures and thoughtfully simplified words, it somehow works. Don't stop them to tell them you don't understand every word—just go along for the ride. For a list of survival phrases, see the appendix.

Note that Italian is pronounced much like English, with a few exceptions, such as: *c* followed by *e* or *i* is pronounced ch (to ask, *"Per centro?"* "To the center?" you say, pehr CHEHN-troh). In Italian, *ch* followed by *e* or *i* is pronounced like the hard c in Chianti (*chiesa*—church—is pronounced kee-AY-zah). Adding a vowel to the English word often gets you close to the Italian one. Give it your best shot. Italians appreciate your efforts.

For more tips on hurdling the language barrier, consider the *Rick Steves Italian Phrase Book* (available at RickSteves. com).

quality wine. (*Riserva* indicates a DOC or DOCG wine that's been aged for even longer than required.)

***Indicazione Geografica Tipica*** (IGT) is a broad group of wines that don't meet the standard for DOC or DOCG status, but have been designated as "typical" of a particular region.

If you're on a tight budget, try looking for a more affordable alternative. For example, in Tuscany, the world-famous Brunello di Montalcino (a DOCG) can break the bank, but Rosso di Montalcino (a DOC)—made in the same zone with similar grapes, in a similar way, but aged for a shorter period of time—costs half as much.

## Staying Connected

One of the most common questions I hear from travelers is, "How can I stay connected in Europe?" The short answer? More easily and affordably than you might think.

The simplest solution is to bring your own device—phone, tablet, or laptop—and use it much as you would at home, following the money-saving tips later, such as getting an international plan or connecting to free Wi-Fi whenever possible. Another option is to buy a European SIM card for your mobile phone. Or you can use European landlines and computers to connect. More details are at RickSteves.com/phoning.

# How to Dial

Here's how to dial from anywhere in the US or Europe, using the phone number of one of my recommended Florence hotels as an example (055 213 154). If a non-Italian number starts with 0, drop it when dialing internationally.

### From a US Mobile Phone
Phone numbers in this book are presented exactly as you would dial them from a US mobile phone. For international access, press and hold 0 (zero) to get a + sign, then dial the country code (39 for Italy) and phone number.
▶ To call the Florence hotel from any location, dial +39 055 213 154.

### From a US Landline
Replace + with 011 (US/Canada access code), then dial the country code (39 for Italy) and phone number.
▶ To call the Florence hotel from your home landline, dial 011 39 055 213 154.

### From a European Landline
Replace + with 00 (Europe access code), then dial the country code (39 for Italy, 1 for the US) and phone number.
▶ To call the Florence hotel from a Spanish landline, dial 00 39 055 213 154.
▶ To call my US office from an Italian landline, dial 00 1 425 771 8303.

### From One Italian Phone to Another
To place a domestic call (from an Italian landline or mobile), drop +39 and dial the phone number.
▶ To call the Florence hotel from Rome, dial 055 213 154.

### More Dialing Tips
**Local Numbers:** European phone numbers and area codes can vary in length and spacing, even within the same country. Mobile phones use separate prefixes (for instance, in Italy, landlines begin with 0, and mobile numbers begin with 3).

**Toll and Toll-Free Calls:** It's generally not possible to dial European toll or toll-free numbers from a US mobile or landline (although you can sometimes get through using Skype). Look for a direct-dial number instead.

**Calling the US from a US Mobile Phone, While Abroad:** Dial +1, area code, and number.

**More Phoning Help:** See HowToCallAbroad.com.

## USING YOUR PHONE IN EUROPE
Here are some budget tips and options.

**Sign up for an international plan.** To stay connected at a lower cost, sign up for an international service plan through your carrier. Most providers offer a simple bundle that includes calling, messaging, and data. Your normal plan may already include international coverage (for example, T-Mobile's covers data and text, but not voice calls).

Before your trip, research your provider's international rates.

## Tips on Internet Security

Make sure that your device is running the latest versions of its operating system, security software, and apps. Next, ensure that your device and key programs (like email) are password-protected. On the road, use only secure, password-protected Wi-Fi. Ask the hotel or café staff for the specific name of their network, and make sure you log on to that exact one.

If you must access your financial info online, use a banking app rather than accessing your account via a browser, and use a cellular connection, not Wi-Fi. Never log on to personal finance sites on a public computer. If you're very concerned, consider subscribing to a VPN (virtual private network).

Activate the plan a day or two before you leave, then remember to cancel it when your trip's over.

**Use free Wi-Fi whenever possible.** Unless you have an un-limited-data plan, save most of your online tasks for Wi-Fi. Most accommodations in Europe offer free Wi-Fi. Many cafés offer hotspots for customers; ask for the password when you buy some-thing. You may also find Wi-Fi at TIs, city squares, major mu-seums, public-transit hubs, airports, and aboard trains and buses.

**Minimize the use of your cellular network.** The best way to make sure you're not accidentally burning through data is to put your device in "airplane" mode (which also disables phone calls and texts), and connect to Wi-Fi as needed. When you need to get on-line but can't find Wi-Fi, simply turn on your cellular network (or turn off airplane mode) just long enough for the task at hand.

Even with an international data plan, wait until you're on Wi-Fi to Skype or FaceTime, download apps, stream videos, or do other megabyte-greedy tasks. Using a navigation app such as Google Maps over a cellular network can require lots of data, so download maps when you're on Wi-Fi, then use the app offline.

Limit automatic updates. By default, your device constantly checks for a data connection and updates app content. Check your device's menu for ways to turn this off, and change your email set-tings from "auto-retrieve" to "manual" (or from "push" to "fetch").

**Use Wi-Fi calling and messaging apps.** Skype, WhatsApp, FaceTime, and Google Meet are great for making free or low-cost calls or sending texts over Wi-Fi worldwide. Just log on to a Wi-Fi network, then connect with friends, family members, or local con-tacts who use the same service.

**Buy a European SIM Card.** If you anticipate making a lot of local calls or need a local phone number, or if your provider's international data rates are expensive, consider buying a SIM card in Europe to replace the one in your (unlocked) US phone or tablet.

In Italy, buy SIM cards at mobile-phone shops. You'll be required to register the SIM card with your passport as an antiterrorism measure (which may mean you can't use the phone for the first hour or two).

There are generally no roaming charges when using a European SIM card in other EU countries, but confirm when you buy.

## WITHOUT A MOBILE PHONE

It's less convenient but possible to travel in Europe without a mobile device. You can make calls from your hotel and check email or get online using public computers.

Most **hotels** charge a fee for placing calls. You can use a prepaid international phone card (*carta telefonica prepagata internazionale*—usually available at newsstands, tobacco shops, and train stations) to call out from your hotel.

Some hotels have **public computers** in their lobbies for guests to use; otherwise you may find them at public libraries (ask your hotelier or the TI for the nearest location). On a European keyboard, use the "Alt Gr" key to the right of the space bar to insert the extra symbol that appears on some keys. If you can't locate a special character (such as @), simply copy and paste it from a web page.

## MAIL

You can mail one package per day to yourself worth up to $200 duty-free from Europe to the US (mark it "personal purchases"). If you're sending a gift to someone, mark it "unsolicited gift." For details, visit www.cbp.gov, select "Travel," and search for "Know Before You Go." The Italian postal service works fine, but for quick transatlantic delivery (in either direction), consider services such as DHL (DHL.com).

# Transportation

Figuring out how to get around in Europe is one of your biggest trip decisions. Cars work well for two or more traveling together (especially families with small kids), those packing heavy, and those delving into the countryside. **Trains** and **buses** are best for solo travelers, blitz tourists, city-to-city travelers, and those who want to leave the driving to others. Short-hop **flights** within Europe can creatively connect the dots. Be aware of the potential downside of each option: A car is an expensive headache in any major city; with trains and buses you're at the mercy of a timetable; flying entails a trek to and from a usually distant airport and leaves a larger carbon footprint. For more detailed information on transportation throughout Europe, see RickSteves.com/transportation.

## TRAINS

To travel by train affordably within Italy, you can simply buy tickets as you go. For travelers ready to lock in dates and times weeks or months in advance, buying nonrefundable tickets online can cut costs in half. Note that the Italy rail pass is generally not a good value, but if your travel extends beyond Italy, there are multicountry rail passes that might be worth checking into. For advice on figuring out the smartest train-ticket or rail-pass options for your trip, visit the Trains & Rail Passes section of my website at RickSteves.com/rail.

## Types of Trains

Most trains in Italy are operated by the state-run **Trenitalia** company (www.trenitalia.com, a.k.a. Ferrovie dello Stato Italiane,

abbreviated FS). Ticket prices depend on the speed of the train, so it helps to know the different types of trains: pokey Regionale (R or REG); medium-speed Regionale Veloce (RV); fast InterCity (IC) and EuroCity (EC); and super-fast Frecce trains.

All trains (except those with Regionale in the name) require seat assignments, which are built into your ticket for a specific date and time. If you're traveling with a rail pass, you'll need to buy a separate seat reservation (see "Rail Passes," later). Regional trains offer only open seating (no assigned seats for love nor money).

The private train company Italo (www.italotreno.it) runs fast trains on major routes serving large cities on the mainland but few small towns. Italo has fewer departures than Trenitalia but its service is comparable to Trenitalia's Frecce service, with similar prices and advance purchase discounts. Be aware that in Naples, Milan, and Rome, a few departures use secondary stations. Italo does not accept rail passes, but is a worthy alternative for point-to-point tickets.

Both train companies have call centers for answering general questions (**Trenitalia:** daily 7:00-24:00, +39 06 6847 5475; Italo: daily 6:00-23:00, +39 06 8937 1892).

Be aware that Trenitalia and Italo don't cooperate. If you buy a ticket for one train line, it's not valid on the other. Both companies tend to ignore the other's schedules.

## Schedules

Check schedules at Trenitalia.it and ItaloTreno.it (domestic jour-

# Italy's Public Transportation

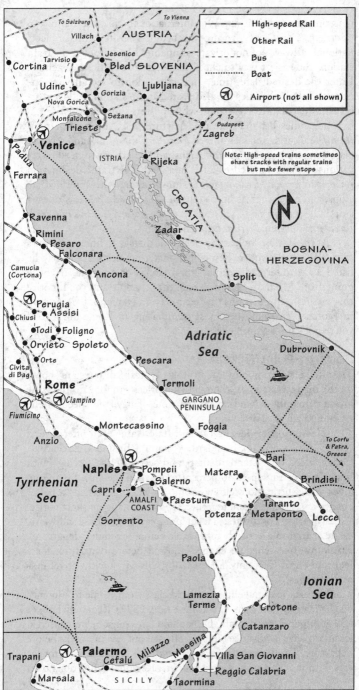

neys only) or use their apps; for international trips, use Bahn.com (Germany's excellent all-Europe schedule website, which reflects national railways but not private companies like Italo). At the train station, the easiest way to check schedules is at a ticket machine. Enter the desired date, time, and destination to see all your options. Printed schedules are also posted at the station (yellow posters show departures—*partenze;* white posters show arrivals).

Schedules list the time of departure *(ora),* the type of train *(treni),* and service classes offered *(classi servizi)*—first- and second-class cars, dining car, *cuccetta* berths, and whether you need reservations (usually denoted by an R in a box). The train's destination *(principali fermate destinazioni)* is shown, along with intermediate stops, and notes such as "also stops in..." *(ferma anche a...),* "doesn't stop in..." *(non ferma a...),* "stops in every station" *(ferma in tutte le stazioni),* "delayed..." *(ritardo...),* and so on.

At the station, look at the electronic display to find your train's track *(binario)* number. Remember that your destination may be listed as an intermediate (not final) stop. For example, if you're going from Milan to Florence, scan the schedule and you'll notice that virtually all the trains that terminate in Naples or Salerno stop in Florence en route (but most terminating in Rome do not). If you're not sure, ask for help.

## Point-to-Point Tickets

Train tickets are a good value in Italy. Typical full fares are shown on the map on page 701, though ticket prices can vary for the same journey, mainly depending on the time of day, the speed of the train, and advance discounts.

**Classes of Service:** Frecce and Italo trains each offer several classes of service (e.g., Standard, Premium, Business, Executive). Other trains offer standard first- and second-class seating (with first class costing up to 50 percent more than second). Buying up gives you a little more elbow room, a snack, or perhaps a better chance at seating a group together, if you're buying on short notice.

**Advance Discounts:** Ticket price levels are Base (full fare, easily changeable or partly refundable before scheduled departure), Economy (one schedule change allowed before departure, for a fee), and Super Economy or Low Cost (sells out quickly, no refunds or exchanges).

For example, traveling Standard class from Rome to Florence on the fastest train costs €50 at Base fare, €39 at Economy fare, or €30 at Super Economy rate. Discounted fares must be purchased at least two days in advance but typically sell out several weeks before departure. Fares labeled *servizi abbonati* are available only for locals with monthly passes—not tourists. Regional trains don't offer advance discounts or seat assignments, so there's little need to buy those tickets in advance.

**Speed vs. Savings:** For point-to-point tickets, you'll pay more the faster you go. Spending a modest amount of extra time in transit can save money on shorter trips. For example, the regional train from Milano Centrale to Stresa takes just over an hour (67 minutes) and costs €9, while the EC train takes just under an hour (58 minutes)—but costs €19.

On longer mainline routes, fast trains save more time and provide most of the service. For example, speedy Florence-Rome trains run about 3/hour, cost €50 in second class, and make the trip in 1.5 hours, while infrequent InterCity trains (only 1-2/day) cost €37 at full price and take three hours.

**Age-Based Discounts:** Discounts for kids don't usually beat the Super Economy rate described earlier. If the cheapest tickets are no longer available, look for deals like "Bimbi Gratis" and "Offerta Famiglia." Other discounts for youths and seniors require purchase of a separate card (€40 Carta Verde for ages 12-26, €30 Carta Argento for ages 60 and over), but the discount is so minor (10-15 percent for domestic travel), it's not worth it for most.

## Buying Point-to-Point Tickets

You can buy tickets online, with an app, at train station ticket windows, from ticket machines, or at travel agencies. For long-haul runs or travel on a busy weekend or holiday, it can be cheaper to buy tickets in advance. But because most Italian trains run frequently and there's no deadline to buy tickets, for the most part I prefer to keep my travel plans flexible by purchasing tickets as I go. (You can buy tickets at one station for several trips when you are ready to commit.)

It's easy to buy tickets **online** at Trenitalia.com or ItaloTreno. it. On either website, choose English and be sure to read the pricing info, as many of the cheaper tickets are not refundable or changeable. You can keep the ticket on your mobile device (either as a PDF or with a QR code), or you can print it out. Or download the Trenitalia or Italo **app** to your phone—both have English versions that make ticket-buying a breeze.

If you instead go to the train station to buy tickets, you can avoid ticket-office lines by using the **ticket machines** in station halls. You'll be able to easily purchase tickets for travel within Italy, make seat reservations, and even book a *cuccetta* (koo-CHEH-tah; overnight berth). If you do use the **ticket windows** (e.g., to buy international tickets), be sure you're in the correct line. Key terms: *biglietti* (general tickets), *prenotazioni* (reservations), *nazionali* (domestic), and *internazionali*. Some big stations have counters (close to the tracks) marked "Last Minute," which let you jump the line if your train is departing soon.

**Trenitalia**'s ticket machines are user-friendly and found in all but the tiniest stations in Italy. You can pay with cash (change given when indicated) or by debit or credit card (even for small amounts, but you may need to enter your PIN—even when using "tap-to-pay"). Select English, then your destination. If you don't immediately see the city you're traveling to, keep keying in the spelling until it's listed. You can choose from first- and second-class seats, request tickets for more than one traveler, and pick seats, when applicable. Don't select a discount rate without being sure that you meet the criteria (for example, Americans are not eligible for certain EU or resident discounts).

To buy tickets at the station for **Italo** trains, look for a dedicated service counter (in most major stations) or a red ticket machine labeled *Italo*.

Some **international tickets** can't be bought online or from machines; for these tickets and anything else that requires a real person, you must go to a ticket window at the station. A good alternative, though, is to drop by a local travel agency. Agencies sell domestic and international tickets and make reservations. They charge a small fee, but the language barrier (and the lines) can be smaller than at the station's ticket windows.

## Rail Passes

The single-country Eurail Italy Pass may save you money if you take several long train rides or prefer first-class travel, but for most people it's not a good value. Most train travelers in Italy take relatively short rides on the Milan-Venice-Florence-Rome circuit. For these trips, it can be cheaper to buy point-to-point tickets. Remember that rail passes are valid on Trenitalia trains but not on Italo trains.

Furthermore, a rail pass doesn't offer much hop-on convenience in Italy, since even with a rail pass, seat reservations are required for InterCity, EuroCity, and Frecce trains (€5-10 each; make seat reservations at station ticket machines or windows). Most regional trains (such as Florence-Pisa-Cinque Terre service) don't require (or offer) reservations. Reservations for berths on overnight trains cost extra and aren't covered by rail passes.

If you're also traveling by train in other countries, consider a Eurail Global Pass. Although it covers most of Europe, prices can work for trips as short as three travel days or as long as three months. For more info, see the sidebar.

## Train Tips

**Validating Tickets:** If your ticket includes a seat reservation on a

# Rail Pass or Point-to-Point Tickets?

Will you be better off buying a rail pass or point-to-point tickets? It pays to know your options and choose what's best for your itinerary.

## Rail Passes

A Eurail Italy Pass lets you travel by train in Italy for three to eight days (consecutively or not) within a one-month period. Italy is also covered (along with most of Europe) by the classic Eurail Global Pass.

Discounted rates are offered for seniors (age 60 and up) and youths (ages 12-27). Up to two kids (ages 4-11) can travel free with each adult-rate pass (but not with senior rates). All rail passes offer a choice of first or second class for all ages.

While most rail passes are delivered electronically, it's smart to get your pass sorted before leaving home. For more on rail passes, including current prices and purchasing, visit RickSteves.com/rail.

## Point-to-Point Tickets

Italian train tickets are relatively cheap, and most include seat reservations, making them the best deal for most travelers. Use this map to add up approximate pay-as-you-go fares for your itinerary, and compare that to the price of a rail pass plus reservations. Keep in mind that significant discounts on point-to-point tickets may be available with advance purchase.

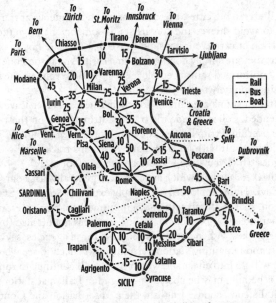

*Map shows approximate costs, in US dollars, for one-way, second-class tickets on faster trains.*

specific train *(biglietto con prenotazione)*, you're all set and can just get on board. The same is true for any ticket bought online or with the Trenitalia or Italo apps (whether open or reserved seating); these tickets are considered already validated.

An open ticket (generally for a *regionale* train) bought from a ticket desk or machine must be validated (date-stamped) before you board (the ticket may say *da convalidare* or *convalida*). To validate it, before getting on the train, stamp your ticket in the machine near the platform (usually marked *convalida biglietti* or *vidimazione*). Once you validate a ticket, you must complete your trip within the stamped timeframe (usually about four hours). If you forget to validate your ticket, go right away to the train conductor—before he comes to you—or you'll pay a fine.

**Getting a Seat:** If you're taking an unreserved *regionale* train that originates at your departure point (e.g., you're catching the Florence-Pisa train in Florence), arriving at least 15 minutes before the departure time will help you snare a seat.

**Baggage Storage:** Many Italian stations have *deposito bagagli* where you can safely leave your bag for a standardized but steep price (€6/5 hours, €12/12 hours, €17/24 hours, payable when you pick up the bag, double-check closing hours; they may ask to photocopy your passport). Due to security concerns, no Italian stations have lockers.

**Theft:** In big cities, exercise caution and prudence at train stations to avoid thieves and con artists. If someone helps you to find your train or carry your bags, be aware that they are not an official porter; they are simply hoping for some cash. And if someone other than a uniformed railway employee tries to help you use the ticket machines, politely refuse.

Italian trains are famous for their thieves. Never leave a bag unattended. Police do ride the trains, cutting down on theft. Still, for an overnight trip, I'd feel safe only in a *cuccetta* (a bunk in a special sleeping car with an attendant who keeps track of who comes and goes while you sleep—approximately €40 or more).

**Strikes:** Strikes, which are common, generally last a day (often a Friday). Train employees will simply explain, *"Sciopero"* (SHOH-peh-roh, strike). But in actuality, a minimum amount of "essential" or "guaranteed" *(garantito)* main-line service is maintained (by law) during strikes. When a strike is pending, travel agencies, savvy hoteliers, and remaining station personnel can check to see when the strike will go into effect and which trains will continue to run. Revised schedules may be posted online and in Italian at stations. See Trenitalia.com, choose English, then "Information and Contacts," and then "In Case of Strike."

If your train is cancelled, your reserved-seat ticket will likely be accepted on any similar train running that day (either earlier or

Tuscan Hill Towns Public Transportation

later than the original departure time) but you won't have a seat assignment. Tickets for cancelled trains should also be exchangeable without penalty ahead of the original departure time, or can be refunded (have an agent mark it "unused," and check refund deadlines). A rail pass works on any train still operating, but partially used rail passes can't be refunded—so make full use of any pass you have to continue your trip.

## BUSES

You can usually get anywhere you want in Italy by bus, as long as you're not in a hurry and plan ahead using bus schedules (pick up at local TIs or bus stations). For reaching small towns, buses are sometimes the only option if you don't have a car. In many hill towns, trains leave you at a station in the valley far below, while buses more likely drop you right into the thick of things. (If the bus stop or station is below town, sometimes an escalator or elevator helps get you up into town.)

Long-distance buses are catching on in Italy as an alternative to the train. Buses are usually cheaper, more modern, and often have free Wi-Fi. They're especially useful on routes poorly served by train, or to allow a direct connection instead of having to change trains (such as from Rome to Siena or Sorrento). Some of the operators you'll see are Flixbus (http://global.flixbus.com) and Marozzi (www.marozzivt.it). In general, orange buses are local city buses, and blue buses are for long distances.

Larger towns have a (usually chaotic) long-distance bus station *(stazione degli autobus* or *autostazione),* with ticket windows and several stalls (usually labeled *corsia, stallo,* or *binario)*—but to save time, buy your ticket at a travel agent or online; many companies use etickets (they'll scan your emailed QR code as you board). Smaller towns—where buses are more useful—often have a central bus stop *(fermata),* likely along the main road or on the main square, and maybe several more scattered around town. In small towns, buy bus tickets at newsstands or tobacco shops (with the big *T* signs). When buying your ticket, confirm the departure point *("Dov'è la fermata?").*

Before boarding, confirm the destination with the driver. You are expected to stow big bags underneath the bus (if the compartment is closed, ask the driver for help; which compartment you use may depend on your destination). If you'll be continuing on later by bus, upon arrival, double-check that the posted schedule lists your next destination and departure time.

Traveling by bus on Sundays and holidays can be problematic; even from large cities, schedules are sparse, departing buses are jam-packed, and ticket offices are often closed. Plan ahead and buy your ticket in advance. Most travel agencies book bus (and train) tickets for a small fee.

## TAXIS AND RIDE-BOOKING SERVICES

Most Italian taxis are reliable and cheap. In many cities, two people can travel short distances by cab for little more than the cost of bus or subway tickets.

## RENTING A CAR

It's cheaper to arrange most car rentals from the US, so research and compare rates before you go. Most of the major US rental agencies (including Avis, Budget, Enterprise, Hertz, and Thrifty) have offices throughout Europe. Also consider the two major Europe-based agencies, Europcar and Sixt. Consolidators such as Auto Europe (AutoEurope.com—or the sometimes cheaper AutoEurope.eu) compare rates at several companies to get you the best deal.

Wherever you book, always read the fine print. Check for add-on charges—such as one-way drop-off fees, airport surcharges, or mandatory insurance policies—that aren't included in the "total price."

## Rental Costs and Considerations

If you book well in advance, expect to pay $350-500 for a one-week rental for a basic compact car. Allow extra for supplemental insurance, fuel, tolls, and parking. To save money on fuel, request a diesel car.

**Manual vs. Automatic:** Almost all rental cars in Europe are manual by default—and cars with a stick shift are generally cheaper. If you need an automatic, reserve one specifically. When selecting a car, remember that larger models won't be as maneuverable on narrow, winding roads or when squeezing into tight parking lots.

**Age Restrictions:** Some rental companies impose minimum and maximum age limits. Young drivers (25 and under) and seniors (69 and up) should check the rental policies and rules section of car-rental websites.

**Choosing Pick-Up/Drop-off Locations:** Always check the hours of the locations you choose: Many rental offices close from midday Saturday until Monday morning and, in smaller towns, at lunchtime. When selecting an office, confirm the location on a map. A downtown site might seem more convenient than the airport but could actually be in the suburbs or buried deep in big-city streets. Pedestrianized and one-way streets can make navigation tricky when returning a car at a big-city office or urban train station. Wherever you select, get precise details on the location and allow ample time to find it. And be aware that most Italian cities have a "ZTL" (limited traffic zone) that's carefully monitored by cameras. If your drop-off point is near this zone, get clear directions on how to get there to avoid getting a big fine.

**Have the Right License:** If you're renting a car in Italy, bring your driver's license. You're also technically required to have an International Driving Permit—an official translation of your license (sold at AAA offices for about $20 plus the cost of two passport-type photos; see AAA.com). How this is enforced varies: I've never needed one.

**Picking Up Your Car:** Before driving off in your rental car, check it thoroughly and make sure any damage is noted on your rental agreement. Rental agencies in Europe tend to charge for even minor damage, so be sure to mark everything. Find out how your car's gearshift, lights, turn signals, wipers, radio, and fuel cap function, and know what kind of fuel the car takes (diesel is common in Europe). When you return the car, make sure the agent verifies its condition with you.

## Car Insurance Options

When you rent a car in Europe, the price typically includes liability insurance, which covers harm to other cars or motorists—but not the rental car itself. To limit your financial risk in case of damage to the rental, choose one of these options: Buy a Collision Damage Waiver (CDW; also called "loss damage waiver" or LDW by some firms) with a low or zero deductible from the car-rental company (roughly 30-40 percent extra), get coverage through your credit card (free, but more complicated), or get collision insurance as part of a larger travel-insurance policy.

Basic **CDW** costs $15–30 a day and typically comes with a $1,000-2,000 deductible, reducing but not eliminating your financial responsibility. When you reserve or pick up the car, you'll be offered the chance to "buy down" the deductible to zero (for an additional $10–30/day; this is sometimes called "super CDW" or "zero-deductible coverage").

In Italy, most car-rental companies' rates automatically include CDW coverage. Even if you try to decline CDW when you reserve your car, you may find when you show up at the counter that you must buy it after all (along with mandatory theft insurance, about $15–20 a day).

If you opt for **credit-card coverage,** you must decline all coverage offered by the car-rental company—which means they can place a hold on your card to cover the deductible. In case of damage, it can be time-consuming to resolve the charges. Before relying on this option, quiz your card company about how it works.

For more on car-rental insurance, see RickSteves.com/cdw.

## Navigation Options

If you'll be navigating using your phone or a GPS unit from home, remember to bring a car charger and device mount.

**Your Mobile Phone:** The mapping app on your mobile phone works fine for navigating Europe's roads. To save on data, most apps allow you to download maps for offline use (do this before you need them, when you have a strong Wi-Fi signal). Some apps—including Google Maps—also have offline route directions, but you'll need mobile data access for current traffic. For more on using a mapping app without burning through data, see "Using Your Phone in Europe," earlier.

**GPS Devices:** If you want a dedicated GPS unit, consider renting one with your car (about $20/day, or sometimes included—ask). These units offer real-time turn-by-turn directions and traffic without the data requirements of an app. The unit may come loaded only with maps for its home country; if you need additional maps, ask. Make sure you know how to use the device—and that the language is set to English—before you drive off.

**Paper Maps and Atlases:** Even when navigating primarily with a mobile app or GPS, I always have a paper map, ideally a big, detailed regional road map. It's invaluable for getting the big picture, understanding alternate routes, and filling in if my phone runs out of juice. The free maps you get from your car-rental company usually don't have enough detail. It's smart to buy a better map before you go, or pick one up at a local gas station, bookshop, newsstand, or tourist shop.

## DRIVING

Driving in Italy can be scary—a video game for keeps, and you only get one quarter. Locals drive fast and tailgate as if it were required. They pass where Americans are taught not to—on blind corners and just before tunnels. Roads have narrow shoulders or none at all. Driving in the countryside is less stressful than driving through urban areas or on busy highways, but stay alert. On one-lane roads, larger vehicles have the right-of-way. (For more on driving in Tuscany, see page 358.)

**Road Rules:** Stay out of restricted traffic zones or you'll risk huge fines. Car traffic is restricted in many city centers. Don't drive or park in any area that has a sign reading *Zona Traffico Limitato* (*ZTL*, often shown above a red circle—see image). If you do, your license plate will likely be photographed and a hefty (€80-plus) ticket mailed to your home without your ever having met a cop. Bumbling in and out of these zones can net you multiple fines. If your hotel is within a restricted area, ask your

hotelier to direct you to parking outside the zone. (Although your hotelier can register your car as an authorized vehicle permitted to enter the zone, this usually isn't worth the hassle.) If you get a ticket, it could take months to show up (for more about traffic tickets in Italy, see www.bella-toscana.com/traffic_violations_italy.htm).

Be aware of typical European road rules; for example, many countries require headlights to be turned on at all times, and nearly all forbid handheld mobile-phone use. Seatbelts are mandatory, and children under age 12 must ride in child-safety or booster seats. In Europe, you're not allowed to turn right on a red light unless a sign or signal specifically authorizes it, and on expressways it's illegal to pass drivers on the right. Ask your car-rental company about these rules, or check the "International Travel" section of the US State Department website (www.travel.state.gov, search for your country in the "Learn About Your Destination" box, then click "Travel and Transportation").

**Drive Defensively:** Italians are aggressive drivers. Turn signals are optional. If a driver is tailgating you on the highway, pull to the side to let them pass, even if that means driving on the shoul-

## Driving in Tuscany

To Venice

EMILIA- ROMAGNA

To Milan

ITALY

To Cinque Terre
(La Spezia)

100 Miles

20 Kilometers

20 Miles

LE
MARCHE

50m · 1h

20m · .5h

Lucca

50m · 1h

Pisa

70m · 1.25h
(via FiPiLi)

Florence

190m · 3.5h

160m · 3.5h

70m · 1.5h

50m · 1h

15m · .5h

60m · 1.25h

55m · 1.5h

Livorno

San
Gimignano

40m · .75h
(via SR-2)

45m · 1h
(via superstrada)

45m · 2h
(via SR-222)

75m · 1.5h
(via A-1)

20m ·
.5h

30m ·
.5h

Volterra

T   U   S   C   A   N   Y

Cortona

Siena

45m · 1h

40m · 1h

40m · 1h

50m · 1h
(via SP-438)

10m
.25h

20m · 75h

30m · 75h

40m · 1h

To
Assisi

25m · 75h

30m · 1h

San Galgano
Monastery

55m · 1.5h

15m · .5h

15m · .5h

Chiusi

Montalcino

Pienza

Monte-
pulciano

UMBRIA

To Assisi

Mediterranean
Sea

210m · 4h

60m · 1.5h

35m · 1h

60m 1.5h

Orvieto

m = miles  h = hours
Note: Your times may
vary based on traffic,
construction, and
road conditions.

Bagnoregio
(Civita)

15m .5h

75m · 1.5h

To Rome

To
Rome

LAZIO

der. If you're traveling in the right-hand lane on the highway, keep
an eye out for slow-moving cars that appear out of nowhere. Also,
if you brake quickly, it's customary to put on your hazard lights to
warn the driver behind you. All this is normal for locals, who may
colorfully gesture at you. Don't take it personally.

Motor scooters are very popular, and scooter drivers often see
themselves as exempt from rules that apply to automobiles.

**Tolls:** You'll pay tolls for some stretches of freeway (autostrada; for costs, use the trip-planning tool at www.autostrade.it
or search "European Tolls" on www.theaa.com). When approaching a tollbooth, skip lanes marked *Telepass;* for an attended booth,
choose a lane with a sign that shows a hand or coins.

While I favor freeways because I feel they're safer and less
nerve-racking than smaller roads, savvy local drivers know which
toll-free *superstrade* are actually faster and more direct than the autostrada (e.g., Florence to Pisa). In some cases, if you have some
time to spare, smaller roads can be worth the extra hassle.

**Fuel:** Fuel is expensive—often about $6.50 per gallon. Diesel cars are more common in Europe than back home, so be sure you know what type of fuel your car takes before you fill up. Diesel costs less, about $6 per gallon. Some pumps are color-coded: Unleaded pumps *(senza piombo)* are green and labeled "E," while diesel pumps *(gasolio;* often yellow or black) are labeled "B". You'll also see the term *benzina,* which is standard fuel. If you are unsure or need help, stop for full-service gas *(servito).* To fill up, say *"Pieno"* (pee-EH-noh). Autostrada rest stops can have full- or self-service stations (open daily without a siesta break). Many 24-hour stations are entirely automated. Small-town stations are usually cheaper and offer full service but shorter hours.

**STOP AND LEARN THESE ROAD SIGNS**

| | | | |
|---|---|---|---|
| **50** Speed Limit (km/hr) | Yield | No Passing | End of No Passing Zone |
| One Way | Intersection | Main Road | Expressway |
| Roundabout Ahead | Danger | No Entry | All Vehicles Prohibited |
| No Through Road | Restrictions No Longer Apply | Yield to Oncoming Traffic | No Stopping |
| Parking | No Parking | Customs or Toll Road | Peace |

**Maps and Signage:** Learn the universal road signs (see illustration). Although roads are numbered on maps, actual road signs give just a city name (for example, if you were heading west out of Montepulciano, the map would be marked "route SP-146"—but you'd follow signs to *Pienza,* the next town along this road). Signs are inconsistent: They may direct you to the nearest big city or simply the next town along the route.

**Theft:** Cars are routinely vandalized and stolen. Thieves easily recognize rental cars and assume they are filled with a tourist's gear. Be sure all of your valuables are out of sight and locked in the trunk, or even better, with you or in your room.

**Parking:** White lines generally mean parking is free. Yellow lines mean that parking is reserved for residents only (who have permits). Blue lines mean you'll have to pay—usually around €1.50 per hour (use machine, leave time-stamped receipt on dashboard). Study the signs. Free zones often have a 30- or 60-minute time limit. Signs showing a street cleaner and a day of the week indicate which day the street is cleaned; there's a €100 tow-fee—incentive to learn the days of the week in Italian.

*Zona disco* has nothing to do with dancing. Italian cars come equipped with a time disc (a cardboard clock), which you can use in a *zona disco*—set the clock to your arrival time and leave it on the dashboard. (If your rental car doesn't come with a *disco*, pick one up at a tobacco shop or just write your arrival time on a piece of paper and place it on the dashboard.) These are generally used in areas where parking is free but has a time limit.

Garages are safe, save time, and help you avoid the stress of parking tickets. Take the parking voucher with you to pay the cashier before you leave.

## FLIGHTS

To compare flights, begin with an online travel search engine: Kayak is the top site for flights to and within Europe, easy-to-use Google Flights has price alerts, and Skyscanner includes many inexpensive flights within Europe. To avoid unpleasant surprises, before you book be sure to read the small print about refunds, changes, and the costs for "extras" such as reserving a seat, checking a bag, or printing a boarding pass.

**Flights to Europe:** Start looking for international flights about four to six months before your trip, especially for peak-season travel. Depending on your itinerary, it can be efficient and no more expensive to fly into one city and out of another. If your flight requires a connection in Europe, see my hints on navigating Europe's top hub airports at RickSteves.com/hub-airports.

**Flights Within Europe:** Flying between European cities is surprisingly affordable. Before buying a long-distance train or bus ticket, check the cost of a flight on one of Europe's airlines, whether a major carrier or a no-frills outfit like Easyjet or Ryanair. Be aware that flying with a discount airline can have drawbacks, such as minimal customer service, time-consuming treks to secondary airports, and a larger carbon footprint than a train or bus.

**Flying to the US and Canada:** Because security is extra tight for flights to the US, be sure to give yourself plenty of time at the airport (see www.tsa.gov for the latest rules).

# Resources from Rick Steves

## Begin Your Trip at RickSteves.com

My mobile-friendly **website** is *the* place to explore Europe in preparation for your trip. You'll find thousands of fun articles, videos, and radio interviews; a wealth of money-saving tips for planning your dream trip; travel news dispatches; a video library of travel talks; my travel blog; our latest guidebook updates (RickSteves.com/update); and the free Rick Steves Audio Europe app. You can also follow me on Facebook, Instagram, and Twitter.

Our **Travel Forum** is a well-groomed collection of message boards where our travel-savvy community answers questions and shares their personal travel experiences—and our well-traveled staff chimes in when they can be helpful (RickSteves.com/forums).

Our **online Travel Store** offers bags and accessories that I've designed to help you travel smarter and lighter. These include my popular carry-on bags (which I live out of four months a year), money belts, totes, toiletries kits, adapters, guidebooks, and planning maps (RickSteves.com/shop).

Our website can also help you find the perfect **rail pass** for your itinerary and your budget, with easy, one-stop shopping for rail passes, seat reservations, and point-to-point tickets (RickSteves.com/rail).

## Rick Steves' Tours, Guidebooks, TV Shows, and More

**Small Group Tours:** Want to travel with greater efficiency and less stress? We offer more than 40 itineraries reaching the best destinations in this book...and beyond. Each year about 30,000 travelers join us on about 1,000 Rick Steves bus tours. You'll enjoy great guides and a fun bunch of travel partners (with small groups of 24 to 28 travelers). You'll find European adventures to fit every vacation length. For all the details, and to get our tour catalog, visit RickSteves.com/tours or call us at +1 425 608 4217.

**Books:** This book is just one of many books in my series on European travel, which includes country and city guidebooks, Snapshots (excerpted chapters from bigger guides), Pocket guides (full-color little books on big cities), "Best Of" guidebooks (condensed, full-color country guides), and my budget-travel skills handbook, *Rick Steves Europe Through the Back Door*. A complete list of my titles—including phrase books, cruising guides, and travelogues on European art, history, and culture—appears near the end of this book.

**TV Shows and Travel Talks:** My public television series, *Rick Steves' Europe,* covers Europe from top to bottom with over 100 half-hour episodes—and we're working on new shows every year (watch full episodes at my website for free). My free online video library, Rick Steves Classroom Europe, offers a searchable database of short video clips on European history, culture, and geography (Classroom.RickSteves.com). And to raise your travel IQ, check out the video versions of our popular classes (covering most European countries as well as travel skills, packing smart, cruising, tech for travelers, European art, and travel as a political act—RickSteves.com/travel-talks).

**Audio Tours on My Free App:** I've produced dozens of free, self-guided audio tours of the top sights in Europe. For those tours and other audio content, get my free **Rick Steves Audio Europe app,** an extensive online library organized by destination. For more on my app, see page 24.

**Radio:** My weekly public radio show, *Travel with Rick Steves*, features interviews with travel experts from around the world. It airs on 400 public radio stations across the US. An archive of programs is available at RickSteves.com/radio.

**Podcasts:** You can enjoy my travel content via several free podcasts. The podcast version of my radio show brings you a weekly, hour-long travel conversation. My other podcasts include a weekly selection of video clips from my public television show, my audio tours of Europe's top sights, and live recordings of my travel classes (RickSteves.com/watch-read-listen/audio/podcasts).

# APPENDIX

## Holidays and Festivals

This list includes selected festivals in Florence, Siena, Pisa, and Lucca, plus national holidays observed throughout Italy. Many sights and banks close on national holidays—keep this in mind when planning your itinerary. Before planning a trip around a festival, verify the dates with the festival website, the TI, or my "Upcoming Holidays and Festivals in Italy" web page at RickSteves.com/europe/italy/festivals.

In Florence, hotels get booked up on Easter weekend, Liberation Day, Labor Day, Ascension Day, St. John the Baptist feast day, All Saints' Day, and on Fridays and Saturdays year-round. Some hotels require you to book the full three-day weekend around a holiday.

| | |
|---|---|
| **Jan** | Florence fashion convention |
| **Jan 1** | New Year's Day |
| **Jan 6** | Epiphany |
| **Feb/March** | Carnival celebrations/Mardi Gras, Florence (costumed parades, jousting competitions) |

| | |
|---|---|
| **March/April** | Easter weekend (Good Friday-Easter Monday): April 7-10, 2023; March 29-April 1, 2024 Explosion of the Cart (Scoppio del Carro), Florence (fireworks, bonfire in wooden cart) |
| **April 25** | Italian Liberation Day |
| **April/May** | Gelato Festival, Florence |
| **Early May** | Lucca Classica Festival (free concerts, www. luccaclassica.it) |
| **May** | Ascension: May 18, 2023; May 9, 2024 Cricket Festival, Florence (music, entertainment, food, crickets sold in cages) |
| **May 1** | Labor Day |
| **May/June** | Feast of Corpus Christi: June 8, 2023; May 30, 2024 |
| **June 2** | Anniversary of the Republic |
| **June 16-17** | Feast of St. Ranieri, Pisa |
| **June 24** | Feast of St. John the Baptist, Florence (parades, dances, boat races, fireworks); Calcio Storico, Florence (Renaissance ball game played on Piazza Santa Croce) |
| **June/July** | Florence Dance Festival (www. florencedancefestival.org) |
| **Late June-early Sept** | Outdoor cinema season, Florence (contemporary films) |
| **July 2** | Palio horse race, Siena |
| **Mid-Aug** | Medieval festival, Volterra (www.volterra1398.it) |
| **Aug 15** | Feast of the Assumption (Ferragosto) |
| **Aug 16** | Palio horse race, Siena |
| **Early Sept** | Festa della Rificolona, Florence (children's procession with lanterns, street performances, parade) |
| **Sept 13-14** | Volto Santo, Lucca (luminaria procession and fair) |
| **Sept/Oct** | Musica dei Popoli Festival, Florence (global and folk music and dances) |
| **Late Oct** | Comics & Games Festival, Lucca |
| **Nov 1** | All Saints' Day |
| **Dec 8** | Feast of the Immaculate Conception |
| **Dec 25** | Christmas |
| **Dec 26** | St. Stephen's Day |

# Books and Films

To learn more about Italy past and present, and specifically Florence, check out a few of these books or films. For kids' recommendations, see the Florence with Children chapter.

## Nonfiction

*The Architecture of the Italian Renaissance* (Peter Murray, 1969). Heavily illustrated, this classic presents the architectural life of Italy from the 13th through the 16th century.

*Brunelleschi's Dome: How a Renaissance Genius Reinvented Architecture* (Ross King, 2000). The remarkable story of how the dome of Florence's Duomo was designed and built.

*The City of Florence* (R. W. B. Lewis, 1994). The author's 50-year love affair with Florence started in the chaos of World War II; this book is both a personal biography and an informal history of the city.

*Dark Water* (Robert Clark, 2008). Florentines race to save seven centuries of human achievement in the face of the city's destructive 1966 floods.

*Fortune Is a River* (Roger D. Masters, 1998). Two geniuses of the Renaissance—Niccolo Machiavelli and Leonardo da Vinci—conspire to reroute the Arno River (unsuccessfully, thankfully).

*The Hills of Tuscany* (Ferenc Máté, 1998). After traveling all over the globe, a writer and his wife try to settle down in the Tuscan countryside.

*The House of Medici* (Christopher Hibbert, 1974). Florence's first family of the Renaissance included power-hungry bankers, merchants, popes, art patrons...and two queens of France.

*Italian Renaissance Art* (Laurie Schneider Adams, 2001). In this well-written introduction to this pivotal period, Adams focuses on the most important and innovative artists and their best works.

*The Lives of the Artists* (Giorgio Vasari, 1550). The man who invented the term "Renaissance" offers anecdote-filled biographies of his era's greatest artists, some of whom he knew personally.

*Looking at Painting in Florence, A Learner's Handbook* (Richard Peterson, 2014). An illustrated interpretive guide to the city's art masterpieces.

*The Prince* (Niccolò Machiavelli, 1532). The original "how-to" for gaining and maintaining political power, still chillingly relevant after 500 years.

*A Small Place in Italy* (Eric Newby, 1994). A young American couple tries to renovate a Tuscan farmhouse in the late 1960s.

*The Stones of Florence* (Mary McCarthy, 1956). McCarthy applies wit and keen observation to produce a quirky, impressionistic investigation of Florence and its history.

*A Tuscan Childhood* (Kinta Beevor, 1993). The daughter of a bohemian painter reminisces about growing up in prewar Tuscany among writers like Aldous Huxley and D. H. Lawrence.

*Under the Tuscan Sun* (Frances Mayes, 1996). Mayes' best seller describes living *la dolce vita* in the Tuscan countryside (and is better than the movie of the same name).

## Fiction

*The Agony and the Ecstasy* (Irving Stone, 1958). This fictional biography of Michelangelo brings to life the great artist's dramatic passions and furies (also a 1965 movie starring Charlton Heston).

*Birth of Venus* (Sarah Dunant, 2003). Dunant follows the life of a Florentine girl who develops feelings for the boy hired to paint the walls of the family's chapel.

*Death in the Mountains: The True Story of a Tuscan Murder* (Lisa Clifford, 2008). Clifford explores the region's humble roots as she re-creates life in the countryside before Tuscany became glamorous.

*The Decameron* (Giovanni Boccaccio, 1348). Boccaccio's collection of 100 hilarious, often bawdy tales is a masterpiece of Italian literature and inspired Chaucer, Keats, and Shakespeare.

*Divine Comedy* (Dante Alighieri, 1321). Dante's epic poem—a journey through hell, purgatory, and paradise—is one of the world's greatest works of literature.

*Galileo's Daughter* (Dava Sobel, 1999). Sobel's historical memoir centers on Galileo's correspondence with his oldest daughter and confidante.

*The Light in the Piazza* (Elizabeth Spencer, 1960). A mother and daughter are intoxicated by the beauty of 1950s Florence (also a 1962 movie and an award-winning Broadway musical).

*Murder of a Medici Princess* (Caroline P. Murphy, 2008). This historical novel recounts the life and death of Isabella de Medici, daughter of the duke who ruled Renaissance Florence and Tuscany.

*Romola* (George Eliot, 1863). In this historical novel set in Renaissance Florence, Eliot depicts the awakening of a young woman in the time of the Medicis and Savonarola.

*A Room with a View* (E. M. Forster, 1908). A young Englishwoman visiting Florence finds a socially unsuitable replacement for her snobby fiancé (also a 1985 movie starring Helena Bonham Carter).

*The Sixteen Pleasures* (Robert Hellenga, 1994). Set during the 1966 floods in Florence, a young student discovers an erotic manuscript banned by the pope and lost for centuries.

## Film and TV

*The Best of Youth* (2003). Beginning in the turbulent 1960s, this award-winning miniseries follows the dramatic ups and downs in the lives of two brothers over four decades.

*Brother Sun, Sister Moon* (1972). Franco Zeffirelli presents a sensitive account of the life of St. Francis of Assisi, including his friendship with St. Clare.

*Medici: Godfathers of the Renaissance* (2004). This PBS miniseries reveals the good, the bad, and the ugly about Florence's first family.

*Tea with Mussolini* (1999). Franco Zeffirelli's look at prewar Florence involves proper English ladies, a rich American Jew, and the son of a local businessman—all caught in the rise of fascism.

*Up at the Villa* (2000). Based on a W. Somerset Maugham novella, the film follows a wealthy young Englishwoman in 1930s Florence who is brutally confronted by the consequences of her whimsy.

*Where Angels Fear to Tread* (1991). In this adaptation of an E. M. Forster novel, a rich Edwardian widow impulsively marries a poor Tuscan but dies in childbirth, prompting a custody battle.

# Conversions and Climate

## Numbers and Stumblers

- Europeans write a few of their numbers differently than we do. 1 =1, 4 =4, 7 =7.
- In Europe, dates appear as day/month/year, so Christmas 2023 is 25/12/23.
- Commas are decimal points, and decimals are commas. A dollar and a half is $1,50, one thousand is 1.000, and there are 5.280 feet in a mile.
- When counting with fingers, start with your thumb. If you hold up your first finger to request one item, you'll probably get two.
- What Americans call the second floor of a building is the first floor in Europe.
- On escalators and moving sidewalks, Europeans keep the left "lane" open for passing. Keep to the right.

## Metric Conversions

A **kilogram** equals 1,000 grams (about 2.2 pounds). One hundred

**grams** (a common unit at markets) is about a quarter-pound. One **liter** is about a quart, or almost four to a gallon.

A **kilometer** is six-tenths of a mile. To convert kilometers to miles, cut the kilometers in half and add back 10 percent of the original (120 km: 60 + 12 = 72 miles). One **meter** is 39 inches—just over a yard.

| | |
|---|---|
| 1 foot = 0.3 meter | 1 square yard = 0.8 square meter |
| 1 yard = 0.9 meter | 1 square mile = 2.6 square kilometers |
| 1 mile = 1.6 kilometers | 1 ounce = 28 grams |
| 1 centimeter = 0.4 inch | 1 quart = 0.95 liter |
| 1 meter = 39.4 inches | 1 kilogram = 2.2 pounds |
| 1 kilometer = 0.62 mile | 32°F = 0°C |

## Roman Numerals

In the US, you'll see Roman numerals—which originated in ancient Rome—used for copyright dates, clocks, and the Super Bowl. In Italy, you're likely to observe these numbers chiseled on statues and buildings. If you want to do some numeric detective work, here's how: In Roman numerals, as in ours, the highest numbers (thousands, hundreds) come first, followed by smaller numbers. Many numbers are made by combining numerals into sets: V = 5, so VIII = 8 (5 plus 3). Roman numerals follow a subtraction principle for multiples of four (4, 40, 400, etc.) and nine (9, 90, 900, etc.); the number four, for example, is written as IV (1 subtracted from 5), rather than IIII. The number nine is IX (1 subtracted from 10).

Big numbers such as dates can look daunting at first. The easiest way to handle them is to read the numbers in discrete chunks. For example, Michelangelo was born in MCDLXXV. Break it down: M (1,000) + CD (100 subtracted from 500, so 400) + LXX (50 + 10 + 10, or 70) + V (5)=1475. It was a very good year.

| | |
|---|---|
| M = 1000 | XL = 40 |
| CM = 900 | X = 10 |
| D = 500 | IX = 9 |
| CD = 400 | V = 5 |
| C = 100 | IV = 4 |
| XC = 90 | I = duh |
| L = 50 | |

## Clothing Sizes

When shopping for clothing, use these US-to-European comparisons as general guidelines (but note that no conversion is perfect).

**Women:** For pants and dresses, add 36 in Italy (US 10 = Italian 46). For blouses and sweaters, add 8 for most of Europe (US 32 = European 40). For shoes, add 30-31 (US 7 = European 37/38).

**Men:** For shirts, multiply by 2 and add about 8 (US 15 = European 38). For jackets and suits, add 10. For shoes, add 32-34.

**Children:** Clothing is sized by height—in centimeters (2.5 cm = 1 inch), so a US size 8 roughly equates to 132-140. For shoes up to size 13, add 16-18, and for sizes 1 and up, add 30-32.

## Florence's Climate

First line, average daily high; second line, average daily low; third line, average days without rain. For more detailed weather statistics for destinations in this book (as well as the rest of the world), check Wunderground.com.

| J | F | M | A | M | J | J | A | S | O | N | D |
|---|---|---|---|---|---|---|---|---|---|---|---|
| 54° | 54° | 59° | 66° | 75° | 82° | 88° | 88° | 81° | 70° | 59° | 52° |
| 37° | 39° | 43° | 48° | 55° | 63° | 66° | 64° | 61° | 54° | 45° | 39° |
| 25 | 21 | 24 | 23 | 24 | 23 | 27 | 26 | 22 | 22 | 21 | 23 |

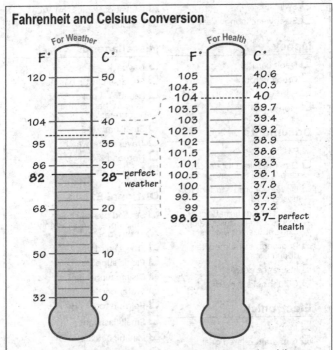

## Fahrenheit and Celsius Conversion

Europe takes its temperature using the Celsius scale, while we opt for Fahrenheit. For a rough conversion from Celsius to Fahrenheit, double the number and add 30. For weather, remember that 28°C is 82°F—perfect. For health, 37°C is just right. At a launderette, 30°C is cold, 40°C is warm (usually the default setting), 60°C is hot, and 95°C is boiling. Your air-conditioner should be set at about 20°C.

# Packing Checklist

Whether you're traveling for five days or five weeks, you won't need more than this. Pack light to enjoy the sweet freedom of true mobility.

## Clothing

- ☐ 5 shirts: long- & short-sleeve
- ☐ 2 pairs pants (or skirts/capris)
- ☐ 1 pair shorts
- ☐ 5 pairs underwear & socks
- ☐ 1 pair walking shoes
- ☐ Sweater or warm layer
- ☐ Rainproof jacket with hood
- ☐ Tie, scarf, belt, and/or hat
- ☐ Swimsuit
- ☐ Sleepwear/loungewear

## Money

- ☐ Debit card(s)
- ☐ Credit card(s)
- ☐ Hard cash (US $100-200)
- ☐ Money belt

## Documents

- ☐ Passport
- ☐ Other required ID: Vaccine card/Covid test, entry visa, etc.
- ☐ Driver's license, student ID, hostel card, etc.
- ☐ Tickets & confirmations: flights, hotels, trains, rail pass, car rental, sight entries
- ☐ Photocopies of important documents
- ☐ Insurance details
- ☐ Guidebooks & maps

## Electronics

- ☐ Mobile phone
- ☐ Camera & related gear
- ☐ Tablet/ebook reader/laptop
- ☐ Headphones/earbuds
- ☐ Chargers & batteries
- ☐ Phone car charger & mount (or GPS device)
- ☐ Plug adapters

## Toiletries

- ☐ Basics: soap, shampoo, toothbrush, toothpaste, floss, deodorant, sunscreen, brush/comb, etc.
- ☐ Medicines & vitamins
- ☐ First-aid kit
- ☐ Glasses/contacts/sunglasses
- ☐ Face masks & hand sanitizer
- ☐ Sewing kit
- ☐ Packet of tissues (for WC)
- ☐ Earplugs

## Miscellaneous

- ☐ Daypack
- ☐ Sealable plastic baggies
- ☐ Laundry supplies: soap, laundry bag, clothesline, spot remover
- ☐ Small umbrella
- ☐ Travel alarm/watch
- ☐ Notepad & pen
- ☐ Journal

## Optional Extras

- ☐ Second pair of shoes (flip-flops, sandals, tennis shoes, boots)
- ☐ Travel hairdryer
- ☐ Picnic supplies
- ☐ Disinfecting wipes
- ☐ Water bottle
- ☐ Fold-up tote bag
- ☐ Small flashlight
- ☐ Mini binoculars
- ☐ Small towel or washcloth
- ☐ Inflatable pillow/neck rest
- ☐ Tiny lock
- ☐ Address list (to mail postcards)
- ☐ Extra passport photos

# Italian Survival Phrases

| | | |
|---|---|---|
| **Hello. (informal)** | Ciao. | chow |
| **Good day.** | Buongiorno. | bwohn-**jor**-noh |
| **Do you speak English?** | Parla inglese? | **par**-lah een-**gleh**-zay |
| **Yes. / No.** | Sì. / No. | see / noh |
| **I (don't) understand.** | (Non) capisco. | (nohn) kah-**pees**-koh |
| **Please.** | Per favore. | pehr fah-**voh**-ray |
| **Thank you.** | Grazie. | **graht**-see-ay |
| **You're welcome.** | Prego. | **preh**-go |
| **I'm sorry.** | Mi dispiace. | mee dee-spee-**ah**-chay |
| **Excuse me.** | Mi scusi. | mee **skoo**-zee |
| **No problem.** | Non c'è problema. | nohn cheh proh-**bleh**-mah |
| **Goodbye.** | Arrivederci. | ah-ree-veh-**dehr**-chee |
| **one / two / three** | uno / due / tre | **oo**-noh / **doo**-ay / tray |
| **four / five / six** | quattro / cinque / sei | **kwah**-troh / **cheeng**-kway / **seh**-ee |
| **seven / eight** | sette / otto | **seh**-tay / **oh**-toh |
| **nine / ten** | nove / dieci | **noh**-vay / dee-**ay**-chee |
| **How much is it?** | Quanto costa? | **kwahn**-toh **koh**-stah |
| **Write it?** | Me lo scrive? | may loh **skree**-vay |
| **Is it free?** | È gratis? | eh **grah**-tees |
| **Is it included?** | È incluso? | eh een-**kloo**-zoh |
| **Where can I buy / find...?** | Dove posso comprare / trovare...? | **doh**-vay **poh**-soh kohm-**prah**-ray / troh-**vah**-ray |
| **I'd like / We'd like...** | Vorrei / Vorremmo... | voh-**reh**-ee / voh-**reh**-moh |
| **...a room.** | ...una camera. | **oo**-nah **kah**-meh-rah |
| **...a ticket to ___.** | ...un biglietto per ___. | oon beel-**yeh**-toh pehr ___ |
| **Is it possible?** | È possibile? | eh poh-**see**-bee-lay |
| **Where is...?** | Dov'è...? | doh-**veh** |
| **...the train station** | ...la stazione | lah staht-see-**oh**-nay |
| **...tourist information** | ...informazioni turisti | een-for-maht-see-**oh**-nee too-**ree**-stee |
| **...the bathroom** | ...il bagno | eel **bahn**-yoh |
| **men / women** | uomini, signori / donne, signore | **woh**-mee-nee, seen-**yoh**-ree / **doh**-nay, seen-**yoh**-ray |
| **left / right / straight** | sinistra / destra / sempre dritto | see-**nee**-strah / **deh**-strah / **sehm**-pray **dree**-toh |
| **What time does this open / close?** | A che ora apre / chiude? | ah kay **oh**-rah **ah**-pray / kee-**oo**-day |
| **At what time?** | A che ora? | ah kay **oh**-rah |
| **Just a moment.** | Un momento. | oon moh-**mehn**-toh |
| **now / soon / later** | adesso / presto / tardi | ah-**deh**-soh / **preh**-stoh / **tar**-dee |
| **today / tomorrow** | oggi / domani | **oh**-jee / doh-**mah**-nee |

## In an Italian Restaurant

| | |
|---|---|
| I'd like / We'd like... | Vorrei / Vorremmo...  voh-**reh**-ee / voh-**reh**-moh |
| ...to reserve a table for one / two. | ...prenotare un tavolo per uno / due.<br>preh-noh-**tah**-ray oon **tah**-voh-loh pehr **oo**-noh / **doo**-ay |
| ...the menu (in English). | ...il menù (in inglese).<br>eel meh-**noo** (een een-**gleh**-zay) |
| Is this seat free? | È libero questo posto?<br>eh **lee**-beh-roh **kweh**-stoh **poh**-stoh |
| service (not) included | servizio (non) compreso<br>sehr-**veet**-see-oh (nohn) kohm-**pray**-zoh |
| cover charge | (pane e) coperto  (**pah**-nay ay) koh-**pehr**-toh |
| to go | da portar via  dah **por**-tar **vee**-ah |
| with / without | con / senza  kohn / **sehnt**-sah |
| and / or | e / o  ay / oh |
| breakfast / lunch / dinner | (prima) colazione / pranzo / cena<br>(**pree**-mah) koh-laht-zee-oh-nay / **prahn**-zoh / **chay**-nah |
| fixed-price meal (of the day) | menù (del giorno)  meh-**noo** (dehl **jor**-noh) |
| specialty of the house | specialità della casa<br>speh-chah-lee-**tah deh**-lah **kah**-zah |
| appetizer | antipasto  ahn-tee-**pah**-stoh |
| first course | primo (piatto)  **pree**-moh (pee-**ah**-toh) |
| main course | secondo (piatto)  seh-**kohn**-doh (pee-**ah**-toh) |
| side dishes | contorni  kohn-**tor**-nee |
| cold cuts / bread / cheese | salumi / pane / formaggio<br>sah-**loo**-mee / **pah**-nay / for-**mah**-joh |
| sandwich | panino  pah-**nee**-noh |
| soup / salad | zuppa / insalata  **tsoo**-pah / een-sah-**lah**-tah |
| meat / chicken | carne / pollo  **kar**-nay / **poh**-loh |
| fish / seafood | pesce / frutti di mare<br>**peh**-shay / **froo**-tee dee **mah**-ray |
| fruit / vegetables | frutta / verdure  **froo**-tah / vehr-**doo**-ray |
| dessert | dolce  **dohl**-chay |
| tap water | acqua del rubinetto  **ah**-kwah dehl roo-bee-**neh**-toh |
| mineral water | acqua minerale  **ah**-kwah mee-neh-**rah**-lay |
| still / sparkling | naturale / frizzante  nah-too-**rah**-lay / freet-**zahn**-tay |
| (orange) juice | succo (d'arancia)  **soo**-koh (dah-**rahn**-chah) |
| coffee / tea / milk | caffè / tè / latte  kah-**feh** / teh / **lah**-tay |
| wine / beer | vino / birra  **vee**-noh / **bee**-rah |
| red / white | rosso / bianco  **roh**-soh / bee-**ahn**-koh |
| glass / bottle | bicchiere / bottiglia  bee-kee-**eh**-ray / boh-**teel**-yah |
| Cheers! | Salute! / Cin cin!  sah-**loo**-tay / cheen cheen |
| The bill, please. | Il conto, per favore.  eel **kohn**-toh pehr fah-**voh**-ray |
| Do you accept credit cards? | Accettate carte di credito?<br>ah-cheh-**tah**-tay **kar**-tay dee **kreh**-dee-toh |
| Delicious! | Delizioso!  day-leet-see-oh-zoh |

For more user-friendly Italian phrases, check out *Rick Steves Italian Phrase Book* or *Rick Steves French, Italian, & German Phrase Book*.

# INDEX

INDEX

INDEX

**INDEX**

# MAP INDEX

# Start your trip at

## Explore Europe

At ricksteves.com you can browse through thousands of articles, videos, photos and radio interviews, plus find a wealth of money-saving travel tips for planning your dream trip. And with our mobile-friendly website, you can easily access all this great travel information anywhere you go.

## TV Shows

Preview the places you'll visit by watching entire half-hour episodes of *Rick Steves' Europe* (choose from all 100 shows) on-demand, for free.

*your travel dreams into affordable reality*

## Radio Interviews

Enjoy ready access to Rick's vast library of radio interviews covering travel tips and cultural insights that relate specifically to your Europe travel plans.

## Travel Forums

Learn, ask, share! Our online community of savvy travelers is a great resource for first-time travelers to Europe, as well as seasoned pros.

## Travel News

Subscribe to our free Travel News e-newsletter, and get monthly updates from Rick on what's happening in Europe.

## Classroom Europe®

Check out our free resource for educators with 500 short video clips from the *Rick Steves' Europe* TV show.

## Rick's Free Travel App

Get your FREE **Rick Steves Audio Europe**™ app to enjoy…

- Dozens of self-guided tours of Europe's top museums, sights and historic walks
- Hundreds of tracks filled with cultural insights and sightseeing tips from Rick's radio interviews
- All organized into handy geographic playlists
- For Apple and Android

With Rick whispering in your ear, Europe gets even better.

**Find out more at ricksteves.com**

*Gear up for your next adventure at ricksteves.com*

## Light Luggage

Pack light and right with Rick Steves' affordable, custom-designed rolling carry-on bags, backpacks, day packs and shoulder bags.

## Accessories

From packing cubes to moneybelts and beyond, Rick has personally selected the travel goodies that will help your trip go smoother.

## Save time and energy

This guidebook is your independent-travel toolkit. But for all it delivers, it's still up to you to devote the time and energy it takes to manage the preparation and logistics that are essential for a happy trip. If that's a hassle, there's a solution.

## Rick Steves Tours

A Rick Steves tour takes you to Europe's most interesting places with great

## with minimum stress

guides and small groups. We follow Rick's favorite itineraries, ride in comfy buses, stay in family-run hotels, and bring you intimately close to the Europe you've traveled so far to see. Most importantly, we take away the logistical headaches so you can focus on the fun.

### Join the fun

This year we'll take thousands of free-spirited travelers—nearly half of them repeat customers— along with us on 50 different itineraries, from Athens to Istanbul. Is a Rick Steves tour the right fit for your travel dreams?

Find out at ricksteves.com, where you can also check seat availability and sign up. Europe is best experienced with happy travel partners. We hope you can join us.

## See our itineraries at ricksteves.com

# A Guide for Every Trip

## BEST OF GUIDES

*Full-color guides in an easy-to-scan format. Focused on top sights and experiences in the most popular European destinations*

Best of England
Best of Europe
Best of France
Best of Germany
Best of Ireland
Best of Italy
Best of Scotland
Best of Spain

## COMPREHENSIVE GUIDES

*City, country, and regional guides printed on Bible-thin paper. Packed with detailed coverage for a multi-week trip exploring iconic sights and venturing off the beaten path*

Amsterdam & the Netherlands
Barcelona
Belgium: Bruges, Brussels, Antwerp & Ghent
Berlin
Budapest
Croatia & Slovenia
Eastern Europe
England
Florence & Tuscany
France
Germany
Great Britain
Greece: Athens & the Peloponnese
Iceland
Ireland
Istanbul
Italy
London
Paris
Portugal
Prague & the Czech Republic
Provence & the French Riviera
Rome
Scandinavia
Scotland
Sicily
Spain
Switzerland
Venice
Vienna, Salzburg & Tirol

HE BEST OF ROME

, Italy's capital, is studded with
n remnants and floodlit fountain
s. From the Vatican to the Colos-
with crazy traffic in between, Rome
erful, huge, and exhausting. The
the heat, and the weighty history

of the Eternal City where Caesars walked
can make tourists wilt. Recharge by taking siestas, gelato breaks, and after-dark
walks, strolling from one atmospheric
square to another in the refreshing evening air.

*Pantheon—which*
*dome until the*
*,000 years old*
*over 1,500).*

*Athens in the Vat-*
*the humanistic*

*diators fought*
*her, entertaining*

*ome ristorante*

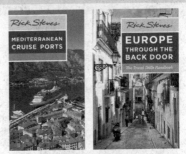

## POCKET GUIDES
*Compact color guides for shorter trips*

| | |
|---|---|
| Amsterdam | Paris |
| Athens | Prague |
| Barcelona | Rome |
| Florence | Venice |
| Italy's Cinque Terre | Vienna |
| London | |
| Munich & Salzburg | |

## SNAPSHOT GUIDES
*Focused single-destination coverage*

Basque Country: Spain & France
Copenhagen & the Best of Denmark
Dublin
Dubrovnik
Edinburgh
Hill Towns of Central Italy
Krakow, Warsaw & Gdansk
Lisbon
Loire Valley
Madrid & Toledo
Milan & the Italian Lakes District
Naples & the Amalfi Coast
Nice & the French Riviera
Normandy
Northern Ireland
Norway
Reykjavík
Rothenburg & the Rhine
Sevilla, Granada & Southern Spain
St. Petersburg, Helsinki & Tallinn
Stockholm

## CRUISE PORTS GUIDES
*Reference for cruise ports of call*

Mediterranean Cruise Ports
Scandinavian & Northern European
 Cruise Ports

### Complete your library with...

## TRAVEL SKILLS & CULTURE
*Study up on travel skills and gain
insight on history and culture*

Europe 101
Europe Through the Back Door
Europe's Top 100 Masterpieces
European Christmas
European Easter
European Festivals
For the Love of Europe
Italy for Food Lovers
Travel as a Political Act

## PHRASE BOOKS & DICTIONARIES
French
French, Italian & German
German
Italian
Portuguese
Spanish

## PLANNING MAPS
Britain, Ireland & London
Europe
France & Paris
Germany, Austria & Switzerland
Iceland
Ireland
Italy
Scotland
Spain & Portugal

# Credits

## RESEARCHERS
For help with this edition, Rick and Gene relied on...

### Cameron Hewitt

Cameron Hewitt was born in Denver, grew up in Central Ohio, and moved to Seattle in 2000 to work for Rick Steves' Europe. Since then, he has spent about 100 days each year in Europe—researching and writing guidebooks, blogging, tour guiding, and making travel TV (described in his memoir, *The Temporary European*). Cameron married his high school sweetheart, Shawna, and enjoys taking pictures, trying new restaurants, and planning his next trip.

### Cary Walker

Cary discovered international travel during college and has been feeding her wanderlust ever since. A former teacher, she believes that Europe is the best classroom for those who travel with an open mind. When not researching guidebooks or leading Rick Steves' Europe tours, she resides in Dallas with her husband Brian and three well-traveled stepsons.

## ACKNOWLEDGMENT
Thank you to Risa Laib for her 25-plus years of dedication to the Rick Steves guidebook series.

Avalon Travel
Hachette Book Group
1700 Fourth Street
Berkeley, CA 94710

Printed in Canada by Friesens.
19th Edition. First printing November 2022.

ISBN 978-1-64171-413-6

For the latest on Rick's talks, guidebooks, tours, public television series, and public radio show, contact Rick Steves' Europe, 130 Fourth Avenue North, Edmonds, WA 98020, +1 425 771 8303, RickSteves.com, rick@ricksteves.com.

**Rick Steves' Europe**
**Managing Editor:** Jennifer Madison Davis
**Assistant Managing Editor:** Cathy Lu
**Editors:** Glenn Eriksen, Julie Fanselow, Suzanne Kotz, Rosie Leutzinger, Teresa Nemeth, Jessica Shaw, Carrie Shepherd
**Editorial & Production Assistant:** Megan Simms
**Researchers:** Cameron Hewitt, Cary Walker
**Research Assistance:** David Tordi
**Graphic Content Director:** Sandra Hundacker
**Maps & Graphics:** Orin Dubrow, David C. Hoerlein, Lauren Mills, Mary Rostad, Laura Terrenzio

**Avalon Travel**
**Senior Editor and Series Manager:** Madhu Prasher
**Associate Managing Editor:** Jamie Andrade
**Editor:** Rachael Sablik
**Production & Typesetting:** Lisi Baldwin, Rue Flaherty, Jane Musser, Ravina Schneider
**Maps & Graphics:** Kat Bennett
**Copy Editor:** Maggie Ryan
**Proofreader:** Elizabeth Jang
**Indexer:** Stephen Callahan
**Cover Design:** Kimberly Glyder Design

# COLOR MAPS

*Florence • Tuscany • Siena*

# Florence

To Fortezza da Basso

ATAF LOCAL BUS OFFICE

Tram T-2 to Airport

VIA ALAMANNI

SANTA MARIA NOVELLA TRAIN STATION **36**

PEDESTRIAN UNDERPASS

Valfonda Line T1

Piazza della Stazione

Alamanni–Stazione Line T1 & T2

VIA NAZIONALE

VIA DELL'ARIENTO

VIA FAENZA

MERCATO CENTRALE **15**

Piaz Merc Centr

BORGO LA

**29**

**BUS STATION 37**

To Airport & A-1 Autostrada (Firenze Nord exit)

tram line

Piazza dell' Unità Italiana

VIA S. ANTONINO

VIA S. AMARINO

Piazza S

MEDICI CHAPELS **13**

SAN LOREN.

VIA DEL MELARANCIO

Piazza Madonna

PEDESTRIAN UNDERPASS ENTRANCE

VIA DE' CONTI

LAURENTI MEDICI LIBRARY

VIA DELLA SCALA

VIA DE CANACCI

VIA DELLA SCALA

VIA DE' BENEDETTA

SANTA MARIA NOVELLA **32**

EXIT

Unità Line T2

VIA DEGLI AVELLI

VIA DEL GIGLIO

VIA DEL

VIA DEI

VIA DEL PANZANI

VIA DELL'ALLORO

ZANNETTI

PERFUMERY **33**

VIA PALAZZUOLO

Piazza Santa Maria Novella

VIA DEI BANCHI

BELLE DONNE

TREBBIO

RONDINELLI

VIA DE' CERRETANI

SANTA MARIA MAGGIORE

P. D'OLIO

OGNISSANTI

Piazza Ognissanti

VIA DELLA PORCELLANA

VIA DI PAOLINO

VIA DEL SOLE

VIA DELLA SPADA

GIACOMINI

ANTINORI

SAN GAETANO

V. CORSI

VIA PECORI

VIA DE' TOSINGHI

VECCHIETTI

BRUN.

Piazza della Repubblica **22**

LUNGARNO VESPUCCI

BORGO OGNISSANTI

VIA DELLA PORCELLANA

VIA DE' FOSSI

VIA DEL MORO

VIA DE' FEDERIGHI

VIA DELLA

RUCELLAI PALACE

VIGNA NUOVA

PURGATORIO

INFERNO

VIA DEGLI STROZZI

PESCIONI

STROZZI PALACE **20**

VIA D' ANSELMI

MONALDA

SASSETTI

POST

Piazza Goldoni

VIA DEL PARIONE

PARIONCINO

TORNABUONI

VIA PORTA ROSSA

VIA PELLICCERIA

**19**

**16**

PONTE ALLA CARRAIA

LUNGARNO CORSINI

SANTA TRINITÀ **10**

Piazza Sta. Trinità

VIA DE'

VIA DELLE TERME

RICASOLI

BOMBARDE

FIORDALISO

CORNINO

MANETTO

L. SODERINI

Arno River

LUNGARNO GUICCIARDINI

PONTE STA. TRINITA

BORGO S. APOSTOLI

LUNGARNO ACCIAIUOLI

VIA POR SANTA M

To Porta San Frediano

Piazza Sauro

LUNGARNO GUICCIARDINI

GEPPI

VIA SANTO SPIRITO

Piazza degli Scarlatti

V. COVERELLI

Piazza Frescobaldi

TORRE DEI BELFREDELLI

PONTE VECCHIO **27**

SAN STEFAN

BORGO STELLA

VIA DE' SERRAGLI

MAFFIA

VIA S. MONACA

VIA SANT'AGOSTINO

OLTRARNO

VIA D. S. MARTINO

VIA DE' VELLUTINI

VIA DELLO SPRONE

TORRE DI MARSILI

BORGO SAN JACOPO

Piazza della Pasera

Piazza S. Felicità

VASAR CORRIDO

VIA DE

COSTA DI SAN GIO

**4**

SANTO SPIRITO **34**

Piazza Santo Spirito

VIA DE' MICHELOZZI

VIA DELVELLUTI

V. SGUAZZA

VIA MAGGIO

VIA TOSCANELLA

SDRUCCIOLO DE' PITTI

SANTA FELICITÀ

GROTTO BACCHUS

VIA DELLE CALDAIE

BORGO

TEGOLAIO

VIA MAZZETTA

Piazza di San Felice

GUICCIARDINI

Piazza de' Pitti **26**

EXIT GARDENS

PITTI PALACE

Boboli Gardens

To Forte di Belvedere

To Porta Romana

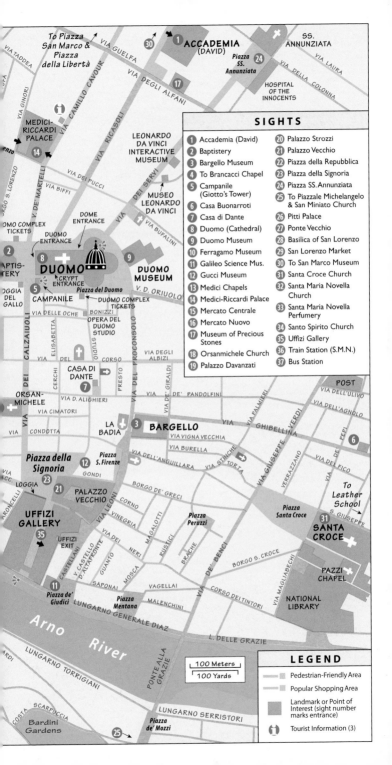

## SIGHTS

| | | | |
|---|---|---|---|
| **1** Accademia (David) | | **20** Palazzo Strozzi |
| **2** Baptistery | | **21** Palazzo Vecchio |
| **3** Bargello Museum | | **22** Piazza della Repubblica |
| **4** To Brancacci Chapel | | **23** Piazza della Signoria |
| **5** Campanile (Giotto's Tower) | | **24** Piazza SS. Annunziata |
| **6** Casa Buonarroti | | **25** To Piazzale Michelangelo & San Miniato Church |
| **7** Casa di Dante | | **26** Pitti Palace |
| **8** Duomo (Cathedral) | | **27** Ponte Vecchio |
| **9** Duomo Museum | | **28** Basilica of San Lorenzo |
| **10** Ferragamo Museum | | **29** San Lorenzo Market |
| **11** Galileo Science Mus. | | **30** To San Marco Museum |
| **12** Gucci Museum | | **31** Santa Croce Church |
| **13** Medici Chapels | | **32** Santa Maria Novella Church |
| **14** Medici-Riccardi Palace | | **33** Santa Maria Novella Perfumery |
| **15** Mercato Centrale | | **34** Santo Spirito Church |
| **16** Mercato Nuovo | | **35** Uffizi Gallery |
| **17** Museum of Precious Stones | | **36** Train Station (S.M.N.) |
| **18** Orsanmichele Church | | **37** Bus Station |
| **19** Palazzo Davanzati | | |

### LEGEND

- Pedestrian-Friendly Area
- Popular Shopping Area
- Landmark or Point of Interest (sight number marks entrance)
- Tourist Information (3)

100 Meters
100 Yards

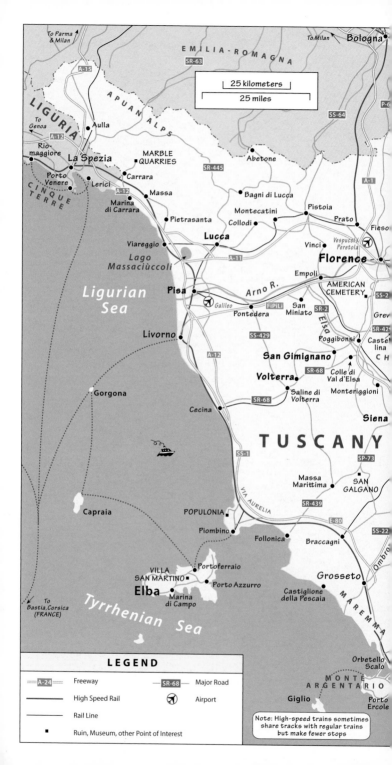

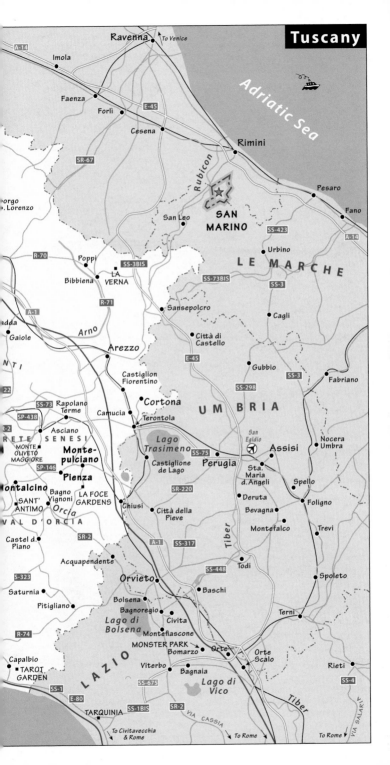

# Tuscany

Ravenna  *To Venice*
A-14
Imola
Faenza  E-45
Forlì
Cesena
Rimini
SR-67
Rubicon
*Adriatic Sea*

Pesaro
Fano
A-14
San Leo
SAN MARINO
SS-423

orgo
Lorenzo
Urbino
LE  MARCHE
R-70
Poppi
SS-3BIS
LA VERNA
SS-73BIS
SS-3
Bibbiena
R-71
A-1
Sansepolcro
Cagli
adda
Gaiole
Arno
Città di Castello
E-45
Arezzo
Gubbio
SS-3
Fabriano
NTI
Castiglion Fiorentino
SS-298
22
Cortona
UMBRIA
SS-73
Rapolano Terme
Camucia
SP-438
Terontola
San Egidio
Nocera Umbra
32
Asciano
Lago Trasimeno
SS-75
Assisi
RETE SENESI
MONTE OLIVETO MAGGIORE
Montepulciano
Castiglione de Lago
Perugia
Sta. Maria d.Angeli
Spello
SP-146
Pienza
SR-220
Deruta
Foligno
ontalcino
Bagno Vignoni
LA FOCE GARDENS
Chiusi
Città della Pieve
Bevagna
Trevi
SANT' ANTIMO
Orcia
Montefalco
VAL D'ORCIA
SR-2
A-1
SS-317
Tiber
Castel d. Piano
Acquapendente
SS-448
Todi
Spoleto
S-323
Orvieto
Baschi
Saturnia
Bolsena
Terni
Pitigliano
Bagnoregio
Civita
R-74
Lago di Bolsena
Montefiascone
Orte
MONSTER PARK
Bomarzo
Orte Scalo
Rieti
Capalbio
TAROT GARDEN
Viterbo
Bagnaia
SS-4
LAZIO
SS-675
Lago di Vico
SS-1
E-80
TARQUINIA
SS-1BIS
SR-2
*VIA CASSIA*
*Tiber*
*VIA SALARIA*
*To Civitavecchia & Rome*
*To Rome*
*To Rome*

# Siena

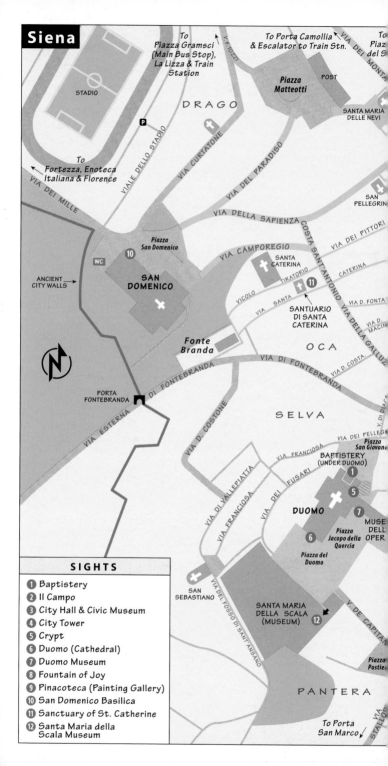

STADIO

DRAGO

To
Piazza Gramsci
(Main Bus Stop),
La Lizza & Train
Station

To Porta Camollia
& Escalator to Train Stn.

VIA DEI MONTA

To
Piaz
del S

VIA F. TOZZI

Piazza
Matteotti

POST

SANTA MARIA
DELLE NEVI

P

VIALE DELLO STADIO

VIA CURTATONE

VIA DEL PARADISO

To
Fortezza, Enoteca
Italiana & Florence

VIA DEI MILLE

SAN
PELLEGRIN

VIA DELLA SAPIENZA

VIA DEI PITTORI

Piazza
San Domenico

10

WC

SAN
DOMENICO

VIA CAMPOREGIO

SANTA
CATERINA

COSTA SANT'ANTONIO

VIA DELLA GALLUZ

CATERINA

11

TIRATORIO

VICOLO

VIA SANTA

VIA D. FONTA

VIA D.
MACIN

ANCIENT
CITY WALLS

SANTUARIO
DI SANTA
CATERINA

OCA

Fonte
Branda

VIA DI FONTEBRANDA

VIA D. COSTA.

N

VIA DI FONTEBRANDA

PORTA
FONTEBRANDA

VIA ESTERNA

SELVA

V. DI DIAC

VIA D. COSTONE

VIA DEI PELLEG

Piazza
San Giovan

VIA FRANCIOSA

BAPTISTERY
(UNDER DUOMO)

1

VIA DI VALLEPIATTA

VIA FRANCIOSA

VIA DEI FUSARI

5

DUOMO

7

MUSE
DELL
OPER

6

Piazza
Jacopo della
Quercia

SAN
SEBASTIANO

Piazza del
Duomo

VIA DEL FOSSO DI SANT'ANSANO

SANTA MARIA
DELLA SCALA
(MUSEUM)

12

V. DE CAPITAN

Piazza
Postie

PANTERA

VIA

To Porta
San Marco

## SIGHTS

1. Baptistery
2. Il Campo
3. City Hall & Civic Museum
4. City Tower
5. Crypt
6. Duomo (Cathedral)
7. Duomo Museum
8. Fountain of Joy
9. Pinacoteca (Painting Gallery)
10. San Domenico Basilica
11. Sanctuary of St. Catherine
12. Santa Maria della
    Scala Museum

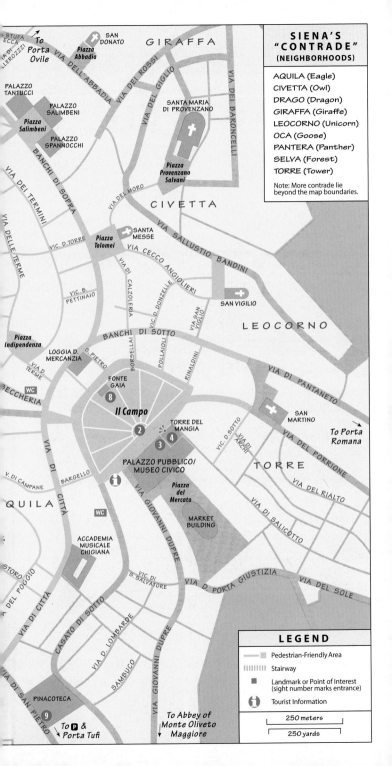

**SIENA'S "CONTRADE"**
(NEIGHBORHOODS)

AQUILA (Eagle)
CIVETTA (Owl)
DRAGO (Dragon)
GIRAFFA (Giraffe)
LEOCORNO (Unicorn)
OCA (Goose)
PANTERA (Panther)
SELVA (Forest)
TORRE (Tower)

Note: More contrade lie beyond the map boundaries.

GIRAFFA

SAN DONATO

Piazza Abbadia

To Porta Ovile

VIA DI LLEROZZI

STUFA ECCA

PALAZZO TANTUCCI

PALAZZO SALIMBENI

Piazza Salimbeni

PALAZZO SPANNOCCHI

VIA DELL'ABBADIA

VIA DEI ROSSI

VIA DEL GIGLIO

SANTA MARIA DI PROVENZANO

VIA DEI BARONCELLI

Piazza Provenzano Salvani

BANCHI DI SOPRA

VIA DEI TERMINI

VIA DEL MORO

CIVETTA

VIC. D. TORRE

Piazza Tolomei

SANTA MESSE

VIA CECCO ANGIOLIERI

VIA SALLUSTIO BANDINI

VIA DELLE TERME

VIC. B. PETTINAIO

VIA DI CALZOLERIA

VIC. D. DONZELLE

SAN VIGILIO

LEOCORNO

Piazza Indipendenza

BANCHI DI SOTTO

S. PIETRO

BORSELLINI

POLLAIOLI

VIA SAN VIGILIO

RINALDINI

VIA DI PANTANETO

LOGGIA D. MERCANZIA

VIA D. TERME

BECCHERIA

WC

FONTE GAIA

**8**

**Il Campo**

**2**

TORRE DEL MANGIA

**3** **4**

SAN MARTINO

VIA DEL PORRIONE

To Porta Romana

SAN MARTINO

TORRE

VIA DEL RIALTO

VIC. D. SOTTO

VIA DI ARCHI

VIA DI SALICOTTO

PALAZZO PUBBLICO/
MUSEO CIVICO

BARGELLO

V. DI CAMPANE

QUILA

VIA DI CITTA

WC

ACCADEMIA MUSICALE CHIGIANA

Piazza del Mercato

MARKET BUILDING

VIA GIOVANNI DUPRE

STORO

A DEL POGGIO

VIC. DI S. SALVATORE

VIA D. PORTA GIUSTIZIA

VIA DEL SOLE

CASATO DI SOTTO

VIA DI CITTA

VIA D. LOMBARDE

SAMBUCO

VIA GIOVANNI DUPRE

VIA DI SAN PIETRO

PINACOTECA

**9**

To 🅿 &
Porta Tufi

To Abbey of Monte Oliveto Maggiore

**LEGEND**

Pedestrian-Friendly Area

Stairway

■ Landmark or Point of Interest (sight number marks entrance)

ℹ Tourist Information

250 meters

250 yards

# Let's Keep on Travelin'

Your trip doesn't need to end.

Follow Rick on social media!